OTAKAR ZICH

AESTHETICS OF THE DRAMATIC ART
THEORETICAL DRAMATURGY

EDITED BY DAVID DROZD
AND PAVEL DRÁBEK

TRANSLATED FROM CZECH
BY PAVEL DRÁBEK AND TOMÁŠ KAČER

CHARLES UNIVERSITY
KAROLINUM PRESS 2024

KAROLINUM PRESS
Karolinum Press is a publishing department of Charles University
Ovocný trh 560/5, 116 36 Prague 1, Czech Republic
www.karolinum.cz
© Edited by David Drozd, Pavel Drábek, 2024
© Translated by Pavel Drábek, Tomáš Kačer, 2024 (with reference
to the unpublished translation by Samuel Kostomlatský and Ivo Osolsobě)
Coverphoto © Gallery of Modern Art in Hradec Králové
Copy-edited by Josh Overton
Set in DTP Karolinum Press
Printed in the Czech Republic by Karolinum Press
Layout by Jan Šerých
First English edition

This book is the principal outcome of the research project *Divadlo jako syntéza umění: Otakar Zich v kontextu moderní vědy a dnešní potenciál jeho konceptů / Theatre as Synthesis of Arts: Otakar Zich in Context of Modern Science and Actual Potential of His Concepts* (GAČR 2016–2018, GA16-20335S), funded by the Czech Grant Agency.

A catalogue record for this book is available from the National Library
of the Czech Republic.

ISBN 978-80-246-5785-1
ISBN 978-80-246-5786-8 (pdf)
ISBN 978-80-246-5935-0 (epub)

CONTENTS

Acknowledgements — 7
Preface — 8

Introduction — 11
Otakar Zich and his Aesthetics of the Dramatic Art: Introducing a Seminal Work After a Century (David Drozd, with Pavel Drábek and Josh Overton) — 12
    The Layout of the *Aesthetics*: Organisation of the Book — 14
    Establishing the Specific Genre of "the Dramatic Art" — 16
    The Audience Perspective: a Synchronous Theory — 17
    Theatre as a Synthesis of the Arts: Critique of the Concept — 18
    An Analytical Approach to the Theatre — 19
    Ostention and Inner Tactile Perception — 24
    The Specialised Skills of Theatre Makers — 26
    Opera as a Dramatic Genre *per se* — 30
    Style, Stylisation and Theatrical Illusion — 31
    Theoretical Dramaturgy and Theatre Studies — 33
    Otakar Zich, a Scholar and an Artist: the Life and Times — 34
    The Arts Around Zich — 40
    Ways of Reading Zich's *Aesthetics*: a Short Catalogue — 45
A Note on this Edition — 47

Otakar Zich: Aesthetics of the Dramatic Art: Theoretical Dramaturgy — 49

An Analytical List of Contents — 50
Foreword — 55
Introduction — 57
THE CONCEPT OF DRAMATIC ART — 59
    1 The Character of the Dramatic Work — 60
    2 The Synthetic Theory — 74
    3 The Analytical Theory — 83
THE PRINCIPLE OF DRAMATICITY — 107
    4 The Dramatic Text: The Playwright's Creative Work — 108
    5 The Dramatic Persona: The Actor's Creative Work — 139
    6 Dramatic Action: The Stage Director's First Task — 183

7 Theatrical Scene: The Stage Director's Second Task	229
8 Dramatic Music: The Composer's Creative Work	270
THE PRINCIPLE OF STYLISATION	333
9 Realism and Idealism: The Basis of Theatrical Illusion	334
10 Dramatic Styles	357

Afterword	375
Otakar Zich in Context: Inspirations, Interpretations and Issues (David Drozd)	376
1 Zich's Intellectual World: Inspirations and Sources	377
Zich as a University Teacher	377
Zich as a Critical Reader	378
Scholarly Sources for Zich's *Aesthetics*	380
Zich and the Formation of *Theaterwissenschaft*	385
Artur Kutscher and Hugo Dinger as Zich's Contemporaries	387
Kutscher's Systemic *Theaterwissenschaft*	391
Kutscher and Zich *vs.* the Avant-Garde	393
Zich and the Intellectual Horizons of His Age	396
Zich and the Case of…	399
…Roman Ingarden and Phenomenology	399
…Aristotle and Structural Poetics	406
… Friedrich Nietzsche and Sigmund Freud	408
The *What If* of Zich's Reception	415
2 Reading Zich in Czech and Beyond: Interpreting the Book	417
…in Early Published Book Reviews	417
…by Structuralists	421
…by Semioticians	424
…by Scholars Abroad	427
…by Theatre Practitioners	432
3 Zich's World of Words in Czech and in Translation	435
A Brief History of Translating Zich's *Aesthetics*	435
Key Concepts in Translation	439

An Annotated Glossary (Pavel Drábek and David Drozd)	446
Bibliography	466
Editors and Translators	472
Name Index	473

ACKNOWLEDGEMENTS

We dedicate this translation to two distinguished scholars, Eva Stehlíková (1941–2019) and Ivo Osolsobě (1928–2012). Ivo Osolsobě was a leading Czech theatre theorist and dramaturg of the operetta. He was a major proponent of Otakar Zich's theory and brought about a renewed interest in his work. Much more should be said about Osolsobě and we do so in the Afterword of this book. Eva Stehlíková was a theatre scholar and classical philologist and throughout her life was of the firm belief that the "family silver" of Czech theatre theory – that is, Prague School theory and Otakar Zich – should be made available to the wider world in translation. Following our *Theatre Theory Reader: Prague School Writings* (2016), the present book fulfils the promise we have given Eva. Without her conviction, resolution and support we would probably never dare undertake this enterprise…

We would also like to thank a great many colleagues who helped along the way – everyone in a different fashion, but all of them crucially: Veronika Ambros, Henry Bell, Martin Bernátek, Lenka Bystrá, Jules Deering, Campbell Edinborough, Šárka Havlíčková Kysová, Jitka Kapinusová, Dita Lánská, Brian S. Locke, Peter W. Marx, Lizzy McEllan, Mark McEllan, Yana Meerzon, Iva Mikulová, Martina Musilová, Petr Osolsobě, Barbora Příhodová, Martin Revermann, Karolína Stehlíková, Eva Šlaisová and Miloš Štědroň. A special thanks to Professor Marie Dohalská, Otakar Zich's granddaughter and professor of French phonology, who has been immensely supportive of our efforts. And of course to our students with whom we have discussed and flexed Zich's ideas – both in Czech at Masaryk University in Brno and in English at the University of Hull.

We would also like to thank our patient families, partners and friends.

We are very grateful to our peer reviewers, Professor Yana Meerzon (University of Ottawa), Professor Martin Revermann (University of Toronto), Professor Peter W. Marx (University of Cologne) and Professor Veronika Ambros (University of Toronto emerita). Their comments have been invaluable and have helped our work very much.

The book is published as an outcome of the research project *Theatre as Synthesis of Arts: Otakar Zich in Context of Modern Science and Actual Potential of His Concepts* (GA16-20335S, 2016–2018), supported by Czech Science Foundation.

David Drozd and Pavel Drábek

PREFACE

This book brings an English translation of Otakar Zich's book *Estetika dramatického umění* – *Aesthetics of the Dramatic Art*. Zich's book is recognised as the foundation of Czech theatre theory. We believe that the importance of Zich's theory reaches far beyond the local context. We argue that it is one of the earliest books (if not the very first) to bring a systematic theatre theory in the modern sense. Zich's *Aesthetics* is the cornerstone of theatre theory in an international context too. It has established theatre theory as such. Zich was the point of departure for the Prague School's Structural-Functional theatre thinking, which in turn influenced several strands of theatre semiotics. Many of their theoretical concepts and the organic philosophical, aesthetic approach to theatre can be traced back to Zich.

Zich's *Aesthetics* continues to resonate with a number of present-day and historic contexts. At the same time, it is a self-standing integral theory of theatre, which is the principal reason why this book needs to be available in the international English-language discourse. *Aesthetics* is unique also in its analytical method: it not only constructs the theory as a system of discrete statements but also takes the audience's perspective as the fundamental methodological approach. For Zich, the theatre is an event that happens in the shared presence of the performers and the spectators, as perceived by the latter. The distinctive feature of theatre is a focus on human interaction. Zich's ideas about performance space are truly revelatory. Very importantly, theatre is an autonomous art form and his theory is an *aesthetic* theory dedicated to the unique principles of this art.

Aesthetics of the Dramatic Art first appeared in 1931 at a time when Central Europe saw the formation of theatre studies (or Drama) as a discipline. Zich's *Aesthetics* as a theoretical system belongs to this historic context and its aspirations. However, its systemic approach and the level of its theoretical thoroughness and rigour surpasses most other foundational works of its time. Together with Prague School theory, *Aesthetics* also had an immense impact on Czech theatre culture and inspired several generations of theatre practitioners, especially theatre directors, such as the Avant-Garde generation of E. F. Burian, Jindřich Honzl and Jiří Frejka, as well as the artists of later decades – among them Otomar Krejča and Alfréd Radok.

In equal measure, if not more, Zich's *Aesthetics* belongs to a European context of theatre. Zich himself comes from a generation of the great Modernist reformers in the theatre that are conventionally represented by the personalities of Adolphe Appia (1862–1928), Edward Gordon Craig (1872–1966), Max Reinhardt (1873–1943) or Konstantin Stanislavski (1863–1938). All their reforms shared an aspiration to conceive theatrical performance as a coherent whole, with a unified (consistent) aesthetic expression, and to establish the theatrical director as the central organising principle of the conception. These reforms simultaneously – and perhaps inevitably – revisited the question of the sources of acting and of the methods of acting as an artistic endeavour. Zich's *Aesthetics* appeared in 1931, at the very watershed moment between Modernist and Avant-Garde concepts of theatre. Appia's and Craig's texts from the turn of the century often took the form of visionary manifestos that proposed novel theatre aesthetics. In comparison, Zich's book systematically reflects and theorises on those visions in application. Zich wrote at a point in history when the Modernist manifestos had become integral parts of theatre practice.

This book presents Otakar Zich as a theorist and outlines his work and the various approaches to it. *Aesthetics of the Dramatic Art* – it needs to be said – is a work of unpreceded theoretical complexity. It is one of those books that acquires new dimensions with the ever-changing contexts of the modern world. Repeated readings often find the text reframed and *Aesthetics* is able to rise to the new challenges of contemporary art. The rigour and lasting applicability of Zich's theory in the face of new readings and rereadings bring proof of *Aesthetics'* usefulness and validity.

Since its publication in 1931, *Aesthetics* has had a long life of sorts, spanning almost a century, and has accumulated a great number of interpretations and critical commentary. The Introduction offers its readers the essential contextual knowledge to approach the text from the vantage point of their contemporary theory and cultural environments. A brief overview of Zich's life appears towards the end of the Introduction – intentionally placed last. We believe that it is Zich's thinking that should be at the forefront of the interest, and only then his personality and the historical context.

This book's Afterword provides the historical and cultural context of the book's 1931 publication, Zich's inspirations and the developing reception of the book. As such, the Afterword is aimed at a scholarly reader who will approach *Aesthetics* as one of the fundamental texts that has so far been under-researched in the international discourse. The Afterword places *Aesthetics* in the historical context of the formation of theatre studies as a discipline and the establishment of theatre theory in today's sense of the word.

David Drozd, Pavel Drábek, Tomáš Kačer and Josh Overton

INTRODUCTION

OTAKAR ZICH AND HIS AESTHETICS OF THE DRAMATIC ART: INTRODUCING A SEMINAL WORK AFTER A CENTURY

DAVID DROZD, WITH PAVEL DRÁBEK AND JOSH OVERTON

Zich's *Aesthetics of the Dramatic Art*, by itself as well as its English translation, has had a peculiar life. Since it was written, it has been widely read, variously interpreted, admired as visionary but also denounced as past its prime or too conservative. Some find the book immensely thought-provoking, others pedantic. Once you have finished reading this Introduction and delve into the work itself, you will also be starting a new chapter of the book's life and of the afterlife of its creator, Otakar Zich.

Why should you read this book? There are several reasons. First, if you are a theatre practitioner, this book can inspire you to rethink the principles of your creative work. Zich offers an attempt at a reflection – that is, he writes a theory, a retrospective from a distance – but constantly has theatre practice and its makers in mind. In so doing, Zich wishes to enhance creativity by gaining a concrete understanding of its principles. Second: there has recently occurred a certain scepticism towards the broader theories of the theatre and of the arts, which are today shattered into numerous partial trends and lines of thought. In contrast, Zich's approach is so old-school that it does not splinter itself: his thinking tends to integrate observations on the form of a work of art, on the creative process and on the effect it has on the spectator. At the very core of his approach is theatre as an art form, and his thinking is holistic, integral and almost universalist. Third: anyone interested in getting to the roots of theatre theory can start here; it is not always necessary to go back to Aristotle; Zich also builds his theory from the basics. Fourth, there is a purely scholarly reason: Zich practises theory in the strict sense of the word – a Theory that tends to abstraction, intelligent differentiation and systemic thought; at the same time, his theory is pragmatic, succinct, parsimonious and unburdened with unnecessary concepts. It may seem that one of the favourite tools of Zich the aesthetician and logician was Ockham's razor.

For any Czech theatre student – whether a practitioner or a theorist – Zich's *Aesthetics* is certainly one of the first theories to read. It is considered an integral foundation, almost a primer of Czech theatre terminology, and Zich's distinctions – especially those in the opening three chapters – are regarded as the absolute basics. A well-used anecdote sums it up: studying theatre theory from A to Z: from Aristotle to Zich. The question of course remains if the fundamental works on the reading list are being read thoroughly. In this Introduction, we will offer a few ways of reading the book that will help the reader uncover individual layers of Zich's opus, a book not to be read but to be studied.

From an outside perspective Zich remains known only to a narrow group of specialists who are able to read his work in Czech. And let's be frank: there aren't that many people interested in the theatre (let alone theatre theory) to begin with, and the proportion of that group that is sufficiently well-versed in Czech language and culture is vanishingly small. For an international theatre scholar Otakar Zich still remains a name in a footnote. The exception that proves this rule can be found with the only notable mention of Zich in the English language. In 1980 Keir Elam in one of the most influential books of theatre semiotics – *The Semiotics of Theatre and Drama* (Routledge, 1980) – makes a decisive declaration:

> The year 1931 is an important date in the history of theatre studies. Until that time dramatic poetics – the descriptive science of the drama and theatrical performance – had made little substantial progress since its Aristotelian origins. [...] That year, however, saw the publication of two studies in Czechoslovakia which radically changed the prospects for the scientific analysis of theatre and drama: Otakar Zich's *Aesthetics of the Art of Drama* and Jan Mukařovský's 'An Attempted Structural Analysis of the Phenomenon of the Actor'. [...] Zich's *Aesthetics* is not explicitly structuralist but exercised a considerable influence on later semioticians, particularly in its emphasis on the necessary interrelationship in the theatre between heterogeneous but interdependent systems. [...] Zich does not allow special prominence to any one of the components involved: he refuses, particularly, to grant automatic dominance to the written text, which takes its place in the system of systems making up the total dramatic representation. (Elam 2005: 5)

On the one hand Elam asserts that Zich is a central figure for theatre theory, but on the other, his knowledge of Zich only derived from secondary sources and depended inevitably on the prevailing narrow reading of his work. Zich's *Aesthetics of the Dramatic Art* (1931) has mostly received mention in connection with the Prague School, especially with its theatre theory. In this way Zich is perceived as a forerunner of the Functional-Structuralist school of thought, or a link between nineteenth-century Czech aesthetics and the modern Structuralist or semiotic theory. This may be a plausible and logical approach, but it certainly is not the only one.

There is a strong link between the Prague Linguistic Circle (PLC) and Otakar Zich's thought that appeared very clearly when we were editing the volume *Theatre Theory Reader: Prague School Writings* (Drozd et al. 2016) given the number of allusions and references to Zich's concepts. We even considered including some selections of Zich's *Aesthetics* in our reader. But fragments can never capture the whole with sufficient accuracy and any selection necessarily distorts the overall image. In the end we decided to translate Zich's *magnum opus* in its totality and publish it as a stand-alone volume. It is only now, when Zich's work is finally available as a whole, that readers can judge for themselves the veracity of the declared table-turning change that the *Aesthetics* brought about on its publication in 1931 – a landmark of modern theatre theory and aesthetics of art.

THE LAYOUT OF THE *AESTHETICS*: ORGANISATION OF THE BOOK

Otakar Zich (1879–1934) was trained as a logician and mathematician, and later added musicology and aesthetics to his repertoire. It is no surprise then, to find that his book is organised strictly and methodically. Zich himself introduces the book laconically:

> This book falls into three parts: the first, entitled "The Concept of Dramatic Art", is basically methodological. The second, called "The Principle of Dramaticity", contains predominantly aesthetic reflections, despite the above-mentioned proximity of both approaches, while the third part, named "The Principle of Stylisation", is dominated by theoretical or art-disciplinary reflections. (58 below)

Zich remains true to his word. In the first part of his book he defines theatre and discusses the dramatic art as a unique art form with its own special laws, logic and conceptual framework. In the second part Zich discusses the specific creative work of individual roles in the process of theatrical creation – the artistic roles of the playwright, the actor, the stage director (and the scenographer), and then examines the specific role of the theatre composer (of opera in particular). In the third part Zich focuses on the spectator's experience and perception, with a special focus on realism, stylisations and theatrical genres.

Zich's method is inductive – starting with simple premises, claims and assertions (similar to basic mathematical axioms), with introspective thoughts and reflections, or with mental experiments (such as "Let us imagine watching an actor whose language we don't understand..."), and then moving on to greater complexity. In this way he builds his entire theoretical and aesthetic system step by step. Zich doesn't approach the theatre from an ideological point of departure; he treats his subject descriptively and analytically. In his own words:

> This is a consequence of the method of *scientific aesthetics*, which derives its findings inductively from the material given by experience, rather than deductively from some *a priori* philosophical principles, as speculative aesthetics does. (57 below)

In its structure Zich's book is less of an aesthetic essay, but rather a "classical" philosophical treatise organised in numbered paragraphs or sections, chapters and subchapters arranged in an exact hierarchy – not unlike the German treatises of Hegel or Kant. Zich approaches the theatre as a subject worthy of treatment in the genre of high idealist, systematically explained, and scientific philosophy.

Zich's commitment to creating a self-standing, integral system comes with a frustrating feature – an almost complete absence of references to other criticism. Early on Zich admits to his inspiration in earlier and contemporaneous scholarship, but he proclaims confidently:

> As for the detailed elaboration of this design in the second part, **the conception and arrangement of the material are my own**. Factually it does not contain – as that would be entirely impossible in a systematic study – only my own thoughts, especially when it comes to spoken drama, which has recently been thoroughly theorised. Nonetheless, specialists will appreciate how many new thoughts and concepts of my own there are here. (*our emphasis*) (56 below)

Zich felt no need to start with an exhaustive critical review of existing scholarship on drama and theatre. This further confirms his commitment to, first, creating a holistic theoretical system that would build on its own principles, and second, Zich expected his reader to be non-specialist, un-versed in aesthetics. (There were very few of that sort in the Czech lands in his time.) Rather, Zich wrote for practical theatre makers or theatre afficionados. The book was to help the reader understand the principles of the theatre makers' own creative work and art, and help the spectator cultivate their theatrical experience. (It is symptomatic that almost all early reviews of *Aesthetics* mention the exhortation that the book should be on the shelf of every actor!)

Nowadays, Zich's book is a challenging, though in some ways foundational theoretical treatise. Despite the passage of time, the exhortation that the book should be read by every actor and theatre maker still stands. When we start reading this book with our present-day mindset, the reasons become clear.

ESTABLISHING THE SPECIFIC GENRE OF "THE DRAMATIC ART"

Zich intentionally starts his book in a naive-sounding and almost banal way:

> Spoken drama and opera – in short, the dramatic work – is what we perceive (see and hear) in the course of a performance in the theatre (60 below).

Today, this opening assertion – one of Zich's foundational axioms – may sound perfectly self-evident. But with this claim Zich revolutionises the incumbent thinking and foregrounds the recipients' perspective. Gradually, with the support of thorough argumentation, Zich rejects the dominant notion (which still reoccurs nowadays) that the theatre is no more than the production of dramatic literature. By the same token, Zich proposes *the dramatic art* as a framing category that brings together spoken drama and sung drama (a term Zich uses as a broad category that includes most prominently the opera), because they share the same fundamental feature: all of these genres and art forms are live works of art performed in a theatre space before a live audience. This feature is much more essential than the relatively partial differences, such as the actors speaking in one, but singing in the other. In this way, Zich wants to put to bed the belief that the theatre – narrowly understood as dramatic literature or poetry – belongs to the discipline of literary studies while the opera is a subject for musicology. It follows logically then that Zich's book proposes a new aesthetic discipline. He calls it *theoretical dramaturgy* and declares the dramatic art as its specific object of study. As such, the book as a whole can be read as an attempt to establish a new paradigm of critical thinking about the theatre. This theoretical approach does not depend on other disciplines but derives its principles from within the theatre in performance as an autonomous art.

Zich's paradigm shift shows most controversially in his view of the dramatic text because he refuses to accept it – just like the score of an opera – as an autonomous work of art. He argues that "a literary or a musical text can at best be called a potential artwork. [...] We have shown, however, that the 'dramatic text' is only a partial record of the dramatic work" (67 below). For Zich, a work of art is something created intentionally – that is, a logically structured/composed whole, while a literary drama is rather fragmentary: it cannot be taken for art in its own right since the images that the process of mere reading evokes are too arbitrary and subjective. If we take as a point of departure Zich's commitment to approach spoken drama and sung drama as one art form, the following comparison arises: Do we commonly read an opera score and claim that we have an aesthetic enjoyment of it? How is it then that the readers of a playscript immediately turn into theatre specialists? For Zich then, the dramatic text is primarily a text intended for a professional reader (the actor, the stage director or other theatre creatives) – a reader capable of "theatrical reading". But the final, fully fledged work of art is the performance and nothing but the performance.

Zich goes against the narrow understanding of drama as literature, a trend culminating at the turn of the nineteenth century when playscripts were published as books with lengthy descriptive notes to facilitate their reading. Some playwrights (Ibsen and especially Shaw) indulge in extending and novelistically elaborating their stage directions and comments, while editors of drama classics – be it Shakespeare or the ancient Greeks or Romans – follow the same trend and insert long-winded, descriptive stage directions. In his rejection of this trend, Zich is truly progressive, understanding the dramatic text as if it were a modern stage script – a mere technical tool, a partial record of the authorial vision or intention, which comes to completion and full creation only in a live performance. This is not to deny the author-playwright their autonomy but rather the opposite: by approaching them as a dramatic author (i.e., an author writing for the theatre), their role in the artistic process is strengthened. This also allows Zich to argue for the unique dramatic talent of the playwright, as opposed to the talents of a poet, a musical composer or a visual artist.

Treating together spoken drama and sung drama as a single performative art form allows Zich to transfer observations from one to the other on the basis of their differences and their similarities. The comparisons of spoken drama and sung drama are especially productive in the first chapter where Zich argues that "acting is not a reproductive art". This assertion logically follows from some of his axioms: if theatre is more than the mere staging of the written letter of a dramatic text (i.e., an interpretation in a musicological sense), it needs to have an autonomous artistic creator – inevitably the actor. This begs the question: to what extent is the actor in an inferior position to the text, comparable to the interpretive musician in relation to the musical score? In his elaboration of the parallel, Zich uses it inventively to deepen his findings. This allows him to identify the minute distinction between the performing musician and the performing actor as to the extent of the autonomy of their creativity.

THE AUDIENCE PERSPECTIVE: A SYNCHRONOUS THEORY

Analysing the theatrical performance from the audience perspective – from the point of view of the spectator – makes Zich's *Aesthetics of the Dramatic Art* a theory in the truest sense of the word: a theory that operates within a single moment of time – a synchronous theory, independent of history. As Ivo Osolsobě points out in his essay "Sémiotika sémiotika…" (2002 [1981]):

220–221), it was customary in the nineteenth century to interpret the theatre through the lens of its history, minimising direct theoretical approaches to the art form in favour of analyses of historical phenomena. This is a trend that starts as far back as Aristotle's *Poetics* and occurs still today – a random glance at any bookshelf of so-called theatre theory will prove the point. We run away from theory to history more often than we dare admit. Naturally, no theatre theory can operate entirely outside of history. Every author operates within their environments and their horizons. (In relation to Zich, we discuss this in greater detail in the Afterword.) Notwithstanding, Zich's work continues to inspire and remains unique in its theoretical rigour and refinement that abstracts (moves independently) from concrete historic varieties of theatre. In that, we argue, Zich's theory can serve as a useful insight to any performance and theatre practitioner, artist and theorist, irrespective of where and when they are.

Zich turns the period perspective upside down and derives all his observations from the viewpoint of the immediate spectator and their real-time perception of actual theatre performance. The historical perspective, the development of the theatre, its art forms and its cultural memory enter Zich's discussions as well, of course, but only in the second and third parts of the book. Nonetheless, Zich incorporates individual historic examples into the conceptual framework he has established in the first part (in chapters 1 to 3). He uses these as minor case studies to instantiate partial theoretical issues. Osolsobě, a prominent Zich scholar, highlights this as a major accomplishment of abstract thinking and Zich's logical mind, seeing it as a manifestation of Zich's mathematical and musicological background. Such an approach stands out uniquely, not only for the time in which it was conceived but more generally too.

THEATRE AS A SYNTHESIS OF THE ARTS: CRITIQUE OF THE CONCEPT

Zich's Chapter 2 discusses the relation between the theatre – or *the dramatic art*, as he calls it – and other arts. Following his methodology and strategy of argumentation, established in the opening chapter, Zich debunks the widespread synthetic theory of theatre, best known in Wagner's concept of the *Gesamtkunstwerk* (or total work of art). Notably, Zich does not reject the theory wholesale but argues the limits of its validity. He states that as far as the creation of the dramatic work of art is concerned, the individual creative building blocks made by distinct artists come together bit by bit. However, the work of art is complete only as the homogenous aesthetic experience of the spectators. Our "analytical" understanding of the theatrical experience (the act of spectating) – one that breaks the work of art up into its individual components – cannot derive from our knowledge of how it was created, bit by bit, in the first place. The dramatic work of art – the theatrical performance – is an organic whole. Zich is very particular about distinguishing between the two perspectives – the process of creation and the act of spectating.

Zich argues that individual tributary arts that collaborate on the theatrical experience – literature, music, visual arts (design, painting, architecture) and acting – cannot just smoothly blend: they always need to undergo transformation, adapt to one another, respond mutually and link up. With his attention to the inner structure of the dramatic work of art, Zich comes close to a structuralist approach to the theatre. The work of art is more than a sum of its parts: it is the specific way of their blending, their mutual relationships and interconnections. The inner hierarchy of the work in which the *dramatic* (i.e., *actorly*) component becomes the dominant force, coordinating all the others to a great extent. This leads to what he calls *theatrical paradoxes*, intimately or intuitively well-known to all theatre makers, but repeatedly surprising to many artists from other disciplines tributary to the theatre (discussed in the second part of Chapter 2), that all the contributing arts must transcend and relent their autonomies for the sake of the dramatic work.

Zich's rejection of the synthetic theory of the theatre is more than a mere part of the period debate on the Wagnerian *Gesamtkunstwerk*. Zich's polemical claims equally apply to many later theories of the twentieth century, which simply assert the multimedia, composite character of the theatre without a greater elaboration of the links between individual "media". To claim that the theatre is a synthesis of various arts is an inefficient and theoretically unproductive approach (see overview of the discussion in Balme 2008: 195–208). Zich's refutation leads to his first theory that methodically treats theatre as a homogeneous perception (the theatrical experience), an aesthetic event practised and perceived in real time. In this way Zich anticipates the *performative turn* and the interest in *performance analysis* in Western theatre scholarship of the 1970s. Theatre as a homogeneous aesthetic perception, Zich's key concept, is the subject of the next chapter.

AN ANALYTICAL APPROACH TO THE THEATRE

Chapter 3, entitled "Analytical Theory", is doubtless Zich's most original contribution and remains highly inspirative to this day. In this chapter Zich takes the most introspective approach. In a sense, he carries out a phenomenological analysis of the spectators' perception, identifies the layers and conceptualises the process of making meaning on the spectator's part – in the viewer's mind. This part represents the methodological core of Zich's *Aesthetics of the*

Dramatic Art. Drifting off when reading this part renders the entire book pretty much pointless.

Zich breaks up the spectators' perception into individual fixed and dynamic (or mutable) components. Gradually, he clarifies and refines commonly used, intuitive terms such as *action, dramatic persona* (character) or *dramaticity*. Zich distinguishes between the spectator's percept – which has objective causes in the action on stage but is perceived subjectively – and the ideas or thoughts that arise in consequence – and these exist solely subjectively in the spectator's mind. In order to do so effectively, Zich introduces the term *conceptual image* (or *image*, for short; *významová představa*). This image is what arises in our mind in response to the question "What is it that we are perceiving?". In the case of art, the question also can be: "What does the thing we perceive represent?". Zich's Czech expression *významová představa* (conceptual, mental or meaning image) is hard to translate. It derives from the German term *Bedeutungsvorstellung* (meaning or semantic imagining). In this, Zich is not entirely original, but his own justification and usage are. In both German and Czech, the term has two components: *meaning* and *mental image*. English moves between the corresponding words *image, idea* or sometimes even *concept*. Here Zich comes close to semiotics – the assertion that an image in our brain carries a certain *significance* or meaning. At the same time Zich respects that this *image* exists only in the recipient's mind, i.e., subjectively. As such, Zich approaches *meaning* not as objective, as something communicated to the spectator and existing autonomously, but strictly as something the recipients (the spectators) actively create themselves. Much more than in any other semiotic theories of the theatre, Zich takes the spectator/recipient as an active co-creator of the meaning – and that meaning is always partly individualised.

Before Zich introduces this conceptual distinction, he works with the preliminary opposition *dramatic character | actor* (*dramatická osoba | herec*). However, a *dramatic character* can be viewed as something closely associated with the dramatic text. Intuitively we often keep referring to it: when reading a play we speak of a role, and when watching a performance we refer to what the actor presented on stage as a role as well, and we do so without distinguishing sufficiently between the *dramatic persona* written in the play text and that involved in a live performance.

In 1981, Ivo Osolsobě wrote with a certain panache:

> Skutečným triumfem Zichovy sémiotiky je však objev, který nám zpětně připadá bezmála jako samozřejmost, který však samozřejmost není a ještě dlouho nebude. Naopak ještě dlouho bude těžko pochopitelný sémiotikům, dokonce i sémiotikům divadla, přestože je to problém ryze sémiotický a specificky divadelní. V podstatě jde o něco velmi jednoduchého: o skutečně důslednou aplikaci rozlišovací síly Zichových pojmových

dvojic "představující/představované" a "významová představa technická/významová představa obrazová" na sémiotiku herectví. Výsledkem nemohlo být nic jiného než stanovení nové, pro sémiotiku herectví specifické pojmové dvojice herecká postava/ dramatická osoba. (Osolsobě 2002 (1981): 231)
[The true triumph of Zich's semiotics is his discovery that may seem self-evident to us nowadays but is far from being so and will remain far from being so for a very long time. It will continue to be hard to grasp to many semioticians and even theatre semioticians, although it's a purely semiotic and specifically theatrical problem. The discovery – or rather, distinction – that Zich makes resides in principle in something very simple: a true and methodical application of the analytical power of Zich's dual terms *the representing / the represented* (*představující / představované*) and *the technical image / the referential image* (*významová představa technická / obrazová*) onto the semiotics of acting. The outcome of this application couldn't be anything less than the establishment of the novel dual terms that are specific to the semiotics of acting, namely *actor figure / dramatic persona* (*herecká postava / dramatická osoba*).][1]

The groundbreaking impact of Zich's concept is in precisely distinguishing individual layers of the actor's creative work and the spectators' perception of the actor's performance. Zich identifies the actor as the creator who uses their bodily material to form the *actor figure*. On the basis of watching this actor figure, the spectator imagines (or creates the image) of the *dramatic persona*. Zich establishes this binary of the *technical* and the *referential* image in Chapter 3 and carries on applying it as a key point of distinction throughout the rest of the book. Occasionally, Zich's own usage of the binary may appear insufficiently sharp when applied to various instances. It is helpful therefore, to emphasise some of the basic principal features. First, Zich finds it crucial and unique that the actor creates their work of art from themself – however paradoxical this may sound. At the same time Zich stresses that there is an essential difference between the actor and the actor figure (i.e., the actor's creative work). Zich elaborates on the importance of the actor using their own personal experience in creating the actor figure. But he also rejects the naive psychological assumption that equates the actor with the actor figure – i.e., the creator with their creation. It follows from here that the actor figure exists objectively while the dramatic persona comes into existence in the spectator's mind, in response to perceiving the actor figure on stage. The actor figure is then an objective phenomenon, while the dramatic persona is a mental image that exists purely as a subjective one. This image is naturally not entirely arbitrary but its formation necessarily incorporates each spectator's personal experiences and associations. This difference between the two

---

[1] Unless stated otherwise all translations are ours and all footnotes are ours.

concepts also stands out in Zich's considered selection of the names: the actor *figure* (*postava*) and the dramatic *persona* (*osoba*). A *figure* in itself suggests something formed, constructed, shaped and intentionally created and built. In contrast, a *persona* evokes a certain degree of psychological complexity that the spectator's *mental image* may acquire on account of the spectator's own experience and imagination. In so doing Zich rejects the naive ideas that appear every now and then from spectators thrilled by the overwhelming performance of an actor: "That Hamlet was so real…". For Zich, only the spectator's mental image can be truly *real* (or genuine), mobilised by an intensive (excellent, accomplished, professional, etc.) actor performance. Treating the actor figure as an objective structure allows Zich to elaborate further: not only how the spectator perceives this figure, but also how the actor themself perceives it.

Referring to the actor as one would to a material should be seen as a purely technical and terminological approach. Throughout the book Zich avoids any prejudicial and primitive views, occasionally found with stage directors who understand theatre making directively and authoritatively, reducing actors to a mere material. It is worth noting: while Modernism is a point that establishes the stage director as the supreme and autonomous creator of the work of theatre, criticism often forgets that this is also the historical moment when modern acting as an art with its theory appears. In this way Zich's contributions to both the modern theory of acting and of stage directing, and the complementarity and synergy of the two disciplines (a rarity for theorists past and present) are monumental and – should one ever be fortunate enough to encounter them – undeniable.

Of course, Zich acknowledges the decisive position of the dramatic text in the creation of the actor figure, but he uses the term *dramatic persona* only reluctantly when it comes to the play text. It follows logically from the above theses that the dramatic text determines the dramatic character only in a fragmentary way, as a potential; a text is merely a set of guidelines or a blueprint for the actor's creative work, and it is only the actor figure that constitutes the artefact as such. The subtlety and methodical integrity of Zich's distinctions appear most clearly when he differentiates between the playwright's and the actor's work in the formation of the actor figure: the playwright provides the words, while the acoustic delivery (including the intonation) is created by the actor. Zich further applies the distinction between the *technical* and the *referential* image to other components of the dramatic artefact such as the costumes, the set (the scene), music and others. Given that in the other components of theatre there is no comparable conflation of the creator and their material, Zich's findings may appear less surprising. But his accuracy in making a difference between the factual (objective) and the imagined (referential) part of any given component is decisive.

In Chapter 3, Zich's discursive method stands out most clearly as he constructs a line of argument from a continuous sequence of theses. The continuity and logical links can make it hard to isolate individual points from their place in the sequence. This difficulty aside, it is Zich's logic of argumentation that makes his book particularly remarkable.

It is perhaps worth commenting on one of the most refined definitions of the dramatic art, which Zich deduces from a series of partial analyses:

> *The dramatic work* is a work of art presenting interaction of personas through the actors' onstage interplay. (103 below)

This characteristically dense sentence captures the very core of Zich's theory. We can divide it into individual elementary assertions. For Zich, the dramatic work (or the theatre as such) is an art. It is remarkable how rarely this aspect receives a mention in the 21st-century definitions. This art *presents interaction of personas*: it follows that it is a *mimetic* art. Simultaneously Zich broadly identifies the subject of this art as *the interaction of personas*. Human interaction is Zich's central category in his concept of *dramaticity*. He dedicates lengthy passages to clarifying what is merely involuntary action and what is interaction in the specific sense of the word. In this respect, Zich is strictly anthropological in that he approaches interaction as intentional, conscious action of beings. In his own words:

> A persona's ostensive activity intended to have and having an impact on another persona shall be called **interaction** (*jednání*). (86 below)

Dramatic interaction is its special variant: it is *ostensive*, i.e., directly available to senses and perception and accessible to the spectator; it is manifest, tangible action. In this way, Zich joins the long tradition starting with Aristotle. Zich's emphasis on interaction and his own concept of action as such correspond with the period reception of Aristotle's assertion that "the first principle and, as it were, the soul of tragedy is the plot [i.e., the imitation of the action], and second in importance is character" (*Poetics* 2018: 105; 1450a). Today, Aristotle's definition is generally understood in normative terms, as prescribing what tragedy (i.e., theatre) is as such. Zich, on the contrary, uses the notion of interaction to specify what the dramatic art is within the broad category of theatre. Unlike later classicist poetics, Zich's point is not to normatively prescribe correct subject matter for certain genres but to capture the specifics of the art form and to derive it from its unique material, i.e., from the performing human: the actor. With a remarkably Aristotelian logic, Zich makes a statement that can be rephrased in today's terms very simply: the dramatic art is uniquely placed to portray human interaction due to its unique material – the human being and the human body behaving intentionally within a situation. This paraphrase consciously leaves out the word *theatre* in favour of Zich's term *the dramatic art*. Since Zich is not prescriptive in his definition, he recognises that *theatre* is structurally and thematically broader than *the dramatic art*. The theatre can be perfectly undramatic – in sidelining action, foregrounding poetry, songs, dance, static images and so on – but it is the specific focus on *the portrayal of human interaction* that makes the difference.

Zich's definition appears timeless. However, significantly, the period context appears towards its end when he refers to the means of representation as *actors' onstage interplay*. In the context of his entire theory it is worth pointing out that he understands the stage (or scene, as he prefers to call it) as principally the end-on stage that is architectonically framed by the proscenium arch, separating the actors from the audience. His aesthetic theory requires an aesthetic distance between the artefact and the recipient. It is worth observing that Zich is writing at a time when the *crisis of representation* was far from a talking point in scholarship. So he may assert uncontentiously that *dramatic art is a mimetic art*. This is a gauntlet thrown at the reader's feet to pick up the debate of *representation crisis* and judge how present-day performative theories and postdramatic aesthetics interact with Zich's claims about the specifics of *the dramatic art*.

The refinement and pregnancy of Zich's 1931 definition of the dramatic art stands out in full when compared with the notorious and much-cited definition by Eric Bentley, who in his 1964 book *The Life of Drama* defines the dramatic situation as follows: "A impersonates B while C looks on" (1965: 150). Bentley's definition has served as a point of departure as late as 2008 in Christopher Balme's *Cambridge Introduction to Theatre Studies* (Balme 2008: 2). This elementary and unhelpfully reductive definition can pass only as a mere and rather intuitive approximation, while Zich's incisive definition, predating Bentley's by well over 30 years, sets the foundation for an entirely novel theory of drama and theatre.

OSTENTION AND INNER TACTILE PERCEPTION

Zich's complex definition above does not include two key terms that play a crucial role in the first part of the book, developing his theory: *ostension* and *inner tactile perception*.

When Zich describes our perception of the theatrical performance and discusses the mental images arising in our mind, he asserts that the images are *ostensive* (*názorné*). Similarly, he asserts that interaction is a persona's *ostensive action* that has an impact on another persona. *Názorný* (or *názornost*) is a peculiar word that is hard to translate into English. Our choice of the word *ostensive* (or *ostension*, respectively) suggests that the theatre is an art that is directly available to the senses – which is the literal meaning of *názorný*. In a clumsy wording, it stands for "made available to sensual perception" – with imperfect synonyms such as *legible, graphic, demonstrative, manifest, evident, clear, visible* or *recognisable*, some of which tackle only one part of the word's significance. Zich also asserts that the images (or ideas) that the art evokes in our minds are *ostensive* – i.e., distinct in that they relate directly to concrete sensual percepts and to real-world phenomena.

The second key term is *inner tactile perception*. Zich often discusses the perception of art as such – which continued to be his central topic throughout his scholarly work. At times he abbreviates it to what we can hear and see (i.e., as audio-visual perception), but where necessary, Zich adds a third aspect – the inner tactile perception. Inner tactile perception plays a significant role in the spectator's relationship to the actor figure. In his pioneering introspective analyses Zich points out that as spectators we can not only hear and see the actor figure, but we also empathise with the actor and their bodily sensations – such as their bodily tensions and efforts. We experience these by means of our inner tactile perceptions. This inner tactile experience (or body image) plays a key part in our enjoyment of the theatrical experience. Similarly, the actor also perceives "from within" the actor figure they are creating through this "sixth" sense. Zich articulates this crucial aspect of the theatrical experience from both the spectator's and the creator's (actor's) point of view and introduces the concept of *inner tactile perception* to account for this psychological process.

Zich's emphasis on *ostension* – that is, the sharp, concrete formation of the theatrical experience – closely relates to *inner tactile perception*. The relationship is firmly rooted in the awareness that all inner tactile perceptions are tangible and physically concrete, which makes them inevitably ostensive. For a spectator to "feel" and empathise, for example, with the heartbreak of an actor's dramatic persona (e.g., King Lear), a simple explanation that the actor is in pain will not do. They must perceive that pain with multiple senses, see the actor shake, hear the discomfort in their speech, etc. The spectator must use their *inner tactile perception* (consciously or not) to "sense" the persona's feelings just as much as (if not more than) they intellectualise the experience.

These two terms reflect Zich's focus on the reception of art (spectator focus) as well as his psychological training – greatly influenced by William James's theories by way of Zich's teacher František Krejčí. *Ostension* and *inner tactile perception* are not limited to visual or auditory features – as later semiotic theory often believes. The ostensive (tangible) quality of the theatrical performance engages another channel that directly relates to the fact that it always happens here and now and it needs to be perceived here and now in physical, bodily terms. This psychological trait counters much of mainstream semiotic theory and shouldn't be neglected. Taking inspiration from Zich, Ivo Osolsobě started to develop his theory of ostension in the 1960s as *communication without signs*, as a direct reaction to and attack on the overwhelmingly linguistic paradigm of semiotics that treats everything as if it were a language (see Osolsobě 2002 [1967] or 1979).

Clearly, there are multiple ways of reading Zich's theory, even when it comes to the opening three chapters. We could emphasise the period context and the conditions Zich was working within, reading the book as a testimony of a certain type of theatre. Or, we can prefer a more semiotic and universalising reading and proclaim the psychological traits as period residues that have outlived their time. Or, we can relate to Zich's effort to approach the theatre in a complex fashion – bringing together not only audio-visual communication but also the inner tactile layer of the experience. This reading of Zich anticipates present-day cognitive theories of embodiment and bodily co-existence in the performance space.

THE SPECIALISED SKILLS OF THEATRE MAKERS

The second part of Zich's *Aesthetics*, called "The Principle of Dramaticity", focuses on individual creators involved in the *dramatic work of art*. He dedicates chapters, in turn, to the playwright, the actor and the stage director – who receives two chapters as the second treats the scenic space, effectively discussing scenography – and finally to the theatre composer (in opera and other types of musical drama), effectively exploring the potential and function of music within the dramatic art. Zich takes as his point of departure his conviction that each artist needs to "think in their own material". The artist is therefore obliged to know their material (their medium), its potential and inner logic (its properties) and make full use of them in their creative work.

Throughout his analyses Zich continues to deploy the terminological apparatus he has established in the first part of his book, using it to get a more analytical and accurate grasp of well-known aspects of theatrical creation. His terminological apparatus allows him to come up with much more precise formulations of theatre's inner logic. While Zich initially gets support from his preceding introspections and abstract thought experiments and psychological analysis, here he introduces anecdotal testimonies from concrete theatre makers. This helps him redirect and refine his understanding of what constitutes the dramatic art. As a matter of fact, by discussing the *dramaticity* (*dramatičnost*; the specifically dramatic quality) of individual components of the theatre, he articulates the functions of individual theatre makers involved in the process of creation and identifies the specific skills (or talents) of these creative artists.

The second part of the book dedicated to the principle of dramaticity covers more than two thirds of the entire length. It would be counterproductive and redundant to give a detailed account of all the paths of Zich's ruminations here (whatever one might say about Zich's qualities, a failure to go into detail is not one of them). It may seem that Zich takes his point of departure from the period predilection for psychological realism in the theatre. This is not entirely fair as he has a great sense of stylisation in art, especially when it comes to the opera. Notwithstanding all objections to his period conditionality, Zich proffers thought-provoking and inspiring observations about the playwright, the actor, the stage director (and scenographer) and the theatre composer. Many of these discussions are among the earliest attempts ever at theorising the point in question – particularly when it comes to modern acting or the scenic space. Let us mention only a few – not just because the second part of the book is simply too long, but also for another reason: in comparison to the general distinctions and concepts of the first part, the second part with its focus on the creative processes derives much more from Zich's personal, critical, practical and artistic experience. Apart from elaborating on additional concepts, Zich also offers in-depth reflections on creative practice. These reflections are designed to engage the readers and provoke them to take their own standpoint – whether they might agree or not. It is worth noting that Zich's approach is born from the potentially narrow vantage point of his own work and his context but his writing always factors in the knowledge that he may be only partially correct on any given subject, suggesting that a reader ought to take what parts of his work they find impactful and discard the rest – an offer that history perhaps took him up on a little too eagerly.

Zich follows the ideal creation of the dramatic work – not just from the first read-through of a play, but from the playwright's initial idea, continuing with the firmed-up dramatic text, the casting process, the rehearsals, up to the opening night. Inner tactile perception accompanies the process at every step. In relation to creative artists, he refers to the term as *mental transfiguration (předuševnění)* – a notion that allows him to articulate the specific skill to capture and imagine the persona of someone else – grasping it not just empathically (through emotions) but also in relation to their ideas, efforts, intentions and aspirations. Mental transfiguration allows the creative artist to conceive of the persona as a physical being – specifically thanks to inner tactile perception or inner tactile imagination. Mental transfiguration is not metaphysical, let alone mystical thought operation but a very specific skill – the creative mind's ability that is crucially connected with the bodily experience. To a great extent it is very much a physiological process. In the case of the actor who is creating from within their own body as their unique material, Zich introduces a logical addition to mental transfiguration: *transbodiment (přetělesnění)*.

The skill of mental transfiguration relates very closely to Zich's premise that may seem counterintuitive: the playwright's creative work doesn't start with the text but with the dramatic situation – or more precisely, with the author's vision (or mental image) of a dramatic situation. In this way Zich completes his own conception of the dramatic text which he conceives of as a tool (or medium) between the playwright's imagination (into which the playwright mentally transfigures) and that which eventually materialises on stage. This is his ultimate debunking of the literary notion of "the dramatic poet" as a master of the word and of poetry. Against it Zich places the necessary skill of theatrical and dramatic perception and imagination as the playwright's principal competency. It is worth pointing out that Zich is analytically so thorough that he distinguishes between several types of playwrights – identifying the visual type, who tends to see the imagined situations in visual terms, and the auditory type, who tends to hear the imagined lines (however, not lines as poetry, but lines as situational dialogue).

In the opening chapter of the book, Zich observes that acting is an autonomous creative art with a unique position in the theatre. Its uniqueness rests in the fact that it is the only art participating in the theatrical process that does *not* exist outside of the theatre as an art form. Zich deduces that acting is theatre's essential component. Chapter 5, devoted to the actor's creative work, further develops his thesis of acting's unique autonomy, analysing its creative variety. Zich discusses the expressive potential of what he calls *mimics (mimika)* – a word he uses as a catch-all for all nonverbal expression from facial mimicry to body language. He also observes that *mimics* is uniquely placed to portray the characters' (dramatic personas') inner processes, emotions and aspirations (or efforts) – because mimic portrayal is always ostensive: externalised, articulated and available to view. Zich argues that *mimics'* ability to convey emotions and aspirations makes it dramatic in the purest sense of the word. *Mimics* refers to the actor's outer work (which is perceptible to the senses). Zich proceeds to the inner processes of the actor's psychological work, culminating in Zich's elaboration of what he calls *the inner logic of actorly thinking (logika hereckého myšlení)*. In the Czech context, this first systematic conceptualisation of acting includes a number of considerations such as an attempt at actor typology or an identification of the sources of actors' inspiration for their creative work. It is worth noting that Zich is writing at a time when the first modern theories of acting are just starting to appear – Stanislavski's landmark book *My Life in Art* appeared first in English in 1924, while his decisive treatise *An Actor's Work* came out in 1938. Naturally, Zich does not present a concrete acting method. While his discussions depart from the psychological acting styles of the turn of the 19th century, his theory can be seen as a basis for an analysis of the fundamental principles of various acting methods and styles in general.

The creative work of the stage director falls into two points – or tasks, as Zich prefers to call them: the construction of the dramatic action (or onstage happenings) and the construction of the scenic space. He dedicates a chapter to each of the two. The stage director's first task pertains to the construction of situations and its necessary layers: the layer of the actors' action and interaction in time. The stage director's duty is to arrange and coordinate this interaction in regards to its tempo, rhythm and dynamics. For that reason Zich metaphorically refers to the stage director as *director-conductor* (*režisér-dirigent*). The second task of the stage director relates to the performance space – from its structure and arrangement, through the use of stage properties, to the actors' blocking and movement in the space. From today's perspective we could say that this approach brings together scenography and the blocking. Zich refers to the function of the stage director in this task as *director-scenic* (*režisér-scénik*).

It is especially in relation to the actors' movement in the scenic space that Zich goes far beyond a mere catalogue of potential stage movement towards uncovering more general principles. He starts with a thought experiment of sorts – trying to describe the inner logic of the actor's movement in the empty space on the end-on (proscenium arch) type of stage. Gradually, he discovers compositional principles relating to the actor's points of entry on the stage or the actor's position upstage or downstage. At the same time Zich analyses the topic painstakingly in dynamic terms – considering not only the actor's movement but also the speed, tempo, continuity or accentuation of the moves. By considering an imaginary empty space – and an abstract space at that – Zich transcends the limitations of the psychological-realistic types of staging, which does, on occasion, narrow down his observations. In the case of spatial movement, the opposite is true: Zich deploys surprising metaphors and expressions to describe the dynamics of individual arrangements, moments and spatial compositions, referring to the dramatic persona as a *centre of force* whose intensity can vary in relation to the actor figure's position on the stage (on the scene) and with it its relative significance for the dramatic action. Zich calls the relations between individual personas *lines of force* that expand and contract within the space. For Zich, the dramatic scene (i.e., the stage in performance) is a *field of force*. Such physical metaphors derived from industry practice and have much in common with the technical language that Avant-Garde stage directors were starting to use at the time. While Zich remained quite sceptical to the burgeoning Avant-Garde, a closer look clearly suggests that his analyses are remarkably similar to Sergei Eisenstein's (1898–1948) concept of the *mise-en-scène* as spatial metaphor composition that dates back to the 1930s. (Unfortunately his writings on theatre were published only in the 1960s in Russian, thus English-speaking academia understands the concept of mise-en-scène only as a part of Eisenstein's film theory, while in the Czech context Eisenstein's theory connects Zich with modern theatre.)

Zich's abstract thinking shows itself in its supreme power. It is highly unlikely that Zich would have influenced or been influenced by the Avant-Gardists. The dynamism of the stage space was the period's writing on the wall that occupied Modernist and Avant-Garde thinkers and practitioners transnationally, starting from Adolphe Appia (1862–1928) and Edward Gordon Craig (1872–1966) to Vsevolod Emilyevich Meyerhold (1874–1940) and Sergei Eisenstein (1898–1948).

OPERA AS A DRAMATIC GENRE *PER SE*

Chapter 8, the last dedicated to creative work, discusses sung drama (opera) – or musical drama as such. However, this chapter addresses much more than mere opera and its musical composition. Despite insisting that those readers interested in the opera absolutely must read all the preceding chapters because Chapter 8 directly builds on them for its conception of sung drama, Zich jokingly points out that readers only interested in spoken drama are free to skip this part. We wouldn't suggest following his advice: in this chapter, Zich does not appeal to music composers only. Given his complex treatment of the theatre, he offers refined insights into the elements and the creative processes in theatre making, so any practitioner will benefit from his reflections on opera and musical drama. Zich keeps referring back to spoken drama and by drawing comparisons continues to hone his own observations about it. The chapter in question is far from just being about opera or musical drama in the narrow sense of the word but simply treats the potential of music in the theatre. Given the role that music plays in theatrical genres today, the entire chapter remains central to the theory. At the same time, Zich in his systemic integrity effectively repeats the line of argumentation of his preceding discussions – this time applied to the analysis of the musico-dramatic theatrical work. In this way, the chapter can be seen as a book within a book – one that sums up but also transcends the complexity of Zich's preceding thinking about theatrical structure and the creative process.

Zich makes full use of his thorough understanding of opera as a dramatic art, based both on his expertise as opera review and experience as opera composer and in doing so he succeeds in demonstrating that sung drama (or opera) together with spoken drama is the principal genre of the dramatic art. Zich's arguments regarding opera composition and the staging of operatic works remain valid as Zich is treating them in their specificity – making a clear and remarkable distinction between music composition and opera composition. The centrality of dramatic action within the dramatic work of art leads Zich to crucially argue that it is not the text that the composer sets to music but the situation. This claim continues to be contentious to this day. Analogically, Zich views the opera singer strictly as a (singing) actor – a provocative requirement in regards to the way opera singers continue to be trained until the present day.

It follows from the above that the creative work of the dramatic composer is specific and requires specific skills. In Chapter 8, for one last time, Zich uses the case study of the composer to revisit what *theatrical reading* of the dramatic text (i.e., the libretto) means. The composer must read and mine the text for its dramatic and scenic potential. At the same time, Zich views the dramatic composer with great complexity of thought, not unlike the playwright. Additionally, Zich identifies what the composer has to summon and capture in their musical score and what that creation further offers to the unique creative input of the stage director and the actor-singer. These passages about the autonomy of the opera director remain valid arguments in today's ongoing debate about the production of opera, and Zich's claims from almost a century ago continue to be incisive and inspirational. Their complexity and subtlety may help refine the ongoing debates. The longevity and adaptability of Zich's thoughts on the matter derive from his skill and experience not only as a theorist but also as an opera practitioner. Zich draws heavily on his own experience as the composer and librettist of three successful operas.

STYLE, STYLISATION AND THEATRICAL ILLUSION

The third and final part of Zich's *Aesthetics of the Dramatic Art* reverts the perspective of his theory and revisits systematically its fundamental audience focus. We re-enter a psychologic-semiotic context, but this time the dramatic work of art (the theatrical performance) is not viewed from the inside but aesthetically, in its overall structure. Zich discusses its impact on the spectator and analyses the relation of the work to the spectator's individual experiences. He treats individual theatrical styles in general terms – less as a classification of concrete theatrical genres but rather as a theoretical discussion of the way these genres are defined. He offers a sort of "typology of typology" or a meta-genre theory. Constantly taking the spectator's aesthetic perception as something firmly rooted in individual experience, Zich describes art on the basis of its distance from real-world, lived experience – both inner and outer. He refers to this distance as (the measure of) *theatrical stylisation*. On the most abstract level, Zich observes a tendency towards realism on the one hand, and towards idealism on the other. In idealism, the work of art with its forms moves away from material/outer reality, and idealistic works of art relate to reality by means of our inner (ideational, psychological) experience. Zich views naturalism not only as an extreme form of realism but already as a unartistic tendency as its way of representation is a mere mechanical (i.e., non-creative) reproduction of reality. In this way Zich's claims about naturalism coincide with period discussions about naturalism in photography, literature and other arts and in the Czech context with the aesthetic views of Otokar Hostinský, Zich's teacher. Both Zich and Hostinský conceptualise realism and idealism as abstract, general aesthetics categories rather than as artistic styles within specific historic contexts, but Zich takes the argument further, elaborating the audience's reception processes. Although today's critical theory conceives of genres differently, Zich's approach to genre classification as built on the interplay of the experience of the recipient (spectator), the creator (theatre maker) and the spectator's knowledge of artistic conventions remains noteworthy. It is a relevant contribution to reception aesthetics in the state of its nascence.

Zich's subchapter on *the theatrical illusion* is also of great significance – it is the only extract that has recently appeared in English in Emil Volek and Andrés Pérez-Simón's (Zich 2019). In this passage Zich carries out his conception of the dual conceptual image (technical and referential) to its ultimate implications. He holds the historic primacy in being the first ever to capture and theorise the mental processes of the spectator being drawn into or lost in the theatrical performance – i.e., experience the theatrical illusion – without being disturbed by the awareness that it is "only" theatre, i.e., "un-real" (or makeshift) reality. Zich argues this seeming paradox on the basis of his analysis of our experience – the paradox is only seeming because the theatrical spectator commonly doesn't perceive it as a contradiction. Zich's argument is rooted in the mind's ability to create and sustain two simultaneous mental images – the technical and the referential one. In other words, we are able to nourish the idea of a fictional world while being aware that we are at a theatrical performance. He comes with this theoretical concept long before modern cognitive psychology arrives with the notion of *conceptual blending*, which was later applied onto the theatrical experience. In one stroke, Zich debunks Samuel Taylor Coleridge's notion of suspension of disbelief as naive and theoretically as well as empirically untenable. For Zich, *the theatrical illusion* is not an onstage accomplishment or an act of self-inflicted mental numbing, but an indelible process of perception that brings together ostensive onstage action and the spectator's own and individualised mental processes.

THEORETICAL DRAMATURGY AND THEATRE STUDIES

Having mapped Zich's *Aesthetics of the Dramatic Art* in its basic contours, let us return to the beginning. Zich gives his book the subtitle of *Theoretical Dramaturgy* and this usage is somewhat surprising to the modern ear. Dramaturgy nowadays generally refers to one of the roles in the creative team in the theatre, but in Zich's time this role wasn't as systematically established as would happen later. At the same time, Theatre Studies (*Theaterwissenschaft*) as a discipline was in a nascent state. It may well be that Zich uses the term *dramaturgy* to refer to a critical reflection of theatre. In this sense, he may be referring back to G. E. Lessing's *The Hamburg Dramaturgy* (*Hamburgische Dramaturgie*, 1767–1769) and in his emphasis on *theoretical dramaturgy* may be suggesting a self-standing discipline that offers a critical reflection of theatre practice in its variety, from the creative processes to performance. From this perspective, Zich's *theoretical dramaturgy* represents a variant of early Theatre Studies as a scholarly discipline – but a discipline that forms itself in a close link with its art. In a sense, the unprecedented complexity of modern theatre necessitates a theoretical reflection and the formation of a special discipline.

Zich emphasises repeatedly that his theory wants to be empirical – deriving directly from experiencing the form, structure and material of the artwork. Zich follows this to an aesthetic analysis that focuses on the artwork's effect – the work's impact on the recipient. In this he follows current trends in aesthetic research, artistic trends and their critical reception.

Osolsobě spells out the particular approaches that Zich takes, stating that Zich's *Aesthetics* could be divided methodologically into theoretical, psychological analyses and analyses of cognitive (noetic) processes (Osolsobě 1986: 335). Osolsobě calls the essay that accompanies the 1986 edition of *Aesthetics* "Zich's Philosophy of the Dramatic Form" (Zichova filosofie dramatického tvaru) – which is another way of summarising the specifics of Zich's approach. Osolsobě highlights Zich's attempt at capturing the general principles of the dramatic art – its creation and its reception – hence *philosophy*. The notion of *form* is crucial given Zich's cardinal interest in the construction, formation and conscious shaping of artworks. For Zich, the artwork is not just an expression of the artist, but Zich argues that the true artists need to understand and be well versed in the art's inner laws and logic – namely, the *material* of the art as such (e.g., space, language, body). Zich writes his *Aesthetics* also as an attempt at educating the theatre artist in the specifics of their art.

OTAKAR ZICH, A SCHOLAR AND AN ARTIST: THE LIFE AND TIMES

Aesthetics of the Dramatic Art came out in 1931 as the last major work of Zich's relatively short life. The roots of the book go back to the early 1920s when Zich delivered a lecture series in the Seminar of Aesthetics at Charles University in Prague. The series was entitled *Theoretical Dramaturgy*.

Otakar Zich had joined Charles University as a student in 1897 – a crucial era that saw the transition from Czech National Revival to artistic Modernism. In 1895, the *Czech Modernist Manifesto* (*Manifest české moderny*) was published and in 1900, the leading Modernist playwright and theatre director Jaroslav Kvapil (1868–1950) became the Director of Drama at the National Theatre in Prague. Kvapil's work brings decisive impulses into the dramatic art – psychological realism, impressionism and symbolism, in a way culminating in his collaboration with the composer Antonín Dvořák (1841–1904) on their opera *Rusalka* (1901), for which Kvapil wrote the libretto. The decades of the 1890s to the 1920s formed Zich's taste and practical experience and his *Aesthetics of the Dramatic Art* bear an imprint of the era. It is helpful to draw the contextual links between this theoretical treatise and Zich's personality, education and preceding scholarly work. Besides, Zich always considered himself an empiricist and constantly projected his theatre going experience onto his scholarly work.

Otakar Zich was born in the town of Městec Králové (80 km east of Prague) on 25 March 1879. He combined two lineages in himself – a generation of schoolmasters on his paternal side and a line of musicians on the maternal. At the age of eleven, Zich entered a grammar school in Prague, and when he was in Year 4 (at the age of fifteen), he became an obsessive theatre goer, especially fascinated by opera. In 1897, he started his undergraduate studies at Charles University at the Faculty of Philosophy – which comprised humanities and natural sciences. Zich read Maths and Physics, concluding his five-year studies in 1902 with a final thesis entitled *Of Singular Integrals*. However, his talents always remained dual – mathematical and musical. He was self-taught on several instruments – piano of course, but also cello and clarinet – and though he was an amateur, his performance clearly surpassed the average. As a university student, Zich played the cello in a string quartet, performing, among others, Bedřich Smetana's virtuoso String Quartet No. 1 in E minor "From My Life" (*Z mého života*). He was also a member of the Academic Orchestra and later, as a grammar school teacher of maths and physics, he led a student orchestra. Over the years, Zich's interest in music took precedence. However, Zich's aesthetics continued to retain the links to rigorous mathematical logic and to the empiricism of physics.

Zich considered his university teacher, the aesthetician, musicologist and critic Otakar Hostinský (1847–1910) to be his greatest influence. Hostinský was Director of the Seminar of Aesthetics at Charles University and a formative figure of systematic aesthetics as a discipline. He was also a prominent theatre and opera critic as well as an opera librettist. Soon after his death in 1910, Otakar Zich took over his chair at the university. Several other leading personalities influenced Zich greatly, prominent among them the philosopher and psychologist František Krejčí (1858–1934) and sociologist Tomáš Garrigue Masaryk (1850–1937), who would in 1918 become the first President of independent Czechoslovakia. The positivist, empirically focused methods that both university professors promoted in their respective disciplines helped shape Zich's theories.

As a composer Zich was self-taught and some reviewers arrogantly referred to him as a dilettante who hadn't studied composition at the Prague Conservatoire, the decisive formal educational institution at the turn of the century. His compositions complied with the period tastes and haven't survived as part of the live musical repertoire. Nonetheless, Zich's musical output is far from negligible or insignificant and plays an important role in the understanding of his creative personality and originality. Zich's first compositional attempts date from his grammar school years when he was seventeen. Over the years, he composed numerous chamber works, a series of cantatas and song cycles. His symphonic poem *Konrád Wallenrod*, based on the classical Polish poem by Adam Mickiewicz, is an important milestone in his creation: writing a Romantic symphonic poem was the necessary task for any aspiring composer of the era. Like any other solid Czech composer (Smetana, Dvořák, Fibich, Foerster, Janáček), Zich also made arrangements of folk songs – in his case mostly from the Chodsko Region of southwest Bohemia where he taught at a secondary school for three years and collected much of his musical material as part of his field work – as a musical ethnographer of sorts. A significant proportion of his compositional work sets lyrics to music – such as folk song arrangements, poems set to music as songs or as melodramas (lyrics recited to an orchestral accompaniment). He was a great proponent of this peculiar musical genre, now obsolete. Apart from Zdeněk Fibich (1850–1900), Otakar Zich was the leading representative of the Czech melodrama, with many of his compositions set to the poems of his favourite author, Jan Neruda (1834–1891). Zich's refined sense of the relationship between lyrics and music shows also in one of his studies about the librettos of Bedřich Smetana's (1824–1884) operas *Libuše* (1869–1872) and *Čertova stěna* (The Devil's Wall, 1880) where he proposed minor revisions to the lyrics which were adopted in later performance practice. Zich's changes proved successful in the singers' delivery. Zich also translated opera librettos, such as his 1914 Czech translation of Mozart's *Die Entführung aus dem Serail*

(The Abduction from the Seraglio, 1782) or the 1932 translation of Mahler's *Das Lied von der Erde* (The Song of the Earth, 1908–1909). One reviewer even declared Zich's translation as matching the qualities of the original – high praise in 1930s Czechoslovakia where the sweeping majority of the cultured public was bilingual in Czech and German.

The attention Zich pays to the opera in his *Aesthetics of the Dramatic Art* comes not only from his interests as a scholar or critic, but also as a creative artist. His involvement with vocal music logically led him towards the opera. His first attempt was a one-act comic opera *Malířský nápad* (The Painter's Idea, 1908) based on the short story by Svatopluk Čech (1846–1908). The opera gained an enthusiastic reception. From the point of view of the dramatic art another two compositions are significant, both based on pre-existing dramatic texts. In 1911, Zich started to work on his new opera from Jaroslav Hilbert's (1871–1936) *Vina* (Guilt, 1896). At the time of writing, Hilbert's play was welcomed as an original Czech attempt at an Ibsenian analytical drama. When Zich completed his opera of the same name in 1915, Karel Kovařovic (1862–1920), Director of Opera at the National Theatre in Prague, rejected it and Zich had to wait until 1926 when the leadership was taken over by Zich's friend Otakar Ostrčil (1879–1935).

Zich's opera *Vina* is remarkable as an attempt at setting to music a closely knit psychological-realistic drama. It explores the ways of stylising musically present day spoken language and of portraying complex psychological processes by means of music. The key part of the opera is a fugue – almost atonal in its harmony – that portrays the complicated emotions of the female protagonist when she is writing a letter to her past lover. Zich tries to use music to externalise the motivations and psychological impulses of the dramatic persona. (Unsurprisingly, Zich dedicated an extensive part of a chapter of his *Aesthetics* to the possibilities of musical mimics.) Zich's last opera is *Preciézky* (1922–1924), based on his own translation of Molière's comedy *Les Précieuses ridicules*. One reviewer summed up the success of the work by claiming that Zich managed to create "a new type of Czech comic opera that brilliantly parodies the drawing room style of plays" (cited in Osolsobě 1986: 396). A tiny piece of evidence relates to this opera's reception by the Prague German critics. In 1930, when the New German Theatre staged Felice Lattuada's (1882–1962) Italian opera *Le preciose ridicole* under the German title *Die lächerlichen Zierpuppen*, the critic did not hesitate to compare it with Zich's opera on the same topic and observed that Zich's version was better, both musically and scenically (Ludvová 2012: 481). We will return to the context and the relationship between the Czech and German theatre in Prague below.

Mentioning Zich's creative work first is our deliberate attempt to prevent it from being sidelined when we come over to his work as a theatre critic and theorist. His creative output, however dependent on period tastes, is much more than a tag-on to his serious work – as one might think at a cursory glance. It forms an integral part of Zich's personality.

His views were formed not only by his theatre-going experience but also by his participation in Czech musical life as a critic and a creator. Interestingly, as far as spoken drama is concerned, his opinions and predilections do not show in his theory very much. However, when it comes to opera, the situation is very different. We can see this particularly in Chapter 8, where Zich is clearly partial to the operas of Bedřich Smetana (1824–1884), given the number of examples he draws from them. Smetana clearly served as the model "dramatic" opera composer. Occasionally, Zich also refers to the operas of Zdeněk Fibich (1850–1900), Josef Bohuslav Foerster (1859–1951) and his friend and conductor Otakar Ostrčil (1879–1935) – the next generation of the neoromantic, Smetanian music. No other Czech composer, except for himself, is included. In this, Zich clearly follows the ideological positions of his contemporary and university colleague, musicologist Zdeněk Nejedlý (1878–1962). (For a critical analysis of Nejedlý's concept of Czech musical history, see Zapletal 2016.) Nejedlý divided Czech music into two lines: he saw one, comprising the Smetanian group, as progressive, while the other – including Antonín Dvořák, Josef Suk and partly also Leoš Janáček – was retrograde, artistically weak and crowd-pleasing. As Miloš Zapletal succinctly summed up: "The progressive line was basically focused on developing programmatic music and post-Wagnerian music drama, while the second focused mainly on absolute music" (2016: 103). Zich's ideological positions kowtow to Nejedlý, who follows the views of Otakar Hostinský, who had taught both of them. "The progressiveness is principally understood in terms of the Beethovenian-Lisztian-Wagnerian-Mahlerian line of German music" (Zapletal 2016: 103). Ideologically, Nejedlý (and Zich in tow) follows Wagner and traces modern, truly dramatic opera to Christoph Willibald Gluck (1714–1787). He takes his positions to the extreme, such as when establishing Zdeněk Fibich as the ultimate creator of the "truly dramatic" melodrama and even awards him a central place in the formation of the genre – in his book *Zdenko Fibich: Zakladatel scénického melodramu* (Zdenko Fibich: the Founder of the Scenic Melodrama; Prague, 1901). From the perspective of period tensions and ideological debates, it is symptomatic that Zich does not draw on a single example from the works of Antonín Dvořák (1841–1904). The "progressive" musicologists and critics of Nejedlý's camp, Zich included, framed Dvořák as an un-Czech, eclectic and therefore unartistic composer – despite, or perhaps because of, his international acclaim. Brian Locke has analysed the ideological fray over Dvořák and the "soul and essence" of Czech music in his chapter "A crisis of Identity: The 'Dvořák Affair', 1911–1914" (Locke 2006: 54–58).

Zich also fails to come to terms with Leoš Janáček (1854–1928), although Janáček's work was complete and gaining international recognition as Zich was finishing his *Aesthetics*. On the basis of their disagreement on the principles of opera, Zich misunderstands Janáček's speech melody theory and views it as a mere mechanical replicating of reality – which in his view was an instance of unartistic naturalism, a view shared by many other critics of the Nejedlý camp (see "Nejedlý, Janáček and Smetana Exhibition" in Locke 2006: 62-64). In brief, Zich's attitude to Janáček resembles his view of the Avant-Garde: he is well aware of both, but neither fit with his aesthetic system. The mismatch between his aesthetics and his appreciation of Janáček is humorously ironic: Zich clearly enjoyed and recognised the dramatic effect of Janáček's *Její pastorkyňa*. In his review, he tries hard to rationalise the impact by framing it as a one-off: an unschooled exception, a spontaneous and idiosyncratic phenomenon that allegedly ignores the cultivated history of Western music.

In the first part of his scholarly career Zich established himself primarily as a musicological and musical aesthetician. He published extensive studies dedicated to the work of his favourite composer, Bedřich Smetana – analysing his symphonic works and operas. It is of significance that unlike Zdeněk Nejedlý, the most influential Czech musicologist of the early twentieth century, Zich never wrote a history of music: his domain lay firmly in the analysis and theory of the work of art. His first major scholarly work was *Estetické vnímání hudby* (Aesthetic Perception of Music, 1910-1911), which also became his habilitation work, submitted for his promotion to Associate Professorship (*Dozentur*). In this work Zich combines musical analysis and experimental psychology to study meaning-making in music. Apart from theoretical and introspective methods he also uses simple experiments: he plays musical extracts to his interviewees and asks them about their mental associations. Zich tries to establish to what extent these mental images and meanings are *logical* (zákonité) and *inevitable* (nutné). The book straddles music psychology and what later came to form music semiotics. Here he first uses the term *conceptual image* (významová představa), although in a simple form. (For a more detailed discussion, see Dykast 2009: 180-181, and Lánská 2016.) Another significant work is *Hodnocení estetické a umělecké* (1917; in English as *Aesthetic and Artistic Evaluation*, 2009, with Dykast's commentary). Zich categorises different types of recipients (perceivers), distinguishing between aesthetic and artistic evaluation. For Zich, the aesthetic evaluation is purely an emotional and subjective response, while the artistic progresses to the inner logic of the artwork and depends on the recipient's experience, knowledge and willingness to proceed to an objective evaluation of the work. Both studies attempt a conceptual understanding of the audience's perception of the work of art – and in both Zich aims at distinguishing between random and purely subjective moments and moments that are determined by an inner logic or law and the recipient's pre-existing experience and knowledge. In so doing,

Zich's objective is to uncover the principles of perception and evaluation (or assessment) of art. It is noteworthy that Zich constantly pays a balanced attention to both these aspects of the reception process – the subjective and the objective (or the aesthetic and the artistic) – approaching them as dialectically complementary. Zich builds on these principles in his *Aesthetics of the Dramatic Art* and draws out crucial consequences from them – in the first analytical part of the book and in the final part devoted to theatrical illusion and the spectator's theatrical focus.

With the arrival of the 1920s, Zich's scholarly output turned increasingly to the opera and the theatre. The first seeds of *Aesthetics of the Dramatic Art* date from as early as 1913 when Zich delivered a semester-long lecture cycle entitled *Theoretical Dramaturgy* – a name that eventually became the book's subtitle. In 1922 Zich adapted the topic when he reached out to a wider audience with his public lecture "Principles of Theoretical Dramaturgy". One of its parts, "The Basis of the Theatrical Scene", came out shortly afterwards – and Zich took it as a basis for his chapter on the scenic space of his *Aesthetics*. The remainder survived only in manuscript before it was first published in Czech in 1997 and in an English translation in 2016 (in Drozd et al. 2016: 34–58). This text provides a very accurate concept of the first part of Zich's *Aesthetics of the Dramatic Art* with all its substantial distinctions. Another of Zich's publications relates to the theatre, namely his 1923 essay *Loutkové divadlo* (Puppet Theatre; for an English translation see Zich 2015). Zich dedicated his essay not only to the study of a much neglected theatrical form but also to the process of audience reception and perception in relation to puppet theatre's visual stylisation, including considerations of scale and abstraction. Although it would take Zich another decade before he would complete his magnum opus – while he continued to elaborate on and refine individual themes and conclusions as part of his university lectures (as we learn from his correspondence) – the formation and the physical publication of the book as a whole obviously took the better part of twenty years.

It is only Zich's unexpected death in 1934 that made *Aesthetics of the Dramatic Art* a culmination of his life's work. It is likely that Zich would have proceeded to write a comparably systematic treatise on another art form. From the point of view of theatre theory we can hold ourselves fortunate that Zich started with the theatre – as the most complex of art forms. Ivo Osolsobě (1928–2012), Zich's best biographer and scholar to date, sums up the final two years of his life:

> Dokončení díla a jeho vydání vytrhlo, zdá se, Zicha z jeho izolace. Udílí interwievy, vrací se ke své bytostné družnosti, přednáší v Kroužku (17. 1. 1933 na téma *Tempo básnického jazyka*), překládá Mahlerovy písně, publikuje stať o fyzikální kauzalitě, intenzivně se zajímá o nové směry matematické, zejména o topologii, připravuje studii o tónovém

prostoru jako topologickém prostoru, koncipuje velkou estetiku hudby, komponuje další písně a sbory k oslavě stého výročí Jana Nerudy, chystá se na další operu, tragickou, o Přemyslu Otakarovi II., přichází však náhlý konec, za slunečního jasu, na venkově, při chůzi po pěšině uprostřed polí…(Osolsobě 1986: 399)

[The completion and publication of his work seems to have brought Zich out of his isolation. He gives interviews; returns to his vivacious sociability; delivers lectures for the Prague Linguistic Circle (on the "Tempo of the Poetic Language"); translates Mahler's songs; publishes an essay on causality in physics; nurtures a vivid interest in new trends in maths, especially topology; works on an essay on tonal space as a topological space; elaborates a concept for a major aesthetics of music; composes songs and choral works to mark Jan Neruda's centenary; makes preparations for another, tragic opera on the medieval Czech king Přemysl Otakar II; but a sudden end comes, in a sunlit countryside during a walk on a path in the middle of fields…]

This very portrait of Zich's final years clearly shows the versatility, variety and inner coherence of his creativity – as an artist and as a scholar.

THE ARTS AROUND ZICH

When *Aesthetics of the Dramatic Art* appeared in 1931, it was partly received as dated or conservative – clearly due to Zich's long-term conceptual work on the volume and his conscious decision to eschew in his theory the most topical and novel trends, such as the Russian (Soviet), French or Czech theatrical avant-garde. Setting the appropriate context for the formation of Zich's views of the theatre – perhaps going as far as the 1890s – plays a crucial role for a thorough appreciation of his *Aesthetics*. Czech culture of the 1890s – including the theatre – absorbed numerous modernist impulses. Henrik Ibsen's *A Doll's House* (*Et dukkehjem*, 1879) was staged in Prague as early as 1887 – at a time when the Prague National Theatre also hosted the international nineteenth-century actor celebrity Sarah Bernhardt (1844–1923) as well as the prime modernist actress Eleonora Duse (1858–1924). When Konstantin Stanislavski (1863–1938) founded his Moscow Art Theatre in 1898, the leading actors of the National Theatre in Prague who tended towards psychological realism – such as Hana Kvapilová (1860–1907) – followed them systematically and found inspiration in Stanislavski's work. Very importantly, during their very first tour the Moscow Art Theatre were invited to perform in Prague in 1906 as well. The staging practice at the National Theatre in Prague showed clear tendencies to move from a descriptive realism towards a more subtle psychological portrayal with frequent forays into symbolism or impressionism – such as in the emblematic stagings of Shakespeare made by the leading impressionist stage director and author Jaroslav Kvapil (see more in Burian 2000: 20–56).

Prague theatre of the time does not mean only Czech-language theatre. Czech and German cultures coexisted and mutually influenced one another. While the history of Czech-language theatre in Prague has received a comprehensive treatment (in English see Burian 2000 and 2002, among others), the historical research into the German-language culture is only in its early phases, given that systematic research could start only after the fall of the Communist regime in 1989. Several case studies appeared in German in *Deutschsprachiges Theater in Prag* (German-Language Theatre in Prague; Jakubcová et al. 2001), and then in Czech in Jitka Ludvová's seminal work *Až k hořkému konci: Pražské německé divadlo 1845–1945* (To the Very Bitter End: Prague German Theatre 1845–1945; Ludvová 2012). What follows relies heavily on Ludvová's research, and while this Introduction has been relatively brief when it comes to Czech-language theatre, the German-language theatrical activities deserve a more elaborate treatment.

When the Czech theatre culture achieved its institutional success with the opening of the independent Czech National Theatre in Prague in 1883, the German community responded by building its glamorous Neues Deutsches Theater (New German Theatre) in 1888, since the preceding venue, Stavovské divadlo (The Estates Theatre), which had opened in 1783, struggled to meet the requirements of the late nineteenth century. The New German Theatre boasted three ensembles: spoken drama, opera and ballet, and the theatre's orchestra also gave philharmonic concerts. Even after the opening of the New German Theatre the Estates Theatre continued to serve as a venue of the German stage.

Between 1885 and 1910, Angelo Neumann (1838–1910) served as the New German Theatre's director. He made great effort to appeal to his audiences with remarkable events. He frequently made use of having obtained the rights to perform Richard Wagner's complete Ring Cycle in an abridged form and he was held in high regard as an authority and a producer of Wagner's operas outside of Bayreuth. Thanks to him, Prague became a Wagnerite centre for a time. This was especially true in the late 1890s, when Neumann produced the complete Ring Cycle six times. Such activities naturally transcended any notion of local culture and German-language as well as Czech-language Prague became an international cultural metropolis.

Towards the end of each theatre season, Neumann organised *Maifestspiele*, the May Theatre Festival that hosted significant events with leading companies. In the decade of 1878–1888 Prague saw repeated visits of the Meiningen Theatre. In 1895, the Berliner Ensemble (Die Moderne), newly formed from a group of actors by Otto Brahm and Max Reinhardt as a touring company, came to Prague and performed a novel naturalistic repertoire with such plays as Max Halbe's *Jugend* (Youth, 1893) and Henrik Ibsen's *Ghosts* (1881). Another remarkable guest appearance – to name one among many others – was the

Deutsches Theater Berlin's production of Frank Wedekind's scandalous play *Frühlings-Erwachsen* (The Spring Awakening, 1891). This took place in the presence of the author in May 1907, only a year after the play's opening in Berlin. Neumann's successors continued in the tradition and the *Maifestspiele* effectively became an annual festival showcasing modern German-language theatre. In 1912, for instance, Prague saw five different ensembles in performance: three from Berlin – the Lessing-Theater, the Deutsches Theater and the Kleines Theater – and the theatres from Vienna and Dresden. Similar guest performances continued after the First World War.

It could be said that the gradual shift of the acting and producing styles from the late romantic, declamatory aesthetics to the more modern styles of psychological realism and naturalism took place simultaneously and in parallel in both leading Prague theatres: the Czech and the German stages. At the brink of the First World War, the German Prague was a centre of the "Schnitzler Cult" – centred around the influential Austrian playwright, novelist and physician Arthur Schnitzler (1862–1931). In 1911, Prague saw the coordinated premiere of his play *Das weite Land* (The Vast Domain), which also opened on the same day in Vienna, Munich, Breslau (Wrocław), Bochum, Hamburg, Hannover and Leipzig. As a follow-up the New German Theatre performed a cycle of 17 productions of Schnitzler's plays in 1912. The plays of the Austrian Modern (Hermann Bahr, Arthur Schnitzler, Hugo von Hofmannsthal and others) had their place in the dramaturgy of the Czech National Theatre under the leadership of Jaroslav Kvapil too. It comes as no surprise then that when Schnitzler arrived in Prague in 1912 to see the production of one of his plays in the New German Theatre, he met with the director of the Czech National Theatre Gustav Schmoranz on the following day and attended Jaroslav Kvapil's rehearsal of Czech playwright Alois Jirásek's historical drama *Jan Hus*.

Prague's German theatre was organically connected with the rest of the German-speaking theatrical culture and many famous personalities started their careers in Prague – among them the actors Ernst Deutsch (1890–1969) and Alexander Moissi (1879–1935) (for the many others, see Ludvová 2012). The German theatre in Prague never had very prominent stage director figures but it retained links with modern trends in other ways. In 1912 for instance, the New German Theatre staged Shakespeare's *Hamlet* using a set borrowed from the newly formed Künstlertheater in Munich and the lead role was played by star actors of the age, among them Albert Bassermann (1867–1952) of Berlin's Lessing-Theater and the above-named Alexander Moissi, who had gained renown as a lead actor in Max Reinhardt's productions. In 1922, the stage director Leopold Jessner came to Prague to stage Shakespeare's *Richard III*, a remount of his 1919 Berlin production. These instances of expressionist poetics in the theatre took place in parallel with the efforts of the leading Czech representative of expressionist theatre, stage director Karel Hugo

Hilar (1885–1935), who promoted expressionist aesthetics in another Czech-language theatre house in Prague, Divadlo na Vinohradech (for more details see Burian 2002: 1–19). Czech theatre critics in Prague followed the opera and dramatic productions of the German stages. And vice versa: if the literary and theatre critic Max Brod had not gone to see the Prague premiere of Leoš Janáček's *Její pastorkyňa* (Jenůfa), the opera would probably never have reached its world-renowned status. While there always existed a certain tension and a sense of rivalry (and often also amicable cooperation), the Prague Czech and German scenes complemented one another.

Given Zich's interest in opera and classical music, one other element needs to be added: the philharmonic concerts of the German Theatre's orchestra. The orchestra appears to have had very high standards and rose to the challenge of performing a modern, fresh and demanding repertoire, such as the works of Gustav Mahler or Richard Strauss, allegedly to the composers' great contentment (Ludvová 2012: 77). The Prague German theatre belonged to the prominent centres of Mahler's music and the interest was met by the Czech side too. This symbolically manifested itself at the world premiere of Mahler's Symphony No. 7 in 1907, performed under the baton of the composer by the Czech Philharmonic Orchestra enriched for the occasion by two dozen musicians from the German theatre. In other words, the musical life in Prague on both the Czech and German sides followed the newest trends, including the more controversial ones. So for instance, Alexander Zemlinsky (1871–1942), who was the musical director and conductor of New German Theatre's opera between 1911 and 1927, staged new operas of such contemporary composers as Paul Hindemith (1895–1963), Erich Wolfgang Korngold (1897–1957) or Ernst Krenek (1900–1991). Zemlinsky's programmes of the philharmonic concerts featured several compositions by Arnold Schönberg (1874–1951) which caused a stir in the audience, no matter if German or Czech. In 1925, Zemlinsky included in his concert programme three scenes from Alban Berg's (1885–1935) ground-breaking opera *Wozzeck*, several months before the planned stage premiere of the entire work in Berlin. Although Zemlinsky himself seriously considered a staging of the opera in the New German Theatre, he gave up on his plan. But it is likely that he gave encouragement to the musical director of the Czech opera in Prague Otakar Ostrčil (1879–1935), who resolved to stage it on hearing Zemlinsky's concert performance of the selected scenes (see Ludvová 2012: 380–383). The production of Berg's *Wozzeck* at the Czech National Theatre in 1926 caused a genuine and far-reaching scandal – probably partly orchestrated. The professional and musical public came to the support of the production in an open letter. Among the signatories was Otakar Zich. (For a detailed description of the *Wozzeck* affair, see Locke 2006: 200–206.)

Even this cursory overview illustrates that Prague's theatrical and musical stages belonged integrally to a European cultural web and reflected all its developments. In the first three decades of the century, when he was working on his *Aesthetics of the Dramatic Art*, Zich was in direct contact with all the dominant artistic endeavours, attempts and trends. While we are lacking exact evidence of what he saw and heard, it is beyond any doubt that his thinking took shape in confrontation with the Czech and German cultures within a European context.

Modernist theatre received the decisive theoretical impulses from Adolphe Appia (1862–1928) and Edward Gordon Craig (1872–1966), who continued to exert their influence on theatre theory and practice. Appia's *La Musique et la mise en scène* (Music and the Art of the Theatre) came out in 1897 (the German translation came out in 1899) and Craig's *The Art of the Theatre* (later called *On the Art of the Theatre*) first appeared in 1905 – and the two works posed the crucial questions of modern theatre: the harmony and coordination of the components of theatre and the consistent stylisation throughout the theatrical work. Appia foregrounds the relationship between music and scenography (and the stage space), while Craig is concerned with the overall interaction within the theatrical work – the domain of the stage director. Is the stage director merely an organiser of the rehearsal process, or an autonomous creator in his or her own right? These questions are in principle remarkably similar to those that Zich asks – especially in the middle part of his book. In a sense, these are the key questions of Modernist theatre. While Appia and Craig are pioneers whose texts are programme manifestos and exhortations, Zich's *Aesthetics of the Dramatic Art* stands at the opposite end of the Modernist impulse – before the theatre became the Avant Garde – and his theory can be viewed as the first systematic reflection of the principles of Modernist theatre. For instance, as far as the art of acting is concerned, Zich formulates his theses side by side and independently of Stanislavski but at the same time Zich was well aware of Stanislavski's innovations and very likely saw the Moscow Art Theatre during their Prague performances.

It is also worth pointing out that Appia and Craig derive their discussions of modern theatre primarily from the opera. Their search for principles of Modernist stage directing goes back to Wagnerian opera. This may seem counterintuitive and surprising since opera today is sometimes viewed as a theatrical genre of the past but Modernist theatre does not start with Ibsen's, Chekhov's or Strindberg's dramas. These become a point of discussion only later. Modernist theatre starts with the opera. On the one hand, Wagner's theory of the complex organism of the musical drama was highly inspirational. On the other, his visionary theories and musical compositions were in striking contrast with his own stagings of his operas, which continued in the late Romantic and conservative staging style. This contradiction between the individual components of the performance and the overall integrity of the theatrical work of art remained a major challenge that Modernists needed to confront. Viewed from this perspective, it is understandable that Zich dedicates the longest chapter of his book to opera. Despite his own suggestion that the operatic chapter could be skipped by readers interested in spoken drama, we could argue that the opposite is true: more than anywhere else, it is in this chapter that the integral principles of modern theatre are foregrounded. It is here that the structural relationships between music, lyrics and the actors' performance in space stand out most clearly.

Zich does not cite either Appia or Craig. Yet, it is apparent from his writing that he was acquainted with their theories and practical experiments. Zich undoubtedly focuses primarily on the questions that had been posited by the two visionaries. If we were to categorise Zich stylistically, we could call him an early Modernist. We could confidently state, with a bit of licence, that by 1923, when the Soviet theatre innovator Alexander Tairov (1885–1950) published his *Das entfesselte Theater* (in English as *Notes of the Director*), one of the key manifestos of Avant-Garde theatre, Zich's *Aesthetics of the Dramatic Art* had been conceptually complete – although it would take almost another decade to write in full and get it through publication.

WAYS OF READING ZICH'S *AESTHETICS*: A SHORT CATALOGUE

This Introduction has been following two principal aims – to present *Aesthetics of the Dramatic Art* as an original system of critical thinking of the theatre as an autonomous art form and to offer a brief overview of the ways in which the book can be read. We have written much on the former point, while the latter has received only cursory and scattered hints. What follows is a more systematic overview.

The era in which Zich was active – as a student and as a scholar – saw far-reaching changes in science and scholarship. The humanities and social sciences especially bore witness to the establishment of new, modern disciplines – a trend that often led to narrow specialisation of expertise, later even rivalry and the fragmentation of knowledge. Otakar Zich stands at the start of this phase: his *Aesthetics of the Dramatic Art* effectively established Czech Theatre Studies. As the head of the Seminar of Aesthetics at Charles University he strove to introduce specialised seminars on the theatre as part of the curriculum – a trend that would lead to the establishment of Theatre Studies as a self-standing programme of studies after 1945 under the leadership of his successor, Jan Mukařovský (1891–1975). At the same time, Zich loved to retain his old-time academic predilections that positioned him clearly as a man of the nineteenth century. Despite his academic rigour, art for Zich remains an act of artistic creation, experiencing and aesthetic pleasure. From today's perspective, Zich straddles several disciplines – but calling his approach interdisciplinary in today's sense would be an anachronism: the separation of individual disciplines was far from complete in his time. What remains remarkable is that Zich does not shy away from close connections to individual artists. Besides, he himself embodied a unique expertise that combined academic qualities and experience of creative practice. Zich managed to wed his powers of abstraction and of systemic thought with artistic intuition and creative talent.

The fact that Zich stood at the early phases of disciplinary diversification in the humanities may – in a way – play to his advantage in the context of our present-day push towards multi- and interdisciplinary work. What today's academics and practitioners try to articulate in such concepts as *artistic research* or *practice-as-research* was for Zich a natural modus operandi – as an artist-cum-scholar. In a way, he captured that mode of working in the subtitle of his book: *theoretical dramaturgy*.

We could view Zich as a liminal phenomenon of sorts – in one sense firmly rooted in historic traditions (with his obsessive interest in the nineteenth-century national giants, composer Bedřich Smetana and poet Jan Neruda) and in another his modernist abilities for abstract thought systems whose universality transcend his era. Ivo Osolsobě refers to Zich as a visionary figure who "would often come up with conclusions that others would arrive at much later" (Osolsobě 1986: 376). Osolsobě wrote this observation almost forty years ago and paradoxically such instances have become even more numerous. Zich's work anticipates many issues that theatre theory has come to address only recently.

There are many ways in which we can read Zich's integral theatre theory. In this introduction we have briefly referred to the structuralist-semiotic interpretation but Zich can also be viewed as a Modernist creator among other Modernists (Musilová 2020) and his theory can be linked with today's efforts at integrating artistic practice and scientific research (artistic research, practice-as-research). A reading that is complementary to a structuralist interpretation may focus on Zich's "psychologism" that relates to the phenomenology of art (see Volek 2012; Etlík 2011) or the recent developments in cognitive theatre studies (see Havlíčková Kysová 2015). Given that Zich's theory of the dramatic art emphasises live performance, his theory can be viewed also as an anticipation of Performance Studies (see Ambros 2020).

What you have read so far have been a few attempts at grappling with the overwhelming scope of Zich's oeuvre. We have hoped to provide a context and supportive framework for chipping away at the mysteries of his thinking. After this 35-page "brief" introduction, we would suggest to the reader to take over the initiative, carve out their own inspiration from his game-changing insights and dive into Zich *an sich*.

A NOTE ON THIS EDITION

Our edition respects the original structure of Zich's text. We accurately follow the diagrams, tables, visualisations and notations. We also respect that certain passages are set in a smaller font. As Zich explains in his introduction, he divides the body of his text into two layers: the passages in smaller font present partial examples and consolidate the material at hand, while the key ideas are always formulated in paragraphs in the larger font. On the basis of our own experience, we recommend that the reader doesn't skip the passages in smaller font as they contain numerous nuanced discussions and detailed historic examples that illustrate and support Zich's arguments.

We also follow Zich's peculiar system of emphasis; his text is awash with italicised or letter-spaced passages, as well as words in inverted commas. We keep Zich's *italicisation*, but replace letter-spaced passages with **bold font**, for convenience's sake. Today's reader may find it strange how Zich uses "inverted double commas": often he places in them formulations that are intuitively clear but work figuratively, metaphorically (i.e., non-literally) and transfer the meaning from natural speech to scholarly language. By placing these expressions in inverted double commas, Zich distinguishes them from accurately defined and established concepts. Occasionally he uses quotation marks to emphasise the expressions. (And we admit that there are occasions where his system totally baffles us.)

We have tried to keep our explanatory footnotes to an absolute minimum. We insert a footnote almost exclusively when Zich draws on lesser-known facts from Czech theatre or musical culture; we do that only when an explanation is essential to follow Zich's argument. We have restricted all our explicit interpretations to our Introduction and to the Afterword. We have retained Zich's original analytical list of contents in its full extent. This preliminary text provides a detailed overview of individual topics and serves, as a matter of fact, as a mental map of sorts that provides orientation in the thematic structure of Zich's *Aesthetics of the Dramatic Art*.

OTAKAR ZICH
AESTHETICS OF THE DRAMATIC ART: THEORETICAL DRAMATURGY

TO THE MEMORY OF OTAKAR HOSTINSKÝ

TRANSLATED BY PAVEL DRÁBEK AND TOMÁŠ KAČER

AN ANALYTICAL LIST OF CONTENTS

Foreword   **55**
Introduction   **57**

THE CONCEPT OF DRAMATIC ART   **59–105**

1   **The Character of the Dramatic Work**   **60–73**
Dramatic art comprises both spoken drama and sung drama 60. *The character of the material*: the dramatic work is the theatre performance 60. Its *first* feature: the union of two heterogeneous components: the visible and the audible 61. Literary drama and concert opera 62. The insufficiency of the mere literary or musical text 63. Performances of the same text are actually different dramatic works 64. Its *second* feature: real performance as a necessary existential condition 66. Causes of a "textual" conception of dramatic works 66. *The text and the work*: the principle of reproductive art 68. Acting is not a reproductive art 69. The problem of fixing temporal arts 70. The relationship between the text and the actor's performance is a relation of artistic correspondence 72.

2   **The Synthetic Theory**   **74–82**
The dramatic work as a union of arts 74. Hostinský's theory 75. The creation of the dramatic work: a consecutive uniting of artists 76. Certain components of dramatic work resemble certain arts 77. Theatrical paradoxes 77. Pitfalls of dramatic practice 80. Theatrical compromises 80. The acting component is specifically dramatic 81.

3   **The Analytical Theory**   **83–105**
Dramatic art is autonomous and unique 83. A *psychological analysis* of the dramatic work; the principle of aesthetic analysis 83. Constant components: dramatic personas and location 84. The changeable component: dramatic action (*děj*) 85. The definition of "*action*" (*jednání*) and, consecutively, the definition of dramatic action (*děj*) and of the dramatic persona 86. The dramatic work is necessarily a collective work 86. A semantic and an affective *analysis* of the "*dramatic*" impression; its motoric basis 86. The popular use of the word "dramatic" 88. Natural and constructed (artificial) dramatic action (*děj*) 89. The functional pleasure principle 90. The *dual* conceptual image: the *technical* and the *referential* 90. Dramatic art is mimetic art 92. The specific qualities of *acting* 92. The concept of actor "figure" and "interplay" 93. The principle of correspondence between the technical and the referential images 94. Acting

is a constant and a necessary component of the dramatic art 95. A definition of the actor 96. *The extent (bounding) of the dramatic art.* Distinguishing it from related arts: the dance 96. The artistes' art 97. The principle of totality of actor's performance: this also includes speech 99. Classical pantomime 100. The scenic space also belongs to acting 100. Spoken drama as purely actorly work 101. The spectacle and the film 101. Sung drama and the scenic melodrama as actorly works "set to music" 102. A *definition of the dramatic work* as such, and of spoken drama, opera and the scenic melodrama specifically 102. The principle of dramaticity and the principle of stylisation 104.

THE PRINCIPLE OF DRAMATICITY 107-331

4   The Dramatic Text: The Playwright's Creative Work 108-138

The meaning of the term *"poetic"* 108. The ideal nature of action (*děj*), time, personas, etc. in literature vs. their real nature in drama 110. A "theatrical" reading of drama 114. *The playwright's creative work.* In the beginning is not the word, but the situation 115. The motoric basis of the dramatist's conceptions 117. An analysis of "mental transfiguration" 119. The conditions of the playwright's mental transfiguration 120. Textual fixing of the dramatic creation 121. Direct speeches (actors' lines) 122. The task of the text in the genesis of the dramatic work 124. A solely textual analysis and assessment of the dramatic work is inadmissible 125. Theatre plays without a text 127. *The dramatic task of the text* 129. The text as a component of the actor figure (role) 130. Speech as a characteristic of the dramatic persona: social dialects 131, psychological dialects 132, the intellectual content 133. The text as a component of the actors' interplay (dialogue) 133. The text as a component of the dramatic action (*děj*) 133. The dynamic and the static effect of speeches in drama 134. Theoretical, narrative and lyrical speeches 135. The dramatic bond 136. The degree of a text's dramaticity 137.

5   The Dramatic Persona: The Actor's Creative Work 139-182

The "foreign actor" experiment as a study of purely actorly components 139. The *dramatic persona* as a sum of percepts with a fixed core 140. The direct and the indirect (associative) factor of impression 142. The work's dramaticity comes from the associative factor 144. The principle of dramatic truthfulness 144. An *analysis* of the associative factor: (1) the fixed set (the wear and the physical appearance). The static characteristics of the dramatic persona 145. The motif of mistaken identities 146. (2) The dynamic set (speech, behaviours, actions). *The expressive capacities of mimics* 147. The dramatic capacity of mimics surpasses the lyrical 151. The dynamic characteristics of the dramatic persona 151. The motif of dissimulation 152. The relation of the persona's mimics and the speech 154. The dramatic persona as threefold characterising synthesis 155. The principle of the dramatic persona's coherence 156. *An analysis of the actor figure*; the figure as a set of inner tactile percepts 157. The mask and the costume 158. Theatrical optics and acoustics 159. Psychophysiological correspondence 160. The figure as a psychophysiological formation 161. The primacy of the physiological set 161. The fixed component of the actor figure 162. An analysis of the actorly focus 163. *The psychology of an actor*. (1) Actor talent: The capacity for mental transfiguration and transpersonation 165. The capacity for expression; the actor and the reciter 166. The actor as a motoric type 167. *The logic of actorly thinking*: the principle of impulse coordination, of actor figure coherence and of impulse exteriorisation 168. (2) The sources of acting: inner experience 170, outer experience; the imitative talent 171. Actorly motifs automised (the actor's technique) 172. (3) The actor's actual creative work 174. The preparatory stage 174. Conceiving the figure 175. Executing the figure 176. Fixing the figure 178. The finalised performance 179. Imaginary mental states 180. Actor types 182. The classification of actor figures 182.

6 Dramatic Action: The Stage Director's First Task 183–228

The conflict about the primacy of persona vs plot in drama 183. An analysis of human *action* 183. Personal action 184. The cause-and-objective nexus of personal action 186. Interaction 187. Agreement and conflict 188. The pragmatic nexus of interaction 189. *The dramatic relation* 190. Types of dramatic relations 191. Changes of dramatic relations over time 195. The *dramatic situation* and the "french scene" (*výjev*) 196. Dramatic situation analysis: the number of personas in it 198. Chorus 198. Plot charts of dramatic forms 199. Monologue 200. Ensemble 201. Personas' weight in a situation 202. Dramatic polyphony 203. Personal concatenation 205. The concealment motif 205. *The manifestation principle* 206. The effect of manifestation 209. *The dramatic plot*: its extensity and continuity 211. Combining ostensive and imagined components; the exposition 212. The idea of a dramatic plot 214. Plot ending. The role of chance in drama 215. *The stage director's task*: the co-adaptation of interplay 216. The synthesis actor figures and the form of interplay 217. The director's *first* task: *director-conductor* 219. Their specific talent 221. *The dramatic form*. A strict temporal bond 222. The transitoriness of the plot 223. The asymmetry of the plot 225. The principle of gradation 226. The dynamic and the agogic forms in spoken drama 226. In combination with the imagined form 227.

7 Theatrical Scene: The Stage Director's Second Task 229–269

The definition of the theatrical scene 229. The delimitation of the scene 230. The structure of its space 231. The extent of the "dramatic location" 231. The segmentation of the scene: the neutral scene 233. The fixed fill of the scene; *scenic objects* in general 234. From the actor to the scene 234. Functional and characterising objects 236. The issue of genuineness of their material 237. The issue of their physicality 237. The *static* scenic qualities; they do not belong to the plastic arts 238. The *kinetic* scenic qualities 240. The scenic situation 241. The positional and motoric scenic qualities 243. Dramatising the kinetic scenic qualities 244. The dramatic scene as a mental force field 244. *An overview of kinetic scenic qualities*. (A) Primary relations. (1) positional 245. (2) motoric 248. (B) Mutual relations. (1) positional 251. (2) motoric 254. (C) Ensemble 258. Chorus 259. *Variable* scenic qualities 262. Scenic lighting 262. The stage director's *second* task: *director-scenic*. Static scenic form 264. Kinetic scenic form 265. The mimetic requirement of the scenic form 265. The summative form of the dramatic work and its segmentation 266. The director-scenic's relation to the author 267. The apron orientation law 268. The degree of the scene's dramaticity. The director-scenic's specific talent 269.

8   Dramatic Music: The Composer's Creative Work · 270–331

The mimetic qualities of the music of sung drama 271. (I) *The pictorial capacity of music*. Portraying external things (tone painting) 273. Portraying inner states (soul painting) 275. The emotional (lyrical) effect of music 276. The aspirational (dramatic) effect of music 277. The similarity of the musical effect to human emotions and aspirations 278. Musical characterisation 282. Dramatising music through the personas' mimics and speech 282. (II) *The expressive capacity of music* 285. Musical quotations: conventional 285, authorial 287. The characteristic reminiscence 288. The characteristic motif (leitmotif) 289. Variations of leitmotifs 291. Motivic work 292. *Singing*. Its relation to speech 293. Opera singing as a type of personas' vocal expression 295. The declamatory principle 295. The national character of declamatory melodies 297. *The polyphony (multi-vocality) of music* 298. Singing and the orchestra 300. Multi-part singing 302. *The dramatic composer's creative work*; not setting the text to music, but the situations 303. Anticipating the director-conductor in the temporal form 305. Anticipating the actor in the vocal expression 306. The opera conductor-director 308. The double invention of the musico-dramatic creative work 309. *The musico-dramatic formations*; the degree of music's dramaticity. The musical persona, its singing task 313. Its orchestral music 314. The musical interplay: situational music 316. Musical motivation 318. Musico-dramatic synthesis 319. Musical manifestation 321. The actor's playing in accordance with the music 322. The operatic ensemble and chorus 323. The scenic tasks of music 325. The entr'acte tasks of music 327. The scenic melodrama 329. Sound and music in spoken drama 330.

THE PRINCIPLE OF STYLISATION · 333–374

9   Realism and Idealism: The Basis of Theatrical Illusion · 334–356

Condition of *resemblance* for the mimetic work 334. The requirement of imitation for the mimetic creative work. Naturalism 335. Realism and stylisation 336. Idealism 337. The principle of artistic empirism; relative realism 338. Subjective naturalism, i.e., illusionism 339. *The theatrical illusion* 340. The theatrical conception 341. The theatrical focus 343. Its psychological analysis 344. The dual theatrical conceptual image 346. The isolation of the dramatic work 347. Separating the stage from the auditorium 349. *The stylistic principles of the dramatic work*: The principle of relative realism 349, the principle of consistent stylisation 350, the principle of artistic economy 351. The principle of subjective realism 352, the requirement of inner truthfulness 354. The audience's experiences and knowledge 354.

10 Dramatic Styles   357–374

The concept of the artistic style 357. *Technical* dramatic styles 358. The primacy of the dramaticity principle over the stylisation requirement 359. *An overview of technical stylisations.* Speech stylisation: the principle of literariness 360. The actor's stylisation 362. The stage director's stylisation 363. The visual requirement of the fixed fill of the scene 365. The stylisation of music; the musicality requirement 366. *Psychological* dramatic styles 370. *Historico-social* dramatic styles; the divergence of individual styles 373. Conclusion 374.

FOREWORD

This book, which I offer here to the public, arose from lectures on the subject that I delivered as a specialised aesthetician at Charles University. My first lecture series on "Theoretical Dramaturgy" took place in the winter semester of 1913–14 and was dedicated not only to spoken drama but, towards the end, also to opera. After a longer break I returned to the subject matter in an effort to find a formulation as generally valid as possible. I presented the results of my reflections at the Philosophical Union in Brno in 1922, in two lectures called "Principles of Theoretical Dramaturgy". One part of the lecture, called "The Basis of the Theatrical Scene", was published in the *Moravsko-slezská revue* 1923; the advertised publication of the whole work did not materialise. I have addressed the problem of the theatrical illusion in the study "The Aesthetic Preparation of the Mind" (*Česká mysl* XVII, 1921) and in the article "Puppet Theatre" (*Drobné umění* 1923) as well as in smaller essays. In the summer semester of 1925 I delivered a special university lecture "The Aesthetics of the Opera". Two samples from it have come out: "The Dramatic Possibilities of the Opera" in the collection *Nové české divadlo 1918-26* and "How Opera is Composed" in *Nové české divadlo 1927*.[2] I gave a similar special lecture "The Aesthetics of the Dramatic Text" in the summer semester of 1927. This is probably all the outer evidence documenting the phases of my work on the subject.

The principal idea of this book is: First, *the establishment of the dramatic art* as an autonomous and self-sufficient art form that would comprise spoken drama, sung drama and the related genres as its special forms. Second, *a formulation of general principles* of this art, from which the principles of the individual genres would follow according to their specific material properties. In brief: a systematic treatment of a new art, on a par with other well-known and established arts. What has led me to this idea, apart from theoretical impulses – and here I would like to emphasise the views of my teacher *Hostinský* – was my own artistic practice. As an opera composer I have always felt vividly and decisively that a dramatist is a *different* kind of artist from a

---

[2] All of Zich's preparatory texts are listed in the bibliography. Only two of them are available in English translation: his 1923 essay "Puppet Theatre" (Zich 2015) and his manuscript treatise "Principles of Theoretical Dramaturgy" (Zich 2016). All footnotes are ours.

poet or a composer, although they could join in a certain personal union. This is the theme of the first part of this book.

As for the detailed elaboration of this design in the second part, the conception and arrangement of the material are my own. Factually it does not contain – as that would be entirely impossible in a systematic study – *only my* own thoughts, especially when it comes to spoken drama, which has recently been thoroughly theorised. Nonetheless, specialists will appreciate how many new thoughts and concepts of my own there are here. In my treatment of sung drama I could also rely on my own compositional experience. I believe that a theory and aesthetics of the dramatic art in a strictly scientific form as I have presented here is a novelty. As for questions of style, discussed in the third part, I have sought to establish a solid bedrock in the jumble of vague, confused and even contradictory views by addressing the issue of theatrical illusion on the basis of psychology, or rather noetics. From this angle I approached other issues, such as the eternal binary of realism and idealism. I cherish the hope that I have brought at least a little light to all these problems, especially in those that are topical in the artistic and specifically theatrical life nowadays. However, theory does not make art; that is what artists are for. But artists need to evolve. A good theory leads well and directly; a bad one misleads. Everyone who has sincerely wished to move ahead has taste a bit of both.

Otakar Zich
Prague, May 1931

INTRODUCTION

This book deals with the *theory and aesthetics of the dramatic art*.

A theoretical study of a particular artistic discipline pertains to a specific *structure* that works belonging to that discipline have; an aesthetic study relates to their aesthetic, i.e., emotional *effect*. In principle, an aesthetic study is broader because even objects that do not count as art could have an aesthetic effect – e.g., natural phenomena or man-made works. If our intent is an aesthetic study of *artistic* works, this selection clearly narrows down the aesthetic study to studying the aesthetic working of the moment that makes these works "artistic" – and that is their specific structure. A theoretical study is also broader because it can morphologically study objects existing outside art; if our intent again is the objects of *art*, a study of the structure needs to respect that this is a structure of an aesthetically effective work. It follows then that in the study of *art* the theoretical and aesthetic approaches *interweave* so closely that it is practically best to combine them, otherwise we would not escape constant repetition and cross-references. This is a consequence of the method of *scientific aesthetics*, which derives its findings inductively from the material given by experience, rather than deductively from some *a priori* philosophical principles, as speculative aesthetics does.

Combining the theoretical and the aesthetic approaches also has the consequence that the material basis of our study will not cover all dramatic works, but only a selection restricted to those that are truly *valuable*. Strictly speaking, such a selection is always subjective but reality shows that one can achieve a significant extent of objectivity from the consensus of many, especially from the consensus of experts, and from the selection done by time, which corrects – sometimes more quickly, sometimes more leniently – the many injustices of contemporaries towards excellent artworks that were rejected by their age as well as towards poor works once admired. What needs to be shunned is a dogmatic selection, done not according to an unprejudiced impression of a work, but according to some norms or proclamations that – as we know – accompany every age of artistic life. There is not only a dogmatism of the conservative type, but also a progressive one. Nevertheless, even from the less valuable works or from works that are weaker in some of their aspects (as is common in dramatic art) one can glean theoretical findings, even negative ones, which are no less important – and we shall do so.

This book falls into three parts: the first, entitled "The Concept of Dramatic Art", is basically methodological. The second, called "The Principle of Dramaticity", contains predominantly aesthetic reflections, despite the above-mentioned proximity of both approaches, while the third part, named "The Principle of Stylisation", is dominated by theoretical or art-disciplinary reflections.

THE CONCEPT OF DRAMATIC ART

1 THE CHARACTER OF THE DRAMATIC WORK

It is a common practice to understand the term "dramatic art" as spoken drama or theatre and to subsume it under literary art (*umění básnické*). As such, its theoretical and aesthetic considerations would belong to poetics. Yet our conception of the dramatic art is wider and also includes opera or sung drama, which usually comes under music – or, more specifically, vocal music – and is therefore habitually the subject matter of musical theory and aesthetics. *Spoken drama (činohra)* and *sung drama (zpěvohra)* are not the only two forms of the *dramatic art* in our sense of the term, but they are the most prominent and artistically developed – one could say, the most representative ones. For this reason, they will be the main subjects of our consideration.

Combining spoken drama and sung drama in a wider discipline of the dramatic art, as we are proposing to do, is not mechanical but organic. It means removing them from the literary and musical arts, respectively, and uniting them into *a new art* which shares many ties and points of contact with them but is nonetheless an independent art in its own right. This is the principal standpoint of this book.

How is it possible, though, to unite artistic disciplines which have been so far – albeit in theory only – divided into two different arts? This unity is the consequence of a fundamentally different view of spoken drama and sung drama in comparison to the view commonly held by existing theories. When a literary theorist speaks of spoken drama, they have in mind a book and its text, and similarly, a music theorist takes an opera for its musical score. They both know that both these works are performed in the theatre, but they still take the two *texts* – the verbal and the musical – for entirely sufficient for their observations. But practice is different. Not only theatre artists but also the theatre audience consider spoken drama or sung drama to be that which is performed in the theatre. This is the only correct standpoint, and we will also assume it. Subjectively – that is, from the audience's point of view – we can formulate it as follows:

Spoken drama (činohra) and opera – in short, the dramatic work – is what we perceive (see and hear) in the course of a performance in the theatre.

The statement that a dramatic work is the theatre performance seems obvious at first sight, almost trivial. Unfortunately, that is not so and the error of viewing the dramatic work merely as its (literary or musical) text is so deeply ingrained that people cannot help but fall for it again and again. In the present study, we shall always understand the "dramatic work" exclusively and systematically in the above sense, and we ask the reader to bear this in mind.

In short, the dramatic work is a work of theatre, and the sum of all dramatic artworks – that is, the dramatic art – belongs to the art of theatre. As we have established, this is the view held by the audience as well as the theatre artists. Those who "make theatre" are – for the most part – convinced that dramatic art and the theatrical art are one and the same thing. This is not the case and we have deliberately given this book the title "Aesthetics of the Dramatic Art", and not "theatre" art, even if the latter might have expressed our above view more clearly. Theatre art has a wider scope than dramatic art; in addition to dramatic art, it includes other art forms that principally do not merit the term "dramatic". We shall return to this problem later, once we have established what exactly the term means. For the time being, we want to point out that the above statement does not provide a definition of the dramatic work, but only its identification. The statement stresses the *true nature* of the dramatic work. From there follow both its typical and specific features – i.e., those that distinguish the dramatic art (or, more generally, theatre art) from all other arts that lack them. What this signifies follows from the following observation:

Every inquiry that aspires to be scientific – such as ours – must employ the empirical method: it must begin from experience and return to it in order to verify its results. In this case the experience is an artistic one: it pertains to artworks we have called "dramatic" and our cultural life surely makes them available to us in abundance. That is the concrete material and its analyses and comparisons will serve to infer the general properties of the dramatic art and the principles that govern it. Understandably the results based on "theatrical" material would simply be different from those based merely on "textual" material – by which we mean both the literary and the musical text. The empirical method will allow us to verify our findings again by means of artistic experiences – and we or anyone else can do that. The principles (*zákony*) of the dramatic art, uncovered in this way, will not disagree with the artistic practice or force it in a particular direction – as so many of the dogmatic theories of various "schools" do – because the principles will have arisen from practice, and so they also apply to it.

What then are the *specific features* of a dramatic work (from our "theatrical" point of view)? When we think of any performance of a drama or opera, we realise that we are not only *spectators* but also *listeners*: both *at the same time*. This union of a *dual simultaneous* perception is not present in any art other than the dramatic one (or, more generally, the theatrical one). In front of a visual work – a building, a statue or a picture – we are only spectators; with a literary (*básnické*) or a musical work we are only listeners. It is true that we can also read literary or works but it seems apparent that what we perceive with our sight while reading – i.e., printed letters or notation – does not belong to that work of literature or music, and we will not take it as such, even though this visual element may itself possess artistic qualities when assessed independently (such as the graphic design of a book). By contrast, that which we can see during a theatre performance is definitely a part of the dramatic work and it forms a component just as essential as that which we can hear. The union of both components – the visible (optical) and the audible (acoustic) – is not only characteristic but also *inseparable* – and that is true specifically in the case of dramatic artworks, unlike the theatrical artworks in general (e.g., ballet). This means that excluding one of these two components and narrowing down to the other component alone feels not only as an impoverishment of the work, but as its mutilation. The work thus becomes *incomplete*.

> Let us imagine that we stop our ears during a performance of spoken drama or opera, so that we cannot hear but can only see. Conversely, let us imagine that we shut our eyes so that we cannot see anything, but only listen (which happens during a radio broadcast of a theatre performance). The omission of one component damages not only the work as a whole, but also the *remaining component* itself. What are these people saying and how? I can see them in a particular situation behaving in a particular way – and they must be saying something! Conversely, how are the persons behaving while saying a particular line or that? And they must be particular persons, but I cannot see them. And what is happening now during this protracted silence? Perhaps something serious, but I don't know what it is! Speech without visible action is somehow more abstract, and visible action without speech is more vague. It is as if we cut up an organism and threw away one half; the remaining half will also be stained with blood, and while it was full of life before, it is now paralysed. Those who do not mind and are satisfied with such a one-dimensional perception of the artwork have no true sense of what real dramatic art is. And that refers, as we shall see, to all those who instead of the dramatic work make do with the mere dramatic text.
>
> However, there are works that will not suffer greatly from a reduction to merely one of these two components. "Literary drama" serves as an example of work that can stand fairly well the suppression of the *optical* impression. They work quite well when we only hear them, and sometimes even better than if we watched them on stage, as some of these dramas are not intended for staging at all. They are poems rather than drama. Another example are numerous old operas, especially Italian operas of the 17th and 18th centuries. Although their staging often offered a splendid spectacle, the optical component was not united with the acoustic organically enough to make its omission result in the aforementioned impression of frustrating incompleteness. If we leave aside the recitatives and spoken passages, we are left with concerts rather than

sung drama and it is sufficient to merely listen to these "*concert operas*" as we may call them. The two examples just given do not represent strictly defined genres, but some of them closely border on spoken and sung dramas. However, even if staged, one can hardly classify them as full-fledged dramatic works.

An opposite example is provided by two genres, which are clearly distinct by the mere fact that they voluntarily forego the acoustic component. In the case of *pantomime* this holds only to a point, because it is usually accompanied by music. Nevertheless, the fact that it does not involve speaking or singing creates the aforementioned impression of a frustrating incompleteness, which intensifies whenever the pantomime attempts to move closer to spoken drama and weakens or disappears whenever it proceeds to pure dance. Film presents an even more striking example. Film must be counted as a kind of theatre art – at least in a broad sense – because a cinema is nothing more than a theatre adapted to the specific conditions of mechanical reproduction. Although film provides a splendid spectacle, we lack the acoustic component of the impression. Our desire to hear the persons that we can see is so great that mere captions with explanatory lines are not enough to satisfy it. It leads towards a desire for sound film.

We need to emphasise one specific circumstance that is included in the above analysis but might escape our notice. There may be the objection that these two essential components, the significance of which we have stressed above, are *both* present when merely *reading* a dramatic text. By following the text and particularly its stage directions, we can hear in our minds not only the personas' speech, but we can see these same personas, their actions and even the scene (the stage) in our imaginations. These are not optical perceptions but mere mental images, however as a result of being ostensive they may surely be sufficient substitutes for a sensory impression. We also can read a poem, and even read it usually *silently*, and we content ourselves fully with our "inner hearing" – and the same is true with music. An expert musician may read the score and is able to hear even a complicated composition in all its detail in their imagination. The only difference between reading letters and reading a musical score is that everyone can do the former, while only a few are capable of the latter, since it requires both a special talent and training. No doubt imagination alone lacks the liveness, the power or the urgency of a sensory experience, but every reader knows this; what matters is that reading satisfies the reader *without causing harm to the work*. Why then should not the reading of a dramatic text serve as a weak but satisfactory substitute for the work in performance?

Such argumentation is valid when it comes to literature and music and one would gladly hope that more people got used to hearing in their minds the poems they read, particularly lyrical ones. In the case of the dramatic art, however, it does not hold, and it would not hold even if the reader of a dramatic text tried to imagine the play scenically – which is otherwise very desirable. The reason is that for the reader of a poem or score, the text *determines* the auditive mental images and as such they are the same for everyone. In contrast: while the dramatic text *determines* the reader's auditive mental images (more or less determines, as we shall see), and so they are almost the same for all readers, the visual mental images are quite *arbitrary* and they are *different* for different readers. This is similar to reading a novel (that is, a literary work) where we often imagine its personas, objects and events, but each of us does so differently – someone does so vividly, another feebly, and yet another imagines nothing at all. But when it comes to a literary work this optical mental vision is the reader's personal addition, which does not belong to the work itself, whereas with a dramatic work it should be the work's *substantive* (*podstatná*) part.

> This difference in the work's optical component will stand out very clearly if the acoustic component is sensory: that is, when we can hear the work actually, not only in our imagination. Let us imagine that we are listening to a story being told and that on this prompt our imagination draws some "pictures". In contrast, let us imagine we are listening to a radio broadcast of a live performance of spoken drama, and that we complement what we hear with visual mental images, even including images of the scenic business. In the former case, our visions are merely a personal experience, but in the latter case they are a substitute for what is actually happening on stage and what those who are present in the theatre can see. How arbitrary this substitution is needs no proof.

Even so, someone could object: does not a similar situation occur when *the same dramatic work* – e.g., Shakespeare's *Othello* – is staged in different circumstances – that is to say, in different theatres, with different cast, directors and so on? Is not even here the optical component – i.e., that which we can see on the scene – different and to some extent also personally arbitrary? This objection conceals circular reasoning because by "the same dramatic work" it clearly means the same dramatic text. But for us who have accepted the "theatrical" conception of the dramatic work it is clear that the performances of Shakespeare's *Othello* are *not* "*the same*" dramatic work but different dramatic works [performances], even though not entirely different. Together, they form *a group* of dramatic works with *the same script* – and naturally written by the same author; when it comes to opera, we also need to add: with *the same music* [score] and the same composer. Logically we refer to such a group of dramatic works by a shared name of the playwright or composer, and by a shared name that they gave to *their textual creation*: Shakespeare's *Othello*, Smetana's *The Bartered Bride*, etc.[3] However, this shared name does not turn

---

3   *The Bartered Bride* (Prodaná nevěsta) is a comic opera by the Czech composer Bedřich Smetana (1824-1884) with the libretto by Karel Sabina. The opera opened at the Provisional Theatre in Prague in 1866 and continues to be a popular title of the repertoire internationally.

the group of dramatic works into a single work. Let us recall our own theatrical experiences of watching such performances of *Othello* or *The Bartered Bride* in different theatres (let us say in Czech theatre only, for now), and in different eras, if we have lived through them, done by different directors and with different casts of actors or singers! What a diversity of impressions! Those performances *hardly shared anything more* than *the bare text* (and not even its delivery!) or the *music*. To say, as is habitual, that these were merely "different performances" (*provedení*) of the same work, would – literally – mean to shut one's eyes to everything else, above all to the whole visible component.

However, can one speak – in line with the above objection – of an analogy with the imaginative complementation of the optical component when one is reading a dramatic text? Certainly not. Optical mental images of different readers are not only different but – as we have pointed out – *arbitrary* (*libovolný*) in the true sense of the word.[4] They are personal associations of each of the readers, arising spontaneously and without any claim to their value (or validity). Such arbitrariness is absolutely not the case with the optical impression of an audience member during a performance, because what the spectator sees is determined by what happens on stage – the scenic action is formed based on *principles or logic* (*zákonitě*), with an artistic intent and with a claim to one's value.

And this has brought us to the root of the matter. The acoustic component of a dramatic work may be imagined based on reading the script, since it is determined by the text to such an extent that even in our imagination (*představa*) it will be logical and artistic. This is not possible for the optical component, because there is no such fixed support (*opora*). In other words, the reading of a literary or a musical text is a sufficient substitute for listening to a literary or a musical (instrumental or vocal) composition, whereas the reading of a play script, a book or a musical score is not a *sufficient* substitute for the experiencing of the dramatic work (i.e., the live performance) of spoken or sung drama, because it does not do justice – in the aforementioned sense – to the optical component of the work, which is just as substantive (*podstatná*) as the acoustic one. It follows from here that a dramatic work can subjectively exist *only as the percept* (*vněm*) of an *actual*, real performance, where both the visible and audible components have *a quality of sensory ostensiveness*. This assertion conclusively justifies our rejection of the "textual conception" of the dramatic work and the adoption of a "theatrical conception". It is also, as a matter of fact, a consequence of the problem of the *fixing* (*fixace*) of a temporal work of art. We will come to it later.

---

4   *Libovolný* means literally *up to one's will*. Our English equivalent *arbitrary* corresponds with its meaning *up to one's arbitration or decision*.

The above analysis, done to identify the specific features of a dramatic work, may be summarised in the following statement:

The dramatic work consists of **two** *simultaneous, inseparable and ostensive* **heterogeneous** *components – the visible (optical) and the audible (acoustic) one.*

We have also arrived at another statement, which is closely related to the above:

A necessary existential condition of the dramatic work is its **actual** *(real) performance.*

The first statement distinguishes dramatic art (i.e., the sum of dramatic works) from arts with a single component – either the optical one (such as the plastic arts) or the acoustic one (such as literature or music). As for dance, the statement applies to it as well if we drop the word "inseparable", because in pure ballet the two components – the visible component of dance and the audible component of music – despite their shared rhythm and mood (their rhythmic and atmospheric union) always retain their independence and self-sufficiency.

The second statement distinguishes dramatic art from literature and music, where an artwork may exist not only as a sensory percept given by a real performance, but also as a mere mental image on the basis of reading a verbal or a musical text.

ः ः ः

With the conclusions of our above findings in mind, we ask: how is it possible that the "textual conception" of the dramatic work has not only come into existence, but has endured and led to such errors as the inclusion of drama in the domain of literature, and of opera in the domain of music? There are two causes.

The first cause is the fact that the dramatic work is a *temporal* artwork. As it exists in real time it acquires it qualities, particularly its *transitoriness* (*transitornost*): its passing nature. Every dramatic work exists only for a given, limited time: it begins at a certain moment, lasts for a given time and ends at a certain moment. Before its beginning and after its end it does not exist. We become feelingly aware of this seemingly commonplace thing for instance when we miss the beginning of a show, because at that point the beginning of the artwork has been irrevocably lost to us. If we miss a performance altogether (say, an opening night), we cannot replace it. Even if there is another night (*reprisa*), it will be different at least slightly, if not a great deal (a different cast, etc.). The same is true with musical and even literary works if they are performed by live musical playing, singing, recitation or narration. But here record (*zápis*) is possible capturing in verbal or musical writing everything necessary. To be sure, such a book or score does not "sound"; it only contains, as we say, "dead" marks that must be "brought to life" by a performance. Nonetheless, the book or score is a *lasting* thing, exempt from time: a thing that can be used at any time to realise the artwork – whether in real (performance), or in ideal terms (reading). By its objective existence the literary book or a musical score resembles a work of the plastic arts, such as a building, a statue or a painting. However, it differs from them – which should not be forgotten – in that *it is not an artwork in itself* but only its *possibility* (potentiality; *možnost*). Thus a literary or a musical text can at best be called a potential artwork. It stands to reason – also with a view to the aforementioned disadvantage of temporal arts and the advantages of "texts" – that the dramatic art also desires such record (*zápis*) and that we feel inclined to see it in the script of spoken drama or the score of an opera – all the more so that the *history* of the dramatic art has left us with little else left but such bare texts. We have shown, however, that the "dramatic text" is only a partial record of the dramatic work.

> The other cause of the above-mentioned errors is that in both literature and music there are *texts* that are *very similar* to the *texts* of spoken dramas or operas. Literary theorists, who are used to assessing works (and righly so) within their field on the basis of the text, assert (wrongly) from this practice that playscripts belong with literary works and that spoken drama – or, as it is commonly called, drama – to literature, forming one of the three main literary genres, alongside lyric and epic (narrative) writing. We have touched on such "seeming likes" in the textual realm before: they are the so-called literary dramas and "dramatic poems". A few examples will suffice: Goethe's *Faust*, Arthur de Gobineau's *La Renaissance* or Adam Mickiewicz's *Konrad Wallenrod*[5]. This is even more apparent in music. Music contains entire musical genres whose scores – since music theorists also deal with texts only – resemble opera scores "like peas in a pod", because they contain not only musical texts (i.e., notation) but also words (lyrics). These are various kinds of vocal music, most prominently oratorios, both sacred and especially secular, then various cantatas, Passion music, ballads and so on. Among the examples are Hector Berlioz's *La damnation de Faust*, Haydn's *The Seasons* and Bach's *St Matthew Passion*. Music theorists find it natural to include operas alongside oratorios in the list of vocal genres, where the above examples belong. Of course they know that operas are "produced" on stage; but it is a given that all music goes hand in hand with "producing". The performing artists are the same in both cases: singers (both solo and choral), orchestra players and a conductor. The fact that in opera the singers are also actors and they perform on a stage is out of the theorists' focus. No matter if a theatre

---

5   *La Renaissance* (1877) by Joseph Arthur de Gobineau (1816–1882) is a historical treatise in the form of a dialogue in scene, featuring five main heroes: Savonarola, Cesare Borgia, Pope Julius II, Pope Leo X and Michelangelo, as well as countless smaller roles, both fictitious and historical.
    Konrad Wallenrod (1828) by the Polish romantic poet Adam Mickiewicz (1798–1855) is in fact a historical narrative poem.

or a concert hall, a stage or a podium – the only difference is that in the theatre there is also something to be seen – but that is outside of music! And so it is that sung drama is neglected in music theory, without the slightest understanding of its dramatic nature.

It is fair to admit that literary theorists do not ignore the theatrical existence of spoken drama to the same extent that music theorists do with opera. The reason for this is that the producing of musical compositions is quite common and their silent reading quite exceptional, whereas poems and other literary works are mostly destined for silent reading and produced, i.e., performed, only exceptionally. That is why literary people find it remarkable that works of an entire branch of literature, namely dramatic poems, are written in order to be produced – performed and that on stage – and that this is commonly done. The analogy with music seems obvious: a body of musicians and singers, led by a conductor corresponds to an ensemble of *actors* led by a director. However, literary theorists pay no attention to the construction of the scene (i.e., to the stage), because they consider it, at best, a question of the visual arts. On the other hand, they have an interest in actors, since it is actors who deliver the text of the dramatic work. Acting for them is a *reproductive art*, necessary for the realisation of a dramatic poem as appropriate – on stage. This approach surely does more justice to the true character of the dramatic work than looking exclusively at the text; a theory of acting can explain a number of the peculiarities that "dramatic poems" have in contrast to other poems, especially the narrative ones. But this approach is opposed by actors themselves, who rightly point out that their art does not merely reproduce, but produces as well; that they do not only carry out what the dramatic text prescribes, but create something new, and that this new thing is the core of their art.

If the following analysis proves that *acting is not a reproductive art*, this is not to suggest that we consider reproductive art to be inferior, let alone semi-artistic. Generally speaking, the artistic value of reproductive art is undoubtedly a match for any other creative art. It is enough to remember the virtuosi of reproductive art in music to acknowledge this fully. Our concern here is a purely theoretical clarification of terms and concepts. And it is not the word that is at stake but the thing. Words may be ambiguous and have a number of different meanings; their significance may be narrower or broader. If we are to approach it scientifically, we must first state *what exactly* we mean by a certain word and *this* meaning we must *keep consistently*. Otherwise every discourse turns into idle talking. We intend to undertake such terminological inquiries throughout and do so quite often since aesthetic and literary critical discussions often deploy numerous words and phrases inaccurately and ambiguously.

What the feature of *"reproductive art"* are can best be seen in an analysis of its model – the reproductive musical art. A composer hears their work in their own imagination; but the composer wants to make it audible for other people – and that requires the co-operation of performing musicians – and he or she also wants to secure its productions

1 THE CHARACTER OF THE DRAMATIC WORK

in the future. For these reasons, the composer must write down as much of it as possible. The musicians' and singers' task is, in fact, to play and sing the notes according to "the notation". What aspects of the notes are captured in the score and how accurately? Their timbre is prescribed by the instrument that should play it – including the human voice. The pitch and the relative duration of the notes are accurately given in the notation. The composer, however, prescribes also the dynamics and the tempo, even though not as exactly as to prevent the reproductive artists from having some freedom of variation. If we add that the artists are also free to alter at will the timbre (by their way of playing and singing), albeit within certain limits, we can see that their creative freedom consists in *nuancing that* which has been *determined by the score*. The reproductive musical art is the art of *nuance*; what is added at will is *homogenous* with what the score prescribes. This is, of course, a mere theoretical statement and not an evaluation, for in these "mere nuances" lies the life of the work. We may even say that it is the minutest, irrational shades that the composer has no way of capturing in the score by marks or directions (as is done with the major nuances) that produce the strongest effect. It is through these minute nuances – their choice and their execution – that the artistic personality of the reproductive musician speaks to us.

The same holds for the reproductive art of literature – recitation. It may seem that a literary text determines its oral delivery much less than a musical score and grants the reciter much greater creative freedom than a musician has. This would wrong. Every piece of literature is always written in a certain language (e.g., in Czech) and every language has *its way of speaking* determined by the conventions of a certain community of people (e.g., Czechs), which determines to a high degree the different aspects of the language, such as the rhythm or the melodic cadence. The poet naturally presupposes that the person who wants to recite the work has a perfect command of the language in which it was written. For that reason the author does not need to capture in the text more than is necessary. The aforementioned conventions nonetheless determine the other aspects to such a degree of accuracy that the reciters who wish to avoid errors and incomprehension have little beyond a limited opportunity of *nuancing* individual aspects of their delivery.

Generally speaking, it can be said that a reproductive artist *performs* what is *prescribed by the text* (literary or musical), adding mere *nuances*, which are homogenous with the given. In contrast with this, what is an actor's performance with regards to the dramatic text – taking only spoken drama for now? The text – the direct speeches of dramatic personas – is really contained in the actor's performance, namely in their speaking. Acting, therefore, in regards to its audible side, could be called a reproductive art – with the two specifications though. First, an actor's delivery is not "recitation" because actors use the aforementioned freedom of nuancing to a different end: to characterise the dramatic persona. Second, the speaking is not the actor's only vocal or audible expression (let us think of laughter, groaning, intentional noises and many other sounds). We will discuss both these points in detail in the chapter on acting. For now, let us say that not even from the acoustic aspect is an actor's performance merely reproductive art. It brings not only nuances – those specifically actorly nuances prescribed by the text – but also a number of other things that are not at all given in the text and cannot therefore be *merely* nuanced, but things that the actor must create themselves. The playwright occasionally indicates by means of *directions outside of* the dramatic text proper that they wish the actor to express something vocally (such as "bursts into laughter" and "weeps"), but such a stage direction is no more than an instruction for the actor to do so at that given moment. It needs to be admitted, though, that all such expressions of the actor are homogenous with their speech – that is, they are also audible.

However, what can we say about the visible aspects of an actor's performance – the actor's mask, mimics, gestures, the way the dramatic persona behaves and how it acts? All this is surely not *given* by the dramatic text in the sense of our analysis above – that is, the text does not prescribe in such a way that an actor's only freedom is in nuancing. Besides, as it is something visible, it is *heterogeneous* to what a performance of a text creates – that is, something audible. It is true that at times the actor's visible performance follows, to a certain extent, the *directions* that the author adds *outside of* the dramatic text. But just like above, these directions are merely the author's wishes and instructions and we cannot even say that the actor "produces" them in the same sense that he or she delivers the dramatic text! Let us imagine that someone commissions a painter to paint a picture and instructs the painter in words or in writing what they want to see in the painting. Will the painter become a reproductive artist by following the instructions? Is it reproductive art when a book illustrator embellishes a novel with pictures based on detailed descriptions of the novel's scenes? Certainly not. Despite all prescriptions and instructions, it is a fully creative art. That fact that visual artists bound by such prescriptions can create artistically valuable works is just as true as that their other, free works may be thoroughly valueless. The question of artistic value is clearly a fundamentally different issue.

We have arrived at a similar, or even identical conclusion as with our earlier discussion of the "reading" of the dramatic text. Someone might raise the objection that aside from the *stage directions* – sometimes not even specified by the dramatist – the actor's audible, but also their *visible* performance is sufficiently determined by the *entirety* of the dramatic text – that it is *contained* in it, even if only *potentially*; and that the actor is only allowed to nuance it – albeit quite broadly. Our experience refutes this assumption: we know well that performances of outstanding actors in "the same role" agree in little more than the mere text, and that they differ – especially in their visual aspects – to such an extent that one could not possibly call them "nuances of one and the same" in the sense of a true reproductive art. Moreover, such an assumption is a *principal* error: while we may visualise a performance on the basis of the dramatic text and its stage directions, such imaginings cannot claim artistic value. While the dramatic text gives an *ideational* directive to the actor's visible playing, it does not *concretely* determine its specific artistic qualities. These qualities are *optically dynamic*.

Ignoring the specific features of acting is the cause of the erroneous views that we criticise here. First and foremost, acting, including its optical side, is clearly a temporal (time-based) art. While a work of the visual arts – a picture, a statue or a building – belongs to the logical category of "objects", *acting as a work of art belongs entirely to the category of "actions"* [events or happenings]. It is not a static but a dynamic thing: the actor's *work* is simply the actor's *performance* – and yet, acting is not a reproductive art.[6] The contradiction is only seeming since the concept of "reproductive art" (*výkonné umění*) is a technical term that assumes a preexisting text, on which the production is based – in other words, "*an execution (výkon) of a prescribed* work of art". However, is not a composer who improvises their own composition a reproductive artist? We could say at most that he or she – in regards to the composition – is a creative artist who also happens to be their own reproductive artist. We could say *the same* about an actor, provided that we replace the words "happens to be" by "is necessarily". The difference between them is that the composer *may also write down* the score of their work *for others* – that is, for reproductive artists in the true sense of the word – whereas the actor *cannot* do so when it comes to the visible aspect of their work.

Failing to realise the *impossibility of fixing* the *variable optical qualities* by any "script" – that is, by *invariable* symbols – is the second cause of the erroneous view that takes acting for a reproductive art. If it were possible to write a score of an actor's performance in the same way that scores of musical compositions are written, it would be evident to everybody that that actor's performances are works of art in their own right. But who would write them down? The dramatist, perhaps, but more likely the director. Actors themselves could hardly do so because such scores would not "match" in the interplay. On the other hand, they would be able to "execute" them just like orchestra musicians or singers execute their parts – that is, free *only in nuances*. Then they would be true reproductive artists. But this is impossible.

---

6   In Czech, Zich uses *výkon*, one of the words for *performance*. *Výkon* refers to something that is achieved, executed or simply carried out. The Czech term for *reproductive art* is *výkonné umění*, which shares the same root with *výkon*. Here Zich emphasises that while the actor's art is their *výkon* (the way they carry out their role), acting is not a *výkonné* (reproductive, executive) art.

Thus, an actor's work of art is a creative work; it is not comprised in the dramatic text, but rather, it comprises the text – and moreover, it is complemented by the actor's own creative work. This creative work is naturally related to the dramatic text, but this relation does not have the character of reproductive art. It is a bond between two artefacts from *different arts* – there is a relation of *"artistic correspondence"* between them.

Cases when a work of art gives rise to another work of art of a different kind, whilst responding to it, are very frequent in art. We have mentioned book illustrations in a novel as an example in the above passage concerning stage directions. In such a case, the correspondence is not only in the contents but in form. Moreover, the correspondence is imperfect, because an illustration cannot tell the novel's plot but merely depict a particular moment. For a correspondence to be perfect – that is, to correspond in form too – it is necessary, if the primary work (the preexisting work) is a temporal, time-based work, that the secondary work (the derived work) is also temporal. Only then may both artworks form a perfect unity. As the *perfect analogy* to this instance, we might mention the act of *composing a musical piece to a literary work* – such as a song with an instrumental accompaniment. Here it is evident that the music which the composer created on the basis of the literary work is their own creative work, which is not contained in the poem but rather contains the text within itself – i.e., in its singing part – and additionally supplements it with something new: the music. Naturally, this music, the tune with its so-called "accompaniment", is not as autonomous as if it were without that text; the music is clearly bound up with it, but not *determined* by it in the above sense of the word. How different such music can be, even if it is composed to *identical* texts, can be interestingly shown in musical compositions to the same poem by different, mostly prominent composers (who surely did justice to the text) – such as Goethe's *Der Erlkönig*, set to music by Franz Schubert and by Carl Loewe, or *Mignon*, in the compositions of Beethoven, Schubert and Hugo Wolf. It is quite the same as with "different castings of one role" in spoken drama. To make this analogy perfect, let us imagine that the composer "sets the text to music" without writing down its score, and now he or she is playing it from memory as if it were an improvisation. Could we call this reproductive art? And yet that is exactly how many people see the more or less analogical act of the actor's performance – which we could call "setting the dramatic text to acting"! The fact that dramatic texts are written for the stage, while lyrical texts are not written for music, is inconsequential for the validity of our analogy. After all, sometimes the situation is reversed in both cases. This merely underlines the *self-sufficiency* of literary texts in comparison to dramatic texts. We will discuss the psychological reason for this situation in the chapter dealing with a dramatist's creative work.

What we have stated in this analysis with respect to the actor of spoken drama applies also to the opera actor. We may also speak about "reproductive art" only when it comes to the audible side of their performance. In other words, the opera actor is a reproductive artist only as long as they are a "singer" – and that merely with the proviso that operatic singing – intent on characterising a dramatic persona – is focused differently to concert singing (analogous to recitation). A detailed examination will follow in our discussion of sung drama. However, apart from singing, opera also involves an instrumental musical component, and the function of the orchestra with its conductor obviously belongs to the category of reproductive art, although even this performance – unlike instrumental concert productions – is governed in its nuances with respect to the drama.

2 THE SYNTHETIC THEORY

Our previous analysis has led to our rejection of the view of dramatic art that sees spoken drama (*činohra*) as part of literature, sung drama (*zpěvohra*) as part of (vocal) music, and acting as a special area of reproductive art. The very separating of two related genres of dramatic art into two different domains of art shows the one-sidedness of such a view, which quite unfairly – or even with a bias – favours *one* component of these works and ignores all others. This incorrect view, which unfortunately still persists and is subscribed to by critics as well as some of the public, could be called *aristocratic* – a purely figurative name, though, for the "aristocrats" in this case are the two front lined art forms, by the common assumptions: spoken drama is – mostly or at least *primarily* – literature, and sung drama is – mostly or at least primarily – music. Both these assumptions have done a lot of harm in artistic practice.

There is a different way of solving the problem of dramatic art theoretically without reducing it to a single art form. This approach comes from the remarkable variety of components in a dramatic work, particularly in sung drama. At the beginning of the first chapter, we established that a dramatic work has two heterogeneous components – the visible and the audible. Both each of these components further subdivide into components pointing to several other arts they resemble. The acoustic component of spoken drama (the actors' speech) looks like literature, and in opera, music joins in too. The optical component resembles the visual arts, namely architecture, sculpture and painting. It logically follows that the essence of dramatic art lies in *combining several arts* (a synthesis of art forms), none of which has aesthetic precedence over the others, since all of them are *artistically equal* in the final work that the audience perceives. This view of dramatic art – which we could analogically call *democratic*, in analogy to the above "aristocratic" label – is surely closer to reality and much more just to the above-mentioned components of a dramatic work.

> Seen in this way, sung drama would unite all of the generally recognised arts and create an *"all-arts work"*. This is Wagner's well-known idea of "Gesamtkunstwerk", as he presented it in his theoretical writings and demonstrated practically in his "music dramas". However, *Wagner's theory* does not stand the test of scientific criticism because it is speculative and dogmatic. It could be called *"communist"* – figuratively speaking, of

course – because it denies individual arts the right to exist independently and requires them to exist only collectively in the artistic super-work, and only sung drama – not even spoken drama – can fulfil that. Wagner argues that humanity's original primal art (a sort of mimic dance with primitive songs and music) was all-artistic, and thus all art forms should remain in this union rather than seek to break free and evolve independently, as has actually happened due to individualistic egotism of some of these arts. However, said "primal art" is no more than a hypothesis. Even if his hypothesis were plausible when it comes to time-based arts, the fact that something had been so does not imply that it should be so now, let alone for ever. This would deny any sense of *progress* (evolution), which manifests itself exactly in the differentiation of tasks and the division of labour between individual arts. Wagner concedes that the emancipated arts have learned something, but in requesting that these arts should now (i.e., in Wagner's time) give up their autonomy, he reduces the value of progress to a mere learning process.

In *Das Musikalisch-Schöne und Gesamtkunstwerk* (1877), Otakar Hostinský has developed a thorough comprehensive theory for combining different art forms. While firmly based in empiricism, which determined his concrete aesthetic formalism, he recognises that each individual art form has the right to evolve independently. To this, he adds the right (that is, not the obligation) to combine with the other forms. He analyses the conditions that allow various arts to merge in an organic union, and argues that literature and music, as temporal arts, cannot combine with the visual arts unless a temporal factor is involved – that is, a change or movement of the visible. For that he introduces the concept of *"scenic art"* as a third party in the combination of art forms; this *scenic art* is characteristic of the dramatic art. A combination of the scenic art with literature produces spoken drama; a combination of the scenic art with music produces pantomime, and a combination of all three arts produces musical drama (sung drama). Furthermore, there is also the combination of literature with music that produces vocal music (as well as melodrama). There are then three double and one triple combinations of arts, and Hostinský asserts and discusses the three conditions of their union: the semantic unity, the unity of temporal progress, and the unity of mood. With a view to temporality, scenic arts divide into two components: one of them is truly changeable – given by the playing actors – while the other is the unchanging contents of the visible scene (the stage set). Hostinský assigns the latter to the domain of the visual arts, but the former constitutes a specific and independent art, namely the *mimics* (or mimic art) or acting.

There are two issues that call for attention at this point. First and foremost it is significant that the earlier vague idea of the "visual arts" participating in a dramatic work has led us strictly logically to the formulation of a *new art* – i.e., acting – *of an equal order* with the other arts. Acting had of course been the subject of numerous theoretical and aesthetic studies, but only as a special kind of reproductive art associated with literature. The second issue is that mimics – but also the "scenic art" more broadly, which Hostinský combines with literature and music – only appears in such combinations but *does not exist* as an *autonomous* art – unlike literature and music, which clearly are self-standing. Mimic art (or scenic art) *must* therefore combine with one other art at least (e.g., literature) if it is to create a work of art known to our artistic experience (in this instance, it is spoken drama).

This theory about the essence of dramatic art as a *union of various arts*, which I will call the *synthetic theory*, leads on the one hand *necessarily* to the establishment of acting as an art, but on the other finds that this art has no independent existence. Acting is therefore an art *necessary* for dramatic art – and as such, it is essential – but it is *not sufficient* on its own!

This peculiarity may be explained by Hostinský's *narrow* conception of acting, for he defines "mimics" as the art "of movement in space" – in other words, only the actor's visible expression – and he subsumes the audible expression to literature. Such an art is an abstraction, a mere theoretical fiction. Isn't this clearly a relic of the "textual" conception of dramatic work as a work of literature? A broader conception of acting that corresponds with reality – taking acting in the totality of an actor's performance – will make acting not only a necessary, but under certain conditions also a sufficient (in spoken drama), art as an essence of dramatic art. This would acknowledge the full artistic autonomy of acting. We will come back to this later.

> Is the synthetic theory correct when it views dramatic art as a combination of arts? Epistemologically speaking this question is wrong. Every theory is developed with an aim to make comprehensible a certain set of facts and for this reason, the theory must necessarily impose certain simplification – in comparison to the facts' real-world complexities. If a theory leads to consequences which contradict experience, the theory is wrong. Such is, for instance, the aforementioned debunked theory of dramatic art based on an "aristocratic" view. If, however, a theory conforms to experience, this does not make it automatically "correct", because we cannot know whether the theory will come to contradict experience – which may happen tomorrow. For this reason, we may say that the theory is "suitable" for the above aim. Yet there may be several suitable theories for a given set of facts; in this case, with a view to the economy principle, we should then choose the *simplest* among them. The synthetic theory of dramatic art *is not* wrong, as it has not contradicted experience, so far at least. When it comes to its suitability though, we need to admit that sometimes it creates rather unnecessary difficulties. It is good to take account of them.

There is no doubt that the *creation of the dramatic work* presents a particularly solid argument in favour of the synthetic theory; least of all in that it proceeds *in stages*. First, an author writes a dramatic text, which sets a case for being understood as a work of literature – as we have already pointed out at the beginning of our inquiry. On its basis the actors with the director create an actorly artwork. If the director cares about the artistic formation of the scene, they engage a visual artist – as well as a tailor, an electrician, a mechanic and others; but we can leave those aside: after all, such and similar tasks come under the responsibility of the head of construction in life, too. In the case of sung drama, this process starts with the composer's work who – following the dramatic text – composes the score and hands it over to the theatre company, who continue in the process outlined above. The musical score is given to the singers (who are also the actors), the orchestra musicians and the conductor, who rehearse and finally perform it in a way that is common when performing large musical compositions. But if we consider this lengthy and complex way leading to the realisation of a dramatic work, a way that is interesting for its *strictly prescribed, irreversible process*, we can see that in fact this is not a combination of various arts, but rather, strictly speaking, a *combination of various **artists***. And this is not the same thing, as the aforementioned "process" shows.

Yet, when it comes to the finished dramatic work – as experienced in performance – the synthetic theory may not be so self-evident. An artwork (a good one, that is) appears as composite, and yet so well *unified* that the separation of its individual components can only be done artificially and forcibly; in short, the individual components are *not autonomous*. When observed in isolation, these components remind us of works from various independent art forms; strictly speaking, they *resemble* such *autonomous* artworks. The synthetic theory, however, asserts that this resemblance is an essential identity. This is to say: all artworks of a given autonomous art follow more or less certain general principles despite their great diversity. These principles are specific to a particular art and each independent and self-contained art follows those principles alone: they are autonomous arts. Formulating the dramatic work as a "union of arts" infers a theoretical assumption – that the principles governing a particular component of the dramatic work are the same as those governing the autonomous art that resembles the component; or – figuratively speaking in accordance with the synthetic theory – the principles are those of the "*mother*" art. But in practice, it is precarious to transfer the principles of the "simple" or "pure" autonomous arts onto the dependent components of dramatic work. These components are, so to speak, obliged to follow the "family tradition", even though they need to combine to form an organic union. What does artistic practice have to say about this?

It is characteristic of every *organic* artistic whole that intensifying any component intensifies the effect of the whole. The synthetic theory of dramatic art requires that such intensification of the aesthetic effect of each component should take place *according to the principles of its "mother" art*. Practice, however, shows that this expected intensification of the overall (that is, dramatic) effect does not always arrive; on the contrary, it often weakens significantly. We can speak of various *"theatrical paradoxes"* (*antinomie*), well known in theatre practice. Let us briefly list them here:

(a) The more *poetic* the text of a dramatic work, the more likely it is that the *dramaticity* of the work (that is, of its performance!) will be *weakened*. By "poetic" we mean the literary qualities of lyric poetry and narrative literature. This is widely known, yet it takes by surprise again and again not only inexperienced authors, but also experienced theatre practitioners. All specifically poetic values that capture and charm us when reading the text – all the subtle nuances of thought and mood, word play, exquisite metaphors and symbolic allusions – all of them fade, vanish and die in stage light. The author feels crushed: the most charming and poignant parts of the text pass without the expected impression, even unnoticed – yet the actors are not the only ones to blame (though this may be possible, too). To add to the confusion, the *opposite* also takes place! Dry passages, without a drop of poetry in them, which we rush through impatiently while reading, suddenly grow large in performance, acquiring profound meaning and unexpected energy. The former loses while the latter gains, and it follows that the above phenomenon – usually called *"theatrical acoustics"* – comes not just from the fact that actors speak in relatively large spaces. What suffers the most is "literary drama", which we have mentioned on several occasions. For example, let us say there is a production of a beautiful work of poetry, such as Goethe's *Faust*. We deceive ourselves in vain that this is a grand impression, for we feel that it is somewhat bland, in places even painfully boring – and we end up admitting grumpily that we should have stayed at home and read it instead. On the contrary, try to read most of Shakespeare's or Molière's dialogues. If you do not happen to know them from the theatre, you cannot even come close to imagining how brilliant they are on stage. The same also holds for a number of more recent plays, especially French well-made comedies, that are neglected by literary critics on account of their "negligible literary value".

(b) The more *musical* the music of a sung drama, the more likely it is that the *dramaticity* of the work will be weakened. We use the word "musical" here in the sense of pure, instrumental music. This particularly holds for purely musical forms that are based on the principle of repetition. In such cases, the composer either disregards the text of the libretto or demands in advance the formation of a text that "suits the music". This is how notoriously formulaic, cliché opera *librettos* are born. We have called them "concert librettos"; they have long arias, duets and choruses, that endlessly repeat even a single sentence; these librettos are quite rightly ignored by literary criticism. That the audience is not as bored by their undramatic character as in the case of the above-mentioned literary dramas, comes from the fact that they find satisfaction in the purely musical impressions, as they know from concert halls – even though they are now sitting in the theatre. But anyone with a little sense for dramaticity feels this shortcoming acutely and it is quite understandable that such operas – and consequently *operas in general* – are scorned by spoken drama practitioners. "Opera," they say, "is no real drama. Don't you dare compare it to spoken drama: the opera's successes in the theatre (often envied by spoken drama practitioners) are not honest: the opera only achieves them with its concert effects." The comic irony is that many "genuine" musicians, particularly lovers of chamber and orchestral music, speak like that about opera music! "Opera", they say, "is not proper music; don't you dare compare it to a quartet or a symphony! The opera's suspect successes (which they envy too) comes from its theatrical effects." – Behold, these are the paradoxes of the "union of arts".

(c) The more *painterly* the scene of a dramatic work, the more likely it is that the *dramaticity* of the work will be *weakened*. By "painterly" we mean here, once again, the treatment of optical values in the sense of visual arts and more specifically, the arts of painting and sculpting, since a "scenic picture" is at work here. An illustrative example of this attitude is the reform proposed by Munich's "Künstlertheater"[7], which strived to stylise the stage according to the principles of a relief, with the actors as silhouettes. The attempt failed just like any other attempts that tried to organise the scene in accordance with the principles of painting and sculpture. Then again, it is well known that many visual artists refuse to have anything to do with the stage; they despise what they call "the panorama" on stage. For these reasons, namely his painterly principles, Arnold Böcklin[8] refused to design the scene for Wagner's operas.

(d) The more *actorly* an actor's performance in a dramatic work, the *stronger* the *dramaticity* of the work! There is no paradox here. We could see inverse proportionality between the component and the whole in all three previous cases. By intensifying the component – in accordance with the principles of the mother art – the whole was *likely* to become *dramatically* worse. In this fourth case, however, we find direct proportionality: that is to say, whenever the acting component intensifies, the *dramaticity* of the whole *reliably* improves as well. This undoubtedly relates to our above discussion of the synthetic theory: acting is not an independent, autonomous art outside the dramatic art; it has no mother art that could advance and improve it further. It can only do this on its own and that exclusively within the bounds of the dramatic art. Our conclusion that *more "actorly" always means more "dramatic"* – which generally cannot be said about the other components – does not necessarily mean that "actorly" and "dramatic" are *identical* concepts. But, within the domain of collective art, as we shall soon see, we will come to that conclusion.

---

7   The Münchner Künstlertheater (Munich Art Theatre) opened in 1908, designed by the architect Max Littmann (1862–1931). The building of a new theatre was initiated by the journalist and playwright George Fuchs (1868–1949). The theatre had a very shallow stage, no orchestra pit and an auditorium seating in an amphitheatre shape. The concept was that stage action was supposed to be arranged visually in the form of a relief, with the actors' action taking place in front of a stylised backdrop.
8   Arnold Böcklin (1827–1901) was a Swiss-born symbolist painter, graphic artist and sculptor. His best-known painting is *Die Toteninsel* (Isle of the Dead), which exists in five versions Böcklin created between 1880 and 1886.

The aforementioned "paradoxes" appear very often in artistic practice – during the creation of a dramatic work, which, as we have already stated, can be rightly viewed from the perspective of the synthetic theory as "a combination of *artists*". Apart from actors, the artists producing individual components in the above-mentioned process recruit from the ranks of their respective "mother" arts. It happens very often that they are gifted for and focused on their own art *exclusively*, and are often unable and unwilling to create outside its bounds. It helps then if such artists are self-critical enough not to take part in the creative process of the dramatic work. Their artistic greatness will not suffer in the least; the dramatic art is, we believe, a specific art of its own kind, and an artist without a talent or even a sense for it may still excel in another art form.

> The many writers of genius who focused exclusively on lyrical poetry or fiction, or great composers who only wrote instrumental or vocal music, are a telling testimony. A lot of them, particularly those of a lyrical vein, have often felt a strong aversion to dramatic art. It is much worse however when such artists, seduced by non-artistic motivations, often a desire for public fame or even material gain, dare venture into creating dramatic works. They then create dramatic works that are undramatic and do not and cannot achieve artistic success. Often these are the romantic beginnings of young artists dreaming of a great tragedy or a grand opera, and they are loath to confirm Weber's quip that beginners' operas are like puppies: to be drowned. To be sure, these are not people without artistic talent altogether, but people who are undoubtedly gifted in arts other than the dramatic.
>
> Herein also rests the apparent precarity of the assumption that the dramatic work is "a combination of arts." Each contributing artist feels entitled to look at the work from the perspective of their art. And it is also clear that what always *suffers* is the creative work of *one particular* type of artists: the *actors*; to the poet they are reciters; to the composer they are singers (and that is what they also are called!); and to the visual artist they are no more than a silhouette or a "colour blot"... This becomes all the more fatal for the actors because within the mercilessly fixed process of creating the dramatic work, they are and need to be the last to join, and this deprives them of any influence on everything that precedes. They have to finish baking what those before them might have burnt a bit, and then they even have to personally present it to the audience.

These difficulties of artistic practice are not an outcome of the synthetic theory, of course, but rather of the artists' human nature: each favours their own affairs. But the phrase "a combination of arts" seems to entitle them to do so. Let each of them do their best on behalf of *their own* art – and that in practice leads to what we have criticised and rejected above as aristocratic. The two aristocrats we spoke about above – literature (in spoken drama) and music (in sung drama) – are now joined by a third, which is visual arts (in both spoken and sung drama); the fourth art, acting, becomes their servant. But the synthetic theory champions a *democratic* notion of *equality* among all arts that are combining in the dramatic work. Artistic practice, as we have seen however, shows that this is impossible; each of the arts (apart from acting) must make concessions in its autonomy if it does not want to damage the dramaticity of the whole (and acting to boot). *The formulation "combination of arts", alongside an acknowledgement of equality among the arts, also means a compromise between these arts.*

> This alone would not be an issue; Hostinský rightly observes that resolving conflicting aesthetic norms that contradict one another in part is common in artistic practice. Theatre practice makes such mutual compromises nearly at every step; it may be annoying but there is nothing shameful about it, as would be the case with a compromise between artistic and non-artistic priorities. It all comes down to having a fortunate idea that can resolve and often even eliminate the artistic conflict. But there is a different issue: If – as we have seen – the individual arts combining in the dramatic artwork must compromise on the very individuality they possess as autonomous arts, are they still the same arts? Are they not then artistic components that merely resemble the autonomous arts? This is no trivial issue but a matter of essential significance: it offers an entirely different notion of the dramatic art than the synthetic theory. Conflicts may only arise during the creating of a dramatic work or with an imperfect finished work. Perfect dramatic works – and only such works are the subject of our study – have no conflicts because the principles (or laws) guiding their components *are not* identical to the principles of the related autonomous arts.

We can also see that the acknowledgement of equality included in the "democratic notion" may be justified but this democracy is not as simple as the synthetic theory makes it seem. The components of a dramatic work are not altogether on a par, of equal status. This is only true for three of the components: the textual, the musical and the scenic, which have – outside the bounds of dramatic art – their own independent arts (literature, music, and visual arts). In practice, these three often show aristocratic desires, but they must eschew them for the benefit of the whole – that is to say, *for the sake of dramaticity*. This does not hold for the fourth component, the actorly, which is at home here and therefore does not need to make any compromises on its unique quality. This component must be respected by the other three, because any disruption to acting disrupts the dramaticity of the whole work. Despite all components having equal value, the *actorly component* is the central and governing component of the dramatic work; not because it is the most important but because *it is the only one* that is *dramatic in the proper sense of the word. The other components are* "**dramatic**" *only in so far as they contribute to the effect of the actorly component*. We shall call this basic principle of the dramatic art the *principle of dramaticity* and will discuss it analytically in the next chapter. For now, we must point out that this principle relates only to the *aesthetic* – that is, the emotional – *efficacy* of the work and not to its *artistic value*. These are two different concepts, for non-artistic things and events – from nature or real life – may have an aesthetic effect, and it is a known fact that we often encounter dramatic events in everyday life. Works of art surely aim at an aesthetic effect and often achieve it, but they have besides this a specific value of their own, independent of their potential effect; put simply, their specific value is their original structure.

> The notion that acting is not only the central but also the *governing* component among all the other components of the dramatic work may be countered by observing that it is the last to join the creative process; how could it govern it then? But this is only a seeming objection, because – as we shall see in the chapter on the playwright's creative work – the actorly component is and must be contained in the author's initial conception.

Taking all this into consideration, we cannot call the synthetic theory incorrect, and yet it is not beneficial for an aesthetics of the dramatic art. Nevertheless, we shall make use of it when dealing with the creation of a dramatic work, particularly in the variant we called "the combination of artists". We shall return to the original formulation – the combination (or union) of arts – when we discuss dramatic style; we shall demonstrate that *artistic* stylisation of a dramatic work depends on a tendency to bring each of its components closer to its "mother art".

3 THE ANALYTICAL THEORY

In order to arrive at a theory of the dramatic art that does not contradict artistic experience but also captures it as usefully as possible, let us reverse the direction of our inquiry. Instead of the path of synthesis that composes the dramatic work from various arts, we shall use analysis. At the opening of this book we defined the dramatic work as a percept [a sensory experience] we have during a theatre performance. It follows from here that the dramatic work exists in our consciousness as a psychological fact. As such, its analysis needs to be *psychological*, and the same holds for a description of the finding we arrive at through our analysis. Since we are dealing with an object of our experience, it is a critical requirement that our analysis should be *free of presuppositions* [assumptions]. In our case this means that we have to study the dramatic work, in the beginning at least, without a regard for art works from other arts, without prejudice, *as if* dramatic art were:

a) *a new, independent* [autonomous] art and not just a special kind of another *recognised* art (i.e., viewing spoken drama as a kind of literature, sung drama [opera, musical theatre] as a kind of vocal music, and scenic art as a kind of visual arts);

b) a *single* art and not a union of *several* arts. The dramatic work does appear to us in our perception [during performance] as composite, and even composed of several synchronous [simultaneously occurring] and heterogeneous components, as we have stressed. However, there are other composite art works, made of components that are consecutive and synchronous, such as musical works. As for heterogeneous components, why could there not be an art with art works consisting of heterogeneous components? We should not reject that possibility offhand.

> A note on methodology first. The dramatic work as a psychological fact can certainly be analysed psychologically. But a dramatic work is also an artistic fact [an artefact]. Would not an analysis, which is always an extraneous thing, destroy its aesthetic nature? This danger would actually exist if we carried out the analysis to the very end, as is done in psychology. But in such case, the results would belong to psychology, but surely not to aesthetics and art criticism. That means we must perform our analysis in such a way and only insofar *that the components identified through the analysis still remain aesthetically effective*. Above all, this means that we must never separate the aspect

of content from the emotional aspect. Analysis directed in such a way is an *aesthetic analysis*.

Let us begin with the analysis of spoken drama (*činohra*), which is obviously *simpler* than sung drama (*zpěvohra*).

The dramatic work – i.e., that which we perceive with our sight and hearing during a performance – appears to us not only as something composed of great diversity but also *changeable over time*. In its constant developments, movement and changes we can nevertheless identify two more or less lasting phenomena, two *relative constants*. They are:

(1) The *personas of the drama*. Clearly they are not entirely stable; the same holds for them as for real-world people. A person's *visible appearance* for all its changes in facial expression, in posture, in movement or in dress still has something constant about it, and that allows us to take them for one and the same person. Even the *audible* vocal performance has something constant about it: the timbre of the voice and the individual manner of speech. So we can recognise a friend by their voice or their laughter even if we cannot see them. However, the changes, especially the visual ones, which are practically the most important to us, are sometimes so great that we can "almost fail to recognise" even a close friend. And yet, there is always something about them that has not changed and that reminds us that it is the "same" person, even though they look "completely different". The same holds for the dramatic personas we got to know on stage. How different King Lear looks over the course of the performance! And yet it is always him. In a strictly noetic sense, such a "persona" – whether from the real world or from a play – is something *imaginary that we add* to the optical and acoustic appearance; it is a mere mental image that we *impose* (foist or hypostasise) upon the appearance (the percept) as its constant and lasting *essence* (substance). We are driven to this by the very fact that the appearance we perceive remains at least partly the same. By equating the mental image with this percept, the mental image gains an ostensive quality. And since the dramatic persona only exists in our mind, albeit on the basis of a percept, we need some lasting markers to be able to think or even speak about it; most commonly we resolve this (just as in life) by giving it a name. This is evidenced in "the list of dramatis personae" common in dramatic texts. It should also be mentioned – although we are jumping forward in our discussion – that the relative stability of the dramatic persona springs largely from being played by one and the same actor. The awareness that behind the dramatic persona there is in fact a particular actor – no matter if well-known or unknown – is specifically characteristic of our theatrical focus (and that is a difference from the real world).

(2) The *location of the drama*. The location is the surroundings of the dramatic personas, given by our optical percept of the scene with everything in it, except for the personas themselves – no matter if we abstract from them or if they happen not to be there. In this the real world also offers parallels, such as a room, a street, a landscape and so on. It is obvious that our percept of the location of the drama is much more constant than our percept of a persona. There is no movement in it and its change limits itself to little more than the effects of different lighting.

The relativity of this constant depends on the changes of location (alongside its invariable features (*výplň*, or *fill*)) on the basis of the drama's division into acts, changes and scenes. In the course of such a unit, the "scenic image" remains fixed in its shape. It lacks therefore the *graduality* of change that is characteristic of dramatic personas – particularly of their movement. It especially lacks any *need* to change; the fill of the scene [the set and the scenic objects] may remain as is for the whole performance, which certainly does not apply to actors. The relative non-participation of the "scenic image" in the development of our overall percept entitles to leave it aside – for the time being at least – while reflecting on the essence of the dramatic work. We may go even so far as to claim that the "scenic image" is not an essential component of the dramatic work. That is because it may be reduced from a maximum variety to a minimalist *mere space* that is only architectonically bounded. A great number of plays – or their parts – are performed on such "neutral scenes" [stages], as they are called, without the least loss to the works themselves. But such an empty space, psychologically speaking, actually belongs to the dramatic personas whom – just like everything else – we must naturally see *somewhere*. What additionally fills the space (apart from the dramatic personas) is not always necessary, and as such it is only optional.

Setting the said location of the drama aside, we find that any changes in our percept – what we have called "the dramatic work" – comes from changes in what we have named "the dramatic personas". It is that which is changeable about them: their behaviour and actions, as well as their speech and their vocal expressions in general. This is *dramatic action* (*děj dramatu*) and we may assert that dramatic action is created exclusively by the dramatic personas. That is to say, the action is not something separate from them, something they would merely "take part in". They *do* it themselves. This active conception stems from the fact that, under (1) above, we have thought of the constants as "personas", i.e., as beings that are mentally organised as we are. Their changes briefly listed above – both visible and audible; in a word, ostensive – are for us *their actions* based on their mental lives, which we understand according to our own *inner* experience. At the same time we can see that these actions are reciprocal (interactive; *vzájemné*); they are the personas' *collective actions and reactions*. They are not only bound, like everything in this world, by a causal relation (causality), but also – specifically because they involve psychological beings – by a relation of purpose (finality). Each of their actions is caused by a preceding action, and usually it happens in order to bring about another.

A *persona's ostensive activity intended to have and having an impact on another persona shall be called* **interaction** (jednání).

Since we are entitled to refer to the personas and the events of a drama (a good one, of course!) as "dramatic", our present analysis leads to the following:

Dramatic action *is that which results from personas' interactions.*
Dramatic persona *is one that interacts with other personas.*

Both these basic elements of the dramatic work are necessary and sufficient for its existence, and they are one and the same thing, only viewed from different angles, like the face and back of sheet of paper. Grammatically, it can be expressed in the following captions:

interacting *people* = dramatic *personas*
people's *interaction* = dramatic *action*

> We have preferred to use the word "personas" rather than "people" because, as we know, there are not only people appearing in drama but also other beings, such as gods, spirits and even animals, but *always* humanised, personified.

Our analysis of the concept of "action" leads to another important quality that is essential for the dramatic work: *it must contain more than one persona* – two at least. That is to say:

The dramatic work is necessarily a **collective** *work.*

"Monodrama" [in this sense] is not drama, no matter how much pathos is involved, unless a second persona were represented by some power, force or another element; that second persona has to be personified, at least in abstraction, i.e., through words – and that would be a *borderline* case of a dramatic work.

It is only now that we may proceed to a critical investigation into what we mean by the scientific aesthetic term "**the dramatic**". As for its semantic, factual content, it is determined by the above "interaction of personas" in the sense of our definition of "action". Let us emphasis – in line with our formulation of the dramatic work – that we are referring to real interaction of real personas: that is, it is action that is perceived by us, not only imagined. As for theory, this definition would be sufficient. However, given that "the dramatic" is an aesthetic term, we need to inquire into what the *impact* of "the dramatic" is and if there are any specifics that belong to it.

In the above analysis of the dramatic work we have repeatedly stressed that we grasp what we perceive during the dramatic work according to ourselves, on the basis of our own inner experience. But what is the psychological nature of our *own* action? Surely, during our own action we can see and hear ourselves at least a bit, but these are only partial and secondary impressions in comparison to what we, so to say, *"feel"* ourselves during the action, and that in a *bodily* (physical) way. Let us imagine that we are in such darkness and such noise that we can neither see nor hear ourselves. And yet we are aware of each of our actions, of the position and movement of our whole body as well as all its parts, such as the face, and particularly of the speech organs, and that with such clarity that we not only know that, for instance, we are smiling or speaking, but also what we are saying – although we cannot hear ourselves. The sensations through which we become aware of all this are called *inner tactile*: we sense the tension in our muscles, the pressure and the pull in our sinews and joints and so on. The most significant sets of such sensations (as there are always many of them at once) are called kinaesthetic or *motoric* percepts. The essence of all our action, from the slightest smile to the greatest effort, is therefore *motoric*. From the moment of birth we accumulate our own experiences in this way and they soon become so common that we are no longer aware of their inner tactile nature, and concentrate almost exclusively on the visual and auditory impressions associated with them.

When observing *other* people's action, be it in the real world or on stage, we spontaneously, unconsciously recall our own motoric experiences; they resurface all the more copiously and powerfully the more we *empathise* with the actions of others – which we surely do when perceiving theatre. It is not only mere motoric images that get recalled in us; we are also unwittingly pulled to imitate what we see and hear – and that happens in certain hints, also known as innervations, which often enough makes us empathise fully with the actions of others. It is this spontaneous motoric component that give our sensory percepts a quality of extraordinarily live and compelling *activity*. It is a characteristic for the impression of "the dramatic" that apart from the visual and acoustic components, there appears the *motoric component* as its *essential* part which pulls into play our entire bodily organism. In our mind, they are mirrored as two emotions (in fact, groups of emotions): the emotion of dramatic *tension* and its release, and the emotion of *excitement* and its calming. They both have an apparent bodily quality and a motoric character. Although these two emotions are very characteristic for our emotional *impression of the dramatic*, they are not in fact specific to it, because they can also be found in numerous other aesthetic impressions. So, for instance, in the visual arts, lines may cause the emotion of tension, and colours may cause the emotion of excitement; similarly in music, melody may bring tension and dissonant harmonies, excitement, and so on.

Everyday speech and literature use the term "dramatic" quite differently to how we established it here. The "dramatic" in *popular* use refers to something that arouses an impression of excitement or irritation; i.e., to something that itself is exciting or irritable, etc., with an apparent flair of unpleasantness to it. That is a definition of the word based on its impression, not in factual terms. "We witnessed a dramatic scene" or "in this dramatic moment" and so on – in all these statements we could easily and without any loss replace the "dramatic" with the word "exciting" (or turbulent). This popular use of the word "dramatic", thought it can be found in literature, seems to aspire to scientific standards (see for instance various essays in journals), but it is incorrect and that for two reasons. Firstly, the term "dramatic" is used too *narrowly*, referring only to violent and at least partly unpleasant impressions, which is probably down to confusing the words "dramatic" and "tragic". Newspaper headlines such as "Two Lovers Drama" refers surely to the couple's "tragedy" – but we know that drama also covers comedy. No doubt there are a number of charming comedies that are not violent or unpleasantly exciting at all even though they are fully dramatic. If a dramaturg returns a script of a tragedy to an emerging author saying "it is not dramatic enough", this certainly does not suggest a lack of excited scenes but rather that he believes the play is not theatrically effective because there is too much talking (and maybe very much and very excited talking!) and too little action. Secondly, the popular use of the word "dramatic" is too *broad* and even vague because it is used to refer not only to human action – as in the above examples – but also to anything else that is agitated or excited. So for instance, a raging storm is a "dramatic sight" or in the context of the arts, the term is often used, with a particular fondness in music. Whenever a musical work is exited, agitated or tempestuous, it is immediately dubbed "dramatic". Even the philosophical theory that drama is a conflict or a clash of two wills gets symbolically extended to "a conflict of themes" in musical polyphony: the fiercer the clash, the more dissonances there are, and so on. As metaphorical expressions one could tolerate it but from a strictly scientific perspective such vague analogies are wholly unacceptable. It is specifically unacceptable to conclude from a composer's ability to produce agitated music that they are able to write dramatic music – that is, that they can write good sung drama. The history of music offers many examples that refute this superficial conclusion (e.g., Schubert and Mahler). It is the fault of this popular sense of the word "dramatic" that many composers, as well as poets, believe that to write an opera, or a spoken drama, respectively, it is necessary and also sufficient to write agitated, pathos-filled music, or speech.

Throughout this book, the word "dramatic" is used *exclusively* in the above precise sense – i.e., to refer to human action. Likewise the term "*dramatic tension*", which appears frequently in discussions of drama, will only refer to that particular kind of mental tension that is caused by our motoric response to an action – as we have laid it out above. It *will not* therefore refer to, for instance, the tension arising from expectation or suspense of the type com-

mon in fiction ("suspenseful" novels!) – and also very common in dramatic works, where its misuse is particularly striking, because those works are dramatically bad.

ଔ ଔ ଔ

It follows from our analysis and definition of *"dramatic action"* that dramatic actions are also possible *in the real world*. This is certainly so and we now need to identify what the specifics are of the theatrical "dramatic actions".

> *Actions (děje) as such* can be purely natural (such as a storm or a sunset), natural with human participation (such as a flood) or only human ones but not in the sense of our definition of human *interaction* (e.g., people working together or on their own). These are all usually non-dramatic actions. On the contrary, all actions resulting from interactions of people are *dramatic actions*. But since we are concerned with aesthetic phenomena, all these actions must also meet the requirement of having an aesthetic effect on us. A general condition of such effect is that we should have no *practical* interest in the action. This means first and foremost that we do not participate in it and we are only its observers; but even then we must be conscious that the action poses no physical or mental threat to us. So we may, for instance, take an aesthetic stance toward some very lively scene in a pub: we enjoy watching the different characters and the original way they interact with one another. But when it comes to a fight, our aesthetic impression is gone, because our survival instinct suppressed it. Even if we were ourselves safe, say watching from a window on an upper floor a public demonstration involving bloodshed, our social instinct of compassion would prevent us from such "aesthetic focus". However, as for the latter example, there are (generally speaking) great differences between people, arising from their individual characters and from their different standards of civility; some people are unfazed and find even horrendous actions a delightful theatre to watch. More favourable conditions for aesthetic focus come from joyful dramatic actions. But this is also highly relative; we know that some people find fun in actions that more delicate people disgustedly turn away from as too brutal.
>
> The above obstacles to the aesthetic focus would disappear for all of us if we knew that the interaction of people we are observing *cannot* bring about anything bad either for us, or for them. What an entertaining piece of theatre for the inhabitants of a tenement house is the row between two neighbours because everyone knows it never amounts to anything. How often have we found in surprise, when we tried to intervene on a boys' scuffle that looked a bit too rough, that it we learned that it was not "for real", but only *"just so"*, that they were only *playing*?

This brings us from *natural* dramatic actions to *artificial* (constructed; *umělý*) ones. Dramatic actions (*děje*) – unlike other actions – are relatively easy to make artificially because people create them with their action (*jednání*). Those who possess the abilities to *represent dramatic personas* and *present dramatic action* are called *actors*. Such dramatic *"performances"* have the advantage over natural, real-world dramatic actions in that they may be carried out whenever we please and may even be repeated. Most importantly, these performances allow for an aesthetic experience of even the most horrendous, even monstrous dramatic actions, which in the real world would have a crushing impact. Such is the case of *tragedy*, one of the summits of dramatic art. It is certainly remarkable that even tragic impressions, which Aristotle called "pity and awe" – that is as emotionally unpleasant impressions – still evoke aesthetic pleasure in the spectator. This mystery, which has been written about and discussed in abundance, was solved by the great French aesthetician Jean-Baptiste Dubos[9] in the early eighteenth century when he discovered the *principle of functional pleasure*. We take delight in experiencing various mental actions (*děje*); the more intensive the action, the greater the pleasure – which particularly applies to passions. Dubos evidences this human desire to experience passions, even *unpleasant* ones, on numerous examples from the real world – a pleasure in horrendous scenes, bloody fights, gambling and so on. According to Dubos, art has the advantage of replacing natural passions with *artificial* ones, which have the same character but lack their destructive effects; they are, so to speak, purified. That it was tragedy that gave the impetus to the *"Dubos problem"* will become clear from what we said earlier above about the motoric character of the dramatic impression. It is enough to imagine the effect that descriptions of a horrendous action in literature has on us, compare it with a portrayal in painting or in sculpture, and finally with a representation on stage. It will become apparent that the theatre has the most powerful effect in that it gets the most "to the quick".

After this analysis of "dramatic action" (*děj*), let us turn to an analysis of the *"dramatic persona"*. This will be more challenging because it is in fact epistemological (*noetická*) and requires a careful and precise distinguishing of concepts.

Early in our analysis we have shown that the "dramatic persona" is in fact *our mental image* (*představa*) that we add in our mind to a relatively constant element of the dramatic *percept* (*vněm*). At that point we also noted that this is like in real life. Each of our relatively constant perceptions evokes in our experience some image on the basis of similarity. This image responds to the most general question: *what is it* that we can see or hear and so on? For this

---

9   Zich refers to the book *Réflexions critiques sur la poésie et sur la peinture* (*Critical Reflections on Poetry and Painting*) by Jean-Baptiste Dubos (1670–1742), published in 1719. Dubos is considered to be one of the founders of modern aesthetics and his *Reflexions* went through many reprints and was also translated to English, German and Dutch. In the French context the book was considered a key work of aesthetics and a popular textbook until the nineteenth century.

reason we shall call it *the conceptual image (představa významová)*. This image does not come to us from the outside but from within, from our experience, and so may be – depending on the quality of our experiences – general, vague and poor, but it can also be specific, definite and rich. Our above example of a real-world dramatic action, the public demonstration, involves rather general conceptual images, which do not assume any extraordinary experience on our part: there are people, young and old, men and women; and more specifically, they might be workers and policemen; and even more particularly, for instance, politician X. What is important here is that the *conceptual image*, underpinning the percept that evoked it on the basis of similarity, merges with the percept itself in such a way that it acquires an *ostensive* quality (*názornost*).

The same holds true for the conceptual image when perceiving artificial dramatic action – the theatre. Such an image may range from general to particular, based on the quality of our experiences (for example, a young man – a prince – Hamlet), and it also has an ostensive quality. But in a theatrical performance, as we have observed, we do not limit ourselves to a single conceptual image. An accurate answer to the question "What is it?" is: what I perceive now is, in reality, *an actor*. This latter conceptual image does not emerge on the basis of similarity with the percept. It is offered by my theatrical experience and that in an abstract way, and against what I perceive: I *know* this is an actor, and even a particular actor A (listed on the poster), although I see and hear someone else, say Prince Hamlet. This second conceptual image therefore does not merge with the perception but remains *abstract*, and even at times when several minor details (such as facial features and timbre of voice) betray and confirm that this is truly actor A. We can clearly see that the conceptual image of a dramatic persona in the theatre is different from the real world. As a matter of fact, the exact question to which the conceptual image responds is not "What is it (this phenomenon)?", but rather "*What does this phenomenon, perceived by us, represent or portray?*". Let us call it the *referential* conceptual image. In contrast to it, let us call the conceptual image of the actor – which comes from our knowledge of the theatre and its practice – the *technical* conceptual image. *Broadly speaking*, the technical image remains abstract, while the referential image, merging with the percept, takes on an *ostensive* quality.

It is therefore characteristic of the dramatic work that in its perception we have **two different** conceptual images **at once**: the technical and the referential. This is an exclusive quality of art in general, but not of all of its disciplines. I walk through a gallery and stop in front of a Cézanne. What is it? A painting, more specifically, an oil painting. What does it represent? A landscape, more specifically, a landscape near Paris. Painting therefore has both the technical and the referential images. I have a walk to Prague Castle. What is it? A building, more specifically, a Gothic church, St. Vitus Cathedral. What does it represent? Nothing whatsoever; the question makes no sense. Thus, architecture only has the technical image. Those art disciplines that evoke the referential image as well as the technical image – and that essentially, not just accidentally – will be called *mimetic arts*.

It follows from the above that *dramatic art is a **mimetic** art and the same holds for acting itself.*

Up to this point it all seems quite transparent, but it becomes more complicated when we examine the specific relations between the technical image and the referential image as it appears particularly in the dramatic art. Their relation is truly complex. To clarify the relation, let us consider the parallel between an actor and a sculptor (for sculpture is clearly a mimetic art, too). We shall *expand* the notion of *the technical image* with a view to the *material* from which the artwork is made – in other words, not only what the artwork is but also what it is made of. The logic of our parallel is as follows: An *artist* creates from some *material* a given *artwork* that represents *some specific thing*. It follows then:

A sculptor uses *marble* (for instance) to make *a statue* representing, say, Heracles.

An *actor* uses **their own self** to make *a figure* representing, say, Macbeth.

This parallel is very instructive because it clarifies the nature of actorly concepts by showing their analogy with concepts from sculpting, as well as the differences between the two. It shows that:

(1) While the statue may be made from "marble (for instance)", which suggests it may be made of other materials too (other kinds of stone, metal or wood), and analogically other visual artworks of other disciplines, acting has *only one single* material: the *live human*. The direct, immediate material is the actor's *living body*, and indirectly also their *consciousness*. If we consider that the word is the only material of literature, and that the note is almost the only material of music, we will understand how exceptional the material of acting is, since it is neither constant nor renewable, but ephemeral. The same material is also used in *dance* art, but dance limits its expressive possibilities to visible movements, while acting also uses audible expressions, and as such makes use of the *full human*.

(2) It is only in acting (and in dance, of course) that *the creating artist is essentially identical to the material* from which they create their work. What this means becomes clear from the absurd idea that a sculptor, for example, would also be the marble from which they chisel the statue. It might seem that a reproductive artist is also identical to their material just like the actor, but this is not the case. The reproductive artist is identical to the *instrument* used to produce their artwork, and that either completely – such as the reciter

and the singer – or at least partly – such as the musician who uses a special, separate musical instrument. In our discussion of reproductive art we have stated that its necessary condition is the possibility to fix temporal art into a "text". When it comes to acting, where only partial fixing is possible, we could say at best that the actor as creator is – also *inevitably* – *their own* reproductive artist. It would follow from such a conception that in acting, too, the *creative artist is identical with their instrument*, usually only *partly* so, because they may also use a mask and costumes as additional accessories for their artwork. But both of these could be viewed as (auxiliary) material of their artwork. Let us also point out that the idea of "instrument" is also a technical image, but this one recedes into the background in the process of perception of the finished work. That is why we have left it out of our above parallel.

(3) The most delicate term is the *actor figure* (*herecká postava*), or *figure* (for short), since it often gets lost in theories of acting. Either it is not discussed at all or it is confused with other concepts. And yet this "figure" (which parallels a sculptor's statue) is the actor's *artwork* proper! The meaning of this concept is best understood by theatre experts who take it as a truly *technical* term.

> It might seem at first that the actor figure is identical with the actor, but this would be a mistake caused by the fact that the material of the actor's work (i.e., the very "figure") is the actor himself or herself. Just like marble alone is not the statue until it has been properly shaped, so the "figure" arises only with the *"fully shaped* actor"; the difference is that this shaping is done by the actor himself or herself – the one that is being shaped.

A much more common, even regular, mistake is to mix up – unwittingly – the "figure" with the "dramatic persona". This wrongly confuses the technical image with the referential image; logically speaking, it is the same as confusing a statue with what it represents. The mistake is caused by the extraordinary similarity between the technical image and the referential image in acting. This springs from the fact that the material of the actor's work, i.e., the material for shaping the "figure", is a live human (the actor themself), and that the dramatic persona (someone "interacting" with others) is also a living creature, often also a human. In no other art are these two images so similar as in acting; perhaps in painting, as long as we are dealing with representations of static and distant objects (such as a landscape). This similarity prompts the tendency towards naturalistic performance in acting, a tendency shared by audiences as well as actors. The representing and the represented are too homogeneous here.

The difference between the actor figure and the persona could be put in common words: the figure is what the actor makes; the persona is what the audience can see and hear. Indeed, they are a single fact viewed from different perspectives: one from backstage, the other from the auditorium.

Psychologically speaking, the figure is the actor's percept, and the persona is the spectator's percept. If we recall the above psychological analysis of the "dramatic", we find that the actor figure is an unmediated motoric percept, while the dramatic persona is an unmediated visual-acoustic percept, and it is motoric only in a mediated way. In a shorthand that allows us to capture the *gist* of the difference, in its most significant aspect, the distinction is that the actor *figure* is a formation of a *physiological* kind, whereas the dramatic *persona* is a formation of a *psychological* kind.

(4) While the parallel between sculpture and acting has been helpful in our distinctions so far – in that a statue in comparison with the figure is a physical formation – it could also be misleading if we took the actor figure as a static formation, like the statue. The technical word "figure" (*postava*) could also contribute to this mistake. It is not so. An actor figure is a dynamic formation: it is the totality of an actor's performance in one artwork. *Structurally* speaking, the *"figure"* and the *"persona" are in full agreement*. This fact, which holds for *all mimetic arts*, will be called **the principle of correspondence** *between the technical and the referential images*. These are in fact the head and tail of the same objective fact. That is to say: it is the same actorly performance viewed either from backstage or from the auditorium. Just like the dramatic persona – which we have defined as an "interacting human" – the actor figure is a formation that changes over time, but it contains a relatively constant feature: the actor's mask and the actor's costume.

By the "figure" we mean the actor's conception and performance of the role; in other words, the way *they play their "persona"*, visibly and audibly. Let us recall what we have established above in our analysis of the *dramatic action* (*děj*). We stated that the action results from the interaction of several personas. This means that the action, itself a referential image, corresponds to the technical image of an interaction between several actors – in a word: *interplay*. We can say that the interplay is nothing less than a **synthesis** of actor figures.

As the following chapters will include more detailed discussions of these issues, let us conclude our argument for now and summarise our findings in a table that will clarify any confusion:

Artist	material	work	image
Actor	the same actor	figure	dramatic persona
Several actors	the same actors	interplay	dramatic action

☙ ☙ ☙

The psychological analysis carried out in the beginning of this chapter focused specifically to spoken drama, an obviously simpler form than sung drama. This was for reasons of style, so that we do not need to add all the time: "as long as we disregard the musical component of the dramatic work". With this caveat, the whole analysis and all its results also applies to *sung drama*. Sung drama also contains the *same* two relatively constant percepts (the dramatic personas and the location) and it also contains dramatic action (*děj*). It is true that in sung drama dramatic personas do not speak but *sing*, but since we stated in our next discussion that the dramatic action of a theatrical performance is not natural but artificial (constructed), there can be no objections if in the dramatic action an actor's speaking is replaced by singing. For that reason those who perform the dramatic action in sung drama are called "singers", but there can be no doubt that they are also actors – singing actors, as opposed to speaking actors. If we subsume both speech and singing under the general term "vocal expression", we do not need to distinguish between spoken drama actors and sung drama actors; all that we have said about the art of acting holds word-for-word for sung drama as well.

It becomes clear that acting is a *shared* ingredient of both spoken drama and sung drama; the actor's work is a *constant* component that participates *in all* works of spoken drama and sung drama. This entitles us to bring together both the disciplines, in spite of their apparent difference (in their texts!), into a single discipline of the "*dramatic art*". We now need to define the *extent* (bounds) of this concept – that is, to find out whether any other forms, similar to them, belong to the dramatic art too. After all we stated at the beginning of the first chapter that spoken drama and sung drama are not the only genres of the dramatic art, but only the most common and important. Indeed, various other genres, especially theatrical ones, belong to the dramatic art even if not without reservation. It is on us to decide which of them belong there and which of them *do not*.

We came to the following statement in the first chapter:
(1) A necessary existential condition of the dramatic work is its *actual* (real) *performance*.

In our analysis of dramatic action in this third chapter we have found that:
(2) A dramatic work presents to us *artificial* (*constructed*) dramatic action.
(3) Those who create the artificial dramatic action are *actors*.

It follows from these three statements that the *actorly component* is a *necessary condition* of the dramatic work. A "necessary" condition is the "conditio sine qua non"; it negatively sets the extent of the dramatic art as a discipline as follows:

A work of art, even if it is temporal or even theatrical, is not a dramatic work unless it is created or at least co-created by actors, and therefore it *does not belong to the dramatic art.*

As the second criterion we will use the finding that came from the concept of "interaction" (*jednání*); it says that the dramatic work is *necessarily* a collective work. This leads to another negative definition:

A work of art, even if it is temporal or even theatrical, if it is limited to a single artist's performance, cannot be a dramatic work. More generally:

The artistic discipline whose works can, without any loss to their essence, be limited to the performance of a single artist, does not belong to the dramatic art.

The latter criterion is of secondary importance and it has *seeming* exceptions – the best known among them being *puppet theatre*. A puppeteer does not represent a persona; each of their puppets does so and the puppeteer lends them their speech and play. Technically, each "figure" is split into two components: a constant one, which is the puppet (made from some material, like a statue); and a variable one, performed (usually for all puppets at once) by the puppet master. Mimetically (*obrazově*) and ostensively, each dramatic persona is coherent and there are more than one of them in the interplay.

The following inquiry begins with a definition of the actor, which follows from our analysis of acting as a mimetic art:

An **actor** *is an artist that represents an intended* (imaginary; *myšlená*) *persona by means of themself.*

There are two artistic disciplines that concern us here in the first place: the art of dancing and – what we might call – the art of *artistes*. Their respective performers are the dancer and the *artiste* (entertainer).

(1) **Dance** is not a mimetic art and *dancers* **are not** *actors* because *they do not represent a persona by their performance*. The dancer does not represent or portray anybody, not even themself as a dancer. A dancer *is* a dancer, just like a joiner is a joiner, a teacher is a teacher and so on – and of course, like an actor is an actor. Logically, a working joiner does not represent a joiner, just as a teaching teacher does not represent a teacher. An actor is *the only one* who represents somebody else, and this can be *anybody*, even a joiner, a teacher and so on – or even an actor (as in *Hamlet*, for example). The actor may also represent a dancer; or their role may simply call for dancing. If this dancing task is small and the actor has the abilities, they can perform the dance themself. But if the task is too huge for the actor to execute it, or even perform it in an aesthetically pleasing way, the only possibility, for *purely practical reasons*, is to call in a professional dancer. An interesting example is Oscar Wilde's *Salome*. The title role calls for an excellent female actor and demands from her the performance of a lengthy and, for dramatic reasons, an outstanding dance; her dance must convince Herod to deliver Jokanaan's head to Salome. If the actor is unable to performing this dance herself, it is necessary to find a dancer with a similar appearance, who – with the same costume

and makeup – will smoothly replace her for this scene. This is all the more necessary in Strauss's opera of the same name, where the actor (or rather, the singer) playing Salome is obliged to sing immediately after a physically exhausting dance, which is technically very difficult. Conversely, when the acting part in a primarily dancing role is small, which is often the case in collective dances in operas, it is unnecessary to resort to such deception and the role may be left to the dancers, who thus become *occasional actors*. So, for example, in Bedřich Smetana's *The Bartered Bride*, members of both the singing and the dancing choruses represent "country people". In Mozart's *Don Giovanni*, there is a scene of a feast to which Don Giovanni has invited the statue of the Commendatore. Apart from the dinner guests, the feast features also invited musicians and ballet dancers. Naturally, the ballet dancers are not played by actors (or opera singers) but by members of the ballet ensemble, who, as it happens, are dancers representing dancers (but not themselves!) and thus become actors in this instance by virtue of their act. This example demonstrates a situation common even in spoken dramas, when professional musicians need to be called in to represent "musicians" on stage, since one cannot generally expect actors to perform special musical acts; and so these musicians also become occasional actors.

The art of dancing does not therefore belong to the dramatic art. This is confirmed by another aspect too: the fact that even a solo dance performance can be an independent and autonomous work of art; it is a lyrical expression, in other words *emotional*, which covers all kinds of emotional modes, even the most passionate and excited ones (those often called "dramatic" in the popular sense of the word). The feature it shares with acting is that the work's creator is at the same time its material. The material of dance art is the live human, just like in acting, but not the human in the totality of their expression, but only in their visible movement. The motoric essence of dance stands out even more clearly than in acting, because the audible vocal expression is *excluded* – at least as long as we deal with cultivated, not primitive dance. On the other hand, dance is nearly always linked with music, no matter how sophisticated. As an art form intended for the sight, dance makes use of specific clothing and even masks, just like acting, but for a different purpose: this is not to enhance the representation of some persona but only to intensify and determine the lyrical mode of the dance performance. When, for example, a dancer performs an "Egyptian dance", she naturally wears an appropriate costume without really wishing to "represent" an Egyptian. Her only purpose is that the dance and the costume have a coherent and illustrative character. The same applies to dance ensembles: both their costume and their mask serve to intensify the lyrical characteristic of the performance proper (known as "a character dance"). We will discuss pantomime later.

(2) The art of **artistes** (entertainers) – such as acrobats, comedians, merrymakers (jugglers), clowns and the like – is not a mimetic art and these **artistes are not actors** because, again, they *do not represent any personas*. An acrobat or a clown does not represent an acrobat and a clown; they simply *are* them – that is their profession. It

would almost not be worthwhile to discuss this, were it not for retrogressive claims in today's theatre that actors and artistes are one and the same just because they were so in the past. We have already pointed out that arguments based on earlier forms are not convincing because they ignore historical evolution. True, travelling comedians, who were the only ones sustaining the tradition of true dramatic art (in our sense of the word) from the fall of the Roman Empire to the beginning of the Modern Age, were mostly actors and artistes at the same time and their art was a diverse mix of both performance types. However, this was a primitive evolutionary stage that gradually differentiated into the art of actors and that of artistes, as we know it at present. This is not to say that we devalue this primitive art that later culminated dramatically in the commedia dell'arte, even if we claim that today's theatre must not return to it as a whole and in principle. Since the division of labour enables specialist perfection, actors and artistes – as well as dancers, as a matter of fact – parted ways, and inevitably so. While the actors have gone to the theatre, the artistes have kept to their arenas, circuses and less demanding venues (such as variety shows).

After all, the artistry discipline is very diverse; one could say that it spans all the way from the borders of dance to the borders of acting. The feats of acrobats, for instance, are of a purely motoric kind and intended for the sight just like dance, yet they differ from dance in that they are purely physiological expressions, but not psychological. At the other end, clowning shows also use speech and have some psychological content, no matter how small. From their pranks and jokes there is a continuous range of performance types to "solo performances" of *comedians* who *represent some personas* (usually stock characters), and they *are* therefore *actors*. The simple possibility of performing artistic parts solo, which is true of both artistes and said comedians, shows that neither the performances of artistes, who are not actors, nor of comedians, who are actors, belong to the dramatic art. It is only through the interaction of such comedians (though not of the artistes) that dramatic action and thus a dramatic work can come into existence, no matter how primitive. An important finding follows:

The actor's performance as such is a necessary, but *a not sufficient condition for a dramatic work.*

All three artistic disciplines discussed above – the art of the artistes, of comedians and of dancers – move smoothly from art to real-world life. Many people are good dancers or welcome comedians at social events; acrobatics is connected to gymnastics and sports. In this case we can speak of "art" in a *broad* sense of the word – an ability to do something ("artistry") that not everybody can do: something that requires special skills and training and thus deserves admiration.

It is obvious that actors participating in a dramatic work must represent all sorts of personas, including – as we have said – dancers, artistes and comedians. Just think of the many clowns in Shakespeare or the comedians in Smetana's *The Bartered Bride*, where the lead comedian has to carry out acrobatics, but also sing. If no actor could be found that would meet the demanding requirements of such an acrobatic role, a professional artiste might be invited to stand in; this artiste, representing an artiste on stage, would be an occasional actor just like the dancer and musician mentioned above.

Now that we have eliminated from acting, and also from the dramatic art, the related disciplines, let us demonstrate that acting is also the *central* component of dramatic art; that is because it contains, in its essence, both the literary and the scenic component of any dramatic work. We have already touched upon both in the above discussions and analyses.

The actor's task is to represent dramatic personas. These personas, as we know from artistic practice, are mostly people; but even if they are other kinds of beings – be they above or below humans – they are always anthropomorphised: made in a human image. For the dramatic action to arise, interaction of these personas is needed; we have defined interaction above as "any personal activity intended to have and having an impact on another persona". What follows from both these points is the requirement that the dramatic personas manifest themselves not only visibly (that is by their movements) but also audibly (that is by their voice: primarily by speech). For it is only the *speaking* human – unlike a "mute creature" – who makes *a whole* human being. It follows from the principle of correspondence between the actor figure and the dramatic persona that *the actor's performance* should be not only visual but also acoustic, which is certainly possible because the material of acting is a living human – the actor themself. Let us call this **the principle of the totality of the actor's performance**. It stands to reason that this requirement is not in conflict with the fact that in a lot of dramatic works there are also "mute roles", usually performed by extras; these are minor exceptions that prove the rule. In a major role, the exclusion of vocal expression must always be justified by some peculiarity of the dramatic persona, as in Daniel Auber's opera *La muette de Portici* (The Mute Girl of Portici): it is clear that in opera, singing is the equivalent of speaking.

It follows that the actor's vocal expression as such (laughter, groaning and so on), but also specific vocal expression such as speaking and singing, *belong to the art of acting*, and that also with its *content*, because actors always say or sing something, namely words and sentences; otherwise it would be *mere vocal* expression, which no other art form claims from the actor. In contrast to this, what the actor speaks on stage is claimed by literature, just because it is "verbal art". This may be so, but it does not hold the other way around: not everything that is spoken belongs to literature, and not even to art as such! The *actor's* speech, spoken or sung, does belong to art, but not to literature, as we have established, but rather to acting. Both artistic disciplines have a *shared layer* and *qualities in common*. This is not uncommon in the arts; for instance, dance, music and poetry share the common quality of rhythm, and there are similar overlaps between branches of the visual arts.

Pantomime, as is well known, is void of any vocal expression such as speech and singing – a feature it shares with dance. It is in fact an intensification of the character dance in the sense that it is its intellectualisation, similar to the way in which "programmatic music" is an evolution of instrumental music. Bodily movements in pantomime should not only be expressive; they should also *mean* something. We shall see later, in our analysis of mimics (facial expression), that its ability to succeed in this intellectual task is weak; not even music, which nearly always accompanies pantomime, is of much help in this respect because here it is similarly powerless. As long as pantomime artists remain mere dancers, we don't mind their restriction to mere visual expression; this is *ballet-pantomime*. However, once they are required to represent personas or even interacting personas – in other words, to become actors, which is the business of the *dramatic pantomime* – the *incompleteness* of their appearance and the *unnaturalness* of their performance immediately stands out. Its popular name unwittingly captures this very well: "the dumb show". This objection does not follow from "realism", i.e., from a comparison with our *real-world* experience, where people speak in such situations; as a matter of fact, our experience also tells us that people do not sing in such situations – and yet, sung drama does not seem unnatural or even incomplete to us. The issue is our *inner* experience, which demands that the expressions of the represented persona be complete and all-round. In *this* lies the trouble; the fact that a dancer wishes to represent a human in action; if he or she remained a dancer, said restriction would not hinder the performance; on the contrary, it would be no "restriction" at all. It would not strike us as odd that the dancer does not speak and is "mute", let alone that we would find this a flaw or misrepresentation.

It is not true then that acting is a mimic performance with *added* speech (as its literary component), but rather, a pantomimic (but not a dance) performance is an actorly performance with speech *taken away*. Herein we may rely on the reader's unprejudiced experience. Do we ever feel in spoken drama that an audible speech is added – as if a top-up – to the actors' visible playing? And do we not, on the other hand, feel very unpleasantly that in dramatic pantomime the performances that are essentially acting, are robbed of speech? We may conclude that pantomime is a *liminal* theatrical discipline between the dramatic art (especially sung drama) and the dance art; this discipline is all the more aesthetically pleasing the closer it is to dance, and all the less so the more it tries to be a dramatic art.

Regarding the *scenic* component of the dramatic work we may draw the following conclusion: Actors representing dramatic personas are real people and must therefore be in a real space where they present the dramatic action (*děj*) through their interplay. This space, appropriately bounded and enclosed, forms the "*scene*", and as such *it belongs with the actors and their performances* – we cannot abstract the space from the actors. The concept of acting thus contains the concept of the scene as an *epistemological* principle (and the above requirement of speech for actors is a psychological principle). This scene (or scenic space) as a technical image corresponds to the referential image of the "location of the dramatic action", as analysed early in this chapter. There must be some "location" because ostensive action – which is what dramatic action is – must take place *somewhere*. It is an entirely different question, however, *how* such a place is *determined* in any particular instance. Sometimes it is not determined at all, but sometimes it is very detailed. In Shakespearean theatre a mere inscription on a small plaque did this, whereas nowadays this is done, whenever necessary, by an ostensive and relatively constant setup (fill) of the scene. It follows from here, that the scene itself – as a space – is necessary, but the said constant scenic fill (*výplň*) is not; the latter is merely *accidental* (occasional; *případná*), whereas its essential and altogether changeable fill of the scene are *the actors themselves*.

It goes without saying that the construction of the scene as the theatre building's interior space (*interieur*) is a task for an architect.

We can summatively see that *the actor's performance contains not only the speech component but*, in its essence, *also the scenic component of the dramatic work*. Actors' performances therefore – *as long as they meet the requirement of dramaticity*, which calls for a "personas' interaction" – are not only a necessary but also a *sufficient* condition for the existence of a dramatic work. The dramatic formation created in this way, and in its essence a product of *merely* the art of acting, is **spoken drama** (*činohra*). *Spoken drama instantiates acting is an autonomous, self-sufficient art.*

> Actions presented by spoken drama must be *dramatic*. In our analysis of this concept we have learned that dramatic actions (*děje*) are a special case of events as such, which can be found in nature, with or without human participation, or among humans, but these without interaction. Examples of such actions, which may even be "dramatic" in the popular sense of the word – i.e., simply exciting – might include the following: a storm, a building on fire, a train collision and so on. These happenings (*děje*), as opposed to human actions (*jednání*), could be called *events*, and as such they can be unpleasant or pleasant, or else emotionally indifferent, like social entertainment or collective works and such. It is understandable that in real life such events and actions, if they involve humans, may include some dramatic elements, just like, on the contrary, many an action unfolds on the background of non-dramatic happenings. What matters is, after all, what is the main event and what is a side event.
>
> Just like dramatic actions, these "events" may also be presented *artificially* (*uměle*): the sad ones for pleasant excitement, and the cheery ones for amusement. If they involve people, it is *actors* who perform them; the rest needs to be left to technology – to stage machinery. These are **spectacular shows** (*výpravné hry*), popular with those audiences that have a desire for *spectacle*. That is why they always involve a rich scenic fill (*výplň*), as their name tellingly suggests. Spectacular shows thus belong to the theatrical art as such, representing a gradual *transition* to dramatic plays, not only of

spoken drama, but also of sung drama (known as "grand opera"), depending on how much the dramatic element (personas' interaction) is at play. From the opposite perspective, spectacular shows make a transition to the arena, to the circus and to real life: such as in various festivities (like the carnival), processions and so on. Here, however, people taking part in them are no longer actors because as a matter of fact they do not represent anybody; simultaneously the distinction between performers and spectators vanishes, which signals the eclipse of "theatricality".

What has been said about spectacular shows also holds for the **film**. Its audible component, if it is not altogether missing, is imperfect so far. Since it is only a moving picture, film has greater technical possibilities and it can be almost endlessly reproduced (cf. graphic art).

And finally, there is the **sung drama** (*zpěvohra*). Obviously, the music we hear in sung drama is not a part of the actors' performance, but it is relatively autonomous: an *addition*. Here we could, as a matter of fact, speak of a "combination of arts", but such an assumption has been refuted by the discussion in the previous chapter. Let us rather assert that unlike spoken drama, sung drama has *two* artistic components – *acting* and *music*. A parallel can be found in vocal music – for instance, in songs or choral music – which contains *literature* and music. As for the relationship of these two components, let us state briefly that they *run parallel to one another.* We will discuss this in detail in the chapter on dramatic music. But their combination is not usually limited to merely *associating* one with the other, but rather, one *permeates* into the other. This permeation pertains to the aspect they share – the sound – and their relation is such that *music affects speech, transforming it into singing*. In this way, the musical component permeates the literary component (in vocal music) and into acting (in sung drama). This process, which we will discuss in detail in the chapter on sung drama, can be called *"musicalisation"* (*zhudebnění*). It is interesting, however, that there are genres in which this musicalisation does not occur and where the two components run parallel to one another and speech is preserved. Such is *melodrama*, both in its concert and its scenic variant. The *scenic melodrama* is, alongside sung drama, a genre of dramatic art, even if not as common, or even rare.

After all these discussions that have analysed various forms of the dramatic art as other, related disciplines, we may finally proceed to a definition of the dramatic art and its forms. We have seen that *actors' performance* is always present and that this is a necessary and even a sufficient condition, as long as it meets the requirement of dramaticity. In order to make the definition easier stylistically, let it be said that:

The dramatic art *is the sum of dramatic works* (meaning stage performances).

The definition may proceed further:

The dramatic work is *a work of art presenting interaction of personas through the actors' onstage interplay.*

> What "action" and interaction mean has been explained above; likewise, we have given a definition of the "actor": an artist representing an imagined persona by themself. Let us also point out that the definition speaks about *actors* – that is, more than one. And finally, we have also laid out what the scene is in its essence: it is the space in which actors perform and *it comprises these actors.*

A specific difference characterising individual forms of the dramatic art comes – as we have established – from the musical component and its effect on the actorly component. Following the above definition of "the dramatic work", let us further define:

Spoken drama is *a dramatic work in which actors speak.*
Sung drama is *a dramatic work co-created by music in which actors sing.*
Scenic melodrama is *a dramatic work co-created by music in which actors speak.*

> If we wished to add *dramatic pantomime* to this list, we would need to say that it is a dramatic work co-created by music *in which actors neither speak nor sing*; this negation would correspond to the actual impression of such pantomime, as opposed to *ballet-pantomime.*

Thus we see that the general definition of the dramatic work is based on its specific material – the actors and their performances. Similarly, individual forms of the dramatic art are defined by their differing materials. All that we will analyse in this book's discussions about dramatic works, their typical qualities and their compositional laws will follow from the nature of this specific material, and all that represents the difference between the forms, primarily spoken drama and sung drama, can be transferred to the partial difference in these forms' specific materials.

Let us also note that the definitions of the actor and the scene do not mention "action", which determines the concept of "the dramatic" as regards to its content. We know from the above that actors' performances do not always need to be dramatic (think the art of comedians), and that all that is shown on stage does not automatically need to be dramatic action (*děj*). When we reflected on "spectacular shows" we stated that they show – through actors and on the scene – non-dramatic events occasionally mixed with dramatic action, and we also observed that spoken drama and sung drama sometimes include non-dramatic events, even if only as side events. Our definition of the dramatic work lays out a theoretical *ideal*, which artistic practice approximates to a greater or lesser extent. If we say about a spoken drama that it is "very dramatic" or that "its performance was exceptionally dramatic" or, on the contrary, that it was "dramatically weak" – the word "dramatic" is used to refer to the dramatic *effect* of the work (the performance) and the artwork is *assessed* with regard to the specific *aesthetic effect* it makes, and a very special kind of effect at that. What is at play is the *psychological efficacy* leading to an experience of aesthetic pleasure. If we claim then that *a dramatic work should be as dramatic as possible*, this is not a tautological statement because the same word is used in the subject of the sentence in the sense of its *material formation*, while in the predicate we use it in the sense of the *aesthetic effect* it makes. This entitles us to require that dramatic works – given that they are artificially created *with an aesthetic purpose* – and as such the dramatic works should fulfil this specifically *dramatic* purpose.

We will call the latter statement **the dramaticity principle**; we arrived at it in Chapter 2 by means of the synthetic method; now we have justified it analytically. The entire second part of this book will be governed by this principle; in it we will analyse what *all* these various components of the dramatic work need to be so that they comply with the stated principle – in other words, so that they are truly "dramatic", both as to their content and their impression – and of course, the whole as their union.

Nevertheless, the requirement of dramaticity, though necessary, is *not sufficient* on its own. If the dramatic work is an *artificial* (*umělé*) artwork, this *does not* say nor guarantee that it is also *artistic* (*umělecké*) – and not even *when the work is truly dramatic and therefore aesthetically valuable*. After all, many real-world events can be dramatically effective! If we were to reproduce such a real-world action entirely faithfully – I would even say, cinematographically and phonographically faithfully – we would get an artificial artwork that is certainly dramatically effective. But would it be an artistic work? Certainly not, just like a photograph of a "romantic" landscape or a cast of a beautiful live model are not artistic works. The dramatic art, as we know, is a mimetic art; and since we take our referential images from our own life experience, this means that the dramatic work has always a relation to our own life experience, particularly to our social life experience. If the dramatic work wants to be artistic, it cannot be a mechanical copy of reality because those who made it (and there are many of them in the case of dramatic and theatrical works) would not be *creative artists*. Artists must transform their experience – and they must do so in a *purposeful transformation* – and we will call this act the (artistic) *stylisation*. There are literally endless possibilities of stylisation in the dramatic art – just like in other arts – with a view to the concrete artworks, i.e., theatrical performances. Which of them will the artist, or artists that create the work, choose? Surely, they choose – or at least they *should* choose – those stylisations that correspond to their personal artistic dispositions. Only then can a particular completed artwork become a signature of their artistic personality, which is usually described as the *originality of a work of art*.

The dramatic work as a work of *art* (as its definition asserts) *should be stylised*, and that should be done *in all its components and consistently (jednotně)*. This **stylisation principle** will be the central idea in the third and final part of this book.

THE PRINCIPLE OF DRAMATICITY

4 THE DRAMATIC TEXT: THE PLAYWRIGHT'S CREATIVE WORK

From an objective point of view, the *dramatic text* is the beginning of a long and complicated process which brings a dramatic work into completion as a theatre performance. From a subjective point of view it is, conversely, the outcome of a mental process undertaken by the author; we shall call it the *playwright's creative work*, avoiding the more customary designation as the work of a "dramatic poet". We have laid out in the first part of the book that a dramatic work is not a product of literature and that a dramatic text is not its sufficient representative as it renders only one component of the actual work; such a representation would be imperfect and only partial. A dramatic text by itself however, *could* claim to be classified as *a work of literature*; this is not only by the virtue of it generically belonging to literature but also because of its formal resemblance to numerous texts that are inherently and legitimately identified as literary (*básnická*) works, such with the so-called "literary dramas" or "dramatic poems".

In order to investigate this issue we must establish – just like when consolidating the aesthetic term "dramatic" – what the exact, critical meaning of the term "**poetic**" is. We shall similarly find that the word has multiple meanings.

> First, there is the *popular* meaning of the word, based on a mere emotional impression of a kind that, while rather indefinite as to its content, is commonly called "a poetic" impression. Poetic is that which produces a poetic effect; however, what is the nature of this poetic effect? In one respect it is the opposite of what popular usage terms "dramatic": the non-arousing but calming; the not dissonant but consonant, *harmonious*. What is meant is a gentle, sweet impression, one that is otherwise called "beautiful" in a narrower, similarly popular sense of the word; and in fact, we could employ the word whenever speaking or commonly writing of "a poetic moment" or "a poetic scene" in life and such like. In these situations we often also perceive a certain peculiarity that could be expressed in words like "enchanting" or "bewitching", such as when speaking of "a poetic voice" or "a poetic appearance". An object or an event evokes somewhat *indeterminate* but very pleasing recollections and images, rippling gently our imagination and transporting us to the realm of fantasy.
>
> This observation brings us to a definition of the meaning of "poetic" impression, that is, to the second meaning of this term. "Poetic" can be a description of such objects

or events that have a direct effect on us in evoking multiple images or, psychologically speaking, multiple *associations* of a vague as well as a concrete nature. Disregarding objects and events of our real lives that often evoke various images and recollections (such as private memories) and capture our imagination, there are especially certain art disciplines able to affect us in such a way. In the first place it would certainly be poetry (or literature) itself that impresses not only by the sound and rhythm of the spoken or read words and sentences but also – and especially – by the mood of the evoked images and thoughts. However, to call the impressions produced by poetry "poetic" would be in fact tautological. And yet, we are drawing on an analogy with poetry whenever we apply the term to visual artefacts that evoke multiple images, talking of "poetic" painting or sculpture – such as with instances of genre pictures or fairy-tale pictures as opposed to the so-called "still lives". The most striking case is the type of "poetic" art in music. Music as an art is the least capable of evoking images other than purely musical ones, and even less any concrete and clear images. Still there are certain conditions under which music does evoke concrete images, as will be discussed later; there is furthermore an entire type of musical compositions that aim at describing or depicting things by means of their tonal formations. These are the genres of the "symphonic poem" or the "symphonic painting" that use the orchestra to this end; which is particularly suitable for this thanks to its colourfulness; such "poetic" pictures and tales are often also presented by piano compositions ("piano poetry"). Due to the vagueness of music in regards to images, it is necessary that the composer should present the so-called *"programme"* of the work in words – which give the technical term of *"programmatic music"* for this genre of compositions. Such a programme may be conveyed by a mere title of the composition, especially if it is comprehensive enough; in this aspect such musical works resemble paintings or statues, which are usually also given names indicating what they represent. It is obvious that the image in this case, whether in visual arts or in music, is not "poetic" in itself; the description "poetic music" and its variants are therefore necessarily reduced to the above popular notion of "poetic impression", not arising this time from the work itself but from the associations it evokes.

The actual, scholarly meaning of the word "poetic" needs to be found not in the subjective impression evoked by the object but in its objective nature; it may be found in its *material* (*látka*). In regards of poetry, what may be called *"poetic"* is anything created by language, i.e., any *verbal formation* on condition *that its effect on us is aesthetic*. It is obvious that its emotive impression may be of any kind: excited or calm, harmonious or disharmonic; a poetic impression is any emotive impression springing from a verbal work of art. It is in this exact sense that we will use this term.

It follows that any utterance, any verbal expression of emotions or any telling of an event may be "poetic" as long as it has an aesthetic effect, and the same holds true when such an expression is written down, i.e., of its *text*. The domain of art is entered once a speech is *intentionally* formulated with the *purpose* of an aesthetic effect. This becomes *verbal art*, or poetry. The two main forms of this verbal art are *lyrical poet-*

ry, depicting emotions (in words), and *epic poetry* (*narrative literature*), telling stories. Dramatic poetry (or dramatic literature) as such *does not exist* because – as has been pointed out in the first part of this work – a dramatic work can not be an exclusively verbal artefact and there is no obligation to identify *pars pro toto*, one part of it with the whole. Only such "dramatic poems" that the author intended as *self-sufficient* texts belong to literature, namely to *epic* (narrative) literature, even though they are written in what is known as the "dramatic form" of direct speeches; this genre will be discussed shortly.

Our exact definition of "the poetic" implies that a dramatic text in itself, considered as a *partial* dramatic artefact, may be poetic in the strict sense of the word as it is a verbal formation; however, this would be so only on condition that the text is artificially formed in order to have – by itself – an aesthetic effect. This condition will be analysed in the third part of this book; at this point the focus is exclusively with the requirement of a dramatic persona.

Theory that considers drama as a genre of literature (*básnictví*) does not content itself with reference to the verbal text. It has reclaimed the *dramatic action and personas,* declaring them to be *poetic* formations since they also occur in literature, primarily narrative literature (epic poetry), and especially in the novel and the short story. Even personas and the dramatic action of the pantomime are also considered to be poetic formations; however, opponents of the view that drama is literature cite pantomime as evidence that a dramatic work may stand even without a text and that a text is not an essential part of drama, only an optional one. The above mistaken view of pantomime's dramatic action and personas probably stems from the fact that an outline of that dramatic action and the description of those personas' use words. In such a case literature would comprise anything that can be expressed through words – that is, anything that can be perceived, imagined or thought about: the personas depicted on visual artefacts would then be poetic; events and people experienced in our real world would be poetic as soon as they started to have an aesthetic effect. All that may be, if we will, described and told in words. However, that would mean a total disintegration of the term "poetic".

Having restricted the concept of "poetic" to verbal formations it is obvious that one can speak of the poetic only once persons or actions have been formulated. Strictly speaking, the persons described or actions told are not "poetic", only *their verbal description and telling*, whether heard or read. Such conceptual differentiation is consequential, not in a dogmatic way but rather empirically. It is commonly found that the same story may be described poetically as well as non-poetically. A narrated plot – and for that matter, a described person too – is neither poetic or non-poetic in itself; it is a mere object, a *sujet*, a motif existing *outside* of poetry and literature, and even *outside of aesthetics* since it is only merely *imaginary*. Given the importance of this point to the current discussion let us analyse it briefly, firstly with a view to the *imaginary* or *ideal action* (please note the distinction from the common word "ideal" in the sense of "perfect").

The opening part of this book emphasised that the necessary existential condition of a dramatic work is its actual performance. This performance or "play" is a *real* event – just like any event in everyday life; that means that it is performed by *real people* (the actors) in *real space* (the stage) and in *real time*. In contrast, a narrated event is only imagined or *ideal*, performed by *ideal persons*; likewise the *location* in which the event is happening is *imaginary* and the action occurs in an *ideal time*. In above all the difference between real time and ideal time is a distinctive criterion for differentiating the two types of action. Dramatic action in the theatre is experienced in the *same* real time in which it objectively takes place (as a play). In contrast, a story that is told or read out is also experienced in real time – that is in the moment of telling or reading – but this real time is *essentially independent of and generally different from* the ideal time in which the described action happens. This is especially true of the *duration* of this action; usually it is longer, often much longer than the time needed to hear of it. A short story that can be heard or read within an hour or so almost always comprises events covering several hours, if not days or more. A novelist may use a few sentences or pages to describe how a person spent a whole afternoon. This can be read in a short while. But what would it look like if it should be played on stage? Exceptionally, the opposite may be found: a brief but important action (for instance an assault) may be described in such detail and extent that can take relatively long to hear it or read it. The writer often recognises this discrepancy and may conclude the description with such words as: "But all of this occurred much quicker than it can be told – almost in a single instant." If this should be played on stage, it could or perhaps had to be performed "almost in a single instant", and we would experience it at that pace. A narrator may take the same license with the *sequence* of action as with duration whereas real time offers only one option: from the past to the future. The ideal time of a narrated action is not bound by this law as evidenced by numerous examples from novels, such as chapters that tell events that took place before or simultaneously with the action of the previous chapter. This is no difficulty to the reader. But would it be possible for a scene or act to present events preceding the action of the previous scene or act? That would hardly be tolerable since these events occur in real time and such reversal of sequence is unthinkable.

The arbitrary disparity between the duration of the ideal *narrated* action and the time we spend experiencing it (either as listeners of a narrator or as readers of a text) stems, generally speaking, from the *incomparability* of words as means of communication to the subject that is communicated. Words and sentences are not commensurate with the action; they only convey a *message* about it, not the action itself, and the relation between words and the actual events is always only generic and conventional. So when reading in a story that someone "approached him and said", we learn exclusively that someone approached and said, but not *how* this was done. Slowly or quickly? In a loud or a soft voice? The writer does say that – and even more: the writer *does not have to* say it if it is of no importance. This is a strength of speech in that it *may* deliberately omit details, remaining general, succinct. Such an option is impossible in real action. Let us imagine the quoted sentence is a stage direction inserted in a dramatic text in the usual format: (*approaches him and says*). Is it possible for an actor to obey such a stage direction *at all*? Surely not: the actor *must* approach and speak *so and so*. There *is no* avoiding the *"how"*; and yet this is not a weakness of the actor's art but conversely the *actor's* strength since it is *exactly this "how"* which comprises the *actor's task*. One could object and suggest that words can also express this "how" and nothing prevents the epic poet from going into details; the writer may state "he approached him hastily and said sharply" or "said with a smile" and so on. However, a recollection of an actual, concrete action of an actor's delivery will expose that this is an error: such a verbal specification of the manner of the action – no matter how detailed – always remains relatively generic and therefore, in comparison with the concrete action, imperfect. The absolute "how" of an action may be conveyed only by its actual presentation as experienced by us; only that comprises everything – and inevitably at that – and in full *continuity of real* time and space.

What has just been assumed about the ideal character of narrated action is also valid for the *ideal nature of persons* participating in such an action and for the *idealness of place* in which the persons and action are. In this case a verbal description is not and cannot be adequate to the object; naturally, it does not even need to be adequate. It is unnecessary for the poet to describe the hero's outer looks; any description is on the author's deliberation as to what should be covered and what left unmentioned. The author may choose to describe the hero's face but not the clothes; or include the clothes but only their shape, not their colour. In contrast, an actor presenting a certain dramatic persona *must* have outer looks and that precisely so and so; it is impossible that the actor's clothes have a certain shape but not colour; it has to have such and such a colour! It is therefore impossible to leave something "unmentioned" like in a verbal description; everything is inevitable, so the artist needs to bear everything in mind – that is the question of the actor's mask (or make-up) and costume, even if the mask is the actor's own face. At the same time it is obvious that even in the most detailed and extensive description – as is popular in naturalistic novels – the writer can never present the personas and places of the action fully and perfectly. In dramatic works the incompleteness of verbal description as to the visuals can be evidenced by comparing stage directions regarding persons and place of action with the persons and places we can see on stage; that is also true even if the stage directions are maximally detailed and the actors and directors comply with them in all aspects. Of course, the art capable of an adequate rendering of visual aspects are the fine arts, especially painting; as for a mechanical reproduction of the original, that is the domain of photography. However, a dramatic work, based on action created by its personas' behaviour, cannot comply in this respect, with the exception of capturing the unchanging set, which is in fact a mere frame. One picture could capture only one moment; there would have to be a great number of them and they would have to follow one after another so densely in order to create an impression of continuity in time and movement. This is, of course, the principle of cinematography – by the way.

> It may seem that what has been scrutinised here is so self-obvious that it is unnecessary to discuss it. In fact, basic things are usually obvious, but only in thoughts, not in words. Words trick reason. Literary theorists claim – as has been the starting point of these reflections – that actions and personas can be equally found in epic genres as well as in dramas. However, we have shown that the *same* word "action" (*děj*) means different things in each case, and *profoundly different*, psychologically and noetically: ideal action in the former, and real action in the latter. How can such error be possible? Very simple. A literary theorist has two books on their desk: a novel and a drama. They read and analyse the former, and they read and analyse the latter – both with the same method: on the basis of the text. That means, in *both* cases their analysis deals with ideal action and ideal persons. This is appropriate for the novel, but not for the drama since in drama, as we know from our theatregoing experience, action and persons are real in both time and space, not ideal. In other words, the literary theorist reflects on something that does not exist in the actual work of art. They consider dramatic action *as* narrated action, a drama *as* a novel with direct speeches; with that literary focus they may conclude that "drama is literature nonetheless", which is an obvious *petitio principii*.[10] They may regret that the beauty of this "dramatic poem" fades in coarse footlights and shrug over the theatrical efficacy of a poetically worthless piece. What a vicious circle!
>
> In actuality there is no greater injustice towards the dramatic work than to replace its real action which appeals to the senses, with merely an imaginary one. Ideal action is in fact no action anymore, merely a concept of action (*děj*) and its temporality is not its inherent characteristic, but only a mere logical feature. If an action is told in detail, there can be a certain illusion of temporality at least due to experiencing the narration (or reading) in real time: we actually do get to know what happened first, what next and so on. Frequently the narrative itself follows the sequence of the ideal action; yet, strictly speaking, this is not a temporal but only a *successive sequence* (as in a row of numbers or letters of the alphabet) and that is enough. The briefer the narrative and

---

10   Or *circulus vitiosus* or *circular reasoning*. Formally a wrong argument in which the reasoner begins with what they are trying to end with.

the more comprehensive in details and condensed in words, the more the impression of temporality is lost, until it disappears entirely when it comes to a single sentence or word. Then it becomes no more than a title for the action and it assumes that we know at least the general outlines of its details and sequence when it comes to a singular action (e.g., "The Defenestration" or "The Women's War"[11]), otherwise we would need to be acquainted with it better. This is action (*děj*) as subject matter (sujet), whether elaborated or not – the differences between them are gradual; their nature is identical (in their very *ideal nature*).

Yet, is it not possible to *imagine* dramatic action even when only reading a text, that is, to see and hear it, though only in one's imagination? Such imagined action would surely be ostensive and occurs in real time. It would certainly be possible but the same holds also for epic action; in that case, as has been shown above, there is a particularly clear mismatch in time. The speed of reading would have to be governed by the ideal time in which the narrated action flows, which does not usually happen and could potentially lead to utter nonsense – so a novel that covers five years of action would need to be read over five years. It is pointless to cite instances of brief descriptions of long-lasting actions; one example will suffice: "Scowling, he crossed the room slowly several times before he stopped and...". If the reader were to visualise this faithfully, they would need to interrupt their reading at that point to gain time for the persona's "several slow walks across the room" and resume only after "the persona stops". This is not the custom of novel reading even for those with the most vivid imagination; readers content themselves with only flitting bursts of imagination during a steady reading: an image of a walking person, an image of a stopping person. Any continuity in time of such images is out of question; there is usually no time for it, or there is too much time if the novel gives a lengthy description of a momentary action. Equally, the narrator is clearly not meant to regulate the speed of their narrative according to the ideal time of the action; the narrator is not going to wait, as in the popular fairy tale, "for the sheep to pass".

In a drama it is different. Its action is conceived in such a way so that its delivery fills the limited space of several hours on stage. When reading a play,

---

[11] Zich refers to events notorious for the Czech reader and every Czech school child. The "Defenestration" refers to a revolutionary moment when a crowd entered the Old Town Hall in Prague in 1618 and representatives of goverment were thrown out of the windows (defenestrated). In fact there were three different defenestrations, in 1419, 1483 and 1618, each in different political circumstances. But the general concept of throwing a figure of power from a window remained the same in principle.
"The Women's War" refers to mythological Czech history: after the death of Libuše (Libussa), eponymous founding queen of the Czech nation, men take over and women are deprived of their previous rights. So they organised an uprising against men. This story was popular amongst romantic artists, including the composer Bedřich Smetana. These fighting women are sometimes called the Czech Amazons.

one can always imagine the dramatic action (and its personas) continuously and fully, in its real time. Such reading is evidently only a *substitute* for its true existential form as a stage performance, and we *have to* imagine it such a way if we are to do justice to a dramatic work. A similar case is a musician reading the score of a composition, with the difference that this is a case of exclusively acoustic ostensive images on the basis of an *exact* notation. With a dramatic work there are *also* acoustic images in regards to the speech and other vocal expressions of the actors; *apart* from them there are also visual images. The first part of this book, in the discussion on "reproductive arts" (*výkonná umění*), has shown how *imperfect* and *fragmentary* a dramatic text is as a basis for the overall visualisation. Such a *"theatrical reading"* of a dramatic text – so called as it requires to imagine the dramatic action of the personas as played *by actors on stage* – necessitates considerable theatrical experience.

But who reads dramatic texts in *this* way? I believe that most readers, even literary theorists – if they imagine ostensively (*názorně*) anything at all when reading – make do with the above type of sketchy reading, characteristic of epic or lyrical poetic works. That is of course utterly unsatisfactory for a dramatic work. A "theatrical reading", based so much on *free* imagination, requires not only theatrical experience but also an inborn *"dramatic sense"*, that is, a sense for the effect of real action and all its specifics – as has been mentioned above and will be discussed in greater detail in the following chapters. Not referring to this as *a* "theatrical sense", however clearer this might be, is because dramatic sense is a *special*, though the most important instance of the theatrical sense.

A "theatrical" reading of a dramatic text is a requirement that *should* be fulfilled *in as many as possible* (and frequent) cases when one has to make do with only a text. There are cases when this requirement *must* be fulfilled *to the full*: such has to be the reading done by the stage director of the play, such has to be a reading of it (or at least its parts) by the actors, and such has to be the reading of the opera text (libretto) by the composer – as shall be discussed in the later chapters. Most importantly and crucially the "theatrical" requirement holds for the *author* of the play. It is therefore relevant to turn to playwright's creative work.

☙ ☙ ☙

THE PLAYWRIGHT'S CREATIVE WORK

Early in this chapter it has been established that the dramatic text, as a literary form, is only seemingly the first stage of a dramatic work. The formula "in the beginning was the *word*", fully valid for all literature, is correct when it comes to a theatrical activity that carries out a dramatic work as a performance. However, it is not true of the preceding creative work of the playwright; that is dominated by a scenic vision, an imaginative visualisation of a concrete dramatic situation where the personas of the play interact. The formula for a dramatic creative work (a good one, that is!) should be in brief: "in the beginning is the (dramatic) *situation*".

This fact is evidenced beyond doubt by the experience of numerous playwrights as far as they are recorded in diaries, autobiographies, theoretical treatises as well as in their statements and views as captured by others. Let me cite the most prominent ones at least. The evidence is that the primary concept of a drama is not verbal but actorly-scenic. *Diderot*, the earliest theorist of the dramatic art and the creator of "bourgeois drama", says: "When playwrights conceive of a persona, they associate it with a concrete physiognomy. The image of a persona acting on the stage must suggest the persona's lines to the author".[12] German playwright and theorist O. Ludwig[13] gives several examples of his plays originating in optical visions of the stage, almost hallucinations, which he describes at length. Generally a theatre persona or a group appeared to him suddenly "in a passionate posture": even before he knew anything of the action, that is how he saw the hero of his play *Der Erbförster* [1845], "with a gesture to accompany the actor's words 'So the beasts should all be shot dead immediately' or later 'A right must therefore remain a right'." Ludwig says: "It is striking that such an image or a group is generally not one of catastrophe…; it is soon followed by several others… until I have the whole play ready with all its scenes, written in great haste… I may rearrange the content of individual scenes as I wish but I am unable to provide a brief novelistic summary. Eventually lines can be found to go with the gestures." Similarly, German playwright W. v. Scholz says that "Drama is engendered in the author's mind as a sequence of scenes in a particular space and time, and these scenes are only later and bit by bit filled with the dialogue of the visualised persons."[14]

---

12 Zich is paraphrasing (possibly via Lessing's influential German translation) from Denis Diderot's *Discours sur la poésie dramatique* (1758), the opening paragraphs of the section "XIV. Des scènes":
Tout peintre, tout poëte dramatique sera physionomiste. Ces images, formées d'après les caractères, influeront aussi sur les discours et sur le mouvement de la scène; surtout si le poëte les évoque, les voit, les arrête devant lui, et en remarque les changements. (Diderot 1875: 360)
[Every painter and every dramatic poet will be a physiognomist. The images formed on the basis of the characters will also influence their speech and their movement on stage; especially when the poet evokes them, he sees them, fixes them before his eyes and observes how they change.]
13 Otto Ludwig (1813–1865) was a playwright, novelist and critic, considered to be one of the first and most prominent German realist dramatists. The quotations are borrowed by Zich from Richard Müller-Freienfels's *Psychologie der Kunst* [Psychology of Art], vol. I (Leipzig und Berlin: B. G. Teubner, 1912), p. 219.
14 Wilhelm von Scholz, "Das Schaffen des dramatischen Dichters" [The Creative Work of the Dramatic Poet], *Zeitschrift für Ästhetik und allgemeine Kunstwissenschaft* IX (1914): vol. 2: 180–181.

4 THE DRAMATIC TEXT: THE PLAYWRIGHT'S CREATIVE WORK

Such evidence shows that the very beginning of the dramatic work lies in optical visions, without lines. This is the case most commonly, though not exclusively. Such playwrights belong psychologically to the "visual type", which is most common among people. More scarce is its counterpart, the "auditive type"; playwrights of this type conceive their plays in words from the start – not in abstract words but in concrete speeches, or precisely in a dialogue (or its extracts), all of which are again in theatrical mode, as if delivered by the actors of the play's personas.

> A telling example of the difference between the two types is the report by the French psychologist *Binet* regarding two popular authors of French comedy: "When I am writing a scene," says Legouvé to Scribe, "I can *hear* it, but you *see* it. Every sentence I write down sounds in my ears in the voice of the speaking persona. You are the theatre itself: your actors walk and gesticulate before your eyes: I am a listener, you are a spectator." "There is nothing more correct," said Scribe. "Do you know where I imagine to be when writing a play? In the middle of the stalls."[15] This quotation seem to point more towards the playwright's execution of the creative work than to its conception; still it confirms obliquely Ludwig's claim: "A lyrical poet feels into themself; the epic poet into their personas; *the dramatist into the actors of their personas*." It should be added that often the playwright's conception grew on very particular actors (a notorious example is Coquelin who served as a model for Rostand's Cyrano). This also confirms the general fact that an artist creating their work do not think in abstract "ideas" but in their material. For a playwright these are *actors* on stage.

A delineation of the above two sensorial types, the visual and the auditive, does not exhaust the psychological characteristics of the playwright's conceptions. The first part of this book, analysing the dramatic impression, has established the important role of the inner tactile (*vnitřně hmatový*), bodily sensations and especially motoric ones. A playwright *empathising* in their visions as intensely as possible experiences also such *motoric sensations* relating to postures, gestures and all imaginatively visualised actions as well as to the speech heard internally. Surely a playwright often – especially in the state of inspiration – will spontaneously imitate the play of their personas or speak out their lines, but that is not essential; it is enough to experience flitting sensations of the actions – mere "innervations" of the whole body and organs of speech. Such *bodily playing out* (*tělové rozehrání*) forms the characteristic *basis* of the playwright's creative work; compared to the above sensorial, i.e., mental visions, it is *physiological* to a great extent. It has been identified in the audience's experiencing and here it is found in the playwright at work; it is

---

15 Alfred Binet, *Psychologie du Raisonnement* [Psychology of Reasoning] (1886), p. 25. This example demonstrating the difference between the auditive and the visual psychological type was quoted quite often, most prominently in William James's *Principles of Psychology* (vol. II, 1890).

therefore present at the start and the end of the process that a dramatic work undergoes. As will be shown below, it is a characteristic base that follows through all phases of that process.

> A true playwright is therefore *"playing out"* in their imagination, not *only* seeing and hearing, as does an epic poet. That is the meaning of the above quotation; the playwright empathises in the actors of the play's personas. This "bodily component" of the creative work has a very characteristic psychological consequence: a peculiar sensation of "reality" of dramatic visions. We know well from our experience that what can be seen or heard is not always the reality but an illusion; in contrast, what can be felt by touch is undoubtedly real. That is why the sense of touch, inner or outer, is the sense of "reality" and this also explains the peculiar sensation experienced by playwrights in their merely imaginary visions. Scholz, cited above, is not a psychologist but captures this sensation in the following words: "[The playwright's visions] reach a state of inner reality, much stronger than with the many imagined events that daily pass through our mind... When intensified, they oust all other outer interests (apart from the fundamental ones) and assume in their events, images and personas such physical (*tělesná*) concreteness for the eyes and the ears, such intensity of emotion and passion that they become as material (*předmětný*) as a half-dream... Long before the performance they are a mixture of a reality happening in space and a manifest onstage play"[16].

Yet another supremely significant feature of the playwright's creative work needs to be stressed. Ludwig's observation that the playwright empathises with the actors of the play's personas means – in line with the accurate distinction made early in this book – that the empathy happens in relation to the *"personas"* of the drama. This act is equally true for the audience experiencing a theatre performance – but with a difference. For an audience, "a persona" is objective: it is the actor figure on stage; it is externally enforced and the audience interpret it imaginatively as a "dramatic persona". In contrast, for a playwright, this "persona" is subjective: it is a part of their mind that shaped the character by the creative process and *identified* it with the "dramatic persona", so these two cannot be separated. In brief, this "dramatic persona" is the playwright's proper "self" that has been *transformed* into a new, *other* "self". We shall call this process **"mental transfiguration"** (*předuševnění*); let us stress that it is different from *metempsychosis* (transmigration of the soul), a well-known teaching of some religions believing that a human soul after death passes to another body (even an animal one) without substantially changing in itself. *The ability of mental transfiguration is a specific quality of the dramatic talent in general*, that is not only *the playwright's talent* but also of those that carry out the dramatic work: *actors, stage directors* as well as the

---

16　Wilhelm von Scholz, "Das Schaffen des dramatischen Dichters" [The Creative Work of the Dramatic Poet], *Zeitschrift für Ästhetik und allgemeine Kunstwissenschaft* IX (1914): vol. 2: 179.

dramatic *musical composer*. For the other theatre makers it is the dramatic text this aids this process. The importance of "mental transfiguration" deserves a more detailed analysis.

What is the psychological basis of "mental transfiguration"? The mental "self" is a sum of a great number of features relating to the imaginative, the emotive and voluntary life of the human individual. These are inborn, that is, inherited *predispositions* or *tendencies* towards particular reactions to the outer world; these predispositions may grow stronger or weaker in the course of life under the influence of the environment, especially the social one; yet these changes are always only partial in regards to their original intensity. Of the greatest interest and importance for the present study of "dramatic personas" are the emotive and voluntary tendencies. A psychological view is that all people have predispositions to all basic emotions and aspirations but they differ in intensity: some of them are well developed, others only rudimentary; the psychiatric view is that we all also have at least traces of all abnormal tendencies but these are entirely suppressed in normal mental states. Individuality may therefore be understood as a unique combination of differently developed tendencies. If these different tendencies are marked with the letters of the alphabet, in lower or upper case, depending on their intensity, a schematic rendering of a particular individual mental "self" could be AbcDEfGh…; another aBcDeFgH… and so on. Since intensive tendencies can be noticed from the outside, the former individuality *appears* essentially as "ADEG…", the latter as "BDFH…", that is, as very different, except for the one shared feature D (for instance, a predisposition to anger). To *transfigure mentally* means to change one's own constellation of tendencies in such a way that some strong ones are suppressed, while other weak ones are strengthened, so that a new constellation is created: a mental "self" other than one's own.

> Preventing or allowing a particular inclination is what people do very often for practical reasons, usually under the influence of the social environment. Habit fixes such balance of one's self, so it is not uncommon to find that someone is "a different person" at home, another in an office, yet another in public and so on. Some of these changes are so great that they may seem to show contradictory qualities in one individual. How amazed are we at times when we happen to get a glimpse of the private life of someone of whose personality we have made a firm judgement on the basis of long-lasting social contact! How we disagree with those who know "our good friend" but differently! One may often ask which one is actually the person's "true face" and generally we opt for the face one wears in an environment that does not require self-control or dissembling.
>
> In such instances mental transfiguration is naturally quite superficial – rather outer than inner. For example, a timid person may put on "a brave face" – being frightened

but not giving it away. Where the person does not need to be ashamed, such as when alone, they give in to their predisposition. However, the situation is different when it is not pragmatic reasons that make one mentally transfigure but *aesthetic* motives. It is the joy of being someone else from who I am (at least in my imagination) and of living a different mental life (outside of reality at least) from the one I lead in fact. Young people especially tend to indulge in such daydreaming, imagining themselves heroic, passionate, tender and so on – in brief, taking on qualities they admire in others but do not themselves possess, unless in a limited way. Such mental transfiguration is deeper, more profound and internalised, or more elaborate; it is not caused by will and habit but by desire and mood. For that reason it is only temporary; it is a departure from the everyday to the realm of dreams.

Mental transfiguration becomes an artefact on two conditions: firstly, if it is freed from self-enjoyment, that is if it becomes *autotelic* (finding an end in itself), independent of a personal wish to become *exactly* such and such. What remains then is only the creative joy of mentally transfiguring in one or another way, with *all variety possible*. This is essential for a playwright; even one single play requires *several* dramatic personas and the playwright must know how to live *with all of them*. The playwright's mental transfiguration into any of them has to be so intense to allow the playwright to assume the persona's standpoint against the others; to seem them with the persona's eyes, not the playwright's own; to love with the persona's love, or hate with the persona's hate – although all the personas are the playwright's creations. Only this will allow the playwright to create autonomous personas and a truly *dramatic* action – and this action, as has been pointed out above, is not only one that personas merely "participate in" but action that they themselves *make* through their interaction (*vespolné jednání*). Based on how *broadly* the playwright's talent fulfils this condition, rests the *variety* of the dramatic personas which the playwright creates for the play and which in themselves should probably be in contrast to one another rather than in agreement. An author who creates "look-alike" personas – which are usually little variants of him- or herself – is surely not a full-fledged playwright. And clearly, dramatists can make projections of themselves in one of their personas; there are several examples of this, especially in Molière's plays.

The second condition is as *complete* mental transfiguration as can be – not only assuming one or another mental quality but the entire set that constitutes an all-around individuality, diverse and yet integral, that is, psychologically coherent. Although this condition is very important for all dramatic artists, it is only relatively rarely found in a perfect form with playwrights. Dramatic personas created in this way have the full concreteness of real people, even though they are only imaginary. Whenever the set of individual predispositions is incomplete, the dramatic persona made through mental transfiguration is less or more abstract, formulaic. It has to be said that an all-around mental transfiguration is essential only for the *main* personas in a play – those that are pivotal in the dramatic interaction and have to act in a versatile way, deploying their various mental features and predispositions. If the playwright fails to live through some of the dispositions, there is a danger that personas behaving according to them will contradict the other features. The crucial importance of mental transfiguration lies in preventing such contradiction; a persona into whom the playwright has mentally transfigured gains *an inner truth*. More on this point will be said in the chapter on actors. Secondary or episodic personas do not require full mental transfiguration – only such that relates to the mental features necessary for their behaviour. Such personas are only sketched or outlined by the playwright.

After an analysis of the important act of "mental transfiguration", a description of the playwright's creative work as such may continue.

Clearly such a large and complex work like a drama cannot come into existence at once, by a single act of conception. More of them are needed and the creative work takes relatively long, even in the most fortunate cases. The individual acts of conception are negotiated in the playwright's artistic reflections, which have become quite prominent in creative practice. Two types of dramatic conceptions can be distinguished: the general and the detailed ones. A *general* conception provides the artist with the large parts or even the overall view of the work, though only in its rough, principal outlines. The following tasks of the creative work is to fill in the gaps with the conceptions of details. An advantage of the general conception is in guaranteeing the unity (*jednota*) of the whole work; but its danger is that an impatient but overly skilful playwright may fill those gaps with borrowed tropes or stories or even routines from one's own life (playwright's "padding" ("*macha*")). A *detailed* conception pertains to particulars; the artist collects them in order to use them in composing the whole. A distinct advantage here would be the captivating and effective moments made possible by this approach in the work; its danger is that the "composite" work may lack unity and coherence, and be patched up and fragmented. Generally – and especially in larger works – the two types of conception complement one another. The number, variety as well as unevenness and ephemerality of the conceptions force the playwright to capture them in hurried *sketches*. This is usually done in words and sometimes in other auxiliary symbols. In this way the playwright sketches out the plot structure, the persons' characters, capturing stage situations, fragments of speeches, gestures or actions.

> The playwrights' keen effort to render as many of their visions as possible often compels especially younger authors to give their personas too much to say. The dramaturg's

pen then cuts out many of them as unnecessary – and the playwrights find during the performance with amazement that they really were redundant. The more experienced playwrights, on completion of their play, make the necessary cuts themselves. On this point, see also František Langer's telling article "The Dramatic Craft"[17].

Critical reflection must overrule improvisation – accepting, rejecting, changing, adapting and creating new versions.

As this kaleidoscopic chaos gradually settles down we can see more and more clearly the proper sense of all creative work: to *fix* one's creation in a firm, *objective record*. Yet, what can the playwright *reliably* render out of this actually imaginary theatre performance? *No more than the words of the personas* – that is, *what* they speak, but not the speech itself and how it is spoken, let alone their play, their facial expressions or the stage business.

Only the personas' words can be counted into "the dramatic text" as the artefact because they alone are reproduced during the performance, forming an actual part of the dramatic work in our sense of the word. This does not apply to the *acting and stage directions* that the playwright sometimes includes in the text (usually in brackets); these do not exist during the performance since nobody voices them. Their significance is purely technical; they are only *suggestions* or hints for the actors and the stage director, or for the musical composer when it comes to a libretto. By means of stage directions the playwright is trying to capture at least some of their inner dramatic vision in the aspects that cannot be adequately expressed in the lines. Different authors make use of stage directions to a different extent: some profusely while others not at all; some only in rough outlines while others in detail. Generally it may be said that recent plays tend to use them more and in greater detail than earlier; that relates to the modern nature of creative work, which – compared to the past – places greater and greater emphasis on the individuality of the author's work. There is no doubt that the conceptions of the earlier playwrights – the good ones at least – was "theatrical" in the sense outlined above; however, they contented themselves with the verbal record of what can actually be captured, leaving the rest to the actors and other theatre makers.

The difference between the personas' lines contained in the dramatic text and the stage directions may be illustrated by the same example that I used when outlining the ideal nature of the narrated action, only this time some-

---

17   František Langer, "Dramatické řemeslo" [The Dramatic Craft], *Nové české divadlo 1918–1926*. Praha: Aventinum, 1927: pp. 122–125. František Langer (1888–1965) was a Czech Jewish playwright, screenwriter and publicist. His most famous play is the socially critical *Periférie* (The Periphery, 1925), which enjoyed immense international popular success.

what enlarged. Let us imagine that we read out from a short story aloud: 'He approached him and said sharply: "So you're not coming?"' – and let us compare it with an onstage situation described in similar words in a dramatic text: 'X (*approaches him, sharply*) So you're not coming?' The radical difference and asymmetry between a verbal description and the actual, audiovisual performance has been discussed. On the other hand, the utterance of the cited direct question will be *essentially the same* in both cases. This important fact is actually self-evident: *speech* may be an adequate means of expression only for *speech*. If read aloud, the cited question will be spoken out in both cases, it will take place as action in real time but that which precedes it will be spoken in the case of the short story and its imaginary action will take place in an ideal time, whereas in the case of drama, those words will not take place and will become real action. This brings up the issue of *"direct speech"* in drama and in epic genres.

> The fact that a dramatic text consist *exclusively* of "direct speech" is so apparent that theorists have been pointing it out for eons; this form of "direct speech" has even been recognised as a *specifically dramatic* form. Clearly direct speech can be also found in epic genres, and though not exclusively, still often and typically enough. Proponents of the "poetic" theory of drama have resolved this by proclaiming direct speech in narrative literature (epic poetry) to be the "dramatic element" associated with the epic. In this vein, for instance, ballads are marked as "dramatic" since they often use direct spech; however, this dramatic quality is also given by the agitated storylines of ballads, which makes them "dramatic" also in the popular sense of the word. In contrast, it would be forceful to talk of Plato's dialogues as "dramatic form" or even as "dramatic" quality although they are written exclusively in direct speech.
>
> Direct speech in an epos and in a drama *is not the same* despite their apparent similarity. They differ in their origin and in their purpose. Direct speech in *literature* is only one of *the effective means* of the verbal art. Its usage is arbitrary because the narrator may always use indirect speech instead. Direct speech is more ostensive (*názorný*) than the indirect in that it is capable of suggestive evocation of the acoustic image. This has physiological and psychological causes. Direct speech has a motoric effect on us; it gives rise to certain perceptions of speaking, known well enough from our own experience. It is enough to compare its effect in reading with the effect of the indirect form of the same speech and it becomes evident that direct speech resonates "with the body". Also psychologically: behind direct speech one senses *a speaker* – not the narrator but a persona of the story. Inadvertently we imagine not only a typical acoustic form (a question, a wish, etc.) but it is also individualised according to the imaginary personas of the narrative. It is well known how the monotonous lull of a narrative suddenly changes when a direct speech appears. Verbal art has a number of similar means of emphasis – for instance, the usage of present tense instead of past enhances liveliness. One instance of a motoric feature of an almost combative kind towards

the reader or listener is direct address (apostrophe) or a rhetorical question; though we only read them, "someone" particular (in this case the author) is sensed behind them.

Effectively, almost all lyrical poetry is the poet's (or the voice's or speaker's) direct speech. It may be asserted that direct speech in literature comes from an intense ostensive vision, especially an acoustic one, and its purpose is to *intensify* the aesthetic effect of the work where the poet *wishes*. If the poet chooses, direct speech may be abandoned; it is merely a certain aesthetic luxury.

"Direct speech" in a dramatic text is, as has been shown, of an altogether different origin and purpose. It is a record of that which may be fixed of the playwright's dramatic conception; bluntly put, it is an emergency tool, the only aid in an artistic crisis – the playwright can do no more for the inner creation of their imagination. Strictly speaking, *it is* in fact *no* "direct speech" at all because this name makes sense only in situations where indirect speech is possible, which would clearly be absurd in a dramatic work. A dramatic text is simply a list of speeches to be spoken in a dramatic work by individual dramatic personas; this is also true in case a drama has a "prologue" or an "epilogue" to be spoken by a persona of the play – though the persona may be symbolic and standing outside the story, it nevertheless remains theatrical.

ෆ ෆ ෆ

A review of what has been stated of the playwright's creative work corroborates the validity of the crucial standpoint expressed at the opening of this book: A dramatic work is the theatre performance, not the dramatic text. This book's first concern was the perceiving of the dramatic work at the end of the long process that gives rise to the work; it could rely on the unprejudiced view of theatregoers who see drama as that which one comes to see in the theatre. *The same* conclusion has now been reached when analysing the early phase of the process in the inner creativity of the playwright: For a genuine dramatist a dramatic work also exists as *a theatre performance*, in the form of an *imaginative* (*fantazijní*) actor-scenic vision (*herecko-scénická vise*). The cause of this correspondence is obvious. A work of art, in its condensed and formalised shape, is there to evoke those mental states (images, thoughts, emotions) that the artist experienced when creating the work (that is, those experienced as a creative artist, not as a human). This double analysis, a certain "cross-examination" (experimentum crucis!), approaching the issue from opposite directions, has shown that a dramatic work is the theatre performance, not the dramatic text.

Clearly the correspondence between the playwright's conception and the performed work pertains particularly to the key aspect of the dramatic work, its "theatricality". With a dramatic work it is impossible to talk of complete *identity* due to the frag-

4 THE DRAMATIC TEXT: THE PLAYWRIGHT'S CREATIVE WORK

mentary and imperfect nature of the *objective fixity* that the dramatic text allows. In comparison with the dramatic art other art disciplines allow more, especially the non-temporal (*nečasový*) arts, that is the visual arts. Such artworks may even be the perfect fixities of the internally imagined work – they are in themselves the complete artefact that either needs no addition (a completed painting or a sculpture), or it can be completed by purely mechanical work (building a house according to the project, casting a statue from the mould, printing a graphic artwork from a plate). The fixed text in literature and music (verbal or musical) necessitates a special reproductive art to bring the work into completion; and yet it comprises *everything* that is essential. The text in the dramatic art renders only one component of the author's inner vision (sung drama also allows the fixity of the musical component). In terms of objective fixity, the least and close to nothing is possible in dance (except for choreographic notation).

The position of the dramatic text in the whole creative process in which a dramatic work comes into existence can be illustrated by the schema below; the arrows indicate the causal connection, that is what comes from what:

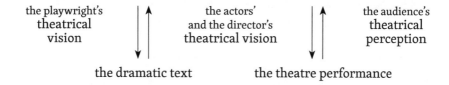

The first row comprises subjective formations; there is a clear equivalence between them in that they contain the entire dramatic work in its mental existence (*psychická existence*). The second row gives *objective* formations and these are obviously not equivalent to one another. The dramatic text is fully contained in the theatre performance but not vice versa: the performance comprises much more. This disproportion causes that only a partial match is *secured* between the two theatrical visions (the playwright's and the actors') – one based on the text. In all other aspects the accord can be only approximate. In contrast, the actors' and the director's theatrical vision, and the audience's theatrical perception are matched – provided the artists are good and able to present what they intend.

The conclusion of the first part of the book was that the theatrical perception (*divadelní vněm*) of the dramatic work evokes a referential image (*obrazová představa*) in our minds that tells us what is "represented" by what we perceive. This rich and complex image is decisive for us as spectators; its basic elements are the dramatic personas and the dramatic action. A literary work (*básnické dílo*) is also a *mimetic* (*obrazové*) work in that it evokes – for instance, when reading a novel – images of personas and action; however, these personas and actions are not perceived but only imagined. The situation is identical when reading a dramatic text; in fact, it is even worse. The narrative text at least depicts the action and often also describes the personas, while that is not the case of a dramatic text as it generally comprises only direct speeches. This shortcoming is often perceived very intensely when reading dramas; however, this cannot be objectively viewed as a shortcoming since dramatic texts are not made to be read like literary texts. The personas and action when reading a dramatic text have to be only inferred. Once this has been done, we have come up with no more than literary surrogates of the personas and the action existing in an imagined time and space only, which *is not the case* in a theatrical perception (*divadelní vněm*) of the dramatic work.

The reading of a dramatic text is an insufficient and misleading substitute for a theatrical perception (*divadelní vněm*) not only because it lacks much of what the theatrical perception offers but also because it contains much that the theatrical perception, that is, the actual dramatic work – at least in that form – does not offer. This implies a principle that we will consistently adopt in what follows:

All reflections, analyses and assessment of the dramatic work relating to its "mimetic" (image-based) qualities that are based merely on the dramatic text are principally inadmissible, since they are uncertain. They may be correct but do not need to be, although one can formally hardly object to them. *They evaluate something that, strictly speaking, does not exist as a dramatic work at all.*

Let me bring up a telling analogy of this principle from singing a folk song. When sung it comprises not only words but also the tune. Naturally, many collectors of folk songs lacked musical background and put down the words alone; so there are large collections of folk songs containing only the lyrics. Even if the tunes have been recorded, literary scholars pass them by, analysing only the verbal texts, that is a fragmentary song. As for the analysis of the songs' semantics, such as ideas and motifs, the conclusion of the research may be correct. However, as for the songs' artistic expression, it is obvious that it depends on the music too and that ignoring it may make the conclusions dubious (for example with a merry dance-like song with a motif of unrequited love). Completely delusional is the metric analysis of folk songs since the rhythm is governed by its musical side. Some of the musical side passes naturally into the lyrics, so such metric research may come to some results; however, these results are inconsequential because there is no such artwork as a spoken folk song. This would be pointless scholarship.

The study of dramatic texts is justified when it deals with the purely *ideational* aspects. Existing theoretical works on dramatic art (or dramatic literature, as it is mostly referred to) predominantly dedicate most space to analyses of ideas, such as philosophical, moral, religious or social. Undoubtedly these essays comprise many correct and ingenious observations but it should not be assumed that these present the *specific* character of dramatic art or its individual works! All that has been listed here is also present – if considering art, not life too – in literature, especially in the novel. This holds also when it comes to ideas that are considered specifically "dramatic", such as the tragic mode. Narrative literature has many a tragic heroes and stories. However, once we come to researching the *concrete* quality of the dramatic work, that is to an inquiry into its *specific structure*, a mere dramatic text becomes an uncertain and often even a misleading basis. How – on the basis of the words spoken – can a persona of the dramatic persona, its coherence, concreteness and inner truth be ascertained if all this is co-created by the actor, who often surprisingly balances and corrects the seeming gaps and inconsistencies of the text – *though not necessarily conceived as such by the author*. How can a motivation of action be studied solely from the words if the behaviour can also be motivated by how a persona says something and how they behave a that moment – or even outside that moment? Could an action not be motivated for instance by a mere gleeful sneer, which the dramatist never even mentioned in the stage direction, although a good actor can find it nevertheless and turn a motivation that may seem "strained", judged by the text, into a perfectly natural one? How can we analyse the construction of the dramatic action, which flows like music in real time and which takes great effect of its dynamic form from this quality, while the only thing knowable from the text is the sequence of events in ideal time? And so forth. And if anyone objects that we can and may analyse the mere text like this – what is the purpose of such study if the text is not yet the real dramatic work?

    Nowhere is the validity of this principle more pronounced than in the *evaluation* of the work's dramatic quality on the basis of the mere text, which is the frequently demanding and truly responsible task of the theatre dramaturg or artistic director. There is not only the risk of wasted effort, time and finances but also the possibility of wronging a talented author – and generally the latter is the option taken. How many seemingly gifted works have disappointed not only the author and the audiences but also experienced theatre makers used to a "theatrical reading" of a text? And conversely how many repeatedly refused works have surprised with their elementary efficacy once they were taken up by a producer with a dramatic instinct? It is almost a general belief of theatre makers that the success of a drama production is unpredictable. To a great extent this is actually so, due to the uncertain basis that a mere dramatic text offers to the dramatic appraisal of a work. The history of the dramatic art provides numerous instances. The outer success in the theatre is often also dictated by other, non-artistic circumstances; that however, never lasts, as evidenced by many cases of rehabilitated dramatic works (though mostly only after the playwright's death), and conversely their well-deserved oblivion. This is equally valid for spoken drama and sung drama.

This critical standpoint towards the dramatic text as a substitute for the actual, i.e., the performed dramatic work does not mean that the dramatic text should be taken as something secondary and inconsequential, let alone meaningless for dramatic art. Such – in opposition to literary theorists – is the stance of some theatre theorists, who argue that there have been numerous dramatic works without a text; the most notorious example is the commedia dell'arte, which appeared in sixteenth-century Italy and spread all over Europe for a long time. Tairov even claims that "periods of *flowering* in the theatre have ensued when the theatre abandoned written plays and created its own scenarios" (Tairov, *Notes of a Director*, Chapter 6, p. 96). This is to argue that the dramatic work is not a literary artefact. Although the thesis is correct, this argument is wrong. By the same token one could argue, for instance, that the folk tale is not a literary artefact since its original form has no written text. And yet, the tales are narrated, just like these unscripted theatre traditions. The lack of a written text is a specific feature of *folk* arts, be it popular literature, theatre or music. The text is substituted here by *tradition*; the objective rendition (*fixace*) by means of text is replaced by *subjective rendition*, which relies on the memory of folk narrators, actors, singers and musicians. They all learn their parts *by direct ostension* (*přímý názor*) from their elders and in the same way pass it onto their juniors; a condition of the tradition is the contact with people in time and space, which a textual rendition does not necessitate – and that is its great advantage. The advantage of subjective rendition is that it is capable of recording *everything*, which is of special significance for the domain of dramatic art: acting performances can be rendered only by that means, which is not only the case now but has always been happening. This upside also has its downside: the rendition is limited to the individual artist and it fades and perishes with him or her, while the objective rendition through text lasts for ages and can be easily distributed.

> Dramatic plays without a written text were a folk, *primitive* stage of dramatic art with all its qualities. It was an insufficiently differentiated art, generally a coarse combination of dancing, acrobatics and slapstick with dramatic art proper. To aid memory certain stock routines had been created for personas, speeches, situations, etc., and those were usually combined in improvisation according to a story outline. The word "improvisation" is still highly rated due to the surviving romantic view of genius; *undeservingly so*, since it is in fact *the most mechanical* method of artistic creation. Valuable improvisation is possible only within a detailed structure of the artwork, not with the whole: the construction of a work that is at least a bit more extensive (such as a dramatic work) requires artistic deliberation, which needs to rely upon a solid, objective record. The development of dramatic art towards a higher artistic level has always necessitated the written text and the history of dramatic art provides evidence that actual *flowering* started generally as soon as dramas started to get written down. This is clearest where dramatic art grew out of live folk plays (secular or sacred), rather than from dead classical texts. Such was the case in Spain (Lope de Vega, Calderón), in England (Marlowe, Shakespeare) and partly also in France (Molière) and in Italy (Goldoni).

4 THE DRAMATIC TEXT: THE PLAYWRIGHT'S CREATIVE WORK

ೞ ೞ ೞ

THE DRAMATIC TASK OF THE TEXT

The above defence of the dramatic text points out its actual significance for the dramatic art. The offered schema of the dramatic creative process (p. 125) illustrates this clearly: although the dramatic text *by itself* is not a satisfactory substitute for the dramatic work proper, it is a lasting *intermediary* between the dramatic author and the interpreters (actors and the director). From the *technical* perspective, though not from the referential one, it is legitimate and fruitful to take it into account. The third chapter of the first part has established that the basic elements of the technical image (*technická představa*) are the *actor figure* (*herecká postava*), corresponding to the referential image of the dramatic persona, and the actors' *interplay* (*spoluhra*), corresponding to the referential image of the dramatic action (*dramatický děj*). With the audience, the said technical image, though it always necessarily exists, is only poorly developed and limited; generally, it hardly comprises more than the mere image of "actors, play". In contrast, the image created by the actors and the director is much much richer and more developed, as will be illustrated in the following chapters. Even the dramatist's own technical image (unless he or she is a practical theatre maker or actor) is often insufficiently developed, with the exception of one component: the *speeches of the personas*, which the dramatist has to work out purposely and in great detail because it is *these and only these* that the dramatist can capture in the text. This is the actual, proper domain of the dramatist's technique; the development of other components of the technical image are left to the actors and the director.

However, the dramatic text as an intermediary between the author and the theatre has a *double* sense in its status, expressed in the following two statements: The author writes for actors and the director. Actors and the director receive it for the benefit of their own creative work. These are clearly two eventualities that are separated both in time, often by several centuries, and in place, commonly "over the hills and far away". They are connected only by this mere, bare text. The text therefore needs to be analysed and assessed from both standpoints, the authorial and the theatrical. From the authorial perspective the question may be: How does the mere text fulfil the two main dramatic purposes of the author, i.e., *how does it characterise dramatic personas and how does it contribute to the dramatic action?* From the theatrical perspective the analogical question could be: *What does the dramatist's mere text offer to the actor figures and to the actors' interplay?* These mutually parallel questions are the boundaries within which the inquiry needs to operate, respecting both, assessing with a view to both, since the former expresses the dramatist's interest while the latter theatre's interest in the same matter, i.e., in the dramatic text; no other interests in it are legitimate since the audience (as well as the critics) are the intended recipients of the fully realised dramatic work.

The text fulfils its proper *dramatic task* as defined by the above questions in two ways: *directly* as a rendering of the *actual, spoken component* of the actor figure (*herecká postava*) and the interplay (*souhra*); and *indirectly* as an *authorised guideline for other components* of the actor figure and interplay. This chapter, dedicated to the dramatic text, will address the former instance, approaching the text as an actual *speech* that can heard from the stage and whose contents the text forms.

The dramatic text – without considering the stage directions (for reasons given above) – consists of words, grammatically speaking, but since it comprises the speeches of the actors as dramatic personas, it is necessary to distinguish its units that have a *relatively autonomous meaning*, be they whole sentences (simple or complex), or mere words and turns of phrase (such as "Coming!" or "In a moment!"). Another, higher and dramatically significant unit of the text is given by the fact that certain sections of the speech belong to a particular dramatic persona and therefore to a concrete actor who impersonates it. In the written text this is indicated by prefixes that precede each paragraph spoken by a persona. This specifics of the dramatic text manifests itself in "*a reading with distributed roles*", which generally occurs early in the rehearsal process. Such a reading would be unthinkable with a non-dramatic literature, and even if it were undertaken, it would be of no consequence since narrative genres (*epos*) always presupposes a single reader or narrator.

Each sentence and *each* phrase comprised in a dramatic text has a *double* dramatic mission. Firstly, it is always spoken by someone, a particular dramatic persona, and the text is to characterise it in some way. Secondly, it is a link in a chain of speeches that run through the whole work and as such is supposed to create a part of the dramatic action. This, however, is only an ideal requirement; in practice, perhaps every play text has individual speeches that fulfil only one of the two tasks – and we're lucky to even have that. In following theoretical reflections it is important to remember this crucial *dramatic duality* of the text (which is also equally valid for the actors' performances, as will be shown).

1. The actor figure (*herecká postava*) is **directly given in the dramatic text** as a *sum of the speeches that the actor delivers as an impersonator of that particular dramatic persona* (*dramatická osoba*). What is known as the "*role*" is handed over to the actor copied out (unless the script is printed) before the start of rehearsal for the actor to learn it by heart, since the lines of the role will have to be *actually* spoken; they will form a part of an actual figure (*postava*).

Naturally, in practice, the role comprises a number of other things to aid the actor's orientation (e.g., in relation to the interaction with others); but this is irrelevant at this point because these will not be spoken aloud by the actor. Similarly the roles handed out to theatre singers comprise a similarly copied out text alongside the notation indicating how it should be sung (which will be discussed below under sung drama); in contrast, the way of delivery of the spoken role is not indicated in the script (or perhaps only general terms) and it needs to be created by the actor herself or himself.

This sum of the actor's individual speeches has to be created by the dramatist in such a way that by itself, through its mere existence within the theatrical performance – that is, irrespective of what the actor adds through delivery, mimics or mask (*maska*) – the role should *characterise the dramatic persona* to which it relates as *an individuality,* which means that it should be idiosyncratic (*rázovitý*) and consistent (*jednotný*). It needs to be stressed in advance that this requirement presupposes that such a textual role exists, i.e., that the dramatic persona in question speaks at all. This is the well-established principle of the totality of the actor's performance; however, it allows for well justified exceptions, such as when it comes to smaller characters. Generally, the speeches of dramatic personas are not a necessary condition, but surely a desirable one; this is all the more so, the more demands are placed on the mental capacity (*duševnost*) of that particular individual.

The characteristic of a dramatic persona is achieved by a particular role, firstly, through the *material* side of the text, i.e., through a specific choice of *words* and *phrases* used by the persona in the play, or to put it more aptly, through *an individualised "vocabulary"*. Even in reality people have their *"personal dialects"* (*idiolects*), their vocabularies are richer or poorer, but always somewhat different from others. The specificity of such idiolects is based predominantly on *how frequently* someone uses words of their vocabulary. Clearly, it is characteristic of certain individuals how often they use a particular word or phrase (such as "I tell you", "actually" or certain swearwords or "what-you-call-its", so popular when it comes to characterisation of personas in comedy). The second, dominant source of specificity of an idiolect is in that it is an individual variant of the language spoken by a certain social class, which I shall call *"the social dialect"* (*sociolect*). Such a sociolect is always idiosyncratic (*rázovité*) through the shared human atmosphere in which it is born and where it lives; this atmosphere seems to soak into its characteristic words and phrases giving them not only its mood but also its particular shade of meaning. Social layers can be classified by various criteria, which even results in overlaps – and these overlaps are also seen in the corresponding sociolects. For instance, country and city languages or children's and adults' languages, which combine into four sublanguages (country children's language, etc.). One of the most general differences is the choice language of the educated layer as opposed to the simple language of the uneducated; its trivial dramatic example are the lords' and peasants' speech. With servants, the situation is different: it shows that some dialects are mixtures of two sociolects originating in environments where a persona has been in turns living. Certain sociolects can be acquired to some extent for occasional use and, again, it is characteristic of the individual of a particular persona if she or he does so or not. Certain administrators may, for instance, speak officially when in the office, familiarly when at home, while others may speak "officially" when at home and yet others familiarly when in the office. Naturally, this is influenced by habit but also by individual inclinations. For the present purpose it is important that a specific feature of a dialect is remarkably *strengthened* when it is used in a different environment by way of contrast: it comes across as striking and inappropriate. In this way, through the mere speech, the *sharpness of the persona portrayal* can be heightened as far as caricature. The pedantic language of a persona kept in a free, leisurely company, or conversely, the free or naughty language kept among puritans (as Shaw loves to do) are two examples to illustrate the commonly used technique.

From a different perspective than was the case of social dialects, one can also speak of *"psychological dialects"* (*psycholects*). These are groups of words and phrases ("vocabularies") that share a uniform emotive accent springing not so much from a societal environment but rather from the sense of words, both literally and figuratively. For a dramatic text the most important are *emotional* dialects. This is what is meant by "the language of passions" or "the vocabulary of love". The most notorious is the typical idiom of anger – swearing. Emotional dialects are notable for their abundant metaphors brought about by the rudimentary nature and intensity of passionate expression, which aims at exaggeration; one can find "You ass!" in one, just like "My angel!" in the other. Through them the dramatist captures the mental states of the dramatic personas – in other words, an actual component of the dramatic action. The characterisation of dramatic personas is achieved through psychological dialects as long as they are a relatively *lasting disposition* of the persona for a particular mental or emotional relationship; the speeches of such a persona *predominantly* consist of a specific psychological dialect as appropriate to the mindset. This builds on an earlier observation on the "abundant" use of certain words by a particular persona; here we are dealing with an entire "vocabulary". In one case this may be the prevalence of effeminate words and phrases of a sentimental mistress; in another, the bombastic hyperboles of a braggart or a moralist; or a flowery speech of a gallant lady, etc.; the traditional stock types (known from as early as classical comedy) are also, clearly, conventionalised textual types. Psychological dialects cut across sociolects, forming certain "sub-languages"; it is noteworthy that they tend, according to the nature of the emotion they express, to socially higher or lower dialects. Love instinctively seeks a more lofty speech, while anger tends to a more vulgar one: the angry Lord Capulet in *Romeo and Juliet* swears like a servant. However, there are personas who are never unsettled from their ways by any passion whatsoever – in their *speech* at least; this changeability or uniformity of a personal idiom in relation to the persona's mental states point to a characteristic of the temperament.

It is a well known fact that *the ideas and intellectual content* of the text belonging to a particular role contribute to the characterisation of dramatic personas. In particular it is significant what the ideas are that drive and motivate the deeds of the leading figures, the "heroes" of the drama. In the abundance of intellectual criticism of dramatic art, so much can be found on this point that it is unnecessary to say more – especially since such intellectual characteristics of the personas are nothing specifically dramatic. But I would like point out one thing particularly important for a truly dramatic characterisation of personas; I will call it the *cogency (pithiness) of speech* and define it as a *ratio between the quantity of words and the quantity and quality of ideas* expressed by them. Someone speaks little; others a lot; someone has many ideas; others only scarcely or none at all, and yet they keep speaking; various combinations create a range of very significant human types: A person of few words and brains, and a taciturn person, who is full of ideas (e.g., Mercutio in *Romeo and Juliet*), and then a mere windbag who keeps milling over the same thing. This type may intensify to empty talk of a mere moralist in whatever sphere of human activity, and even the pathological state of the speech that lacks any sense – a crackpot's talking. Conversely, there can be speeches that are only seemingly nonsensical (as is brilliantly evidence by Shakespeare's fools), which brings us back to a type of clever person who enjoys speeches full of quick-witted paradoxes.

2. *The actors' interplay* is **given directly within the dramatic text** as *the sum of speeches spoken by all actors as they perform the dramatic action*. That is, the *entire* dramatic text, naturally without the stage direction as these are not supposed to be spoken. This sum of all speeches have to be shaped by the playwright in such a way that they – irrespective of what the actors add to them in the way of delivery in speaking and physical action – form an actual *component of the dramatic action*.

Since we have defined dramatic action – in agreement with a majority of drama theorists – as the interaction of personas, we have to face the question if *mere speech* can constitute *action*. At the same time, speech or action must not be taken in the narrow sense that automatically excludes one another – as when we say that someone "is all words, but no action". What is meant in that sense is that someone says what needs doing and how but never does it. Action here is understood in a narrower sense – as physical acts or deeds. However, if someone by using words moves a crowd to mutiny, is that speech not an action in itself? If someone offends someone else with a word, is it not as if one was struck? If someone, in a surprising twist, discloses an important circumstance that is meant to remain concealed, do we not say: "What have you done?" These examples show that mere speech *may* be action; however, not every speech is action. The conditions are comprised in the definition of "action" (*jednání*) provided in Chapter 3 of the first part. What follows from it is: *The speech of a persona becomes action if the persona wants to, and does, have impact on someone else*. Such speech can be called *dramatic speech*.

A brief note: This distinction between "action" and "acts" or "deeds" might seem pedantic word-splitting; in the real world this is often not distinguished. However, the issue here is not the word but the *concept* that is used to define dramatic action (as dramatic persona) and that comprises more than what is communicated through "act" or "deed". We have called the concept "action" (*jednání*); who finds this word inadequate should abandon it but will need to find a new name for this concept.

The above delineation of dramatic speech actually includes *two* distinct conditions (just like the definition of action itself): the intention to have effect and the actuality of this effect. Out of these, *intention* is a specifically dramatic moment because it is happening between personas, that is, between thinking beings. However, it is not necessary that the intended aim should be fully aware; the intent may be only instinctive. The simplest case is when the effect of a speech *agrees* with the intention; a typical instance is slander – and it may have tragic effect (Shakespeare's *Othello*) or comic effect (Sheridan's *The School for Scandal*). Often, the two *disagree*, as when the intended effect brings about a different, unintended or even contrary outcome. A classic example is Cordelia's sincere speech towards Lear, which triggers an uncontrolled anger in him. There are clearly two extreme (i.e., one-sided) examples of dramatic speeches. Either the speech was made almost completely without an intention, "just saying", and yet it has a strong effect; this is a "slip", sometimes funny, sometimes fatal. Or the speech, although starkly directed, has almost no effect on the opponent; it fails and lapses in its effect, irrespective of what the reasons are. This outline will suffice; a more detailed analysis will be given for action as a whole, not just for speech itself, in the chapter dedicated to "dramatic action" (*dramatický děj*). It has been previously noted that the effect of a speech is determined not only by its contents but also by the way in which it is delivered.

The efficacy of dramatic speech on the *audience* is *double*. Firstly it has a *direct* impact, as a verbal expression of ideas, emotions and aspirations; such is the impact of every speech, even a non-dramatic one, as long as it has some effect at all. A *specific* efficacy of dramatic speech is *indirect*, deriving from the fact that we can see its *workings on stage*, coming into being *among dramatic personas*, and that we sense that these workings have effect on us. Dramatic speech seems in this way as mental energy springing from one persona and affecting another; it generally returns from the other person to the first, or is as if reflected towards other personas. This is the basic form of dramatic speech – *dialogue*. Recalling what has been said in the first part about the motoric basis of all dramatic workings, it can be posited that dramatic speech has a *dynamic* effect on the audience. Conversely, an undramatic speech – i.e., that which does neither spring from a persona's intention to influence someone else, nor has an effect – may affect an audience only as itself, that is, like a recited or read-out speech would. It informs us of something, it may bring up a mood, lift our spirits, but this efficacy is only *static*.

One may ask now which types of speeches are dramatic and which are not; the answer cannot be determined in advance. *Any* type may be dramatic or not: it depends only and exclusively on us, sitting in the auditorium, observing them as having effect – not from the stage on us but *on stage* among the dramatic personas, from one to another. If we do not sense this effect on stage, that is, if it is not there for us, then it naturally does work on us and we have to be content with a mere static efficacy of the speech *on us ourselves*. A surprising thing can be stated, one that has been confirmed by experience without fail: the static, especially the atmospheric effect of speech from the stage is weaker and fainter than in reading. This phenomenon, sometimes called *"theatrical acoustics"* will be discussed later. It has been and always will remain a tumbling block for many authors with an outstanding poetic talent and for their dramatic (and yet undramatic) works.

An especially frequent is the error that emotional speeches are more dramatic than intellectual ones. This is caused by judging drama from the effect it has in reading, where the atmospheric effect is great, while the indirect, springing from the situation hardly registers in our imagination. So we confuse static efficacy with the dynamic, mixing them up and believing that the drama is "powerful". In performance we are amazed at the outcome, so contrary to our expectations; naturally so, since the static efficacy of speech grows faint, while the dynamic efficacy stands out with extraordinary clarity and power. This is equally true about individual acts and scenes as well as moments. A dry announcement may have the most fierce dramatic impact because – as can be seen – that is how it works on stage; conversely, a long lyrical stretch of text fails to move us if it fails to move those on stage. A joke directed at another may entertain us (Beatrice and Benedick!) because it entertains the stage; but "a joke in itself" evaporates before it gets to us.

> **Undramatic** speeches come across in performance as something isolated, standing on its own; they do not hurl like a ball or a spear from one dramatic persona to another, dancing or rampaging on stage, but vanish like smoke directly into the auditorium. They do not serve the dramatic action but serve only themselves; they are *self-serving* and as such do a disservice to themselves in the theatre. Undramatic speeches should therefore not appear in the play script; however, certain types are admissible under certain conditions.
>
> First is the purely *theoretical* type of speeches, ruminations and reflections relating to some moral, social, philosophical or religious ideals and such like; understandably, what is meant here are not speeches made to have effect on others but such that are spoken "for their own sake". These are particularly frequent in "ideological" dramas and it is evident that the author has made use of the theatre as a forum to communicate them to the public. Nonetheless, such speeches, though they are undramatic in themselves, may has a certain mission in drama in that they characterise the persona who

delivers them – but not as an active agent but as a reflective persona. Therefore there should not be too many of them and they should be limited to one persona only; the "*raisonneur*" of French social dramas is an example. It is bad if the author forgets about the personas for all the ideas; the resulting play then is little more than an abstract treatise about one thing or another, and then it would have been better if the author had rather written a theoretical tract. It is hard work for the actor to create a concrete figure for such a role; it is hard and unrewarding as the actor knows he or she will be boring.

A second type are speeches describing or telling some phenomenon or story, in short: *narratives*. It is assumed by many that they are a necessary evil for drama and it is somewhat true. Limited by real time to only a couple of hours, drama has to give a condensed *fraction* of a story, usually its last phase. In order to understand the story, it is essential to know much of what has preceded – and that can only be retold. The same holds true for events occurring in between the acts and those taking place off stage. However, these two can be avoided, with scene changes. In contrast, the first task, retelling the preceding story, forms – if necessary – the complex problem of the drama's "*exposition*". A successful solution is principally possible if the author sets up the situation in such a way that one dramatic personal tells the story to affect another and that the narrative actually does have such an effect. Usually this develops itself into a dramatic dialogue. The presupposes that the second persona does not know the story or that the narration serves to evoke some long-gone and emotionally powerful memories. Masterful examples of this can be found in Ibsen. However, wherever it is clear that the narration has no effect for the other persona because they know it or do not care, the dramatic effect is gone; this is not because we feel that all this is done for us but because it is done *exclusively* for us. These are then epic weaknesses of the drama, which can be excused only when there is no other option. For instance, in classical Greek tragedy, which knew no scene changes, everything that has taken place off stage needs to be announced through the speeches of messengers; but even here one can find a successful tendency to transform a messenger's monologue into a more dramatic dialogue. Otherwise it would be better for the author to write a narrative poem, a short story or a novel rather than a play.

A third type are *lyrical* speeches – that is, a verbal expression of the sentiments possessing the persona – again, only as long as these are not action in themselves (which would be the case of a confession of love, for instance). Due to the psychological relationship between emotions and aspirations (which will be analysed further in the chapter on dramatic action), there are many lyrical speeches that are undramatic in themselves, and yet are *dramatically bonded* in that they either form an *introduction* to action, or conversely its *outcome*. To link it to the above discussion: an example is a verbal expression of the captivation by a woman's beauty (followed by a courting of her favour) and the expression of happiness when the love has been achieved. There are many instances of such lyrical monologues and even dialogues – since one's sentiment may be shared with another person. In sung drama, where lyrical passages are well supported by music, the typical examples are "love duets" – next to arias of course. It is imperative that such dramatically tied lyrical speeches should not be too long, otherwise as the audience we may *lose* the impression of such a dramatic bond – the speeches become self-indulgent for us (and in fact). This *dramatic bond* is also true in the preceding two types, though less so. Nonetheless, even "loose", self-indulgent lyrical speeches can be tolerated in drama for two reasons: Firstly, they have at least an indirect dramatic effect in that of all speech types they provoke the actor's performance most – both verbally and mimically. Secondly, through them certain dramatic personas can be characterised, as has been observed when discussing "emotional dialects". However, it is not advisable that there are too many of them, or the drama will become too "lyrical" and too little dramatic. The author should then rather opt for a lyrical poem or for prose.

This has brought to an end, in rough outlines, an inquiry into the dramatic text. In conclusion, we can proceed to its *evaluation* – but that from a *dramatic*, not an artistic angle, which will be the topic of the third part of this book. So far we have referred to the "dramatic text" in sense of "text for drama, for a play", not in the sense of "a text that is dramatic" – that would have been pointless to analyse when a dramatic text is dramatic. The text a dramatist writes for their play is a *literary work* and the name "dramatic" in the strict sense of the word (cf. our definition in the first part of the book) can be given to it only because it *forms the content* of speeches that we can *hear* during a theatrical *performance*. It *can* be given to it – that is, only if it fulfils those particular conditions that have been analysed above. If those conditions are not met, the text is not dramatic; if it meets them only partially, the whole is *less or more* dramatic. In such a case the term "dramatic" is an *evaluation* – and a special aesthetic evaluation at that. That this is in perfect agreement with the artistic experience is evident; the proof of this can be seen in the amount of written or printed plays that theatres accept – and while some of them are dramatically powerful, others are weak, and yet others wholly undramatic. How difficult and responsible it is to appraise them in this way on the basis of the mere text, has already been stated; the analysis that has been undertaken here is therefore not only of theoretical importance but also of practical consequence. The findings can be summed up as follows:

The text of a theatre play is all the **more dramatic** *if it fulfils the following dramatic tasks:*
a) *directly, as a (spoken or sung) speech: to characterise dramatic personas and form the component of dramatic action;*
b) *indirectly, as a text: to be a basis and a directive for actors' figures and actors' interplay.*

The condition b) will discussed in the following chapters. Its extension to the case of the opera libretto will be addressed later with music theatre. The condition a) will remain the same since the word "speech" means here and everywhere else *that which* is spoken, not *how* it is spoken, which is what we refer to as "delivery" (*mluva*). Delivery forms exclusively the actor's component of a figure in spoken drama and *its* counterpart in the opera is singing.

5 THE DRAMATIC PERSONA: THE ACTOR'S CREATIVE WORK

Imagine that a play is performed on stage and that one of the performers is a foreign actor. The actor is performing in their mother tongue, which we *do not understand,* and yet we are present and curious about the actor's art. This example, which is far from uncommon, is a definitive test for the *purely actorly art* since it is isolated from the dramatic effect of the art of the author (i.e., the dramatic text that the playwright has created for the actor to perform, without its performance). We the audience can see and hear the actor, and this visual and acoustic perception is for us the basis on which we create the mental image of the *dramatic persona (dramatická osoba).* In the above case of the foreign actor, what kind of perception exists, and how much basis does it offer us for this mental image?

Let us imagine the curtain goes up on the scene in which the foreign actor first appears on his or her own. What captures our attention first is the *costume* and the *physical appearance of the actor.* We can see clothes of a specific colour and shape – perhaps modern dress, period costume or fantasy clothes. The actor's body may be slim or fat, upright or stooped; their hair dark or grey, thick or wispy; their face pale or ruddy, plump or wrinkled, beautiful or ugly, smiling or serious... All such perceptions – most of them *visual* – are specific in that they are *fixed;* they do not change during the play or its coherent part. This is particularly true of the appearance of the body and face (*physiognomy*), which may undergo *partial* changes – perhaps through age, illness or some other suffering – though such changes also take effect for a relatively fixed time, e.g., for an entire act. This can be seen for instance in Rostand's *Cyrano de Bergerac,* in which the protagonist is many years older in the final act than in those earlier. Similarly, we can see Dumas's *La Dame aux Camélias* progressively ruined by consumption, or watch the transformation of Shakespeare's *King Lear* as he descends into madness. By contrast, the change of costume can be absolute and is much more common; but still the clothes are part of the impression of the "persona" for the duration of the persona's continuous presence on stage.

The second component of our perception are *dynamic* impressions, which vary over time. Again, these are predominantly *visual;* their *behaviours* and *actions.* We can see the persona on stage take a few steps or even run, turn or bend; we can see the persona waving arms, threatening or hitting someone. Besides these larger bodily movements there are smaller ones pertaining to particular body parts, especially to the hands, such as a nervous fidgeting of fingers or clenching of a fist. Most prominently, we can see the face as each part of it changes: a fleeting smile on the cheek, a narrowing of the eyes, the movement of speaking lips and so on. The second group of dynamic impressions is *acoustic*, created by the *vocal* expressions of the persona. This comprises not only the persona's *speaking* (or *singing* in the opera) on the purely acoustic level (as we do not understand the foreign actor's words in our imagined scenario), but also inarticulate sounds. We can hear the speech melody rising or falling, the voice getting louder or softer, down to a tiny whisper; we can hear a cry, a laughter or a sigh. Finally, it is necessary to include other, non-vocal sounds, such as the clapping of hands, stamping of feet, the fist hitting the table top and such like.

Naturally, the alternating and changing visual and acoustic perceptions bear on the fixed perceptions all the stronger: it is understandable therefore that it is the fixed visual perception – especially that which we have called "physical appearance" – that we associate with our image of the "dramatic persona". From the point of a noetic analysis, we form a conviction that behind this fixed set of perceptions – which we will call (F) – there is *something*, some kind of substance that carries certain qualities and attributes that we ascribe to this substance on the basis of our own experience. The dynamic group of perceptions (D) leads us to believe that this "something" is not only physical but also psychological – that it is a live being with a body and a soul – in short, a *persona* (usually a human, exceptionally other creatures, lower or higher than humans, but always anthropomorphised).

The dynamic group of perceptions (D) goes further than the process of "bringing to life" that the fixed perceptions of (F) evoked in us. We have asserted above, during our analysis of the theatre experience, that the dynamic element on the stage offers an audience dramatic action. Here, we limit ourselves to the part tied to one particular persona: this set (D) gives us only a part of the dramatic action, the one created by the one dramatic persona – that is the "personal" component of the action (*děj*): personal action (*jednání*).

Sitting in the theatre, we find that this group of *personal* dynamic perceptions carry something *fixed* itself, despite its changing nature. Over time, one can find certain *aspects* or *features* that are *of a specific kind*. And if not always, then *mostly* – which is a rule with only few exceptions. This is most obvious in vocal expressions. The timbre of the voice is always the same and the way of speaking is generally identical. The voice can be a sonorous bellow, generally deep, or else sweetly whispering or grotesquely squeaky. The laughter of one persona may be croaking, of another it may be giggly. The same is true for a persona's visual impression. One may have a wobbly way of walking, while another may walk in a military style; one may be clumsy in their movement, another elegant. The facial expressions of one may be bluntly straightforward, another fawningly feline. One persona laughing may be grinning boisterously, another may hardly move the lips. Clearly, we might also list such expressions as "a smiling face", which we have subsumed under the fixed set, because even this "eternal smile" may eventually fade in the course of the play (e.g., when frightened or in pain); the transition between the two sets is obviously fluid. To these features "of a kind", it is necessary to add tiny expressions that are not fixed but frequently repeated and characteristic of a particular persona. These are a certain *"repertory of motifs"* of a purely *actorly* kind, analogical to characteristic words or phrases, which we mentioned in the analysis of the dramatic text; for phrases, such as "I tell you" or "actually", the way they are said is more significant than what they say. Vocal expressions offer actors the most rewarding material, e.g., typical speech cadences of a "singsong" voice (not a sung voice), especially for inarticulate expressions, such as "hum", "ha" and "er", guttural sounds, snorting nasal sounds, giggling and such like. Less conspicuous but no less characteristic are personal characteristic motifs that are only visual: hands in pockets, drumming with fingers, twirling one's moustache, pursing one's lips and so on. Their stereotypical nature suggest that they are unconscious habits and therefore they are of a physiognomic nature, which makes them even more significant for the persona's individuality.

What has been discussed so far may be summarised in the assertion that from a *purely actorly* perspective – that is, excluding the contents of the language – the *dramatic persona* is given *to the audience* as *a sum of all visual and acoustic perceptions* pertaining to the *most fixed* of them: that is, to the physical appearance of the persona. This set of perceptions stimulated from the outside is complemented by a set of *inner tactile* perceptions caused by our *empathising* in a certain dramatic persona, and the instinctive inner imitation of their standpoints, movements or speeches. As has been highlighted above, this motoric set of perceptions contributes exceptional liveness and plasticity to our impression of the dramatic persona, and this is especially typical of our experience of drama. Most significantly, this inner tactile set is the the *central* conduit which allows access to the *inside* of the dramatic persona: to the persona's *emotional and aspirational* (*citový a snahový*) mental life – but not to their thoughts, which are communicated by the contents of the speeches, as we have seen in the analysis of the dramatic text.

It is revealing to confront these assertions with the real world. It may be said that we function in the theatre as we do in the real world, with the exception of (a) our suspended awareness that the onstage persona is an actor (a qualitative difference) and (b) the intense impression caused by the powerful participation of our inner tactile perceptions (a quantitative difference). In both cases we get to know some personalities (irrespective of whether they are fictitious or real) and our psychological processes are essentially identical as long as we do not enter into direct personal contact with the real personas. Take, for example, a person I observe from a distance somewhere in a society, in the street, at a concert or around the neighbourhood. What is a *directly*, i.e., *outwardly*, acquainted persona? A set of visual and acoustic impressions, a visual and acoustic memory simplified in fixed moments. The visual image has decisive preference over the acoustic: when recalling someone, we can see them in our mind, with all the peculiarities of their appearance (including perhaps their typical dress), their movements and behaviour. Vocal expressions may also by typical (I can recognise my acquaintance by their voice, for example), but they are secondary. The cause has been identified: physical appearance is fixed and therefore a sound basis for a persona's image as its substance. Voice is only an attribute of this substance, it is not "something", but a significant *feature* "of something". I need to see this "something" – i.e., the persona – so that the vocal expressions gain concreteness. The vocal expression alone is abstract, as can be evidenced by the *"voice behind the stage"* during a theatre performance. However, the abstract nature does not necessarily weaken its effect; on the contrary, it gives the vocal expression a flair of mystery by a certain "dematerialisation".

We have assumed that the dramatic persona is *"given"* for the audience as a certain set of *perceptions*. This posits two important facts: firstly, that a dramatic persona as a perception is given from the outside, as something *external* to us. It is easy to figure out what this something "external to us" actually is: it is the actor playing on stage – in our terminology, the *actor figure (herecká postava)*. Only the actor figure exists *objectively* on the stage; the dramatic persona *is not* on the stage: it exists only within us – that is, it exists subjectively in our mind.

> This fact is not changed by our habit to ascribe objective reality to our perceptions, which may often result in errors of judgement. These errors are sometimes used productively by theatrical practice, for instance when we are presented with an apparition of a ghost by means of a projector. This is, however, rather exceptional, often out of technical necessity, where the actor would be insufficient – such as in supernatural size, strangeness, mobility or torpidity of the apparition. The speaking of this being is generally taken over by a hidden actor – but even that could be replaced by a recording, if a superhuman intensity of voice were needed. But these are exceptional cases, at least as far as people are concerned; when it comes to stage business, such tricks are much more common; I mention them here to illustrate the subjective nature of the "dramatic persona".

The second important fact is this: if the "dramatic persona" is a sensorial perception of a purely psychological nature, it is far from limited only to this perception. It is merely "given" by it, i.e., determined from the outside. This perceived outer component is complemented by the inner component – the *images* in our mind (*významové představy*) that are created on the basis of *our own experience*. The miscellaneous interpretation of this complicated and yet in many ways unified perception is down to us; the very thought that what I can see and hear of a person is *my* interpretation, similar to those I constantly make in everyday contact with people. This is all the more true when it comes to all the details of the persona's features and actions. It may be said that the "dramatic persona" consists of two components: one is the above perception and the other is the complex mental image, that is, a set of images that the perception evoked, i.e., recollected in my mind. And consequently the *aesthetic effect* that this dramatic persona has on me is also dual: one comes from the perception itself – which we will call the *direct* or guiding *factor* of the impression, following Fechner's terminology[18] – and the other originates from the images evoked by the perception – that is the *indirect* or associative *factor*. It is understood that in the aesthetic enjoyment both emotional effects merge into a single impression; however, our critical analysis needs to differentiate between the two. The reasons for this will be seen below.

In order to illustrate the effect of the *direct* factor we need to assume the role of a spectator or listener who is totally naive, though not primitive, but fully prone to any sensory impressions. For such a person, the "dramatic persona" would be truly *no more* than a set of perceptions containing *colours, forms (shapes), movements and sounds* that are totally "devoid of meaning". It does not follow of course that the spectator would have no benefit from these perceptions. These perception sets, as long as they are *logically arranged,* carry *a meaning of their own* – one that is so rich and emotionally profound that it can constitute an entire art form. Our "naive person" is entirely fictional, but there are certain artistic disciplines that force us to assume – at least a little – *such a naive* approach: that is, to leave all our foreknowledge aside and retain only that which we have called "technical image". In architecture and applied arts, our aesthetic enjoyment is fulfilled by colours and forms that are artistically conceived – think, for instance, of an ornament. The same is true in pure dance – where we enjoy colours, forms and movements – and equally in music, where we enjoy sounds, and more specifically notes. In all cases, these are non-mimetic art disciplines; but it is clear that this direct factor is at play in all arts that depict or represent something, including the dramatic art. So a colour by itself has an effect on us, for instance when it is red or black for instance – and it may be that a red tint has a piercing and agitating impression, or that a black tint has a duller and more sombre effect. However, if we assert on the basis of our experience that a certain black dress is appropriate to take out to a society, this impression of "elegance" of its black colour is an associative factor. As this part of the book is concerned with the dramatic principle, we will satisfy ourselves for now with the suggestion of the direct factor in the impression of the dramatic work; its proper moment is in the domain of artistic stylisation, which is achieved through *its* principled composition (*utváření*) – which will be discussed in the final part of this book.

---

18   Gustav Theodor Fechner (1801–1887) was a doctor, physicist and psychologist, and one of the founders of scientific and experimental aesthetics based on empirical research of the recipients' experiences. In his other works, Zich refers mainly to Fechner's *Zur Experimentellen Ästhetik* (Towards an Experimental Aesthetics, 1871) and *Vorschule der Ästhetik* (A Preschool of Aesthetics, 1876).

The *dramaticity* (*dramatičnost*) of a work of art is determined exclusively by the *associative factor*; that is, all of the images (*představy*) that are evoked by the perception, according to the familiar psychological principles. Therefore, these images have to pre-exist in our minds: they are all the experiences we have ever had, acquired either externally, or internally. *Outer* experience – from our environment, from life, from what other people told us, from books, etc. – constitutes predominantly (though not exclusively) *pragmatic* knowledge; in a psychological sense, this is knowledge of imaginations in regards to their content. *Inner* experience – i.e., the experiencing of various mental states and processes – gives us predominantly the knowledge of all aspects of *mental* life – of our own emotions and aspirations, but also those of others, indirectly, as we empathise with their inner life. Here, our inner and outer experiences clearly combine; this is the only way of knowing other people as psychological beings, which is the most important condition for the understanding of dramatic art. Unfortunately, this exclusive way is often also very hypothetical: we judge people's inner qualities by their outer features and expressions, which tacitly assumes a consensus between their psychological setup and ours. The second condition is met generically – we are all humans – but when it comes to detail, everyone is different. The disagreement or tension between the outer and inner aspects of people – involuntarily or intentionally – is what we experience on a daily basis. In life, we are subject to many errors and misunderstandings regarding these aspects. But how do these circumstances take shape when we are looking at dramatic personas? Let us answer this question before the following analysis: *A dramatic work must never delude us* (the audience); on the contrary, in all its components *it has to be created so as try and eliminate even our subjective misunderstandings*. Let us call this assertion **the principle of dramatic truthfulness**. This truthfulness principle does not apply to the stage but for *the relation between the stage and the audience*. The reach of this principle – which holds equally for all mimetic arts (*obrazová umění*) – will be discussed in the chapter on realism and idealism. However, it must be understood here because it will justify some of our current conclusions.

ଓ ଓ ଓ

Let us now turn to the analysis of the *indirect* (i.e., associative) factor evoked by the appearance and behaviour of the dramatic persona on stage. We shall consider both the fixed set of perceptions (F) and the dynamic set (D) in regards to their *meaning*. Elements of (D) also pertain to dramatic action (*děj*) in that they amount to the dramatic persona's individual contribution to it, so our will also be relevant for the following chapter. As we have stated, the focus of the present chapter is the "acting persona"; the next is about "the personas' actions". There is also an objective significance to the present discussion because dramatic persona and action (*děj*) are given from the stage point of view by the actor figure and play (*hra*). We may succinctly say that our present discussion focuses on *the expressive abilities of elements of the actor's art* – especially since our analysis still excludes the content of what is spoken (i.e., the dramatic text); our concern for the time being is "pure" acting.

(1) *The fixed set of perceptions* (F). We have already established two categories: the *costume* and the actor's *physical appearance* evoke specific images in the spectator's mind. This happens on the principle of association, as we search for similarities between what we can see on stage and what we know from elsewhere. Instead of 'Who?', we ask 'What is represented by what I can see?'; the answer may be very general but it can also be very specific, even to the point of singularity. At its most generic, we can see it is a human or some other being. Since the person (the actor) that represents this persona is also human, the emphasis in the latter case shifts to the clothes because physical appearance cannot easily change, and the features of such a being (gods, angels, fairy tale beings, animals, etc.) need to be conventional because we know them only from myths, folklore, art, etc., and not from life. A general and given feature of a person is their *sex* and – approximately at least – their *age*. Although some dramas ignore it, many of them also require another feature: their *status*, which is generally done through costuming. If the setting is the present day and our environment, this places no special demands on our experience; it becomes more difficult when it comes to a period setting and unfamiliar countries. This will be discussed in the third part of this book. The physical appearance also gives us *directly* a number of the *outer qualities* of the dramatic persona: this is a healthy and strong, or a weak and ill person, or even lame or blind, etc. Another important quality of the dramatic persona is their beauty – especially a woman's beauty because in many dramas it is the main lever of the action. The same is sometimes true of ugliness, if it is repulsive or ridiculous (Roxane, Cyrano and Christian).

In contrast, we may only *indirectly speculate* on the persona's *inner features* from their appearance and clothes. A very important function here is the persona's facial appearance or *physiognomy*. The study of the relation between physiognomy and a person's mental qualities or state, known as physiognomics, has been well elaborated and evidenced (at least in part) by scientific studies. Our physiognomic speculations are typically intuitive, uncritically based on our (often insufficient) individual experience; we often end up finding that we have been deluded in our impressions. And yet it is admirable how convincing certain physiognomic features may be: when we talk about "gaunt" lines in someone's face, a "bold" forehead or "sensuous" lips, we are certain that they harbour these mental qualities. Among the most interesting are someone's "animal-like" physiognomy that evoke the characteristic qualities of individual animals (a bulldog, a ram, a bird, etc.). We may assert the first application of the principle of dramatic truthfulness: the physical appearance of dramatic personas should facilitate our intuitive interpretation *in agreement* with the psychological qualities that a dramatic persona is supposed to have. Only then will the appearance of the persona be significant. Our judgements of the persona's psychological qualities that are based on the person's clothes are of a more rational nature since we can follow the causal relation between them. One usually chooses one's own clothes, so we can deduce the vanity or plainness, particularity or negligence of their character. The same principle applies here; the assignment of costume should suggest the persona's status.

Since both these characteristics of the persona depend on fixed elements (appearance, costume), we shall call them *the fixed characteristics*.

> Seemingly contrary to this principle of dramatic truthfulness is a case that is common and popular in dramatic works: *mistaken* or **exchanged** *identities*. These relate to physical appearance and costume. In the first case, which I will call "quid pro quo", two dramatic persons are so similar in appearance that they are mistaken for one another: which is which? From Plautus' *Menaechmi* to the present, there are numerous such *doppelgängers* in dramatic literature, sometimes even with two such pairs of twins (as in Shakespeare's *The Comedy of Errors*), which cause the merriest situations and most unheard-of plot twists. A costume and a mask offer the motif of *"disguise"*; a dramatic persona may pretend to be somebody else, often someone unknown or even – with the help of twilight, for instance – someone known, as in the evening rendezvous in Mozart's *The Marriage of Figaro*. The motif of disguise is even more frequent and varied than the previous motif of *"quid pro quo"*; a popular variant is the crossdressing disguise of a woman into a man, as in Beethoven's *Fidelio* (Leonora) or Smetana's *Dalibor* (Milada). Disguise differs from *quid pro quo* in that it is an intentional exchange rather than a chance one, and the persona has to "disguise" their way of speaking and behaviour too. Both motifs may also be combined, as in Shakespeare's *Twelfth Night* (Sebastian and Viola).
>
> On closer inspection, these exchange motifs do not contradict the principle of dramatic truthfulness but *comply* with it. The exchange holds true only for the onstage world, among the dramatic personas, but not for the audience. Indeed, the spectator must always and securely know who is who on stage *"in truth"*, otherwise the exchange motif would lose its principal charm as well as its entire purpose. The audience is amused by knowing what those on stage fail to understand. The playwright as well as the actor need to make sure that the audience is properly appraised of what is going on in the exchange, which is usually explained in the dramatic text. Otherwise a confusing and a principally misunderstood situation might occur, which the stage direction

has hard time resolving, for instance through some distinguishing feature. One such embarrassing example (for Czech culture) is the faulty *quid pro quo* in Smetana's opera *The Devil's Wall* (Čertova stěna, libretto by Krásnohorská), which is somewhat corrected by the composer's musical distinction.[19] From a psychological point of view, the exchange motif is interesting in that we spectators sustain *two referential images*: the first, suggested by the perception, is visible and yet "false"; the other, which only we know about, is abstract but "true". Necessarily, this is before we take into account our technical image of the "actor", which is different from the others. Our mental processes in this case are fairly complex. From a more profound point of view, the exchange motif is an artistic expression of a *noetic* truth that an entity (in this case a person) is not a phenomenon we perceive but the substance with all its attributes that we associate with that phenomenon. It is therefore always our *fiction* and it does not even need to be based on a misleading assumption. This third type can be found for instance in Gogol's *The Government Inspector* where the townspeople take Khlestakov for the government inspector who has arrived incognito and in disguise. What we find in some of Pirandello's works is no more than a variant of this type, original in that it is conceived terrifyingly seriously and consequentially. If a persona is the product of my imagination, it may also be imagined differently by someone else, and becomes, despite its physical appearance, a mere apparition (*Right You Are (if you think so)*). Such apparitions, almost non-entities, are also insane dramatic personas, especially seemingly insane, as can be seen in Pirandello's *Henry IV.* or in Shakespeare's *King Lear* (Gloucester's son Edgar). Naturally, language and behaviour, especially the way of speaking, are major contributing factors here.

The exchange motif is specifically a dramatic, i.e., theatrical one. Since its principle is a contradiction between the perceived and the imagined, in reading it is bland but on stage it is very ostensive and lively.

(2) *The dynamic set of perceptions* (D) is more difficult to analyse. It contains *two kinds* of perceptions: the acoustic (the persona's *speech* and other vocal expressions) and the visual (the person's *behaviours* and *actions*). They may be summarised in the word "*mimics*" (nonverbal expression) in a broader sense, i.e., all that which can be seen and heard (the narrower sense refers only to the expressions of the face). It is sometime metaphorically referred to as "body language" as opposed to speaking (or language) in the narrower sense, which is an an unhelpful broadening of the concept that is given by its name. Let us remember that by "speaking" we refer now only to the way of

---

19   Zich is refering to the fact that the character of Rarach (the Imp) from Smetana's comic opera *Čertova stěna* (The Devil's Wall, 1882) disguises himself at times as a shepherd or takes on the identity of another character. In some cases it is not clear from the libretto whether it is Rarach in disguise who is on stage, or the actual character. Smetana as a composer partly addressed this confusion by introducing a leitmotif for Rarach to mitigate the librettist's failings.

speaking, not the content of what is said. What are the mental images evoked by the rich and various elements of mimics?

THE EXPRESSIVE CAPACITIES OF MIMICS

(a) As for the purely *intellectual* images (i.e., ideas), the expressive capacity of mimics is minimal, linked almost exclusively to images of certain activities, especially "tasks". We realise that what we see is walking or running (such as an escape from someone), sitting down or falling (when passing out or dying), a fight (e.g., fencing), the killing of someone and such like. As for the speaking (remember our "foreign actor"!) we recognise a question or command, or else when someone is called for – why and what about, we do not know. From the gesticulation we can hardly learn more than "yes" or "no", "come here" or "go away". Aside from these natural and generally comprehensible gestures there are a number of *conventional* ones that depend closely on the social habits: different kinds of greetings, a kiss, ceremonial or liturgical rites (e.g., blessing with a cross), etc. And even these expressions contain emotional or aspirational elements that may be given live or deadened by empty form – one may recall, for instance, the range of kisses, from sensually passionate to coldly officious, or the range of refusals, from a calmly gesticulated "no" to an angry rebuttal.

It is apparent that this limited intellectual concept of mimics fails to express more complex ideas and concepts; the realm of contemplations and epic narratives is almost entirely beyond its reach. That is a significant weakness of *dramatic* pantomime, which has to resort to imitative or conventional gestures in order to attempt to express complex concepts it ultimately isn't equipped to. Criticising pantomime for its conventionality is useless and unjust; this conventionality is in fact *necessary* if the audience is supposed to understand the pantomime's intellectual aspect – and dramatic pantomime must at least aspire to this. By the same token it condemns itself from a dramatic point of view.

(b) The situation is very different when it comes to the communication of *emotion* through mimics. The expression of *emotions* is its true and natural domain. Certainly, the aesthetic term *"expression of emotions"* scientifically, that is in terms of psychology and physiology, refers particularly to the bodily movements and processes that accompany emotions, both internally (circulation of blood, breathing, etc.) and externally (gesticulation and vocal expressions). The James-Lange theory of emotions[20] goes as far as to claim that bodily processes do not accompany but *cause* emotions and that

---

20   The theory was proposed independently by psychologist William James (1842–1910) and physiologist Carl Lange (1834–1900) in the 1880s, and became very influential in the psychology of emotions. The starting point of the critical discussion and the ensuing debate was a paper by W. B. Cannon entitled "The James-Lange Theory of Emotions: A Critical Examination and An Alternative Theory" (1927). Zich is evidently aware of the limitations of the James-Lange theory, so he does not take its application to any extremes.

emotions are perceptions of these bodily processes. This is captured in part by the cliche "we don't laugh because we are merry but we are merry because we laugh". The approximation is incomplete however, since such laughter is only the most apparent link in a chain of ever tinier and even microscopic bodily activities, which can be traced only experimentally (in "joy" it is the intensifying and quickening of the pulse, breathing becomes faster and less deep, etc.). This *straightforward* sensory interpretation of emotions has been seriously criticised, but there can be no doubt that inner bodily perceptions and impressions strongly and characteristically colour each emotion; the stronger the emotion, the more prominent this colouring becomes. This is particularly clear with passionate emotion, either vivid (joy, anger, etc.) or feeble (sadness, fear, etc.).

The visible and audible expressions of both bodily movements and inner bodily processes in other people give us a *sign* – and a *natural* sign at that – of a particular emotion; we know from our own experience that these expressions typically (and involuntarily) accompany the emotion. It is well known that the suggestive effect of these emotional expressions on other people is extensive; not only do they make us recall the memories of our own emotional experiences – often intensely – but compel us to inadvertently imitate them internally, evoking these emotions in reality (albeit only through suggestion). This is what brings about "sympathy" (feeling) for someone else. We can see an example of the signposting of emotion when we consider how intolerable it is for us to listen to even pained groaning, even if we know that it is not cause by any particularly big pain: we find such moaning and sighing especially disturbing. The other case, of inadvertent imitation, is also commonplace: yawning, laughing, weeping, shivering and such like are "contagious" – both in their expression and their emotional fallout.

As far as the expression of emotions of onstage dramatic personas is concerned, these may be limited only to those bodily motions that the actor can control. They cannot, for instance, force their blood pressure to rise or fall, though they could express such changes outwardly (e.g., turning red with anger, going pale with shock). Most significant are those expressions that the audience can easily observe. From these visible expressions it is those that change the physical appearance most clearly that are of most use; the amazingly rich range of mimics, including the countless nuances of smiling, various expressions of pain, horror, contempt or anger. These are accompanied by coarser gesticulations, especially of hands (clasping or wringing of hands, clenching of fists, etc.) and expressive movements of the whole body (tightening up, collapsing, stamping, jumping, etc.). Much finer emotional nuances can be expressed though speech and other vocal sounds because they appeal to hearing, which is sharper in observation: this leads to a greater intensity of inner effect. An involuntary sigh, a mild trembling in the voice, its dropping or sudden breaking immediately suggest even those emotions that the persona wished to conceal. But the most significant power of acoustic impressions (even over the visual) is the *irresistibility* of their emotional effect on the listener; this is equally true of music and vocal expressions. It may be said that they truly "penetrate the heart", and so may be used to take immediate effect and securely control the emotions they evoke. A single terrifying cry from a dramatic persona will evoke the impression of horror better than several sentences about it and will immediately put a stop to a merry situation, just as a tense atmosphere lights up with a brief outburst of laughter.

Despite these outstanding abilities, the mimic expression of emotions has its limits, mostly caused by its above-mentioned intellectual paucity; it cannot tell us the *content* of the emotion, i.e., the ideas from which it flows. We can see a smile on the face, we can hear an angry voice, but we cannot know from such mimics what caused the joy or the anger. Sometimes we can infer from the situation, e.g., when the other persona is ridiculous or behaves adversely, but that is exceptional and uncertain. A reliable message about the root cause can only be given by the content of the lines delivered by the dramatic personas. Mimics is only self-sufficient therefore when presenting emotions that are free content – that is to say, with moods. Such moods, not caused by ideas (at least not consciously) are in fact a mental reflection of the bodily state and express themselves through the entire organism, through speech and behaviour. Take for example a contented, joyful, low or excited mood, or else states that are physiologically caused, such as by exhaustion or drunkenness.

(c) Just like emotions, mimics can also express *aspirations* or efforts, be they intentional – i.e., desires – unintentional or instinctive. We may also say that it can do so to an even *more perfect* level since it is not so hampered by its intellectual limitations. This is for two reasons: firstly, every aspiration stems from a particular emotion; this happens so immediately that they almost merge into one. What is a desire or a revulsion? It is both an emotion and an aspiration. There are also manifestations of the will that are seemingly "cold" or "emotionless". The idea or thought that guides them always has to have an emotional element, although sometimes it does not show so clearly. Even the person who "reluctantly wants something" is experiencing conflict between two emotions, one of which – a "sense of duty" for instance – will take precedence. An expression of will is an outer suggestion of emotion, at least to the extent that it does not turn another person into a mere automaton without a will. In many cases, however – especially in drama – an aspiration is merely instinctive, i.e., it stems *only* out of emotion. Since mimics can express emotions excellently as it can represent ostensively (*názorně*) the inner motivation of an aspiration. Secondly, an aspiration that is unhampered or unstifled by contrary thought develops into action. This action, as something outer, can be directly presented on stage and its intellectual meaning, as we have seen, will be usually obvious to the spectator. This also determines the purpose of the aspiration, which becomes doubly clear to the audience. See the diagram below; the brackets signal that the mental image is only possibly present in the actor's awareness:

(mental image) — emotion ⟶ *aspiration* ⟶ action

The outer expression of the aspiration fluidly transforms into action, which is no more than an escalation. Desire draws one person to another, extending their arms towards them; its fulfilment is achieved when one person comes to the other and holds them. Mimics will tell us if the driving force has been love or hate, and the action – an embrace or an affront – will show what the objective of the aspiration was.

Mimics is not limited by its intellectual paucity in the expression of aspirations as it is in the expression of emotions; it may be said that in expressing aspirations mimics is *self-sufficient* – it does not depend on speech. From the definition of "action" (*jednání*), as formulated in the first part of this book, it follows that the above diagram serves as a diagram for any action, and that any aspiration – whether intended or instinctive – is its *central* element. We can therefore critically claim that the ability of mimics to express human aspirations is a *dramatic* ability. If we label as *lyrical* the capacity of any art form to express emotions, this analysis has brought us to conclude that *the dramatic ability of mimics surpasses even its considerable capacity for lyricism*.

After this general discussion of mimics, let us return to the main aim of this chapter with the following question: how does the dynamic set (D) contribute to the meaning of the *dramatic persona*? If we recall the example of the "foreign actor" from the opening of this chapter, we can see that it is the dramatic persona's *overall manner* of speech, behaviour and actions that *remain as their constant feature*. The set constitutes many of the persona's outer qualities and from these we indirectly judge their inner, i.e., psychological qualities. So we learn, for instance, that one person speaks *generally* loudly, another softly, that another behaves clumsily, another nimbly, etc. It is remarkable that this general feature does not relate only to one aspect of behaviour (to speech for instance) but to *all* or at least most of them. A "burly" person not only speaks loudly but also laughs loudly, walks loudly and generally behaves loudly, whereas a "timid" persona is equally soft in all expressions as they are in speech. When it comes to using these outer qualities as a basis for our judgement of the inner qualities, it must be noted that such they are usually ambiguous. The "timid person" may be such because of their humility or coyness, or else because of their wariness or "slyness". It is only on the basis of the whole set of outer qualities that we may judge some of the psychological features unambiguously; the conclusiveness of such a judgement is based not only on intuition – as is the case with appearances – but also on rational reflection. It is not only the unrationalised "impression", which often leaves us with only a painted portrait, but also knowledge *evidenced* by speech, behaviour and actions. In this case we are even inclined to equate the inner with the outer, however the speech suggests. We may tend to read "proud cheekbones" as a metaphor but not "a proud walk". A proud walk not only *testifies* to a person's pride; it also somehow *contains it* – the person's pride "manifests itself" through the walk.

Psychological features, judged on the basis of this dynamic set, are therefore of a different kind: they are expressions of life and determine the *dynamic* character for the persona as opposed to the *static* character given by their fixed appearance. The notorious four "humours" can serve as examples; they are given by an individual's different reaction to outer impulses, and can be elaborated on to a greater degree of nuance. Dramatic art offers an endless range of such dynamic types, generally in a combination with static types: a fat hedonist, a scrawny miser, an attractive belle, an ugly prankster, etc. Many of them are ancient (originating in Hellenistic New comedy, as far as we know) and they have been made so conventional by centuries of use that they have come to be well-known "stock characters" (see also below). It would be useful to classify the *types of dramatic personas* from a modern point of view. They could be reduced to fewer basic types with many variants, which in turn would lead to an interesting study of their genealogy. Unfortunately, this task has to be abandoned here as it is too special and extensive.

We judge people's psychological features from their speech, behaviour and actions in keeping with our own inner and outer experience; that is, our experience of ourselves and of others. This judgement is subjective and often found faulty in reality when checked by new, contrary experience. "He seemed so modest to me, and yet..." The principle of dramatic truthfulness is valid for dramatic personas too: their speaking, behaviour and actions need to be arranged so that our interpretation is in line with the mental qualities these personas should possess. This is the requirement of the *dynamic characteristics* of a dramatic persona.

> We stated at the opening of this chapter that the dynamic complex of perceptions (D) that pertain to a particular persona are also a component of the dramatic action – indeed, they form that individual's contribution to it. We will approach (D) from this perspective in the following chapter. However, let us mention here an instance that seemingly contradicts the principle of dramatic truthfulness; it is supplementary to the "exchange motif" – discussed above with the fixed complex (F) – and significantly contributes to the characteristics of the dramatic persona. The *motif of* **dissimulation** is of a mimic type; the persona's speech and behaviour suggests psychological qualities and a worldview different from those that the persona actually possesses. Usually, dissimulation is corroborated by the contents of the speech, i.e., the lines, as given by the dramatic text, and so the pretence is associated with lying in the broadest sense of the word. On the contrary, the person's actions go against the dissimulation, corresponding to what the person is "indeed" (i.e., *in deed*), so they can lead to their discovery: "Ye shall know them by their fruits" [Matthew 7:16]. The word "dissimulation" is commonly used in the sense of intentional pretence, and so it is a parallel to the motif of "disguise". It is natural then that its purpose is to look better to others, pretend a friendship, evoke sympathy and so on. If it is driven by self-profit, it is sycophancy;

if by a wish to bring harm to someone, it is *intrigue* – which can be a comic plot – or serious scheming. These are purely narrative motifs. Dissimulation can also be unintentional, motivated by a drive to ingratiate oneself with someone or by a simple social convention; in such a case it is a character feature of the persona, either inborn or received under the influence of the environment. Much rarer is the instance when the persona tries to look worse in language and behaviour (also in what they say) than they actually are. The causes are much more varied, often very complicated (Molière's *Misanthrope*).

The motif of dissimulation – especially in connection with intrigue (which can also stand on its own) – is one of the most common dramatic motifs; it can be found in a majority of dramatic works, in tragedies and comedies, and often as the main motif. It has contributed to a countless number of specific "hypocrites", among them perhaps most prominently Shakespeare's Iago and Molière's Tartuffe. The principle of dramatic truthfulness is not disrupted by it but rather confirmed because the errors caused by the dramatic persona's dissimulation hold only for the stage world, i.e., for other dramatic personas, but not for the audience. The playwright and the actor once again have taken pains to make the dissimulation clear to the audience, otherwise the motif could lose not only all its interest, but also its entire purpose. The means to do so are many: sometimes the hypocrite himself or herself casts off their mask when on their own or with an intimate friend; or another dramatic persona "sees through" them, etc. The "discovery" of the dissimulation must always be only for the stage world, not for the audience.

This has concluded the analysis of the "dramatic persona" on the basis of the fictitious "foreign actor". We have adopted it to eliminate provisionally the dramatic contribution of the words, i.e., of the dramatic text. Now we may return to the standard type, i.e., "our" actor, whom we can understand, and attempt a synthesis.

As for characterisation of the dramatic persona by means of the text alone (or by a textual role), that was covered in the preceding chapter and there is little to add, apart from a minor observation. Theorists who study drama only on the basis of the text consider the "characteristic of a dramatic persona" to be a description or an account (mostly brief) that is given by another dramatic persona. That is a gross error because that clearly is not the playwright's own characteristic. Such a characteristic – or rather *critique* – of a dramatic persona makes sense only as a part of the dramatic action, i.e., as an action (*jednání*) by which the speaking dramatic persona wants to influence others. Therefore it does not have to be correct but is often exaggerated, whether towards praise, or towards slander, e.g., with the intention to win someone's favour, convince someone for or against a proposition, gratify someone or offend them. It tends to characterise the speaking person more than the persona that is spoken about. Even the actual characteristic of a dramatic persona has to be seen from this dramatic perspective. An account of a person alone can only be found in narrative literature, but not in drama; it is redundant to listen to someone's description of a person that I can see and hear on the stage for myself. Similarly, the above-mentioned clarification of the motifs of exchange or dissimulation for the sake of the audience – if it is done by words spoken by personas – needs to be done through dramatic speaking.

It is necessary to comment on the *relation between mimics and language* in a dramatic work. We have seen that the expressive abilities of mimics are excellent but limited when it comes to expressing the intellectual aspects of a persona. In that respect the abilities of language itself to make meaning, irrespective of delivery, are greatest. Language is a system of audible notes (or markers, *značky*) with a conventional, contractual significance; that is why we have to learn a language, i.e., create the necessary associations on the basis of the reproductive principle of simultaneity; for that same reason words and sayings may have any meaning, including non-ostensive (*nenázorný*), i.e., general or abstract. The core of the expressive abilities of language is in the fact that it can communicate the contents of mental images, ideas, thoughts, in short that which mimics – or even music, as we shall see – is unable to do, except insufficiently and vaguely. The relation between language and mimics in a dramatic work is that they *complement one another* and their combination is capable of evoking in the audience a perfect and *complete referential image* (*obrazová představa*).

As far as the *inner* life of dramatic personas is concerned, their thoughts can be communicated to us (i.e., the audience) only by means of language, not by mimics. Their emotions and aspirations can be shown very suggestively by mimics but the content needs to be provided by speaking alone; that is how we learn of the causes of the emotions or the purpose of the aspirations, specifically whenever this differs from the appearance. That is the case of abstract thoughts (the love for one's country, a desire for glory, etc.) as well as in situations when the object of the emotion or the aspiration (e.g., the beloved person) is not present on stage, so it cannot be perceived directly. Only the visible deeds and actions of dramatic personas need no explanation through language, not even as supplements, since they speak for themselves. It betrays a playwright's limited talent if they make their personas say what they are doing; that betrays the playwright's literary orientation and the performance proves its redundance and even ridiculousness of such speechifying.

The *findings* of our discussion can be presented in the following diagram:

Objective and ostensive:	—	mimics	mimics	actions (*činy*)	⎫ of a
Subjective:	thoughts	emotions	aspirations	—	⎬ dramatic
Objective and imaginary:	language	language	language	—	⎭ persona

Individual columns show that the thoughts of dramatic personas are made manifest through language, emotions and aspirations through mimics and language, while actions manifest themselves directly.

It is understandable that this natural psychological relation, studied from the audience point of view, is equally valid for the very dramatic persona – as we know from our own experience: mere thoughts can be expressed by language without any apparent mimics; emotions and aspirations make a greater call for mimics, while the needs for language diminishes; and in actions (deeds) that need entirely disappears. The above diagram *justifies psychologically* the principle of the *totality* of the actor's performance, which we asserted in the first part of this book, including its consequences.

The dramatic persona presents itself to us eventually as a *product of three syntheses* that the audience undertakes. Two of them are based on the display (*názor*) proffered by the actor, and the third on the imagined content of the lines written by the author for this persona. As has been stated, the actor's characterisation is static and dynamic, either based on the physical appearance and clothes, or by language and behaviour. Similarly, the textual characteristic could be distinguished on the basis of how we judge the persona's language: the persona's speaking ("from the way they speak they must be someone learned") or they way they behave, but the distinction is not very clear because it is broadly the same material. A purely static characteristic could be given by any undramatic speeches, pertaining *exclusively* to the characteristic of the persona (reflecting, lyrical). In brief:

The characteristics of a dramatic persona	ostensive	1. static:	through appearance and clothes
		2. dynamic:	through speaking and behaviour
	imagined	3. textual:	through language

Each of these characteristics has to be *coherent*, not only in regards to its minor components but also over the *course of time*. This is a psychologically mandatory condition, otherwise it *could not* evoke for us an image of a "dramatic personality". In the case of the actor's static characteristic, this stability over time is taken for granted. The other two characteristics require it necessarily; it is an *absolute* requirement that must not be broken, except seemingly (cf. the motifs of exchange and dissimulation), and it is equally binding for the playwright and the actor. We (as the audience) grasp the coherence of the dynamic character intuitively, i.e., by living through it; the coherence of the textual characteristic rationally.

The required character coherence does not mean its utter *fixity*; it allows *change* and *development*, but *only gradual*. Everything is exclusively dependent on our synthesis, or as we could say: "to let us piece it all together". So any *jumps* in characteristics must be avoided, i.e., those that "would not go together" and would be inadvertently perceived as character incoherence. This is true not only for the dramatic art but also in life. We may hear, for instance, that someone we know as a gentle and kind person behaved in a rude and vulgar way. We are amazed: "Impossible – that doesn't sound like them at all!" And then we learn the details, from the person themself for instance, and *we understand them*: they were provoked by something far beyond *their normal* way. That is why we need to be cautious in judging the characteristics provided by the playwright only by means of words; it is down to the actor to portray the persona with their seeming character leaps in such a way that we experience the persona as suggested by the actor's performance and *through this experiencing we can understand* him or her. Clearly, this is again the issue of *"mental transfiguration"* that was described above in the discussion of the playwright's creative work. Here it is the matter of the audience and apparently the process takes place only whenever the persona's character is presented in a consistent (unified) way. Let us call this rule of character coherence over time more generally *the principle of the dramatic persona's coherence*, which covers both the options: complete fixity and gradual development.

> There are also "dramas" that do not allow the actor to sustain this character coherence since it simply contradicts psychological laws; the best-known example is the notorious *sudden* (and allegedly lasting) transformation of a complete villain into a perfect angel, with moral inclinations and guaranteed praise from all virtuous souls. We are not going to believe it, neither will the actor, because it is psychologically impossible.

The three listed characteristics relate to one and the same persona so they should also agree with one another. This need for *agreement* or *overall* coherence is logical but since it is not justified psychologically, it is not mandatory. The cause is that the means of these three characteristics are different and generally independent of each other. This agrees with our real-world experience. A person sharp with words is commonly of an intelligent appearance but not always; neither does their behaviour need to be sharp and nimble, nor is an exquisite dress a safe guarantee of an exquisite mind. The principle of dramatic truthfulness requires that there should be such an agreement because *an all-round consistent* characteristic is not only more effective but also more convincing. A person who is energetic in speaking should be energetic in all behaviour as well as in appearance. Excellent clothes should be accompanied with excellent speaking, etc. However, this requirement is only *aesthetic* and therefore only *relative*.

There is even an entire dramatic style typical for breaking this requirement: *dramatic comedy*. The most effective comedy is achieved when the three characteristics are mutually at odds. It is funnier if silly nonsense is uttered by a persona behaving seriously than with laughter (e.g., Constable Dogberry in *Much Ado About Nothing*); it is merrier if a clumsy persona is dressed in splendid rather than plain clothes (e.g., Malvolio in *Twelfth Night*). An appropriate choice of such odds is the fathomless source of true *actorly comedy* which – unlike literary comedy, especially word play – never tires and never gets old. Here rests the mystery of all great actor comedians in contrast to the coarse jesting of comedian clowns who rely only the physiological suggestion of the facial grimace.

෴ ෴ ෴

THE ACTOR FIGURE

Leaving the auditorium behind, let us enter "into the wings" of the stage in search of the *actor* and look at the actor's art through their eyes. The actor's task in the dramatic work is to create a certain "figure" in the play. What is this *actor figure (herecká postava)*? In the first part of this book we have asserted that the material out of which the actor creates his or her artwork, and the tool with which he or she creates it, is himself or herself, i.e., their *own live and discerning body*. This has two crucial consequences. Firstly, the actor as a creative artist perceives their artwork, i.e., the figure, *differently* from the audience: for the actor the figure exists *primarily* as *a bodily percept* (*tělový vněm*) and only secondarily as a visual and an acoustic one. Secondly, the figure is neither of a purely mental nature, as literary theorists take it, nor of an exclusively physical one, as some theatre theorists would like to have it, but *both at once*.

From the point of the technical image (as opposed to the referential one), the components of the actor figure (as opposed to the clothes, the physical appearance, the behaviour and the speaking of the dramatic persona) are *costume, mask, playing (hra) and delivery (mluva)*, which for the sake of brevity comprises other vocal expressions too. Additionally, the contents of the delivery, i.e., the dramatic text, belongs here, but that is not the actor's creation but the playwright's. Especially *acting (hra)* clearly shows that it is for the actor a *system* of purely bodily (i.e., *inner tactile*) perceptions through which the actor becomes aware of his or her movements and postures – just like we are aware, for instance, in perfect darkness how we hold our hand or what movement we make with it. As for visual perceptions, they are fragmentary and imperfect; if available at all, they only serve to double-check other perceptions. Facial mimicry cannot be seen by the actor at all; even if it was rehearsed in front of a mirror – as beginners tend to do – the actor has to go by "muscular memory". Other movements (of arms, legs, the whole body) can be seen but only in part and skewed, i.e., from the actor's own viewpoint. The actor never sees *their acting (hra)* the way the audience does and that is decisive: it is only the acting of others that an actor knows the art and can use that experience in their own study, purely theoretically. *Delivery* is the same case: it is also little more than a system of perceptions pertaining to the speech organs; through them the actor perceives their movements and positions, both in relation to the sounds as well as the breath. We all perceive our speaking in situations where we cannot hear ourselves and our *vocal* sensations give us a sufficient sense of orientation. It is true that an actor can hear what they say – but only once they have spoken out; the acoustic perceptions, again, can only double-check if they have spoken well, or if "they adopted a false tone", which could then be set right in what follows. Again, the same is true here: an actor can never hear himself or herself the way the audience hears them.

The costume and the mask seem to be an exception here since they are not a part of the actor's live body, but an unlive accessory. This is only a seeming exception though. Firstly, we should not take *mask* to refer only to the wig and other such outer accessories that modify the actor's appearance; they are not used in all instances. If make-up is used, it is clearly modifying only the outer appearance – and sometimes not even that is necessary. A lasting aspect, e.g., frowny, smiley, dull, etc., may be achieved purely physiologically, i.e., by a sustained contraction of facial muscles. If the body is to be corpulent, it can be padded up, but if it the figure is meant to be hunched, it can be achieved with the body. That is to say, the "mask" in its broader sense – corresponding to the mental image of a "physical appearance" – contains much that the actor can perceive as an inner tactile sensation of a fixed type (the perceptions of "postures" as opposed to movements, e.g., a constantly open mouth, etc.).

Any extraneous and mechanical additions (i.e., additions to the organic body) are dictated by practical reasons; from a technical point of view, these components should logically be counted as a part of the costume. The actor wants to look in such and such a way; whether the means to that end are of one or another kind is all the same. But since the actor wants to look one way and soon another way, their body should make that transformation possible: it should be average, normal, so that it can be adapted in one or another way. Individual beauty, body size, etc. are surely beneficial but only on a personal level, not artistically. The actor's choice of the repertoire of characters is important here; for the comic genre, relative ugliness or minor physical disability are not an obstacle. A "mask" in the broader sense can effect a huge change, not only actually but also seemingly, through an optical illusion (making a figure taller by means of a long robe, etc.). The same is true of voice: a strong organ is a certain technical advantage with a view to the large space of the auditorium, while a sweet voice affects a personal rather than an artistic success, which requires a rich variety of vocal modulations. Training plays an important role here too.

Not even extraneous, inorganic additions that the actors uses to make a figure, such as a *costume*, a wig, etc., are exempt from the sphere of "bodily perceptions". All the accessories *extend* the actor's *bodily self*. We all know how we feel at one with clothes we are used to. They are as if parts of our body. This is all the more true for an actor. Splendid and long locks of a wig may press on them a suggestion of vanity, as if one's own; a knife, which is an extension of one's arm, adds courage. We can still amusingly observe the process of clothes becoming part of the actor's physical persona in "grand opera", for instance, where swashbuckling with a cloak and a rapier retains the features of the Spanish comedies *de capa y espada* (also known as cloak and dagger drama). And since the actor's visual perception of their mask and costume during performance is equally imperfect as that of their acting, lacking even a chance of double-checking on them, we may assert that subjectively, i.e., for the actor, *the actor figure is a set of all inner tactile perceptions* an actor has in the course of his or her performance, presenting a certain dramatic persona. This set of perceptions – just like all perceptions – is of a psychological nature, but since an actor feels the movements and states of their own organism, we may take this set as a *physiological* one; our live body is truly halfway between a purely mental and an outer, purely physical world.

> The movements and postures of an actor's body, which he or she experiences in the way we have just described, are not subjective in themselves but objective, since they can be perceived – differently, i.e., through sight and hearing – by others, namely the audience. For the audience they constitute a certain dramatic persona in its outer form. *Subjectively*, there is a sharp difference between the actor figure (*herecká postava*) (the actor's inner tactile perception) and the "dramatic persona" (*dramatická osoba*) (the audience's audiovisual perception). We know that the audience has a certain motoric perception but that is of secondary importance, only an accompanying thing, just like the actor's audiovisual perception is a secondary perception. Neither do these two constructs match objectively, which may seem paradoxical given that they relate to one and the same performance of an actor on stage. However, this performance appears one way to the stage and another to the auditorium. It is an error of an inexperienced actor to assume that the way they look, speak and play is exactly how the audience sees and hears them; likewise an inexperienced spectator is mistaken to assume that the way they see and hear a dramatic persona is the identical to the way they actually look, speak and play. This difference is known under the name of "*theatre optics* or *acoustics*" and stems from a relatively large distance between the actors and the audience, from a particular lighting of the stage, the acoustics of the stage and the auditorium, etc. The actor figure needs to be, in brief, *usually transposed higher* in order to appear to the auditorium as it should. Whoever sits close and can see well can often observe that in the

actor's mask, esp. in the make-up. If the person who asks actors to speak "naturally", i.e., like in the real world, once went into the wings, they would be amazed how "supernaturally", i.e., exaggeratedly the actors have to speak to make it sound "natural" to the auditorium. This observation is made to demonstrate the objective difference between the actor figure and the dramatic persona. For the time being this is of no further importance since during the perception of a dramatic work this difference *does not exist*. In contrast, in the artistic stylisation of the dramatic work the principles of theatre optics and acoustics play a certain role, which will be discussed at a later point.

The actor figure is not *exclusively* a physiological formation. Firstly, the actor understands the language they speak, which evokes many associations, especially of an intellectual type. The same is true of the actor's costume and mask, which suggest to the actor that they are, for instance, an old king, etc. and bring about certain mental states; among them, the emotions and aspirations are further enhanced by the actor's way of speaking and the physical action. Let us recall our analysis of the expressive abilities of mimics complemented by words. If it held true from the audience, it is also valid for the actor; from the emotional and aspirational point of view, this is even more intensive because the actor experiences all of this somatically (*tělesně*). If the actor has a rather imperfect mental image of the dramatic persona, in comparison to the audience, he or she has an all the more intense image of the persona's inner being, an image that grows emotionally and aspirationally to a real inner perception. In brief, *the actor figure* is for the actor also *a set of mental states* that he or she experiences during the performance; it is therefore a *psychological* formation.

The actor figure is then a formation of a *dual* kind: *primarily* physiological and *secondarily* psychological. These two formations are not dependent on one another but rather closely interconnected since every single element of the physiological set corresponds to an element (or elements) from the psychological set. So, for instance, a certain movement of the speech organs is sensed by the actor alongside the sound of the word, evoking a certain mental image (the meaning of this word), while it is simultaneously co-determined by the delivery, e.g., spoken in a loud voice. The furrowing of the forehead, sensed by the actor, evokes a sense of discontent. Even the costume worn by the actor, e.g., a loose and long gown, is not only physically sensed by the actor, making him move in a measured and distinguished way, but also evokes certain mental images that are appropriately emotionally coloured (the office of a judge for example). Such similar connections are generally a *given* (*zákonité*), stemming from the actor's inner and outer experience, be it naturally (a loud voice – emphasising the significance of the word; furrowing the forehead – a sense of discontent) or artificially, through conventional association (a word – its meaning; a gown – a judge's office). We shall refer to them as **psychophysiological correspondences**.

By way of summary of our investigation we may assert that *an actor figure is a sum of all psychophysiological correspondences* that can be found in the actor's given performance. If we refer to physiological elements as *f*, and to psychological ones as *p*, and symbolise their relationship – the psychophysiological correspondence – by a horizontal line (the conventional mathematical symbol for ratio), and use the sign + to symbolise their sum (we use both these signs in the logical, not arithmetical sense), we may express the definition as follows (while retaining the primacy of the physiological elements):

$$\text{actor figure} = \frac{f_1}{p_1} + \frac{f_2}{p_2} + \frac{f_3}{p_3} + \ldots = \Sigma$$

The symbol Σ signifies synthesis, a set.

From what has been said, the psychological sum $p_1 + p_2 + \ldots = \Sigma\, p$ comprises not only the actor's perception of the sum of the physiological $\Sigma\, f$, but also the mental image of its meaning (*významová představa*), the *associative factor* – analogically to the way we described it in our analysis of the dramatic persona. This associative factor, in brief, refers to the *inner* life of the actor figure as opposed to its outer life, given by $\Sigma\, f$. For the actor, this inner life of the actor figure is *identical* with the inner life of *the dramatic persona in the way the actor understands it*. More cautiously, one could say that the actor tries to make it identical and achieves full artistic satisfaction only once they are able to say: I have delivered the persona of the drama the way I wanted it, i.e., the way I inwardly understood it. So what is the condition of such success? There is only one. We have seen that the set $\Sigma\, p$ is yoked through psychophysiological correspondence with the set $\Sigma\, f$; it is *on this*, i.e., on the outer performance of the actor that everything depends. The *specifically actorly problem* does not lie in the way the actor embraces the *inner* life of their figure and simultaneously their dramatic persona. This is a necessary condition but it is not enough; anyone with a sufficiently vivid and intensive inner life can do this. But to make this figure, to embody one's idea (*představa*) – that is not what anyone can do but an actor must be capable of it, if they want to be called *an actor*.

The *primacy of the physiological set* is given not only psychologically but also *artistically*. For, what is the ideal mode of perception every work of art? To experience it like the creator. Clearly this ideal can never be reached because that would presuppose that the recipient is identical in all aspects with the creator, which can never happen; still, that should be the objective. This means in our case that the inner life of the dramatic persona as it is understood by the audience should be as close to the inner life of the persona as it is understood by the dramatic persona's creator – the actor. The only bridge that spans both leads over the pillar of the actor's delivery, i.e., over the said physiological set which is jointly perceived by the actor as well as the audience – although either of them do it differently (inner tactile for the former, audiovisual for the latter) – and with a result as identical as can be.

It would be a big mistake to assume from the above that we belittle the psychological set of the actor's art. Its necessity has been emphasised in asserting the psychophysiological correspondence as the central principle. The physiological set has primacy because it is *specific* of the actor's art – just like, let us add, in the case of dance art; there, however, the psychological set is much leaner, especially when it comes to mental images, because dance is not a mimetic art (*obrazové umění*). The above argues that the psychological set by itself is not sufficient, which does not mean it is not necessary. On the contrary, it is without fail needed in acting, which is – in presenting persons – a mimetic art. It must not lack in dance performance either, although it is almost entirely narrowed down to emotions and aspirations. Its bare minimum can be found in the art of acrobats, which is almost entirely physiological; but an acrobat is not an actor, as we concluded in the first part of this book. An actor who would content themselves with the physiological set only would not stand up to the challenge of playing (presenting) people; such an actor would present not more than empty "ham", which is unfortunately often the case in practice, especially with so-called virtuoso actors. Their performances may dazzle or even delude one to believe that they are soulful (*oduševnělý*) but we eventually feel that they lack an inner charge, that they are not "lived through". What is meant by this "living through" (*prožití*) will be clarified in the analysis of the actor's creative work below. For the time being, let us formulate the conclusion of the preceding discussion: The principle of psychophysiological correspondence requires the *necessary coexistence* of the physiological and psychological sets in the actor's performance because *the physiological has to be internally propped up by the psychological, and the psychological externally expressed by the physiological.*

Our psychological analysis of the "dramatic persona" has shown that it contains two components: the fixed one (the dress and the persona's physical appearance) and the dynamic one (the persona's speaking, behaviour and actions). Similarly the actor figure, which is a kind of reverse side to the dramatic persona, and contains a fixed (the costume and the mask) and a dynamic component (delivery and acting). The parallel goes even further. We have identified some stable features in the dynamic part of the perceived dramatic persona, such as its overall way of speaking, etc., which we then ascribe to the dramatic persona, based on the continuous perception, while we grasp the changes themselves as the personal part of the dramatic action (*děj*), which is constructed by the interaction of the personas. The same needs to be true in the case of the actor figure; the figure's delivery and acting – though they are a dynamic set of inner tactile perceptions – also need to have something lasting, *stable* in them, which we ascribe to the actor figure proper, based on the costume and the mask, especially as a kind of *organic* part of that mask. The remainder of delivery and acting, a truly *variable* part of component of the figure, is an individual part of the actors' onstage interaction. As far as that is concerned, it is a clear matter. An actor, for instance, shouts, stamps their feet, waves their arms, puckers their face – that is a dramatic persona's outburst of anger, perhaps towards another. The actor's voice sinks into a whisper, their body collapses and trembles, their face narrows and their eyes stare – that is the dramatic persona's fit of fear, perhaps from another. What is then the basis of the stable part of the actor's delivery and acting, that "organic mask" (as we have called it), on which we base the dramatic persona's psychological profile, temperament and character?

There is little doubt that it is of a purely physiological kind. It is based on certain *predispositions* of psychological states, not the psychological states themselves. Let us connect it to the two above examples: what is irritability or fearfulness? An irritable or a fearful person is not the one who is angry or afraid but one who has a *tendency* towards one or the other. An irritable is irritable even if they are not being angry; a fearful one is such even without being afraid. So these "psychological qualities" are not connected with psyche but they are predispositions whose basis is physiological. Let us analyse their condition.

A person can be irritable or fearful – let us stay with these two examples – from their birth. But these qualities may also be acquired, permanently or temporarily. If someone has suffered a bitter disappointment and ingratitude from people, for instance in a public activity, they may withdraw deeply hurt, become embittered and full of malevolent aversion to people; the person may become stern, irritable – at least for a time. Whoever has gone through some awful horrors will be affected even if the horrors pass. The person's nerves will weaken, they become easily frightened, fearful – we have seen many such cases during the Great War. In these cases, said qualities have been acquired through a natural way. But they can also be acquired artificially, because only then it is of worth to acting. This can be done in two ways.

> Let us say, I come to a person to get something important from them, which they deny me. I know from elsewhere that the person can be managed only roughly, by force; but I happen to be a mild person. What can be done given the thing is so important? I shall resolve with utmost determination to be as stark in my behaviour as can be and shall not put up with anything but rather tell the person, etc. Resolving on this I can feel that a strange state takes hold of me, a kind of irritation, which is not yet anger but it is

short of flipping into it. I am *ready* for anger. The fact that this readiness is of a purely physiological kind can be seen from the opposite: calming one's anger often requires literally physical exertion. If I am trying to tame my anger, I place all my bodily impulses forcefully against it; if I am trying to get ready for it, I release them, clearing the path for them. This example of "getting ready", by which I have become "irritable" only through my *will* is not entirely perfect; it does not always come off the way we want and often fails in the crucial moment: In the evening I am in a country pub; although it is getting dark I want to get to the next village, about an hour's walk through the woods. At that point I hear the guests say that there are travellers around and it is not really safe. I happen to be a courageous person, so I go anyway. But what a strange state has taken hold of me on suggestion by what I have heard. I do not feel fear but I am *focused* on it. Against my will I have become fearful, but only for the duration of the journey, and then I admit: "I wasn't afraid but neither was I at ease!" This "focus" was not caused by my will but by *suggestion* from the guests' stories, and that is why it is near perfect. Also here is the basis of the state of a purely physiological kind; all the paths of the impulses connected with fear (e.g., heightened alertness of sense, readiness to dodge) are free. This is analogical in other cases too.

Actors combine both the above ways. They purposely *prepare* the means that would allow *suggestion* to make them achieve the physiological intentness of a particular quality of the dramatic persona. Such means are of very diverse kinds and can be loosely grouped as special, designed for a particular focus, and general, which focus actors overall – for whatever may be needed. The special foci are given by the text of the actor's role, which they have to memorise, but also by the costume and the mask in which they perform. I have already noted how certain clothes, a wig or even a prop (a dagger) inspire the actor with particular qualities. In the age of the commedia dell'arte, taking on a *typical* dress, e.g., the harlequin's, caused the donning of the entire focus for the typical qualities of that particular figure. For actors, the general means of suggestion are the stage and everything on it, especially other actors. The actor, who has only just cracked jokes in the wings, enters onstage on prompt from the stage manager and appears face to face with their partner, now livid or cowardly – whatever is needed. *The actorly focus* arises – apart from the partner's influence – *through a purposely prepared self-induced suggestion.*

The significance of the focus as a *stable* component of the actor figure is in that it *guides*, i.e., selectively adjusts the figure's *variable* component, which forms part of the interaction. A constant focus on anger or fear necessarily causes typical changes in delivery and acting even if the anger or fear themselves are not being presented: in the case of anger, harsh, sharp, loud delivery, a frowning face, fierce and aggressive movements and gestures. In the case of fear, soft, faltering delivery, staring eyes, uncertain movements as if defensive, etc. And of course, if the persona is one of anger (or fear in the other case,) even if that emotion is unnecessary or excessive in a given situation, these changes in delivery and acting will be all the more pronounced. The audience perceives this then as the "general way" of speaking, behaviour and action, mentioned above, characterising a given dramatic persona.

These discussions have brought us to the research theme of extreme interest: the **actor's psychology**. There are two issues that we wish to analyse here: *the conditions of the actor's creative work* – and these conditions can be inner (talents) or outer (sources) – and *the actor's concrete process of creation*.

C₃ C₃ C₃

Actor's Talent. In our discussion of the playwright's creative work we identified as a specifically dramatic talent the playwright's ability of *mental transfiguration*, outlining the basis of this process. This ability needs to be shared by everyone who co-creates the dramatic work: not only the writer but also the stage director, composer and necessarily also the actor. Preceding discussions make it clear that this ability is not sufficient on its own but needs to be complemented by the ability of **transbodiment**; in *it* lies the *specific* feature of actor's talent since the other mentioned artistic roles do not need them. The substance of the transbodiment act may be formulated in brevity: it is the actor's *combined bodily focus* on the qualities that the actor needs for his or her dramatic persona and that make the persona sufficiently characteristic for the performance. Let us emphasise that the ability of transbodiment, although it is central for the actor, needs to combine with the ability of mental transfiguration – in a relation of psychological correspondence. If we call this double act **"transpersonation"**, it may be rendered symbolically in keeping with our above convention:

$$\text{transpersonation} = \frac{\text{transbodiment}}{\text{mental transfiguration}}$$

It is apparent that the ability of transpersonation contains another necessary feature of the actor's talent also *a sense of psychophysiological correspondence* (see the section "Sources of Acting" below).

In the above analysis of the actor figure we have stated that the changeable way of speaking and acting contains a certain fixed component pertaining to the dramatic persona and its own variable component pertaining to the individual participation in dramatic action. Transpersonation clearly pertains to the dramatic persona. In order for the actor to be able to express their part in the dramatic action, they need another ability, which is generally taken for a sufficient feature of an actor's talent. It is the ability of *bodily expression of psychological states*, especially of *emotions* and *aspirations* (*efforts*); this ability is in principle of a physical nature but encapsulates also a sense of psychological correspondence. It is only with this in place that an actor is able to suggestively deliver not only, for instance, a burst of anger, joy, anxiety and others, but also drunkenness, dying, etc. This ability is necessary for an actor but it is not specific for this profession since others – in their particular way – need to have it too: dancers and interpretive artists (reciters and instrumentalists). The bodily expressive ability means *generally* an ability for performance feelingly lived *through oneself*, whereas acting requires performances feelingly lived *through the dramatic persona* presented by the actor – a persona into which the actor first needs to transpersonate.

> A suitable example is the difference between *an actor's delivery* and *recitation*. A reciter delivering a lyrical poem or narrating a story speaks as the author's *surrogate*, not as the author's impersonator. The reciter could say to the audience: "The poet should actually deliver this on their own but it's impossible; so that's why I come *in their stead* but I am not *them* and don't wish to *play* them." So reciters deliver everything in "their" own voice and the nuances of their delivery are an expression of the emotions that the poem has evoked in them. The poem is the *cause* of their emotions: "The words are here in readiness, I the reciter am raptured by them". Being merely interpretive artists for the poetic (i.e., literary) work, reciters limit the expressions of their emotions to speaking. Mimics are excluded entirely, with the exception of those that arise spontaneously through the reciter's actual emotional experience of the work. Only in the case of the orator is mimics an integral part of their performance since *their* "speaking" is action (*jednání*) that is meant to have an effect on the audience – but also this mimics and gesticulation are the orator's personal expression. Whereas actors are not the author's (i.e., the playwright's) surrogates but *impersonators* of the dramatic personas they are *playing*. The actors are not here instead of the author or of the dramatic persona but they are that persona, thought fictively. Not even in the exceptional cases when a dramatist calls for such personas as an "author" or "manager" do actors deputise for them but impersonate, i.e., play them. Therefore actors do not deliver everything in "their own" voice but with their "persona's" voice and the nuances of this delivery are not an expression of the actor's psychological states but of those of the persona. For a harsh persona they speak harshly; for a gentle one gently; for the one, when angered, they will "thunder", for the other they will squeal. Of course, actors may choose their own "organic mask" to deliver a particular persona but that does not change anything in principle. In such a case, the dramatic persona speaks – exceptionally – like the actor himself or herself; but who in the audience can know that?
>
> Moreover, actors have to speak in such a way that the speaking of their dramatic persona is a *consequence* of its psychological state (not of the actor's). In other words: "emotional and aspirational rapture is here, behold the *words and delivery that they give birth to*". This act of (only seeming) *birth* of the words spoken is an important dramatic requirement and pertains not only to the actor, who needs to be able to speak once

as if "searching for words" and then spout them out at once, but also to the author of the dramatic text. The dramatic personas' lines need to be formed in such a way as if they were a direct consequence of their psychological state, whatever it is. Through its content and delivery the lines have to create an impression of improvisation; only then can they give us the impression of being spontaneous. A brilliant example are the words of Shakespeare's personas; there are also modern realistic dramatists who fulfil this requirement, observed from life – recently O'Neill for instance. The principle itself is not realistic but psychological – generally human – and does not prevent stylisation. This principle is confirmed even in the special case when the persona created by the playwright is characterised as a speaker of clichés and only says words that have been "learned by rote".

Both the ability of transbodiment and the ability of bodily expression show that actors belong to what is known as the *motoric* or *visceral (pohybový)* type of people, which is the most common among the three sensory types – the other two being the visual (optical) and aural (auditive). These types only signify which sense an individual *predominantly* relies on in their sensory life and may be variously combined or specialised. The musical type is a special case of the acoustic type; similarly, a specialisation of the motoric type is the *oral (mluvní)* type. The characteristic of the motoric type (just like of the other two) is defined by three moments. People of the motoric kind have an outstanding *bent* for physical and generally *inner tactile* perceptions, through which they learn of the movements and postures of their bodies. They automatically dedicate intense attention to them and their combinations, arising in any more complex procedures – just like people of the other two types take especial note of visual or aural perceptions. The interest relates either to movements of the whole body (gymnastics, dance, sports) or to their part, especially to organs of speaking (or singing) and hands (writing, drawing, playing musical instruments, various handicrafts). Closely connected with this is a *fondness* for any such procedures: inner tactile perceptions evoked by them are for such a person a source of extraordinary pleasure or even bliss. "I love doing this," they say. Thirdly, connected with bent and fondness is an extraordinary *memory* for inner tactile perceptions and *especially for their complex combinations*, so they very easily learn physical procedures – they are agile and dexterous – and remember them very well.

This memory for inner tactile impressions is surely the most significant moment; it should be emphasised that the memory does not only pertain to the elements but also to the complex combinations and it follows that it also applies to *relations between inner tactile elements*; it is therefore connected with *a sense of these relations and their specific kind* and accompanied by a strong fondness stemming from these relations. The importance of such a *talent for relations* is in that it brings us to the artistic sphere; it is a necessary condition for an artistic talent in general, as we shall see from examples derived from the other two types. A painter as a predominantly visual type needs to have not only an interest in, fondness and memory for individual colours but also – and even especially – for their relations, i.e., colour harmonies, just like a musician, a special aural type, needs to have it not only for tones but also for their relations, i.e., harmonies and melodies. This *"sense of relations"* of sensations and perceptions, for *the specific kind and logic (zákonitost)* of each of them – since there are very numerous relations even within one discipline – is a necessary and sufficient condition for their *organic syntheses*. As parallels with the syntheses of abstract mental images, i.e., with logical thoughts, let us call them *ostensive thoughts (myšlenky názorné)*. A painter thinks in colours and shapes; a musician in tones; *an actor in inner tactile perceptions*. Each of them understands the *order* or *principles* of their ostensive relations, which are the glue of the artist's synthesis, as an *artistic logic* of their discipline.

It is impossible to discuss the *logic of **actorly ostensive** (názorný) thinking* in detail; let us only identify its main principles. The first is the principle of *coordination of inner tactile impulses*. It applies equally to both personal and the action-related *(dějový)* components of the actor figure. A human organism is a unit that is coherent as a whole; if an impulse of some sort arises in any of its parts, it has a tendency to and does indeed spread out to all other parts. The impulses may manifest themselves differently to the outside but still we can feel a unity in its basis. So, for instance, the so-called "proud" posture is caused by certain energetic impulses in the muscles that rapture of the entire organism and bring about not only an energetic gait and "mighty" gestures but also a sonorous voice. As observers we can *feel* through empathy – and not only from our own experience – that "these belong together". I shall call this logical relation *"a harmonic affinity"*. Often we use the same word for all these manifestations although they are basically different ("proud" gait, proud gesture, proud way of speaking). Such a principle gives the actor a personal *unity* of the actor figure, which is defined (as we know) through the actor's *multiple* simultaneous foci. Since each of them raptures the entire organism, they cannot be combined to oppose one another. It is obvious that, for instance, a "proud" bodily focus is incompatible with an "anxious" one because their characteristic impulses are mutually in contradiction; they cannot be brought together even partially, e.g., anxious mimics with a proud tone of speech. However, it is possible with a proud *content of the lines* (i.e., the dramatic text): cowards can utter the most heroic words. Referentially, for the dramatic persona, this corresponds with the afore

The second is the principle of *coherence of the actor figure*. A figure has to be coherent across time, always the identical. This is brought about not only by costume and mask but also – and especially – by the focus on the chosen personality feature. A particular fixed bodily focus brings about *congruous modifications* of all the dynamic displays, speaking and delivery, and therefore we take these displays relatively, judging them in relation to the focus. So, for example, an irritable focus tends to loud speaking, which then becomes as if normal for that persona. If the persona is supposed to speak softly in a particular moment, the actor needs to suppress that focus obviously; this appears to the viewer as a noticeable "tempering" of the voice, although in absolute terms the voice is still rather loud. Conversely, a situation that requires a strong, resounding style of speech from an actor with a "timid" focus would mean a straining of the voice, apparent also to the viewer: for *this* persona it amounts to shouting. In this way we can feel the fixed focus in all outer manifestations, even those that differ from it. The dramatic persona remains "the same" whatever they are doing; its character is coherent or coherently changing. This logic of a consistent focus of speaking and delivery, brought about through the bodily focus, could never be achieved by the actor through rational deliberation only. Image-wise, this also corresponds to the previously emphasised dramatic persona's coherence.

Finally, the third is the principle of *exteriorisation of inner tactile impulses*. It concerns the temporal coupling of elements and is valid for the variable component of speaking and delivery, i.e., the *personal action* component (*osobně dějová složka*). Every inner bodily impulse has a tendency to spread out *centrifugally*, from the inside out, to the surface of the body and on to the surrounding space. At the same time, remaining basically identical, it *develops* intensively and extensively. Let us take anger as an example: first takes form in minor inner tactile perceptions, corresponding with fierce and irregular bodily vibration – that is an irritable mood. The impulse spreads outwardly, displaying itself in spasmodic activity in the face, irregular outcries, disorderly movements of the stamping feet and flailing of arms, culminating eventually in a violent act. All the activities are clearly parallel in their spacial and temporal (i.e., rhythmic) forms, only gradated in intensity and size. If we take into account the corresponding mental states (mood passing on to passion and through an aspiration into a deed) and if we reflect on the following formulation that states this coupling in the words "out of anger he beat or killed him", we can see that the coupling given by the third principle is *an ostensive organic causality* (*názorná kauzalita organická*), i.e., physiologically lived through, as opposed to mechanical causality that governs machines – which can also be ostensive (*názorný*) but only optically, e.g., when we can directly "see" the effect of a lever on another lever. Referentially, this corresponds to the causality of personal action (*osobní jednání*), which shall be discussed in the next chapter.

The Sources of Acting. After this outline of "actorly logic", let us inquire into the *sources* from which an actor draws the *material* of their art. This material on which actors synthetically create their art is comprised of generally *dual* elements, as we have seen: of the links of physiological with a corresponding psychological element. We have used the symbol f/p and stressed that neither *f*, nor *p* on its own is sufficient for an actor but the actor is specifically interested in their relation. As for the sources, there are two of them: inner experience and outer experience.

1. *The actor's **inner** experience.* This one is the best source since here the actor can *directly* observe both the parts, the psychological and the physical (through inner tactile perceptions), as well as their psychophysiological correspondence. An abundance of matter is offered by the actor's inner life, responding sensitively to their surroundings, be it nature or people, the arts, especially literature, and other cultural things. In this way an actor can gain a rich psychological experience, which is not limited only to emotions and aspirations (*snahy*) that the actor is prone to on account of their individual character, but are also enriched – especially under the influence of the arts – with those that are alien to the actor's character since the actor's creative work needs all of them. This is done – as we have analysed in the case of the playwright's creative work – by imaginatively the germs of such emotions and aspirations that are otherwise underdeveloped or suppressed in the actor's character. It is specific for actors that they are not primarily interested in the mental states *in their own right*; that is an exclusive purpose of the *lyrical poet*, who aims at expressing them verbally. Actors are most of all interested in their *bodily expression,* which they simultaneously live through; this is the main focus of their attention. Therefore actors do not immerse themselves in their soul but rather *step out* of it as outside observers – a stance they may feel as a *bifurcation* (*rozdvojení*) of their self. This is certainly the utmost case of self-observation, where the observer stands against the observed almost estranged, critically, although both are the one and the same person. A spontaneous assuming of such a stance towards oneself (let us call it "actorly self-observation") in any suitable situation is a certain sign of an actor's talent.

Olga Scheinpflugová writes elegantly about such a mania in her essay "The Actor and Their Shadow"[21]: "It is awful that the actor's curiosity goes shopping and inquiring so close that it concentrates mostly on ourselves. I mean the sensitive, subconscious control to which we, actors, subject our entire private life. Acting is a cursed hungry shadow that obsessively follows us anywhere we go, even to the most common of everyday situations, listening greedily and slyly like a paid spy, taking down every event in the notebook of subconscious memory, adding it to the storehouse to be exploited

---

21   Olga Scheinpflugová, "Herec a jeho stín" [The Actor and Their Shadow], *Nové české divadlo 1918–1926* (Praha: Aventinum, 1927), p. 115–116. Olga Scheinpflugová (1902–1968) was a Czech actress, playwright and novelist. She spent the main part of her career at the National Theatre in Prague, where she worked from 1929 till her death.

when the time comes." She goes on to describe an interesting story from her childhood, when her mother died. "I was ill with genuine pain and numb with weeping – and yet I remember well how, walking behind the hearse, I became aware of myself and the whole situation, how I could hear myself cry violently and shatter my breath with pain... That's how we cry when we are deeply unhappy – I was saying to myself then. And now, of course, this comes about much more often."

Aesthetics (specifically German, starting with Dilthey) tend to exaggerate the importance of live experiences for artists, especially if assuming in a dilettante way that such an experience will make its way somehow fluidly into the work of art. This is not so even in lyrical poetry; even here it has to be "translated" into language and this very act of "translating" is the very *essence* of art – i.e., in the form, not in the content. Live experiences mean the most for actors but only as material out of which something has to be made. And here it is not only the mere mental state but its simultaneous embodiment that are stored in the actor's memory. For emotions cannot be remembered at all, only felt. A memory of an emotion is a memory of its accompanying bodily expressions; if this memory is live, it can bring about the emotion itself, although in a weak form. That is true for all of us and especially so for actors. If the actor has not noticed the bodily expression of their mental experience, then this experience – however intensive and peculiar – is dead capital for them.

2. *The actor's **outer** experience.* This type of experience pertains obviously to other people and is utterly *indirect* and therefore imperfect. While the actor can see and hear the people in their expressions, sight and hearing are not an actor's specific senses. Therefore this experience cannot be as fulfilling for actors as it is for a narrative writer or a painter; the *actor's* sense is the somatic (*tělový*) one. So actors need to be able to feel with their bodies what they hear and see – i.e., literally "go through" it. The mediator here is the *imitative instinct*, one of the basic tendencies of man as well as of higher organisms. Actors as motoric types are marked with such a prominent *imitative talent* that lay people often assume that the imitative abilities and acting talent are one and the same – and this assumption is also captured in the word *mimics* as a generic name for the art of acting (from Greek *mimesis*, i.e., imitation). Although Nietzsche calls actors "ideal apes", his theoretical view is not only superficial but altogether incorrect. The imitative ability is necessary for actors but not sufficient, as can be seen from the numerous imitators whose performances are often striking in their faithful accuracy and very amusing. However, this is only craft, not art; if you will, it is only an *initial stage* of acting and actors need to progress to a higher level, even in the simple collection of their material. We know that the elements of actors' art – let us call them "*actorly motifs*" – are dual in kind, comprising both the physiological and the psychological part as well as their mutual correspondence. With the outer experience, an actor needs to respect the mental state of the observed people, which is possible only if the actor *not only* observes the outer expressions but also *feels him- or herself into their soul* (*nitro*). This is a reverse requirement to that made with actors' inner experience; however, with a view to actors' instinctive physiological focus there is a danger that the outer

experience will result in the actor only observing the outer show, without penetrating into the soul. Many actors actually do this; they can of course make use of such material but their performances will not be satisfactory and convincing because they lack sincerity. Such an accumulation of motifs is flawed.

In the era of psychological naturalism, the actor's outer experience was given great significance and actors studied in this sense with untiring and careful commitment. Nowadays, with the opposite trend of idealism, this source is considered to be of little importance. This is a wholly unjustified neglect. The tremendous importance of outer experience for actors lies in that their inner experience is expanded in ways that they could never do by themselves. Through it, an actor as creator of the figure gets to know a great number of alien individualities – provided it is processed appropriately, as mentioned above. Clearly, the purpose is not to copy them but to create independently, *after them*. If an actor is creating a personality type, they need to have something to work from: how should they, for example, perform the *type* of a phlegmatic or the *type* of an alcoholic, the *type* of an adolescent or the *type* of a diplomat (I have purposely selected types defined by different aspects) unless by synthesis derived from a *range* of people of one or the other kind? The actor should make this synthesis independently without comfortably making do with an individual they discover of that type and simply copying him or her. After all – in spite of all theories and their developments – all actors exploit the outer source *spontaneously*, perceiving the world, whether they want it or not, with their "actorly sense", i.e., with the inner tactile sense, although the mediators in this case are their sight and hearing. This *specialised* focus on the outer world is true of other artists too: a painter sees everything like a painting; a novelist like a part of a novel; however, an actor sees it like a piece of theatre. It often manifests itself – like with the specialised inner focus mentioned above – from an early youth as a sign of a particular talent and becomes later, with the help of will and habit, a true mania that can make the artist even suffer (Flaubert).

It is necessary to count into outer experience also that which actor, especially beginning actors, receive from other, more experienced and especially excellent actors. There is little doubt that this is significant material for actors but it is also very dangerous. This material is already artistically stylised and tempts one to adopt it only in its outer form, without living it through psychologically. Nevertheless, it must not be ignored; its significance is extraordinary. Actors, like any artists, *must proceed* from a model that serves as example and encouragement. Only a weak talent drowns itself in epigonism; a strong one progresses and creates an idiosyncratic variant. That is how *acting schools* – though unofficial – are formed under the influence of an actor genius, and over the course of time, an *acting tradition*, which is an essential basis of a dramatic culture of a particular nation. The performances of a great actor cannot be fixed like the works of other artists; they perish each night and the actor's whole art disappears with their death. It can live on only through those who continue in the path set out by the actor.

Actorly motifs, acquired through either of the ways outlined here, are stored by actors in their memory. This *motoric memory* is of a very special kind as compared to the memory of perceptions of other senses, and this needs to be examined. Inner tactile perceptions, corresponding to the irritations of sensory nerves, are linked with bodily *movements and postures* that came about through the irritations of the motoric nerves. Motoric memory is after all a memory of movements, i.e., an ability to *repeat* the same movement whenever necessary; the said perceptions are only intermediaries. To remember a movement faithfully is therefore possible only through accurate repetition – *by practising* that movement. At the same time we can observe a very strange procedure: the more the movement has been practised, the more our perception of that movement recedes into the background. As if our sensory nerves have switched off more and more, leaving the activity entirely to motoric nerves – until they switch off entirely: the movement has become *automatised*. In reality, the inner tactile perception does not fall away completely; it is only *simplified to the minimum*. We can say of an automatic movement, I know *that* I have made it, I know *what* I have done, but I do not know *how* I did it.

Movement automatisation is an extremely important mechanism of our organism, showing *the principle of economy*, valid also universally in the world. By suppressing the inner tactile perception, our aware mind is relieved and given the chance to devote attention not only to the movements but also to other necessary tasks. We speak, write, etc. and think about what we are saying and writing but not how we are doing it. The same is true of acting. The inner tactile perceptions of complex physical performance become with practice merely indicative shorthands. It is justified therefore that we have called the motoric inner tactile elements *physiological*: they are such when automatised. As for the accuracy and infallibility of automatic movements, there is no need to lose words about it; it is a generally known fact.

The actorly motifs stored in the actor's memory are automatised; that means only that they are (almost) deprived of their sensory components – *"desensualised"* – but not that they lack the corresponding psychological components. Through this process, the physiological – one could say, the almost physical – becomes for the actor, a mere *token*, a *symbol* of a particular mental state or event. The sum of these tokens creates *an actor's personal technique*. Naturally it grows not only through study but also through artistic practice itself. It needs to be distinguished from "actor" technique in a general sense, which is any system of actorly motifs used for training purposes. Their motifs are conventional movement routines and the appropriate "meanings", made by flattening and schematising a former (perhaps) psychophysiological correspondence. These sets have discredited the word "technique" – not only in acting but also in other arts – so dilettantes talk of technique as something inferior, only mechanical and skill-based. A true personal technique is not skill but a substantive part of the artist's creative work; the fact that in acting – though not exclusively – it is so physical, so corporeal, cannot be taken as its weakness. It is through technique that an artistic idea is embodied because *every true artist thinks in their own material* and their *ostensive artistic ideas* are tantamount in value to any other abstract notions. Artistic ideas do not need to pad up their value by being stuffed with sublime notions; this is done only by those who fail to understand their specific value. If artistic technique is a skill, then it is a sacred skill.

> A general "actor" technique, as long as it forms a good and educationally useful system, should not be looked down upon; its value is, however, only pedagogical. Just like a beginner needs to start learning from someone, so they also need to start learning from something. In this respect, acting is at a disadvantage as compared to, for instance, the systematic training in musical performance or in dance. Even non-actorly training of the body – the actor's instrument – has a fully justified practical significance.

☙ ☙ ☙

The Actor's Creative Work. Let us turn to the description and analysis of an actor's particular creative work, i.e., to the genesis of a specific actor figure. The variety of this process is vast, not only with different actors but also with one actor in different cases. Nonetheless, certain typical *stages* can be identified here; these follow theoretically in a specific sequence but in practice, given the extent and variety of the process, individual processes may appear earlier or later and they may even intertwine.

Let us first say that a "dramatic persona" as it is given by the playwright's text (see the preceding chapter) is *the controlling idea* (*řídící představa*), a regulating force for the actor's whole creative work; nothing more but also nothing less, especially considering that the textual role is also contained in the figure's speaking.

(a) *The Preparatory Stage.* The starting point for an actor is the textual role, which needs to be memorised. From the many lines of the text the actor gets a sense not only of the expression of speaking but also the accompanying mimics as well as the way they can play it. Certainly they adopt any available playwright's instructions in the stage directions; these can be pragmatic ("aloud", "sits down") or pertaining to mood, commonly phrased figuratively ("bitterly", "as if absent-mindedly"). The psychological process is that the lines (and the directions) evoke distinct *actual* (*reálné*) psychological state that create the actor's speaking and delivery, as this diagram shows:

(I) text ⟶ actual psychological events (*děje*) ⟶ physical performance (*výkon*)

The arrows symbolise the causal relation, i.e., what causes, evokes what.

Two things are characteristic for this stage: firstly, the above physical performance (acting and delivery) correspond (to some extent) with the partial dramatic action (*děj*), but not yet the dramatic persona; and secondly, this is the actor's individual performance, i.e., they speak and play *on their own behalf*, not on behalf of the dramatic persona they are to present. This performance is more like a reciter's performance expanded by mimic display (in the broader sense). Many dilletante performances stop developing at this stage, leaving the formation of the actor figure to the mask and the costume.

(b) *Conceiving the Figure*. The desire of true actors extends to the creation of a figure that would be a picture of a particular dramatic persona. Whereupon actors start the creative act only with the *conception of static* elements that determine the figure.

> The great German actor Friedrich Mitterwurzer says on this account: "I immerse myself entirely in the poem. If it has its effect on me, I am soon overtaken by a strange state in which I can see my figures alive, palpably, in their described and undescribed manifestations – but not *before me* but *in me*. What I should be and how I should be it stands ready in its substantial forms, replenished with its emotional content, before my soul in fact at once, at a stroke. That's how I find that I can play that role."

Generally there are more of these conceptions, partly developed; like all conceptions they appear suddenly and entirely randomly over a time, illuminating like electric sparks the creative process sometimes until its very end. The above quotation suggests that they are of an *inner tactile* nature; they relate to what we have called the actor's "organic mask" – that is, the physical *"focus"*. We have previously seen that all these fixed elements of the figure correspond to particular qualities of the dramatic persona, both outer and inner. If they are to be secure, the actor need to know the *entire* text of the play, not only their role, which could lead to a mistaken conception that would later – in rehearsal – be hard to correct.

> So, for example, numerous lines suggesting anger may lead to the assumption that the dramatic persona is irritable. But that does not need to be the case – it may well be a good-natured person who is constantly faced with many causes for anger (fathers of ungrateful children!). Only when the person bursts into anger for minor reasons (e.g., Lear in the first part of the play) is it an irritable persona.
>
> Let us not assume that actors come up with their conceptions through such intellectual reflections – those are often favoured by stage directors, who then expound them to their actors unnecessarily and pointlessly, because actors work intuitively. An actor who immerses themself in their play finds it natural, for instance, to burst out

angrily after an offensive line from their onstage partner, while in the case when the script directs them to react angrily to a harmless line, they feel intuitively that they need to increase their irritability throughout, i.e., assume a "peevish" focus. If actors need some instructions for their conception, it is helpful if they are given some characterisation, even a popular one ("he is a hothead", "she keeps snarling"); that is why they welcome author's notes that are atmospheric and metaphorical rather than matter-of--fact – however surprising this may seem at first sight. Sigmund Bytkowski (in *Gerhart Hauptmanns Naturalismus und Drama*, Hamburg, 1908) is wrong when he mocks as mostly nonsensical all the plentiful and detailed descriptive directions written by dramatists; he forgets that these are not intended for the audience (the theatre audience, not the readers of the text!), but for the *actors*. He cites for instance Hauptmann's stage direction from his play *Before Dawn* (*Vor Sonnenaufgang*): "On the path from the inn to the house a dark figure becomes visible... It is Farmer Krause, who, as always, has been the last to leave the inn," and asks if one can actually see the "as always" on stage. One cannot, and yet one can: the actor who reads this "as always" knows how to be leaving better than if the dramatist gave a matter-of-fact detailed description. Conversely, factual descriptions, especially mimic, are often anathema to the actor as they may feel like it is not *their* mode of expression. Dramatists use stage directions to capture their scenic vision as completely as possible. Therefore the actor should obey these directions *without exception*, but only in the sense of their *intention* – otherwise the actor is free in carrying them out. In other words the well known rule "follow the spirit, not the letter".

Partial conceptions that govern the actor figure may pertain to the mask in the general sense of the word (e.g., a constantly gloomy face) but also in a narrower sense (such as a pointed beard), even pertain to the dress. How closely these moments correspond with the actor's physical focus has been mentioned earlier. It is also necessary to count in the conception of "actorly motifs" that characterise the persona by their frequent use.

This and other *controlling ideas* are usually *ostensive* (*názorné*) and predominantly inner tactile. This is simply "transbodiment" (*přetělesňování*). Only exceptionally can the actors see themselves in their mind's eye in some mask or dress. All partial conceptions of the figure that the actor makes in the creative time are great and joyful discoveries; however, literary theorists who require deep philosophical concepts often find them entirely "banal". It is told, for instance, that Rostand's Cyrano was born out of Coquelin's immense desire to play a role where he would be able to – twirl his moustache.

(c) *Executing the Figure*. Also the preceding phase matches the above psychological diagram (I), only assuming a static nature:

(II) text (entire) ⟶ psychological character ⟶ transbodiment (*přetělesňování*)

The farther the figure's conception progresses, the more the actor feels that the lines of the role are something very external. So actors concentrate in this phase on their figure, trying to *unify* it, follow through the figure's fixed components and *focusing* the dynamic component – the playing (*hra*; or *play*). This activity of the actor is predominantly *reflexive* but the thinking behind it is not abstract but *ostensive*, firmly rooted in its proper artistic material. We have already outlined its key principles and clearly the unification of the figure, i.e., the synthesis of partial conceptions, takes place in according to the principle of the coordination of inner tactile impulses, and its result is the actor's complete transbodiment. The focusing of the acting delivery follows the principle of the coherence of the actor figure, transposing the actor's delivery proper (from the first phase) by means of transbodiment into another, desirable key. That is not only how the prospective "dramatic persona" comes into existence but also its *personal* part of the dramatic action (*dramatický děj*), which also becomes consistent while the actor is forming their physical expression according to the principle of the externalising inner tactile impulses, and ostensively living through the action's causality. This is significantly influenced in this phase – the phase of group rehearsals – by the contribution of other actors, i.e., their figures, especially their acting and delivery (*mluva a hra*). This pertains primarily to the actor's delivery and acting that forms in response to the causal chain of action and reaction, but sometimes the actor needs to adjust the figure's conception. However, that influence is mutual and we could call it *co-adaptation*. What is created here is the actors' interplay (*spoluhra*), which gets influenced by the stage director, who makes sure that the resulting dramatic action is effectual.

> It is a good practice if actors appearing in the same play are in contact from the earliest production phases. That is why the "first readthrough after casting" is a commendable thing; the actors not only get acquainted with work itself but even more importantly with one another.

All this suggests that although this third phase is predominantly synthesising, it also has an analytical purpose in helping the *elaboration* of the actor figure, naturally within the framework of the overall conception. From the governing conceptions follow ever new details, developed through an ostensive (*názorný*) logic and enriched by other impulses from the interplay with others. Actors need to use the interplay to fill in those moments of their onstage presence when they do not lead the action and make their acting coherent (*souvislý*). It is self-evident that the *actor's technique* – in the sense outlined above – plays the foremost role here. An actor's personal technique is the most secure source of their artistic creativity and just like any true artist the actor also has the most and the best ideas when working and least in theorising.

From the psychological point of view, this phase completes the actor's mental transfiguration (*preduševnění*). The sensation of psychophysilogical correspondence between mental transfiguration and transbodiment culminates here; the overall composition of the figure deepens and refines relationship that earlier, during the mere reading of the play script, remained hidden from the actor and that now, in interplay, stand out clearly and require embodying (*ztělesnění*). The creative process in this phase takes on multiple forms and cannot be easily rendered in a single diagram – as was done in the previous cases. Thus much still holds here that the impulses for the actors' physical action stem from their *real* mental processes, whatever their origin.

(d) *Fixing the Figure*. This phase belongs in equal measure after the second as after the third phase; it is actually a conclusion of either. An actor fixes their conceptions, recording them – metaphorically speaking – in *their* memory, i.e., in their motoric memory. Just like a painter captures the colour or shape of their idea with a brush or a pencil to steady it for their next creative steps, so does the actor. An *actor's sketch* is made in an actorly material, i.e., the inner tactile one, in the actor's own body. In other words, it is a *subjective* fixity and actors achieve it through *automatisation*, as we have described in the above analysis of the actor's "technique". The painter analogy can be taken even further: the fixities of actor's inner and outer experiences described earlier are *an actor's study sketches* just like a painter or a sculptor make their study sketches: the purpose of both is to collect material for future creative work as well as train one's technical skill. Actor's *conceptual* sketches are of two kinds: an analytical one capture a particular detail, e.g., a "characteristic motif" for a particular figure, while a synthetic one fixes a particular lasting feature, especially a particular "focus".

In the same way, through automatisation, actors fix their creations, i.e., compositions and adaptations of their figure, in the accomplishing phase, developing it to perfect completion, again similar to a painter who completes their canvas on the basis of the earlier drafts. But here again the actor's "painting" is inner tactile and is "completed", i.e., automatised in their own body; it also needs to be noted that the memorisation of the lines, which we assigned to the first phase, becomes for the actor a matter of motoric memory, specifically of the *oral* one, rather than of logical memory. This specific nature of their fixity is identical in the case of actors and interpretive artists, particularly the musical ones, among whom, in part, actors and opera singers should also be counted.

> Our discussions so far make it clear why the actor's perfect technique is of such overwhelming significance for their creative work. Naturally, a new figure asks new conceptions of the actor but their fixity is all the faster, easier and more accomplished,

the more numerous and varied the actorly motifs are, obtained through the actor's personal experience and automatised by their motoric memory. This is even more true of the phase of "accomplishing the figure", where the task to memorise, i.e., to automatise the entire actor figure, command it with confidence to the last detail, is very demanding. An outstanding ability of motoric memory is a very welcome gift for an actor; however – just like in other art disciplines – it does not free this technical talent from training, but rather obliges to it. It is the most opportune condition for an *actor's scope*, i.e., the ability to create figures that are as varied, dissimilar to one another or even contending.

The most significant feature of automatisation for the actor's concrete creative work is the above-mentioned *economisation*, achieved by means of simplifying the *psychological* side of the actor's performance. Starting with the second phase, the more the fixity process of the actor figure progresses, the more the psychological moment moves into the background. We have pointed out in the first and second phases that the causal primacy is with the actor's actual psychological states, which bring about the actor's physical performance. The actor's mind is entirely overtaken by them. However, the more automatisation progresses, the more the actor's attention is *relieved*, which is the only way the actor can split their mental "I" into two: the *observing* and the *observed* one. This is a necessary condition of actors' *self-awareness*, which is essential for them to have. This splitting and to some extent even a mutual alienation of both the parts of the actor's mind is the most demanding process and is made possible by the fact that the observing I is the actor's own self, while the observed I is mentally transfigured and in that way already relatively alienated. On the other hand, the progressing fixity makes the actor's actual psychological states, practically speaking, redundant as agents of creation; and once the fixity is complete, which generally coincides in standard conditions with the dress rehearsal, they can be abandoned altogether. This is the state achieved by a *virtuoso actor* who usually limits his or her repertoire to several excellent roles. The psychological schema corresponding to this is actually not psychological but is very simple: bodily (automatic) reproduction.

(e) *The Finalised Performance*. Leaving aside the difference between objective and subjective fixity made it possible to draw a parallel between the creative work of an actor and a painter. Both operate with study sketches, concept sketches and eventually with the final fixity of the artwork. This is where the parallel needs to end and a basic difference appears between the plastic artwork as non-temporal and the actorly temporal artwork. When a painter finalises a painting, their work as a creative artist is finished; it is the painting that is sent to be exhibited, not the painter. The actor, on finalising the fixity of the figure through automatisation, needs to send him- or herself onstage because the actor figure is not only inside but needs to be lived out both in space as well as in time. In this the actor resembles the composer who, having composed a piano piece, for instance, goes onstage to perform it. From the first part of this book we know that the composer is in such a case (but not inevitably!) the interpretive artist to themselves. The same is true of the actor in this final phase, which generally starts with the opening night of the production: on completing the fixity of the figure the actor is *their own reproductive artist* – but in this case inevitably, just like a dancer because they lack a special notation that could sufficiently fix their artwork objectively, i.e., for others.

Tairov is therefore mistaken in assuming that an actor must create whenever it is needed, and that in a timely fashion – today from seven to ten – and not when they would like themself. In course of the above four phases of the actor's creative work, the actor prepares, conceives, accomplishes (subjectively) and fix their artwork. In the fifth phase, the actor actually becomes an reproductive artist – to themself; with a view to the analysis of the reproductive art (*výkonné umění*) we are not going to say that the actor merely reproduces their artwork but *finalises it* in its rationally automatised form *by means of irational nuances*. Where does this source spring from? From the actor's bodily performance.

We have repeatedly referred to the mysterious link between a person's psychological state and their bodily expression. I have also pointed out the James-Lange theory opposes the common belief that emotions are the cause of the expression: an expression is the cause of emotions, since the perception of such a bodily expression is an emotion. This is a hypothesis; the only fact is that the process of perceiving makes a bodily performance evoke the corresponding emotion in a measure that is especially conspicuous when it relates to perceiving *one's own self*. Try this, for instance, in a state of complete serenity: wrinkle your forehead, cry out, start waving your arms, stamp your feet! You will feel immediately how our consciousness is entered by something like *anger*. This is not actual, real anger, only a phantom or a shadow; at the same time, it not entirely unreal and imaginary because we actually experience it, although it is only in a hint, in a kind of transposition to an imaginary world. It is difficult to find the right name. It is not a "seeming emotion" because we actually feel it. It is supported by actual inner tactile perceptions that stem from our performance and they hover above them as a kind of reflection. The difference between a "true" emotion and this one is roughly such that between perceptions and our imaginations, a difference that is minimal or non at all when it comes to bodily impressions. Let us call such emotions and the psychological states formed in this way *imaginary*. The process that gives rise to them is clearly *autosuggestion*. Similar psychological states felt by the audience are the result of suggestion from the actor's performance, internally imitated by the spectators.

Actors who are ready for their performance with their artwork perfectly fixed are, as we have seen, psychologically so relieved and freed that they can be not only a critical observer of themselves, i.e., their "figure", but they are also free to choose when and how to *empathise into* their bodily performance and so rouse in themselves the above-mentioned imaginary psychological states. These imaginary states, which substitute the earlier, real states that were subdued through automatisation, *function* similarly like they did: naturally they cause only *minor changes* in the actor's bodily performance – mere irrational nuances that would be too subtle for the actor to fix; they are just momentary *improvisations*. Nevertheless, as is true of all reproductive art, which we have called "the art of nuances", these minor shades have an overwhelming impact on the audience, because we can feel in them the soulfulness (*oduševnělost*) of the actor's performance. The psychological schema of this final phase of an actor's creative work is this:

(III) (autom.) bodily performance ⟶ imag. psychological states ⟶ improv. performance nuances

One of the popular questions of actor theory since the 18th century has been: should the performing actor be "in the role", or "above the role"? It was Lessing (in his *Hamburg Dramaturgy*) who resolved it fully in the above sense: "I should say that if the actor is able to imitate all outer signs and expressions, all the transformations of the body of which he has learned from experience that they express something psychological, then the impression created by the senses brings his soul to a state that corresponds to his movements, postures and habits. To learn this in a manner that is to some extent mechanical but based on certain unchanging principles, is the only and true way for an actor to study."[22] Our discussion and diagram make it clear that an actor needs be in that typical split of the mind not only sufficiently distant from their figure to be able to control it but also sufficiently connected to it so that the figure can overwhelm the actor's mind and bring about a certain secondary, derived soulfulness. The intensity of the overwhelming nature of this depends not only on the actor's sensitivity but also on the momentary dispositions. For that reason the individual shows of a production run are very different in this respect, some of them even better than the opening night, some notably worse, although the actors' performance stays roughly the same. It depends on what actors call "the mood". Sometimes they "get into the mood" before entering the stage, sometimes later and sometimes never at all. The mood in the auditorium contributes to this significantly – just like a given actor figure, even when it is

---

22 Osolsobě and Procházka point out in their Czech edition (1986) that such a passage can't be found in Lessing but the ideas agree with Lessing's Essay No. 3 of *Hamburg Dramaturgy*. However, we have to concede that we were unable to identify the exact passage. Just like in his quotation from Diderot above, Zich is paraphrasing.

dramatically good. An actor may cling to some, while find no friendly way to others – just like with people.

Actor types from a psychological point of view follow from the above description of the actor's creative work and they have been touched upon there too. A dilettante actor who makes do with the phase (a) is the extreme type of the *emotional* type, creating only on the basis of real emotions. A virtuoso actor who ends with the phase (d) is, on the contrary, a purely *intellectual* type – in the sense of the ostensive (*názorný*), i.e., inner tactile reflection. Between these two extremes stands the actor artist as the *mixed* type, who uses the imaginary, artificial emotions for the final phase. On the basis of the *"actor's scope"* we can formulate the *universal* type, who is able to deliver figures that are very diverse; it has to be emphasised that this is not only in the rich ability of mental transfiguration but also – even primarily – in the wide-ranging ability of transbodiment. That is why an actor's repertoire changes at least partly with age (but even an older actor can play younger figures!) and that is the much more frequent type is the *specialist*, who limits themself to a narrower range of figures of a kind. However, it is not necessary (although it is quite common) that these figures are of the same kind as the actor him- or herself: it is well-known for instance that the greatest comic actors generally are not people of a cheerful nature and amusing behaviour in society. It has to be stressed that actors of *either* kind can be artistically outstanding; after all, the differences in the actor's scope are continuous, so for instance, the above special type of comic actor can also cover a range of other very different figures.

The classification of actor figures would be an equally thankful task as the parallel classification of dramatic personas, which would agree in a number of points but would not match, since the classifying criteria would be different, not based on referential images, but on technical ones. So for instance, figures can be divided according to the actorly focus into all-round and one-sided, which only roughly corresponds with main and side personas (a division on the basis of the personas' significance) and rather more with personas that are "fully fledged" and only "sketched", appearing in episodic roles that can be acted by the actor with only one, but distinctive focus. The famous "masks" of the commedia dell'arte are in fact types of actor figures, not of personas, since each of them is defined by a set mask and costume but is able to represent very different dramatic personas. Of great interest is the relation between a *particular* dramatic persona, e.g., Hamlet, and the actor figures that different actors make of this role. This richness of meaning (in which is also the appeal of "new casting") is a consequence of the fragmentary textual fixity; it is not a weakness but rather an asset of good dramatic works. Those are then the famous types of dramatic personas that live in thousands of shapes a truly immortal life.

6 DRAMATIC ACTION: THE STAGE DIRECTOR'S FIRST TASK

What is *principal* for a dramatic work? Is it dramatic personas (*osoby*), or dramatic plot (*děj*)? This long-lasting dispute among literary theorists is characteristic of a "literary" approach to drama placing it as "dramatic literature" *alongside* narrative literature and trying to locate the difference in the primacy of either the personas, or the plot, because narrative fiction (a novel, novella or a short story) also includes characters and a plot. It was assumed in the past that plot was primary in fiction and characters secondary, while in drama was dominated by personas – or *characters*, as they are often called. The plot is there merely to manifest personas' activities, which is what makes them "dramatic" in the first place; the plot is therefore only a means to an end. Recent theorists have adopted the opposite view: personas are crucial for narrative fiction, plot for drama. This shift was surely prompted by changes in the nature of modern narrative literature, i.e., the novel, which has been mainly concerned with the psychological analysis of its characters while often neglecting the outer plot, as well as developments in modern drama, which mostly lacks "heroes". What has also been decisive was the generally accepted formula that the essence of drama is *struggle*; in this view, drama's task is to present the plot as a struggle between two conflicting sides and its personas are just a means to this end.

The very existence of *both* these *opposing* views (and, we must add, both are partially justified) shows that this is not the way to determine the difference between narrative fiction and drama. As we know already, the difference between them is in their essence: they are two different arts and to compare one to a *part* of the other is a fundamental error. Fiction and drama differ noetically, i.e., by the form of their existence – the form in which they present their materials to us. Clearly, a novel can also contain characters in the dramatic sense and a plot as a struggle – but these characters are only described there and the plot is only narrated, whereas in drama, personas are presented and the plot (*děj*) performed. This *basic* difference leads to all other differences as its secondary derivations.

The central concept of the dramatic art is *human action* (*jednání*), which we have defined as a persona's action that aims to and does have an effect on another person. The requirement for drama to include action is not only a necessary condition, but it is also a sufficient one; in principle, this is what fully captures the content of drama. Surely, narrative fiction can also include action (*jednání*), but there it is only accessory, not necessary. A novel may also describe persons that (or when) do not interact with each other, and may tell stories that do not result from interactions between "characters" – and none of this will harm the novel's essence. This is why "characters" and "plots" in narrative fiction are much more autonomous and independent of each other than "characters" and "plots" in drama. Let us not be deluded by the sameness of the words! There are no characters in drama but dramatic characters (personas) and plots in drama are dramatic plots – and this special quality is down to action (*jednání*). Both these elements of a dramatic work are so linked together by the attribute of "action" that as concepts they are *interrelated* (*souvztažné*), i.e., one cannot exist without the other. Dramatic personas are those that interact with others; and it is this interaction of theirs that constitutes dramatic action itself. One could object that even in drama there are sometimes personas that do not act and plots (*děj*) that do not result entirely from interaction (*jednání*). This is true, but all such instances are undramatic. Naturally, artistic *practice* brings us works that are more dramatic or less so. A theory must be derived from the entirely dramatic ones.

Let us now turn to the analysis of dramatic action and primarily to a psychological analysis of *human action* (*jednání*) as its basis, always bearing in mind that we are dealing with dramatic action that is presented, that is to say: ostensive. What is ostensive about it is only its underlying material, perceived by us as the audience: speaking, behaviour and actions of the personas, who also present themselves to us ostensively through their physical appearance. This is accompanied by our own interpretation of this perception: *the referential image* (*obrazová představa*), which reveals meanings and emotions of the whole, thus disclosing the inner side of the outer dramatic action. How is this image of the dramatic action (*děj*) – associated with said perception – evoked in us as the audience?

PERSONAL ACTION

Following up on the previous chapter, let us first analyse "*personal action*" (*jednání*) – that is, the mental process of a persona that acts towards another persona. This first persona (I) is active, while the second persona (II) is passive for us, at least at this point – or rather, seemingly passive because we are not concerned with their activity yet. Personal action can be illustrated in this diagram:

$$I \longrightarrow II$$

It is a one-way relation that comes *from* I and aims *towards* II; it is also asymmetrical because it cannot be reversed: action of I towards II is not the same as action of II towards I.

Let us remember that according to our definition, Persona I's action could not only be a deed but also behaviour and speech, as long as Persona I aims to and does have effect on Persona II; and we must ask, what is the cause of Persona I's action? A *direct* cause or an *incentive* (*motif*) of action is always an *emotion*; the *aspiration* (*snaha*) associated with the emotion is only its motor reflex, and already its focus on another persona constitutes action, though a rudimentary one that only needs evolve to be observable to others. A mental image or thought is very often a *secondary* cause, but it always must be emotionally tinted. What is called "cold action" is also motivated by emotions but ones that are externally subpressed – which is not to say that they must therefore be any weaker than an externally apparent passion (for example hate as opposed to anger). If in contrast, the mental image in question is unaware, the action is impulsive or instinctive – as is common in plays. An image is often associated both with an emotion and with an aspiration; it is the image of an object the aspiration aims to, and of an effect that the action should cause: that it the *purpose* (or *objective*) of the action. An aspiration that is aware of its purpose is called *will*, and action resulting from it is intentional as opposed to spontaneous, which has no conscious objective.

Intentional action, controlled by will, is the most advanced kind of personal action and it rightly plays the greatest part in dramatic works. It may involve a very rich and complex mental image or idea of purpose, comprising the various means to be used to reach the objective or even means that will serve the persona as interim milestones towards an ultimate goal. The psychology of a fully conscious action can be illustrated by the following diagram:

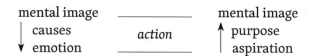

Both referential images, quite complex in themselves, merge into one whole, which is the *intellectual* aspect of the action that is carried on by the *emotional* component, made of emotions and aspirations. Even the mental image of the purpose itself, which anticipates the desired effect of the action, must always appeal to emotions – otherwise the persona would not act in that way; that image thus becomes a secondary motivation of the action, superseding the original motive. So, for example, someone's offence provokes a persona's anger and the aspiration to take revenge; the idea (the image) of this "sweet" revenge nourishes the entire action that follows. The summative image, no matter how complex, always contains a central idea that is of utmost importance to the acting persona. We will call the core of this summative image "*the idea of personal action*" – that is to say, the actual idea, since there can also be an idea that the persona only pretends to have; or even a false idea, if the acting persona is mistaken about it. The principle of dramatic truthfulness requires that the dramatist's concept as well as the actor's delivery should make *obvious the true* idea of the personal action to the audience; as for the pretended or false ideas, the dramatic persona will tell us, the audience, always enough about them.

We will not analyse in greater detail the intellectual side of a will-controlled action, which is often so complex in drama – think of the intrigues in many comedies – that the audience finds it hard to find their way through the maze of such "intricate" action with concealed or pretended motivations, with seemingly innocent means ("ruses"), and with secret or planted motives. It is characteristic of all such actions that the said summative mental image, in which the acting persona is becoming aware of the cause and purpose of their actions, reveals to us, the audience, the *"cause-and-objective nexus"* (or *"causal nexus"; kauzálně finální nexus*) of personal action, namely of the *inner* kind, pertaining to the acting persona. However, such *intellectual* explanation of the nexus, which answers the questions, "Why this action?" and "To what purpose?" cannot in itself satisfy us as the audience. We need to experience the nexus ourselves by *mentally transfiguring into* (empathising with) *the dramatic persona* in question. The actor's task is to carry us away by their suggestive performance and bring about this mental transfiguration. Only then do we "grasp" the persona's action no matter how incomprehensible it could have been on the outside – the actor has convinced us about it.

> The necessity of this "mental transfiguration" becomes all the more evident in cases, which are not at all infrequent, where the intellectual component is insignificant in a dramatic persona's actions. A persona acts based on emotions and aspirations, but is unaware of why or what for, or both. Such action is instinctive, springing from a deep physiological root of the personality and relates to impulsive actions or actions coming from acquired and habitual fervours and so on. Often these are actions where it makes no sense to ask, "To what end?", and where it is also rather hard to find an answer to the question "Why?". And yet, even if the personal action had no purpose, it surely always had a cause, and we, as the audience, must understand this inner causal nexus. Since the dramatic persona is not conscious of it, since it lacks the intellectual explanation, we can only experience or live through this causal nexus, and that not as ourselves but only by means of perfect mental transfiguration into the dramatic persona. We have to be transfigured so perfectly that we even see other dramatic personas through this persona's eyes. Many examples of actions that are difficult to grasp intellectually, often pathological cases, can be found in Ibsen (Brack in Ibsen's *Hedda Gabler*: "Good God! – people don't do such things!").

We call the actions that lack the intellectual component *immediate* (*bezprostřední*) – often, they are little more than mere reflexes. To them and to the *conscious* actions may be added a third important class: *split* actions characterised by an inner conflict between the intellectual and emotional components – or, as is often said, a conflict between reason and passion. Strictly speaking, it is a conflict between two emotions because the idea that stands against emotions must also be rooted in an emotion, albeit of a different kind; the aspirations resulting in the two opposing emotions go different ways. This split, dual mental state might be called a "struggle" in a figurative sense; however, it is not in itself dramatic in the same way as a "struggle" between two personas. It only becomes a true struggle when it materialises in action towards other personas. If the intellectual or emotional motive won, it would not differ from the previous cases. Its specific feature is that once one of them wins (i.e., it results in certain action), the other wins another time, so the action is random or even indecisive and hesitant.

> Shakespeare's Hamlet is the classic example of this. Modern drama is full of characters suffering from an inner conflict and falling under the weight of irresolution. As for modern playwrights, they are clearly in favour of emotional or, let us say, "natural" action; they consider the opposite, intellectual action, a capital lie, which eventually leads either to a persona's ruin (Ibsen) or to their merciless or even burlesque unmasking (Shaw).

INTERACTION OF TWO PERSONAS

Personal action is a one-sided relation between *two* personas. It follows from here that in interaction there are generally *two* actions going on between these two personas – i.e., the action of Persona I towards Persona II, and the action of Persona II towards Persona I:

These two actions *differ* from each other although the two personas involved are the same. Yet the actions are not alien to one another; after all, they involve personas (that is, psychological organisms) that are not only aware of their own but also the other persona's actions. Persona I's actions towards Persona II are, in part at least, the cause of Persona II' actions towards I, and vice versa. Thus, both personas have a *shared idea* of action, no matter how differently they reacted to it based on their own interests. We will call this interlocked couple of personal actions *interaction* (*vzájemné jednání*); it is clearly the *ultimate elementary type* of interaction, and thus also of dramatic action. Let us also point out that this element, when it comes to the dramatic text, is called *the dialogue*; here we comprise in it not only the words and speaking but also the acting of both actors.

If one were to take Persona I's activity as an action, we must ask what is Persona II's response to it – that is to say, what II's reaction to I's action is. If we disregard the option of complete passive inaction, which is rare in drama, there are three types that can be distinguished.

First, Persona II *submits* to Persona I's action, so its action by way of response (or a change or discontinuation of previous action) is, as for its purpose, identical to Persona I's. Depending on the hierarchy between the two personas, Persona II either becomes an executor of Persona I's will (e.g., master and servant) or their ally. Their interaction turns into joint action and the two dramatic personas become in fact a single persona – a collective dramatic persona – in regards to *this particular* idea-motivated action. From the point of view of its dramatic effect, this type of interaction is the least intensive one.

Second, Persona II *resists* Persona I's action, unwilling to act accordingly or stop their own course of actions (e.g., Antigone and Creon). This generally intensifies Persona I's subsequent actions, and often also Persona II's resistance. This type is therefore more intensive regarding its dramatic effect, and it may reach a climax, where Persona II is either forced to submit to Persona I, or is defeated, provided Persona I does not abandon their intention.

The third type is the most explicit: Persona II responds to Persona I's action with their own action aimed against it, but this action is in itself autonomous. It clearly is goaded as a reaction to the other persona's action, but this is true of both actions. This is a true *conflict* or *struggle* between two opponents over an issue, and it can only be resolved by *one side's* defeat – whether with a tragic or comic effect. It is understandable that the dramatic effect of this type is very intensive, although not necessarily greater than the previous type – which, after all, often fluently turns into it. "Struggle" (or conflict) is by no means a general formula of dramatic action (*děj*), but merely a special case, and any generalisation of its specific features (the two personas' equivalence, a symmetrical interaction, etc.) for the dramatic structure as such (e.g., in having an exclusively dichotomous and symmetrical arrangement of characters in *every* drama) is dogmatic and speculative.

On the other hand, the first type of interaction, where Persona I's and II's actions are in agreement, cannot *in itself* constitute dramatic action and plot because from a dramatic point of view – i.e., in regards to this interaction – the two personas in fact make up a single collective dramatic persona. Their joint action becomes a collective personal action, which may have dramatic significance only when it relates to a third persona – but this persona must not submit to it, interacting either according to the second or the third types above. We may therefore reformulate in more detail the *principle of the collective nature of a dramatic work*, outlined in the first part of his book: *For a dramatic action, at least two autonomously interacting personas are needed.* To reach a full agreement in the personas' action therefore means the end of dramatic action and thus of the dramatic work.

We have identified the relation of the two personal actions in interaction as action and reaction. This is a new causal bond, distinct from the above cause-and-objective nexus that occurs within a single persona's mind, may be called the *outer causal nexus* (*kauzální nexus vnější*). Such relationship is only rarely exclusively physical, for example when a persona coerces another to do something by force or prevents them violently from doing it, such as when killing them, an action very prominent in drama. Usually it pertains understandably to *both* personas' minds, as the cause of the action is in one, and the effect in the other. Although the action originates with one of the personas, it exists somehow *between them*, being observable, i.e., objective, for both the personas – and also for the audience. At the same time, the effect of the action in the other persona's mind is at least a partial cause of their own action. For that reason it would be simpler to call this whole inner-outer nexus *pragmatic*. Directly – i.e., ostensively (*názorně*)– this is actually available to us (as the audience) only in the *ostensive* action, such as language, behaviour or deeds; however, the causal bond resides within the minds of the one and the other persona. This explains why the purpose of a persona's action does not necessarily need to agree with the effect it has on the other persona. The action is successful at one time but unsuccessful at another; on another occasion, it may even go amiss when the effect the action actually has on the other persona is not the intended one but entirely different and unexpected one.

It follows that as the audience we should empathise with both the interacting personas and we should do so fully, by mental transfiguration, in order to understand the bond between the two personal actions. Although the transfiguration is usually partial – becoming empathetic with that particular feature of a persona that plays out in a given situation – a complete mental transfiguration into both personas is impossible at once (e.g., one of them irritable, the other timid) and it can only be done in turn. We usually empathise with the persona that leads the interaction at a given moment and we judge the other persona through their eyes; at other times, it can also be the defeated persona. All this also depends of course on our sympathies – some spectators experience a whole play along with "their" chosen persona – and especially on the mesmerising force of a particular actor's performance. In fact, the former attitude is actually unartistic, subjectively human, while the latter may become unartistic if the actor egotistically asserts themself throughout, even when they should make room for others. Therefore each long dramatic scene should be conceived by the playwright and performed by actors in such a way that its weight does not rest with one and the same persona the whole time, but takes turns in shifting from one to another, which spontaneously leads the viewer to shift their attention, and so their experience, to one or another persona in turn.

☙ ☙ ☙

The Dramatic Relation. The mutual *relation of personas* in a drama is not limited to their interaction, although that is their basic relation as it is constitutive of dramatic action (and plot). Besides this *dynamic* relation of characters, there are also other relations, of a *static* kind; out of these, the only ones relevant for drama are those that are in a causal relation to action – either through causing, or through being caused by, this action. *A sum of personal relations, which are action, a cause of action or an effect of action, shall be called a dramatic relation* – and that of an *elementary* kind when it is a relation of *two personas*, and of a *complex* kind when it involves *more than two* personas.

> A particular dramatic work determines which *static* personal relations will be included in the dramatic relations of two personas – not any possible relation but only such that are a causal nexus with the action in any given case. The best known and most common of them is amorous passion aroused by another persona's physical appearance. Like other static relations, it often becomes the *initial cause* of personas' interaction. An example of this is the beginning of Romeo and Juliet's tragedy, where this relation is moreover reciprocal, and all their actions that follow spring from here. A similar case, though only one-sided, is Mortimer's relation to Mary Stuart in Friedrich Schiller's tragedy. In comparison, Mary Stuart's beauty leaves Mortimer's uncle Paulet cold, and thus it plays no role in their dramatic relation. It gains prominence only later in the relation between Queen Mary Stuart and Queen Elizabeth in exactly the opposite way – in their hatred. It is clearly not the objective physical appearance or manner of speaking or behaviour (unless the latter two are seen as action in themselves, which we leave aside in this case), but rather a subjective impression that these aspects of one persona evoke in another. What is at play here is the both the image of the persona and the emotions and aspirations evoked by that image. Understandably, the emotions and aspirations associated with the persona's image manifest themselves on the outside and are directed towards *that objective persona*: this could be the love or the hatred towards them, desiring after them, etc. We shall call this important static relation between two personas' *viewpoint* (this term may seem somewhat too sober for personal relations between characters, but at least it is general). Rather, it should be *"personal viewpoint"*, analogous to "personal action", for it is also a unilateral and asymmetrical relation. Persona I's viewpoint of (though I would prefer "towards") Persona II can be illustrated in this diagram:
>
> I ⟶ II
>
> Its complement is Persona II's viewpoint of Persona I, which gives us a complete, two-way relation of *"mutual viewpoint"*:
>
> I ⇌ II

It needs to be stressed that this "viewpoint" is our own image, which we project into personas' minds on the basis of our own life experiences; as such, it is a referential image (*obrazová představa*) based on our perception of the stage. (There is no need to point out that this viewpoint does not objectively exist, since it is a fictional dramatic action (*děj*) represented by actors). A persona's viewpoint of another persona is *for us* the main (though not the only) *cause* of their action towards that other persona, but also, conversely, an *effect* of the latter persona's action toward the former (though not exclusively of that action, of course), since the effect of an action does not always have to manifest itself in an active reaction, at least not immediately.

It is certainly very strange that all we perceive directly from the stage we interpret with the help of something that is not directly presented to our senses, but what we only imagine, and that entirely *on the basis* of what is ostensive – and these perceptions are therefore psychologically primary. In a simple reading of a text, which lacks the ostensive perception, the true relation between the two components – the ostensive and the imaginary – does not become sufficiently evident to be thoroughly appreciated. This is different at a theatre performance: everyone will agree based on their experiences that the *ostensive perceptions are* clearly *primary* here. It is therefore necessary to point out another static relation between personas, which is ostensive in its nature. It is a persona's language, behaviour and even deeds towards another persona that does *not constitute actions* directed at them; in other words, when these are not motivated by an aspiration to affect the other persona. Let us call this summatively *"behaviour"* (*chování*), which may certainly be used for "innocent" dialogue (e.g., light conversation) or insignificant deeds (e.g., social niceties). What has been said about "viewpoint" also applies to this relation: "*personal* behaviour" is a unilateral, asymmetrical relation (Persona I's behaviour towards Persona II), while "*mutual* behaviour" is a two-way relation; the diagrams illustrating it would be the same as above. Let us not forget that a persona's behaviour is ostensive both to us as well as, we may assume, to the persona towards whom the former persona behaves. Its interpretation is therefore also our referential image (*obrazová představa*).

Types *of the Dramatic Relations.* For those reducing dramatic action to "struggle" (or conflict), the types of dramatic relations are very simple. Any two personas in a drama are either *antagonists* or *allies* in one and the same cause, which may eventually produce two groups of allies who struggle in a conflict against one another. We have said already that this desire for symmetry of a dramatic relation is dogmatic. Dramatic literature brings ample evidence showing that besides the relations of mutual opponents and allies, asymmetric relations are very frequent: for instance, someone has a friend who sees them as their enemy. Take for example Othello and Iago: Iago is Othello's enemy all the time, while Othello see Iago as his friend until the final discovery. Depending on the *viewpoint* (and there also on the action), there are three dramatic relations; in the diagram, a friendly viewpoint is symbolised by *f*; an enemy viewpoint by *e*:

$$I \xrightleftharpoons[f]{f} II \qquad I \xrightleftharpoons[e]{e} II \qquad I \xrightleftharpoons[n]{f} II$$

Clearly, this is only a very rough distinction, for there are various degrees of friendly and inimical viewpoints in drama, from ardent love and hatred to moderate sympathy or antipathy. If we refer to the the lowest degree, which is neither friendship nor enmity, as "indifference" (which of course does not preclude action), symbolising as i, we would get three more relations: one symmetrical and two asymmetrical:

$$I \xrightleftharpoons[i]{i} II \qquad I \xrightleftharpoons[i]{e} II \qquad I \xrightleftharpoons[i]{f} II$$

Yet another differentiation is necessary. The above example of Iago's relation to Othello shows that one may view another as an enemy, but behave as a friend. Such personal dramatic relation contains a contradiction between how a persona ostensively (visually and auditively) appears, and what the persona "truly" is – a well-known motif of dissembling. Let us point out that the above asymmetrical relation between two personas is not actually conditioned by dissembling – for example, in the relation between Othello and Desdemona in the final act, Othello is inimical both in viewpoint and behaviour, while Desdemona is friendly towards him. If we bring into our diagram of the personal (i.e., one-way) dramatic relation of *both* the aspects – viewpoint and behaviour – we will get two personal types: an "open" personal type when both aspects agree; and a "secret" personal type when they contradict one another. In other words, on the basis of how they *appear* (not what truly *are*), we will get a "manifest" type and a "seeming" type. The diagram below employs a double arrow, where the first half symbolises a persona's viewpoint, the latter their behaviour towards the other persona:

$$\text{open, mutually manifest} \begin{cases} \text{enemy } I \xrightarrow{e} \xrightarrow{e} II \\ \text{friend } I \xrightarrow{f} \xrightarrow{f} II \end{cases}$$

$$\text{secret} \begin{cases} \text{enemy} \\ \text{friend} \end{cases} \text{mutually seeming} \begin{cases} \text{friend } I \xrightarrow{e} \xrightarrow{f} II \\ \text{enemy } I \xrightarrow{f} \xrightarrow{e} II \end{cases}$$

As far as "indifference" is concerned, its manifestation in behaviour means "usual behaviour", and this aspect does not add anything substantial to the above four types. This is because a persona's "indifferent viewpoint" of another persona means that their "friendly" or "inimical" behaviour towards them becomes merely smooth or rough behaviour, respectively; as such it contributes to the persona's characteristic rather than to their relationship to the persona (unless, of course, it turns into action). As for indifferent behaviour, a secret enemy's or a friend's "seemingly indifferent behaviour" is, in a way, a "weakened" variant of the third and fourth type, respectively – or it can also be viewed as a repressed variant of the first and second type (repressed by convention or the persona's character).

It is evident that the first two types as well as the third (and especially that one) are extremely frequent in dramatic works. The fourth type can also be found quite often, as in Petruchio's relation to Katherine in *The Taming of the Shrew* or Don Cesar's relation to Donna Diana in Moreto's play[23]. This type is more varied and psychologically more interesting than the third type. The egotistic instinct compels one to appear friendly to others. It is therefore natural to purposely mask one's hostile viewpoint by friendly behaviour; however, the opposite is not natural and needs a specific and intricate justification. Nonetheless, there are numerous instances of this type, where hostile behaviour is not dissembling but rather a reaction to the other persona's unpleasant action; but the persona's friendly viewpoint moderates their reaction, so they are content only to react with hostile behaviour. Examples can be see in the well-known dramatic relation of the good-natured father to his good-for-nothing son, of the testy wife to her weakling husband or of the kind-hearted master to his rogue servant – mostly motifs popular in comedy because they do not develop into serious action. What is more, such hostile behaviour can be actually a twisted manifestation of unacknowledged sympathies, as in the relation between Benedict and Beatrice in *Much Ado about Nothing*. It is only when the other persona's action becomes too nasty – whether actually or seemingly – that the persona's viewpoint changes, becoming inimical; more commonly, it only *splits*: the most common motif in this instance is jealousy. Such split viewpoint of the other persona cannot be found with the other types; as such, they could be considered developmental variants of this fourth type.

Let us take the four personal relations and combine them in pairs into mutual dramatic relations. This will give ten different cases, four of them symmetric:

$$\text{I} \xrightleftharpoons[e]{e} \xrightleftharpoons[e]{e} \text{II}$$

(1) mutually manifest enemies

$$\text{I} \xrightleftharpoons[f]{f} \xrightleftharpoons[f]{f} \text{II}$$

(2) mutually manifest friends

$$\text{I} \xrightleftharpoons[f]{e} \xrightleftharpoons[e]{f} \text{II}$$

(3) mutually seeming friends

$$\text{I} \xrightleftharpoons[e]{f} \xrightleftharpoons[f]{e} \text{II}$$

(4) mutually seeming enemies

---

23   Agustín Moreto y Cavana's Spanish Golden Age comedy *El desdén, con el desdén* (Disdain Upon Disdain) was adapted in 1816 by the Viennese playwright Carl August West under the name *Donna Diana*. The titular Diana is proud of her great learning and dismissive of any advances. Don Cesar (who is called Don Carlos in Moreto) adopts her strategy as a countermeasure: haughty disdain. West's adaptation was popular throughout the nineteenth century and was produced also at the National Theatre in Prague in Czech (in 1885).

The remaining six case are asymmetric:

$$I \underset{f}{\overset{e}{\rightleftarrows}} \underset{f}{\overset{e}{\rightleftarrows}} II \qquad I \underset{f}{\overset{e}{\rightleftarrows}} \underset{e}{\overset{e}{\rightleftarrows}} II$$

(5) manifest enemy – manifest friend   (6) manifest enemy – seeming friend

$$I \underset{e}{\overset{e}{\rightleftarrows}} \underset{f}{\overset{e}{\rightleftarrows}} II \qquad I \underset{f}{\overset{f}{\rightleftarrows}} \underset{e}{\overset{f}{\rightleftarrows}} II$$

(7) manifest enemy – seeming enemy   (8) manifest friend – seeming enemy

$$I \underset{e}{\overset{f}{\rightleftarrows}} \underset{f}{\overset{f}{\rightleftarrows}} II \qquad I \underset{e}{\overset{e}{\rightleftarrows}} \underset{f}{\overset{f}{\rightleftarrows}} II$$

(9) manifest friend – seeming enemy i (10) seeming friend – seeming enemy

I have used the names above on the basis of how these relations ostensively appear to us, but what they "truly" are (in our thinking).

We can add the personal type of "indifferent viewpoint, any behaviour", which will give us the following diagram:

$$I \xrightarrow{\quad i \quad} \xrightarrow{\quad i \quad} II$$

This would give us another symmetrical relation, i.e., mutually indifferent viewpoints, which is common in drama but dramatically unimportant, and another four asymmetrical relations of much greater dramatic importance, which can be easily added to the list. The total number of relations will come up to 15.

Examples of *all* the stated types of mutual dramatic relations can be found in dramatic works – or it would be more accurate to say, in individual scenes as a particular relation hardly goes unchanged during a play. True, some of these types are more frequent than others. That depends not only on how psychologically natural they are, which of course differs for each type, but also on how interesting and dramatically productive individual types are. After all, each of these theoretical types is only roughly outlined above and in practice has has so many varieties and nuances in regards to their intensity and the quality of the "friendship" or "enmity", as well as such a variety of motivation for behaviour in those instances where behaviour does not correspond with the viewpoint, that a particular instance may easily belong to more than one type. The most common types are 1, 2 and 8, of course (the schemer!); type 3 is also quite common (e.g., two enemy diplomats, such as in Eugène Scribe's comedy *Le verre d'eau*[24]). Masking one's hostile viewpoint in type 6 is usually a "ruse" or a "stratagem" or may even come from fear; it applies to a relation of someone weaker to someone stronger.

---

24 *The Glass of Water: or, Effects and Causes* is an 1840 five-act comedy by the French dramatist Eugène Scribe (1791–1861). It is set at the court of Queen Anne of Great Britain during the early eighteenth century. The play is a prime example of a well-made play or *la pièce bien faite*.

In type 10, which is similar, it often comes from greed. In contrast, type 4, seeming enemies of one another, requires personas who are more or less equal: quarrelling couples, friends or lovers who have fallen out, and similar pairs that are especially suitable for comedy. It is understandable that this relation may easily slip into type 7, when one of the couple starts "taking it in earnest" – with *The Taming of the Shrew* offering a good example. In contrast, type 9 offers a certain "tragic comedy", with one side openly friendly: persisting suitors (as well as husbands) are an example and *The Midsummer Night's Dream* makes a masterful use of this type. Yet again, it is difficult to determine when this type slips into type 5 – the least natural of all the dramatic relations, in which an open enemy stands against an open friend, e.g., a despised lover. Do examples of jealousy, such as that of Othello and Desdemona towards the end of the tragedy, belong here? An example of sorts is the relation between Mína and Uhlíř (after his arrival) in Jaroslav Hilbert's *Guilt* (*Vina*)[25]. This type is in principle purely tragic and does not last long in a drama: it is either set right (if a mistake has occured!) or it breaks.

A principal feature of a dramatic relation is that it generally *changes* with the *course of time* of the dramatic action (*děj*), which is causes these changes. This is a specific feature of the dramatic art as temporal art, which is further enhanced by the fact that in drama – unlike in narrative literature – the dramatic relation itself as well as its change are made ostensively clear to us.

It is very rare that all personal relations in a drama remain unchanged, in their kind at least – that is, keeping within one of the above types. Sophocles' *Electra* is one such example. In those instances relations among the main personas change in their intensity, both in the viewpoints and in the behaviours of both sides. As mentioned in the above analysis of action, there is a whole scale of tension and agitation manifest in speech and behaviour, and *culminating in a deed* – if it ever comes to a deed, especially with personas with an inner conflict.

Direct ostensive deeds aimed at the other persona can only be expected from "open" personas, whose viewpoint manifest itself in their behaviour: a deed is an escalation of their behaviour. On the other hand, "secret" personas must keep their deeds secret, unless they finally stop hiding their viewpoints – which would, effectively, change the type of their personal relation. Such changes of behaviour (that is to say, action) that

---

25　*Guilt* (*Vina*) is an intimate psychological tragedy by the Czech playwright Jaroslav Hilbert (1871–1936). The main protagonist of the play, a young woman called Mína, commits suicide because she is unable to cope with her guilt: the fact that she is no longer a virgin as a result of her former secret relationship with Uhlíř. The main conflict of the play starts with Uhlíř visiting Mína's family by coincidence at the very moment when she plans to get married to another man. The relation between Mína and Uhlíř is very complex and dynamic, as he manipulates by means of the guilt, which only they two know about. The play opened at the National Theatre in Prague in 1896 and was lauded as a Czech attempt at psychological-realistic drama in the style of Ibsen. Zich based his opera *Vina* (1915, premiered 1922) on Hilbert's play.

turn secret friends and enemies to open ones (cf. Mortimer's romantic relation to Mary Stuart) are much more efficacious thanks to their ostensive character than changes of viewpoint – unless these are immediately accompanied by behaviour and thus made ostensive, because otherwise we would often only have to guess at them. Changes of viewpoint are sometimes gradual, but mostly they are sudden – because there is little time to spare in drama – which creates a significant demand for their motivation: usually a persona is either deluded or freed from a delusion, and that by actions of others (intrigues!) or by chance. For example, the intrigue in *Much Ado about Nothing* turns Claudio into Hero's open enemy for a time (with the situation culminating during the nuptials), only to revert to the original relation soon thereafter. Since Hero's relation to Claudio does not change, in our system this is a change from type 2 into type 5 and back again. The personal relation between Othello and Desdemona is also a change from type 2 into type 5; yet the change is gradual, proceeding step by step and covering almost the whole play, and of course it never reverts. We may say that exactly this *change* of one relation into another is the subject of the play, as it is in most drama, at least in regards to their main personas.

However, these relational changes "in their kind" mostly do not happen in leaps, but gradually, in a sequence of nuances in their intensity as well as their *quality*. As we have pointed out said above, for the sake of simplification the terms "an enemy" and especially "a friend" are intentionally so general that they, in actual fact, stand for whole sets of sentiments. They would hardly suffice for a play of the most elementary emotions, let alone satisfy the needs of modern psychological drama. They are no more than basic patterns and theoretical types to process the subject in rough terms. Let me emphasise the embryonic dramatic relations that have resulted from our use of the even broad notion of "indifferent" viewpoint and behaviour. This is not some middle-point on the scale of friend-enemy, but something qualitatively rather different. Especially modern plays often present a *gradual* change of what we might call "relations of indifference" into relations of friendship or hostility and vice versa (Ibsen). However, the aim of this book is not the study of the psychological evolution of personal relations, even less so since the perfect artistic tool for such a soul-searching analysis is doubtless the novel. The primacy of the dramatic work is ostensive perception: that is what theatre lives by. Let us therefore turn to this dramatic reality.

೧൭ ೧൭ ೧൭

THE DRAMATIC SITUATION

For dramatic personas to be able to interact, they must spend some time together in the same place – which is self-evident. Thus, a necessary condition of dramatic action is the dramatic personas' *shared presence in time and space* perceived by us as the audience; technically, this means the relevant actors being together on stage. This shared presence naturally keeps chang-

6 DRAMATIC ACTION: THE STAGE DIRECTOR'S FIRST TASK

ing during the play as actors enter and leave the stage. As entrances are more important for them for practical reasons, dramas are usually divided into "full scenes" (*výstupy*) for technical reasons. Since actors' exits are also important, bringing about a change in the shared presence, we will use both entrances and exits to subdivide the play into *"french scenes" (výjevy)*.[26] During a *french scene*, the same actors are on stage; and from the audience's point of view, the same dramatic personas are at the same location represented by the stage scene. Each *french scene* presents to us ostensively (i.e., visibly and audibly) the dramatic relations between specific dramatic personas.

French scenes may largely differ in duration, and dramatic relations between the personas may *change* during them – especially during the longer ones – and they change in their intensity at the very least. For the sake of this analysis, let us therefore further subdivide each *french scene* into such temporal units that allow us to *consider a relation between all personas as constant*.

Let us call *the ostensive setup of dramatic relations at a given while within these limits a dramatic situation*. We could also say "at a given moment", and it is often necessary to literally talk about a "momentary" dramatic situation. In some cases, however, the unit of time is comparably longer, so the general word "a while" is more suitable.

There are two implications of this definition. First, each dramatic situation may be, *ex definitione*, considered as *more or less constant* and as such, it can be handled more easily. Second, it follows by the same token that *two consecutive* dramatic situations always differ in personal relations manifest in them. If these differences are small and merely relate to their intensity, we speak about a *transition* or *development* of one dramatic situation into another. If they are substantial and affect especially the qualitative changes of personal relations, they signify a *turn* of the dramatic situation. Only this method, which divides a ceaselessly changing dramatic action into a series of constant dramatic situations, makes it possible to handle the complexity of its dynamic temporal form. In this way, the drama as a whole as well as each of its parts turns into a *successive synthesis of dramatic situations*. In this sense, a *"french scene"* is a successive synthesis of dramatic situations with the same *personas*. We could call this method "cinematographic"; as a matter of fact, "cinema" differs from it only by structuring the action only into moments, whereas we divide it into differently long whiles, during which the dramatic situation remains unchanged.

In regards to the *"dramatic situation"* let us introduce one simplification: while studying the shared presence of personas at a given space and time, let

---

26   There is no English equivalent for *výjev* (or *die Auftritt* in German) to differentiate it from a full scene (*výstup*). We have opted for an idiosyncratic solution and refer to it as *the french scene*. See also *scene (II) in the Glossary.

us – for the time being – disregard the spatial relations between the personas and take for a fact that they are ostensive. The position (or blocking) of actors on stage and the corresponding spatial relations between the dramatic personas in a given while, when they remain unchanged, will be called analogically *"a scenic situation"* – and we shall closely discuss it in the next chapter. We perceive scenic situations exclusively by sight.

> It will be beneficial if we support the discussion that follows with a visual aid. For that reason, we present schematic *charts of the temporal forms* in two plays: Ibsen's tragedy *Ghosts* and Shakespeare's comedy *Much Ado About Nothing*. The former has only a few characters and simple plot; the latter has many characters and a much more complicated plot. They are divided into *french scenes* (and further into scene changes and acts) and their respective widths correspond in proportion with the actual duration in performance (2mm signify about 2 minutes). Thick lines indicate which personas are present on stage.

DRAMATIC SITUATION ANALYSIS

The first feature of a particular dramatic situation is the *number of personas* involved. Since a dramatic situation is merely a temporal segment of dramatic action, it is not limited by the same restrictions that apply to a play as a whole, i.e., the need for at least two autonomous personas. It may involve only one persona, which we shall call, following the opera, a "solo" or two personas (duo), three (trio) and so on up to a great number of personas, which is practically limited only by the size of the stage. Although it is a good dramatic rule that all personas in a *french scene* – i.e., the sum of subsequent dramatic situations with the same personas – should have some dramatic purpose and do something, dramatic situations as such do not necessitate it and may involve both active as well as variously passive or static personas, who are in turn active in another situation or *french scene*.

From a technical point of view, personas that act independently anywhere in a play, no matter how small their part may be, are played by actor *soloists*. Personas that are merely static within a play are assigned to *extras*, who usually perform in a group as a collective persona, a *chorus*, under a *single* name (attendants, citizens, etc.), by which the playwright indicates their loss of individualities to a mass individuality. Their task is usually limited to *characterising* a social *environment* of the dramatic (soloist) personas proper – additionally, they also have a visual effect on stage. We also need to consider the option that a crowd take action – but that would be as a collective persona towards an individual one. The difficulty in spoken drama is not so much joint action but joint *speaking*, which is hard to achieve without compromising

6 DRAMATIC ACTION: THE STAGE DIRECTOR'S FIRST TASK

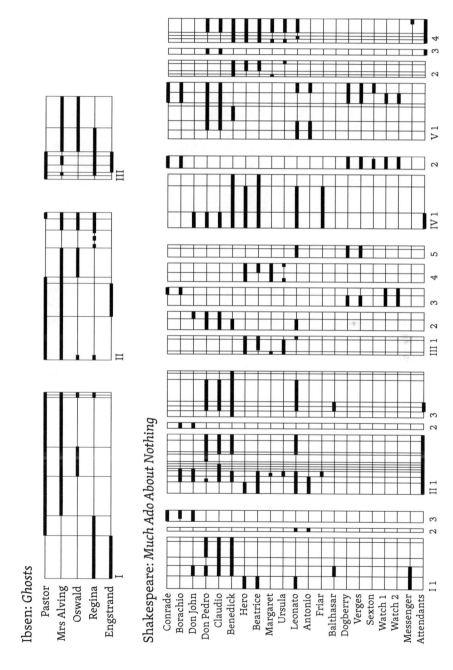

TEMPORAL CHARTS OF PLAYS

Ibsen: *Ghosts*

Shakespeare: *Much Ado About Nothing*

comprensibility. For this reason, collective performance usually limits itself audible to expressions where the exact words do not matter very much (such as expressions of consent or protest); alternatively, the obstacle is overcome by the crowd being spoken for by a leader. In sung drama joint singing does not compromise comprehensibility, so the chorus as a collective persona has a much more prominent function, as we shall see later. A crowd may be divided, of course, when divided in opinions, which may lead to various manifestations – quite often, we get two crowds in fact, which stand one against the other and at the same time, each behind their leader or more generally behind persons they sympathise with. When several personas step out of the crowd in a soloist fashion, particularly in speaking, it suggests that a differentiation begins from a collective to individual personas. This type exists on a gradual scale, useful also in spoken drama, that can grow into another: a *group* of personas that retain their individualities within the collective; they have individual names and in other situations may behave autonomously.

> *Much Ado About Nothing* provides an example of such partially collective personas. *The Ghosts*, in contrast, is an example of a play with exclusively individualised personas and very few of them at that. Most sung drama would be structurally similar to the latter, only with an even greater use of the chorus.

Since the dramatic situation does not present only action but also a dramatic relation, which is a more general notion, it may certainly also present us with only a *single* persona. On the level of the text, this is termed a *monologue*, and that means not only solo speaking but also acting. As far as this solo acting is concerned, it has never received any theoretical objections; however, naturalist theory denounces solo speaking (soliloquy) as unnatural and false because it does not occur in the real world. This argument is completely naive: we established early in this book that a dramatic work presents *constructed* events, that is such that do not or even cannot occur in the real world. The same argument would reject all verse drama and even all operas, because people in the real world do not communicate in verse or in singing. However, if we consider inner, psychological truthfulness, which is the only one respect unconditionally in art, it is a fact that we engage such soliloquies, in our minds of course, very often and that in circumstances closely connected to our actions, either when getting ready (making decisions), or in the aftermath (doubts, regrets, etc.). Such monologue is therefore psychologically fully justified and there is even no need to point out that there are instances (e.g., in agitation) when soliloquies actually happen aloud in the real world. If a dramatic persona's monologue is in *a causal relation with their following or preceding action*, it agrees with the dramaticity principle and is therefore *fully justified* both in spoken drama and in opera, where it is usually referred to as an "aria". Even a monologue that merely expresses sentiments, i.e., the lyrical monologue, is admissible, provided it is *dramatically bound* to the context and not too long to put the action and plot to a halt. It is deficient, i.e., undramatic, only when the expression of sentiments is its sole aim – that is, when it is purely, self-indulgently "lyrical" (see p. 136).

If a dramatic situation shows more than one persona, as is usually the case, its complexity increases immensely with the number of persons. We have pointed this out in our analysis of the elementary dramatic relation, between two personas; there we had to take into account both their ostensive relation (their speeches and behaviours) as well as their viewpoint of their relation (their views of one another), for these components may agree or disagree. Consider that with three personas there are three mutual and six personal relations; with four personas there are six mutual and twelve personal ones, and so forth!

Fortunately, such a "*complex* dramatic relation" gets simpler since some personas are in a friendly relation, and openly so, as allies in their actions. A dramatic situation that presents only such allies makes a *harmonious* impression; these are generally situations of striking a deal between two, three or more personas, and conversational dialogues, spiced only with minor skirmishes and disagreements. *Disharmony* enters the dramatic situation with the appearance of a secret enemy as soon as their seemingly friendly action causes negative effects on another persona – for example, in the scenes of Othello and Iago, who are seemingly friendly. The impression of disharmony escalates when it comes to open enemies, since our feeling of *agitation* combines with dramatic *tension* evoked by the conflict of two opposing aspirations. The personas involved in the dramatic situation are clearly divided into two camps, which enhances the dramatic contrast *quantitatively* too; it is interesting though that what is crucial for the tension in a scene is not their absolute number but rather the numeric *ratio* of the two sides. An individual standing against several people perhaps makes a more powerful impression than several against several, because we measure that single will against the will of more people, which enhances the intensity.

It has to be said that a conflict of two sides does not exhaust the potential of a dramatic situation. With three personas, each of them may well be independent – or the third person can view the conflict of the other two independently. There is also the simple case when the third persona is neutral in spite of interfering in the conflict (otherwise the third persona would not matter). But the third persona may have their own aims, either hidden or open – as long as they are clear to the audience – and that turns such a "*dramatic triangle*" into a highly complex relation. Consider that even a conflict of two personas makes us identify with them *separately*; as shown in our analysis of action, such a split mind is psychologically possible, though difficult. But to identify with *three* personas borders on the limits of a viewer's mental capacity, even for the most dedicated or determined one. The playwright must offer us some help in such a situation by making one – or even two – of the personas *step back* for some time; and the actors must adjust the intensity of their performances accordingly.

This gives us another important point about dramatic situations, namely the varying *dramatic weight* of each persona that makes up a situation, and consequently the *dominance* of one of them. Such dominance shows purely in dramatic terms, i.e as a persona's initiative and actual effect of their action on others. This dominance occurs in a conflict not only when the other side clearly "succumbs", but also when personas agree to accept another persona's lead. In a given dramatic situation one persona usually dominates over others, but there may be also two of them of equal weight – especially in a disagreement. Each persona in a dramatic situation becomes, as it were, a kind of centre of mental force, each of different intensity and different direction. These forces arrange themselves according to the dominant one, working against the opposing force – or a composite of opposing forces – or even meet a passive resistance. This feature of a dramatic situation is not ostensive on its own, of course. An actor may indicate a persona's dramatic weight by intensifying their performance, but we as the audience will recognise it on the basis of its *outer effect*, showing on other personas that seem to be suppressed by the dominant persona. A persona's dominance can be shown directly only by scenic means, which we shall discuss later. The dominance over others may remain unchanged over the course of a situation; it may also grow (or even come into existence) or dwindle (or pass altogether). These changes of dominance sometimes happen gradually, sometimes abruptly. A sudden change is dramatically more effective, of course; it is usually caused by the discovery of something that has been unknown to the others. For example, in Hilbert's *Vina* (Guilt), after a long struggle between Mína and Uhlíř in the second act, Uhlíř gains dominance at the instant moment when he learns that Hošek does not know about Mína's "guilt". Understandably a change in the dramatic weight on one side leads to a change in weight on the other; these are swings of a psychological scale of sorts, hovering over the dramatic situation. When the dominance passes from one dramatic persona to another, the dramatic relation is changed to such extent that a new dramatic situation arises. However, it is necessary to distinguish in this case – at in many other cases – between an actual dominance a persona wields, and a *seeming* dominance that they merely assume for themself. The difference is manifest in the discrepancy between the persona's demanding, externally intense action, and that action's negligible effect. The impression of a seeming dominance is usually comic, but when it is well conceived, it may also be tragic (cf. King Lear's actions toward his two elder daughters).

DRAMATIC POLYPHONY

This concept, adopted from musical terminology, can sometimes be found in drama criticism. It describes the fact that dramatic works mostly involve multiple *actions* (*děj*), of varying importance, *running simultaneously* and forming various relations and combinations. This resembles the specific form of *musical polyphony* – several melodies playing simultaneously, which we can hear together with the relations between them. On closer inspection, however, this analogy is only generic and vague. Musical polyphony (see Chapter 8) is composed of real, i.e., actually sounding and simultaneously audible "voices" – and each of these voices has one melody. In contrast, each action (*děj*) in a dramatic work is only imagined: consisting of several personas' action, it exists, as it were, "between them" and it is carried by a specific abstract idea. This polyphony of actions (*děj*) is therefore not a true, ostensive polyphony but rather a combination of ideas. The concept of dramatic polyphony is, once again, a mere product of a "text-based" view of dramatic works; by the same token, one could also use it to discuss narrative literature such as the novel, which nearly always involves actions (*děj*), often intricately intertwined.

But why is the idea of polyphony used with drama in particular? There certainly is something deserving of that name, but the above conception (together with a vague understanding of musical polyphony) is misleading. However, as soon as we visualise any dramatic scene on stage or approaching the above charts of plays with a view to their progression in time, we will be able to identify the actual polyphony.

Every scene presents several personas (very exceptionally just one) engaged in interaction; each persona's personal action is real and ostensive, continuous and taking place in real time. To be precise, only a persona's acting is continuous in *spoken drama*, not their speech, as personas need to take turns – for the sake of comprehensibility, if nothing else – which is not completely necessary in sung drama. These ostensive personal actions take place *simultaneously in real time* and we actually *perceive* them as such. This analogy with music is sufficient to justify our use of the musical term for drama – in the sense that *dramatic polyphony is the ostensive temporal simultaneity of personal actions*. Adoption the term should not mislead us to transfer all other characteristics of musical polyphony to dramatic art. Let us consider without prejudice which features are shared and which are different.

First, there is an interesting correspondence in the *interrelation* of the components regarding their progression in time. Two musical voices either progress in the same direction (both rising or falling) or in the opposite one: the former is similar motion, the latter is contrary motion. If similar motion is parallel (e.g., in music, a progression in thirds), the two voices are not considered autonomous from a musical point of view, but rather as a single voice that is doubled (or tripled, etc.). Similarly, personas' actions are either in agreement, or go against one another. If they agree entirely, the actions are considered as one collective action, that of allies – as we have observed above. As in music, actions of all personas in a given scene are *generally* grouped into two collective actions that go against one another. All possible instances of dramatic polyphony can be visualised in the following diagrams; individual action is symbolised by a single line, while group action (irrespective of its size) by a double line:

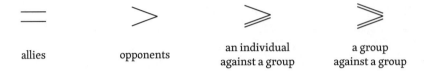

allies   opponents   an individual against a group   a group against a group

In fact, another single line should be added for a solo action, which is a liminal case of dramatic as well as musical polyphony.

> However, this is where the analogy based on "movement" ends. We have seen that two contrary actions can be joined by a third autonomous action, i.e., one that does not take sides with either of the other two. If the third action is neutral, the musical counterpart could be in oblique motion or a drone, where one of the voices sustains a note (this happens with two voices as well, of course); but there is no musical counterpart for three autonomous and more or less contrary actions. The reason is that the movement of a musical voice, as actual movement, has limited possibilities: it can either rise, or fall, but nothing else. For this reason there is only *one* kind of movement "against one another". In contrast, when we speak of personas' actions moving "together" or "against one another", the expression is figurative; there is no actual movement involved. In this sense, dramatic polyphony is *freer* and *richer* than musical polyphony. In music, there is also no analogy for the another feature common in drama: the difference between open and secret action (e.g., seemingly *for*, in reality *against*). In music, all voices are "openly manifest".

A second correspondence between musical and dramatic polyphonies concerns the varying *weight* of the components in a polyphony. One voice is usually dominant over secondary ones (in music too), which is accomplished by intensifying that voice (since there is nothing like illusory dominance in music). But there are frequent examples of two voice of equal importance, usually in contrary motion – like two opposing actions of equal dramatic weight in a dramatic scene. In music, the weight can shift from one voice to another, temporarily or more permanently, just like in the polyphony of personal actions where, sometimes, a previously secondary persona standing aside of the action intervenes for a brief moment, but with great intensity. As to the *number* of personas or voices, the analogy is truly remarkable. The terms we have used in analysing dramatic situations – such as solo, duo, etc. – are in fact adopted from musical terminology, applicable also to purely instrumental music. A collective of solo actors may be called an "ensemble" just as in music, and an actor's "solo" may be understood in parallel to music as a genuine solo of a single actor (i.e., a soliloquy) but also as an outstanding "solo performance" on the background of other actors' "group" performances – as a kind of actorly *concerto* for one actor (occasionally two) on a principally static background formed by other solo actors or chorus of extras. Gloucester's wooing of Lady Anne in Shakespeare's *Richard III* and the meeting of the two queens in Schiller's *Mary Stuart* may serve as telling examples.

Let us say a few words about the polyphonic *connection* of two *consecutive* dramatic *french scenes* within the same location (i.e., in unchanged scenery). A glance at the above chart of our two plays (or any others) will show us how they are usually connected. Either the *french scene* starts with the entrance of a new persona (or a group), joining the previous company; or a persona(s) exit; or some personas enter while others exit. Usually, at least one persona *remains* and *carries over* in the following *french scene*. This form of dramatic polyphony – which I will call the *personal concatenation* – effects an ostensive *connection* between the *french scenes*. It is only exceptionally that all personas exit a scene and a different set enters in the same location; this form causes a conspicuous division of the dramatic action, and it usually comes with a pause, however short, with an empty stage.

At the start of our discussion of the dramatic situation we asserted that we perceive the number of a scene's participants by sight and hearing. That is the standard case. However, we must also mention a non-standard case that is not uncommon, when we perceive a persona by our *hearing only* and not by our sight, because we cannot see them. The actor may be on stage but hidden from view, or they are within, yet in a way that the dramatic persona is engaged with others, either by talking to them being overheard by them. In this case, the "location of action" extends beyond the stage and the personas within must be counted into the dramatic scene, although their ostensive presence (though not necessarily their efficacy) is weakened for the audience. Sometimes the dramatic relation between personas hidden and visible to the audience is one-sided: those on stage know about those within (whom they can hear), but not vice versa. For example, this happens at the end of the first act of *Ghosts* (when Oswald and Regina are in the "next room").

> This relates to an interesting motif, analogous with the disguise and dissimulation motifs discussed above: the **concealment** motif, a very popular dramatic situation, especially in older comedies. A persona in a dramatic situation is hidden, but not from the

audience but from the other dramatic personas, who are not aware of them. Usually, a secret is overheard and so revealed, which then has implications for the following action, often decisively. Overhearing the secret may be intentional or by accident, such as under the cover of darkness, like in *Much Ado About Nothing* where the Prince's watch learns about the intrigue against Claudio's fiancée Hero. Another well-known example is Molière's *Tartuffe*. With this motif, as with the previous two, it is necessary to follow *the principle of dramatic truthfulness* and let the audience know about this concealment, not just to understand the situation, but also to enjoy effects of this motif, especially when those who were overheard remain unaware of it for a time; it is particularly enjoyable to watch the effect of the overheard speech on the secret listeners.

In *Much Ado About Nothing* Shakespeare deploys an ingenious variation of this concealment motif – and that happens twice. Both Benedick and Beatrice are disingenuously induced to listen in secret to what is said about them, while those who are speaking about them *know* they are being overheard, and so they speak accordingly. It is a *"perverted"* concealment motif, trapping those who think they are setting a trap themselves. A comparable "perverted" motif of disguise appears in Jaroslav Vrchlický's comedy *Noc na Karlštejně (A Night at the Karlštejn Castle)*[27], where Charles IV sees through his wife's disguise but he does not show it (which is exactly what matters) and plays with her like a cat with a mouse – a very ingenious motif with a refined comic effect. A "perverted" motif of dissimulation, in which one persona sees through another persona's dissimulation without giving it away, is more common and often reciprocal, e.g., in the two diplomats' brawl in Scribe's *Le verre d'eau*.

ଔ ଔ ଔ

The Manifestation Principle. The motifs of mistaken identities and disguise as well as the motifs of dissimulation and concealment demonstrate with characteristic and well-known examples that dramatic action often contains moments about which some dramatic personas are *ignorant* or *mistaken*, taking them for something else than they truly are; on the other hand, there are some dramatic personas that *know* the real state of things and or even know about the mistakes or ignorance of others – especially if they themselves are the deceivers, whether by accident, or (mostly) intentionally. What is typi-

---

27   *Noc na Karlštejně (A Night at the Karlštejn Castle)* is a 1884 historical comedy by the Czech playwright and poet Jaroslav Vrchlický (1853–1912). It depicts an apocryphal situation from the life of Charles IV, fourteenth-century Czech King and Holy Roman Emperor, who was dubbed the "father of the country" by the Czech National Revival Movement. The fabricated history says that Charles IV was such a pious Christian that when he built the Karlštejn Castle, the seat of the imperial regalia, he forbade the admission of women to the castle, which was to serve as a place of contemplation and prayer. Legend has it that the only woman to break the rule was Elizabeth of Pomerania, Charles's fourth wife, who was known for her extraordinary physical strength and bravery. She snuck into the castle disguised at the King's page to find out if her husband truly loved her.

cal of the countless variations of these motifs is that the dramatic personas' mistakes are caused by a mistaken *perception*. The same perception is also the basis for the audience's understanding of the dramatic action. As we have iterated in the analyses of our examples above, the principle of dramatic truthfulness requires that the audience must not fall victim to the mistake but know the real state of things like the deceiving dramatic personas. As the audience we must not be *deceived* and nothing must be *hidden* from us; we as observers *see through* everything, even that which seems different, and we *know everything*, even that which is secret. Dramatic action lies open before us, without folds or impenetrable shadows, as if in broad daylight; in other words, dramatic action is always made entirely *manifest* to us as the audience.

Not everything that a dramatic work ostensively presents to us is always so ambiguous; we have seen in our analysis of personal dramatic relations, for instance, that it is necessary to distinguish "open" and "secret" relations of one persona to another. Likewise, the "perverted" motifs show that some deceived personas can see through the trap. From a psychological point of view, this is our situation as the audience: anything we perceive – personas, their actions or dramatic situations – is always accompanied, as we know, by a *conceptual,* more particularly a *referential image* in our minds, based on sensory perception (after all, we are observing actors and their performance), and that image interprets it all for us. But it happens sometimes that, for certain reasons, we need to add *another* interpretation that contradicts our perception, or rather with its first, direct interpretation. In such cases we have *two referential images*: one is based on the ostensive and a second that is non-ostensive: we can see and hear one thing – but we know something that goes *against* it.

This *contradiction* between *perception* and knowledge gives us great pleasure of a *specifically dramatic* kind: it never stands out so pronouncedly when reading a play text, when we may only get a rather vague idea in our imagination of its ostensive qualities, and not even when reading a narrative literary work, which may be rich in such motifs, but *all these* are merely narrated. The important point for us here is that we project both of our referential images onto the *dramatic personas* of either kind: we are aware that while we are not being misled, some of the personas are, and that we know something that they do not. This awareness of our omniscience, accompanied by a peculiar sense of our heightened position *above the dramatic situation*, is the true significance or raison d'être of *the manifestation principle (princip zveřejnění)*.

This "*manifestation*" does not only concern the above cases of "deception" in dramatic action, where we need to hold *two* conflicting referential images – the seeming one and the "*true*" one; in such cases, the need for manifestation follows from the principle of dramatic truthfulness. Additionally, manifestation has broader significance, pertaining to the very *essence* of the dramatic work as a *performance*. A novel's narration has unlimited possibilities to evoke any referential or conceptual images, to inform us of all that is necessary, and most importantly, to tell us in the greatest of detail what happens in the characters' inner lives. That is not so with a dramatic work. We have seen the limited possibilities of non-verbal expressions and we know that they need the support of language, and that, in drama, can only be personas' "direct" speeches. The manifestation principle requires that we know all the mental states of the dramatic personas whenever necessary, and that concerns the states that are in any causal relation with the dramatic action (*děj*) – that is to say, with the personas' interaction.

Thus, manifestation turns into a *"mimetic" requirement* that is determined by the character of all the material that the drama uses, and it applies to the playwright first, and then to the actors and their coordinator, i.e., the stage director. Whatever a dramatic persona is hiding, as well as anything that would otherwise remain secret, must be made manifest as soon as it is needed to understand the action – that is, from the *governing principle of dramaticity*; and conversely, when it is not needed, the thing does not need to be and even should not be, made manifest, as it is serve no purpose.

It is this logic that gives the dramatist the full justification to use a monologue whenever certain of a dramatic persona's mental states must be made manifest for dramatic reasons (but only for those reasons!), and when there is no other way to convey them, such as in a dialogue with an ally. This extends to the justification of *"speaking aside"*, used to expose a persona's true relationship to another persona in their presence, when the fixed sequence of scenes prevents the dramatist from postponing it until the persona is alone or with friends. Of course, the audience is expected to imagine that what they can hear is not overheard by the other persona on stage. For this, it is enough if the actor changes the way they speak and if the director makes appropriate blocking (we will speak of this later); a theatrically focused audience will make do with such hints.

As far as actors are concerned, the manifestation requirement is in fact the *technical principle* of their performance, i.e., the governing idea of their *figures*, which must be focused on the audience – while dramatic personas must be focused on one another. The actor's task is therefore twofold – or rather it becomes twofold once these two directives are in conflict. In such cases, performing for the audience needs hints at least – unless the dramatist's text helps – as a kind of "performance aside", in order to show the true side of things to the auditorium. We can see again, as in the previous chapter, that the technical image of the actor figure and of the acting, although it corresponds with the referential image of a dramatic persona and the action, is not always and fully identical with it. Theatre is a constructed thing and it may use corresponding means – which is its privilege – and the audience must be aware that they do not face a life's reality, which in turn is an advantage to them.

The actor's task of making a dramatic work manifest necessarily brings them into *contact with the audience* and it is well-known that all "born" actors are in this contact while performing and that they feel well in it. On entering the stage, transbodied and mentally transfigured, they feel as if attracted by the dark mass of the auditorium behind the footlights. It is for them that they play and improvise, although they do so in interplay with their stage partners. To clarify: actors *do not manifest themselves*, but their *"persona"*. All the notorious excesses of vainglory, playing for applause, chewing the scenery, "grand exits", "microacting" and so on are not governed by the manifestation principle; it is, as it were, also "playing to the audience" but in the wrong sense of the word because there the actor cares for their own little self and not for their dramatic persona – which is utterly unprofessional and un-artistic. Like any other artist, the actor also has the right to be proud of their creation, but not of themselves: their personal kudos will come from the performance they deliver.

Of great psychological interest is the specifically dramatic *effect* that *manifestation* has on the audience. We have already discussed its intellectual effect, based in making the audience completely and correctly informed of the dramatic action; we are now interested in manifestation's *emotional effect*. It has been often claimed that actors "prostitute" their inner selves on stage. This is a mistaken view since even the most intimate stir of the soul that the actor manifests, is not theirs, but belongs to the dramatic persona they represent. More precisely: they *do not feel* it as something of their own – of course, with the exception of the "dilettante actor", discussed in the previous chapter. So, if anybody prostitutes themself at all, it is the dramatic persona that exposes their inner self by what they say and do – but the persona does not manifest themself because they only interact with the other personas. However, as we have asserted above, a dramatic work must also manifest those personas' inner states that are in a causal relation with their actions. And that is the very aspect we are pursuing here. If a dramatic persona exposes their inner self, under what circumstances does that happen? They do so only when the emotions they foster – and emotions are surely the most intimate thing one has – tend to incur aspirations and actions, i.e., to show outwardly. An expression of such emotions or ideas related to them, thus fully corresponds with the manifestation principle. But there are also emotions that lack this tendency and are therefore not dramatic, since they do not lead to action; an expression of these emotions, when voices in speech, is *purely lyrical* and their exposure is psychologically contrived. When inadvertently manifested in the theatre, such purely passive lyricism ends up being killed off: we fail to even recognise passages of the dramatic text we had read before. Their mood is thwarted, their poetic sheen, as it were, brassly obliterated. But how is it that footlights do not scorch every lyricism? Why do they do no harm to the active type that forces its way from the soul? Some emotions flicker only in twilight; in the full light of manifestation they fail to even register.

One could object that a reciter also exposes feelings expressed in a lyrical poem without weakening the effect of its mood, not to mention the unabated effect of the musical mood mediated by a reproductive musician artist. But there the situation is completely different as we have shown in our comparison of recitation and actors' delivery. The reciter and the musician express *their own* emotions evoked by the *work of art* they are performing, which is not the actor's case: there feeelings are expressed only by the dramatic personas, performed by the actor, and that happens not through a work of art but directly in human terms; and we measure these expressions also in human terms. This is the point where manifestation begins to work destructively against emotions that cannot endure it: all delicate detail is lost, all intimacy sounds weird, and sadness sentimental.

This specific change of the impression of mood, caused by manifestation, does not affect intimate and delicate aspects alone. Interestingly, all that is *crude* also changes its effect in manifestation, and that in the opposite direction: it is not subdued but becomes even *cruder*. It is well known that ugly, horrid and repulsive actions or things may be described and related, but how it is unbearable to see and hear them on stage. It is also well known how this has been abused in the artistically monstrous works of dramatic art. There are eras that require, and strata of the audience that hunger, after such crude sensations, and there are dramatic genres and types of playwrights that cater to such drives. However, even where the author's intentions are artistic, one should beware of the threat that the stage might untolerably magnify what is bearable on the page. Naturally, the director is a decisive element in this; such things may be presented on stage openly or covertly. It is certain that the sensory character of perceptions contributes to the amplification of such crude motifs in contrast to mere play of imagination (e.g., in a novel); however, the crux lies in manifesting something that does not tolerate it. An illustrative example is the piercing effect of vulgar or obscene words and sayings on stage, which become jarring and shameless although we merely think of what they mean. The larger the theatrical public, i.e., the more numerous the audience we are part of, the more insulting these things become.

But it is not only these deformations of the emotional impression brought about directly by manifestation that are characteristic of a work's dramatic effect. The mere intellectual effect of manifestation, referred to above as the audience's "omniscience", leads to a range of typical emotions that are mostly *mixed* feelings because they spring from the conflict between what we perceive and what we know. And this does refer only to the emotions we feel over all the deceptions (i.e., those transparent for us): mistaken identities, disguises, dissimulations, concealments and such. Because we know *completely* everything, each stage of the action, we view many scenes with different eyes than we would if – like the personas in the scene – we had no idea what had just happened. This is how we feel, beside the simple emotions evoked by the scene itself, other, contrasting emotions that colour our dramatic impression with a peculiar, specifically dramatic kind of impression, which comes from the conflict between emotions from perception and emotions from our "awareness". So, for example, even if we were not familiar with the historic Wallenstein's fate, we can see Wallenstein overshaded by the impeding death in the last two acts of Schiller's tragedy, beginning with Butler and Gordon's dialogue; and so every word of his last scenes, with Wallenstein talking to Seni, Gordon and a servant, will acquire a different, special colour for us ("Good night! I think to make a long | Sleep of it."). This can culminate in tragic irony and tragic humour – merriment of those ignorant of an approaching catastrophe. And conversely, the most menacing situations in comedies, driving the afflicted persona to despair, is lightened up in a smile of sorts by our awareness, based on previous experience, that things are actually not that bad, that it is a "light-hearted tragedy".

There is nothing more complex, dark and intriguing than what comes from human interaction. *How did this or that really happen* is a question that cannot be fully answered even by a direct participant; they would need to be omniscient and omnipresent. Only dramatic art, on account of its manifestation, offers an ideal insight into the most convoluted of events. We do not need to become a miraculous reporter following all the personas of the action, infiltrating ourselves into their most secret meetings – the personas themselves come before our eyes to the action's location, which automaticaly changes whenever the action shifts elsewhere. The dramatic work in fact meets, by artistic means of course, the ideal of historiography, whose partial, dubious and even fraudulent documents it substitutes with complete evidence that is irrevocable since we witness it with our own eyes and hear it "authentically" with our own ears. We may conveniently observe this difference in history plays that are based on actual historical events. Does history really know that much about what "really" happened back then? But we, after the play, do know for certain: *that* is how it was – of course, only "there on stage". What matters here is not the historical truth, which is always somewhat hypothetical, but the artistic truth, which is always categorical.

The Dramatic Plot (*děj*). We asserted at the beginning of our discussion of dramatic polyphony that what is usually called "dramatic action" – or more correctly the dramatic plot or the plot of a play – is an imagined, ideational formation that can also be found in narrative literature. Still, let us briefly consider these plots in relation to the ostensive foundation that is provided by a theatre performance and on which we imaginatively construct these plots. The components of this foundation are *ostensive personal actions* in a particular dramatic situation. These simultaneous actions always have some idea in common as their core, around which they turn; understandably, this idea relates to the personas who act in its name and who are affected by it to a greater or lesser extent – although it also often relates to personas that are absent from the given scene. One such idea could be the idea of power (e.g., the usurpation of a throne by removing its incumbent) or the idea of love of one persona towards another. This *idea of action (děj)* is the glue holding together the simultaneous action and often remains so even if the personas partly exchange with the next scene. Nevertheless, nearly every play gradually arrives at a scene in which personas no longer deal with this idea, but with something else; in other words, the presentation of the current plot is interrupted, usually for a certain time, before it comes back on the scene again – i.e., the previous idea is resumed and so is the action related to it, and that by partly the same personas as before. It happens often that the personas from before are joined by new ones, or some may drop out, which changes – as we will call it – the *extensity* of the plot.

We may therefore define *the dramatic plot (děj)* in the common, abstract sense as *a sum of simultaneous and consecutive personal actions pertaining to one and the same idea, and at least partly to the same personas*. As for the notorious requirement of *the unity of the plot*, it is given by *the constancy of the idea* governing the plot, and indirectly and relatively by the constancy of the personas acting in the name of that idea. The nexus bonding all the personal actions is, as we have seen, not only causal, but also final – and we will see below that it is only a relative requirement. Likewise the requirement of the unity of the imagined plot is only relative, because strict stability of the idea of plot is impossible, as it usually develops with the action, broadens or narrows down; in short, it changes – and that always in *connection* to its previous state. For that reason we will formulate this requirement more loosely, yet precisely on the basis of artistic practice as *the requirement of ideational plot continuity*.

Both these plot features, extensity and continuity, are only imagined. How does the actual "*dramatic*" (i.e., ostensively presented) action comply with them? No more than imperfectly. Firstly, scenes that would include *all* personas of a given plot are very rare; dramatists tend to save such scenes for climactic moments (viz Shakespeare's "finales"). Usually the playwright presents us with only some of the plot's personas, e.g., two of them scheming against a third; this third persona, who is spoken about, is not ostensive in this situation, but only *imagined*. Secondly, the ostensively presented plot tends to be broken up, even when the dramatic plot is as simple as can be. This could be suitably observed in our charts above if we, for example, used different colours to differentiate personal actions (symbolised there by thick lines) on the basis of their governing ideas. So in Ibsen's *Ghosts*, we would immediately see that the plot line of Engstrand's plan is limited to the first scene of Act I, and returns only in Act II and especially in Act III, where it wins over Regina, too (and that only after Engstrand's exit!). There are many more interruptions of ostensively presented action in plays with more complicated plots, such as *Much Ado About Nothing*. But what happens with a particular plot when it is not being presented to us? The general answer is: it develops in an *imagined* form. Principally, two cases must be distinguished here.

(a) A particular plot that has been presented to us in real time is *replaced* by another one, which now also unfolds before us in real time, until the former plot returns before our eyes. How it has continued in the meantime we cannot tell from our ostensive observation, but we can fill in the gaps because the dramatist must somehow inform us of everything important that has occurred in the interim. Either we had learned what was about to happen, or we find out ex post what has meanwhile happened, and most often both. This *imagined* segment of the plot is usually important and sometimes even crucial, though resistant to manifest onstage presentation, but we insert it within a *real* time sequence, during which another action took place, filling in the interim period. Thus, the duration of both parallel actions, the ostensive and the imagined, is identical, which obliges the playwright to attempt at least some verisimilitude, although one can rely on a certain illusion of time on the audience's part. One cannot believe, for instance, that a persona, within a short absence, would manage to do some time-consuming task. We will return to this point when dealing with the realistic style.

(b) Like any other extensive temporal work, a dramatic work is also divided into parts separated by *intervals*, during which the performance is halted. In the time of an interval, no ostensive dramatic action occurs; the time is our standard time; for the dramatic work, this time is *dead* and does not count. Theoretically speaking, intervals do not necessarily interrupt ostensive action: the second act could well begin at exactly the point where the first act ends. In practice, however, some discontinuity always occurs, especially because the interval often comes with a change of location. What the continuation of the plot (and in fact of all the plots) has been in the meantime, we learn in the same way as in the previous case; the difference is that we place *these* imagined interim actions into an *imagined* time, because the interval time does not apply to it. This allows the playwright to make this imagined time period any length they wish (e.g., months or years). It follows that the notorious *unity of time*, or rather *the continuity of time*, in a work of drama is an unjustified and redundant requirement – on the condition that it does not disrupt the continuity of the plot, even though the interval is filled in purely by imagination as for its content and its time. Let us symbolise ostensive action presented in real time with a thick line; the imagined segments unfolding in real time (while we are watching another action) with a thin line; and the imagined segments in imagined time (i.e., during intervals) with a dotted line; a particular plot line of a play in its *complete continuity* may be schematically shown as follows (e.g., in a play of three acts, where the second act does not open or close with our plot line, and the third act only begins after a longer time period):

This diagram includes a dotted line (i.e., purely imagined action) before the beginning of the first action that is presented, that is to say, in imagined time that belongs not to an interval but, as it were, before the performance as such. This relates to the issue of *exposition* in drama, which we addressed in the chapter on the dramatic text. Only rarely is the first ostensive action, given to us by the dramatist, also the true beginning of the plot. Usually, a part of the plot took place before and the action presented to us is its continuation, or at least some events happened that influence the evolving ostensive action. The reason why these passages are omitted is usually their lengthiness, which the strict economy of actual stage action does not tolerate; but there are other reasons, such as that they are uninteresting, inappropriate or impossible to present on stage. Occasionally, the dramatist turns them into a précis and presents them as a "prelude". The actual presentation of the action itself usually begins when the plot is well underway or gains momentum fitting a real time presentation. Such entrance "in medias res" is not a rule in drama, but it is certainly characteristic. All that has preceded must be filled in ex post – of course not ostensively but in an abstract account, that is in speech. We have already said that these verbal accounts, in fact narrations, should be as dramatic as possible. There are plays, such as Ibsen's *Ghosts*, where the entire dramatic action is in principle nothing but this retrospective disclosure of past events, i.e., of action that the audience only imagines. In fact, even when the action proper starts at the moment of performance, there always are some past moments that we need to learn about because they co-determine the present action. In contrast, the end of the performance concludes both the ostensive and the imagined action. After all, we often need to know what has gone before, but not at all how things will be next.

We can see then that the *"plot of a dramatic work"* (i.e., the theatre performance) is not *just* the ostensive sum of simultaneous and consecutive personal actions linked by a single idea – i.e., the "dramatic" action proper (as presented to us and perceived by us) – but it also includes numerous *imagined* parts that we do not know from direct ostensive perception; these parts pertain to a particular plot by their *relationship to its overall idea*. But since we are informed of these imagined parts by language (and occasionally also by non-verbal expressions) of the acting personas – and these are in our perception – it follows that *the dramatic "plot" is an ideational sum of the parts of dramatic action selected according to this idea from all the dramatic events*. This has two implications:

(1) This *idea* may be and often is *complex*. In addition to images of the dramatic personas involved and the objective that each of these personas connects with it, it also contains a number of imagined *means* to achieve the given objective. Such a means (e.g., removing a person standing in the way) may itself be a *provisional* goal of the action, which subdivides the plot into *successive* steps. On the basis of the personas and their investment in the central idea, the plot can be divided into personal goals – provisional and final – and these personal goals divide a given plot into *simultaneous partial* phases. With a view to the temporal progression of the overall action, various forms emerge that we could call *plot line polyphony* (not dramatic polyphony!), bearing

in mind that the name is figurative and that components of this polyphony – partial plots – are not only imagined, but also composite in that they comprise interactions of several personas, not individual personal actions. A more suitable visualisation would be a line: just like any line, so a plot line can fork off into branches at a certain moment and then these branches may unite again, or cross each other, while some may run out sooner than others and so on.

(2) There may be *several* such governing ideas, and so *several* plots in a single play. Unlike the above "partial" plots, these are *autonomous*, i.e., mutually independent plot lines. Nevertheless, there still must be a link between these plots if the drama, just like any other complex work of art, is to be an organic whole. This link may be based on the mutual relationship between the governing *ideas* of these plots. There is a whole range of instances, from complete unrelatedness to close affinity, corresponding to a range of entirely "autonomous" through to "partial" plots. Of great dramatic importance is a *personal* bond between such autonomous plots. Obviously, one single persona can participate in several plots, always with a different set of personas (partly different at least). It happens then that some personas are, so to speak, in double or even triple "employment" in a play, while others appear only in one plot. This is how the "principal" and "supporting" personas of a play should be defined, and not on the basis of their ideational weight: there are a number of plays with a multiply active servant or another subordinate character (such as the standard-bearer Iago), which makes them dramatically the most important persona. A "titular" hero is not always, in this sense, the most main dramatic persona of a play. As for the mutual relations of several plots, they are commonly distinguished as the main plot and the subplot on the basis of the weight of their ideas. But this is also only partly justified: what matters most is the *extent* of each of the plots presented in the work. A fundamental feature of the *main* plot line is that it *ends with the ending* of the dramatic performance, which is not necessary in the case of subplots even if dramatists like to intensify the conclusion of a play by making "all of it" conclude there. In contrast, it is not necessary to open a performance with the main plot; in fact, plays usually start with a subplot, as in Ibsen's *Ghosts*, where the subplot (between Regina and Endstrand) concludes before the main plot. The fact that dramatic plotlines, in spite of their autonomy, often cross and influence one another is logical, with a view to the persons they share.

Theorists of drama usually list in their definitions of drama the claim for a *"closed"* plot. We have omitted the word "closed" from our definition because a "work of art", by definition, must always be closed – which means, in the case where the work consists of a plot, that this plot also needs to have an *ending* – an *ideational* one of course. The only question then is *when* a plot concludes; and the answer to this question when it comes to dramatic action, i.e., personas' interaction, is very simple. The dramatic plot concludes when all the personas' aspirations are over. These aspirations pass, firstly, when they are fulfilled; secondly, when the relevant persona abandons for whatever outer or inner reason; and thirdly, when these aspirations are made impossible, which means either by violence, by mental disintegration, or by death. The first option prevails in comedies, in combination with the second, such as in voluntary surrender (e.g., an older suitor gives way to a younger one); the third option appears in tragedies, but only for some personas, while for others the first two options apply. The definitive ending of a tragedy remains to be the physical or at least mental death, whereas other endings are of thwarting aspirations, or of abandoning them, which may also turn out to be only provisional, which brings about steps of the *seemingly* concluding action, followed by a twist, which is often surprising.

This brings us to the last issue that we wish to address: it is an essentially philosophical issue of *chance* in drama. In the real world, chance appears as a disturbance in the causal nexus that binds individual parts and events. Chance, in this, becomes another "primal cause" of a new causal chain. It is, in short, the opposite of natural laws; it is something irrational. As chance plays such an immense role in our lives, we try to rationalise it, i.e., to understand it as some higher, metaphysical *finality*. This is all the more true for a dramatist in their works because art as such purports to *ostensively* present to us the world's *laws* (in this case, the principle of human social interaction), a task *theoretically* handled by scientific research. Therefore the requirement for the action (*děj*) presented to us by a playwright to be entirely causally bound, is merely relative and it allows for chance to intervene; but this chance must be construed to correspond with some higher law. The most common term for this is "fate" – be it lucky or unlucky, which is often underpinned by religion (gods' decree, God's will; demons' wrath, a curse) or by philosophy (world order seen optimistically or pessimistically, revenge for a guild). In modern drama, this function is taken over by natural laws, such as heredity or social pressures; yet the difference is just seeming because it is chance again that subjects an individual to the powers of nature, and the moral explanation that is missing here cannot always be in the former instance either (e.g., the guilt afflicting the whole house of Tantalus). Comedies usually make do with the popular philosophy notion of "luck" ("devil's luck") that someone enjoys – not always deserved.

૭ૹ ૭ૹ ૭ૹ

The Stage Director's Task. To the audience a dramatic work appears as a series of dramatic situations, each being, as we know, a spatio-temporal gathering of dramatic personas. Objectively, this corresponds to a technical image of a *spatio-temporal interplay of actors*, of a few or many. To create this interplay as a *spatial as well as temporal synthesis of figures* performed by individual actors is down to one person: the *director*. The need for a director comes from the fact that the dramatic work is principally a collective work of art.

That does not mean, however, that the director is there *only* to bring the performing actors together, although that is also necessary. We have asserted that the playwright should make the personas of their piece as different from one another as possible; the more the playwright succeeds in it, the better they are. That these personas achieve perfect interplay in the dramatist's imagination is a matter of course. On the basis of the textual roles from the playwright's imperfect rendering of this interplay, several actors create their figures: this guarantees the diversity of the dramatic personas and even enhances it, because (good) actors imprint their personas with a seal of their own individuality. This gain is nevertheless accompanied by the difficulty of the actors' interplay, when it comes to its precision as well as its unity and balance, because it is only human that each actor wants to assert their own conception – and themself. This necessarily leads to numerous discrepancies in the interplay. In the chapter on the actor's creative work, we pointed out how important the interplay with the stage partner is, through which the actor corrects and complements their conception. But here the question arises: which of them will comply in one thing or another? It might seem to be an issue of respect towards one another's artistic mastery, i.e., their artistic authority. This becomes even more pressing when more actors are involved. Mutual adjustment, the *co-adaptation* of the actor figures and especially their playing must be left to a single artist: that used to be one of the performing actors; now it is the director. Nonetheless, the co-adaptation of interplay is only the primitive, purely practical task of the director's.

The director's *artistic mission* is to create a *synthesis* of actor figures, which is more than their adjustment: the director must create the *form for the interplay*. The task is to balance the discrepancies between individual playing, but not only as a referee, but according to the firm plan the director designed earlier. This plan is *the director's* creative work, carried out on the basis of the playwright's text. We know that this text (with its stage directions) renders the playwright's vision only imperfectly, so there are multiple ways the work can be realised. If we claim that the director's work must be conceived to the *author's intentions* without exception, it means we still allow the director the freedom afforded by the multiple significance of a mere text, but we withhold from the director the right to ignore or change anything the author explicitly calls for. Some directors like to do just the opposite of everything prescribed by the dramatist, which does for a very cheap originality.

The afforded freedom of the director's creative work is also limited from another side: in regards to the actors' creations. It might seem from the above that the director has the right to require the actors to comply in their performances to his or her conception. Surely, the director does have this right – otherwise, no *consistent* work of art would be created – but they are also required to *conceive the dramatic work according to the actors*. This requirement is in no way a limitation to the director's artistic freedom; on the contrary, it is a purely artistic requirement of the *material-governed style*, which applies to every artist. Once a sculptor chooses marble or bronze, the choice determines the characteristic form of the sculpture in regards to the different techniques with these two materials; but this does not "limit" the sculptor because a true artist always thinks through their material. To impose the bronze forms on marble would be not only technically clumsy (at times even impossible), but it would be an artistic error. *The actors are not the director's material*, as many theatre theorists believe: every actor is the material to themselves, creating "figures" in that way. It is only these *actor figures that are the director's material*. Put simply: the director has no right to the actor's play but only to their interplay.

This claim may seem to contradict the above right afforded to the director to adjust, i.e., to change any actor's creative work; but this is only a seeming contradiction. We know that co-adaptation is necessary, since the dramatic work is collective; the director *organises it systematically*, and that happens by modifying the changes that the actors themselves need to make to fit one another's performance, into changes that match the *director's* plan. Let me give a simile: if we want two clocks to run exactly the same, we either synchronise them one way or another, or adjust each of them to a third clock; the latter way has the advantage that each clock will run together but also with "*our*" third (the director's) clock, which we take as the best. Clocks are, of course, dead mechanisms while actors are living individualities; so *the economy principle* requires that the sum total of the changes in the actors' performances should be *minimal*, i.e., that the actors' original conceptions should be preserved as much as possible, while at the same time broadly agreeing with the director's plan. The above sculptor's analogy offers a key to this charade, from which two necessary conditions for the director's creativity follow:

(1) Just as a sculptor needs to know the character and the techniques of working with marble, bronze, wood and so forth, so a director needs to know the character and working technique of the actors cast in their production and to know them to the level that the director may imagine approximately what figures these actors will create. This is a substantial requirement as it entails knowing many people (i.e., their artistic individualities), but it is achievable. After all, the second condition makes it easier:

(2) Just as a sculptor often decides with their first concept of a future work that "this must be done in bronze", so the director too: on getting a broad conception of the dramatic work, the director generally knows already *which* actors would be best to create this or that figure and the play. It follows then that the *director* should have the right to *cast the roles* for a piece they will direct, because this guarantees the above minimum of changes needed for a perfect and unified interplay. This will also maximally preserve not only the individual performances of all the actors but also the director's individual conceptions, because clearly the director also needs to adjust to the actors' artistic requirements, provided the unity of the director's plan remains intact.

Unfortunately, many directors – especially contemporary ones – are so conceited that they ruthlessly manipulate the actors they are supposed to direct, and whenever they can choose, they pick those with the least artistic individuality in order to mould their "material" exclusively into the shape of their plan. That casting roles is a task of *supreme artistic responsibility* is obvious from the above stated; that it is also humanly responsible needs no elaboration. Biographies of actors, even of the great ones, offer very clear evidence – and often a warning.

The director creates the *spatio-temporal form* of the dramatic performance. This is a very difficult task because the form is a combination of two heterogeneous dimensions – time and space, which is itself three-dimensional. In comparison, a poem's ostensive form is only temporal; a visual art is only spatial; a musical composition combines the temporal dimension with tonal (pitch), but both of them are simple, linear. The complex dramatic form may be decomposed into two forms. The first, a purely temporal one, where we somehow abstract from the scenic space where actors perform; this may be called the ostensive *dramatic* form in the narrow sense of the word *dramatic* (or, *dynamic*). In contrast, the other form, pertaining to the actors' positions on stage, is not purely spatial, because the positions change in time, but rather spatio-temporal, and it is this *shared* temporal dimension that binds it with the first form. Let us call it the *scenic* form, which we shall be discussing in the next chapter.

The director's **first** *task* is then to give the actors' interplay a *dramatic* form, which the director has conceived from a basis of the dramatic text and which he or she realises through the performances of the actors', the creators of figures. The material out of which the director shapes it (but the director themself does not shape the material!) is the actors' vocal and physical delivery – the physical one only to the extent that does not relate to the scenic space, which means primarily mimics (non-verbal expressions). It follows that the ostensive quality of this form is composite visual-acoustic, while the ostensive quality of the scenic form is only visual. Since in opera, the music not only complements but also transforms the acoustic component of the dramatic form, we will be limiting ourselves to *spoken drama* and *the spoken drama stage director*.

The dramatic form pertains to *two aspects* of the interplay, each of which has its specific dramatic effect. Firstly, this is the *intensity* of vocal and physical delivery (speaking and playing) as it leads to a perception of *tension* in the audience. Its diverse, yet designed variations over the course of the performance create the *dynamic* form of drama (in the narrow sense of the word *dynamic*). Secondly, this is the *speed* of vocal and physical delivery, which brings about the impression of *agitation*; we will call the designed form created by its temporal variation the *agogic* dramatic form. Both these forms (dynamic and agogic) incessantly combine in performance, so the resulting dramatic form together with the effect on the audience is not just a sum total, but a product of these two forms. We will call the stage director in this, their *first* function – to create with the actors the *dramatic* form of the work – the **director-conductor** (*režisér-dirigent*).

The parallel with music is striking here. A musical composition – in performance, that is – has both a dynamic and an agogic form given to it, on the basis of the musical notation (with occasional composer's notes), by the performing musician artist. The performance of a composition is not necessarily collective, but often requires more than one artist. As a matter of fact, the number of performing musicians is a criterion in categorising a piece as a *chamber* composition with a few soloist performers (or even just a single one, e.g., a pianist) or an *orchestral/choral* piece with many performers, either orchestral musicians or choral singers, or both combined. Habitually, chamber works are performed without a conductor, who is only present for larger (orchestral or choral) pieces. However, this distinction, justified practically by the smaller number and greater skills of the soloists, is only superficial. In chamber performances, there always is single person who determines the dynamic and agogic forms of the work – it is one of the performers who conducts rehearsals and then imperceptibly also the production, whereas the conductor is separate from the musicians or singers, and their only task is to conduct in full view. It is true that in the past, one of the performers used to be the conductor; the conductor's autonomy was necessitated by artistic development that tended to deliver the best possible performance in both of the forms (dynamic and agogic).

The spoken drama *director-conductor* could also be one of the actors in a small ensemble of solo actors; that would even benefit the work in a way. Eva Vrchlická articulates this well in her article "The Poet, the Actor and the Role": "We are doing Paul Raynal's *The Unknown Warrior* [*Le Tombeau sous l'Arc de Triomphe*]. It only has three characters carrying the whole piece. Nobody should interfere with them. It is inevitable but the director must act too. Fortunately, this is has happened: Václav Vydra is directing and acting."[28] An acting director is like the first violinist in a string quartet: conducting in rehearsal as well as in all the performances, while a director only conducts rehearsals, but *they cannot conduct performances* as an orchestra conductor would. The director must rely on the actors's *"subjective fixity"* of all that has been rehearsed; but that is, as we know from the previous chapter, each separate actor's fixity of their performance, and it is natural that the interplay is what most easily loosens in performance, especially when there is an understudy to replace one of the actors.

---

28 Eva Vrchlická, "Básník, herec a role" [The Poet, the Actor and the Role], *Nové české divadlo 1918-1926* (Praha: Aventinum, 1927), p. 64-66. Eva Vrchlická (1888-1969) was a Czech actress, translator, playwright and novelist. From 1911 until her death, for almost all of her active acting life, she was an actor at the National Theatre in Prague. Her colleague Václav Vydra (1876-1953) was an actor and director, working at the National Theatre from 1922. In Raynal's intimate play for only three actors, Vydra was cast as the Father, but as Vrchlická claims, he started directing the interaction of his colleagues. No other director was included in the production.

A partial recasting therefore uncompromisingly requires a new rehearsal process, if the dramatic form is not to fall prey to personal improvisations.

It follows from here that, unlike the actor, the *director of spoken drama* may be called a *reproductive artist*, but *only* in regards to this *conductor* function – which is not their only one. The director's "art of nuances" is much wider and freer than that of a musical director. Musical scores, especially modern ones, render the dynamic and agogic forms of a composition much more accurately, not only in the many articulation marks but also in the notes themselves (their duration). Moreover, each musician has their own part before them, which enhances the precision of the interplay and facilitates chamber performance "without a conductor". In this respect, the directors is more like a reciter; the director creates the dramatic form of a performance on the basis of a dramatic text, making use of any of the playwright's stage directions, while also considering in rough outlines the expected playing of the actors and their probable conceptions of the figures. That in itself contains so many irrational aspects that the director's conception must bring in much more of their own creativity than just reproductive interpretation. With sung drama, as we shall see later, the situation is entirely different.

It is transpires from the above that a *director-conductor's specific talent* is more related to the playwright's than the actor's. All three of them must have a dramatic sense and the ability of mental transfiguration. The actor and the director must be capable of a "theatrical reading" of a dramatic text; from this moment, however, their creativities burst in different directions: the actor's leads to the figure (*postava*), while the director's to the interplay (*souhra*). The director revives the playwright's theatrical vision and its realisation is finalised on the basis of the imaginative visions of individual figures. That is why it is imperative that the director understands actor performance, but there is no need for the director to be able to perform them, just as it is unnecessary for a musical conductor to be able to play musical instruments (let alone all of them) in their orchestra. The director does not need to have a specific actor talent: the ability of transfiguration, the reproductive technique. And if they have this talent, it better not be too great, otherwise it could limit the director's necessary ability to empathise with all the actors, who are a set of very diverse artistic individualities. After all, a director, as a director, does not act with the actors, but stands separate; and if the director is acting, they carry out two, strictly distinct functions.

It does not follow, of course, that the director-conductor should not be able to act; surely it is only to their benefit, especially in practical terms in rehearsal, where they can more easily express what they want by example rather in words – especially to beginning actors. But that relates to the director's mission as a teacher, which is not the subject of this theoretical study.

THE DRAMATIC FORM

We have asserted that the dramatic form of a performance is *purely temporal*. Since, as we know, dramatic action runs in real time, all principles of the form are come from the axiomatic qualities of real time.

The basic quality of dramatic action is its *strict temporal continuity*. This does not only mean that dramatic action lasts exactly the same as our perception of its performance on stage, but also that *all* (even the tiniest) *phases of this action fall into specific moments of the passing time, and they do so in a specific order* corresponding to *a continuous flow of moments from the past, through the present, to the future*, and that *at a sequential speed exactly determined by the content of the action at any given moment*.

That is to say, it is not possible, first of all, to randomly *shuffle* individual segments of the dramatic action in its temporal sequence. To give a trivial example: it is not possible in the theatre to kill someone in one scene and start to plan the murder in the next scene. We have established this in our discussion on the ideal (imagined) time of narrated action, where this is possible (see Chapter 4). What is new here is that any given segment of the dramatic action must be presented *only at the speed it requires* and no other. So a dramatic situation, for example, may require fast speech and swift acting, while another needs slowness. It is *artistically impossible* to perform the former slowly and the latter quickly; when done this way, the situation is ruined, its meaning mangled and its effect upturned. Certainly this does not mean that a dramatic situation does not allow variation of some "one and only correct" speed of delivery, which would probably be the speed imagined by the play's *author*, without of course being able (in spoken drama) to prescribe it precisely. Nonetheless, a dramatic situation is so *sensitive to the speed* of its delivery that even minor variations from the "right" speed result in a *marked change* in its character and effect. Such minor variations in speed are acceptable perhaps as *possible interpretations* of the situation by individual directors. It is interesting that some situations are less sensitive to the speed of their progression, allowing relatively greater variation, which other situations would never tolerate; similarly, quite some situations still allow relatively rougher speed variation, even though this changes their character significantly, while this would be quite impossible in others, unless as a caricature. Comedy in general tends towards extreme speeds in delivery: very fast and excessively prolonged – both of which is quite uncommon in everyday speech and behaviour and so it easily becomes funny.

> A comparable sensitivity to the tempo of delivery can be found only in music, where the right tempo puts in effect all its beauties to a surprising level, while an "impossible" tempo not only kills them but also proves that the conductor has failed to understand

the composition, or that they have a weak musical sense – just like a director's suitable or unsuitable choice of the pace for the action testifies to their great or poor sense for drama.

Our assertion of the *strict temporal continuity* of dramatic action (*děj*) was made from a noetic standpoint of the so-called practical realism, which states that real time exists on its own and so do real actions that are located "in it", as if in some kind of vessel. From a psychological point of view, we as the audience are offered only a chain of percepts, i.e., dramatic situations, and "time" is no more than a perception of a *specific sequence* of these percepts – that is to say, a mere, but specific relation between them. Apart from a sense of this temporal relation, we must also acknowledge a sense of the *speed of the temporal sequence*, which presupposes some subjective standard according to how we measure what is fast and what is slow. This standard actually exists: it is physiologically given by the periods of blood circulation (the pulse) and psychologically by the related periodisation of our attention. A sequence that runs faster or slower than our pulse has on us the impression of haste or slowness, respectively; between them is an impression of moderate speed. The impression of subjective *duration* of ostensive action (*děj*) is a product of this impression of speed and of numerous percepts that we received in the course of the action. This is what causes the well-known *relativity* of one's subject assessment of time as opposed to objective duration, e.g., measured on a watch, and the *temporal illusions* that results from it ("Where did the time go!") – and each dramatic performance has many of them.

Real time, in which the audience experiences dramatic action, is therefore not objective (physical) as is the time running in the actors' performance on stage, but rather *subjective* (psychological); as such, it belongs to the referential image, not to the technical one. In fact, its real character resides only in the ostensive temporal relation between individual percepts that the onstage play gives us. In other words: the way it seems to run, that is how it "actually" runs (for us), although it may in actuality (i.e., on the stage) run very differently. *This difference must be apparent*, be it intuitively, *to the director when creating the temporal dramatic form.*

Another, no less important quality of real time is *transitoriness*. A certain element of the perceived action (the dramatic situation) is in my consciousness at a particular moment; but it soon loses its sensory liveness, having become a mere mental image that quickly fades, until it disappears from my consciousness altogether. Naturally we can recall it since it stays in the memory and we actually do recall it as soon as any following situations prompts us to it. That first element is immediately replaced by another, new percept in its full sensory liveness, which pronouncedly contrasts with the previous, now faded percept, which *has been*, whereas this one *is*. And this repeats on and on. If we call the moment when we have a percept "the present", then we can say that this *present* tirelessly and greedily *runs* on the ostensive elements of the dramatic action, devouring one after another and immediately casting them out into *the past*, where the elements *accumulate*.

To synthesise such a temporal series of situations makes an *exceptional demand* on our mental activity, permanent straining of attention, careful storing of all that has been in our memory; because that will never come back, yet we must remember it. It is therefore necessary that extensive dramatic action should be *divided into sections*, each at least relatively rounded up and with a length appropriate to our ability to summarise its details into one whole. These are *acts* of a play; experience dictates their length, as we know, between half an hour and an hour. Only in one-act plays can we cope with more because all is over when it ends. Also, the sum of all acts, which we also need to synthesis, has certain length limits of about three hours. Surely we can endure an even longer play but then we feel the palpable aspiration needed to summarise the action, not to mention the pure physiological tiredness that arrives, especially with works that force us to engage intensely. But each act, especially the longer ones, also needs clear subdivision. This is done in *french scenes*, each of which has, as we said above in our discussion of the dramatic situation, a specific and constant number of personas that we as the audience perceive on stage. From scene to scene, this number changes: once there is an entire crowd, then just a few persons, often only two or even just a single one. This quality of dramatic action (or rather its elements: dramatic situations) will be called *quantity* and it is obvious that it has a very specific, unique impression on us – which is also influenced by the size of stage, as we will see later. An extreme case of quantity is surely *no persona* on stage, i.e., the empty stage, which occurs at least for a short while whenever all the personas of a given scene exit and before new ones enter. Although this brings about a palpable division of the dramatic action, which is halted for a brief moment, such a *pause* in the action is different from an *interval* between acts in that running of real time does not stop but continues. The time during a pause is thus "live time" with its dramatic content, be it merely in our imagination (disregarding the percept of the empty stage). Either the pause resonates with the impression of the preceding intense scene, or it is filled with our anticipation of what the next scene would bring. The above subjectivity of dramatic time explains why the length of the pause is such a sensitive issue; by the right length the director may achieve an immense effect (especially when anticipating something bad) and an unsuitable length may do much harm. It is only when the exchange of scenes goes with a change of set, that this results in an actual interval, known as *"scene change"*, on technical grounds.

Let us remark that the scenes' quantity must be distinguished from the extensity of the plot (imagined action), which we have defined as the number of imagined personas participating in a given plot. These plots, as we know, also have their parts, but these are only imagined and they only accidentally, not principally agree with the ostensive division of the dramatic action into *french scenes*. As a reminder: dramatic action usually consists of alternating parts of individual plots (imagined action), and as such it forms a *"temporal mosaic"* of sorts, made of different interspersed plot lines. The director-conductor creates the temporal form of ostensive *dramatic* action, as we suggested in our two charts (of *Ghosts* and *Much Ado*), laying out the structure in proportionate lengths of scenes and acts, and not the temporal form of the plot lines, which are – even in performance – only half imagined.

A third quality of real time that takes effect in a dramatic work is *asymmetry*, the *one-directionality* of its progression. Time is one-dimensional like a line, which is often used to symbolise it; to delimit both of them fully, *two* extremes are necessary. However: both extremes of a line segment *a–b* are of equal value, since a line runs in both directions from *a* to *b*, and from *b* to *a*:

In contrast, both "ends" of the time from *b* to *e* have a completely *different* value, because this time runs only in *one* direction, from *b* to *e*:

The progression of time cannot be inverted, its *beginning* and *end* cannot be swapped; each of them has a completely different meaning than the other, as we all know well.

For this reason, the requirements on the *beginning* and the *ending* of dramatic action or its self-contained, parts, i.e., defined by intervals, are entirely different. I repeat, we are not talking here about the "beginning" and "end" of the self-contained *imagined* action (*děj*) – as discussed above; in plot, only its imagined ending needs to coincide with the ending of the ostensive dramatic action (at least when it comes to the main plot line). At this point, we are concerned with the beginning and ending of the ostensive performance or its part, and so the requirements on them derive from the psychology of perception.

It follows from the transitoriness of time that at the beginning of the dramatic action, we still have *nothing* in our consciousness, apart from the first percept, while at the end we have *everything* that has happened, though only as a memory, crowned with the very last percept. The *opening* must therefore be such as to awake our interest and put us in the desired mood – which is not easy as it must drag us out of the everyday life and its impressions, of which we are full upon arrival in the theatre and which also possess us during the intervals. However, there is no need for the impression of the performance opening to be too strong, because we are still fresh and ready for artistic impressions from a world different to the one outside. In fact, it is not advisable to have an overly strong opening, because the *ending* must top it significantly in order to overcome our mental weariness after so many impressions we have just experienced, and our listlessness towards their effect, which makes us especially impatient if it is "the same thing again and again". For the worst devaluation of a work of art is when it is boredom. That is why dramatic action must *intensify* (*stupňovat*) from the beginning to the end, and this *principle of gradation* (*princip gradace*) also applies to individual acts (and scenes) as much as it does to the whole. What is at stake is always the *concluding culmination*, of which the last must be the greatest.

To arrange this gradation is the task of the director, who employs to that end any available means, actorly as well as scenic. However, the basis for this must be found in the dramatist's text; if there is no such option available in it, the director will have a hard time mending it.

> The requirement of *the concluding culmination*, seemingly very simple, is very complicated in any dramatic text; whoever is able to achieve it, is a true master of the dramatic art. There are many plays with several strong dramatic situations, and yet their overall impression is weak because these scenes are not placed in the work according to the concluding culmination principle, but rather – of a grand opening. A strong start, good early acts, then the weaker ones, with perhaps only the last one boring and a bland ending – and the work is killed. Interestingly, if the distribution of *the same* effects was reversed, the play would work well. The cause is probably that these authors think of their plays only theoretically, as if it were a novel, instead of imagining the progression of their play ostensively, theatrically; they would intuit then that in real time one sequence is not like another. It is always better if the author first thinks of the ending, to which the beginning "leads up", than of the opening, to which they "make" the ending. *Finis coronat opus* – the end praises the work.

In our discussion of the gradation principle we have come to a borderline, where dramatic stylisation begins. Let us return and say a few more words about the character of both kinds of dramatic forms.

The dynamic form is built on the differences in the force of vocal delivery and the power of gestures. There are noisy dramatic situations with big gestures, but also quiet ones with minute mimics. The former prevail in burlesque comedy but also pathetic tragedy, for instance, while the latter in intimate or mystical plays (Maeterlinck). Most places invite a certain medium force, with intensity *highs* and *lows*, efficaciously distributed or simply alternating for the sake of contrast. Of special significance are minor accents in certain moments, achieved by vocal delivery or gesture. In performance, they create two sets – acoustic and visual – with naturally tend to collapse into one but are generally autonomous: often a mere gesture achieves a climax.

The agogic form comes from the differences in the speed of vocal delivery and gestures. What also contributes is the speed of personas' movement on stage, which actually belongs to the scenic form, namely the kinetic one (see the next chapter), which defines the connection between the two forms – the dramatic and the scenic. Again, we can distinguish dramatic situations fast in speech and swift in movement, as opposed to situations slow in speech and casual in movement. The former prevail in numerous comedies; the latter in grand plays. In performances of moderate speed there are certain moments that suddenly speed up, and even more those of absolute calmness, silence and inertia, when the run of the dramatic action *comes to a halt*, but the action itself does not *cease* – in contrast to the above-mentioned pauses with an empty stage – because in these reposes, similar to the fermata in music, the personas remain on stage.

Combinations of both these forms produce four basic types of the ostensive character of a dramatic situation: loud and swift; loud and slow; quiet and swift; and, quiet and slow. The last of these is dramatically the weakest of the four, and as such depends most on a *static, lyrical* effect on the basis of vocal delivery supported by the actors' mimics as well as the static qualities of the scenery.

Here we have touched up the emotional effect of a non-ostensive, *imagined (ideational) form* of the action (*děj*) – that is to say, effects coming from referential images, which the perception of the scene evokes in the audience, and which come primarily from grasping the dramatic text – and as such those images can be obtained just from reading. Nonetheless, the manner of delivery and performance contribute to them on the emotional from in a significant and self-sufficient measure, as we know from our analysis of the "foreign actor's" performance in the previous chapter. The *ideational* content of the action has its own specific emotional effect which is presented to the audience by its manifestation in the ostensive dramatic situation. This effect is down to the playwright, who has written the text in a national language, and to the actors, who produce the international language of non-verbal expression (broadly speaking). The director has no part in this, creating only *the summation of actor figures* – that is, the technical image – albeit this always *according to* the referential image.

In broad terms, there is no parallelism between the ideational (imagined) and the ostensive forms; they may be identical or they may differ. An intellectually immense effect of a specific moment can be delivered in forceful, but also in weak dynamics; the latter option even brings about a uniquely peculiar simultaneous dramatic contrast – as in, for instance, a violent, yet quiet conflict, or a noisy, yet intellectually light jollity. Similarly, a quick sequence of ideationally significant moments, such as in a *catastrophe*, makes us sense the passage of dramatic time as it mercilessly speeds ahead, whereas a sequence of ideationally unimportant moments – the moment of delay, known as *retardation* – creates the impression that time drags on horribly. Through the adoption of an effective dynamic and agogic ostensive form, the director has the creative liberty to interpret the ideational form of the dramatic work – *dramatically*, i.e., with a view to its overall aesthetic (but not yet artistic) *effect*.

So, *the spoken drama director-conductor* appears to be an artist whose place, figuratively speaking, is somewhere on the proscenium, on the dividing line between the stage and the auditorium: still among the actors, directing their interplay, the director is also in the midst of the audience as the first of them – long before the theatre fills for the opening night. Only then does the director diseappear, having completed their task, only to stay on invisible in the same place.

7 THEATRICAL SCENE: THE STAGE DIRECTOR'S SECOND TASK

This chapter is not called "The Dramatic Scene" primarily because the word "scene" has two meanings, signifying not only the stage but also an episode of dramatic action, and it is the latter sense in which the expression "the dramatic scene" is used. Additionally, we also wished to indicate that we are only going to discuss the stage form that we find in modern theatre, not others, such as the arena of the ancient Greek theatre, the circus and so forth. Naturally, we will only consider the stage (in this book) when it is used for performances of dramatic works and not others, such as ballets; in this function, we call it the scene (scéna).

The scene (of a dramatic work) *is the room where actors perform.* This is its *technical* definition, where the word *"room"* refers to an *enclosed* part of space. The creation of such rooms is obviously the task of *architecture*, and the architect designing a theatre building designs, alongside other interior rooms, the stage and its accessory, the auditorium. The stage is designed with a view to satisfy its future purpose, just like, for instance, the assembly room of a town hall is. As a technical image, the stage belongs to architecture. Yet, there is a difference.

The stage becomes the scene *only when it is being acted on* in a dramatic performance. The actors, real people, *therefore inevitably belong to the scene*, forming an *essential* fill (*výplň*) of its actual space. This does not apply to any other room: the above assembly room is not an assembly room only when the town councillors are actually in it, but also they are *imagined* to be there. This is not just a superficial difference but a fundamental one, since actors on the scene *represent* some dramatic personas and, through their interplay, *show* some dramatic action. The said technical image gets accompanied by a *referential image*, and that also relates to the scene: **The scene is a room** *representing* **the location of dramatic action**.

No other architectonic room has this quality; the assembly room, for instance, does not represent an assembly room, but it is one – and it does not represent anything at all. Architecture is not a mimetic art and it evokes in us merely a technical image; the scene there cannot be counted into architecture; by its essence it belongs to a mimetic art. That the mimetic art in question is the dramatic art, is self-evident. The scene is a component of the dramatic work and it only *resembles* architectonic creations in *some* of its features, nothing more. Nevertheless, even this similarity, as we shall see, has significant implications for its formation.

A complete definition of the scene respecting *both* the associated images, technical and referential, is this: *The scene is a room in which actors as dramatic personas present, through their interplay, a dramatic action.* The formation of the scene must therefore observe the *correspondence* principle between the technical and the conceptual images; the actor must do that (in the actor figure – dramatic persona correspondence) and so does the director in their first task (the correspondence between the actors' interplay and the dramatic action). This process of formation is shared between the architect and the director in their second function, as the director-scenic (režisér-scénik). Let us first discuss those features of the scene that mainly fall to the architect. These are firstly *the delimitation* and *the segmentation* of the scene, and also the non-actor *fill* of the scene, which are merely optional.

DELIMITATION OF THE SCENE

The primitive stage is delimited from below by the physical ground, which is either fenced off like in a circus, and so somewhat lower than the auditorium, or elevated, forming a floor ("a world on the boards"). The stage room is simply the spatial column above this ground, of an indeterminate height. The audience looks at the scene *from all sides except one*, where the scene is likewise physically delimited from a room from which actors enter the scene and to which they then exit. Different spectators see this scene differently depending on where they are looking from; for the audience *as a whole* this type of scene differs only in the direction "below – above", and not "right – left" or "downstage – upstage". In those directions all parts of the scene are of equal value, i.e., its space is *homogeneous* – it is, in brief, an *objective* (i.e., super-individual) space.

The modern theatrical stage is principally different. It is also delimited from below by the floor, but as well as this it is delimited *from above and on all sides except one*, from which the audience is looking at the scene. This delimitation is provided by a physical, architectonic frame, constructed in front of the scene, which limits the view of the scene from both sides and above. This is the *optical* delimitation: the scene extends in its width and height only as far as we can see from the auditorium through an opening in the frame, the proscenium arch. Covering it with a curtain means closing the scene completely for the spectators – then, the scene does not exist for us. This happens not only outside the performance but also during the intervals.

Despite the diverse seating in the audience, it may be said that this scene is available to their sight only from one side and it offers more or less *a single view* to all. This scene is differentiated for the audience as a whole not only in "below – (and especially) above", but also "right – left" and "downstage – upstage". The audience's eyes pierce the scene in one *in-depth* direction, stopping only at the physical boundary of its background. This scene, designed for a unified view of the entire audience, may be called *perspectival*, although its qualities are not perspectival in the strict sense, which would require not only a single side but rather a single point to look from. For the audience, the theatrical scene is not an objective space, one that is more or less the same for any spectator, but rather a *subjective* one, and that, specially, *visual*. Its first characteristic is that its non-see-through objects that are closer hide the more distant ones. Second, all that we can see in it has only a seeming size, which *changes* along with its depth, diminishing according to the well-known perspectival principle. The actual size of the objects can only be guessed based on their distance from the border of the scene, which is – in regards to the scene's physical separation – only *imagined*: it is an imaginary surface defined by the front rim of the floor, known as the foot of the stage, and the architectonic frame (the proscenium arch). For a reference we need a measure, well known from experience; and that is *the human figure*, which is present on the scene in all situations. The human figure is also a measure for the *size* of the scene as such; it is certainly possible to narrow the frame of the scene by suitable means including architectonic ones (e.g., drapes), which reduces the scene width and height; also moving the physical background closer can make the scene shallower. Especially a shallow scene offers great technical advantages of its acoustic qualities both in spoken and sung drama.

The scene delimited in this way represents the *location* of the dramatic *action*, with such specificity as the author of the drama wishes. If the location is defined only in general terms, as any location *where* particular dramatic personas interact, these personas will suffice as the scene's fill and the delimitation of the scene may be merely architectonic, i.e., representing nothing in itself – just like, in the visual arts, the frame of a painting or the plinth of a statue. Such a scene is called *neutral*. Usually, though, the location of the action requires greater specificity. In such cases, even the delimitation must be made by objects that represent something, defining the location of the action as needed.

However, the location of action is not delimited by the boundaries of the scene, but extends to its surroundings, and that in all directions. Particularly important is its extension into the depth. Sometimes, a drama requires the stage to represent a location that extends much farther than its actual depth, e.g., a street or even an open landscape stretching all the way to the horizon. Since, as we know, the space of the scene is, for the audience (i.e., visually speaking), an optical space, governed by perspectival principles, it is possible to use perspectival (optical) illusions in that case. The space of the scene will transition in the in-depth direction to an *illusory* space. A more rapid reduction of, for example, the houses forming a street will achieve an impression of a much greater depth than what it actually is (this illusion is also used in architecture); the crucial point is that the distant space seems to us so foreshortened that it may be simply replaced by a surface at the back – irrespective whether it appears as a mere skyline (a curved backdrop, i.e., "cyclorama" is used here with great effect) or displays various objects that are very distant and only *painted*. The scene, which at times may be closed, now appears to *break out* into an unlimited space, which belongs to the "location of the action", but not to the scene, because the action of course does not take place there. The art of painting is used here for purely practical reasons, in order to achieve an illusion of an open space that the author requires and that certainly has a different mood than an enclosed space. More about this will be said when discussing "the fill of the scene".

> Apart from this *ostensive*, though illusory extension of the location in depth and partly in height and sideways (especially when a curved backdrop is used), the location of the action always extends beyond the boundaries of the visible scene *in our imagination*. Adjacent sections of the stage, technically referred to as "backstage", always represent the adjacent places of the location, for this is where dramatic personas enter from and where they exit. So, for instance, when the scene represents a forest, we imagine a forest on both sides as well; when it represents a room, there are other rooms to the sides and perhaps an open area (a garden, a street) behind a back wall. When the scene is made smaller with a built set as in the case of a room, we may get a glimpse of these spaces (through windows or an open door), thanks to which they become ostensive at least in part, and as such they become part of the scene. Often significant moments of dramatic situations are shifted to them – usually only in part – even when one cannot see but only overhear what happens there; this has an eerie, mysterious and therefore suspenseful effect (this is often done by Ibsen, for example). To an imaginary space behind the scene are shifted those scenes that would be too awful to show (but different eras and environments are not equally sensitive about this) – and naturally those events that cannot be satisfactorily realised for technical reasons (e.g., arriving on horseback, etc.).
>
> Less common is extending the location to the space below the floor (one such example is in Schiller: Leicester's scene during the execution of Mary Stuart in the room below) and above, beyond the visible scene. In magical plays, and especially in operas, supernatural creatures arrive from there, both chthonic (through the trap door) and otherworldly (from the fly tower); not to mention spectacular shows (in Shaw's *Misalliance*, entirely "natural" people arrive in a plane from above). Much more common are entries from an invisible depth in the background, such as when the scene represents a hill top; or a tragic departure when there is a river or an abyss in the back into which the dramatic persona throws themself. In the present day, we have seen entries from the depth in front; one might object that this interferes with the delimita-

tion of the scene by the stage front. But this is a moot point because the space to which the scene expands does not belong to the auditorium; it is the space of the orchestra pit, which can be – if it is empty and darkened – effectively used for such an (partly ostensive) extension of the location.

Segmentation of the Scene. It is necessary to distinguish two principally different ways of segmenting the stage according to its different relationships to the conceptual image of the "location of action".

The first type of segmentation is radical, as it divides the stage space into parts representing originally different and unrelated locations. As such, it is a *division of the stage* into two or even three autonomous scenes. This segmentation is possible only along the in-depth axis because it is the only one, as we know, that offers heterogeneous spaces of the "background" and "forefront". The simplest type is an autonomous scene at the back, with its own architectonic frame or even a curtain, capable of all the functions of a normal scene and representing any required and specific location. The forefront of the stage forms in contrast to the neutral scene, delimited only architectonically (both at the front and the back). When the action occurs at the back, the space of the front scene *merges* with that of the back scene, which then determines the location of both scenes whenever necessary; however, when the action takes place only on the front scene, its location is autonomous and the back scene, closed off by a curtain, is out of play. This is the principle of what is known as the *Shakespearean* stage, only adapted to our requirements of an ostensively determined scene.

Fundamentally different is the type of *scene segmentation* in the usual, narrower sense of the word: the stage room is divided into different parts representing different locations, but these locations are dependent on one another and as such they comprise a single aggregate location. It observes a *"unity of place"*, though in a different sense than is meant by the classical requirement that forbids even a successive change of location within acts or scene changes – which is a requirement that is unjustified and dogmatic. The unity of the scenic space segmented in the present sense not only allows the action to develop in different location one after another but also to do so simultaneously – which, as we shall see later, is especially consequential for music drama, which makes two simultaneous actions possible also from the acoustic point of view.

This type of scene segmentation can occur not only in the in-depth dimension, i.e., on the forefront and the background, but also in width, i.e., on the right and the left, and in height. Sometimes it can even be triple, especially in width (e.g., a street and rooms inside houses adjacent to it), combined in all three dimensions of the scene (balconies!). The means of achieving this are diverse: it depends on what the scene is supposed to represent. The means can be diverse objects placed in the scene, many of them flat (partitions, drapes and so on), but also adjustments of the floor's height. So the background (upstage) area is commonly raised over the forefront (downstage) area, simply to make it visible.

THE FIXED FILL OF THE SCENE (PEVNÁ VÝPLŇ SCÉNY); SCENIC OBJECTS IN GENERAL

The fundamental fill of the scene, as we know, are live actors representing personas of the dramatic action. But numerous dramatic works ask that the *location* represented by the scene should be determined in a much more concrete and detailed way than by dramatic personas and their actions alone. After all, dramatic action to be fully realised often requires – besides personas – a great variety of objects. We can thus commonly see the most diverse kinds of *objects* in the scene, generally with two kinds of purpose: firstly, the *characterising* purpose, i.e., to define personas and the location effectively, and secondly, the *functional* purpose, to participate in the dramatic action. However, it is not possible to separate objects according to these two purposes because for the most part they serve both, even though in an unequal measure. Yet, some of them are there for the purpose of characterisation only, which is in particular true for those that signify the location as a specific *environment*.

> The motley collection of all these objects may be arranged, from a technical point of view, to form a *continuous* scale *"from an actor to the scene"*. In our early discussion of the actor figure, we observed that between the actor's *mask* – partly identified with their body – and the actor's *costume* there is a continuous scale (e.g., a wig). Separable parts of the costume, such as a cloak, a cap, a sword, etc., are halfway towards so-called props, which actors use in performance; other objects are already stand-alone, such as a goblet, a book and other petty things, typical for their mobility. Props can also include such objects as a chair, which an actor sits on, but that already is halfway towards immobile objects filling the scene, because while an actor may move a chair to another place, the same cannot be said about a bench in front of a house that serves the same purpose. Furniture in the scene determines the location not only as a room as such, but also – with a view to the play's intentions – as a very specific room, e.g., a plain chamber in a farmhouse; a similar purpose is assigned, for instance, to trees, bushes or boulders (which may also be sat on, if necessary) to determine the location as a specific kind of landscape. This brings us to objects so large that they not only fill the scene but also create its boundaries. These are the *fixed* components of the scene, which do not change during a given part of the dramatic action. We will call them *decorations*, broadening the technical term generally used for painted objects, just like we have broadened the word "props" to include even such objects as furniture and others; the coarse distinc-

tion between the two groups of objects – bearing in mind the continuous scale between them – is based on their mobility or fixity, and partly by size. Considering their concrete use in a given performance, these are, however, only relative differences.

All objects on our scale "from an actor to the scene" have some qualities in common and follow the same rules, which we will briefly outline. Firstly, they are, technically speaking, predominantly *inanimate* objects, that is to say mere *things*, in which they fundamentally differ from actors. That immediately brings up the question as to what *stuff* (or combination of materials) they are made of and what are the laws of their production? At first sight we might conclude that they belong to *arts and crafts and the industry*, and sure enough they do when we consider them on their own, e.g., when they are in a theatre storeroom. However, when we look at them as the fill of the scene during a performance – which is the only appropriate attitude towards these objects – we will realise that that is not the case. They are clearly a component of the dramatic work, but dramatic art is a *mimetic art*, and that as a whole, in *all that it involves*. We have acknowledged that an actor represents a dramatic persona and that the room of the scene, which we initially wanted to assign to architecture, does not belong there because, in performance, it represents the location of the action. The same is true for all objects that we grouped among these two fundamental elements of dramatic art, because these objects also *represent something*. In contrast, arts and craft products *do not in principle represent anything*, and in that they belong to constructional works, with which they are logically often categorised in the single discipline of *architecture* in the broadest sense of the word.

A green carpet in my room does not represent a carpet; it is one. In contrast, a green carpet in a scene, representing a clearing in the woods, is a carpet as well, but additionally it represents grass. Someone might object that a carpet in a scene showing a living room or a parlour, does not represent a carpet because in this case it actually is one. But this is wrong: even this carpet represents something, namely a carpet on the floor of this parlour, say, in late nineteenth-century Paris. What deludes us is that in the former case, the technical image of the *material* (what was it made of?) and the referential image (what is the material of the represented object?) are *different* (fabric and grass), while in the latter case the two mental images are the *same* (and additionally the idea of its purpose is the same: covering and decorating the floor). It is true that in mimetic arts (painting, sculpture) the technical idea and the conceptual idea of the material are always *different* (barring trivial exceptions, such as a wooden statuette of a fisherman with a wooden oar), it is a feature of the *dramatic art*, as we have pointed out in the first part of this book, that there is a *material correspondence* (látková shoda) between the work of art and what it represents, because the material of both the actor figure and the dramatic persona is a living human body with its performances. This correspondence, principally valid for the fundamental component of the dramatic art, i.e., acting, is not obligatory for any fill of the scene, which we are considering now, yet it is acceptable and even (somewhat dogmatically speaking) desirable. The material of the objects intended for the scene *may, but does not have to be, the same* as the material of the objects they represent in the scene; if it is or not, is dictated by purely pragmatic reasons.

> While Hamlet's velvet beret will most likely be also made of velvet, his stepfather's golden crown will hardly be of gold; who could afford it? The skull Hamlet talks to may be of bone, but the sword he stabs Polonius with must not be made of steel to prevent injury. A chair in a townspeople's room may be wooden, but a boulder in the woods cannot be real stone: how would anyone lug it there? And so on and so forth. It is all so simple that it makes one wonder why so many complicated and contrived studies have been written about it. Philosophical meditations of the *falsity* of theatrical objects have no solid ground, and the theoretical requirement of *genuine materiality* in the scene is entirely unjustified. Falsity exists only in non-mimetic arts (e.g., faux marble on buildings), but not in mimetic arts. Why does no one wonder, for example, that a porcelain puppy is not made of "genuine" material?

Nonetheless, the mimetic character of scenic objects that allows for an arbitrary choice in their material also creates certain conditions that the objects must meet. Their task is to evoke a referential image in us – and since what is at stake is specifically the mimetic art of drama, this *referential* image must be *focused dramatically*. And that, as we know, applies in two ways: first, in characterising the dramatic persona and especially the location, and second, in taking part in the dramatic action. Two rules follow from this regarding the choice of material and the object's making. As for the former task, all scenic objects do that, albeit not to the same degree; the latter applies only to some objects.

A scenic object with a characterising function does not evoke in us the relevant referential image on its own; the image is evoked in us by *a visual percept* that we have of the object while sitting in the auditorium. The first rule follows from this:

1. The **characterising scenic object must** *have an appearance* **that evokes in us the desired referential image**. No more but also no less. That is to say: it does not need *to be* what it represents. But still it *may* be like it! Theoretically speaking, it is all the same. On the other hand, it *must* look like it, otherwise it would not evoke the desired image and thus it would be *dramatically* invalid. And that is an existential issue of stage stylisation, as we shall see in Chapter 10.

A scenic object with an active function in the dramatic action is a somewhat different case. It is present now only for our eyes, but also for those performing the dramatic action, i.e., the actors: actual people who come in contact with it and use it for some purpose. A second rule follows from this:

2. **A functional scenic object must** *be able* **to fulfil its real function in the dramatic action**. The function of an object is in fact a particular *relation* between the object and the *persona* that uses it for some purpose. If there is an object before us that obviously "intended" to be used by someone in one way or another, its functional relation is only imagined; it is only when the persona actually uses it that the functional relation becomes real (actual), by being showed as such. In real and ostensive dramatic action, functional relations may only be real. A sword, for example, as a component of a dramatic persona's costume, is a functional object only if the persona uses it in action; a sofa in a room becomes functional only when sat or laid upon during the action – otherwise, they are no more than characterising objects, the former of the persona and the latter of the location. The real dramatic relation is clearly an asymmetrical and bilateral relation: a *persona* uses an object for... (actively); an *object* serves a persona to ... (passively). So far, we have only considered the passive form.

The first rule determines the choice of the material and the shape of practically every object; if the object is functional, then also the second rule applies, which usually changes – and even significantly complicates – the technical aspect of making the object.

> Our above example of a boulder in a gorge in the woods will serve. We have said that it cannot be made of stone for practical reasons; this is not necessary after all as long as it has the *appearance* of a boulder, which may be achieved by using greyish paper, for example. However, if the author or director want a dramatic persona to sit on it, it must be fortified to make it possible. If its only task is to characterise the location, it may even be painted only, provided that it obeys certain perspectival conditions.
>
> This brings us back to *painting* as an art form that helps in building the scene. This time, we do not deal with an illusory space, but rather with an illusory *physical* form.

The requirement of the *physicality of scenic objects* – that is, only of those that the referential image needs to be physical – comes from the fact that an actor – the essential fill of the scene – has a real, three-dimensional corporeality not only as a technical "figure" but also as a referential "dramatic persona". Exceptions, such as a projection of supernatural beings by a *sciopticon* (a kind of magic lantern), are justified by the exceptionality of a dramatic persona, which is in that case only an *apparition*. Thus, the above requirement is theoretically fully justified, especially since the space in which the actors perform is also real and three-dimensional, and *appears* as such to us as well. We estimate the depth of the space we perceive from the objects we can see in it, on the basis of our perspectival experiences. However, we have asserted that the optical space is not homogeneous in its in-depth dimension: actual physical objects seem three-dimensional only in close quarters, and the farther they are, the flatter they appear, until they seem entirely flat. Let us apply these specific findings to the first rule discussed above:

A scenic object must be made so that it (at least) *appears* **to be physical.**
It follows from this that in close quarters, which means that part of the stage where the actors are, all objects must not only appear, but actually *be* physical, otherwise next to the actors they would not look physical but flat, which would be unacceptable in regards to the *referential* images they evoke. It is only in the distance, which means in the illusory space that extends the location optically beyond the scene, that it is acceptable and even desirable that the objects that would otherwise be physical, should be flat, i.e., painted.

The real space of the scene does not well tolerate painted perspective (e.g., on the side wings), because it is the same for the entire audience, whereas the perspectival images of physical objects always differ a little for each seat in the auditorium. Even the aforementioned artificial deepening of the location by foreshortening objects more towards the upstage is problematic because the actor cannot shrink in this way. It is acceptable only if actors never enter these distant places; on the other hand, this device may be used to create an illusion of a large dramatic persona that will appear only in these areas, because there the persona will seem supernaturally big. In short, *the unity of the optical space must be preserved for the entire location.*

THE STATIC SCENIC QUALITIES

If we consider the scene without the actors performing in it (which in itself is inadmissible) and focus only on its *fixed fill*, we must say that from the point of view of a spectator, who perceives the scene as "a location", the scene – despite being an optical and static formation – *does not belong to the visual arts* but to the dramatic art, as its component. When we say "a scenic *picture*", we use the word only figuratively. It is clearly not "a picture" in the sense of a painting, which is technically a planary work that *only* presents to us an illusory space and illusory physical shapes, even if it does not remain visually in one flat surface. The art of *painting*, as we have seen, does not participate in dramatic art as a component of the dramatic work (i.e., of the performance), but is external to it as an *artistic craft*, participating in the *technical* creation, just like various other crafts, e.g., costume making. This is by no means to belittle scenic painting artistically, but only to define its place within dramatic art. In brief, the scenic painter works for the stage, that is to say for the director, and not for the auditorium, i.e., for the audience. The painter's creative work is painting, not a picture.

Let us briefly mention the theory of the so-called *relief stage*, used without success at the Künstlertheater in Munich. It is (cf. p. 79) a telling example that illustrates how principally incorrect it is to apply the laws of an independent art to a component of the dramatic art on the basis of its seeming similarity. A relief is more than a mere flat surface, like a painting, but it adds protruding real physical shapes, contained in a certain shallow spatial layer. The idea was that as a similar layer one could take a sufficiently shallow stage, whereupon the artistic laws of the relief could be applied to it. However, as soon as we look at a relief as a work of mimetic art, we realise that the spatial layer in question does not have a normal spatial structure because physical objects are always flattened here to various degrees; in a flat relief this is almost complete flatness. This means that the depth dimension in a relief, viewed as a painting, is invalidated. If it was required accordingly that, on the relief stage, one should neglect the depth dimension, which would limit the actors' stage business to height and width, the absurd character of this dramatic scene becomes immediately evident. The actors' playing is thus not only unnecessarily impoverished, but also significantly weakened because – as we shall see later – it is most effective particularly in the in-depth direction.

The British theorist Edward Gordon *Craig* even considered the actor a part of the visual arts. It is no wonder then that the requirement of stylisation led him to the puppet.

When it comes to the *aesthetic*, i.e., emotional *effect* of the objects filling the scene, the same holds true with what we established in the chapter on dramatic personas. The *dramatic* effect of all these objects springs from the emotional effect of the *referential images* they evoke in us. They are evoked on the basis of our life experiences, which have created associations between the perceptions of certain objects and certain mental images – or even entire clusters of images – with one or another emotional colouring. To put it in other words: the dramatic effect of scenic objects does not depend on the direct, but rather on the *associative* factor of our perceptions. As for the conditions securing the dramatic quality of this effect, there are two. One: the effect the objects have must get *integrated* into the effect of the dramatic situation. This applies, naturally, to all functional objects, in particular props. A lifted sword in the hand of a dramatic persona has a different effect than a lifted cup, depending on the respective dramatic situation. A bench on which lovers sit down has a different mood than a piano, on which one of the onstage company plays. And two – which applies to objects that characterise the location: the objects' associative effect must *intensify* the dramatic scenes that take place in the given environment. A different mood flows from a parlour with old-fashioned furniture than from a prison cell with bare walls; a different emotional accent comes from trees and shrubs in a landscape than a deck of a ship with its rigging. But since the emotional impression of such a static "scenic picture" is unchanging, it creates in fact a *constant accompaniment of the changeable* effect of the part of dramatic action that takes place in it – sometimes agreeing, at other times contrasting with it. We shall therefore refer to the associative (ideational and emotional) qualities of these relatively constant fill of the scene, intented to characterise the location, as *the static scenic qualities*.

> Here again, just like with dramatic personas, it is necessary to distinguish the *direct* effects that these scenic objects have on our mood *immediately* (i.e., unmediated), that is not as representations of something else, but by their own optical qualities, colours, light and shapes. In practice, especially in every-day life, these effects on the mood merge with the former ones, but for the sake of theory, we must distinguish them because these mood impressions may be artistically controlled by the stylisation of objects in the above aspects. This is what painting achieves according to its own specific principles and what the dramatic art must achieve according to its own. These mood qualities – in this case not the ideational qualities, because they stem directly from the percept – can be best perceived by us when colours and shapes are stylised so intensely that we do not recognise what the objects are representing. Since these direct effects do not come from the conceptual image, these purely optical qualities are not *dramatic qualities* despite the fact that they affect us directly from the scene; we will refer to them as *the pictorial scenic qualities* (*scénické kvality malebné*) – that is to say, not "painterly" scenic qualities, because they differ from them in their scenic structure. We shall discuss them later under dramatic stylisation.

෴ ෴ ෴

THE *KINETIC* SCENIC QUALITIES

We have shown that the scene, *potentially* filled with immobile, lifeless objects, does not belong to any branch of fine arts. One could object that it creates a *new, autonomous* kind of fine art, a kind of *"mimetic architecture"*. However, this view necessarily fails too once we take into account the *fundamental*, i.e., necessary and sufficient, fill of the scene – live people, i.e., the actors, or rather (from the point of the referential images) the dramatic personas. This is the *dramatic scene proper*, i.e., the *location of the dramatic* action. As such, there is no grounds to include it in the fine arts because all artefacts of the fine arts are immobile and therefore purely spatial, whereas the form of the dramatic scene for all its visual form is permanently *changing*. It is a *spatio-temporal* object, with nothing akin to it to be found in the fine arts, but rather in *dance*, which in its pure form, again, is not a mimetic art.

Strictly speaking, the dramatic scene in its totality is the *optical component* of a dramatic work – as a spectator would perceive it if they could only see it, without hearing it. Although the overall perception of the work would be much impoverished (distorted, in fact), what would be left of it – the dramatic scene – is still so immensely complex that it almost defeats theoretical analysis on account of its irrationality. Therefore, simplification is necessary on several fronts. We have achieved one simplification by discussing in isolation the static component of the scene, which contrasts conspicuously with everything else that changes in time. In what follows, we will thus disregard this component *as if* it were a neutral scene of sorts. Observing changes in an appearance of such a scene, we find that they are caused by *movements* of the actors (or rather, dramatic personas) taking place in the scene. However, no task of the study of art is more difficult than a theoretical treatment of movement. Let us just consider that it happens in up to three dimensions and what is more, in the temporal dimension too! There is no notation that can summatively and perfectly capture the data of all four dimensions, which would systemise movement for theoretical inquiry. Luckily, when it comes to the dramatic work, we may simplify movement in the scene by disregarding all *minor and partial* moves the actor makes and by limiting the purview to the *major* ones relating to the body *as a whole*. For example, an actor walks across the stage, then sits down and remains seated for a while. For the sake of our scenic analysis, this will be two movements only: walking and sitting down, followed by a rest, although the actor may be speaking, smiling and gesticulating all the way. We may ignore such minor movements for now, since we consider mimics (non-verbal expression) under the actorly component of the work; as such, we have analysed them from a dramatic perspective in the previous chapters, mainly in Chapter 5.

In order to capture this simplified – and yet, due to its variability, still tangled – **"dramatic scene"** in the narrow sense, let us *subdivide* it into temporal sequences – moments during which *the arrangement of actors in the scene remains more or less unchanged*. This gives us "scenic situations", analogical to "dramatic situations", which served as subdivisions of the dramatic action. These two types of situations do not generally match each other in time; on the contrary, they often cross one another. Usually scenic situations are much shorter than the dramatic ones. Only exceptionally do they last longer (e.g., a longer dialogue between seated figures); on the contrary, the scene often gets so busy that its appearance changes with every new moment. Since spatial movement is continual, a *continuous* sequence of scenic situations arises, each of a specific duration. Such a detailed subdivision is artificial but necessary in such cases: it is the well-known principle of the cinematograph.

In this *temporal change* of the scene – sudden, abrupt or even temporarily suspended – is its true sense as the *dramatic scene*. Obviously, the appearance of each scenic situation – during which the positions of personas do not principally change – has its own dramatic values; at the same time, we also assess each situation as a *transitional point* between the situation that preceded and that which will follow – at least as far as we can expect. For this reason, we will refer to *all* the qualities presented to us by a dramatic scene (in our reductive definition) as scenic *kinetic qualities*, in contrast to the static ones discussed in the previous section – and we will further distinguish between *positional* scenic qualities, as presented by each scenic situation, and *motoric* scenic qualities, which arise through the temporal sequence of scenic situations, i.e., by changes in the positional qualities.

Positional scenic qualities, given the relative stability of each scenic situation, are in fact only spatial; they might seem to belong to the *static* qualities of the scene and it is true that they often merge with them in a single "picture" for us as the audience. The main difference is that they merge with them *only for a while*, only as long as the given scenic situation lasts. As soon as the scenic situation changes, they visibly separate from the true static qualities. Secondly, we have already noted that we understand the positional qualities *kinetically*: they are an outcome of the preceding movement and the starting point of the following one, and that gives them different meanings even if they retain the same appearance. When I see two personas on stage standing a few steps apart, I understand their position differently if I know that they were farther apart before and that they have been coming together; and yet again differently if I know they have both approached one another, or just one of them; and differently again if I know that they were together and they have moved apart, either both at once or just one of them. If I see someone standing by a door on the side when the curtain rises, I understand the position differently when I find out if they have just entered or are about to depart. Why do I not make such nuanced distinctions while perceiving the positions of scenic objects? Simply because I know that the scenic objects are not alive, while personas are live creatures, with autonomous movement and with mental capacity, whose positions *result from purposeful* movement, irrespective of whether they are aware of the purpose or not. It is only when I can see in the scene an inanimate object in an unusual position that I consider it kinetically: a knocked-over chair in the scene is a result of a movement probably performed by a person, a "trace" of their anger or shock and so on.

As for *motoric* scenic qualities, in another aspect, namely in the *speed* of scenic movement of personas, they merge with the *agogic* qualities discussed towards the end of the previous chapter – relating to the speed of delivery as well as to the speed of the visible play, non-verbal expressions and gestures. However, they differ from them in their changing position within the scene; that change is determined by the *trajectory* of their movement in the scene. The fact that we perceive and assess their speed suggests that motoric qualities also have *strict temporal continuity* (see the end of the previous chapter).

The scenic kinetic values may be considered purely technically. In this case they appear to us as *relations* between actors – or more precisely, between *actor figures and the scene* as the room in which they move. We will call them *scenic relations*, keeping in mind that they are variable in time and only of relative stability within one scenic situation. Since there are generally several personas in the scene, these scenic relations are composite (manyfold); therefore we need to subdivide them into the *elementary* ones, expressing individual persona's relation to the scene, and the *complex* ones, expressing the relations between the primary scenic relations; the simplest of them is the *mutual* scenic relation, which determines the scenic relation of *two personas towards each other*.

This concludes our analysis of the dramatic scene, which we have deconstructed from two different viewpoints – one could say from two intersecting directions: according to time into the scenic situations, and according to the number of personas into primary scenic relations. The former are simple when it comes to the number of personas, but variable in time, while the latter are complex in the number of personas, but temporally stable. It is only exceptional, in a solo performance, that the scenic situation contains an elementary scenic relation. Let us also emphasise that scenic situations and scenic relations, as relations between optical percepts, are *ostensive*.

The analysis of the dramatic scene needs to go beyond the technical aspect because a dramatic work is a mimetic work of art. Actor figures represent dramatic personas, their acting represents dramatic action, and the scene represents the location of this action. *Scenic relations*, which we perceive as the audience, *are ceaselessly joined by dramatic relations* – of which we become aware from our audio-visual perceptions of the actors' performances (interpreted by referential images), as well as from the meaning of their speeches delivering the dramatic text. This is how the *dramatic* qualities (this is to say, referential images) *permeate* the scenic kinetic qualities, which *by themselves* would lack them – as can be seen in clasiccal ballet, which contains scenic kinetic qualities but is devoid of referential images – especially of the dramatic ones – because the dancers do not represent anyone (in contrast to the pantomime, especially the dramatic one). Scenic kinetic qualities *become dramatic* by means of this psychological process. This process can be schematically outlined as follows:

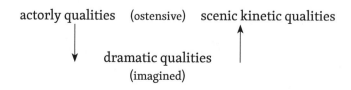

As can be seen, the scenic and the dramatic qualities, which combine here, are by their origin autonomous and independent of one another: they simply exist side by side and the resulting *dramatic impression* is a product of their *co-existence* – whereas there is a causal relation between the actorly and the dramatic qualities. The impression from the same scenic situation differs substantially depending on a given dramatic situation; and vice versa, a particular dramatic situation may be strongly influenced depending on the varying formation of a given scenic situation.

> So for instance, we see two personas on stage approaching one another from opposite sides. How different our impression can be if we know whether they are friends or enemies! If friends, they may seem to be attracted to one another by some fluid sympathetic force; if enemies, they are driven by a brutal force of vengefulness that overrules their mutual antipathy. Additionally, what nuances can be brought into either dramatic relationship by slowing down the pace, even if temporarily, or even by coming to a complete halt, whether by both actors, or just one!

Dramatising scenic relationships induces in them an entirely new and unexpected element – a *dynamic* element, which enters into both positional and motoric qualities. However, this dynamism is not of a mechanical but of a mental (psychic) kind. The metaphorical expressions of being drawn to someone, of being pushed away or of rushing "on the wings of love", acquire a *symbolic ostension* here. Indeed, does it not seem to us that two lovers, left on stage free and alone, are yoked together by some mental force that drives them with irresistible power towards one another? And do we not feel how hard it is for them to part and what effort they must sever this invisible but strong thread of their sympathies? Can we not all but see how an angry gesture or just someone's mere glance gushes forth a mental stream that makes the other persona bolt in headless retreat or at least an involuntary step back?

The dramatising of scenic kinetic relations *transfers* in our eyes to the *stage space* itself. Dramatic personas, represented by actors, are a sort of *force centres* of varying intensity, depending on the dramatic weight of the persona in a given dramatic situation. Their dramatic relations, determined by the situation, are then *force lines* of sorts that expand and contract between the personas. A dramatic scene, filled with such a network of force lines and *motoric tracks* created by them, is then a *force field* of sorts, variable in shape and the the force of its individual components. The effects coming out of this dynamic field transfer to the auditorium, on to the audience. This is the *dramatic tension of the scene*.

> It is noteworthy that a similar formation can also be found in the visual arts. Every architectural work is likewise such a dynamic field and a network of force lines. However, these are *mechanical* forces: the physical weight of the mass, which shows

as pressure and traction, and the solidity and elasticity of the material that resists it. These forces and counterforces are in perfect balance: a pillar may support the mass of an arch, but the pillar props it up and bears it. Therefore, if the sight of architecture (especially the Gothic style) evokes in us a tension of the forces involved, the resulting impression is one of serenity, not of movement. Movement within a force field comprising mechanical forces could be found, for instance, in an engine room. A motoric field of organic forces (albeit merely physiological, not mental) can be found in purposely shaped spaces of circuses and variety theatres where acrobats and other artistes perform. The so-called *constructivist stage* transfers this formational principle on to the scene of the dramatic work of art (i.e., theatre), which is incorrect, since it is one-sided. We emphasised the physiological side of an actor's performance when discussing the actor's creative work; this side used to be overlooked due to the excessive psychologism of the naturalistic scene. At the same time, we did not fail to point out that it would be equally incorrect to suppress the psychological side: the basis of dramaticity is in *psycho-physiological correspondence*, and that applies to the formation of the scene as well. Even a scene that is designed purely for dance (ballet) respects this correspondence, affording both motoric pathways and mental dynamism. However, given that dance is not a mimetic art, it narrows its remit to the purely emotional side of psychology and correctly leaves out the mimetic and volitional aspects, as these are the domain of drama.

An overview of kinetic scenic qualities. In order to illustrate the great number and variety of qualities produced by the relation between the actors and the scenic space, let us provide their *systematic* overview – which, to the best of our knowledge, has not yet been available. We will not include all individual qualities as there are too many of them, let alone their even more countless combinations, but only the main *kinds*. In doing so, we will take into account both the objective scene as is, and the subjective one – that is, as the audience sees it, which is one-sided and perspectival, as we have made clear. Although this is a technical overview, it will also include by way of example, a few modifications of these qualities created by the dramatic conceptual image. There are also so many kinds of dramatic relations that a complete list of the main scenic-dramatic combinations would be immense.

A. Primary kinetic relations, as they arise for each figure on the scene.
(1) **Positional qualities.** We understand them not only on their own, but also as results of the preceding motion.

(a) **The placement** *or the position* of the actor on the scene, differentiated by its direction. The principal difference is in the downstage–upstage direction: *downstage* or *upstage*. This comes from the relation of the figure to the audience. An actor downstage appears bigger, and their visible and audible expressions (speaking, singing) stand out more clearly than upstage, where the actor appears smaller, with their acting less distinct and their speaking or singing weakened to an almost critical level, especially if the stage is deep. The downstage position gives the actor *weight*, whereas upstage "drowns" them; and this transfers to the dramatic persona. As for the right-left direction, the *centre-stage* position is the prominent one. Both sides off the centre, *left* and *right*, are of equal importance as long as the scene is segmented symmetrically. If the scene is asymmetrical, the two sides have different positional meanings. Both sides have a somewhat lesser value compared to the stage centre, because they are a mere step to the offstage – but also from offstage to the onstage. Significant weight can be afforded a figure by elevating it above the level of the stage floor: this not only makes the actor's body stand out over others, but as we know from experience, such a dramatic persona has dominance over the surroundings. Differences in height appear most clearly in the downstage level; moving upstage the stage floor seems to raise perspectivally. The fact that a rake, the elevation of upstage, is used in almost all theatres has an optical reason: it ensures that persons upstage do not get blocked by those downstage. At the same time that elevation does not emphasise their higher standing.

The actor's *bodily posture* may be a mimic quality, yet most of these qualities have a positional significance, not unlike the elevation discussed above. It relates specifically to those qualities that differentiate the position of the *head* as the representative part of the body that comprises sensory and speech organs. The normal bodily posture is the standing position with the head at its highest point. The head can get even higher only by stepping up to an elevated part of the scene, which further obviates the connection of both qualities. *Sitting down* takes away from the weight, since the head appears lower. This is even more so with other postures such as kneeling, squatting and even *lying down* on the ground. These postures differ also in varying levels of activity, which is the highest in standing; diminishes in comfortable sitting down; and so forth, down to passive lying down, which suggests tiredness, sleep, faintness, or even *death*. In death, so to speak, the kinetic quality is zero. It tends to end the persona's play.

Even when we cannot witness with our own eyes how a dramatic persona has reached their place, such as when the curtain goes up on a scene, we always imagine the movement that has preceded. Wherever they are now, they must have entered from somewhere, and if they stand in an elevated place, they must have climbed there. We generally derive bodily postures from the standing position: if the persona is sitting, they must have sat down; if they are kneeling, they must have kneeled down.

The modifications of all these postures by referential images are immensely diverse. Apart from dramatic relations between individual personas, these modifications stem from *functional* relations with other objects that fill and constitute the scene. If a persona is standing next to a door, they have just entered or are about to leave. At the beginning of Act I of *The Marriage of Figaro*, Susanna is sitting next to a mirror: she is trying on a new hat. Argan in Molière's *Le Malade imaginaire* spends almost the entire play where his armchair is; he even seemingly dies in it and only leaves it at the end of the play, when he has been completely "cured".

As an extraordinary (abnormal) case, let us mention the placement of the actor *offstage*. It is abnormal or extraordinary because the scenic relation is not completely ostensive, as we cannot see the actor, only hear them. Notwithstanding, we generally can recognise through mere hearing where the persona is, whether behind the stage, on the left or on the right, and more rarely under the stage or above. For us, the dramatic persona appears in the appropriate part of the imaginary action, as we have discussed it above. We learn what they are doing there from their auditory expressions or from the words of other personas that observe the offstage persona from the scene – a phenomenon also known as teichoscopy, to be found for instance in the third act of Zdeněk Fibich's and Jaroslav Vrchlický's scenic melodrama *Námluvy Pelopovy* (Pelops's Courtship).[29] In such a case, we guess the persona's place from the behaviour of the personas on the scene.

(b) *Turning* the actor along the depth axis of the scene – that is, as facing the *audience* – falls into three types: *facing*, *sideways* (with two possibilities) and with their *back* towards the auditorium. Facing the audiences is by far the most efficient as it shows not only the most important mimics, i.e., facial expression, in its fullest, but it also maintains the full strength of speech and singing, which is particularly important in sung drama, where the singer needs to compete with the sound of the orchestra. The gestures are also more effective in this position: they point directly at the audience, in "mimic apostrophes (addresses)" of sorts. Little wonder that facing the audience is what actors' desire and strive for the most! Turning sideways makes the speech and singing weaker and makes the facial expressions less distinct. It is far more efficient to turn at least "three-quarters sideways". Turning with one's back to the audience is the worst: instead of to the auditorium the voice escapes backstage; the face is entirely out of sight and what remains are gestures sideways. Nevertheless, we should not reject this position entirely as it conveys a peculiar kind of estrangement from the audience, and a certain beauty of concealed mimics that we only guess at on the basis of the delivery. If there is no danger of drowning the speech or the singing, one can be successfully used on occasion – just like any other specialty.

If actors were like orators, reciters and concert singers, they would certainly never opt for any other position but the frontal facing towards the audience. Unfortunately, they all – including theatre singers – *represent* dramatic personas that *interact* in a certain *location*. For that reason they need to turn around to face other personas in the action as well as to various objects that they functionally relate to. They are therefore far from free in choosing their position and direction, even when they are alone on the scene, not to mention being there with others. What remains on such an occasion

---

29 *Námluvy Pelopovy* (Pelops's Courtship) is one part of the melodrama *Smrt Hippodamie* (The Death of Hippodamia, 1889–1891), composed by Zdeněk Fibich (1850–1900) and written as a dramatic trilogy by Jaroslav Vrchlický (1853–1912). Zich refers to the scene in Act 3 of the play, where a chorus of old men describes vividly the offstage carriage race between Pelops and the king Oinomainos.

is to resolve the only conflict that appears at the core of the dramatic art: the conflict between the requirement of dramaticity and the manifestation principle. The actor's positions and directions combine most productively with their diverse positioning on the scene. Both positions coexist by necessity: whenever an actor finds themself somewhere on the scene, they must face a specific direction.

(2) **Motoric qualities** as a continuous transition from one position to the next.

(a) *The actor's scenic appearance* (*scénický výjev*) begins with the moment the actor *emerges* on the scene. Depending on the weight of the place where the actor appears, their entry is more significant or less – for now without regard to the dramatic situation. The entrance usually takes place on the level of the stage floor, from the right or left side (from "backstage") or from the background upstage. This means, from the point of view of the referential image, that a dramatic persona enters from a respective part of the extended location of action. Much rarer is an entrance above, which usually happens from the upstage rake in the background; sometimes on the sides (such as on a balcony of a house) and occasionally even in the middle, as if "from the heavens". The counterpart to the latter is an appearance from below, "from the ground" – that is to say, from the pit through a trapdoor; we have mentioned both in our discussion of the scene. Entering from the depth of the upstage is characteristic for the figure's gradual, rather than sudden appearance. We have also mentioned the entrance from the depth of the downstage – that is, from the orchestra pit. It is characteristic for the fact that the persona enters with their back to the audience – unlike the other cases. Other factors constitute the impression of an actor's appearance: the actor's bodily posture (walking in is not the only way) and of course their bodily appearance, including mimics (and facial expression). There is a difference in Molière's *Les Précieuses ridicules* between the smiling and beautifully dressed Mascarille and the livid Gorgibus entering with a stick in his hand. The onstage "emergence" fulfils an important function in any dramatic situation, especially when it is surprising – that is, when other personas do not *expect* it. Clearly playwrights like to use this kind of emergence, both in comedies and tragedies. But it is also dramatically delicate: for us at least, such an emergence "just in time" (*deus ex machina*) must have plausible motivation, especially in a serious play. (Compare this with our discussion of "chance" in the previous chapter.)

The next point is the actor's *duration* on the scene. Generally speaking, it consists in their movement throughout the scene. We will discuss this movement at a later point; for now, let us emphasise that an uninterrupted passage – a mere *crossing* of the scene – is quite rare. Usually it is interrupted once at least; the figure halts and this relative *calm* stands out prominently in contrast to the preceding and following movement; it may also contrast the movements of other figures. Such a *halt* is characterised by its *duration*; clearly it is very different if it is only momentary, or if it is sustained. The longer the duration, the more prominent the actor's positional qualities become, such as their placement and orientation, and especially their bodily posture. With the exception of standing straight, the bodily postures include a certain tendency to remain calm. For that reason, sitting down momentarily tends to be a sign of disquiet or restlessness.

The kinetic significance of halts – disregarding their mimetic, dramatic meaning – rests in that they *subdivide* the actor's movement on the scene, and in so doing segments the actor's sojourn on the scene into phases. These phases are purely scenic and as such need distinguishing from phases of the dramatic action. All the actor's movements from their emergence to the first halt – no matter how short – counts as the actor's emergence on the scene; as such, it comprises the aspect of speed: the actor either *walks in* or *rushes in*. Similarly, the actor's movement from the last halt to the actor's disappearance is their *departure* or their *fleeing away*. The actor's position in relation to the centre stage has an important function in the final impression: the actor's movement from the sides to the centre creates an impression of "ascending", while the direction from the centre to the side that of stepping aside. It is apparent that all said relations may radically change the referential image of the given dramatic situation.

The final moment of an actor's scenic appearance is their departure or *disappearance* from the scene. Just like their emergence, their departure is characterised by the spot where it happens, both technically (on the side, upstage, etc.) and referentially – that is, *where* the dramatic persona has gone (to the next room, to the underworld, etc.). However, it follows from what we established at the end of the last chapter in our discussion of the asymmetry of temporal progression, that departure is not just a pendant to emergence but something substantially different. We could not see the actor before their emergence but we necessarily can see them afterwards. On the contrary, the case with departure is reversed: we can necessarily see the actor before their departure, but not afterwards. For that reason, the impression of the actor's sojourn on the scene, and especially in its last moments, sinks in more naturally and deeply, culminating in the moment of their departure. This relates to the purely kinetic aspect (such as walking away, retreating and fleeing) as well as for the dramatic one. When a despised persona departs, the scene appears to feel relief too, and with the departure of a loved one the scene also feels the weight of the sorrow. *The empty scene*, as a consequence of the last persona's departure, adopts the atmosphere linked to their exit. After joyful scenes it is full of cheerful memories; after sad scenes it seems to be lying under a shadow. But it can also breathe calmly now, in contrast to the preceding stage business – just like a person who needs a little rest. And yet, after a while, we can feel the eerie sensation that the scene seemingly grows insatiable and longs for the presence of personas to populate and fill it with new stage business. The empty dramatic scene seems to be attracting new personas, mindful as it were of its mission up to the point when the curtain covers it.

(b) **The actor's movement on the scene** refers to the continuous change of their placement on the scene. As such, we may also call it *progression*. The following aspects should be distinguished: Primarily, the *manner* and *speed* of the movement, which partly depend on one another. The actor's normal manner of movement is *walking*, that can intensify gradually into *running*. Walking consists of *steps*, which offer a chance to work with rhythm. With height differences, walking is *ascending* or *descending*. To which we may add the much rarer *jumping*. Walking generally involves a forward movement (progression), but there is also *retreating*, stepping back or jumping back or aside, which are dramatically particularly evocative. There probably is no quality in the dramatic art that would be more varied and more finely nuanced than walking. By walking, the actor may not only characterise the individuality of their persona (for example, as an energetic or vain person), but also to express their current state (the walk of an angry, worried or drunk person) – all of which in great detail. Some of the exceptional types of scenic movement include *crawling*, appropriate for fairy-tale monsters (Caliban), and various passive kinds: *being carried* on a stretcher or in a litter (very popular in older plays) or in a carriage or a vehicle, such as on a boat (in Lohengrin). As for *speed*, we sense well the kinetic *energy* it involves ("he thrusts himself on the man"). However, we measure the speed of walking or running by the temporal speed of the paces rather than by spatial speed – which in turn may be achieved by making longer steps. We know well from experience that the speed of pacing gives us the impression of a "dragging" or "urgent" walk. Especially on a scene that is relatively small (in comparison to the location it represents), one needs to take advantage of this "illusory speed". Since the steps can be heard as well, walking also becomes a part of the agogic dramatic form.

Another two aspects of the actor's movement on the scene are the *direction* and the *range*. Both are practically determined by the trajectory of the movement – an imaginary line that may be straight or curved, connecting all the stopping places: as such, it is a *purely spatial* form. This feature of the trajectory renders it suitable for writing down as a record of the movement, especially when the movement is two-dimensional, i.e., on the stage floor. Unfortunately, this eliminates the possibility to capture the temporal element, because such a line does not show *when* the moving person was where. This will stand out particularly in interactive movements.

The direction of the movement is given by the direction of the trajectory as any of its places. When the trajectory is more or less straight, we can roughly speak of three main directions, each of them two-way. First, there is the *depth direction*: the actor passes either upstage or downstage. These two differ in how it gives the actor their scenic weight. Also, in walking downstage the actor faces the audience, while they face the other way when walking upstage. For that reason it is much more common to retreat upstage by walking backwards, particularly if the actor is not to depart. Second, there is the *width direction*, again in two possible ways: to the right or left. On a neutral scene both directions are equivalent and any differentiation comes with the scenic objects that fill and complete the scene. Since these represent something particular, the scene then differentiates the two possible ways functionally and referentially. The third is to the *height direction*, which is of a secondary importance only; its two alternatives, up and down, differ greatly.

When the actor's trajectory is markedly curved or even broken, then its direction varies significantly too. We can view such a movement as a composite of several simpler ones. The extreme case is the actor's *return* to the point of departure along the same path, which has great dramatic significance. As for the *range* of the movement, it may be short or long (counting the progression between two halts or stops). The longest available direct movement is from an upstage corner to the opposite downstage corner or the other way around. We may in fact measure the range of the movement by the range of the stage. With a view to its illusive size it is better to count it in the steps the actor made – which then create the illusion of a long progression along a trajectory that is actually short. The shortest possible range of the movement is a single step (forward or backward).

(c) **A *change of the actor's bodily positions and orientation*.** Transitions between the actor's *bodily positions* (see above, towards the end of the A(1)(a) section) are measured against the standing position, which carries the greatest weight and is the most active of all positions. A change from the standing position to another, such as sitting or kneeling down, means a decrease of the scenic weight and creates an impression of calming down, while the opposite change means an increase of weight and brings an impression of activation. When someone sits down, we expect them to stay, and when they stand up, we expect them to be going. The character of these relations changes according to *how much* lower or higher the actor's head moves, as well as the *speed* of the change. There is a difference between sinking into an armchair or to the floor, and between getting up slowly or springing up. The differences serve to characterise the intensity and suddenness of a persona's state of mind. We should also point out the conventional symbolic values of certain movements, such as lowering the head, bowing or taking a knee.

The change of the actor figure's *orientation* (see section A(1)(b)) seems to be of small significance, but it has great technical significance in that the actor turns away from or comes to face the audience, as well as dramatically: the actor turns towards or away from an object or persona on the scene. As far as its range is concerned, such a *turn* may be partial (a quarter turn) or full (an about turn), which applies also to walking. Particularly, a full about turn signifies the persona's tendency to return (and even if the persona doesn't return, they halt at least) and offers a beautiful moment in the course of departure. A weakened, but dramatically very effective form, is *looking around* or *looking up*. The speed of this move – whether a slow turn or an abrupt swerve – is kinetically significant and all the more so dramatically.

B. MUTUAL (OR RELATIONAL) KINETIC RELATIONS emerge between two figures on the stage.

(1) **Positional qualities.** We understand them, again, as a result of preceding movements.

(a) **Relational distance between actors** on the scene. Its minimal variant occurs when the two personas stand next to each other. From a referential point of view, this however suggests a maximum dramatic relation between the personas, and it can grow further only by physical contact – friends holding hands, lovers embracing or enemies being violent towards each other. When this relation lasts for some time at least, especially while moving together on the scene, then the two personas make an ostensive unit – *a couple* or *a pair* – united both physically and mentally. The greater the *distance* between the two personas, the weaker their ostensive unity. The space between them seems to alienate them and to reduce the influence of one on the other. We know from experience that the greater distance significantly weakens for us the effect of the visible appearance and mimics as well as the audible speech and other vocal expressions. Just like everything on the scene, even the distance between personas is only seeming and *relative* to the location that the scene filled with such or such objects represents. The maximum distance possible between the personas – that is, diagonally across the whole scene – must often stand for their complete spatial separation, as far as their vocal contact is concerned, so the only remaining option is eye contact. In the case of "asides", an even smaller distance combined with the persona's turn aside needs to suggest that the other persona cannot hear what we can. Let us not forget that the scene is a constructed (*umělý*) space, completely different from the auditorium, and we must use our imagination to bring ourselves into it. The different optical link, given by the personas' distance, undergoes further change by various mental links of the dramatic relation that currently exists between them. We have already discussed how actorly means *represent* this mental link on the scene; we have called it the mental force line.

It follows from our discussion of the nature of the dramatic relation in the preceding chapter that these force lines – despite being symbolic only – are also always two-way. They either express an agreement that draws the two personas together, or a disagreement. When a persona is disinterested in another, they seem to lack this force line. When a persona dissimulates, their force lines agree with their mental states and they find themself in a strange, almost ostensive conflict with their behaviour. A persona that is torn has a force line consisting of two forces at once – for instance, love attracting them to someone, and shame that prevents them. Very strange, but well known from our experience, and therefore plausible, is the fact that the intensity of the repulsive mental force (even if one-sided) grows with the persona's nearness, whereas the intensity of the attractive force grows with their distance on the scene. The *separating function* of spatial distance may be further amplified by visible obstacles (even a third persona) placed in the space between the two personas.

(b) **A relational orientation** of actors on the scene. We seemingly might have called it "relational turning away" but in fact the issue is not whether the actors face the *audience* but how they are facing *one another*. This is an entirely separate quality and it is autonomous in relation to the audience. For that reason we opted for a different name. This relation is limited to the scene only (where we as spectators mentally place ourselves) and its great dramatic significance lies in showing us ostensively the event of the dramatic personas' mental contact. It reaches its maximum intensity in the personas standing *face to face*. The audiences know this well to be the necessary condition for the personas to see and hear each other as best they can. This is particularly necessary when they are further apart to make it clear to the audience that there is contact between the two personas at that particular moment. The reverse, standing *back to back*, suggests that there is no contact or that it is negative in kind – the personas do not want it, which is particularly true when they stand close to one another. One person turned to the other (but not returned) suggests a one-sided mental link: the other persona does not know or does not wish to know. Standing *"behind a persona's back"* is typical of a dramatic scene, being a weakened variant of the well known "concealment" motive. Of special value are incomplete forms of *"asides"* – either of both personas facing one another, or only one towards the other. They often appear on the scene due to the necessary compromise between the dramatic requirement of "facing each other" and the technical requirement of facing the audience. For short periods of time, these half-positions may be sufficiently substituted by turning one's head.

(c) **The relational position** of actors on the scene refers to the *directional* relation between the two personas' placement, both in relation to the scene and to the audience. The main types are: (i) *Next to one another* in the sideways direction, either closer or further, downstage or upstage. This relational position presents an *equal* scenic weight for both figures, and thus also for both dramatic personas (provided they are on the same height level). The relationship between the personas' direction and their relational postures is intriguing. If we designate the two dramatic personas D and E, where each letter's vertical shaft stands for the person's back (viewed as if from above), the scene needs to respond to two technical needs:

for the stage D Ǝ   for the auditorium ᗡ Ǝ

This conflict can generally be resolved by having both personas – or at least the one that is speaking or singing – make a "three quarter" turn towards the audience. (ii) The second type, standing *behind one another* along the depth direction – no matter if centre stage or to the side – is characteristic for the *unequal* scenic weight of the two personas. Out of the two, the one at the back faces the danger that they will be blocked by the one in front, even though they are standing higher upstage. The conflict of the technical needs is as follows:

for the stage Ǝ/ᗡ   for the auditorium Ǝ/Ǝ

This conflict, however, is unsolvable because the first requirement needs the downstage persona to have their back towards the audience, while the second needs to have the upstage persona face the other's back. This is suitable only when they shouldn't or don't need to be seen by the downstage persona. (iii) The third position has one persona standing *above* the other, with the upstage persona being scenically dominant. This is rarely literally *above*, but rather diagonally, both in the width direction and the depth direction (which also then defines the relation of the personas' position and orientation towards one another). The first two types often get combined (on the stage level), but in fact all three types may be.

The *relational bodily position* of actors regarding the height at which their heads stand can have two forms. This is either the *coordinate* level, where *both* actors are standing or sitting, etc. Or it is the *subordinate* level, where one head is lower – with a sitting persona against a standing one, or someone bent or even lying down. Its dramatic significance is well known and widely used even on a symbolic level (a winner standing above the vanquished, a deep bow in homage to a sitting ruler). Nevertheless, the difference in the personas' activity does not necessarily mean a real dominance of the standing persona; it may only seem so – such as when the sitting persona seems confident about their cause.

All three positions discussed above (a, b and c) always get combined in one way or another, because they need to co-exist side by side. When there are two actors on the scene, they always are standing at a certain distance from one another, at a certain relational posture and position.

(2) **Motoric qualities** are, once again, a continuous transition from one relational position to another.

(a) **Actors' relational scenic appearance**. Both actors may *appear* on the scene at once or successively. *Simultaneous* emergence varies significantly depending on whether the actors-personas enter together or, at least, from the same side, or if they enter from different sides. Visually this suggests a great difference of their first relational position (and its distance); dramatically, it tells us whether these personas have associated with one another before or not. That is why a simultaneous entrance from different sides is surprising for us and the personas ("What a coincidence!"), even when it is an arranged meeting. In the case of a *successive* emergence, it depends on, first, whether the second persona appears soon after or after some time; or second, whether we know that they are expected or not, or when they enter unobserved, how long they will remain unnoticed – whether for a while (in the case of surprise) or never at all (in the case of spying). The first persona may also hide on hearing the other approach. Third, it also depends on whether the second persona enters from the same side or from a different side than the first, because we remember very well where each persona entered from and where it would exit. The first relational position of the two personas tends to be different, because the first persona rarely stays where they enter. It is all the more conspicuous if the second persona enters from where the first one did: Were they together before? Why is this persona delayed? As the entrance of a new persona signifies the beginning of a new *french scene*, two successive entrances thus present two *french scenes*, both dramatically and scenically. The first *french scene* presents one persona on the scene *alone*; as such, it is an actor's "solo" and only the primary kinetic relations (A) apply. With the entrance of the second persona the first one gets a partner, and it is only at this point that "dramatic action" in its true sense as interaction (*vespolné jednání*) may unfold. It is also only at this point that mutual relations (B) are formed alongside the primary ones.

This latter type of relations arises during both personas' *sojourn* on the scene – both mutual positional relations (especially when the two personas do not move) and motoric ones, which we will come to later. Regarding the personas' halts, we may repeat what we have established in the above paragraph on "the actor's scenic appearance" (A (2)(b)).

Our above observations also hold for both actors' *disappearance* from the scene, especially when they exit *simultaneously* – either together or to different sides, which often makes a significant difference scenically as well as dramatically. Successive exits involve significant moments that depend on whether the first persona leaves for real or only seemingly (i.e., they remain hidden on the scene); how much later the second persona leaves and whether they leave on the same side, that is "after the first", or leave another way. The successive exit divides the *french scene* into two; the second one is characterised by one persona abandoning the other, leaving them alone on the scene. This *solitude* renders the chances for interaction impossible (and in that way, the dramaticity of the scene), but it allows the second persona manifest what they think and feel of what preceded. This kind of scene is common and popular as a lead-in to a soliloquy (typical of Shakespeare) and especially to an aria (such as Jeník's "Jak možno věřit" (How Can One Believe) in Smetana's *Bartered Bride*).

If one persona leaves only for a *brief moment* (such as to the next room) and they come back again, the scene is divided into three *french scenes* but it feels like one with a short break in the middle. A reciprocal case is when a second persona enters for a brief moment before leaving again (commonly when servants make an announcement). This also makes the impression of a single *french scene* only momentarily interrupted (in both cases, more personas may be involved). Logically, such an *episode* is more conspicuous than in the previous case because the entrance of a new persona attracts more attention for us as the audience and on the scene too, than the exit of an old one.

(b) **Actors' relational movement on the scene** is the most difficult theoretical problem of scenic kinetics. It *generally* occurs whenever actors change their place on the scene. We say "generally" because one actor may remain static in a special case, which is a theoretically much easier case. We will call it a *one-sided* movement in contrast to a *two-sided* one, when both actors are moving. Nevertheless, even in the case of *one-sided* movement, the *distance* and *relational position* of **both** personas change – generally. In some cases, the distance between the actors does not change. One such instance of a one-sided movement is when one persona is circling around the other. In the case of two-sided movements, both actors move in parallel (especially the movement of a couple) or when one is being followed by the other (the latter behind the former). The relational position of both actors does not change in the special case when one or both move along an imaginary line towards or away from one another (e.g., both actors downstage). When the said simultaneous or successive relational movement makes a straight line, neither the distance between the actors nor their relational position changes: both actors appear to create a moving unit – provided they move at the same speed. The movement of a couple may be viewed in fact as the movement of a single (collective) persona.

If we examine the actors' relational movement on its own – i.e., disregarding the orientation of the scene towards the audience – it is characterised primarily by the *changing distance*. Omitting the above case of unchanging distance, there are only two possibilities – both visually and dramatically different and even contrary: the two personas *come closer* or *move away* from one another – be it one-sided (and it is telling which of them moves and which static) or two-sided. Logically, this two-fold nature appears the most when the two personas find themselves next to each other at the beginning or the end of a movement. This is *meeting* and *parting*, the most common scenic kinetic relation, dramatically inconceivably rich in nuances. It is apparent that speed of movement is of great significance: the personas can run or dawdle, possibly halting for a while (or even retreat upon departing), and they may do so in the same way or each differently. Yet there are many movements that *combine* approach and departure; theoretically these can be divided into a sequence of both. For instance, two personas meeting and passing by, one-sided as well as two-sided – if linked with only a short meeting of the two personas or even with a hint of contact – it is practically divided into two sequences.

If the movement is two-sided and at least approximately straight, it may also be categorised according to the mutual relation of *directions* of both the *trajectories*. The movement happens either in correspondence or in the opposite direction – no matter if the trajectories are more or less parallel (occasionally identical), or if the trajectories run in various directions (occasionally intersecting), which presents convergent or divergent movements – and in case of intersecting trajectories (on the scene that is), both approach and depart take place. At the same time we must distinguish the directions of trajectories and the directions of movements within them, as there are two possibilities in each. Even in the equal proportion of relational trajectories, this offers four kinds of movement – as illustrated below; the arrows mark directions of the two simultaneous movements:

Such sketches inform us of the personas' relational position and distance at any given moment only if both personas are *moving at the same speed*. If their speed differs, the result will be different than the sketch may suggest. For example, the relatively simple situation of one persona following another changes depending on the different speed: the follower may lag behind, come close to or catch up with the persona in front or overtake the persona – while they are all on the scene. Similarly, when the trajectories intersect (for example, one running from left to right and the other from the back to the front), it is not always certain that the two personas will meet at the intersection: one may rush past the other or slip behind their back (as is common in comedic genres). For the sake of theoretical reflection, we need to subdivide the duration of the mutual, especially the two-sided movement into sequences – i.e., moments in time in which, first, both personas are in some significant mutual position, and, second, one of them or both come to a halt, even though for a while. Such moments in time are the beginning and the end of a movement (and of course, the two personas do not need to begin and end their movements simultaneously), and then any moments in between. Numbers can be used to mark their sequence and be placed on the trajectories on the basis of where each persona is at a given time: if one persona comes to a halt, that place on the trajectory is marked with more numbers. If such a diagram becomes too complicated, another one can be used for the following movements.

Since this diagram only captures the ground plan, it cannot capture the *vertical* dimension of the mutual movements – which the spectators can observe very well from the auditorium. Some of it can be assumed from the vertical arrangement of the scene itself. The vertical mutual movement can be *one-sided*, in which a persona descends from or ascends to the other persona's level or away from it, or *two-sided*, in which the vertical positions of both personas change, either in the same, or the opposite directions, at the same or at differing levels. When these movements are sequential, the overall movement becomes a combination of one-sided and two-sided movements. The vertical movement often combines with a movement in the upstage-downstage direction or from side to side.

As for the dramatic significance of mutual movements, some of the analysed kinetic relations are typical of certain dramatic relations between personas, but in general terms they can carry many meanings and only acquire different significances on the basis of the different mental relations of the personas who perform them. The above-discussed "mental force lines" are at play here. Their relation to *motoric trajectories*, which we have just analysed, may differ. Often these imaginary force lines that link personas run *along* the motoric trajectories, as if they symbolically caused the movement. They may also *cross* the trajectory and cause a change in the movement's direction – such as when two personas who were about to meet end up avoiding one another.

(c) **The change of the mutual bodily position and of the actors' mutual positions.** With a reference to the above sections A(2)(c), B(1)(b) and the conclusion of B(1)(c), we may cover this topic only briefly. *Changes of mutual bodily positions* may be classified exactly like the changes of actors' vertical positions in the preceding paragraphs. What may also contribute to the change in the scenic weight between the personas is a change of their mutual activity in relation to their postures. So, for example, one persona or both may sit down, or one or both may get up and so on. The dramatic expression is usually very specific, such as an invitation to start or stop a conversation, or to interrupt it by one of the personas and the like.

There are several *changes of mutual position*. If we take facing one another as the normal, starting position, then one type of change is one persona *turning away* from the other partially or completely (with their back on the other), or both personas turning away from each other simultaneously. These changes may signify an interruption or termination of their mental contact, while the opposite – *turning towards* one another – signifies the establishment of such a contact, if not in speech, then by eye contact at least. *Meeting each other's eyes* is a dramatically very significant moment. It may happen by a simple turning of the head, such as when a persona looks back over their shoulder when leaving or simply by lifting one's eyes. We may say that, symbolically, these acts set up mental force lines between personas, as well as cancel them or transform them in their tendencies. It is obvious that the mutual position changes frequently when the personas are moving, be it abruptly (turning back) or slowly (moving in a curve). This change often becomes a cause for the appropriate movement itself. All this may be easily put down in a diagram using the signs D and E.

C. The Ensemble and the Chorus

(1) With more than two personas on the scene the number of kinetic scenic relations between them grows rapidly, as we have observed when analysing dramatic relations: there are three mutual relations for three figures, six of them for four and so on. Besides, *new* scenic qualities arise as a result of the growing number of actors on stage. Let us borrow the word **ensemble** from music drama to refer to numerous actors who represent *individual* dramatic personas.

> Following the discussion of quantity of a *french scene* as established in the previous chapter, we may also speak about the "quantity" of a scenic appearance (*scénický výjev*), which shows in how "populated", i.e., how *full*, a scene is. In a sequence of *french scenes*, the quantity may remain unchanged – with only some of the personas replaced by others – or it may increase or decrease. The personas that remain on the scene create an ostensive bond between individual scenic appearances; they become a "relatively static" element of the scene. The contrast between a full and an un-full scene can be enhanced by deployment of the chorus. There are authors who love scenic appearances with a full scene, such as Shakespeare. Other authors use scenes that are almost always "thin", such as Hebbel's. (Hebbel's *Maria Magdalena* has 11 personas and consists in total of 19 mostly long *french scenes* with 1–2 personas and only 5 shorter scenes with 3–5 personas on the scene.)
>
> New **positional** qualities arise if we view the ensemble as a *whole in itself*. These qualities are in fact *synthetic* and they contrast with the analytical ones that arise from relational combinations between the ensemble's individual members. The synthetic qualities become more apparent as the ensemble becomes more numerous. These qualities then also often operate when it comes to the chorus. The first synthetic quality is the ensemble's *density*: its extreme cases are when the actors are *scattered* all over the scene, and when they are *concentrated* in one place. In that way the ensemble forms a loose *assembly* or a tighter *huddle*. A denser ensemble shows a clearer *shape* in the arrangement of its members. Next to a *group* (in the narrow sense), concentrates

generally around its leader, a *line* is a frequent shape, which is usually placed on the stage from side to side. Finally, the ensemble may form a spatial *split*: an individual may stand apart from the collective and at a distance comes to create a pendant, also in a dramatic sense. Alternatively, the collective splits into two small groups, standing apart at a distance and occupying separate places. An ensemble split in such a way is in a sense a variant of "two personas", and as such, we may apply the mutual positional relations (B1) in the same way as the primary positional relations (A1); these treat a compact ensemble as a single persona consisting of multiple bodies. Naturally, we may subdivide the qualities further still. A threefold form, even if consisting of only three individuals, is usually located along the width of the stage: one in the middle and one on either side. Dramatically speaking, a collective, and even a huddle (which may be further subdivided, as shown above), signifies a *belonging* of personas who are close spatially; in other words, they signal a friendly relationship, either real, or pretended – such pretense of relationships is only directed at personas on the scene, not at the audience. In such cases, an actor can manifest the true thoughts of their persona to the audience by stepping away temporarily from the group. There is of course a hostile huddle – a fight. The scattering of the ensemble commonly signifies mutual estrangement or indifference among the personas. It needs be said that the dramatic weight of individual parts of a split ensemble depends on their placement, especially its depth or height, but not on their number. On the contrary, a single individual often dominates over all others. If they are evenly placed on the two sides of the stage, this produces a strange contrast in regards to the uneven fill of the scene.

New **motoric** qualities of the ensemble arise from changes in the above positional qualities. They include a *change of density*: dispersing or concentrating, regrouping the ensemble, or *arranging* in a group or a line and breaking up such formations; and finally *dissolving* the ensemble into parts or *merging* partial or autonomous ensembles or groups into one whole. A *quantitative change* arises when individuals break away from a group – disregarding whether they stay on the scene or not (which decreases the quantity); or conversely, when they join the group – disregarding whether they have been present or just entered (which increases the quantity). Again, when it comes to a split ensemble, our earlier observations about the mutual motoric relations (B2), and even the primary motoric relations (A2) apply in an equal measure. The dramatic significance of all these motoric relations is wide-ranging: concentrating an ensemble or merging two into one, for instance, may manifest a friendly belonging as well as a hostile confrontation. *After all, the objective of every dramatic action is to bring dramatic personas present on the scene closer to –* and even *"into" – one another.*

(2) We shall use the term **chorus** to describe a larger number of actors who represent dramatic personas *whose individualities are lost in their collective*, i.e., the *crowd*.

Scenically the chorus tends towards the highest possible density; it usually appears *compact* (within the limitations of the perspectival stage space) and it literally *fills* the assigned place. This determines its *quantity*, which is in its low range higher than the ensemble's quantity (we referred to an ensemble starting with three actors), but it also greatly depends on the size of the scene – or, more accurately, on the section of the scene assigned to the chorus. Fewer persons are enough for a smaller scene to create an impression of a crowd than on a large one. Yet the referential image sometimes requires a large number of chorus members in absolute terms (for example, for an army or a crowd of people); but we may always assume that there are more of them in an adjacent space, out of sight (i.e., behind the scene), where the crowd has entered or is entering from.

Since the chorus is *always* a unified whole, its positional and motoric qualities are *only* the *synthetic* ones – that is, those we identified as "new" when discussing the ensemble. We have noted the chorus's high *density*; it cannot change too much. Only exceptionally can the chorus scatter, and then it signifies its end: it dissolved or broke up. Conversely, the chorus may materialise when individuals regroup or come together from different corners. The chorus always forms a compact "body", and as such always has a *shape* – that of a "layer" whose height is determined by people's postures. Usually, everyone is standing, but they may also be sitting, kneeling or even lying down. Different parts of the chorus may take different postures, subdividing itself into sections; the lowest one naturally cannot be behind everyone else. Changes in postures change the height of the chorus. Other than that, the shape of the chorus is in its ground plan: it is planary, areal and very varied. Its principal features are a two-dimensional group (in the shape of a square, circle and so on) and a one-dimensional line (single, double and so on). Transitions from one shape into another happens by individuals moving, but that movement always happens *within* the chorus: the shape does not move, it *only changes* (transforms). Let us call this special and specific kinetic quality of the chorus the *flux* of the chorus; we become aware of it most clearly when a line is moving ahead while its shape remains unchanged. In contrast, a transversal movement of a line or group is an ordinary advance, no different from an individual's advance, because there is no inner movement within it. A line can also bend, form a circle and so on.

Finally, the chorus may be *divided* spatially. With a view to size, it may be divided into two or more partial choruses, placed in different locations on the scene. These partial choruses may move and transform the shape independently or again, regroup and merge in a variety of ways. Choruses may be *subdivided* not only spatially, but also based on *colour*, which depends on what the chorus represents. The chorus, as a "collective persona", tends towards a uniformity of expression as well as a uniformity of costumes. As such, its overall colour should be of *consistent* (*stejnoměrná*), no matter whether monochromatic or multi-coloured. Nevertheless, some differentiation in colour is necessary even within a single chorus, e.g., distinguishing men and women, the young and old and so on. These distinctions show in the difference of their acting, and as such should be visually expressed in differences of colour. This is even more important with two choruses, often representing conflicting groups, which may mingle temporarily. In the case of a chorus that represents an assorted crowd gathered from all sides, or a collective consisting of people from different social classes, a differentiation in costumes to reflect this diversity of personal attitudes is appropriate. The requirement for a *uniform* chorus is only *relative* – especially if we consider that there is a *smooth transition* without a sharp boundary between the chorus and the ensemble. It depends on the measure of individuation that the author allowed or withheld from the dramatic personas that comprise the chorus. We will return to this question in our discussion of the music drama where the chorus has a much more significant function than in spoken drama.

The chorus's *appearance* and *presence* on the scene depend on the dramatic function it has in the given scene. It may be more or less passive and serve to *illustrate the environment* in which the dramatic personas live; in that way they are characterised by the chorus too. In such cases, the chorus's place is in the background or on the sides (a split double chorus). The chorus also enters from those sides even if it isn't given a separate *french scene*, as would be the case in sung drama (prominently, for instance, in Schiller's *Wallenstein's Camp*). In such a case it fills the entire scene and is often richly differentiated. The chorus is often on the scene when the curtain goes up in order to set the mood by short stories or by singing. The more dramatically active it is, the more it moves downstage and its entry becomes more prominent. It often intervenes in the proximity of the soloists, and in so doing visually and dramatically threatens and suppresses them (such as it enters from a downstage door). In such cases the chorus may serve to hide horrific acts on the scene. Placing the chorus downstage centre turns it into the situation's collective hero. The chorus's appearance and disappearance are determined by the speed of the action and its duration, which depend on the chorus size. Except for the situations mentioned above, the scenic relation of the chorus to the soloists is subordinate. Both the dramatic relation and the clarity of the manifestation require that the soloists and the ensemble stand apart from the chorus: they need to be visibly separate and appear in places with a greater scenic weight – such as in front of the chorus or even above it. In contrast, leaders of a mob need to always remain in an ostensive contact with the chorus. Powerful impressions arise when the crowd swarms and swallows an individual, or, conversely, when the crowd retreats from the soloists in fear, such as in Wagner's *Tannhäuser* (a scene at the end of Act II, when the company of knights is horrified by the hero's confession). Naturally, we must not forget the smooth transition between the ensemble and the chorus; the above differentiation showing in costume is not as strict. Nevertheless, the extremes of the transition – the *principal* personas and a *mere* crowd; i.e., technically speaking, soloists and the extras – must always remain distinct scenically as well as dramatically. Finally, let us point out that the chorus may be placed behind the scene, unseen but heard; its dramatic effect upon us may still be very powerful exactly thanks to its hidden quality, whether permanent or temporary (such as an approaching or retreating chorus).

Variable *scenic qualities*. In connection with the ensemble we have pointed out certain spatial qualities such as density, shape and splitting; their changes, caused by the movement of individuals, are not movements themselves, but *changes* (or transformations) in the narrow, qualitative sense. When it comes to the chorus, these qualities – let us call them *variable* – manifest themselves very prominently given the quantities of individuals in a chorus: rather than individual separate points (i.e., individual bodies on the scene), the homogenous surface of the body of the chorus with its inner movement comes into play. The chorus resembles a liquid on a plane: it flows in a stream, spreads out, branches out in meanders and merges again, and pours from one place to another. The impact of these changes on the appearance of the scene becomes apparent particularly in moments of temporary calm. But the main thing is that this change in the scenic picture relates not only to shape, but also to its *colour*. A single individual's movement already changes the colour of the scene's appearance, even if just in part and in details; with the ensemble the change of the scene's colours may become more apparent, and with the chorus even striking. Let us note that the inner flux within a chorus that is varied in costume, may change the chorus's colour appearance even with its shape unchanged. It can also change the *structure* of its appearance through acting while remaining in a state of calm – for instance by raising arms. This structure can change both in colour and in movement, within the surface of the chorus. Through its kinetic structure, this surface may assume different appearances: it may appear serene, mildly ruffled or even fiercely violent. Let us call all variable qualities that are produced this way, *variable kinetic qualities*; they are, after all, always caused by movements of individuals, of live people.

> As for inanimate objects on the scene, they remain at rest as a rule. In the case of dramatic works, this is correct because it is dramatic personas that are the main thing on the scene; it is their movements that should contrast with the static quality of their surroundings (cf. the neutral scene). The movement of scenic objects would distract our attention from the main action to the secondary one. For that reason, we find more prominent movement of scenic objects in scenic spectacles that present "actions" as such – especially in cinema, where personas and things (objects) are of equal importance. In spoken drama and in music drama, the movement of scenic objects should remain an exception, acceptable only if these actions take place apart from the personas (e.g., clouds rolling in the sky) or only very briefly, often foreboding a catastrophe (e.g., the collapse of Armida's palace at the end of Gluck's opera).

There are also *variable static qualities* that do not arise from movement but from a purely qualitative change; they do not relate to shapes but only to colours. The magic is produced by *scenic light*. The reason is that light, which fills the scene and in fact creates it for the audience by enabling their visual perception, is as *real* as the scenic space and the actors in it. Scenic light is not merely painted like a landscape or a painting of an interior. By the same token it may also change. Given that it is, technically speaking, artificial light (with the exception of openair stages), it may change as necessary – that is, in keeping with the flow of the performance.

Works of architecture in shaping its spaces also make use of light, both natural and artificial. But architecture only uses light to segment its spaces (e.g., well-lit and shady places determined by the position of windows in a cathedral or by the placement of chandeliers in a hall) and disregards temporal changes; even if light changes over time, it is irrelevant to architecture. Theatrical light also has the task of segmenting space by its spatial distribution on the scene – that is, its *static* task. In contrast to architecture, theatrical light relates to the temporality of the dramatic work. Theatrical light (most commonly electric) is fully operable today and it *may* and *must* change along with the changes of the dynamics of the dramatic action. This is its *dynamic* task. The changes relate primarily to its intensity (i.e., brightness) as well as its quality (i.e., colour). It goes without saying that these changes effect *changes in the colour appearance of the scene*, both statically and dynamically, alongside the objects placed on it. These changes affect the whole scene or one of its parts. And naturally, they purposely affect the personas moving on the scene. These changes may be gradual or abrupt. In this way light participates in shaping the temporal form of the dramatic work.

> From the dramatic point of view (i.e., in regards to dramaticity), we are only interested in the referential, i.e., associative significance of the scenic light. It has great variety. White theatrical light represents sunlight, of the broad day, of a murky dusk or even the dead of the night – which may never be absolute, otherwise the scene would disappear from our view (a full black-out is used as a short break to allow for quick changes). Minor colour nuances represent the moonlight, glorious sunsets, firelight and so on. In a small scale, lights represent sources of light, lightnings, etc. In a large scale (in a full wash), lights represent the sky in any appearance whatsoever. Light often illuminates only a part of the stage – for example, a throw of moonlight streaming through a window, casting deep shadows. Its brightness changes gradually, such as when dusk sets in during the play and we suddenly realise that the action that began in broad daylight ends in darkness. At other times, the change may be abrupt, such as when a door suddenly opens to a broad landscape. The impact of all this on the *mood*, based on impressions familiar to us from everyday experience, is very powerful and it enhances the dramatic action in its highs and lows as effectively and captivatingly as only music can.

಩ ಩ ಩

The director-scenic (režisér-scénik). The stage director's first task is to conceive the dramatic form of the work. Their *second* task is to conceive the *scenic form* of the performance. For that reason, we have been referring to the director in their second function, which is basically *identical* for spoken drama and sung drama, as the director-*scenic*. The scenic form is of two kinds: *static* and *kinetic*.

The *static scenic form* is to some extent "non-temporal" as it relates to the scenic space and its fixed fill (the objects filling it) in the sense of our discussion early on in this chapter. The director must choose a certain *shape* and *size* of the scene for each continuous section of the performance – its acts, scenes and scene changes – in keeping with the playwright's stage directions at the start of each section. Alternatively, whenever the author does not do so, the director needs to determine it with a view to the requirements of the dramatic action, the number of personas, the presence of a chorus, etc. In the case of a neutral scene, the director determines the shape and size by architectural means (narrowing down the proscenium, shifting the backdrop downstage to achieve a shallow scene and so on). In the case of a scene that has been specified more in the stage directions, the director does so by adding suitable objects (e.g., by walls and a ceiling to construct a small chamber or a large hall; by house front in a street scene, etc.), or perhaps by a perspectival illusion of elongation in the distance upstage. The *segmentation* of the scene is crucial, both in the ground plan and vertically. If the author has not specified this, the director conceives this by planning out the blocking of individual personas in individual phases of the dramatic action. The director does this by adjusting the levels and heights of the floor and by placing objects within the scene. This creates *partial* spaces in the depths (downstage and upstage, e.g., behind a house), on the sides (wingside spaces that often extend visually offstage) or in the height (e.g., a balcony). This is contributed to by the fixed fill of the scenic spaces – that is, objects that are purposely placed so that they can be used in the action or help characterise the location. All of this, with its suitable shape and colour, gives the scene a static form – not unlike the visual form of an architectural work, yet with a different, referential task. The aesthetic significance of this form consists in its temporal stability – even though it is relatively stable: it forms a stable background that contrasts with the dynamic dramatic action, whose constant changes are, in turn, given *integrity* by the unchanging frame, like a melody over the drone of a deep tone. As such, the static scenic form has a *synthetic* task within a given section of the performance; it provides it with a uniform *resonance* in mood. Nonetheless, the said stability is not absolute outside its static shapes. As we have observed, it may change in colour with *lighting changes*, which we need to take into account here as a factor of further segmentation of the scene. By means of this bond between the static (i.e., non-temporal) form and the variable (i.e., temporal) form, the overall static form comes close to the dynamic dramatic form.

The *kinetic scenic form* amounts to the director's shaping of kinetic qualities, which we have listed above. It is a specifically dramatic spatio-temporal form. In fact, the positional form (the blocking) of actors on the scene becomes for the brief, unchanged moment a stable form that becomes one with the said static form. Again, we sense this best when the scene is calm for a short while: at that point the actors in their blocking, their shapes (given by mimics, postures and their orientation) and colours (of the costume) blend in with other objects arranged around and filling the scene. Especially when it comes to such dramatic situations, which are nearly always significant, the director needs to keep in mind when it comes to the colour concept of the scenic fill and the actors' costumes. The director must remember that the impression is only fleeting and passes with the next movement, and that the "picture" should not sacrifice the functional values of said objects. This applies even more to the *variable* kinetic *form* that blends in with the static form *for a moment* – which may be quite long when the chorus is involved. It can conspicuously change the appearance of the scene. In regards to the motoric form, the director works very carefully with the passage of time. We have pointed out with its *speed* the motoric form integrates into the *agogic* dramatic form; the two forms must agree in a *strict temporal continuity* (see the end of the previous chapter).

Since the dramatic art is a *mimetic* art, the director is *absolutely* obliged to *make all scenic concepts represent something* – or more precisely: to evoke in us (as spectators) referential images that are purposeful for the dramatic action – that is the *dramaticity* principle applied to the scene. First, the said *static* form of the scene must characterise the location of the action with the level of clarity as called for by the author or the work itself. This also applies to spaces adjacent to the scene. It should not happen even with the neutral scene, for instance, that the director allows a persona to leave on one side to re-enter from another; wherever the persona exited is the *place assigned to them* and they the persona must re-enter from there – unless the persona explained to us why they returned from elsewhere. The objects that fill the scene must be made to serve their function and characterise the environment to the smallest detail. In order to do so we must recognise them – otherwise the associated image and the mood linked to it will not arrive. Second, the *kinetic* form must always follow the dramatic action; this is certainly possible thanks to its temporality, which adheres to the same laws that we have ascribed to the dramatic form at the end of the previous chapter.

The director-scenic's task is surely to *transcribe the dramatic action into the scenic space*. That means in fact that the dramatic situations and the scenic situations must *correspond* without having to be identical always and entirely. Quite the contrary, this is a question of the basically independent *coexistence of the dramatic and the scenic qualities*. Their *free* combination will produce the overwhelming richness of resulting nuances that are evidence of the director's inventive imagination, whereas a dogmatic translation of the dramatic qualities given in the script into the scenic idiom usually produces mere clichés. Certainly, there are some fixed relations between the two, but these are not absolute.

> For example, a persona's *dramatic weight* within a scene thus *usually* corresponds with their scenic emphasis. But there are instances when it is preferable for it to occupy a prominent place on the scene (e.g., an elevated spot) with a persona of a lesser dramatic importance while weakening the dramatically strong persona scenically: the persona will stand out by means of this contrast. The same applies to the placement of an entire ensemble of personas within a scene. The director therefore must consider well where to concentrate this or that *french scene* or how to distribute it on the scene, so that the ensemble has a purposeful freedom of movement. The *segmentation* of dramatic situations does not generally need to be identical with the segmentation of scenic situations: on the contrary, they are often in conflict. It is unnecessary, for example, that a dramatic change be accompanied by a kinetic scenic change. It is often enough when it is manifest in acting, speech and gestures. Conversely, the situation may change scenically even when it remains more or less the same dramatically; the scene acquires a further fine segmentation (e.g., one persona standing up) or gradual nuancing (e.g., by a slow passage of all personas to another place on the scene). The kinetic scenic changes come to form an autonomous system that unfolds parallel with the changes in the dramatic action – sometimes abruptly and at other times gradually. In moments when they correspond, this has a profound impact on the overall segmentation. Finally, the same applies to *gradations* in the dramatic and scenic forms; the latter mostly relate to changes in lighting and the fullness of the scene – which, apart from the adjustable size of the chorus, is already prescribed by the playwright. Finales, especially in sung drama, tend to be culminations in both the forms – as can be seen from our diagram of *Much Ado About Nothing*. In Ibsen's *Ghosts*, in contrast, the dramatically powerful ending only involves the two remaining personas.

In the previous chapter, we used the transitoriness of time to justify the *necessity to segment* dramatic action. The same applies to scenic action. Within an enclosed section of the dramatic performance, such as an act, some of the segments need to be *connected* as well. We have seen above that the dramatic and kinetic scenic forms fulfil this function complimentarily to each other in a certain *concatenation* (or chain), even including connected intermissions; whereas the static form – disregarding any segmentation by means of light – unifies the duration of the entire section. This diagram visualises the connections:

7 THEATRICAL SCENE: THE STAGE DIRECTOR'S SECOND TASK

```
dramatic form         |    ||    ||    ||    |
kinetic scenic form   |__||___||___||____||__|
static scenic form    |_____|
```

The *simultaneous* welding of two changing forms occurs by virtue of the *strict temporal bond*.

Between individual sections of a performance, divided by *breaks* (or intermissions), there *is no* ostensive continuity *at all*, merely an ideational one. One act tends *to differ* from another in their static form of the scene and the director-scenic must also respect their succession. In so doing, the director-scenic creates a kind of *non-continuous variable form*. There are numerous plays that call for a change of location even after a short time – even after a single scene. But this *"transformation"* requires a break, because the change of scene will not take place before our eyes but behind the lowered curtain or at least in a total black out. When too frequent, one feels that such breaks disturb the continuity of the dramatic action and *mince* the performance – especially since they often reveal the "plotline mosaic" of the dramatic action – discussed in the previous chapter – which would stay unnoticed in a scene that remains unchanged. This was probably the main reason for the "unity of place" requirement, which otherwise has no justification and is, in regards to the entire work, even excessive. Only one thing may help: make the breaks for scene changes as *short* as can be. That is a task for theatrical practice. If a neutral scene may be used, a twofold scene will serve the purpose well. Otherwise, theatre machinery has to come to the rescue (e.g., a track system or a revolve).

Following logically from the above discussions, the director-scenic, both in spoken drama and in sung drama, has *more freedom* in their conception than the director-conductor. They both are bound by the author's "stage directions". But if these are not entirely generic, they only define the location to any level of detail: that is, they specify only the static qualities, but not the personas' movement in space, i.e., not the positional and motoric kinetic qualities. The director-scenic's especially beautiful task is to "translate" the *dramatic polyphony* into the *scenic space*, into the same number of positions (or more motoric trajectories), for which the director-scenic has three dimensions available. It is only in the spatial ostension (*názor*) that the dramatic polyphony's various forms come to full realisation. This is especially true of the segmented forms, such as a two- or three-fold dramatic situation that unfolds all *at once* – either with the ensemble or also with the chorus, etc. In opera, which allows multiple dramatic actions at the same time, the director-scenic has a great many tasks to handle.

Many authors describe the opening location in great detail. By extension, prescribed places for functional objects often determine the actors' positions. To what extent should the director comply with these prescriptions? Our answer is: as much as possible, since these are (with a good dramatist) a record of the author's vision of the scene. Only the practically impossible does not bind the director, naturally. But that is relative. A stage production that is impossible in a particular theatre today may well be possible tomorrow or in another building. Great care is therefore necessary when assessing drama in this respect. There are frequently dramas that "cannot be staged" according to the author's wishes. Such plays are either rejected or staged differently. If that is the *only* flaw of the drama (and we are referring to nearly all so-called closet dramas, but also to the whole of Shakespeare), to reject or change would be an incorrect intervention for the director to do. Much (if not everything) depends on the director's *scenic creative idea* or invention (*nápad*); an "impossible" task inspires the most original conceptions and leads to progress in art in general.

> The director-scenic's freedom mentioned above sometimes misleads the artist to *add* to the scenic form a lot of *useless* detail "from their own head". This includes the so-called "livening up" of the scene by episodic action for the extras that is supposed to "paint" the environment, but actually distracts our attention from the dramatic action proper. More consequential are the additions that overfill the scene with objects that are not functional, i.e., not necessary, and are redundant in characterising the location. Here, the general principle of artistic *economy* applies: the unnecessary becomes harmful because it damages the true mission of the work. The mission of the dramatic work is its dramaticity.

The requirement of the scene's *simplicity* also follows from the manifestation principle that requires *clarity* (*zřetelnost*) of everything we can see on the scene. Too subtle features, be they static or kinetic (which also pertains to actor's playing), will either vanish in the distance, or come across as finicky niceties that pointlessly blur the large features: this is what "theatre optics" means. But the manifestation principle has a decisive impact in creating the scene, in that it makes the scene, which is to be viewed from the one direction of the auditorium, *streamlined in that one direction*. Whenever constructions are erected around the scene, the one side must remain open: for example, a room must lack the front wall – it is as if the ideal plane of the apron (proscenium) "cut through" it. Objects on the scene must *be turned* (at least half-way) towards the audience just like actors – as we have pointed out repeatedly in the above overview of the kinetic qualities.

This *apron orientation law* results from the manifestation principle and sometimes clashes with the mimetic dramaticity principle (viz our discussion of the "mutual orientation" of actors). In this, the apron orientation law is something specifically theatrical. The *apron (rampa)* is the weir that channels the stream of optical and acoustic impressions into the auditorium, but the *apron* is also the rampart breach through which the audience's hungry eyes and ears reach onto the stage. That is why the audience views the scenic space right behind the apron edge as dynamically the strongest. This *"scenic valence"* diminishes progressively the deeper we view into the stage. Just like an electric conductor moving within an electromagnetic field acquires varying levels of potential energy, so does the actor, closer to or further from the apron, acquires or loses dramatic energy.

If we are asking then at what point the theatrical scene on which the director-scenic carries out their dramatic work becomes dramatic, we may summarily answer in this way:

*The scene is **dramatic** when it efficiently manifests, by its kinetic form, the dramatic action and when it characterises, by its static form, the location and the ambience of the action in the appropriate way.*

A few words need saying about *the director-scenic's specific talent*. Clearly, the director-scenic must have sense for *spatial* qualities, but not only for them as such but also for their *changes*, which is not a mere combination of space with time but a *specifically new thing*. The director must be capable of ostensive imagination in space and time *at the same time*. They also must have a talent for *inventing* these qualities in such a way that they *correspond with the dramatic ones* that they discovered as the director-conductor. It is only secondary that they have a sense for the static qualities of the scene and be inventive in them. Because this needs a sense for space as well as for colours and shapes – and much more than just a sense, but also inventiveness in those areas – directors habitually call on the help of an architect – or, more accurately, a visual artist with an architectural talent for the static conception of the scene. It is necessary, however, that this helping artist had at least an elementary sense of a work's dramaticity, so that they could reach an agreement with the director who is fully responsible for the main task, which is to conceive the kinetic scenic form. In contrast, a painter – or, more precisely, a visual artist with a talent for painting – cannot be the designer of the fixed scene because they would not be able to rise to the challenge of the real space, which constitutes its essence.

8 DRAMATIC MUSIC: THE COMPOSER'S CREATIVE WORK

[Editor's note: In his discussions of spoken drama, Zich's opinions and predilections do not show themselves very much. However, when it comes to opera, the situation is very different. We can see this particularly in Chapter 8. He is clearly partial to the operas of Bedřich Smetana (1824–1884), given the number of examples he draws from them. Smetana clearly served as the model "dramatic" opera composer. Occasionally, Zich also refers to the operas of Zdeněk Fibich (1850–1900), Josef Bohuslav Foerster (1859–1951) and his friend and conductor Otakar Ostrčil (1879–1935) – the next generation of the neo-romantic, Smetanian music. No other Czech composer, except for his own work, is included. In this, Zich clearly follows the ideological positions of his contemporary and university colleague, musicologist Zdeněk Nejedlý (1878–1962). (For a critical analysis of Nejedlý's concept of Czech musical history, see Zapletal 2016.) Nejedlý divided Czech music into two lines: he viewed one, comprising the Smetanian group, as progressive, while for him the other – including Antonín Dvořák, Josef Suk, and partly also Leoš Janáček – was retrograde, artistically weak, and crowd-pleasing. As Miloš Zapletal succinctly summed up: "The progressive line was basically focused on developing programmatic music and post-Wagnerian music drama, while the second focused mainly on absolute music" (2016: 103). Zich's ideological positions kowtow to Nejedlý, who follows the views of Otakar Hostinský, who had taught both of them. "The progressiveness is principally understood in terms of the Beethovenian-Lisztian-Wagnerian-Mahlerian line of German music" (Zapletal 2016: 103). Ideologically, Nejedlý (and Zich in tow) follows Wagner and traces modern, truly dramatic opera to Christoph Willibald Gluck (1714–1787). He takes his positions to an extreme, such as when establishing Zdeněk Fibich as the ultimate creator of the "truly dramatic" melodrama, and even awards him a central place in the formation of the genre – in his book *Zdenko Fibich: Zakladatel scénického melodramu* (Zdenko Fibich: the Founder of the Scenic Melodrama; Prague, 1901). From the perspective of period tensions and ideological debates, it is symptomatic that Zich does not draw on a single example from the works of Antonín Dvořák (1841–1904). The "progressive" musicologists and critics of Nejedlý's camp, Zich included, framed Dvořák as an un-Czech, eclectic, and therefore unartistic composer – despite or perhaps because of his international acclaim. Brian Locke has analysed the ideological fray over Dvořák and the "soul and essence" of Czech music in his chapter "A crisis of Identity: The 'Dvořák Affair', 1911–1914" (Locke 2006: 54–58).

8 DRAMATIC MUSIC: THE COMPOSER'S CREATIVE WORK

Zich also fails to come to terms with Leoš Janáček (1854–1928), although Janáček's work was complete at the time Zich was finishing his *Aesthetics*, and gaining international recognition. On the basis of their disagreement on the principles of opera, Zich misunderstands Janáček's speech melody theory and views it as a mere mechanical replicating of reality – which in his view was an instance of unartistic naturalism, a view shared by many other critics of the Nejedlý camp (see "Nejedlý, Janáček and Smetana Exhibition" in Locke 2006: 62–64). In brief, Zich's attitude to Janáček resembles his view of the Avant-Garde: he is well aware of both, but neither fit with his aesthetic system. The mismatch between his aesthetics and his appreciation of Janáček is humorously ironic: Zich clearly enjoyed and recognised the dramatic effect of Janáček's *Její pastorkyňa*. In his review, he tries hard to rationalise the impact by framing it as a one-off: an unschooled exception, a spontaneous and idiosyncratic phenomenon that allegedly ignores the cultivated history of Western music.]

This chapter, though it does not require a specialist's knowledge of music, is nevertheless intended for musicians. Whoever is interested exclusively in spoken drama may skip it. On the contrary, whoever is interested only in sung drama (opera, operetta, etc.) needs to read the preceding chapters of this part too because almost everything covered in them also relates to sung drama. Even the basic points of difference between spoken drama and opera, i.e., speaking versus singing, are so closely interconnected (setting aside the genre of the scenic melodrama) that it is useful knowledge even for those only interested in sung drama. In short, this book as a whole is an aesthetic of sung drama.

Sung drama (zpěvohra), as discussed in Chapter 3, is a dramatic work co-created by music. This *music* – created by the opera composer and performed by an *orchestra* (leaving aside singers for the time being), directed by the conductor, in a designated space between the stage and the auditorium – may at first seem to belong to the domain of musical arts. However, that is not the case. Mere music, or absolute instrumental music, is *not* mimetic art (*obrazové umění*) because it does not represent or portray anything. In contrast, operatic music is a component of *mimetic* dramatic art and as such it *needs* to evoke both technical images and *referential images* (*významové představy obrazové*). It is therefore "*mimetic music*" (hudba obrazová).

This is analogous to the scene (*scéna*), which with its frame and contents seemed to belong to architecture, but we have asserted that it is distinct from architecture in that it *represents* something – the location of the action. It was impossible to describe the stage as "mimetic (representative) architecture" because it changes and develops in time, unlike architecture. Another difference is that works of architecture *generally* do not represent anything, whereas there is a group of instrumental compositions that portray something. This group forms the category of *programmatic music* which includes such forms as the "symphonic poem" or the "symphonic tableau" (*symfonický obraz*). Since *vocal music* is so closely connected to poetry it always needs to portray something, the category of mimetic music is rather broad and dramatic music constitutes only a particular part defined by its special task to evoke a specifically dramatic referential image (*obrazová představa*). It could therefore be summed up: *mimetic music* is such music *in which a particular* **technical** *image* (i.e., a purely musical one) *is* **logically interconnected** (*zákonitě spojena*) *with a certain* **referential** *image*.

Clearly, all mimetic music, comprising the same sonic material as pure music, can technically differ from it only in its *structure*. This structure must contain conditions that *enable* it to evoke referential images, but not just in any way, i.e., *nonspecifically and randomly* – any music can do this depending on the listeners' individual fantasies – but the structure needs to evoke images in a *governed* (logical, principled) way (*zákonitě*). That is, the evoked images need to be as specific and certain as can be, so that the work of art can operate with them as with objective factors, i.e., those that transcend individuality. Let us first analyse this *mimetic capacity of music* with a particular view to dramatic referential images (*obrazová představa*).

From a psychological point of view, this is an inquiry into what is known as the *associative factor* that is governed by two basic principles of image reproduction: the principles of *resemblance* (*podobnost*) and of *concurrence* (*současnost*). The former is almost the exclusive guiding principle in the perception of the visual arts of painting and sculpture. I see a pink blot and it evokes a rose, because the blot has the colour and shape resembling a rose. I know: this is a *picture* of a rose. The latter principle is at work especially in poetry and in mimics. I hear the word "rose" and an image of a rose is evoked because I have seen a rose in the past while hearing its name. I know: the *meaning* of the word (in any language I understand) is "a flower that looks like this or that". It is worth noting that in both principles the *conditions of successful reproduction* are *entirely different*. The former necessitates that the picture and the object are *similar*; the more, the better, because the evocation of the referential image is all the more certain. And that is all that is needed – surely there is no need for me to see a rose and a picture of it concurrently. (Its name has no function here since I can recognise even a flower that I have seen without knowing what it is called.) Conversely, the latter case necessitates that I have seen a rose at least once and *concurrently* heard its name. And again, this is all that is needed – since there is no need for the appearance of the rose and the name "rose" to be similar. On the contrary, with the rare exception of onomatopoeic names, there is usually no similarity and the word spoken or even written is merely a *sign* for a certain image. The *bond* between the

8 DRAMATIC MUSIC: THE COMPOSER'S CREATIVE WORK

sign and the image associated with it is mostly *artificial*, conventional, as evidenced by the different names for the same things in different languages. It can also be *natural*, as we know from our earlier analysis of mimics: our experience shows that a smile, for instance, "means" or "expresses" joy since we experience their simultaneity.

It follows from this substantial difference between the two types of associative factors that it will be necessary to separate our discussion of the mimetic capacities of music into two. The first, investigating music's mimetic capacities in the narrower sense, will be called the *"pictorial"* (*obrazivá*) capacity; the second – analogously to our analysis of mimics – the *"expressive"* (*vyjadřovací*) capacity of music.

I. THE PICTORIAL CAPACITY OF MUSIC depends on the extent of the similarity of musical formations to our experiences.
A. **Portraying external things** that are known to us from nature or life (*tone painting*).

Naturally this is first and foremost the case of *sounds* (acoustic phenomena), since music itself appeals to our hearing. Sounds that nature and life bring (with the exception of music itself or singing, of course) are mostly nonmusical or at least imperfectly musical, while the materials of music are *tones* of musical instruments with the minor and negligible exception of a few percussion instruments (drum, triangle, etc.). With this distinction in mind, the similarity between natural sounds and music can only be *approximate*. Music can imitate these sounds either in its quality, such as its pitch, intensity or especially *timbre* – and therefore it is *orchestral* music that can do this best – or in its temporal progress: in its speed, rhythm and melodic formation. Different acoustic phenomena fit different instrument families; wind instruments have the greatest capacity. The potency and accuracy of the *pictorial* effect of such *"tone painting"* also depends on the extent to which the sounds themselves are acoustically distinctive and unique, or if they are only generic, and thus not so expressive, allowing for a number of interpretations. The most distinctive as well as most popular is the portrayal of birdsong. The flute passage in Act II of Bedřich Smetana's opera *Tajemství* (*The Secret*) effectively portrays a nightingale's song. The rustling of the forest is also common, portrayed by polyphonic undulations of strings *con sordino* (as in Richard Wagner's *Siegfried*). A beautiful example of a combination of winds and strings is Přemysl's "Lime Tree" song ("Ó, vy lípy") in Smetana's opera *Libuše*, portraying the humming and rustling of the crown of the lime tree[30]. As an example of human-made sounds I might give the stamping of feet signalling the arrival of people offstage, which is used

---

30 Zich refers to the situation in Smetana's opera *Libuše*, where Přemysl praises the monumentality and peaceful beauty of lime trees – which are the Czech national symbol. Right after this aria, envoys from Libuše arrive to announce to Přemysl that she has chosen him for her husband.

often (for instance, right after Přemysl's "Lime Tree" song, the pizzicato in strings announces the coming of Libuše's envoys). Evidently, music is capable of effectively portraying *movement*, although only indirectly, by portraying the sound caused by it. Other examples might be the whirring sound of the spinning wheel, portrayed by a viola trill, which accompanies spinning songs, such as in François-Adrien Boïeldieu's *La dame blanche*, Wagner's *Der fliegende Holländer*, Zdeněk Fibich's *Pád Arkuna* (*The Fall of Arkona*)[31] and others. With soundless movement, music can only share the speed of the sequence of notes, which is a similarity too abstract in order to achieve effective reproduction of the image: we do not know what it is that moves.

In the depiction of *visual* things music is generally inefficient. It is true that notes and their combinations evoke a range of images of lights and colours for some people (this is known as *photism* or *synaesthesia, audition colorée*) but this is strictly individual and cannot be taken in objective terms. However, it is true that qualities of pitch and timbre have a particular *character of mood, related* to the moods associated with certain perceptions of sight and touch, and these are the same for everyone. The very names that are transferred from these sensory fields to music bear witness: high notes, we say, are "clear" and "sharp", low notes are "dark", "flat" or "dull". Effects of light can therefore be characterised by means of music to some extent, such as the full sunny daylight portrayed by high violin notes ("noontime" in the aforementioned scene from Smetana's *Libuše* with Přemysl in Act II), the transition from darkness into day ("the dawn" in Smetana's opera *Hubička* (*The Kiss*), portrayed by growing and intensifying orchestral sound from the low to high register) or the dimming of day (when Alberich snatches the ring in Wagner's *Rheingold*), moonlight portrayed by the dark timbre of flutes and *sordino* violins (with many examples, such as Wagner's *Lohengrin*) and others. On this basis music can depict noiseless movements also, such as lightning (naturally with the roaring of thunder) by accented high notes, by a "pointed" figure in the flutes and violins, or blazing flames (the well-known "magic fire music" in Wagner's *Der Ring des Nibelungen*) and such like. We could also add the characteristic of spatial movement from heights to depths, especially if it is accompanied with growing darkness (see Smetana's portrayal in the opera *Dalibor* of Dalibor's descent into the prison cell by descending notes through the orchestra, down to the lowest range in the double basses).

Since these sonic qualities are always present in music, the listener needs to be given an adequate impulse to start picturing the appropriate optical images, and also some directives of what kind those images should be. This is also true in the numerous instances of *actual* tone painting – that is, one based on similarities of sounds, not only of moods. Tone painting based on moods could therefore be called *figurative*.

---

31   *Pád Arkuna* (The Fall of Arkona, 1899) is the last opera of the Czech romantic composer Zdeněk Fibich (1850–1900). The story is taken from Slavic mythology.

Even with this proviso one could say that the external pictorial capacity of music is limited and pertains only to some types of acoustic phenomena and a very narrow range of optical ones. Music can call up *images of objects* – that is of live and inanimate things – with at least some certainty only *indirectly*, by portraying the *qualities* that are *typical* of them, especially acoustic and, to some extent, visual. The resulting extent of the image depends on the scope of this characteristic: music can portray a nightingale's song or birdsong in general, moonlight, etc. The same is true of the images of *events*, especially of movement. If things and events do not have sufficiently characteristic and specific qualities, especially acoustically, then it cannot be expected that they will be evoked; although music can achieve a similarity in sound, we will be unsure what is being portrayed. If a thing or an event is "silent", its musical portrayal is *entirely impossible* (apart from a modest figurative illustration). Music is therefore incapable of picturing such things as a house, floating clouds, a person glancing back and thousands of other *ostensive* facts that are easily portrayed by visual arts (although with only an illusion of movement). It is therefore almost impossible that music could evoke abstract images, since these cannot be portrayed at all, except for ostensive features. Music is not a "language", as people often metaphorically say; music is – with the exception of the above exceptional cases – *devoid of concepts*.

Still, it is said that music is not the language of ideas but *a language of emotions*. This common and popular view should be critically analysed, which has been done in principle by Otakar Hostinský (in *Das Musikalisch-Schöne und das Gesamtkunstwerk vom Standpunkte der formalen Aesthetik*, 1877).

B. **Portraying inner states**, especially emotions and human aspirations (*soul painting*).

There is a fundamental noetic difference between images and emotions in that images, although they are essentially states of our mind that refer to something outside of us, to various objective "things"; they are in fact reproduced perceptions (*vněmy*), which we generally assume with certainty are evoked by various external objects (this is known as "practical realism"). On the other hand, I cannot understand emotions arising inside me as anything but something exclusively mine, something purely subjective. This is also reflected in our language in the transitivity of verbs; in Czech, we say: I can see *something* (vidím něco), I can imagine *something* (představuji si něco), but this makes *me* happy (raduji se), and this makes *me* angry (zlobím se).[32]

There is only one instance – frequent but still special – when I can think of emotion as something objective: when I take the mental state of an object

---

32   Zich makes an observation on Czech reflexive verbs *radovat se* (to rejoice) and *zlobit se* (to be angry). Like in their French equivalents, *se réjouir* and *se fâcher*, they have the *self* (conveyed by the particle *se*) as their object – as if we said *I make myself merry* or *I anger myself*.

to be *outside myself*, be it perceived, imagined, or only hypothetical. It is clear that – apart from mystical interpretations of the world – the only such object can be *a live being*, usually *human*. Only poets invest "inanimate" things with a soul.

Nonetheless, I am unable to perceive the emotions of such a being directly because they cannot be seen or heard – and so music is also unable to portray emotions directly. I can only perceive the *displays (projevy)* of emotions and aspirations – by sight (such as a smile), by hearing (e.g., a sigh) or even by touch (a handshake); but this is irrelevant to our present purpose. Anyway, these displays or *expressions* of emotions and aspirations are nothing other than what we discussed in Chapter 5 as *mimics*. We have established that the psychological process is such that the mimic expression we perceive *evokes in us* a particular emotion on the basis of our experience, which we then *project* onto the being we observe as *their* emotion or aspiration.

It follows then that there are three *conditions* for a musical *"soul painting"* (as we shall call it in brief):

1. Certain music needs to be capable of *evoking* an emotion or an aspiration in us (a kind of "mental stirring").
2. This emotion or aspiration has to be similar to the emotions or aspirations experienced in life by us as well as by other beings that are similar to us.
3. Simultaneously with the music we must have a perception (or at least an image) of some being onto whom we may project said emotion or aspiration as pertaining to it.

1. As for the *first* condition, it is always fulfilled in good music, and to a particularly excellent degree at that; however, these evoked emotions are, generally, purely musical ones.

> There can surely be no doubt that music *by itself* is capable of arousing *emotions* not only of a great variety but also of uncommon intensity, *enrapturing* us so irresistibly and immediately like no other art – perhaps with the exception of vocal mimic expressions, as we have previously observed. To some extent it is a quality of all acoustic perceptions that they have a more powerful and inescapable effect on us than, for example, visual perceptions. The difference between acoustic mimics and music is in that the emotions evoked by mimics are the result of *associations* based on our previous experience – so they are *human* emotions (a certain sound denoted as laughter is naturally an expression of human joy); whereas music does so *directly*, without mediating an experience, and evokes in us multiple emotions linked to notes and their forms. These are purely *musical* emotions, unknown to us from other lived experience. Music is devoid of concepts. In contrast, human emotions – unlike "moods" (generally of somatic origin) – always have some imagined content (I rejoice over something, I grieve for something), although the content may be rather vague or no longer conscious.

Logically then, the emotions evoked by music seem as if distant from anything human, "unspeakable", mystical, cosmic, metaphysical, etc. – as evidenced by all the adjectives used to celebrate them. The cause is very simple: they are distant from our life experience because our life experience is also distant from the material of music, notes and their combinations, since these are entirely *artificial* formations. Only the emotional accent linked to the pitch, volume or timbre of every *note* is entirely of its kind. This is all the more so when it comes to *harmonies*: the emotions accompanying groups of notes are specifically musical, and this also applies to an extent to *melodies*, although here the notes do not sound simultaneously, but rather one after another. All these notes are not random but are selected from the pool of all possible notes according to harmonic principles and arranged into scales. Apart from pleasant consonances there are less pleasant and entirely unpleasant dissonances, both in chords and in melodies. We will call all this emotional effect of music *static*.

The overwhelming emotional effect of music has caused music almost universally to be considered a *highly lyrical* art form. This assumption is taken to imply that the participation of music in a dramatic work is not particularly welcome. Music, it is assumed, *lyricises* too much, emphasising the dramatic work's static moments as opposed to its dynamic ones; it makes it lyrical so powerfully and extensively that it weakens or even kills its dramatic qualities. This view is almost universal; it is held both by audiences and by critics; often opera composers believe it too, using the allegedly exclusively lyrical capacity of music in composing their works in such a way that these may be beautiful to listen to but are more fitting for the concert hall than for the theatre, where their effect is weak. This belief in the *exclusively* lyrical qualities of music is a mere myth. We shall prove that the *dramatic capacity of music is as strong as the lyrical one, and in some ways even stronger*. This is where the *raison d'être* of dramatic music lies: its necessary existential condition.

Let us start with examining if music is as capable of evoking *aspirations* as evoking emotions. The answer to this question is affirmative without any reservations. The basis of an aspiration is motoric; clearly, there is no doubt of the immense *motoric* effect of music by itself – it has this effect on animals too! The moments that determine this effect are contained in the *temporal progression* of music: it is the variation in intensity and speed in the sequence of notes or whole chords – in musical terminology: the *rhythm, dynamics and agogic stress* of music. The irresistible effect of rhythm on listeners is well known; it often makes one's head, body and especially legs move (as in a march or a dance). Heavy accents cause one's entire organism to jerk, affecting breathing, which follows every dynamic change throughout the piece (such as when we hold our breath during the gradual crescendo of the orchestra). All these bodily effects of music are aspirations in their motoric principles, albeit in combination with their mental counterparts, which express either agitation or calm on the one hand, or tension and release on the other. Another example to add are *melodic* dissonances known as "suspensions", where we feel an aspiration to resolve to a consonance. They intensify the *kinetic* nature contained in any melody, especially in their "leading notes". All these *aspirational* effects of music, as briefly outlined here, are again *devoid of ideas*. And yet they are not as distant from human aspirations as the above static musical emotions, of which their deep-seated somatic basis is the cause. This makes them seem much more "human" and in some coarse rhythms (as in all kinds of marches) they may even come across as too human and too physical – since their effect is predominantly physiological. Their link to our life experience (albeit to an extra-musical one) is based on the similarity of experiencing various bodily activities, many of which even have regular rhythms originating with the motoric mechanisms – such as different kinds of manual work, various types of gait, gymnastic movements and even the most daring of them: dance. The popular link of such activities to music is therefore as natural as one could wish. That these activities pertain predominantly to the motoric effect of musical rhythm is clear from the fact that primitive forms of this link are associated with extra-musical sounds (clapping of hands, stamping of feet, drumming and so on, in folk dances or in marches). There is no need to waste words on the mental aspect of the rhythmic effect, especially in more refined and artificial rhythms. We will call all this aspirational effect of music *dynamic*.

Recalling what we established in Chapter 3 about the *"dramatic effect"*, we can see that it is essentially identical to what we have just discussed. What is characteristic about it is its *motoric* component, which manifests itself specifically through its feeling of "dramatic excitement" and "dramatic tension". So, if we disregard any ideational content and its effects, we will see that the motoric and dynamic effect of music – musical excitement and tension – is the same as that of dramatic effect, and that music by itself has the full *capacity* for its effect to be called *dramatic*. In order for this to happen, other conditions have to be met, as follows.

2. The first necessary condition for the dramaticity (*dramatičnost*) of music is that the emotions and aspirations evoked in us by music have to *be similar* to *"human"* emotions and aspirations, known to us from our own (extra-musical) experience. This can be achieved either by an appropriate choice of musical (*tónový*) material, or by its effective forming (*utváření*).

> As far as determining the emotion from its *static*, i.e., purely qualitative side is concerned, this is firstly a matter of choosing the instruments with their specific *timbres* and of using the high or low *registers* of notes. As we know, the emotional impact connected with these qualities is so specifically musical that it barely reminds us of a distinct real-world emotion. To some extent one could use the certain clarity or darkness of high or low registers to symbolise a "bright" mood, that is, joy, a blissful rapture of the mind, etc., as opposed to a "dark" mood, that is, sadness, hopelessness and such like. However, all this also depends on the other components of such music. An example of

this could be the opening of Act III of Wagner's *Tristan*, where the continuously deep register has a depressing effect on us.

It might seem that the *harmony* of musical consonances offers a more secure characteristic for the quality of emotions, since the distinction between consonance and dissonance (disregarding their more minute differentiation) means the basic emotional distinction of pleasant/unpleasant. The notorious opposition of major and minor chords is a characteristic symbol of human joy and sorrow, or melancholy at least; depending, of course, on whether the chord appears in the tonic key or a secondary one. Their contrasting nature best stands out if they follow one after another (over the same root), even unexpectedly; a well-known example is the victorious emergence of the major chord in second inversion after the preceding minor chord, e.g., the finale of Act I of Smetana's *Dalibor*, alongside Jitka's text "do žaláře mu svitne záře" (and light will shine into his jail). Among the most basic dissonances, an unpleasant emotion is characterised, for instance, by the diminished seventh chord or the especially "foreboding" augmented chord, e.g., during Chrudoš's rant against the Queen in Smetana's *Libuše*. As for harmonic sequences, an especially important one is the "resolution" of dissonance into the following consonance, which follows the emotional pattern of "tension–release" and suggests the satisfactory resolution of an unpleasant matter. Conversely, a continuous sequence of dissonances is similar to the frustrated extension of something unpleasant.

Such numerous correspondences between the types of emotions evoked by musical *harmony* and human emotions is rather relative. From a historical point of view, the development of harmony over the last few centuries has progressed from consonance to ever harsher dissonances, reaching – in our times – a culmination in "cacophony". We now find many dissonances from earlier eras to be very pleasant and even sweet chords (such as the dominant seventh chord and especially the dominant ninth). The notorious "tragic" moments of older operas that used to have a horrifying effect in their time (such as the Tartarus scenes in Gluck's *Orfeo*) now seem harmonically quite tame – we are used to other dissonances nowadays. This is a matter of habit, which blunts the edge of impressions; we ourselves find some dissonances that used to be unbearable quite acceptable now. The second cause of uncertain interpretation of the emotional quality of musical harmony is in that a musical idea regularly *alternates* different harmonies, consonant and dissonant, so the overall impression depends on which of them are prominent, or rather which of them we emphasise more, so it may be either pleasant, or unpleasant. I have found empirically that the same music that actually portrays the despair of a dramatic persona (the end of Lukáš's scene in Act II of Smetana's *Hubička*, The Kiss), when played on its own, seemed to express despair to some, but exultation to others (see "Estetické vnímání hudby", in *Česká mysl* XI).

As far as *melody* is concerned, emotional interpretation – disregarding its rhythm and tempo for the time being – may pertain to its harmonic qualities, whether real (i.e., resounding in the underlying harmony) or imaginary (i.e., the imagined accompaniment to a solo melody). What has been said about the interpretation of harmony holds here as well, though all the more strongly influenced by the vagaries of taste over the course of music's development. On the one hand, there may be a clear distinction between joyful melodies in major scales and sad melodies in minor. However, a major melody in a broad tempo can be very serious, while a minor melody in a lively tempo may seem even frivolous. More distant transitional modulations in the melody evoke the impression of imbalance, suggesting human passions. Very important are the leading tones in melodies, which may be emphasised in their dissonance by placing them on downbeats; the harsher their dissonance, the more the melody acquires a painful nature – sometimes even obtrusively so. Conversely, "sweet thirds" (or sixths) of two melodic lines may even come across as sentimental – as in older Italian operas.

However, it is in connection with melodies that another factor comes into play: besides the direct effect, there is the *associative* factor arising from the similarities between musical melodies and *human vocal expressions* of the inarticulate kind (laughter, groaning, etc.) and the articulate one (speech). We have not discussed this instance in our analysis of tone painting where it would logically belong; this was not only because of its special significance for musical melody but also because the associative effect is generally *not entirely conscious*. The *image* of such an associated vocal expression is almost never evoked clearly, except as a *mood* that is connected with human emotions and aspirations as their audible expression. There are instruments reminiscent of the human voice in their timbre and the way they sound (musical articulation): this is true of wind instruments such as the oboe (giving an impression of female voice) or numerous brass instruments (Purkyně[33] made a witty comment saying that the "trumpet speaks the most"); there is a basic general melodic similarity between any instrument and the human voice. In this way certain melodic features acquire their own distinctive mood-like trait. This is most marked in chromatic melodies because the semitone sequence is closest to the continuous melodic progression of speech. A descending chromatic melody is "plaintive" like human lamenting; an ascending one evokes desire, the rising voice of the supplicant (cf. the two main motifs of Wagner's *Tristan*, which carry this dual symbolic meaning). In contrast, melodic leaps over large intervals suggest the passionate voice of a rejoicing, infuriated or despairing person. In brief, what we call an *"expressive"* melody is mainly based on an acoustic analogy with audible human expressions; that is, with *vocal mimics*. It should be noted that music never determines the emotion with certainty on the *qualitative* side – as can be seen from the given example of a "passionate voice"; music still retains its essential lack of ideas in its content. Though a melody may weep, rejoice or yearn, we can never tell from the melody itself why or what for. The same is true of vocal mimics, as we have seen.

---

33   Jan Evangelista Purkyně (1787–1869) was a Czech natural scientist, poet, translator and philosopher. In his research he lay the foundation of the biological study of cell tissues (cytology). His research also included the physiology of hearing and sight. Among his many achievements is his creation of Czech terminology for natural sciences. He was also a theatre and opera enthusiast.

Determining the emotion or aspiration from the *dynamic* side – i.e., the way it unfolds over time – is a different case. Recalling what has been said above of the motoric and dynamic effect of music, we can see that music is *perfectly* capable of expressing the duration of time – i.e., variation in intensity and speed – characteristic for certain emotions, aspirations and their combinations, particularly apparent in passions. Our mimetic interpretation necessarily has to be unambiguous, since the mediating link between them is the *bodily* expression of emotions and aspirations, and this expression is in perfect agreement with the time progression in the mind. Let us remember that this correspondence in the time progression between the bodily expression (which we know from our own experience) and the musical rhythm is based in temporality, which is equally valid for music. That means that calm music can only be an image of a calm state of mind, and agitated music of an agitated one. The well-known strategy of dramatic music, the tremolo in strings, corresponds directly to the shivering of our body – whether we tremble for fear (tremolo in the lower register) or for mystical excitement (Wagner's tremolo in the high register of violins). Rhythmic irregularity, especially syncopation, corresponds with both physical and mental unease (a beautiful example is Anežka's aria from Smetana's opera *Dvě vdovy* (*The Two Widows*) with its irregular rhythm in the horns' accompanimental chords). Heavy timpani strikes resemble the effect of a sudden shock or surprise; there is often a series of further, echoing hits, progressively quieter and slower (numerous examples, such as Senta and the Dutchman's first encounter in Wagner). Music can capture with equal perfection the rhythmic nature of different human activities, but it cannot tell us what kind of work it is, unless this can be done through sound imitation (tone painting). That is the only aspect where mimics is superior to music; however, the range of images that mimics can portray is relatively small and music can make up for this in its specific capacity for tone painting.

What has been concluded in this and the previous section is the following: On account of the pictorial capacity of music embedded in its very structure it can be said that *music is sounding mimics*. It is equally *poor in images* (ideas) and equally *rich in emotions and aspirations*. As for the extent of its *sensory* effect on the audience, it is at least equal to audible mimics (the actor's vocal expressions) and certainly exceeds visible mimics (the actor's physical play or mimics in the narrow sense).

The cause of music's supremacy with regard to its *dramatic* effect lies in its translation of motoric qualities from the optical realm of visible mimics to its own acoustic realm. We have already noted that the sensory impression of hearing is more intense than of sight, which is always more discrete. Clearly we are affected when an actor's gloomy face on stage suddenly lights up in a smile; but when sombre music lights up in a sweet harmony, the effect is greater. If a sitting actor suddenly leaps up with a fierce gesture, it is an effective expression of shock; but how much more effective is a sharp and loud dissonant chord of an entire orchestra! It is like an enhanced outcry of horror.

It is clear that the task of *all* mimetic, programmatic, vocal and dramatic music is to use its capacities as described above to serve necessary, concrete purposes. This is the requirement of *musical characterisation* and is also valid for *dramatic* music where its application is specific to the principles of dramaticity, as we will discuss. It can be summarised in general:

A musical **characterisation** means *shaping the chosen sonic material so that it evokes*
a) *images that are similar in sound or mood* to a certain number of acoustic or visual phenomena that operate here (*musical tone painting*);
b) *emotions and aspirations that are similar statically* (i.e., through their quality) *or dynamically* (i.e., through their development) to *human* emotions and aspirations that are at play (*musical soul painting*).

It is obvious that this second requirement is a principal, or rather, *necessary* condition of *dramatic* music. It must be emphasised that even when the best possible similarity with human emotions and aspirations is achieved, there is still something *non-human* in the impression made by music; herein lies its *purely musical charm*.

3. We have defined the *objective* condition of musical *soul painting*; for it to apply, the *subjective* condition also must be fulfilled: the listener, while perceiving music, needs to perceive (or at least imagine) a *live being* as an imagined *bearer of the emotions and aspirations* that are evoked by the music. In this sense, mimics is in a good position since it is performed on stage by an actor and we project the emotions or aspirations, evoked through mimics, onto the dramatic persona the actor is portraying. The *very same condition is principally fulfilled in dramatic music* and we are able to project the emotions and aspirations, evoked in us by simultaneous *music*, onto the given dramatic persona by the same principle that mimics had evoked emotions – on the aforementioned condition that they are characteristic. In fact, it is the ostensive existence of a dramatic persona that serves as the *actual impetus* to interpret some *orchestral music* as soul painting rather than otherwise, e.g., as tone painting. (We will discuss singing later.) Thus, "tempestuous music" heard by itself may be interpreted as a natural storm or a "storm" inside a human mind, such as anger. The former, tone-painting interpretation would occur if prompted by the *appearance of the stage* (as in the finale of Act I of Boïeldieu's *La dame blanche*). Given there are often more personas onstage, the issue is *onto which of them* we should place the musical soul painting. We are governed in this by the *correspondence* between the emotions or aspirations evoked by *orchestral music* and the emotional and aspirational *mimic* expression (including *singing*) of a particular dramatic persona. We should bear in mind that musical polyphony allows several characterisations simultaneously – as we will discuss later in more detail. It needs to be stressed

that the requirement of correspondence between mimic (including singing) characterisation and musical characterisation (i.e., in the orchestra) *is not absolute*. What is meant here are not only the instances when music takes its own course independent of the dramatic personas – which is typical, for instance, of the operetta, where a persona may be despairing "to the sound of a waltz"; that is an example of non-dramatic music. But there are *exceptional* cases where dramatic characterisation requires the portrayal of disjointed mental states. (We will return to this later.)

> There is generally a qualitative and temporal correspondence between both mimics and music; such correspondence results in an *extraordinary intensification* of the overall impression. This is a generally accepted advantage of sung drama over spoken drama and the lion's share in this is down to music – that is, music that follows the dramatic characterisation without drowning in lyricism. Mimics does important service to music too, in giving things *greater concreteness*, wherever it is capable of doing so. This is specifically true of the *quality* of emotions, which mimics communicates very clearly. The example above – of the empirical finding that tempestuous music, interpreted by some as despair, but as exultation by others – would not apply if we simultaneously perceive the music and the onstage action, because despair and exultation look mimically very different; in that case, we have the least doubt that Lukáš (in Smetana's *Hubička*) is despairing. Given how relative the effect of harmony on us may be, the qualitative concreteness of emotions or aspirations provided by mimics is very important – especially in modern opera, where dissonances are overwhelmingly present. The *permeation* of mimic impressions into musical ones actually takes place in our minds and it is so perfect that it creates the illusion that all of this is already contained in music. We might call this the *dramatisation* of (orchestral) music through mimics.

The combination of orchestral music with *mimics* on stage has great advantages; however, it is frustrated by a weakness that they both share: their *poverty in ideas*. It is only through outer actions of dramatic personas – characterised by music wonderfully, but without concrete ideas – that concrete referential images are evoked in us (such as an embrace, a fight and others); their inner thoughts and imaginations remain concealed – as can best be seen in *dramatic pantomime*. This is where the requirement of the total actor comes into play, asking actors to perform people *in their entirety*, i.e., with their *language*. This language then provides by its content (i.e., the dramatic text) *all the thoughts and imagined ideas* that cannot be expressed by mimics or music (especially abstract ideas), but which are necessary to understand the dramatic action – *both in sung drama (zpěvohra) and in spoken drama (činohra)*. And this still disregards the emotions that the language *by itself* evokes (as opposed to the reading of a dramatic text); however, we need to know what it says in the first place.

The rich expressive capacity of language makes it even possible to place the emotions and aspirations evoked by music *onto an entirely fictitious persona* – that is, one that is only *spoken about*. This is quite a common occurrence in opera. It is in fact necessary for an onstage dramatic persona to describe another (usually absent) in such a way as to give rise to the soul painting of this *second* persona. However, it is usually true – due to empathy – that the mental state of the onstage persona (who is describing the other) is more or less the same, so the soul-painting relates to both. In all the instances when the onstage persona's description is emotionally tainted (for instance by hate towards the other person), the ongoing soul painting relates to the onstage persona that is present – and that is the most common occurrence in dramatic works.

> A combination of (poetic) language and music is common in vocal music, by which we mean instrumental music that accompanies singing. Because this combination takes place in real time and in strict simultaneity, the sung lyrics perfectly define the referential image of simultaneous or unfolding time in all its aspects. As for the final condition of soul painting, there is a significant difference to dramatic music, analogous to the difference between a reciter and an actor, as discussed in Chapter 5. In brief: a concert singer is a "musical reciter", an interpretive artist substituting the composer (and indirectly also the poet whose lyrics the composer set to music). We project the emotions evoked by vocal music onto the singer but only as emotions that were *evoked in the singer* in his or her delivery. They are not *referential* emotions because the singer does not represent anyone; the singer is actually on an equal standing with us and is – we assume at least – as captivated by the composition as we are, with the difference that the singer performs it under that impression. An exception here are songs that quote the speech of a living being (as in Franz Schubert's ballad *Erlkönig*); in that case we project our emotions onto the imagined persona just like we do in an opera, but in this case as exclusively that person's emotions, because the singer stands outside that imaginary world. This is (or should be) also the case in programmatic music; unfortunately, there is no real connection between language (i.e., the programme) and music, since the combination is only imagined and the simultaneity is somewhat uncertain (cf. the soul painting in Smetana's symphonic poem *Šárka*[34]).

---

34 *Šárka* (1875) is third part in Bedřich Smetana's famous cycle of symphonic poems *Má vlast* (My Country). The orchestral poem deals with the mythological legend of the Women's War, also called the Czech Amazons. The aforementioned soul painting refers to the story of Šárka, one of the rebel women who want to take revenge on the menfolk, so she uses her beauty to entrap the warrior Ctirad. Ctirad falls in love with Šárka, and when he falls asleep, Šárka and her fellow Amazons capture him and eventually torture him to death. Smetana paints through Šárka's and Ctirad's emotions: hate, love, passion and vengefulness.

It is equally obvious that the stage scenery, as the *location of the action*, significantly contributes to the *concreteness and certainty* of our interpretation of musical *tone painting*, especially of the figurative kind (visible phenomena), which would otherwise be uncertain. This is conditional upon the characterisation of such music; however, the interpretation itself is mostly caused by the appearance of the scenery (and by the speeches that personas deliver on it). The above example of the nightingale in Smetana's *Tajemství* does not need such support given how characteristic the sound is. In contrast, the music accompanying Gluck's Orpheus entering Elysium stands out clearly as tone painting (rustling of trees and birdsong) only once the scenery shows "a garden in paradise". This is all the more true of the aforementioned "dawn" in Smetana's *Hubička* when it is simultaneously accompanied by lighting changes. The *correspondence* of the stage scenery and music has a very strong effect, just like in soul painting.

II. THE EXPRESSIVE CAPACITY OF MUSIC is based on the association principle of simultaneity. If we have ever experienced an extrinsic impression or image (even an abstract one) while listening to a particular piece of music, it will remain associated with that piece of music; whenever I hear the music later, the image is recalled too. That piece of music has become a certain *marker* (značka) for that image or idea, similar to a word in language. This is clearly a very significant aspect of music: its *intellectual* capacity; given that music of itself is devoid of ideas, it can be *arbitrarily expanded* in this way to a great extent. Naturally, the *emotional* accent of the associated image, which is intense in itself, enriches and governs the purely musical effect. On the basis of the *initial* association of a piece of music with an image, two basic types of such "musical quotations" may be distinguished.

1. **Conventional musical quotations.** In this case, the first connection of a particular piece of music with particular images is not established in the work itself but is known to the listener from elsewhere, from their life experience.

> The composer may be quoting a tune of a song whose lyrics are well-known to the listeners, so both are evoked at the same time. So, for instance, during in Smetana's *Libuše*, during Libuše's prophecy, after her words *"jen oni pevně jdou"* (only *they* firmly march), the orchestra plays the choral *Ktož jsú boží bojovníci* (Ye Who Are Warriors of God). Whoever knows the song will know immediately that *they* refer to the Hussite reformation uprising of the early 15th century and to their battlefield chant that always led them to victory, etc. A fragment of the song would be enough for this, even musically altered, as long as we could recognise it. However, whoever does not know the song will not respond to it – and these are the limitations of such special quotation. The limits broaden once the quotation is of a more *general* kind, such as when it relates

to the practical use of music for specific real-world occasions. Depending on different circumstances and purposes, these may be connected with the use of particular musical *instruments* and particular *conventional forms*, especially of a rhythmic, but also harmonic or melodic kind (originating mostly from a specific mode of playing these instruments). It is not only the complex images of such "real-world occasions" but also their rich *texture array of moods* that influence the musical formations that are associated with them. For instance, simple tunes on the oboe or clarinet remind us of shepherds playing the shawm, strongly conjuring the atmospheric images of an idyllic life, of mountains, etc. Fanfares of horns suggest hunting and forests; flourishes of trumpets (often with the rumbling of timpani) in a moderate tempo suggest a ceremony, a court trial, a royal entry (a beautiful example of a royal entry is in Smetana's opera *Dalibor*), and in a fast tempo, an army and a war. Minor chords in the trombones at a slow tempo evoke gloomy images: a funeral march, a burial, death. We are in fact dealing here with musical *types* which are conventionalised in some ways, while in others they are open to the composer's invention. For instance, a polyphonic texture of music suggests the mood of sacred music and everything associated with it, even when it is not played on the organ (and if it is, all the more so), but by an orchestra that only imitates the organ's sound – that is how Smetana ironically portrays the hypocritical dealings of the monk Beneš in his opera *Čertova stěna* (The Devil's Wall). This is also true of the use of church modes. Often it is a matter of a certain type of rhythm or tempo, while the melodic, harmonic or orchestrational aspects are entirely free. For opera, an important example is the *march* (or a promenade) and especially *dance* in all its countless variants. This pertains both to formal (*umělé*) dances that can characterise a particular society or era, as well as to folk dances that can characterise a simple countryside environment or even, very importantly, a *nationality*.

A study of this motif in opera would require a special, dedicated and extensive treatise; for the present purpose, let us rest on a few examples taken from Romantic operas where the folk element and nationality were first emphasised. Carl Maria von Weber's *Der Freischütz* contains a folk (farmers') march and a dance (the German *Ländler*). Georges Bizet's *Carmen* is replete with Spanish dances even more than Daniel Auber's *La muette de Portici* with Italian ones. Smetana's comic operas importantly feature the polka, the *skočná*, the *furiant* (as in *The Bartered Bride*) and the *vrták* (the Dudácká in *Tajemství*). Foerster's opera *Eva* alludes to a Slovak dance song (the *Kysuca*)[35] – to name but a few. We need to bear in mind that despite their rich varieties all dances share one

---

35   *Polka, skočná* and *furiant* are typical Czech folk dances. Smetana himself made several arrangements of these dances in his works. In *The Bartered Bride* the use of the dances help to characterise the location of the story in south Bohemia. Foerster's opera *Eva* (1899) is located in a village on the border of south Moravia and Slovakia. Here Foerster uses the Slovak folk dance *kysuca*.

feature; they are predominantly joyful, "dance-like", and so it would be entirely absurd to characterise something *exclusively* by means of a typical national dance. Naturally, one has to assume that the national origins of a particular dance are known to the audience, otherwise it will be taken only as a generic, though specific dance.

2. **Authorial musical quotations.** In this case, the first connection of a particular piece of music with a particular image or impression is established *by the composer* and *in the work itself*. This association is not conventional but arbitrary and *authorial*, which gives it – within the boundaries of the work – a full artistic justification. In dramatic music, such an original connection offers itself automatically because music progresses simultaneously alongside dramatic action (visible and audible) and one of its components is constituted even by language based on the dramatic text. In vocal music, this relates only to the simultaneous lyrics, though this is sufficient. Whenever the same music returns, the correct identity of the evoked *image* is guaranteed perfectly within the composer's intentions; with it, the intended impression of mood is also evoked once more, which *immensely* intensifies and enriches the direct effect of the music itself.

In Smetana's *The Bartered Bride* (Prodaná nevěsta), when I see Jeník and Mařenka on stage singing of their true love ("Věrné milování"), a connection is established between the music that accompanies it and the image of the scene and the meaning of the lyrics I hear. When the same music returns in Mařenka's confession "mám už jiného" (I have someone else now), I recall the previous scene and the effect of that moment is greatly heightened – since this new dramatic situation is no more than a type of eavesdropping. An even stronger effect is achieved in the second return of the music in Act III, accompanied by the heartbroken Mařenka's words: "Sám přísahal, že celý svět by obětoval za mne" (He swore himself that he would sacrifice the whole world for me). The contrast between the sweet music that exalts the memory of past happiness and the young woman's current state is supremely effective here. Words themselves are unable to achieve this because their recollection can be no more than a pale image. In a dramatic work, neither is there need for words to create an association; a picture suffices. When in Act I of Smetana's *Dalibor* I see Dalibor arrive for his trial, the brilliant music that accompanies it becomes linked to his chivalric appearance, which overwhelms even his own accuser Milada. When in Act II the Jailer asks the disguised Milada, "Ty znáš rytíře?" (Do you know the knight?), the beginning of the aforementioned music passes through the orchestra like a light shadow – and Milada quietly answers: "Viděl jsem jej pouze jednou" (I have seen him only once). This is a masterpiece of dramatic soul painting that shows how greatly an authorial association can enrich the expressive capacity of music.

From the viewpoint of psychological analysis, the process that, for us, activates authorial associations takes place first *in the composer's mind* during its creation. Be it a place in the text (in a vocal composition) or a dramatic situation (in opera), the composer conceptualises the music to make it as good and poignant as possible. It is therefore understandable that it (i.e., the image content) connects with the given place *for themselves* so firmly that their own music is evoked anew as soon as another place or situation recalls the previous place or situation. During composition, the composer themself forms *a dual image* (or *double idée fixe*, as Berlioz called it in the programme for his *Symphonie fantastique*), which contains primarily an idea – either ostensive or imaginary, i.e., governed by a picture or a word – and that idea is always extra-musical; secondarily, it contains a musical idea associated with it. This dual idea *recurs* later in the course of the composition as soon as its primary component (objectively defined in the poem or drama that serves as its source) gives the composer the appropriate stimulus. Let us call this logical correlation *the principle of musico-poetic* or *musico-dramatic* **parallelism**. This principle is *an extension of the principle of musico-poetic* or *musico-dramatic characterisation* as discussed above in the section on the pictorial (obraziva) capacity of music – with the addition of the above *conventional characterisation*.

This extends the characterisation principle in the sense of *the temporal progression* of a poetic or dramatic work *alongside its musical component*. If a particular image or idea has been musically characterised in a particular way, it is psychologically natural and logically consistent that it is characterised in the same way whenever it recurs. As listeners we feel this to be natural and consistent: it appears to us as if the return of an idea directly *incurred* the return in music. However, it has to be *the same* idea; if it is *partly modified*, then the principle of musical characterisation requires that the music is also *partly modified*. The parallelism principle does not limit itself to the instances of *perfect return* but also covers *modified returns*. From this point of view, authorial quotations may be divided into two distinct groups, despite the continuous transition between them. (Let us focus only on sung drama (zpěvohra).)

a) *Characteristic reminiscence*. This pertains to an actual memory of a *concrete and unique* situation that has been established previously by performers and stage action, with or without words. For that reason the relevant music is *repeated faithfully*, without any changes, or only with minor ones. A reminiscence always repeats *an autonomous and longer* musical passage, though often abbreviated. This can be likened to a quotation of a whole *sentence* in speech, even with a few opening words modified.

> Both the examples given above (from Smetana's *The Bartered Bride* and *Dalibor*) are instances of characteristic reminiscence. The latter, as appropriate for the situation (a sweet memory), modifies the music's dynamics (and thus its instrumentation also),

while retaining the melody, rhythm, harmony (this time sounding over a dominant pedal, which gives it the air of instability) and even the key.

b) *Characteristic motif (leitmotif)*. The idea or image associated with music is of a *more general* and therefore *more abstract* kind, although it is often established ostensively, such as by the appearance of a particular dramatic *persona*. In fact, it is a set of qualities of the persona that we imagine and bestow upon the persona on the basis of its conduct in the dramatic action. This is similar to an idea of *an event* (incident or dramatic plot), established by ostensive dramatic situations, which we then interpret in our minds. Often this idea is co-determined by lines delivered simultaneously – and sometimes even exclusively by words, at which point the idea is entirely abstract. A characteristic motif is established musically by a relatively *short* but self-contained theme: a true "motif", which does *not need* to be principally an autonomous, self-standing piece of music, but only a component or even an element of it. It can be solely melodic, irrespective of its harmonisation or instrumentation (Libuše's motif in Smetana's opera is an example), or it can be solely harmonic (e.g., the Pilgrim's motif in Wagner's *Siegfried*) or even just rhythmic, so that it can be quoted only by percussion instruments (Hunding's motif in Wagner's *Die Walküre*). It is common that *all* musical components participate in the nature of the motif, though one or two of them may be more dominant on the basis of the kind of idea *that this motif is meant to characterise*. In contrast to all the previous partial ones, such a characteristic motif will be called a *total* motif. Since the *overall* nature of such a motif always depends on the co-existence of all its components, any *modification* of the less dominant components will result in a particular *nuance* in its musical character without losing its basis. It is still "the same" motif but *characteristically modified on the basis of the modification of the idea* to which it corresponds and which surely undergoes changes in the course of the dramatic work – as has been stressed in the preceding chapters in relation to both dramatic personas and the dramatic relations between them or even the ideas of the dramatic action (*děj*).

> The oldest variant of a characteristic motif is *instrumental*, which comprises changes in timbre and pitch as well as changes in volume. Such a modification is actually not taken to be a modification in music but only in sound; nevertheless, the motif's nature and effect change immensely (e.g., the Grail motif in Wagner's *Lohengrin* in the violins' high register, then in the brass). Certain motifs have originated from the techniques of individual instruments, and so they are tied to them, as it would be difficult to transfer them to other instruments (e.g., the trumpet motif of the upcoming verdict in Smetana's *Libuše*, which opens the overture; similarly, Wagner's motif of the Flying Dutchman in the horns). In these cases, instrumental characterisation occurs in pitch

and intensity, both directly and associatively (according to convention). *Harmonic* changes are musically more noticeable, often resulting in melodic changes as well (to which can be added changes of key, which are believed by some to each have their own character, though this could only be possible with orchestras containing instruments of prescribed tuning). A different harmonisation will change the nature of the motif greatly (e.g., the minor motif of old Tantalus in Zdeněk Fibich's *Hippodamia*[36] changes into major when he speaks of his youth). Many motifs retain their original harmonies, corresponding to the associated idea (so the motif of Libuše's upcoming verdict in Smetana's *Libuše* is always in a major key, while Morana's motif in Fibich's *Šárka* always in minor[37]). *Rhythmic* changes of motifs are pervasive; *motoric* changes, pertaining to the overall *pace*, are related to them and they can change the motif either through a different tempo or even different note values (i.e., augmentation and diminution) beyond recognition (the Master Singers' motif in Wagner in its elaborate and minimal variations). A true rhythmic change, together with a change of metre, goes to the very roots of the musical motif (Smetana's *Tajemství* offers beautiful examples in the changes of the motif of the secret; see below). The *melodic* changes of a motif are sometimes so substantial that they actually create a *new* motif, which is *related* to the previous one. The most apparent are the changes that enrich the motif internally by adding secondary notes into the melody (the verdict motif in *Libuše*). The inversion of the motif (Eva's motif in Foerster's opera[38]) also belongs to the category of melodic changes. The question of whether it is still the *same motif* is further complicated if the variation occurs in two or three of the above components at once; what remains as a link between these motifs is only a thin line, mostly melodic or rhythmic. Here are three (of the many) variants of the main motif from Smetana's *Tajemství*:

Smetana: *Tajemství* (The Secret)

36 The three-part melodrama *Smrt Hippodamie* (The Death of Hippodamia, 1889–1891) was composed by Zdeněk Fibich (1850–1900) to the dramatic trilogy by Jaroslav Vrchlický (1853–1912).
37 *Šárka* (1897) is Zdeněk Fibich's late romantic opera about the mythological Women's War and the so-called Czech Amazons. In Slavic mythology Morana is the personification of Death. In Fibich's opera Morana's leitmotif foreshadows the tragic fate of the main characters.
38 Eva is the eponymous protagonist of Josef Bohuslav Foerster's (1859–1951) opera, which premiered at the Prague National Theatre in 1899. This tragic opera is set in a Moravian village and is based on the realist play *Gazdina roba* (The Housewife's Maid, 1889) by Gabriela Preissová. It teels the story of Eva, a seamstress who leaves her husband to join her love and work with him in Austria. She endures prejudice and scorn. But when she realises that her lover will never divorce his wife and marry her, she drown herself in the Danube.

This shows that melodic variation may arise when motifs start identically but develop differently; this case, given the continuous flow of music, is very common.

Following the sum of *all* variants of "*the same*" characteristic motif in opera (or in vocal or programmatic music), we can see that, from a musical point of view, a characteristic motif is *a general musical idea* that comprises in itself all the individual formations in which it appears; in this way, it becomes an abstract notion in a sense. It is in fact given by the coexistence of its five components (as discussed above), any of which may principally be modified. Let us abbreviate these components in simple letters: *i* (instrumentation), *h* (harmony), *p* (pace), *r* (rhythm) and *m* (melody). The variants of characteristic motifs can be schematically expressed as follows (the brackets symbolise coexistence):

$$\begin{bmatrix} i \\ h \\ p \\ r \\ m \end{bmatrix} \begin{bmatrix} i' \\ h \\ p \\ r \\ m \end{bmatrix} \begin{bmatrix} i \\ h' \\ p \\ r \\ m \end{bmatrix} \begin{bmatrix} i \\ h \\ p' \\ r \\ m \end{bmatrix} \begin{bmatrix} i \\ h \\ p \\ r' \\ m \end{bmatrix} \begin{bmatrix} i \\ h \\ p \\ r \\ m' \end{bmatrix} \text{etc.} \begin{bmatrix} i' \\ h \\ p' \\ r' \\ m \end{bmatrix} \begin{bmatrix} i'' \\ h' \\ p' \\ r \\ m' \end{bmatrix}$$

The first schema symbolises the "original" motif (i.e., the one that came first), the next five symbolise changes in one of the components. Of the numerous multiple-change variants, I offer two that correspond to the variants in the above motif of the secret from Smetana (the melodic changes pertaining to different endings).

Such a musical motif is perfectly capable of corresponding with the *general*, extra-musical idea or notion with which the composer linked it; this is similar to a *word* with its many morphological and semantic variants (such as *mysterious, mystical...*) but surpasses it by its ability to characterise its idea in all of its variants directly, i.e., through sound. A *characteristic motif* is basically *a characteristic musical sign* for its associated idea; by its means, music acquires an unlimited expressive capacity.

It may sound paradoxical, but it is effectively true: it is the intellectual poverty of music that allows the composers to associate its formations with any ideas, even abstract ones, as long as they fulfill the principle of characterisation. *Music is intellectualised by means of characteristic motifs* without necessarily losing its emotional effect; the emotions and aspirations thereby acquire a certain content. This certainly offers immense *benefits* for music with a mimetic mission (including dramatic music), as will be seen in the following analysis, but this also presents a certain *danger* in using characteristic motifs. This is especially true of motifs that are musically fixed, invariable and connected therefore with an exactly defined and identifiable idea. Such *stable* motifs may be simply quoted with the simultaneously running dramatic text – they are its musical translation.

> With a handful of characteristic motifs and a bit of tone painting, it is possible to "set to music" any text or programme almost mechanically and with a minimum of invention. In opera, this quotation method leads to the setting to music of texts that we identified in Chapter 1 as particularly undramatic: theoretical treatises and narratives. A warning example is the operas of Wagner, starting with *Der Ring des Nibelungen*, which contains lengthy and dramatically dead philosophical sections and particularly tedious narrations with a summative overview of all the motifs from the start to the end – such was Wagner's zeal, markedly apparent that this also reduces the musical inventiveness of the work.

In contrast to this, *variable* motifs require ever fresh invention, although only partially so, since they have to change hand in hand with the characterisation. In opera, such motifs perfectly reflect the variable flow of the stage action, and yet we feel their *unity* like a *firm skeleton* of the work's musical component. Being connected with a variable idea, they can be identified only with difficulty and approximately, a task that has value only for musical theory and analysis (where such variants often require a variety of names). It is interesting that by means of some variants, a link is created between two different characteristic motifs that are, nonetheless, mutually related; and this musical link generally parallels a link in the ideas – though certainly this often happens *without* the composer being *aware*. For example, in Smetana's *Hubička* (The Kiss), the motif of reconciliation (C) is musically related to both the second variant of the conflict motif (A) and the motif of the kiss (B), which caused the conflict. The example below includes the theme from the overture, which helps to make the relation more obvious (symbolised by lower case letters):

Smetana: *Hubička* (The Kiss)

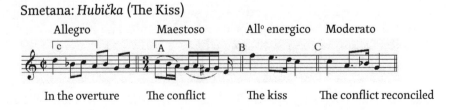

Tracing the "motivic work" in the composer's creation in this way (as we will see, e.g., in relation to polyphony) is one of the most interesting tasks of music psychology since it allows us to penetrate deep into the composer's working methods and often into the unconscious. One other substantial quality of characteristic motifs follows from the above: the *consistent* use of a motif throughout the dramatic work, from the moment of its first appearance –

which derives from the principle of musico-dramatic parallelism. From the outside, a characteristic motif can be recognised when it returns after a long passage of contrasting music or even in another act. The decision as to when and how a characteristic motif should recur is down to the composer; it is in no way governed solely by the dramatic text – as we will see later. It needs to be stressed that *the first appearance* of a characteristic motif needs to happen not only *simultaneously with its idea*, whether ostensively or communicated to the audience in words, but it must also be *foregrounded and emphasised* so that the music itself and the connection is automatically imprinted in one's memory. Music is equipped with ample means to do so.

☙ ☙ ☙

Singing. The definition of sung drama (*zpěvohra*) given at the start of this chapter was given in an incomplete form, since it lacked an addendum: Sung drama (*zpěvohra*) is a dramatic work co-created by music, *whose actors sing*. So far we have studied music performed by an orchestra. Let us now turn our attention to *singing* performed by *actors on stage*. They are commonly called *singers* – and specifically, *operatic singers*, in contrast to *concert singers*, whose performances are purely in singing, without acting.

What is the point of such singing in a dramatic work? Its impulse clearly comes from the combination of music with the work. But is it *necessary* that the actors should also sing? Surely not. We know that in a dramatic pantomime, actors (who are in fact dancers) are mute. But we also know that the principle of the totality of actor's performance is that the actor representing a dramatic persona makes use *of all vocal expressions* to that end. However, the mere combination of a dramatic work with music does not itself necessitate singing. It is well-known that in the melodrama (whether scenic or concert), words are spoken to music and this form is artistically valuable and effective. The singing of the actors is therefore not a necessary requirement, only a desirable one, since it corresponds to the aesthetic principle of *unity* – a unity of *material*, or rather of *material non-contradiction* (*látková bezespornost*).

> Vocal expressions, especially speech (language), are acoustic phenomena as much as music. If we listen to them *simultaneously* – as in the case of melodrama – we find that these simultaneous acoustic perceptions contain many *discrepancies*. These discrepancies come from the fact that speech contains many extramusical sounds (consonants), even though music, whose principal material is musical (notes), also makes use of extramusical sounds, albeit more sparingly and mostly just to strengthen the rhythm. The extramusical sounds are of such a different nature to the musical ones that they do not get in each other's way; many notes are frequently accompanied by soft noises

(the scratching of the bow, the breathy quality of flutes, etc.). But speech also contains musical sounds: tones on which vowels of speech are conveyed. These *tones of speech* may and often do clash with the notes of the music. Although both of them are tones, they differ greatly in the following points:

1. The tones of speech are rather undefined and fluctuating in their pitch, while musical notes are clearly set and consistent (for their entire duration).
2. The tones of speech *fluently* pass from one to another, while musical notes are distinct, i.e., *separate*, so they can only change from one to another. This is also true for their closest succession, semitones.
3. The tones of speech are *arbitrary* as to their pitch, while musical notes are *selected* based on harmonic principles and *arranged* in scales. Notes outside these scales are perceived as "incorrect" (not "dissonant"!) and they are not acceptable in music.

Music could tolerate the second of the above points since it is used *exceptionally* where it is technically available (glissando in the strings, portamento in singing). It is an extramusical tool, although an effective one (thanks to its similarity to language); but it should not be overused. However, the third point is unacceptable for music; the attempts of language at correcting the first flaw (trying to fix and firm up the tones of speech) further bring out its arbitrariness of pitch, i.e., how off-key they are in relation to the accompanying music. It would therefore be necessary that the speaker simultaneously adjusted the pitch of their tones with regard to the harmony of the music also. However, the speaker is not authorised to do so because the adjusted spoken tones would become a component of the harmony and would assist in determining the quality of the chords. That means the pitch of these tones needs be adjusted by the author of the music, the composer, by means of musical symbols: notation. Such *tonalised* speech (as we may call it) is *singing* and it creates, from the viewpoint of pure acoustics, *one of the components of the musical whole* – and it became an integral part by means of the aforementioned adjustment. Singing is therefore speech *set to music* through tonalisation.

There can also be (and often is) a discrepancy between the *temporal progression* of speech and music sounding simultaneously. Each speech not only has a specific *speed* in both its succession of syllables and a certain relative duration of syllables (short and long); these, in connection with word stress, which is also given, create a certain *rhythm* of speech (prosody). However, this rhythm is much looser and more irregular than the comparably strict rhythm of music. It is true that speech acquires a more accurate metrical rhythm in verse; still, it proceeds in combination with the music, carried out in strict temporal unity, so that they agree in both speed and rhythm – unless they are to each "go their separate ways". This is also the task of the composer, who solidifies in notation both the rhythm as well as the duration of syllables (as we know from contemporary music); and this rhythmicisation of speech completes its transformation into singing.

8 DRAMATIC MUSIC: THE COMPOSER'S CREATIVE WORK

Dramatic works that are co-created by (orchestral) music and pursue the aesthetic requirement of material non-contradiction to such an extent that they transform the actor's speech by tonalisation and rhythmicisation into singing, are called *sung drama (zpěvohra)*. It follows that the *singing* of the operatic actor is analogous to the *speaking* of the actor of spoken drama. Singing and speaking in dramatic art are thus *two types of vocal mimics* and they are *part of the technical image that we have called "the actor figure"*.

> Both these types are *fundamental* and have *variations* with transitions between them. Apart from *speech* proper (i.e., non-rhythmic prose speech), there is the rhythmic speech of verse or *declamation*; compared to it, *"parlando"* singing is tonalised but is delivered somewhat inaccurately as to pitch, half-spoken to distinguish it from *singing* proper. Both these types of music differ from the previous ones in that they are strictly bound to the temporal progress of music. As for other vocal expressions, such as laughter, cheering, sighs and so on, in opera they could and should be set to music only if they contain clear tonal elements; in the least, the composer must determine the place exactly (by a symbol in the musical score), when these expressions should appear in the course of music. This is true of any other sounds appearing in opera, such as knocking on the door, bell ringing, etc.

However, dramatic art is a mimetic art, and we are not content in perceiving it solely by its technical image, for we add a referential one to it. This holds true for the singing of operatic actors too. Just as an actor figure *represents* a dramatic persona, so does its *singing represent a certain kind of vocal expression of the dramatic persona*. In fact, a dramatic persona in opera *does not sing* (it is the actor who sings), but rather *"speaks"* (or "expresses him- or herself", if you will), though in a manner that is special and different from the "speech" of a dramatic persona in spoken drama.

> This is not a petty distinction but the *essence* of the matter. The mixing up the technical "figure" with the referential "persona" in opera leads to misleading views, such as that "singing in opera is unnatural because in life (which is also only "represented" in the theatre) people do not sing", or that "opera is not "faithful" to life and it has to be systemically corrected by turning it into a melodrama," etc.

From the above correspondence of the technical and the referential images it follows that operatic singing as *a type of vocal mimics* has to fulfil the same task as speaking, that is, to characterise the dramatic persona. This means, with a view to our analysis of the expressive capacities of mimics, that operatic singing needs *to be an expression of psychological states*, especially of *emotions and aspirations*. The spoken words (text) carry the ideas irrespective of being spoken or sung. Singing that fulfils this task can be referred to as *dramatic singing*. We have seen that the "expressions" of emotions and aspirations are evoked on the basis of our inner and outer experiences that we project onto dramatic personas as if they were properly theirs. If singing is to do this too, then its acoustic forms need to be *similar* to the analogous forms of speech; otherwise it would not evoke "human" emotions but only "musical" ones, as we have established above. In keeping with Leoš Janáček's term[39], let us call these acoustic forms *speech melodies* (*nápěvky mluvy*), to differentiate them from sung "melodies"; speech melodies are different in their imperfect tones and rhythmic looseness. The rule is: the composer should conceive sung melodies to *imitate* the melodies of speech – of course, a speech of the most refined and cultivated declamation. This is the psychologically justified **declamatory principle** of singing; thanks to it, sung melodies acquire genuine *expression*.

> The declamatory principle is commonly understood as a naturalistic aspiration to bring the sung melody *closer* to the speech melody; this (misunderstood) trend is rejected by some, but praised by others. Janáček himself recorded speech melodies as accurately as musical notation allowed. He confusingly called such a record a speech melody too – although it is no longer a speech melody but a true melody, however accurately rendered. In actual fact, the declamatory principle calls for the exact opposite of this naturalistic tendency.

The declamatory principle requires that the *dramatic* composer, in setting an *operatic* text to music, should *take speech melody as a starting point* in a particular place in the text, though not from actual speech, but rather from the *imagined speech of the dramatic persona* to whom this line belongs. The composer's task is *to set this speech melody to music* – that is, to *depart* from it in any way they choose, provided that the new melody *evokes* a semblance of the original speech melody. As we shall see in Chapter 9, the declamatory principle is a principle of (relative) *realism*. The speech melody is no more than a source and directive of invention, while the outcome for any text may be rather diverse. Similarly, speech melody is never *entirely* fixed and different actors – depending on their interpretation – will use different ways of delivery for the very same text.

Nonetheless, there are certain melodic patterns that are in their expression comprehensible to *everyone*; in connection with the dynamics and tempo of speech, they characterise certain emotions and aspirations: a calm message, passionate upbraiding, a question, a command and so on. Understandably, singing should retain this soul painting function, as is guaranteed by

---

39   Leoš Janáček (1854-1928) was a Czech Moravian composer of Silesian origin, musical theorist, folklorist, publicist and teacher, and currently the most popular Czech opera composer worldwide. Janáček based the vocal melodies in his operas on patterns of speech intonation as they relate to psychological conditions, rather than on a strictly musical basis. For a more detailed treatise of Janáček's theory of speech melodies see Wingfield (1992), Christiansen (2004), Štědron (2006) and Tyrrell (2007).

8 DRAMATIC MUSIC: THE COMPOSER'S CREATIVE WORK

the declamatory principle. It has been assumed that the "expression" of an instrumental melody comes from its similarity with speech, which does not need to be consciously recognised, but has its effect. Let us add that the origin of these "expressive" melodies is vocal, having transferred to instrumental music much later – as can be seen from the historical prominence of vocal music. It is not in fact impossible that the composer should use instrumental melodies to compose for the voice, but it is necessary that their own expression should *agree with* the expression called for by the dramatic text. That is to say, the vocal line needs to be *psychologically true* since it is part of the mimic performance. Let us not forget that the character of instrumental melodies is given by the technical parameters of the instrument for which the melody was conceived. And that is the second reason for the application of the declamatory principle in singing. This requirement (principle) based on the specifics of the material: let us call it the *material style* (*látkový sloh*).

Human vocal folds are also a musical instrument (belonging to the family of wind instruments) and have their own technique that determines the character of melodies that vocal folds can create. While vocal folds may be trained to do what other instruments do, with the exception of range and dynamics, still we can clearly see that they are better for some uses than others. In special cases this can be unpleasant but is tolerated in principle, since melodies in compositions are commonly passed between different musical instruments.

Singing is never the vehicle of any "language itself", but always of a concrete language: the dramatic text may be in Czech, Italian, etc. Each language has its specific principles of prosody, pertaining to lengths and stresses of syllables – that is, to rhythm. These need to be followed by the speaking actor as well as by the singer, *without exception*. That means that they also need to be followed without exception by the composer in crafting and notating the melody. A concrete language is effectively a material of specific qualities that *must be* respected, regardless of who uses the material in question. A true artist thinks in the material that he or she has chosen. The declamatory principle is a special manifestation of this assertion. Naturally, declaiming a sung melody *correctly* is not the only guarantee of its artistic quality. However, it is a *necessary* condition, naturally followed by all good composers: a *conditio sine qua non*.

> The artistic significance of the declamatory principle is also in that vocal melodies created from it have their *national character*; that transfers to orchestral music, which often comprises vocal melodies. Language is a principal and one of the most concrete features of national art; its prosodic specifics are *directly ostensive*. So, for instance, Czech is characteristic for its falling rhythm of words regardless of the syllable lengths (commonly v́– and v́–v), which results in melodies without upbeats, etc. The signifi-

cance of the declamatory principle for Czech music has been emphasised by Hostinský in his numerous theoretical essays (O české deklamaci hudební [On Czech Musical Declamation] (1886), among others).

What has been said here about singing, particularly on account of the declamatory principle, applies not only to dramatic but also to vocal music, with the above-noted distinction that a concert singer is a variant of a reciter; that is, concert singing is recitation "set to music". The composer of vocal music (in performance represented by the singer) sets *his or her own* speech or declamation of a *poetic* text to music. Here, too, the declamatory principle is based in the *material style* (leading back to the national character of such singing) as well as in the *characterisation* principle – in this case of a *poetic* kind. We project the emotions evoked in us by such singing onto the singer, but such vocal singers do not represent anyone and their singing is *only* theirs – unless they sing direct speeches of personas appearing in the poem.

The polyphony (multi-vocality) *of music*[40], one of music's *fundamental* qualities, has a wide-ranging and profound impact on the structure of opera. Apart from singing, this is the second-most distinctive difference from spoken drama. It is important to discuss it from a technical aspect, if only briefly, since the analysis below will discuss polyphony's mimetic, which is to say, dramatic uses.

A special quality of notes is that we can hear *several simultaneously*, and so *clearly* and *distinctly* that we can tell not only how many there are, but also what the pitch relations (intervals) between them are. This is true provided we have a *musical ear*. The formation of multiple simultaneous notes is called *harmony* and its structure is referred to as *harmonic*.

Since music occurs in time, it creates a continuous *progression of harmonies* that change with the changes of notes. Their relationships within their progression is also harmonic. Let us illustrate this in a diagram: the vertical dimension represents *the relative pitch of the note*, and the horizontal shows *the passage of time*, the temporal dimension. (Clearly, *new* notes do not have to arrive all at the same time.)

$$\begin{array}{cccccc} x_1 & x_1' & x_1'' & . & . \\ x_2 & x_2' & x_2'' & . & . \\ x_3 & x_3' & x_3'' & . & . \\ . & . & . & & \end{array}$$

---

40 There are two overlapping meanings of *polyphonic* in English: (1) having more than one musical line or voice, i.e., more than *monophonic* (an unaccompanied solo); and (2) having more than one line or voice in a texture, i.e., more than *homophonic* (or chordal), a usage closely synonymous with *contrapuntal*. Even though Zich never mentions it explicitly he understands polyphony always as contrapuntal and uses *polyphonic* always consistently in the second sense.

The notes x, x', x"..., are different in pitch but are connected by one *timbre* arising from the musical instrument that plays them. The timbre's *"voice"* is either *instrumental* or *vocal* (in the former case, the word "voice" is used figuratively); and we understand this "voice" as a musical *manifestation (projev)* of the instrument. It follows from this that music is *principally polyphonic*; monophony (i.e., the sequence x, x', x"...) is similarly a special case, as is *one* single, unchanging harmony or *chord* (for example, $x_1, x_2, x_3...$).

One of the challenging questions of musical aesthetics is when a musical voice becomes a *melody*. Generally, it can be said that this occurs once there is some *overall* logic between individual notes that create the melody (that is, it is not *only* the progression from one note to another; that would be the intervallic voice leading (*zákonitost intervalová*)). It could be compared to the overall relationship between words in a sentence, which gives them the "meaning" by making the sentence an expression of some logical idea. Similarly, a melody is a *musical idea*. Just like we consider a sentence's meaning to be difficult or simple, depending on how difficult or simple the connection between the words is; so we understand a musical voice better or worse as melody, depending on how clear or hidden the overall relationship between its notes is. That is why the general public refers to "melodies" only when the logical organisation of the musical voice is at its most elementary, and thus its most comprehensible – such as in popular (folk) songs or arias from older Italian operas. In other words, recognising a musical voice as a "melody" is rather relative; it depends not only on the individual abilities of the listener, but also on convention and on the historical development of music. When Mozart first appeared, he seemed "unmelodic" to most of his audiences, whereas nowadays most people understand even Wagner's melodies.

Despite all the other exquisite qualities of music, *melody* in our sense of the word can be declared music's principal and fundamental quality. With the help of the above diagram, we can distinguish three types of textures when it comes to melody:

(1) *None* of the musical voices is a distinctive melody. We understand such music as a progression of chords: it is a *purely harmonic* music. Impressionistic soundscapes can serve as an example of this.

(2) *One* of the musical voices is a more prominent melody. This is often the top voice, the most audible one, but it can often be the lowest one (such as when a bass is singing), although it is often somewhat covered by the higher voices. As in the previous type, we understand the other musical voices as a progression of chords, which we perceive as a *"harmonic accompaniment"* of said melody. We call such music *homophonic* (that is to say, single-melodic).

(3) In this type, music contains not only the principal melody but also another. It is important that this second melody is more than a mere copy of the first, such as running in parallel thirds or sixths. If that were the case, we would take such "connected voices" as a *single* melody, and music that has no other melodies to be identical to homophony. If the second melody is at least partly independent, we speak of *polyphonic* (multi-melodic) music. Clearly there can be more than two of such melodies. However,

following them simultaneously is gradually more and more difficult because we have to divide our attention: the upper limit is four- or five-part polyphony. Obviously polyphonic music can also contain voices that play not a melodic but only a harmonic role (especially the bass).

From a technical point of view, *specific forms of dramatic music* (leaving aside other vocal genres) based on their *multivocal* quality are these:

(1) *Singing and the orchestra.* The relationship between singing and the orchestra in opera is special and fundamentally different from vocal music. The principal difference is in that both the components, despite their musical unity, are significantly distinct in their location: we hear the singing voice from the stage while the instrumental voices (with the exception of onstage musicians) arise from the space dedicated to orchestral players between the stage and the auditorium; this is usually lower and sometimes even covered. A more substantial difference is that the actors' singing has a direct mimetic (and especially *dramatic*) significance in that it *represents* the vocal expression of the *dramatic personas* whose action we can simultaneously see on stage. On the other hand, the orchestral music in a dramatic work has a mimetic function of plural significance: it may illustrate the psychological states of dramatic *personas* (soul painting) but it can also depict images through sound in a broad sense, including motoric and optical qualities or the overall mood of *a scene.* The orchestra's task can be therefore seen as much more abstract than that of the singing. Singing is *directly attached* to specific visible objects (i.e., the dramatic personas), while orchestral music relies on us to find its corresponding visible object on stage; and even if we feel that we have found the corresponding onstage object, the music always retains some of its "objectlessness" (abstraction; *nevěcnost*), characteristic of all auditory sensations. We take such impressions only indirectly as manifestations of "something", whereas optical sensations are directly that "something". This can be shown in the case of speaking – and even more commonly of *singing – from behind the stage,* when the persona is only imagined by us.

> There is ample criticism on the relationship between singing and the orchestra. The orchestra's task has, for instance, been compared to that of the chorus in classical Greek tragedy; however, this does not say anything particular, since the function of the chorus changed over time and its early developments are hypothetical. Besides, the chorus used words, and so was capable of philosophical reflections, whereas music as such is incapable of it. Other critics emphasise the "metaphysical" task of the orchestra. As we have observed, the direct (that is, not the associative) effect of music on our emotions is of a non-human variety, but that is simply because music evokes musical emotions based on the relations of real tones, which in itself is not metaphysical. Additionally, we have observed that mimetic music and especially dramatic music, has a tendency

to make these emotions as human as possible – and that is specifically the requirement of the dramatic principle.

As for the location of melody in this coexistence of singing and the orchestra, we can discern the following two instances:

(a) *The melody is in the singing voice*, while the orchestra is its harmonic accompaniment; *the whole is homophonic*. This is very common, particularly in older operas, and it is the simplest type, especially if the sung melody is straightforward. Technically, i.e., *musically*, the *orchestra is subordinate to the voice*. This relationship is sometimes taken for an operatic law (or a principle at least), arguably on account of the dramatic persona being the main thing in opera. Although this is true, it does not follow that the persona's singing is necessarily always the main thing too; although it comprises a text, it is (as we know from Chapter 5) only one of the components of the dramatic persona, apart from their looks and especially their acting, which is continuous and sustained, while the vocal expression is intermittent, often staying silent for a longer period. The aforementioned principle stems from the overrating of the text in drama as well as from conflating dramatic music and vocal music. From a mimetic, i.e., a *dramatic* point of view, the orchestra is principally *on an equal standing* with singing because it can, and often does, convey the dramatic characteristics through harmony, rhythm, dynamics or instrumentation (e.g., the accompaniment may be dissonant or consonant, calm or syncopated, loud or soft, in trombones or in string tremolos, etc.).

A special case, common also in early opera, occurs when *the singing voice is in itself not coherently melodic*, composed of no more than melodic fragments. This is known as the "*recitative*", or in its simplest form the "recitativo secco", accompanied by no more than chords from the harpsichord. It was used in the dramatic moments in opera at a time when the only object worthy of musical execution was lyrical expression. Present-day recitative, used in exulted speech, is much richer in the orchestral accompaniment.

(b) *The melody is not only in the singing* but simultaneously also *in the orchestra*, and that melody is not identical, since that would only mean reinforcement (or parallel duplication) of the sung melody, which is common as a way of supporting the singer. The melody in the orchestra can be in imitation (e.g., played a bar later), or it can be a completely different tune or even several tunes; such *a whole is polyphonic*. In this instance, the orchestra is musically *on an equal standing* with the singing; the task of the orchestra is then often very important and diverse, as will be discussed below. A direct musical and dramatic dominance of the orchestra over the singing – although not over the overall action of the actor figure and the dramatic persona – occurs when the singing is purely recitative while the orchestra is melodic. In early opera, this was known as the "recitativo obbligato", while in modern opera this is the standard. This has reconciled the great musical difference between the melodically scant recitative and the melodically rich aria (or duet, etc.) of early opera. If a difference between melodic and recitative singing (with the numerous transitions) is dramatically necessary, at least the orchestra remains *consistently* melodic: this is known as *"through-composed"* opera. This task of the orchestra becomes especially prominent when singing is silent for a while; at that point, the orchestra is the only musical presenter of the onstage dramatic action. It should also be stressed that vocal melodies, in their entirety or in part, could be taken over by the orchestra, which would create not only musical but also dramatic coherence. These melodies were originally linked with the sung text, turning them effectively into "authorial quotations", not only "reminiscences", but even *leitmotifs*, provided that our above conditions are met (a well-known example is Elsa's "forbidden question" motif in Wagner's *Lohengrin*, "Nie sollst du mich befragen").

(2) *Multi-part singing*. Simultaneous musical voices are so distinct for a musician that one can easily *hear and understand the sung text*. This is an invaluable quality of opera that makes it possible for more than one actor to express themself *at the same time*. From the dramatic point of view this enables such a range of possibilities that the operatic structure is significantly and very *characteristically* different from the structure of spoken drama. Dramatic polyphony, discussed above in Chapter 3, is enriched in its ostensive, visible component by an acoustic component, even with its contents and ideas present in the dramatic text.

The objection that in the real world people do not speak all at once is just as naive as the objection that people do not sing in the real world. For one, people speak like that in heated situations, but that creates confusion, and that is the *only* thing that limits using this in spoken drama. We have observed in our earlier discussion of the manifestation principle that actors may and should express even the thoughts of the personas they are playing to the audience if the drama requires it. In spoken drama, actors can do this only separately (in soliloquy, asides), while in opera they can also do this *all at once* because the personas they represent are all surely thinking at the same time. It is the task of the librettist (the author of the opera's text) to find such dramatic situations that would naturally lend themselves to it, and the same holds for crowd expressions, which have no limits in opera. As for their dramatic significance, let us refer back to our earlier observations about the ensemble and the chorus in Chapters 6 and 7; we will revisit them further below.

From a technical point of view, we can distinguish between the *music ensemble* that consists of solo singers (duets, trios, etc.), and the *music chorus*, consisting of choral singers. The former is more often polyphonic than homophonic, whereas the latter is more commonly homophonic (or even just harmonic) than polyphonic [i.e., the chorus merely harmonises, supplies chords below the melody], unless it is divided for dramatic reasons. Since simultaneous singing is rhythmicly strictly controlled by adherence to time (in practice: by the conductor's baton), it is perfectly in the composer's power to determine whether individual syllables sound simultaneously or consecutively. It is possible then to sing simultaneously in the smallest detail (i.e., in syllables), such as in a duet of two solo voices (the famed parallel thirds or in unison) or chordally as a chorus. Here it is necessary that *the text be identical* (or only with minor variations) because in simultaneous harmonies the consonants of syllables merge (since they are non-musical sounds), which renders the text incomprehensible. During melodic polyphony, in which each part has its own rhythm or starts at different points, the texts may be different. The musical agreement or disagreement corresponds here with an agreement or difference in the dramatic quality.

With regard to the relationship of the orchestra to multi-part singing, a particularly important point is that the multi-part ensemble (and even more so the chorus) may be *self-sufficient* and do well without the orchestra; at those moments, the orchestra can fall silent. This brings sublime moments, especially for the chorus (also known as "a cappella", without accompaniment, for instance the crowd's prayer before the breakout of revolution in Auber's *La muette de Portici*) or the chorus together with the ensemble. Generally the orchestra accompanies not only ensembles with a smaller number of parts (especially duets), which essentially follows the principles discussed in the preceding essay, but also large or full ensembles. The orchestra often reinforces and supports the singing parts, but sometimes also carries its own voices, whether differing only slightly (in any type of figuration, often motivically) or more subtantially, in coherent, independent melodies that frame the whole (as Smetana likes to do in the broad cantilena of the violins). This "ensemble and chorus" with the orchestra, combining all the musical tools to a single dramatic end, is among the most monumental forms available to the dramatic art.

☙ ☙ ☙

The dramatic composer's creative work. It might seem that a composer setting an opera libretto to music does in principle the same thing as a composer who is composing to any sort of poem: both of them aim at writing music that would characterise the *given* text as best as can be. Often even composers themselves hold this view. And yet, the two kinds of composition are *principally* different and said view is true only for the vocal composer. In the preceding chapters we have observed so much about the significance of the dramatic text for a dramatic work that we can formulate a principle defining the specific intent of the dramatic composer:

The dramatic composer does not set the dramatic text to music, but rather the dramatic **situations**. Naturally *the starting point* is with the text of the libretto, but it should not *remain* there. This text is no more than the foundation and directive for their imagination to visualise the dramatic situations in their development and sequence, just like actors do when creating their dramatic personas – and it is *only that* which the composer sets to music. At the same time, said text is *included* as part of the composer's vision, but only as *one* of its *components*: the vocal one. For the composer's *musico*-dramatic conception the text is consequential only when it has *bearing on* the dramatic situation, thus only indirectly. Everything that follows is merely an analysis and elaboration of the above principle, which we shall call *the musico-dramatic principle*.

Taking for granted (theoretically) that the composer has *musical talent*, let us analyse what *else* they need to have to successfully become a *dramatic* composer. Let us refer back to what we observed in Chapter 4 about the dramatist's creative work in comparison to the poet's. With rare exceptions, the composer works with the dramatic text provided as a libretto by another author; the first condition that follows from this is the composer's *capability of "theatrical reading"* of the text, as we named it above.

> The illustrious example of Wagner led to the belief that a perfect opera can be created only when the composer is also the librettist. This is preposterous, for the vocal composer would then also need to be the author of the poem and the director of a spoken play would need to be its dramatist. If an artist finds impulse for their creative work in another art form, it presupposes their *sense* for this other art form, but not necessarily an ability *to create* in it. That is also true if they join the two works of art (their own and the other) in one. There are examples of artists talented in several art forms but they are rare and often not balanced. Wagner himself was a musician and poet, and he was also gifted with a sense for the theatre rather than specifically for the dramatic; this can be seen in the many lengthy passages of extended narration or of philosophical reflection in his later works, which a dramatist would cut in the poet's work because they often have an effect of excessive stagnation on the dramatic action.

The opera composer has the capability of "theatrical reading" in common with the *actor* and especially with the *stage director*, who is also concerned with the entirety of all the personas. At the same time, neither the composer nor the director need to be able to effectively embody the envisioned dramatic persona. The composer does not even need to envision the actor's performance visually, but it is *necessary* that the composer imagine it as distinctly and in as much detail as possible when it comes to its *acoustic* and *motoric* side, because it is these that the composer *sets to music*. It is *beneficial* when the composer's dramatic vision encompasses the kinetic (if not the static) scenic qualities – in short, that which is the task of the director-scenic. We know for instance that Gluck, during the composition of an opera, used to have chairs situated in his room to stand in for his dramatic personas. It is *absolutely necessary* that the composer imagine as vividly as can be the *dramatic qualities – both the dynamic and the agogic* ones. We have said that their conception is the task of the director-conductor and it is *these qualities* that the composer *needs to* **create** *by means of music*.

During our above discussion of the "strict temporal bond" (*přísná vazba časová*) that is at play in real-time dramatic action (see end of Chapter 6), we observed that the same or an even tighter bond is present in music. The choice of the tempo in the performance of a musical composition as a whole and in its details is a rather sensitive issue; greater deviations from the "correct" (i.e., authorial) tempo will ruin the composition straight away because it forces upon it a form of movement that is not appropriate to it and goes against its logic. However, there is a great difference between the temporal form of dramatic action and of music, regarding its *fixity*. Dramatic action cannot be fixed objectively when it comes to time and tempo; it can be done only by generic words (e.g., quickly, casually, lazily, etc.). The stage director has to content themself with subjective fixity in the actors' memories, in the way they practised performing it in rehearsal. In contrast, the temporal progression of music is fixed through notation, not only in its order but also in its speed, because the time signature of the notes gives it a metre. At first glance, this only means that only a relative speed is given accurately, while the absolute speed is only given by the "tempo". But it is the specific feature of music that, despite the generic descriptors provided by the composer (e.g., allegro, moderato, lento, etc.), this *tempo* is determined by *the very musical structure* of the composition so perfectly that it allows only for mild fluctuations.

The opera composer characterises the *real-time dramatic action* by means of an art (music) that is *so sensitive* to its speed and temporal progression, in addition to being fixed in the score; with that in view, the opera composer clearly cannot be satisfied only with the characteristics of the contents (the emotions and aspirations) but has also to respect the temporal aspect of the action – that is, *the changes* in its dynamics and speed. That is, in other words, nothing other than the "dramatic form" of the work (dynamic and agogic), which we acknowledged as the creative task of the director-conductor (in Chapter 6). *The opera composer therefore anticipates the director in their first function* by *creating the dramatic form of* the work *through the temporal form of* the music, *fixing it* through notation so perfectly that the production can no more than vary it *in nuances*. This is done by the artist who controls the musical performance, executing through the music's temporal form the overall dramatic form as well: the *orchestra conductor*, who is thus also the *conductor of the entire performance*.

The function of the spoken drama "director-conductor" ultimately shifts in sung drama to the *opera conductor*, who is a surrogate of the composer. The opera conductor has a right *to nuance* the tempo, just like any other performing artist (which is part of *their* creative work); however, unlike the concert conductor, the opera conductor nuances it in their own original way, not according to the music alone, but also to the *dramatic situation*. Thus, exactly like the author-composer, they are governed by the principle of dramaticity as the supreme authority.

The *creative* work of the *opera director* is therefore limited to the second task: creating the scenic form of the work. The opera director has the function of the *director-scenic*, and that function is principally no different from the function of the stage director of spoken drama, except that they *are tied*, by the strict temporal *bond of the music*, to the kinetic and agogic qualities as well.

Considering what we have stated about singing as the "actor's speech set to music", it transpires that the *opera composer anticipates the actor's vocal expression* by *creating* the acoustic form of this expression in the singing voice and *fixes it* in pitch and rhythm (in a word, in its time progression) by means of the notation; this fixity is so perfect that the performing actor can no more than provide *nuances*. The operatic actor is, therefore, as far as the vocal aspect of their figure is concerned, a true "singer", as they are called anyway. However, this is only one component of the operatic actor's creative work and neither they nor the audience should forget that they are *an actor* overall – that is, a singing actor, an actor-singer. Unlike the concert singer, the opera singer assumes their right to *nuance* their vocal expression (that is, their singing) by means of an *actorly* conception of their singing; and that needs to be in *constant unity* with their "figure". What this means has been discussed above in our analysis of the actor figure and the logic of actorly thinking in Chapter 5. Nuances of pitch are not allowed because these would go against the tonality of music; naturally, the actor-singer must not sing wrong notes. In other aspects – such as timbre, articulation or expression in general – the performer is as free as the spoken drama actor, only directed rather than defined by the composer's instructions, which are often more numerous in opera than in spoken drama.[41]

---

41 In this respect Zich speaks as a composer of the early modernist generation, which tended to exert increasing control over the musician's breadth of interpretation. From Wagner to the High Modernists of the 1950s there is an increasing amount of authorial instructions in regards to the interpretation of the score. It is apparent in Zich's own opera compositions, especially in

All in all, the actor-singer has *only* this liberty to nuance; the composer has delimited the rough outlines for the performer. This has a substantial consequence for the actor-singer's overall conception of the actor figure – though only in its kinetic aspect, not in the static ones (such as appearance or costume). The spoken drama actor *freely* conceives both the audible speech and the visible action of their figure, directed only by the playwright's abstract text; and both these aspects must encompass a coherent whole. The operatic actor also needs to conceptualise their roles, but the vocal expression is *determined* by the composer in the vocal part. So it is not the actor, but firstly the composer who is directed by the dramatic text in this (and only this) aspect of the eventual performance.

The *coherence* of the actor figure must be secured, and thus the conception of *the actor's performance* (hra) must obey the vocal part and it is *bound by it to a great extent*, especially in its *temporal progression*. It is a well-known fact that the range of tempi in singing is much wider than in speaking, and that singing is often (and even commonly) slower than speaking. (Nevertheless, comic operas offer examples of extremely fast singing, sometimes even faster than one is able to speak.) It follows that the speed of the accompanying *mimic play* needs to adjust to the speed of singing and be therefore generally much slower in opera than in spoken drama. The peaks, accents, rests, etc., in the vocal part give the opera singer indications of where exactly to perform a necessary accompanying gesture (however, what kind of gesture is the actor's decision).

However, this is not everything. We know from our discussion of the multivocality of music that the orchestra takes an important part in characterising the dramatic persona, both in connection with singing and sometimes independently of it. The singer therefore needs to conceive the action of their figure with the orchestra in mind – that is, as long the orchestra's music relates to the dramatic persona that the actor performs. Here, once again, the actor is *bound* in time, speed, the temporal placement of gestures and other aspects. In other words, logically, the operatic actor needs to create the conception of their figure not only on the basis of their vocal part, but also according to the orchestral music that sounds while the actor is on stage – because they need to act even if they are not singing.

---

the score of *Vina* (Guilt), where his musical articulations and phrase markings are particularly detailed. In other eras, such as with Rossini, Handel or Monteverdi, the performer is often expected to make a creative contribution to the interpretation, almost like a co-creator. Since Zich is writing from his own perspective as a practising composer, his view of the preceding historical eras of opera composition is necessarily biased. In this passage he is very close to formulating his own or his era's artistic ideal.

It might seem that the above constraints on the opera singer are excessive in comparison to the spoken drama actor. However, it does not pertain to the qualitative aspect of the actor's play; there, the operatic actor is as free as that of the spoken drama. The only difference is that the conception of the figure is directed not only by the dramatic text but also by the music pertaining to the dramatic persona – as we shall see below. Additionally, the above-mentioned temporal bond benefits the whole, perfecting both the interaction and the dramatic form to the utmost. It is the musical component of the work, created and fixed by the composer, that deserves thanks here. In concert music, it is a common fact that the conductor *directs* the work even in its performance (and not only in rehearsal), determining the tempo and its changes, giving "cues" to players and singers, etc. This fact becomes supremely significant in opera. While the spoken drama "director-conductor", as we have stated towards the end of Chapter 6, *disappears* with the opening of the show, the *opera "conductor-director" remains* and directs all the performances, reproducing the composer's dramatic form in their personal interpretation.

The opera conductor does not need to assume the function of director-conductor in any special way; they are one by virtue of their role already. It follows than the opera conductor is *obliged* to take note of both the singing and the acting of their "singers" in rehearsal and to point out the moments when the music requires them to do something. In the end, who knows the score better than the conductor? And just like cueing them to start singing *in performance*, the conductor should also give cues to the agreed mimic action required by the music – especially when the actors are not singing. All this is clearly given by the conductor's score. Examples: Walter's mimics in the opening church scene of Wagner's *Die Meistersinger von Nürnberg*; in Act III of Foerster's *Debora*,[42] the title heroine's entrance coinciding with the dissonant entry of the basses; or Milada's disappearance at the very end of Act II of Smetana's *Dalibor*, coinciding with the sudden fortissimo in the orchestra. Naturally, the conductor only determines the "when", not the "how" of such mimic action, since that is the actor's call. The same is true of the way of singing, as long as it is not infringing upon the temporal progression. Here, the conductor needs to respect the singer's individual interpretation, unless it is entirely mistaken, especially in regards to the singers' personal and general habits and mannerisms (the drawing out of melodies, fermatas, etc.). What was stated at the end of Chapter 6 regarding the "stage director's task" applies here identically. The opera conductor also has the right to choose their singers, and since the conductor's task is also a dramatic one, they need to take the singers' individualities into account – in other words, to "think with and through the material", both in musical and in actorly terms.

It follows from the above that the dramatically well-crafted opera has long discovered and practised (let us say, since the time of Gluck) what contemporary spoken-drama stage direction aspires to: a considered formation of speech (the significance of

---

42   *Debora* (1893) is an opera by Josef Bohuslav Foerster (1859–1951) based on S. H. Mosenthal's popular play *Deborah* (1848).

its speed, intensity, pauses, melodic cadence, etc.) and a purposely structured dynamic and agogic performance from the actors. Opera, which used to be despised by spoken drama in the era of dramatic naturalism, could now be its teacher.

We have now articulated two implications of the "musico-dramatic principle" – a principle followed by the composer in their creative work. These implications are the *specific* difference between the creative work of the operatic actor-singer (otherwise in keeping with Chapter 5) and an extension of the *primary* task of the director to the opera conductor-director (see end of Chapter 6). Let us turn briefly towards the *psychology of musico-dramatic creative work*. It follows from the above musico-dramatic principle that *the conceptual work and invention of the opera* composer needs to be **double**. The composer of vocal music is *directly inspired* by the text for their musical conception; they only need *musical invention* (and, naturally, a sense for poetry, which may be understood as a sign of general intelligence). The composer of dramatic music is also inspired by the text but for a *dramatic* conception, which in turn needs *dramatic invention* (which is itself non-musical). The composer has this in common with the director-conductor. It is only by this *theatrical vision* – that is, through its mediation – that the composer is inspired for a *musical* conception, for which they need *musical invention*. To be sure, during the creative process the two conceptions run together, but the dramatic one needs to come first and the musical one follow.

> Ill fares the opera composer if they are composing music *immediately* from the text. (However, if they have dramatic instinct, they often do not realise that their composition is mediated by a dramatic conception of the text.) If that happens, the composition is no more than a musical illustration of the text, and although it may be musically good and even evocative in character – such that we enjoy listening to a playthrough of the score (or the piano reduction) – it eventually *disappoints* in theatrical performance. Sometimes people say that a particular opera "has only the libretto to thank for its dramatic effect". However, this is wholly ignorant view, stemming from the habit of reading dramatic works "textually". The dramatic qualities of a text are latent, as we have seen: *it is the actors and the director who give shape to them*. We have asserted that the composer anticipates the actors and the director by a good half. If a composer does not "ruin" the dramatic text with their music, it is the same as the actors and the director not "ruining" it in spoken drama; it means then that the composition is dramatically good. What its purely musical qualities are is another matter. In the operatic repertoire there are many works that are better dramatically than musically, so they come to life on stage (such as Lortzing's operas). There are also works that are better musically than dramatically; such works do not appear in the repertoire, say exceptionally, out of respect – just like closet drama (*Lesedrama*). However, if the libretto is dramatically weak (in the sense of our definition at the end of Chapter 4) or even confused, there is

little that even a supreme musical dramatist can do with it, apart from details; sorry examples of this are Mozart's *Die Zauberflöte*, Weber's *Euryanthe* or Smetana's *Čertova stěna* (The Devil's Wall).

The "poetic qualities" of the *dramatic* text are even less important in opera than in spoken drama, perhaps with the exception of lyrical (i.e., undramatic) passages, which are intended as moments of relief in the dramatic action. Smetana's *The Bartered Bride* is a case in point. This is not to say, of course, that the poetic qualities are undesirable, but it is the dramatic quality that has primacy. It is a *conditio sine qua non*.

Just like the playwright's conceptions (see Chapter 4), so are the composer's conceptions a double set: detailed and general. The *general* conceptions are *decisive* for a *dramatic* work since they capture the dramatic form of a particular situation or their sequence. So the composer knows, for instance, that the music of a certain passage will be soft but fast, that it will be only in strings, that it will have this rhythmic basis, that there will be a sudden crescendo, that something portentous will enter with the full power of brass instruments and so on – while they may not know yet what the music will be (melodically). At other times, the composer knows the melodic structure of a passage, incorporating other details into it later, even such things as recitative-like fragments of sung dialogue.

A beautiful document of this is Mozart's letter to his father, where he writes of the broadly envisioned gradation of Osmin's F-major aria in Act I of *Die Entführung aus dem Serail*, describing Osmin's conflict with Pedrillo (I cite in brief): "The 'D'rum beim Barte des Propheten' is indeed in the same time, but with quick notes, and as his wrath gradually increases (when the aria appears to be at an end), the *allegro assai* follows in quite another measure and key, which must insure the best effect; for as a man in such a violent fit of passion transgresses all the bounds of order and propriety and forgets himself in his fury, the same must be the case with the music too. But as the passions, whether violent or not, must never be expressed so as to become revolting, and the music even in the most appalling situations never offend the ear, but continue to please and be melodious, I did not go from F, in which the air is written, into a remote key, but into an analogous one, not however into its nearest relative D minor, but into the more remote A minor."[43]

As far as *detailed* conceptions are concerned, these are minor musical ideas, mostly of a melodic kind, sometimes relating to harmony or instrumentation, which *always* appear in connection to a particular moment of a certain dramatic situation, either with (sometimes only with) or without singing. Their

---

43 The English translation is cited from *The Letters of Wolfgang Amadeus Mozart (1769–1791)*, vol. II., trans. Lady Wallace. New York: Hurd and Houghton, 1866: p. 82. Available in the *Internet Archive* at: https://archive.org/details/lettersofwolfgan02moza/.

peculiarity is in that they are not born in the order given by the plot, but at random – presuming, of course, that the composer knows the whole libretto well enough. It may often happen, for example, in the course of continuous compositional work on the first act that this double conception appears from a following act. This almost always relates to a dramatically significant moment; it is therefore more likely to be the ending of a scene or act rather than its beginning. It isn't always necessarily a culmination, but also a repose as a bridge between two situations. The fact that this idea often turns into a leitmotif or a reminiscence motif is at least psychologically understandable, as we have seen.

> Let me cite examples from my own work. The first idea I had for my opera *Vina (Guilt)* long before starting to compose systematically was a moment from the middle of the third act when Mína, in a frozen, rigid moment, confesses her *guilt* to her mother and brother. It was the vocal melody for her confession ("I am a fallen, unclean girl…"), together with the orchestral music, that logically then became the "guilt" motif throughout the entire opera, reappearing in multiple *variants*, which the audience hears before its *original* form – which agrees with the dramatic idea of the work as a whole. An even greater interchangeability in the order of composition occurred in my work on *Preciézky (Les Précieuses ridicules)*. Wishing to write a comic opera, I carefully read a number of comedies, especially Molière's, with this intent. It was at that point that I had an idea for a tiny *andantino* motif. When I eventually decided to work on *Preciézky* and was translating this comedy, I realised that my motif "belongs" to the moment when the disguised Mascarille meets the *Précieuses* Madelon and Cathos. I was so captured by this realisation that it was from this point – that is, roughly from a third of the way through the play – that I started to compose, and it was only after I had finished composing this long scene (for three characters) that I returned to the beginning, which is in effect no more than an exposition to that moment.
>
> The cases when a composer uses an older musical idea for the composition of an opera are very frequent. This is possible precisely because music lacks idea content, so it is enough if certain music characterises, in its emotions and aspirations, a dramatic moment for which it can be used. There is interesting evidence of this in Smetana's sketchbook of motifs. There is a melody dated October 1862 to which Smetana added the note "chorus (for) comedy"; he used it only after finishing his opera *Braniboři v Čechách (The Brandenburgers in Bohemia)* – thus after April 1863 – for the opening chorus "Proč bychom se netěšili" (Let's rejoice and be merry) in his *Prodaná nevěsta (The Bartered Bride)*. In the very same scene of the opera he also used a dance melody (in the clarinet, then in the violins) that characterises folk music ("Pojďte s námi", Come along), which he had composed back in 1849 for his *Svatební scény (Wedding Scenes)* for piano. It is advisable to use only motifs that can be formally adjusted to fit the dramatic action, rather than longer pieces of music that already have their final form.

Since the days of the ingenious dramatic composer Weber, the inventor of "the leitmotif", this musical device has been gaining weight in opera, and one can even speak of systematic "work" with this device in modern opera, which uses it consistently in keeping with the dramatic action. This happens not only in connection to the text: it is significant that Samiel's famous motif in *Der Freischütz* is first used in the monologue of the despairing Max – at a moment when Samiel makes *only a brief appearance* in the background, without any verbal mention in the text. The composer's work with leitmotifs – which are often created beforehand – has not only a dramatic but also a purely musical significance, in that they shape the overall (ideational) musical form, *unifying the music* of the entire opera, albeit from a dramatic point of view.

> This was beautifully expressed by Smetana in his letter to Svatopluk Čech in which he objects to the cuts in *Hubička* (*The Kiss*): "It is particularly these passages marked for deletion that are important, especially because they relate to earlier motifs. This is the unifying style which […], if it should be left out, would leave nothing in my opera that one could call *style*, because then the individual numbers would be sung as an assortment, not as a unity."

It is musical polyphony in particular that offers the composer a wide range of possibilities of working with leitmotifs. Very importantly, they can be combined *simultaneously*, which has a corresponding dramatic significance. (In this vein Smetana combines Libuše's motif with Přemysl's at the end of Act I, when the people have accepted her verdict, or Šťáhlav's with Chrudoš's at their reconciliation.) Melodic leitmotifs can also be incorporated in musical polyphony as their voices – in short, they can be treated as purely melodic themes. The earliest such usage of "leading themes" (as one could call them) occurs in Wagner's *Tristan*, combined with the well-established techniques of reiteration and variation.

In summary, it can be asserted that composer's *dramatic originality* rests in the ability *to use* certain musical techniques (sometimes entirely generic, common or elementary in music) *in order to* characterise a specific dramatic moment in an unprecedented and, in its precision, surprising way. Dramatic originality is therefore in the originality of the *relation* between the musical and the dramatic imagination; as such, it needs to be distinguished from a purely musical originality.

> From an infinite number of examples, many of which have been cited in our previous discussions, let us give only one, remarkable for its simplicity in an otherwise musically complex opera. When in Strauss's *Elektra* Ägisth, urged on by Elektra, enters the house in which his avenger Orestes awaits him, the silence charged with a dramatic tension is broken by a soft, E-major glissando, from a low E upwards over five octaves,

8 DRAMATIC MUSIC: THE COMPOSER'S CREATIVE WORK

where it is sustained by a *pianissimo* tremolo in the violins. Musically, this is a common thing, but the dramatic effect is immense; its originality lies in its use for this situation.

☙ ☙ ☙

Sung drama (*zpěvohra*) has been defined as a dramatic work *co-created* by music. That is more than "characterised" by music. It means that music itself – that is, as a technical image – contains the same two *basic formations* that can be found in the actor's technical image. For the actor, these are the "actor figure" and "actor interplay"; for music, it is the *"musical persona"* (*hudební postava*) and *"musical interplay"* (*hudební spoluhra*), dividing further into *"musical situations"* (*hudební situace*). *The better* the music realises them, *the more dramatic* the opera is. What is meant by these concepts?

(A) **The musical persona** *is the sum of all the music that characterises a specific dramatic persona*. It can be subdivided into two components:

(1) *The singing task of a specific actor-singer*; that is, a "singing role", which the actor-singer is assigned to learn, just like an actor gets a "textual role", which is in fact fully contained in the former. (We have analysed the textual role in Chapter 4.) Referring to the discussions in Chapter 5 relating to the actor's speech, singing is an expression parallel to it and thus, we can be brief.

> The composer starts characterising a specific dramatic persona by the overall choice of the typical *singing voice*. It is well known that spoken drama's lines of business (*emplois*) are paralleled in opera by *voice types* (*Fach*) with very specific dramatic distinctions, e.g., the dramatic soprano or soubrette, the heldentenor or the lyrical tenor, the basso buffo and others. It is certainly a conscious characterisation when Mozart goes against the convention by making the lover Don Giovanni a baritone, or when Bizet writes the passionate Carmen for a mezzo-soprano.
>
> If the choice is influenced by the composer writing for a specific singer, this is another proof that composers think with and through their material as concretely as possible. And so Smetana composed some (additional) arias for Josef Paleček or Josef Lev[44]. This is common practice for composers, since they have to respect the ranges and technical specifics of individual musical instruments. In the above voice types, this is not only a matter of the pitches and ranges of the voices but also of their technical specifics. Thus the dramatic soprano is stronger (richer) and even heavier (more resonant) than the coloratura soprano, which is very agile, similar to a flute, etc.

In the section on singing we have said that vocal melodies, similar to melodies of speech, are a general expression of certain emotions and aspirations. In

---

[44] Josef Lev (1832–1898) and Josef Paleček (1842–1915) were leading opera singers at the National Theatre in Prague, often taking the lead roles in the first productions of Bedřich Smetana's operas.

dramatic singing this needs to be supported by the individual characteristics of dramatic personas, into which the composer *mentally transfigures*. What is at stake are the personas' individual nuances in their vocal expression, given by their continuous psychological traits, which the composer needs to focus on – as if the composer were an actor. And so a particular singing role, despite all its variety corresponding to various situations, must have certain continuous or at least dominant characteristic features.

> Thus the vocal part of an agile chatterer is predominantly fast-paced and full of repeated phrases and words (Rossini's Figaro or Smetana's Kecal, who keeps saying "Všechno je hotovo"; "Job done"), the part of the flirtatious lady is replete with ornaments and coloratura (Mozart's Donna Elvira or Rossini's Rosina), while the parts of villagers are simpler (Mozart's Masetto). This individual differentiation can be wonderfully seen in opera *ensembles*; Mozart's and Smetana's are especially masterful in this regard. So, in Act 1 Scene 3 of *The Bartered Bride*, the simple and calm melody of the Krušina couple ("Vaše chvála mnoho platí"; "Your praise is very valuable") is in counterpoint with the agile voice of the chattering Kecal ("Není velký ani malý"; "He is neither big nor small"). In the ensemble before the final scene-change of Act 1 of *Don Giovanni*, the sombre Ottavio sings distinctly and simply, as does Anna, who betrays her true passionate nature by a single eruption, while the light-hearted Elvira engages in a coloratura play of tones.
>
> It follows from this that Janáček's *speech melody theory* is dramatically completely misguided. He requires that opera employ speech melodies as spoken by country ("uncorrupted") folk. But these could only be used for dramatic personas from the folk and only for mental states and situations identical to those in which they were recorded. That is a narrow and unreliable usage. What is exaggerated, or even dogmatically prioritised here, is the national character of folk speech melodies. If the author of the opera is Czech and is composing to a Czech text, the speech melodies of the personas, with whose character and mental states the composer is empathising, will be also Czech – and furthermore, dramatic. It is clear that this theory is also unartistic, as evidenced in its extreme naturalism: these are sort of musical photographs and can serve as no more than study material.

(2) *The orchestral music apparently characterising the dramatic persona*, both with and without its singing. It cannot be generally said with any certainty; it has to be judged case by case and the judgment is not always certain. Two instances are highly likely:

(a) Music that accompanies the *solo expression* of a specific dramatic persona. These are almost certainly arias from older operas and often also parts of duets or even ensembles – in other words, any more or less extensive passage where the weight of the situation shifts to the persona who is singing or even just acting. These can also be passages where a persona implicated in a situation is absent but is cited by others. All such passages, especially arias (in modern opera: longer musical monologues, even those delivered in the presence of others), are supposed to convey a certain *significant feature* of the persona, *highlighted by its individual reaction to a given situation*. With leading personas these can often comprise *several* features, irrespective of whether their character appears dramatically multifaceted.

So, for instance, in Mozart's *Le nozze di Figaro*, Cherubino is perfectly characterised as a pubescent boy in two of his arias: the fast E-flat-major aria conveys the passion of his eroticism, and the B-flat-major Canzona shows the sentimentality of his desire. We have mentioned the characterisation of Kecal's agility and verbosity; this is complemented by the sober reasoning of his monotonous aria "Každý jen tu svou" ("Everyone's girl is the one and only"). Sometimes the characteristic is more external, relating for instance to one's profession; such is the marching aria of the officer Georges in Boïeldieu's *La dame blanche*. But this aria excellently conveys his recklessness also, which combines with sentimentality, as his nocturnal aria at the castle shows.

(b) *A personal characteristic motif.* Given that the leitmotif always contains something fixed and even musically commonplace, as we know, it could be compared to the fixed component of the actor figure, i.e., with the mask, especially if it remains predominantly unchanged. In that case, the leitmotif is a more-or-less external characteristic, though often a rather succinct one. However, if dramatic personas are undergoing changes – either circumstantial situations draw out certain features of their character, or they appear differently to other dramatic personas – then then it is necessary that their leitmotif should also undergo changes, characteristically. The leitmotif needs to be sufficiently plastic then. If no special emphasis is placed on the individuality of a persona, then the characteristic motif is reduced to a *characteristic structure (faktura)* of its music – which is subsumed under (a) above. Most operas combine both characteristics because a single leitmotif, however variable, is often insufficient to characterise the leading personas.

Since the personal characteristic motif belongs to the dramatic (i.e., acting) persona, it pertains also to that persona's dramatic relations; it therefore has some ideational content, and its variants can be apparent ideational motifs (cf. earlier reflections on the challenges of its name).

So, for instance, Samiel's motif in *Der Freischütz* is a personal one but also a motif of "evil power". The motif of the secret in Smetana's eponymous *Tajemství* (The Secret) is also the motif of Friar Barnabáš, sounding solemnly in people's reminiscences but merrily in the friar's appearance in Kalina's dream. Dalibor's motif has a chivalric bombast when he appears before the court, but is mellow when he is remembering his friend. The minor-mode variant at the opera's outset suggests the trial of Dalibor, while the brisk and fast-paced one at the end of the act, accompanying Jitka's singing, symbolises the plan to free Dalibor. All these variants proceed systematically throughout the opera. In Smetana's *Čertova stěna* (The Devil's Wall), Rarach (the Imp or Devil) has *two* distinct motifs: the first is an augmented chord ("diabolicus"); the second is pastoral, characterising him in his shepherd *disguise*. Tristan, disguised as Tantris, is characterised by Wagner with an inversion of his motif. – Examples of mere characteristic musical structures (*faktury*) are the undulating passage in Weber's *Euryanthe* that accompanies the sly Eglantine or the pizzicato accompaniment with the declamatory motif of "jářku" (quoth I) for the bricklayer in Smetana's *Tajemství*.

It would be worthwhile to follow the types of musical personas in their historical development, e.g., the chatterer type, whether sly or dull (Figaro, Van Bett, Kecal, Mumlal,[45] etc.), the demonic women (Armida, Englantine, Ortrud, Kundry, etc.) and other types.

(B) **Musical interaction** *is the sum of all the music that characterises the dramatic action.*

Since we have defined dramatic action as the interaction of personas (*vespolné jednání osob*), musical interaction comprises all musical personas in regards to singing and music, but – strictly speaking – only those passages that form a musical ensemble, starting with duets and on up to any number of personas, including the chorus as a collective persona. As far as singing parts are concerned, the case is clear: they contain the expressions of emotions and aspirations, which are individual but stem from the mutual dramatic relations between personas. The orchestral music within opera is a different case. Regarding the musical persona, we have asserted that it is *never certain* which musical passages pertain to it – which is true whenever there are more than one personas on stage. On the contrary, much of the music that sounds in those situations does not relate to one dramatic persona or another, but to the dramatic relations *between them*. This "interpersonal" music needs to be counted as "musical interaction", or rather: its *specific* component truly characterises the "dramatic action" as personas' *interaction*. Whereas the core of the musical persona was its singing, the core of musical interaction lies in the orchestra – and that trend is, with a view to the history of opera, progressively more and more decisive. This could also be expressed by asserting that music often characterises a *"dramatic scene"* in the sense analysed in the preceding chapter: by its *psychological atmosphere* (*psychická atmosféra*), which has come about from the joint effect of all onstage personas but is simultaneously "above them". A section of music with roughly the same musico-dramatic structure will be referred to as a *"musical situation"*.

---

45   Van Bett is a character from the comic opera *Zar und Zimmermann* (Tsar and Carpenter, 1837) by Albert Lortzing (1800–1851). Mumal the gamekeeper appears in Bedřich Smetana's *Dvě vdovy* (The Two Widows, 1874).

It is interesting to observe, for instance, how differently Smetana (and others) treats "love duets"; they may be identical in their text but vary according to the situation (if only in tempo). It would be worthwhile to compare different settings of typical stage events, such as a fit of madness, a death, a curse, a combat, etc. Smetana refused to compose *Wallenrod*[46] because it contained a trial, which he had composed so many times that he would not know how to do it again, but differently!

Of special importance are cases when none of the onstage personas is prominent enough to impress *their singular* dramatic atmosphere onto the situation, even for a short while. In such instances, the orchestral music becomes *autonomous* and the characterisation of personas shrinks to their singing; it frequently contents itself with the declamatory form of recitative.

This is typical, for example, of all "conversational" moments in opera generally – with light social conversation as well as with calm or even agitated moments. A composer wishing to compose more elaborate music for the personas' lines would be entirely lost, since such passages are mostly not worth any "lyrical" composition because they are entirely "prosaic". Masterful examples are the hurried duet in Act 2 of *Le nozze di Figaro* between Susanna and Cherubino, who then jumps out of the window; or the humorous scene between Vendulka, Martinka and the frontier guard in Act 2 of Smetana's *Hubička* (The Kiss): the music to the latter scene is perfectly autonomous and uncovers (as one voice) the merry variant of the smugglers' leitmotif. As far as scenes of "social conversations" are concerned, Mozart's influence brought about a tradition in such settings: this was followed by Auber in France (e.g., in his *Fra Diavolo*), by Lortzing in Germany (*Zar und Zimmermann*) or by Smetana (*Dvě vdovy*, The Two Widows) and Foerster (*Jessika*)[47] in our country. The form is often more complex and the personas more differentiated, each in turn coming to the forefront, but it always follows the principle of relatively autonomous music, spanning even longer and quite varied scenes. The variety of what can appear *in the text* of the dialogue could be illustrated by Ostrčil's *Poupě* (The Bud)[48], where the ensemble starts debating social issues upon Kučina's arrival, or in my *Vina* (Guilt), where Uhlíř, early in Act 2, speaks about his work

---

46 *Konrad Wallenrod* (1828) by the Polish romantic poet Adam Mickiewicz (1798–1855) is a historical narrative poem.

47 *Jessika* (1905) is a three-act lyrical opera by composer Josef Bohuslav Foerster (1859–1951) on the libretto by Jaroslav Vrchlický (1853–1912), based on Shakespeare's *The Merchant of Venice*. In Vrchlický's version the comic and lyrical aspects of the story are foregrounded and Jessika becomes the central figure. The opera is a sentimental love comedy, which offer ample material for the composer to portray social conversations.

48 *Poupě* (The Bud, 1911) is a one-act chamber opera by Otakar Ostrčil (1879–1935) based on a play by F. X. Svoboda. It includes only four characters (the widower and landowner Klán, his daughter Anežka and two young men, Ladislav and Kučina). The entire opera is a continuous series of informal and realistic conversational dialogue in one evening. The adolescent Anežka (the "Bud" of the title) has attracted the attention of two young men and in the end she finds out which of them she loves the most. At the time of its creation, *Poupě* was considered an exquisite case of modern Czech comic opera.

in the sugar factory. The music only captures the dramatic situation, which in the latter case, despite the speaker, is rather tense; this is conveyed by the polyphonic structure in the orchestra, which is split into two groups.

Wherever the dramatic action surges energetically ahead – thanks to the strong impulses of individual personas – and the situation changes, the music must not remain unaffected by this change. It changes therefore; but that places it in danger of losing its purely musical unity and fluency, becoming "fractured". On the contrary, the dramatic action, which the music follows, is *coherent and pragmatic*, being bound by the logical chain of cause and effect. The question arising here is the extent to which music itself is capable of capturing the *motivation of dramatic action*, i.e., of human action. Let us rely on the psychological analysis of "action" from Chapter 6.

Firstly, music is capable of the *emotional* justification of an action. We know that all action stems from emotion. However, we have seen that music is capable of *portraying* the mood, emotion, passion and aspiration leading to the action, especially by its rhythmic and overall motoric aspect. It is the contents of the emotions – i.e., the mental image or idea that evoked this emotion – that music is unable to express unaided; however, this is also beyond the capacities of mimics (i.e., without words), as we know. Music is therefore particularly suitable as motivation for unwitting, instinctive actions that are not fully conscious of their cause or the purpose of their aspiration. For conscious actions, controlled by will, music would need words: and these are provided by fully associated mimics: acting with singing. Older opera contains *only* this type of musical motivation; and so does modern opera – the principle will forever be valid.

Secondly, music is capable of the *ideational* justification of action; in this it surpasses simple mimics, at least with regard to the abstract idea. This is thanks to the *ideational leitmotif*. However, we know that music does not have this capacity inherently – it needs to be linked, at least *initially*, with certain speech (or merely a situation), in order to associate them. But then it will be self-sufficient. The ideational leitmotif that appears in dramatic music is always an *interpersonal* one, corresponding to a specific *dramatic relation* because the idea that is linked to the music must propel the persons affected to interaction – otherwise it would not be dramatic. There are a number of bridges between the personal and the ideational leitmotif (as we have observed), both in their variants and in musically autonomous versions. A special kind is the *"object"* leitmotif (i.e., of an inanimate object), similar to the personal motif; it is an instance of a certain personification.

> An example of an ideational leitmotif is the aforementioned forbidden question motif from Wagner's *Lohengrin*; it is in fact between Lohengrin and Elsa, but Ortrud and Telramund usurp it too for their intrigues. In this way it becomes a true leading "motif"

of the whole plot. Motifs express the subjective feeling of a particular persona, e.g., Chrudoš's love for Krasava in Smetana's *Libuše*; they are semi-personal. In contrast, Friar Barnabáš's motif in *Tajemství* becomes, in its many variants, the "secret" of almost everyone in the opera. Examples of the object leitmotif are the ring motif or the sword motif in Wagner's *Der Ring des Nibelungen*: even these have a dramatic relation to specific personas (the ring carries Alberich's curse and the sword is Siegfried's legacy). Wherever such relations to personas are missing (e.g., the Valhalla motif in the same operas), the leitmotif is *nondramatic*, carrying a different message, such as an epic or a philosophical one.

Musico-dramatic synthesis. So far we have only demonstrated how music *enhances* the causal coherence of dramatic action by associating itself with its elements; the dramatic coherence is, however, only in the action (i.e., in human action). Let us recall our schema of action and further symbolise the music that characterises individual elements of action (mental image, emotion, aspiration, deed) by the sequence m_i, m_e, m_a, m_d:

$$\begin{array}{lllll}
\text{action:} & \text{(mental image)} & \text{— emotion} & \text{— aspiration} & \text{— deed} \\
& | & | & | & | \\
\text{music:} & (m_i) & m_e & m_a & m_d
\end{array}$$

The question that arises here is whether there is a line of coherence between the musical elements that corresponds to the coherence of action. Only then will it be possible to assert that music *co-creates* dramatic action – that is, that *the musical* component of action is *synthetic in its own right*, not only analytical, as a mere illustration of the action that follows it step by step. In this discussion we can omit m_i, which can only pertain to the characteristic motif (always founded upon an associated idea), at least initially.

It is obvious that the musico-dramatic synthesis

$$m_e - m_a - m_d$$

is not founded on a causal bond because there is no such thing in music: we do not consider the second bar of a musical idea to be a consequence of the first bar, nor the first to be its cause. The bond is purely musical – one of *musical logic*, a special case of the most general principle of *identity*, through which the human mind organises and unifies everything; in a sense, the above causal principle is a specific type of this general principle. The systematic study of musical logic belongs to the domain of music theory and aesthetics; for our purposes, let us mention only a few instances typical of musico-dramatic synthesis.

The above example presents only one, though very common, case of action: instinctive or passionate behaviour. Here, a specific emotion is characterised by its dynamic progression over time, being embodied in an aspiration as a rhythmic leitmotif. This characteristic rhythm will be retained in the deed that resulted from the aspiration – this is the principle of exteriorisation of inner tactile impulses (as discussed in Chapter 5). Music, as we have seen, is perfectly capable of portraying the dynamic progression of emotions and the motoric rhythm of the aspiration stemming from that emotion; that rhythm, though gradually intensifying, must be sustained for the deed that was caused by the emotion. The composer, having selected a specific figuration to characterise anger, for instance, will *carry it through*, though perhaps intensified, for the action that followed from this anger. Other aspects of the music can be changed; but in spite of the overall diversity we can sense the logic, thanks to the rhythmic coherence. The nexus (cluster) of psychological causality corresponds with the nexus of *rhythmic identity in music* (*svazek rytmické identity hudební*). And that is the *autonomous synthesis* (*autonomní syntéza*).

> Thus, in Smetana's *Hubička* the music characterising Lukáš's irritation at Paloucký's behaviour ("Nuž rád či nerad"; Whether glad or not), his later, anger-filled breakup with Vendulka, and finally the shameful scene at the end, is all principally the same. The germ of that rhythmic motif develops fully in the mocking song, "Hrajte mi tu nejskočnější" (Play me the merriest of all songs).

This is not the only synthesis. Music has its own *harmonic logic* (also known as chord affinity), which is more a tendency than a rule. There are harmonies (such as the dominant seventh chord) that we expect to be followed *by a specific* harmony; if it does not come, we are disappointed – known as a false ending. If a harmony is followed by one that is too distant, and the affinity is not very clear to us, it seems illogical, random and arbitrary. It is obvious that similar relationships often appear in dramatic action as well. Let us recall Mozart's letter. Although harmonic principles are very liberal nowadays, we still feel the "more or less" of affinity. A sudden, strange or prolonged modulation always signals that the "musical situation" has changed.

The same holds true for other aspects of music. Whenever I hear music of a roughly identical melody, instrumentation or tempo, the situation will seem the same. If the music has changed in part, so has the situation. If the music has suddenly changed completely, the situation has also changed at once and entirely.

A special significance in the *unity of melodies in singing voices* (*identita melodií ve zpěvních hlasech*). It always signifies the alliance of these personas. There are numerous *homophonic* passages in love duets, such as parallel thirds or sixths or even unisons (for instance, the prison duet of Milada and Dalibor). Besides the simultaneous unity of voices, there is also sequential unity: *imitation*. It can often be found at the beginnings of ensembles, such as the G-major quartet in Act 1 of Beethoven's *Fidelio* or the A-flat major one in Act 1 of Smetana's *Dvě vdovy* (The Two Widows: "Ó jakou tíseň"; Oh, what distress).

In the famous duet from *The Bartered Bride* ("Znám jednu dívku"; I know a maid), melodies enter in imitation at six, then four bars, then finally at the half bar. Here, the personas' "alliance" is indeed only a pretended one.

After this analysis of the basic dramatic features of opera, let us discuss – with a continuing view to Chapters 6 and 7 – some dramatic moments that are created, in contrast to spoken drama, by means of the *musical composition*.

Musical manifestation (*hudební zveřejnění*). By means of the manifestation principle in Chapter 6, we justified the monologue as the dramatic persona's spoken expression of ideas, emotions and aspirations. The same is true in opera, where the task is taken up by *arias*, sung either in solitude or at least apart from others. Thanks to the intense emotional effect of music, which has helped us formulate the claim of its unique lyrical qualities, it can be explained why arias that are based on reflexively lyrical texts are so frequent and lyricism is so predominant in them. Nonetheless, they need to be understood as dramatically justified with a causal bond to what precedes or what follows; in other words, if these arias are an outcome of, or a reaction to, the previous action, or a preparation for the next.

> So, for instance, in Smetana's *Dalibor*, Jitka's "Rek ten mne…" (That hero has…) in the middle of the first scene is a reaction to the surrounding situation, while the concluding number ("Do žaláře mu svitne záře"; Light will shine into his jail) is a preparation for her future action. Milada's aria at the trial, having pleaded for Dalibor's pardon in vain, is a continuation and clarification of what preceded it (from "Ó jaká to bouře…"; Oh what tempest, to "Onť láska má"; He is my love). Similarly, in Act 2 of *The Bartered Bride*, Jeník has been abandoned after the duet with Kecal ("Znám jednu dívku"; I know a maid) and he reacts to it with his aria ("Jak možná věřit"; How can one believe).

This last example demonstrates the importance of manifestation for the instances where a dramatic persona is undergoing a change – through words, mimics, or both. This also pertains to the "vocal aside", which is very frequent in opera. In spoken drama, when manifestation is impossible by means of words, it has to be achieved by mimics. Not so in opera: opera has the precious means of manifesting whatever is unspoken or insincerely spoken in its *orchestral music*. This is the specifically *"musical"* manifestation we are discussing here: in many ways it even surpasses mimics. Mimics often has to hide or even deceive, since we understand it as a *direct* expression of the dramatic persona towards others – it is thus very *personal*. In contrast, the orchestral music does not need to hide and is incapable of lying, because we associate its visual images *only loosely* with a specific dramatic persona while always perceiving music as something *impersonal*. For that reason, its emotional effect is not subject to the changes outlined in Chapter 6. *Musical manifestation is the most discreet of the three that dramatic art is capable of*, i.e., over manifestation via words and mimics. Even *unspoken* ideas or thoughts, which mimics is unable to express, can be conveyed by music in the orchestra (that is, impersonally) by means of ideational leitmotifs. This refined capacity of musical soul painting is especially prominent in psychological music dramas; the best tool for it is musical polyphony, especially in states of dilemma.

> A few varying examples: in Gluck's *Iphigénie en Tauride*, the exhausted Oreste sings a broad melody to a soft accompaniment from the strings: "Le calme rentre dans mon cœur". Only the ringing syncopation in the violas betray his self-delusion (Gluck said of this, "He's lying"). In Smetana's *Libuše* (Act 2, the scene at the burial mound), Krasava begs Chrudoš for forgiveness in an ardent cantilena ("Ó pomni"; Oh, remember). At that moment, Chrudoš's motif of love towards Krasava sounds in the orchestra, here and there interspersed by Šťáhlav's motif, betraying his jealous suspicions. In *Hubička*, Vendulka, recounting superstitions about widowers, explains to Lukáš why she still refuses to kiss him, for fear of his deceased wife; simultaneously a short leitmotif sounds in the orchestra. When, a moment later, Vendulka is almost convinced, saying "svou krev i duši vypustím, když tebe z žalu vyprostím" (I'll lose my blood and soul if I free you from your sorrow), Lukáš asks: "Však hubičku?" (But the kiss?) – the motif of superstition breathes in the orchestra – "Ti nedám" (I will not give it to you), answers Vendulka. There is an infinite wealth of such psychological portraits painted through music in Smetana. Let me cite my own practice; the main impulse to set Hilbert's drama *Vina* (Guilt) to music was the idea of Mína's "guilt", to which she constantly alludes in words and which haunts Mína and renders her unable to confess it to Hošek – and Uhlíř bases his action upon this – and yet, her guilt remains unspoken for two long acts but it pervades the atmosphere. That was the music's task.
>
> In contrast, it is naive to cite the music of whatever is just fleetingly mentioned on stage as a leitmotif. Such "pleonasm" stems from "purely textual" composition. Only that which has effect on stage is worth setting to music.

Given that the composer composes before the actor, the actor – as we have said – needs to follow the composer's instructions not only in singing, but also in music to some extent. The actor must also respect each and every musical manifestation pertaining to their persona, as far as mimically possible. How this is to be done, whether by the mimics of the entire body (which is in movement), or only of the face (which is more discreet), is a matter of the actor's invention and, indeed, taste. One should caution the actor not to follow the example of dancing by mirroring *all* the impulses of the music in their physical movements. The above discussion of how "rhythmic identity" of music manifests human action reveals that it is impossible to know for certain when the composer portrays physical movement or a mere mental state; the composer might, for instance, only be portraying someone's anger teeming inside. Music and its material are such a refined means of expression that movement and bodily mimics cannot emulate them. It is completely impossible and ugly to capture *each and every* detail of music through movement even in dance, especially if it is not dance music ("dancing Beethoven!"). For an actor, this would be pointless and, if done methodically, altogether *stylistically incorrect*, because an actor performing a dramatic persona is not a dancer, whose expression is limited only to bodily movements.

Which music belongs to which actor can best be decided by the director-conductor. It is hardly ever easy or certain, except for moments when the actor is alone on stage. If there are more actors present, the only signal for certain is the leitmotif; otherwise, not even the music to which the actor sings *has* to be "theirs" – and all the less so if the actor is not singing. Conversely, it could be theirs even though they are not singing. It is helpful whenever the composer has marked this in their score.

> An instance where a persona sings but the accompaniment does not belong to them is the above example of Krasava and Chrudoš. Similarly, in Act 2 of Fibich's *Nevěsta messinská* (The Bride of Messina)[49], Don Cesar makes his love confession to Beatrice through his impassioned melody, while the basses in the orchestra portray the girl's creeping horror.

The operatic ensemble and chorus. We have often touched upon the operatic ensemble when analysing the musical persona, especially its interaction. Let us now discuss it in connection to the chorus. We have established that the reality of vocal polyphony turns the chorus into a perfect "collective persona", even capable of speech, complying fully with the actor's totality principle (*postulát herecké totality*). The operatic chorus fulfils three tasks. Sometimes the chorus is *entirely* dramatically passive, merely creating the environment for the play – an environment in a rather *decorative* sense, both visually and musically speaking. It is then in fact only a *singing component of the set*, often not even encountering the soloists. This is often the case of operas adapted from spoken drama, which only added the chorus for its musical effect, or the case of operatic spectacles; whenever the chorus appears alongside the soloists, it merely creates their *musical backdrop*. The second type is when the chorus creates a *dramatic persona*, but a *passive* one at that; it *contributes* to situations with individual personas, but does not create dramatic action (děj). This fluently transitions into the third type, where the chorus is *an active dramatic persona* that makes dramatic action on its own – together with

---

49   *Nevěsta messinská* (The Bride of Messina) is a tragic opera in three acts by composer Zdeněk Fibich (1850–1900), premiered at the National Theatre in Prague in 1883. The libretto by the philosopher, aesthetician and Zich's predecessor Otakar Hostinský (1847–1910) is adapted from Friedrich Schiller's play *Die Braut von Messina* (1803).

individual personas. The dramatic texts of the latter two types are true opera librettos, conceived with the chorus and ensemble in mind.

> The very first modern opera, Gluck's *Orfeo ed Euridice*, offers examples of all three choral functions: in Act 1, the chorus partakes in Orfeo's mourning for Euridice; in Act 2, the chorus of Furies prevent Orfeo from entering the underworld; in Elysium in Act 3, the chorus only creates a scenic background. The chorus plays an excellent, active role as the crowd in Auber's *La muette de Portici* (the revolution) and similarly in Smetana's *Braniboři v Čechách* (The Brandenburgers in Bohemia).

Although the operatic chorus represents a single collective persona, it generally has several singing voices and is only exceptionally in unison. These voices are commonly "choral": each of them is sung by several people, which is a well-known phenomenon. This is what makes the chorus *audibly* distinct from *an ensemble of soloists*, not only in cases where they represent unnamed personas only acting together, in fact "*a chorus of soloists*" (e.g., the Pages in Wagner's *Tannhäuser* or the four harvesters offstage in Smetana's *Libuše*). In opera, the distinction between the ensemble and the chorus is much more pronounced and varied than in spoken drama. Naturally, the chorus can also bring forth such "unnamed" soloists, who otherwise do not appear elsewhere in the opera (for instance, the two prisoners from the crowd in the Act 1 finale of Beethoven's *Fidelio*); the next step is that these people also act autonomously throughout the play (e.g., the leaders of the people in Auber's *La muette de Portici*).

The chorus can often be split further, representing several collective personas. The most natural division, by sex, gives the opera an exquisite musical differentiation, into women's and men's choruses, timbrally distinct, which can further be divided by register into sopranos and altos, and tenors and basses – which often visually means division by age (e.g., a chorus of old men, judges or children). Women's and men's groups may also appear separately, with the task of representing the most varied personas (spinners, soldiers), but they can also appear together as a double chorus (e.g., at the opening of Act 3 of Wagner's *Der fliegende Holländer*, there is a chorus of Norwegian sailors and a chorus of girls bringing refreshments). The chorus can also be divided into two homogeneous groups, such as two smaller mixed choruses or two men's choruses (as happens in the above scenes in *Der fliegende Holländer* when the girls leave; the Norwegian sailors encounter the Dutchman's sailors). In those cases, the distinction needs to be at least musical, and thus polyphonic, which is often supported by a distinct scenic realisation. Similar to the solo singing voices, as we have asserted, the same holds for the chorus: a homophonic texture always suggests an affirmative attitude of the crowd, while a polyphonic one, unless it is merely imitative in nature, is capable of expressing differing views of the group, let alone of two distinct groups (the double chorus) – which, on reaching agreement, can merge into a single chorus again. Apart from portraying the dynamic (i.e., action-related) characteristic of the chorus, the composer needs to take into account the static characterisation of the chorus as a "persona", albeit a collective one. Gluck was the first to do this, musically distinguishing (vocally and orchestrally) the choruses of the Greeks and the Barbarians.

Since even the expression of "one of the crowd" is often distinct from the chorus – in time, by alternating with it, or by polyphonic means if they sing at the same time – this needs to be the case all the more so whenever individual personas appear together with the chorus. It is only in moments of perfect agreement that the ensemble sings what the chorus does (for instance, at the end of an opera); otherwise, it is polyphonically distinct. The soloists generally sing the melodies to the harmonic background of the chorus (as in "Jsme svoji"; We are one another's, in Act 1 of Smetana's *Hubička*). The musical differentiation needs to be all the greater, the more a persona is at odds with the chorus; this is surely aided scenically by blocking, with the soloists downstage and the chorus in the background. Some exquisite examples are: the Act 1 finale of Weber's *Oberon* (Rezia against the chorus of the Harem Guard) and Act 2 of Foerster's *Debora*[50] (Debora against the chorus singing in the temple).

> The form of the *operatic* ensemble, and even more so of the *operatic* chorus, is capable of an almost unlimited development. However, this requires that dramatic text (i.e., the libretto) offer an original impulse, not only a cliché. For instance, collective drama, which in spoken drama is doomed to no more than glimpses via a "speaker" in the crowd, could be perfectly realised in opera. Here, the "people" could be the true hero of a drama, as can be seen from several operas where the crowd interferes in the action. Operatic technique allows the deployment of the chorus to be gradually increased dynamically in dramatic scenes, both visually and acoustically. Among the most powerful examples is the immense, gradual build-up in the second half of Act 1 of Smetana's *Libuše*, where Libuše's verdict receives a growing response from the lords (ensemble) and from the people (chorus).

The scenic tasks of music. Proceeding from the chapter on the theatrical scene, let us first focus on the musical characterisation of the *static* qualities, i.e., of the *location of action*, represented by fixed components of the stage (at most nuanced by means of lighting). The character of such a "scenic image" is captured musically by tone-painting means (e.g., Elysium in Gluck's *Orfeo*) or by conventionalised semantic means (such as the opening of Act 2 of *Tristan*

---

50 Zich alludes to a scene from Foerster's opera *Debora* that portrays a conflict between the Jewish Debora and the Czech villagers, who are Catholic. The chorus is singing an Easter prayer that contrasts with Debora's aria.

with French horns in the distance), even using such things as scenic "fill-ins" (e.g., pastoral music and song after the scene change in Act 1 of *Tannhäuser*) or merely the musical atmosphere. Music can do this both with an empty stage and also with personas present, especially individuals who can respond to the atmosphere of their environment in song or action. This is also one of the ways in which opera creates passages where the orchestral music does not belong to a musical persona envoiced by singing. There can be an agreement between the mood of the persona and the scene, but also a disagreement (such as that of Přemysl in Act 2 of *Libuše*: "Jen v mých ňadrech nepokoj"; But for the disquiet in my heart), which is also often conveyed by orchestral polyphony. The atmospheric power of music allows the elaboration of such scenic intermezzos in much broader passages than spoken drama would bear (e.g., the moonlight intermezzo towards the end of Act 1 of Foerster's *Eva*). Nevertheless, with a view to the purely lyrical manifestations of music in opera, one should take care that the music does not become *self-sufficient* and risk *disrupting* the coherence of the dramatic action.

As far as kinetic (and truly just *motoric*) scenic *qualities* are concerned, music is fully capable of expressing them; moreover, music productively supports them with its own motoric effect. This is, then, a true "*scene*": which is to say, live and created by people. Since the motoric aspect of the personas' action relates directly to the dramatic action and is therefore encompassed in the "musical interaction", what is at stake here is only the musical portrayal of the *human environment* – the same as the task of the chorus (or the "chorus of soloists", as we have called the collective of all such episodic personas) – in its aspect of movement; in brief, it concerns the *motoric*, not the dramatic, scene with its accompanying mood. The musical depiction is often left exclusively to the orchestra, especially in preludes and postludes to such scenes; occasionally, they are accompanied by the singing of the chorus or its individual members. Music often derives here from a characteristic rhythm of some particular type of labour, such as rowing or hammering. It is the task of the *director-scenic* to give shape to the *scene* (in our sense of the word) according to the music. In this, they have to see to any cue provided in the composer's stage directions, and *these must be followed unconditionally* (just like everywhere else), because the composer created the music according to the libretto or added them as instructions to the score. The *director-scenic* in opera has essentially the same function as in spoken drama.

> Thus, for instance, the opening of Act 2 and in the second scene of Act 3 of Auber's *La muette de Portici* portrays the vivid hustle and bustle of the fishing folk on the coast and in the marketplace. In Scene 2 of Charpentier's *Louise*, the environment is created by a chorus of female soloists (seamstresses). Or in Wagner's *Das Rheingold*, on descending into the realm of the Nibelungs, we can increasingly hear their hammering. However,

it is *not only* a matter of live movement or exclusively of motoric musical characterisation, but rather a combination with the aforementioned static characteristics, i.e., of tone-painting and conventional semantics. Such is the case of the Smugglers' chorus in Act 2 of Smetana's *Hubička*, where their furtive steps can be heard only in the basses of the orchestra, which otherwise depicts the mood. The same takes place in any procession, ceremony or festivities with fanfares and other characteristically musical elements; these often acquire an almost static quality (e.g., sacrifices to gods, honours paid to rulers and so forth). Music draws on the broad genre of *marches* of all kinds, from the energetic military march to the plodding funeral march – as it does in daily life, the more so in opera. This is even more true of the genre of *dances*. If in the former, the vocal chorus is enriched by supernumeraries, in dances it is joined by dancers. In these cases, as we know, dancers – in contrast with ballet itself – are *actors representing dancing people*, and this *mimetic* specification needs to be obeyed both in costume and in the manner of dancing. Dances in opera, however frequent, are mostly undramatic in essence – unless the dramatic action takes place in the presence of others (such as in the Act 2 finale of Marschner's *Hans Heiling*[51], where the contrast between Heiling's pain and the exuberant merry-making of the folk is particularly effective). And yet, provided they do not become too self-indulgent, dances are much more acceptable in opera than excessive lyricism because their motoric effect *covers* and *supplants* dramatic stagnation. We know well that the "dramatic" effect contains a strong motoric element. The means of gradual intensification that dance can become, in connection with the vocal chorus, can be seen in the Act 1 finale of *The Bartered Bride*.

The entr'acte. The "*impersonal*" quality of *orchestral* music in opera (in contrast to singing on stage), as we have stressed when discussing "musical manifestation" as a principle, allows for a very strange thing: music can also be performed during the *breaks* in the dramatic action when the real-time dramatic action stops *altogether* (as we have observed in Chapter 6). That would mean then that such music, played while the curtain is down, *is not dramatic*, and perhaps not even *mimetic* (*obrazová*), but mere music. As far as the music played before the performance – known as the *overture* – that is always the case.

The *overture* has the sole psychological task to *make us ready* for the show. The original overtures were no more than fanfares announcing the festivity, which is what an opera was. We can find this also with the overture to *Libuše*, of which Smetana wrote that it was "not an opera, but rather a *grand tableau*". In later times, the overture, composed strictly in the musical forms common in their era, were designed to set the general mood of the piece – i.e., different for serious and comic opera. Since opera composers almost exclusively write the overture only *after completing* the work, it is psychologically understandable that they often inserted pieces of music from the

---

51 *Hans Heiling* (1833) is a German romantic opera in three acts and a prologue by Heinrich Marschner (1795–1861) with a libretto by Eduard Devrient (1801–1877).

opera itself – whether as a free-form introduction (Mozart's *Don Giovanni*) or as the main or secondary themes of the following fast number. In this way, starting with Weber, leitmotifs and musical reminiscences of the opera began to appear in the overture. Naturally, such formations may well have a *purely musical significance* here. Each leitmotif is no more than a simple musical theme; it is only on a second listening to the opera that they can assume their referential meaning. Such use of one's own operatic music is acceptable because the overture prepares us both for the mood as well as for the *music*, acquainting us with the themes that will have a role to play later – which is specifically true of characteristic motifs. The modern overture often has a loose form, reminiscent of a symphonic poem – although, as we have seen, it is not and can never be one.

Of particular interest are Smetana's overtures to *Prodaná nevěsta* and *Tajemství*. The former makes use of music that occurs in the finale of Act 2, when the bride is bartered. The latter develops the "secret" motif. These two overtures are in fact "musical mottos" of the two operas.

The *preludes* to following acts and *interludes* during scene changes are a *substantively* different case. These numbers can make use of the music that we have heard in a scene and deploy them as reminiscences and leitmotifs, because the necessary associations have already been formed. They can be, and often are, proper symphonic poems – that is, programmatic, *mimetic* music. To name but two examples: Wagner's prelude to Act 3 of *Tannhäuser*, depicting the knight's journey to Rome, and Smetana's entr'acte music for the second scene change in Act 2 of *Dalibor*, depicting the descent into Dalibor's cell.

It is obvious that the music depicting such action – even of a psychological kind (the prelude to Act 2 of *Hubička*), ceremonial (the funeral march in Fibich's *Nevěsta messinská*) or naturalistic (the Tempesta in *Il barbiere di Siviglia*) – runs in real time, but we imagine the action it depicts in an *ideal* (imaginary) time, just like any action that occurs in the breaks between acts (cf. Chapter 6). In such instances, the music of preludes and interludes has not only significance for the action, but it also *links up* the acts of the work. If it plays throughout the break intended for a scene change, it establishes a *continuity of the dramatic form*, which is very desirable, as we know, especially where multiple scene changes are needed.

Prelude and interlude music, being generally *mimetic*, becomes specifically *dramatic* as soon as the curtain goes up, and it can fluently transition into the ensuing scene. Shorter interludes of this kind are often no more than atmospheric or musical preparation (scene-setting) for what is to follow. Great examples of this are the contrasting preludes to Acts 2 and 3 of Beethoven's *Fidelio*. Of greater interest is the case when the overture directly transitions into the ensuing scene. In such instances, when the curtain rises, we have to transform our purely musical understanding into a mimetic one. An exception to this is the tone-painting overture, which is of course mimetic too (as in Gluck's *Iphigénie en Tauride*, which depicts a storm at sea). This is comparable to instances where we can hear sounds from the scene (e.g., laughter, hammer strikes) before the curtain goes up. The fact is that the *musico-dramatic work of art begins at the moment when the music starts, regardless of the stage being visible or not.*

ଓ ଓ ଓ

The scenic melodrama. Although there is only a single scenic[52] melodrama that is a true dramatic work, Fibich's monumental *Hippodamia* trilogy, we need to devote attention to it as a theoretically possible genre of dramatic art. We have defined it as a dramatic work *co-created by music* with *speaking* actors. This principally established that it is not "spoken drama with music" since the musical component truly "co-creates" it, just like drama does in opera – that is, the scenic melodrama creates not only musical personas but also musical interaction. However, the musical persona lacks the *singing part*, which creates its axis, as we know; what remains is only the orchestral part, but this is as binding for the actors as it is for the actor-singer in opera. The actor in the melodrama must conceive their figure according to the music (led, again, by the director-conductor, i.e., the conductor of the production). As far as the spoken part is concerned, the temporal bond with music is *not as strict* as in opera, although the bond exists, since the dramatic form of the work is completely determined by the music – that is, by the conductor's interpretation.

As for the acoustic aspect of the speech, there is – as we asserted in our discussion of singing – a *discrepancy* between the speech and music; this is the *only* weakness of melodrama – as acknowledged by Hostinský, an eminent theorist of the genre. This discrepancy does not pertain to the non-musical elements of speech (consonants), but of the musical ones: vowels are imperfect tones and therefore clash with the tones of the music. Hence the requirement, stressed by Hostinský, which contradicts the common assumptions: that the actor *should not* try to adjust melodically to the music to gloss over that discrepancy, but *on the contrary* the actor should retain the *independent character of speech* (excepting the moments that might call for it) with its specific tonal imperfections of the vowels as much as possible. Conversely, the actor would be randomly and arbitrarily trying to do what the composer could do, but *intentionally did not want* to do; in other words, the actor would be contravening the composer's intent. Similarly – with the appropriate exceptions (such as choral recitation in melodrama, just as in spoken drama) – the actor should retain the *rhythmic* imperfection of speech without trying to adjust it, randomly, to the rhythm. Melodramas in general, even concert ones, are an independent genre and do not tolerate a wilful approximation of speech. Even when a certain symbolic notation suggests a seeming melody (as in Schoenberg's *Gurre-Lieder*), this is only an indication of a *speech melody*, not of a musical melody proper.

---

52   This point illustrates Zich's prejudice in his aesthetic taste, by elevating Fibich's *Hippodamia*, written in a post-Smetanian style, as the only true *dramatic* melodrama. On melodrama, see the Annotated Glossary.

With these limitations, the same holds for scenic melodrama as for opera. A particularly interesting instance of this is the partial use of melodrama in Smetana's opera *Dvě vdovy*; Smetana makes use of simple *speech* as *another* kind of vocal expression, different from *singing*, to characterise the *reading* of Ladislav's letter to Anežka *aloud*.

Sound and music in spoken drama. Substantially different is the task of music in *spoken drama*. It cannot be said that it co-creates the dramatic work; it merely *prepares* or *supports* its *atmospheric effect* on the audience. One use is in *overtures* and *interludes*, but these – unlike in opera – cannot rise to dramatic significance because they lack the ostensive connection to the dramatic action. Another use is in the variety of musical *inserts* into the action itself: songs, choruses, melodramatic moments, marches, dances, etc. All of these are also used in opera and it is *always* necessary not to weaken the dramatic action too much by them.

Of principal difference is the use of music *on stage*, which corresponds to the functions of music in the real world. These are, for example, serenades, dances, funeral or military marches, church music (organ) and so on. Unless the musicians are hidden (off stage), they need to appear *as actors representing* musicians, or an illusion is used where an actor pretends that they are playing an instrument (a guitar, a piano, etc.), while the actual playing happens off stage (or in the orchestra). The principal difference is in that such music is *part of the dramatic action*, although it often serves no more purpose than heightening a lyrical moment. It follows that the primacy is with the associated *referential image* (*obrazová představa*) and *its* mood; the true musical mood is secondary. Based on the principle of dramaticity, there is no substantial difference between such music and the *nonmusical sounds* used in spoken drama (excepting, of course, the vocal expressions of individual actor figures). The howling wind, the roaring thunder, the trumpet fanfare, the beating of drums, weapons clashing, gunshots and so forth – all these primarily have an atmospheric effect based on *what they mean*, and only then a purely acoustic effect (which can be rather negligible anyway). So for instance, a mere knock at the door is nothing on its own; what affects us as an audience is the image associated with it: someone is coming – and that image is very different, depending on whether we anticipate a pleasant or a foreboding visit.

We have established in our previous analyses that the direct atmospheric effect of most *acoustic perceptions* is very intense and that the associated images are often not excessively concrete and clear, as long as these perceptions are on their own without auxiliary visual perceptions – which gives them a flair of mystery. It is understandable then that if spoken drama does not wish to overuse the aforementioned applications of music, which would turn it into a semi-dramatic genre of *"play with songs and dances"* (comparable to the "dramatic spectacle" or "melodrama" overusing stage technology), it will try to support its dramatic effects by making use of such nonmusical sounds that "do not mean anything"; they have a purely acoustic effect. With a view to the immense variety of sounds, this is surely a beneficial and productive thought. However, we must not forget that spoken drama, like dramatic art in general, is principally a *mimetic* art.

If we hear a (seemingly) *inexplicable* sound *from the scene,* where the scene *represents* the location of a dramatic action presented by actors *representing* certain personas, it is logical to ask: what does the sound *represent*? Since our experience has no answer, we have to assign the sound a *symbolic* meaning, in keeping with the sense of the action. The use of such sounds in spoken drama is therefore limited only to symbolic plays; opera does not need them at all, since its music will fully meet its needs.

THE PRINCIPLE OF STYLISATION

9 REALISM AND IDEALISM: THE BASIS OF THEATRICAL ILLUSION

In the first part of this book as well as in the second, we have frequently emphasised that dramatic art is a *mimetic* (*obrazové*) art, i.e., its works represent, picture something. It is not the only art of such kind: consider sculpture and painting, and in a sense also literary art (*básnictví*), especially of the epic kind (e.g., the novel). It is common to all these art forms *that their works* – whether things (e.g., a statue) or actions (e.g., an actor's playing) – *resemble certain objects* (things and actions) *from nature or life*. This resemblance is different in *degree* – sometimes great, sometimes small – and different in extent, pertaining to mere details, to certain units comprised in the work or even to the entire work. This resemblance can always be ascertained and it constitutes *an objective feature* of every mimetic work of art.

> Having discussed this literary art in the chapter on the dramatic text, it is clear that the resemblance in literary works is not *ostensive*, but only *imagined* (*myšlená*). When a landscape, a persona or an action are described, the similarity does not pertain to the *words* that are used to depict them but of that which is evoked by the *meaning* of those words, compared to what we know from our experience. In contrast, in painting, it pertains to the depicted landscape or persona, and in acting to the performed persona or action – that is to say, to the visible and the audible that I can *directly* compare with my memories (which are also ostensive).

Surely such an outer resemblance *in itself* evokes a pleasurable emotion in us – and it is all the more intense, the greater the resemblance. We recognise the *agreement* between a constructed work of art and something that we know from elsewhere from our own experience. The agreement with experience is what defines *material truth* as such (as opposed to formal truth, i.e., inner logical coherence); such works evoke the impression of *outer truthfulness* – which grows when resemblance is greater. To viewers unwittingly comparing the work of art to a similar object, it may seem as if the representation were a *copy* and the object that it resembles were the original. They may contentedly observe that the trees in the landscape or the fruit in a "still life" are painted "faithfully" and the joy of the agreement reaches its peak whenever the "original" is singular and known to us – for instance, in the case of a portrait. We also know the pleasure caused in society when someone excellently imitates the way of speaking and behaviour of a well known person. If the pleasurability of the agreement can be psychologically explained, so can the displeasure from a *disagreement* between a "copy" and an "original"; the work is then assumed to be unnatural, untruthful or altogether "failing" – as if it were a revealed truth that the artist wanted to copy nature or life. However, this is already shifting from a mere *fact* that mimetic works of art *are* resembling objects of nature or life, to a *requirement* that such works should *resemble* them and *as much as possible*. Such normative conception of works of art is called **naturalism**. This term, of course, relates only to mimetic arts; it would have no relevance to non-mimetic arts (such as architecture).

> The pleasure caused by the agreement between the copy and the original is not the only emotion evoked by naturalist works of art. Another is the emotion of *admiration* for the *craft* of the creator, who made a work that resembles some original so excellently. That is certainly not an ability everyone has; so, the above imitator of a known person's behaviour earns our praise not only for their creation but also for themself – they can do something not everyone is able to do. However, if we say that it is an *"art"* to do something like that, we are using the word in a *very broad* sense. "Art" is then also a juggling trick, a sports achievement, a medical operation and many other activities. It has to be remembered well if a certain achievement or work belongs to an artistic discipline. Drawing someone with a pencil or imitating someone's speaking and mimics to resemble them perfectly *is not by itself* an artistic feat of the visual arts or performance, respectively. That requires more, namely *creative* activity.

It is unsurprising then that for the basis of *artistic creation* in the mimetic arts a theory has formed that sees it as an *"imitation"* of nature or life. Let us remember well that the motto of *"naturalist creation"* (just like in the public's "naturalist understanding" of an artwork) turns around not only the requirement that the work should resemble something from our life experience (which is clearly necessary with mimetic artworks) but also the requirement that the work resemble it *as much as possible*. In other words, it is a creative *trend*, a *tendency* to *come as close* to nature and life as possible.

> It has to be noted that our definition of "naturalism" does not entail the association it habitually has, that it portrays only ugly things and actions. If naturalism has often done that it was because it found the life it embraced to be more bleak than shiny and because it was always intended as a reaction to the beautiful template of idealism. Of course it is possible to also portray naturalistically the many beautiful things that can be found in nature and life.
>
> It is no difficult thing to show that the naturalist motto is *entirely wrong* when it comes to artistic creation as well as to the conception of works of art. First and foremost, naturalism cannot apply to several major arts disciplines: architecture and construction (with its crafts and industry), music and dance. They have nothing to imi-

tate. And even if there were something to imitate, as is the case of mimetic arts, their material is so inconvenient that it renders a faithful imitation difficult and limited. Why should graphic arts exist when sculpture can faithfully deliver even the colour of the objects? Why are sculptures, naturalistically, not painted too? Why does music try, on occasion, to "paint" with its tones when it is much more easily done with other sounds? It is true though that in dramatic art – and more specifically in acting – the material is most convenient for a faithful imitation: a live human portrays a live human. A naturalist conception and creation in this instance suggest themselves the most. Let us therefore consider it in general terms.

The principal reason lies in the basis of artistic creation: *the more naturalistic an artist's work is, the less creative they are*. The most accomplished naturalism would therefore be entirely uncreative because it can be made *mechanically*, with the help of a machine. Instead of an etching or a painting, a photograph of a convenient object (even in full colour). Instead of a dramatic scene, a filming of a convenient event from life. However, nobody considers this a work of art although it is undoubtedly the summit of outer truthfulness.

In the history of art, nonetheless, the naturalist motto of "imitating nature", "a return to nature", etc. has appeared from time to time. True, after a while a reaction to this trend comes along but it represses it only temporarily: it would reappear again, as a reaction to the governing template. It should be considered that many major artists have been advocates of said motto and that their artworks are of supreme artistic value. How is this possible then? What could explain it? The cause lies in the incorrect theoretical formulation of the issue. It is in fact a case of *returning* to nature and life, but not of *imitation*.

Nature and life – which we consider here, of course, without the *art itself*, although its works influence artists too – are for said artists no more than *a source of their invention*, a source so endless that each of them can exploit it anew for their entire lives without depleting it for others and for the future. Nature and life contain an infinite amount of artistic values but their *regularities* (zákonitost) are occluded by the immense complexity of things and by random influences that almost totally disrupt them. In order to arrive at these values, artists must simplify and purify the natural and real-world phenomena by selecting and highlighting only that which captures their interest, while overlooking the rest. Everyone sees something different in it depending on their inclinations: it is not dissimilar to the impressionist dictum that it is "nature seen by a temperament". The movement of artistic creation that *proceeds* from nature and life *moving away* from it by *purposely changing* the chosen objects, without disrupting the resemblance with the "original", is called artistic **realism**. The basis of realism is, again, in a tendency, a trend of creation: to *move away* from nature and life only as far as the mimetic art allows, while the often-quoted "similarity" remains a necessary requirement.

This is a tendency opposite to that of naturalism, which attempts, despite the limited means of each art form, to move closer to the objects given by our experience. This can be expressed in a schema:

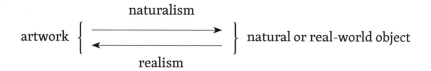

Realism is a fully *artistic* movement because the above "moving away" – that is, the *change* of the objects given by our experience, a change that is not only necessary, i.e., given by the techniques of an artistic discipline, but also *free*, determined by the artist – is the *creative* moment of the artist's work. Despite this freedom of creation, the change is not arbitrary or blind, but purposeful (*účelná*), aiming – as we have seen – to present in the work of art and as best as can be, the *ostensive regularity* (*názorná zákonitost*) of a chosen section of the artist's experience. We will call this purposeful change the *artistic **stylisation*** of the objects portrayed by the artist.

There is yet a second method of artistic creation, which would best be called "expressionism" if that word had not already been taken – just like impressionism – to mean more narrowly a specific historic style; let us use the word that has a more general meaning: **idealism**.

> Neither here are we using the word *idealism* to refer to something beautiful, our "ideal" (cf. the above narrow concept of naturalism). The artist's idea of something does not always have to be "beautiful" in the narrower sense of the word, but for instance, chararacteristic.
>
> Idealist artists do not proceed from their outer experience but from their *inner one* and they form their artworks according to their fantasy, that is with utter freedom. That is surely also the way artists create in non-mimetic arts (architecture, music, dance), but also many of those in mimetic arts. Such art works are entirely *dissimilar* to any natural or real-world things. Such creative method might seem principally different from the preceding one; when it comes to mimetic arts, which requires "similarity", it might seem entirely inadmissible – if it were entirely true what we have written of their "dissimilarity". In fact, the difference is gradual (in degrees).

No artist can create only from themself. Their material must be given by *outer experience* – both directly, i.e., ostensively, and indirectly, mediated through certain ostensive markers (*značky*), especially through speech. As far as non-mimetic arts are concerned, this material is provided by their artistic disciplines, e.g., music; in the case of literary art, it is in fact life itself who teaches us by speech. For mimetic arts, the source of invention is also the appropriate artistic discipline; apart from that, the source is in other outer experiences, nature and life. The only difference is in that the idealist artistic – in contrast to the realist – uses *only* minor *elements* of their outer experience, only as mere "material" out of which they compose *wholes* through fantasised combinations; these wholes are *new* and cannot be found in nature or life because they do not exist there. In *objective* terms, idealist creation differs from realist creation only *quantitatively*: the former appropriates *only* details, the latter *also* the wholes. They differ therefore not so much in degree but rather in the *extent* of similarity of their artworks to nature or life. There is also a *psychological* difference in that the empirical *origin* and *relation* to outer experience is conscious for the realist and unconscious for the idealist – which is, with a view to their comparison, completely understandable. To the outside it appears as if the realist worked according to a specific *model* (or models), while the idealist without them (apparently at least).

> For instance, Shakespeare's Falstaff is a realistic persona; although it may not seem so to us, it certainly did to Shakespeare's audiences, who – jointly with the author – knew many such companions from life. However, it is not impossible that Shakespeare *compounded* the features of several persons and created a type. Similarly, it would also have been possible that there he had a particular model in mind that compounded all of these features already. Is not this similar to Strindberg's Miss Julie in our times? In contrast, Shakespeare's Caliban is surely no realistic persona and there is nothing in our experience that is or could be similar to him. And yet – we are well aware that Caliban is a *combination* of several low human features and animal qualities; both of them are well known to us, but not their compound. This monster is neither "truthful", nor *"verisimilar"* – which is how the realist requirement is often formulated. Despite all this, Caliban is composed of elements of outer *experience* just like the above personas *because there is no other way.*

The psychologically self-evident principle asserting that if not all *objects*, then certainly the *material* of the artist's creative work (i.e., the elements that compound objects) originate *always and exclusively* from the artist's *outer experience* will be called *the principle of artistic empiricism*. When it comes to the artist, outer experience needs to be divided into two: their experience of *art* – which is essential for an artist who creates *non-mimetically* – and their experience of *nature and life* – which is essential for artists creating *mimetically*, i.e., including *works of dramatic art*. Mimetic artworks always retain a relation of similarity with their corresponding natural and art objects, but its extent and degree varies; that is, the *distance* (the moving away) – what we have called *stylisation* – is lesser or greater. In a diagram:

```
natural or            ────────▶  a realist mimetic work
real-world object     ────────▶  an idealist mimetic work
```

It would be enough to add other dramatic personas to our examples above to see that they will form a continuous range in which the degree of similarity and with it the reciprocal degree of distance from life will change *gradually*. The very word "similarity" suggests a partial identity – and *simultaneously* a partial difference, while it is the former that is stressed. Since the principle of artistic empiricism stresses in *mimetic* art the necessity for this *natural and real-world similarity*, we can refer here to the imperative of "relative realism". When applied to dramatic art, this is the principle that follows: *All creators of a dramatic work – the dramatist, the actors, the director and potentially the dramatic composer – must be* **relative realists**.

Analogous conclusions as with our discussion of artistic creation will be arrived at when studying the *artistic perception* of mimetic artworks. That is completely understandable because perception is in fact a mental process reversing the creation of the work (from the artist's mind to the work, from the work to the viewer's mind); the ideal outcome is that the beginning and the end of this dual process should agree as much as possible. The principle of *artistic empiricism* is valid here too: if an artwork is to *evoke* in us a referential image (*obrazová představa*), this mental image *must be in our mind* – if not in its entirety, then in its details or components at least. Otherwise the image would fail to be evoked. That is psychologically self-evident. This mental image or its parts can be gained only through *outer experience* – either directly (through ostension; *názor*) or indirectly (communicated by others), which in fact takes us back to ostension again, since that was how we once learned speech – our primary means of communication.

If we turn to the *ostensive* outer experience as not only the original, but also the experience particularly crucial for art, we can conclude: apart from the above *subjective* condition that requires that the needed referential image be present in the observer's mind, the *objective* condition needs to also be met, that the artwork is *ostensively similar* to this image as a whole or in its parts, because its *direct* evocation is only possible on the basis of the associative principle of similarity. If I see something on stage that should represent something, for instance a tree, I must not only know from my own ostensive observation what a "tree" looks like, but the onstage object must *resemble* a tree. That is clearly a *principal* thing, because it is the condition necessary for creating the referential image. What the *degree* and *extent* of this similarity should be is not principally set – apart from its boundary: the similarity must not be so small as to stop being a similarity; no referential image would then be evoked.

It is surely natural that whenever the scenic object in question (to stay with our example) will evoke the mental image of a "tree" in the spectator, the image will become the *leading* norm, which will serve as an "original" of sorts against which the scenic object is measured as a "copy" of a tree. The requirement following from such a unilateral understanding of the arising relation of similarity "from a (remembered) original to a (seen) copy" would be that the copy should resemble the original as much as possible. Such a tendency, as we know, means naturalism. However, in comparison to *objective* naturalism, requiring that the copy *were* like the original, what is at play here is *subjective* naturalism, which requires that copy *looked* like the original. That is in itself a sufficient condition since the entire reproductive processed (itemised above) takes place in the observer's consciousness. This subjective naturalism pertaining to the perceptions of the artwork (or of its parts) will be called *illusionism*. A copy must evoke a *seeming*, an *illusion* of the original. And since the original is given by a memory of an object from our outer experience, that from "real" life, the illusionist requirement can be formulated as a requirement that the mimetic work or its part must evoke *an illusion of reality*. Perhaps there is no other discipline of mimetic arts where this requirement is more obvious than in dramatic art – or generally, in theatre art. And yet it is, as we shall see, as incorrect as the requirement of objective naturalism. This is again down to the unfounded formulation that refers to "reality".

☙ ☙ ☙

THE THEATRICAL ILLUSION

The peculiar mental state we are in while watching a theatre performance has been the subject of many studies. The most common is the view that it is an unceasing *wavering* between a belief that what we can hear and see is reality, and a disbelief incurred by realising the "true" reality that we are in the theatre (Hippolyte Taine). One speaks of moments that support the illusion and those that disturb it, and of our *conscious* suppression of disbelief, of our self-delusion (Carl Lange). The illusion is fed by everything that increases the similarity between what I can perceive from the stage and reality. The illusion is disturbed by everything that reminds us of the theatre, such as the frame of the stage (the arch), the proscenium, the auditorium, our neighbours, etc.

The psychological falsehood of these theories of wavering between our consciousness of reality and unreality can be easily demonstrated when observing oneself during a performance – or even just by remembering our experience of a show. However much we are enthralled by the scene, we do not *at all* hold the consciousness, conviction or belief that what the actors are playing is "reality". Consequently, we cannot and do not hold the idea that this *is not* reality. This much is certain: the perceptions offered by the scene, by virtue of their similarity, evoke in us mental images we have from outer experiences (i.e., from "reality") and we compare the two. But this is only with a view to their *similarity*, not their *reality* – and that is a different thing. Similarly, a water sprite appearing on stage may recall a memory of a similar water sprite painted by someone (e.g., by Schwaiger[53]). If occasionally we do get an idea that "this is like for real", such as when the similarity is striking, it is no more than a theoretical reflection – a critique and a thoroughly *unartistic* one at that – and this thought leads us away from the scene. Even an audience that has an inclination towards such judgements (cf. our discussion of the pleasures of similarity) prefers to leave such comments for the interval. This never occurs to us when we are riveted by the performance, but only later, when the thrill subsides. In other words, the most perfect dramatic enjoyment occurs without any thought of reality – whether positive or negative.

What takes place on stage is neither reality, nor unreality for us, but a *different* reality from the one we live: it is an artistic – in this case *theatrical* – reality. In aesthetics this other reality is often referred to as "*apparent* reality". This concept, although metaphysically often discussed, has not been so far sufficiently studied from the point of psychology. Let us ask therefore what is to the *perceiver* the difference between this "apparent" and the "real" reality? How do my impressions differ if I have, for instance, overheard a quarrel between two people as a chance observer, and as an audience member watching it on stage? Let us assume that I have observed only these two people, not their environment – at least not the more distant one (which is, in the latter case, the "theatrical framing"). It is only with this assumption that we can arrive at the true cause of the different impression – since here the *perception is identical, and yet* the impression is different.

We could assume that the perception of theatre, which we certainly had *before* the start of the show, associates as a recollection (a remembered image) with all the consequent perceptions coming from the stage, although we no longer notice the "theatrical framing". This could perhaps explain the difference between the two impressions – but we are unaware of any of this, particularly not if we are truly absorbed in the play. Here and there some detail may remind me of "being in theatre", but it is exactly this *reminding* that shows that I am not aware of it all the time. Besides: this association with "being in theatre" would not be enough to explain the basis of the "apparent" reality. If the actors take their bows together with the author, this is not only an apparent reality for us – and this is the same if I am watching a pure ballet (i.e., not a dramatic pantomime) or a theatre concert with the orchestra on stage, even if I were constantly aware of the fact that all this is on the theatrical scene.

---

53   Hanuš Schwaiger (1854–1912) was a Czech painter and graphic artist. Apart from a series of portraits and paintings with historical and etnographic themes, he is best known for his illustrations of Czech mythology and fairy tales.

If the difference is neither in the perception, nor in the associations, it can only be in *a different conception* of the same perception. In one instance I conceive said quarrel between the two people like everything in the real world, i.e., as something real: this is the *actuality* conception (*skutečnostní pojetí*). In the other instance, as something that is presented, played: this is the *theatrical* conception. This latter is a special case of a *mimetic* (*obrazový*) conception, which is found in all mimetic arts, and it is only a *different* kind next to the above actuality (or real-world) conception, but not *opposed* to it, i.e., not "unreal". It is a mental state in which we neither think of reality, nor have a special *"sense of reality"* (that is, *outer* reality), which otherwise accompanies us throughout most of our lives, being absent only in certain abnormal circumstances, for instance when we are extremely tired (not to mention certain illnesses). It may happen then that everything we perceive – especially what we can see – passes us by as if in alienation and at a distance, and everything seems "like a dream", as we say. Dreams are not the same because we can often have a very intense sense of reality in dreams – and we are often glad to awake, relieved that "it was not really true in the end".

There are also mental states when the sense of (outer) reality is not entirely suppressed, but only weakened. The above example of states of tiredness surely reminds everyone of many similar instances, only without the exhaustion. These are certain states of *daydreaming* or *contemplation* incurred in us by objects we perceive and immerse ourselves in – e.g., a landscape, the interior of a church and others. Clearly, this is an *aesthetic state* evoked in us by beautiful objects. The sense of reality is significantly weakened but does not pass entirely: it remains as if in the background and re-enters as soon as our aesthetic perception is over, and we "return to everyday reality".

> What is this sense of outer reality psychologically? Without any doubt it is closely linked to our sense of our *own* reality – or more accurately, the reality of our *"physical self"*, which is a sum of all our somatic perceptions, because our physical self belongs half to the "outer world" and half to the inner one; it is half object, half subject, and therefore a mediator between the two. Our inner somatic percepts are what evokes a sense of our reality (though only of the physical one) and all the perceptions that fit among them – primarily the *haptic* ones – acquire the same character of reality (of the external kind). Acoustic perceptions and especially visual ones (unless they are too intense) do not have the said somatic character – and therefore not the one of actuality. For that reason, art – which aims to evoke aesthetic states in us – limits itself to the visual and the acoustic. For that same reason, they play a key role in natural beauty too.

We have stated that the aesthetic state is evoked in us by beautiful objects. However, this process is not as exclusively passive as it may seem from this sentence. It is just like with unwitting and intent attention: *we ourselves* can bring ourselves to the aesthetic state if we wish to do so; a beautiful object is what prompts it. This is how *aesthetic focus* (*estetické zaměření*) as such arises; depending on its object, it may further specialise into an *artistic focus* (*umělecké zaměření*) or even more narrowly to *mimetic* focus (*obrazové zaměření*), or ultimately – in our discipline – to a *theatrical* focus (*divadelní zaměření*). Let us discuss only the last two.

Mimetic focus as well as its special case, *theatrical focus*, differ from general aesthetic focus in two aspects. First, if the focus is perfect, the sense of reality is *entirely suppressed*. Second, as we have seen previously, in this focus our interpretation of the perception is *twofold* because what is evoked in us is a *technical* image (*technická představa*) as well as a *referential* image (*obrazová představa*). Both of these aspects are interconnected; in fact, *two* different interpretations happening *at once* in a conception of "actuality" would be contradictory.

> The fact that *my* (i.e., subjective) perception *X* is "actually" *A* signifies my conviction of the objectively real existence of this *A*. The same is true if the same perception *X* is "actually" *B*. Given that in *viewing* they have to be *singular* concepts, which being subjected to their shared concept of an *actually* existing thing, necessarily exclude one another, there can only be disjunction between them. For example, I see something dark in the twilight of the wood. My interpretation is twofold: "It is (some actual) bush", *or* "it is (some actual) tramp"; it is either one, or the other, but not both. If I accept the latter, I exclude the former. If I conclude eventually that it is the former, the latter is untrue – it was a *delusion*. Delusion therefore always has a relationship to reality. On the contrary, if I see a statue, I assert: "It is a statue" *and* "it is some person", because these concepts are not of the same category of actually existing things (that is only true of the statue), and therefore they *do not exclude* one another. Said "some person" belongs to the category of things that exist only ideally (in thought) – in my mind. That and *only* that is what I express when I say that "this is a statue representing a person". I have no thought of reality or non-reality here as long as I am *aesthetically focused*. The case would be different if focused on the statue *only technically*; in that eventuality I would view it in no way differently than an artificially shaped column of marble – which naturally does not represent anything.
>
> In dramatic art, I can therefore say: this is actor *A* and *at the same time* King Lear, because this is *a mere interpretation* of the perception, whereas I have no thought of real existence during the performance itself (and it is only the "actor" who has such real existence). There can be no talk of "delusion" here because said interpretation is already twofold and makes no claim to empirical truth value, i.e., correspondence with reality. For that same reason it cannot be said that actor A is an "*untrue*" king. That could only be said of an impostor who pretends to be a real king without being it; we would then believe either one thing, or the other about him, but not both at once. A considerable grace of the actor's art is that they can be someone other than they are without lying.

It could possibly be said that this actor is an *"apparent"* king, but not with the negative connotation of the word, suggesting that he *is not in reality* what he appears to be, but only in the sense of a *mere appearance*, without any relation to reality, because to our sense he actually *does appear to be king* in that he resembles him in all his appearance (optically and acoustically). Everything on the scene is "apparent" in this sense, but not "apparently real" nor "false". One can speak of "false brilliants" only when someone wears them in society, but not if they are worn by a dramatic persona; they are, just like the persona, only apparent. Their actual genuineness, and for that matter, *the genuineness or falseness of all onstage objects is a moot point*; that is only a practical question. Similarly, just like "being apparent" we also need to narrow down the broad sense of the word "illusion" or "illusiveness", which is often evoked exactly in relation to reality.

It follows from our discussion: *The basis of the so-called theatrical illusion lies in the theatrical focus, which – as a special case of the mimetic focus – suppresses the sense of reality and evokes to perceptions a dual conceptual image, the technical and the referential.*

That this is in no way an illusion in the sense of false reality can be seen particularly clearly in that the onstage world of the theatre that appears before us deploys such illusions – delusions. These are the notorious motifs of dissembling and especially *disguise*. Consider Shakespeare's *Twelfth Night*: an *actress* represents *Viola*, who disguises herself as a *noble gentleman*. Our perception evokes three mental images: the technical and then two referential images. It is clear that the relationships

actress – Viola
Viola – noble gentleman

are not of the same kind. Only the gentleman is "false" and Viola's act is a "delusion", but not Viola and the actress's act. The other dramatic personas surely know nothing about the actress (unlike the other actors), while we are aware of her all the time.

An analysis of the theatrical focus

We can illustrate the process of the theatrical focus tellingly with this analogy. Composers record their musical ideas by means of notes placing them on a five-line staff. Their position determines the pitch relationships between individual notes: what these notes are is indicated by the "clef" at the start of the staff. Since there are many notes, more clefs are needed too, most commonly the violin clef and the bass clef. Depending on which clef stands at the start of the line, we read or play differently what looks like *the same* notes (i.e., the same perception), and the melodies or chords are different. How is that possible? It is due to the different *notation focus* that we acquired in our musical *training*. First we learned to read notes in the violin clef by associating each note with a certain idea of the played note (e.g., the note on the second line from the bottom is g on the piano or the violin; the one on the top line is f and so on). This is how we secured a firm *set* of double associations (a note in a score with a musical note), which we committed to memory; we shall call it the "violin" set. Later we similarly learned how to read the bass clef, often confusing it with the preceding "violin" conception of the same notes. Eventually we established a new "bass" set and also committed it to memory. Whenever we read notes, we recall the notes on the basis of the set as signalled by that clef or another. Physiologically, this different focus could be explained as somehow *opening up* a different path leading to the brain cells in which that set is fixed, while *closing down* the path to the other set. This physiological process can explain an otherwise very peculiar fact that we are able to conceive of *the same notes* once in one way, and then in another, *focused* towards it by the clef, which we then no longer think of – unless it changes and with it our conception changes too.

This outlined conception of notes according to their clefs may seem distant from theatrical conceptions, but both the cases are very similar. The only difference is that with notes both the conceptions are conventional, both requiring certain training and mental preparation. In contrast with theatre, only one conception is artificial, the theatrical conception, which requires a certain mental preparation and a special focus; the other conception, the *actuality* conception, is known to us commonly from our lives. The "clef" (or "key") to the theatrical focus is everything we perceive before the start of the play and often also during its opening: entering the theatre, the auditorium filled with the audience, the stage arch with the curtain, which *goes up at a given signal*. So the musician who has spent a long time reading notes in the violin clef is led by the prescribed bass cleff to read other notes differently although *they greatly resemble the previous ones* – which is equally true of theatrical perceptions, which greatly resemble our real-world perceptions. Just as musicians are kept in their new conception by recurring signals (the repetition of the clef at the start of each staff and other special indices), so are the theatrical spectators sustained in their conception by occasional observations (e.g., the stage frame, the proscenium arch, etc.). However, both musicians and spectators are merely *kept* in their focus – although even that is *unnecessary*. It will nevertheless be clear from what we have discussed *why* the above observations (which are often joined by others from the stage itself) that keep reminding us that we are in the theatre *are not* moments that *disturb* the "theatrical illusion" (as some of the above theories would like to claim), but rather enhance it because they keep us in the theatrical focus. And finally: just like when a musician comes across the violin clef and abandons the current conception of notes and returns to the first conception, so does the theatre audience recognise certain perceptions – *the closing of the scene by the lowered curtain*, the noise of the audience leaving the auditorium and others – as impulses to abandon the current theatrical focus and return to the usual conception of actuality.

As soon as we understand the issue along these lines, the difference between reality and theatrical illusion shifts to a difference between two sets of conceptual images that govern one or the other conception. As we have asserted, the actuality conception requires no special mental preparation and therefore no *special* set of conceptual images: that comes together with *all* the sets of images that we have acquired from life (that is, naturally, with the exception of the theatre!). The only issue at stake then is the set of images that controls our theatrical conception. The situation is very simple: we acquire a set of these images through contact with the *theatrical* or *dramatic art*.

Attending theatrical performances we get acquainted with a great number of dramatic personas and dramatic events (action) and their "locations". They are mostly *imaginary* although they remind us, in details at least, of many things we know from our real-world experience. The difference between the above "musical note" set and this acquired "theatrical" set is not only a greater complexity of the mental images but principally the fact that each theatrical perception is associated with two conceptual images (*významová představa*): the technical and the referential. This generally means the following associative bonds:

(1) "*actor figure – dramatic persona*" (acronym: f/p)
(2) "*actor interaction – dramatic action*" (i/a)
(3) "*theatrical scene – location of action*" (s/l)

Each of them further breaks down into many more detailed bonds, discussed in our analyses in Chapters 4 to 8.

> Since we are experiencing dramatic works as specific performances, between many of these specific bonds there is only *partial* identity or at least similarity, according to which they are grouped more narrowly. In this was all f/p and i/a bonds that have *the same dramatic text* (literary or even musical) grouped very tightly together. Such groups then receive a name from the author of a text, a title and its personas. For example, Shakespeare's Iago or Smetana's Kecal (played by anybody), Goldoni's *The Fan* or Mozart's *Die Entführung aus dem Seraglio* (irrespective of the production). In comparison to this, every specific artwork of such a group differs significantly when it comes to acting or the staging, unless the author has equipped the text with many stage directions that must be respected by the actors and the directors. Specific f/p bonds can also be more narrowly grouped by *the same actor* (or singer), e.g., Eduard Vojan's or Emmy Destinn's personas[54], and finally the i/a and the s/l bonds can be grouped by the *same stage director*, potentially with their scenic collaborator (scenographer) or more

---

54 Eduard Vojan (1853–1920) was a leading Czech actor and the foremost representative of the psychological-realistic style at the National Theatre in Prague. Emmy Destinn (Ema Destinnová, the artistic name of Emilie Paulina Jindřiška Kittlová, 1878–1930) was a world-renowned Czech opera singer, a dramatic soprano, who sang in leading opera houses in Berlin, Bayreuth, London and New York, and eventually also at the National Theatre in Prague.

broadly by the same theatre company, e.g., Stanislavski's productions, Mahler's opera productions at the Viennese Burgtheater, etc.

The fact that the above bonds also contain the technical images, especially images of actors known and unknown, but also images of scenic objects, helps explain the often experienced thing: that our "theatrical illusion" not only tolerates the awareness that the imaginary persona is played by an actor, that the house on the side is a stage wing and so on, but that we can also dedicate a great amount of attention to the performance of that specific actor without any disturbance – although it should actually ruin our illusion, alerting us to "reality". Our theatrical focus is not disturbed by any of this, but rather enhanced – unless of course our interest suppresses the referential image too much into the background. That does occasionally happen to theatre professionals when watching a performance: their perception is then (almost) exclusively technical, just like when merely watching ballet.

The Isolation of the Dramatic Work. If we have asserted that the theatrical focus is evoked in us by forming a (probably physiological) connection with the "theatrical set" of the images acquired through our theatrical experience, then this seems like a vicious circle. What stands at the start of such an experience? If someone came to the theatre for the very first time and without preparation, where would they be getting their theatrical conception from, which is based on the *double* image of what "is" and simultaneously what is "represented"? Would they be looking at the performance only in the sense of what it "is"?

We could point out that such double conception is present with all mimetic arts, and that it is well known and common to all of us for instance from sculpture and painting. But in these disciplines the difference between the technical and referential images is so great that they cannot be mistaken for one another, let alone taken for being identical. No one will think that a statue actually *is* the young man it represents or would take even the most realistic painting of a landscape for the landscape itself – unless in a momentary lapse. In comparison, the image of the actor figure agrees with the image of the dramatic persona to such an extent that the said mistake is easily possible; we asserted in the opening part of this book that these two images are often mixed up in *theory*. Not so in practice, unless in error. Travelling theatre troupes have frequently had the experience with very primitive audiences, who were so seduced by the naturalism of their performance that they, for instance, considered the actor playing a villain for a truly evil person and then endangered him with life threats. They identified the figure with the persona.

This can also explain why *primitive, folk* theatre tends to a more marked *ostensible* difference between the figure and the persona, the interaction and the event (action), and especially between the scene and the location of the action than in the culturally more developed theatre. In other words, this is what the *mistaken* claim says – a mistake caused by the illusive view of dramatic art – that primitives will make do with a mere *hint* of reality, which can no longer satisfy us. Another *mistake* is to praise those who profess an entirely stylised theatre, pointing to primitives as their models. As we have emphasised in the chapter on the dramatic text, when discussing improvised plays, this is an issue of the *development* of dramatic art. Its beginnings *need* this ostensive difference of the technical and referential images, approximating dramatic art (in this aspect) to the *visual arts* (*výtvarné umění*). It is enough to remember the motionless masks and the almost entirely neutral scene of classical Greek drama and so on.

The best known example of this is our *puppet theatre* with its many variants. Here the actor is made of wood, its play is incomplete and mechanical; the difference between the figure and the persona is maximal. One can therefore distinguish two possible alternatives of the conception and the impression from the side of the audience. Either we emphasise that that "figure" is unlive and mechanical; then the fact that it represents a live being has a laughable effect. This is the common *comic* type of puppet theatre (the funny persona of Kašpárek). Or we emphasise the live dramatic persona; then the fact that the figure is unlive and only mechanical has a peculiarly uncanny or even horrid effect (cf. the tale of the Golem). This is the second, *mystical* type of puppet theatre, such as for Maeterlinck's plays. That puppet theatre can be exquisitely stylised in a visual way is therefore apparent (cf. page 96).

Each of us has had a primitive preparation for the theatrical focus since our earliest childhood. It arises from the imitative instinct as well as from the pleasure of mentally transfiguring into others, as we have discussed in Chapters 4 (the dramatist's creative work) and 5 (the actor's creative work). Children play mum and dad, soldiers and gangsters, shopkeepers, school and so on. They play themselves and can see others play too. What makes do for their "properties" and their "stage" is well known. The *bifurcation* of one's "self" into the player and the played, and in their own effort into the performing and the performed is intuitively known to them, and they also understand it in others. The difference between a boy "doing" a soldier and a stage supernumerary playing a soldier is not substantial, but only formal; perhaps the boy even feels more courageous in his "role". So even a child knows these preliminary "actorly" and "theatrical" impressions from their own experience, so they will not find themself confronted with something entirely new when they enter the theatre. The child might be surprised by the excessive similarity with reality, which was not the case in child's plays; but it is enough to tell the child that this is "just a play" – and the orientation is in place. The child immediately knows how to conceive of it because they remember from their past a set of such *double* images, creatively constructed by the child and others.

Nonetheless, with a view to the desirable and necessary similarity between the technical image of the work and the referential one – which also necessarily derives in its details from nature and the real world – it is *essential* with every mimetic work to *isolate it* (or set it apart) from its environment to indicate visibly to everyone *how far this mimetic work extends* and where it is no more. This *isolation* from its non-mimetic environment is secured for a statue by its plinth and for a painting by its frame. In dramatic art this is defined by the *framing of the scene*, which is done (from the audience's perspective) by the proscenium arch and the curtain, and once the curtain is up, by the ideal space extending from the *proscenium*. What is before the proscenium or before the neutral space of the orchestra pit is the real world. Whatever is behind the proscenium is a world that is not unreal but *exempt from real-world actuality* as something *apart* from it. If we wish, we can refer to it as the world of another, artistic and specifically "theatrical" reality. It is an actuality that is parallel with real-world actuality, corresponding to it, but *noetically other and heterogeneous*.

> It is *completely inadmissible* to mix the onstage world with the auditorium world. If French courtiers once used to sit on the stage, it was only dull etiquette. If experiments are done nowadays to have actors appear in the auditorium, it is an artistic absurdity. Only the spaces for the orchestra can be used in one way or another because it is neutral. We addressed this when discussing the scene, and we also observed in our analysis of orchestral music that while it can be linked to dramatic personas, it still retains a certain impersonal quality. Actors in the auditorium cease to be dramatic personas; they are entertainers. Combining the stage with the auditorium creates a space that *does not represent anything*; it simply *is*, and little more than an interior where people, lay and professional, entertain themselves. Dance art would tolerate this but not dramatic art, which is mimetic: that simply *vanishes*, turning into actual, though aesthetically modified life – like in a carnival, for instance. Such experiments did not arise from art but a social ideology: "art for life". Fair enough, but if art is to be for life, then *it must remain art*, not *turn* into life.

೦೪ ೦೪ ೦೪

What are the *stylistic principles* that govern the entire *creation of a dramatic work* with a view to its relationship to nature and the real world? We have already asserted the first one:

(1) *The principle of relative realism.* In this principle we have claimed that the technical components of a dramatic work *must* generally *resemble* certain natural and especially *real-world* phenomena, but the degree of their resemblance is *arbitrary*. Only such dissimilarity is inadmissible that would fail to evoke a referential image and such similarity that the artwork would only be

a copy of reality, i.e., it would be naturalistic. This applies to *all* components of the dramatic work apart from music (that is, in opera): as we have seen, music as an entirely constructed material delimits any such resemblance; this is compensated by the fact that a referential image can be evoked according to the principle of concurrence. This is all the more true of language, but that can be counted as a real-world phenomenon.

> The assertion about the "naturalistic" artwork needs to be taken carefully. Many great dramatic works were seen as naturalistic by everyone, even by their creators: in the era when this movement was dominant, this was an expression of praise, but when the counter-movement arrived, it was its shame. It was only the third period that acknowledged that they possessed great creative values and that they clearly stylise – in short, that they are realistic works. This is likely also for those components that they neglect. Knowing that some great actor of the past would once *have an immense effect* on their audience, their performances could not have been naturalistic, although people called them that. The name by itself does not prove anything.

The *degree of resemblance* and its opposite counterpart: the *degree of stylisation* is determined by what the *author* of the work fixed in the *dramatic text*. As for the degree, the author was *free* to decide, but for everyone else this degree of stylisation is obligatory and must be respected. As for this requirement that follows from the principle of a work's *stylistic consistence*, let us call it the principle of **consistent stylisation** (*princip stejnoměrné stylisace*). Again, we need to qualify it for the musical component because for music, which is detached from the real world, the range of the stylisation scale occurs in *a different niveau* than other components, as we shall see below.

Since the *musical-dramatic text* (i.e., the score of an opera) fixes the composer's creative work together with the librettist's, the degree of *its* stylisation is obligatory for the stylisation of the opera's other components, especially since it also fixes aspects of the stage director's and actors's creative work.

The principle of consistent stylisation, as self-evident as it is, is very often sinned against by theatrical creative work in the narrower sense of the word, i.e., by actorly and scenic creative work. This work is obviously "of its age", that is creative work of *the presence*. It therefore complies with the style incumbent in its age or – if these are experimental artists – by the desired style of a future age; however, it is always with one single style, which said artists believe to be the exclusively appropriate style. Dramatic texts – literary or musical – that serve as a basis for such theatrical creative work are not taken only from the present era but also from the past, governed by a different style. So it happens almost by default that in the time of governing realism, let alone naturalism, even idealist works are played and staged naturalistically or illusively, and conversely, when the idealist, stylised style governs, textually realist works get stylised – both of this is *equally unjustified* and often dramatically completely nonsensical.

The principle of consistent stylisation is given not only aesthetically but also *psychologically*: by the *consistency* and the *persistence* of our *theatrical focus*. So, for instance, if the first impression of the personas is idealistic, we will start summoning the necessary referential associations from the set of experiences distant from the real world, which immediately come to create a kind of "ready-at-hand". We do not mind then if the other component, e.g., the scene, is also stylised and we are unsurprised by "the most impossible" action (e.g., in a fairy tale). However, if the first impression is realistic, this activates sets of images close to the real world; it is understandable then that, for instance, a stylised location of action finds itself in *contradiction* to the associations of *exactly these* sets, which leads to an impression of awkwardness or even incomprehensibility. Both applies for the duration of the work, or at least for its continuous section, because the transition from one focus to another is difficult for us – an interval is needed here (e.g., in Hauptmann's *Hannele*). The transition from an *idealistic* to a *realistic focus* is easier because the realistic is easier and more common to the audience. However, this also depends on the conventions of a certain era. In contrast, the idealistic focus tolerates realistic features more easily because they give no rise to contradictions. Either of the two foci can be of a different *degree* (cf. the realism-idealism diagram on p. 339) and looks to sustain it.

A naturalistic play and an illusive scene suffer from an excess of *details*, for instance, arising from the fixed idea "like in reality!" But detailed and secondary features threaten to obscure and occlude the features that are central and pertain to the whole. The *principle of artistic economy* requires that the artwork should be as simple as it possibly can be; it is therefore only relative but it expresses a *tendency* that has to be respected by every artistic creative work, including the dramatic. If the above mentioned details are such that the *dramatic action* fixed *in the text* is enhanced by them, such details are appropriate, irrespective of whether it was the author who suggested them in the stage directions, or the actors and the stage director added them of their own accord. If such details do not support the action, let alone if they harm it, they are inadmissible even if they originated with the work's own author because the author is also bound by the creative economy principle.

> This applies to the excessively detailed descriptions of personas and places of action in naturalistic dramas – not to those that are allegedly "impossible" (that is the stage director's task to make it possible) but to those that are of no use to the personas and the action. Among such unnecessary details are the many "nuances" of naturalistic actors – of course not those that elucidate the dramatic persona and become *incorporated* into the action with that irresistable impression of the matter-of-fact or even necessity

(as we know it so well from the performances of great actors), but those that are *added* as if extra, self-indulgently, for the actor proper. As far as stage directing is concerned, this applies also to the notorious "bringing the scene to life" by various stooges and types that "illustrate the environment" just like plenty of decorative onstage objects – only because that is what happens in the real world. In respect of the theatrical scene (set), which is in its fixed part generally only a circumstantial, not a substantial component of the dramatic work, it is especially important that it do not impose itself too much – also when the scene is stylised.

It is understandable that realist plays have relatively numerous details even if they are limited to the necessary ones. This is not a concern because the audience's focus is closer to actuality. With idealist plays, which would even make do with a neutral scene, there are even in absolute numbers only very few details and they should not be multiplied, not even if they caused the work no harm. This is because the economy principle is very strict: applied to a dramatic work it requires only that which is *dramatically essential. Whatever is dramatically useless is also harmful*. In Sophocles's *Electra* or Smetana's *Libuše* the heroine *does not need* to be as psychologically elaborate as Ibsen's Hedda Gabler or the Electra of Richard Strauss; and therefore she *must not* be.

The issue applies also in reverse, which needs to be stressed especially nowadays. The details required by a realist dramatic work *must not* be left out and simplified because they are the integral parts of the dramatic personas and action. The structure of the theatrical scene, as required for instance by Ibsen's *The Wild Duck*, is connected to the action in all its details to such an extent that the objects that constitute it need to be seen as "functional". It cannot be simplified as one does, for example, with Maeterlinck's play *Pelléas et Mélisande*, not even to a "neutral" scene.

> A telling example are Wagner's operas, especially *Der Ring des Nibelungen*, which – although a myth in its subject matter – was written as well as composed by its author with a certain idea of illusive scene, and it is a continuing problem of opera stage directing to stylise it scenically – almost in contradiction to the author.

The second principle is actually a continuation of the first, presupposing as well as *narrowing* it:

(2) *The principle of subjective realism*. Let us recall what we have asserted of *"illusiveness"* as subjective naturalism in opposition to objective naturalism. If our first principle states that the resemblance between the dramatic object and our experience is necessary but its degree is arbitrary, then the second principle states that this resemblance is only *subjective*, i.e., that irrespective of its degree it is *the relationship between the percept and* **the audience's** experience. This then states two things:

(a) The dramatic object (persona, action, scene) does not need to *be* similar as a necessity, but must only *appear* to be so. The *audience's percept* must be similar; that is enough. This brings the difference between the technical and referential images, which we have previously touched upon when speaking of *"theatrical acoustics"* and *"theatrical optics"*. If an actor wants to be heard in a particular way, they need to speak differently; the scenic space might have only an illusion of depth and so on. Another consequence affects the material genuineness of the scenic objects and so on, as we discussed in detail in Chapter 7.

> It is well known to what absurd extremes scenic naturalism used to run, such as when requiring that the scenic objects in history plays were "genuine" as if they were museum artefacts.
>
> A very peculiar naturalist requirement was that the duration of the dramatic action should *exactly* match the time it would take "in reality" (known as "second-for--second style", e.g., in Strindberg's *Miss Julie*). First of all, this (exact!) action does not exist in reality but only in the theatre – so there is nothing to compare it to. This is also true even if the story is from reality. So for instance, the issue is not the history of Wallenstein, but Friedrich Schiller's Wallenstein. Besides, how much ideal (imagined) action, and therefore imagined time falls into the intervals! Second, we have shown that in experiencing the theatre, we do not think of actuality. This is self-evident with idealist works. With *realist* works, it might apply to shorter actions, whose objective duration we know from our experience. However, even in the real world we *measure time subjectively*; in the theatre we exclusively do so (see the section on "Dramatic Form" above, p. 223). The issue then is that the actor (or stage director) should *not obviate* the possible mismatch between the *technical* (a certain action of the actors) and the *referential durations* (the corresponding interaction of the personas). This then is a certain kind of "theatrical optics", which can deploy certain temporal delusions and illusions (e.g., the time packed with events seems longer). A precarious situation arises when we can *compare* in the theatre two *simultaneous* actions whose temporal *relation* we know from our experience. But even then the issue is that the difference should not be too obvious (e.g., the well-known instanteneous writing of letters). See also the chapter on "Dramatic Action" (p. 213).

The consequence relating to the above mentioned *details* is important. Nuances of speech and playing and scene finesses that the audience cannot observe from the auditorium are worse than useless: they simply *do not exist* for the audience. This is also how the requirement to *simplify* can be justified. This justification is psychological and has only relative validity. Which audience do we have in mind here, in the stalls or on the gallery? If it is said that for this reason everything should be played big, "al fresco", a large auditorium is presumed. But what should be done if the play is realistic and *requires* such details? It is clear that the primacy of dramaticity applies in such cases: the details need to be deployed, i.e., the play has to be produced in a small theatre, on what is known as an "intimate" stage.

(b) The relation of required resemblance is between the percept and the *audience's experience*. The efficacy of the dramatic work therefore depends also on that experience. This simple fact is well known to every actor but few dramatists or stage directors, who tend towards ideological concepts. But what is this "audience's experience" given that an audience comprises many individuals with personal experiences that are widely different? Clearly this can be no more than some average experience, common to all or at least most. Let us try to analyse it briefly.

Experience can be divided into *direct* – comprising all experiences that we gathered ourselves – and *indirect* – containing the experiences of others communicated to us in speech or writing: let us therefore rather call them "*learned knowledge*". Direct experiences can then be subdivided into inner and outer.

Inner experience is our *emotions and aspirations* that we have ever experienced. Education has little currency here, except for some special, elaborate mental states; the simple ones are common to everyone. What is needed to understand dramatic work is the causal bond between mental states that shaped the individual steps in our actions (behaviour). This bond as experienced by us has always appeared to us as *intuitively self-evident*. I told him in anger what I would otherwise never have said. Why did I act that way? I cannot say but I still feel that I simply *had to* act like that. This self-evidence of inner experience participates in the perceiving of dramatic work in my *empathising with* the dramatic personas' actions; it is the actors' task to *suggest* this experiencing to me. If they succeed, then the dramatic personas and their dramatic action have *an inner truth*. If they do not, they are not only untruthful but *entirely incomprehensible*. The requirement of **inner**, *psychological truthfulness of the work* is therefore **absolute**, not because the work's realism would require it (the work may well be most idealistic), but because it is required by the *identical (jednostejný) psychological organisation* of the audience, i.e., of humans in general.

Our *outer experience* is also subjectively self-evident but not the judgement that I derive from it in relation to something outer. We say "I have seen it with my own eyes, heard with my own ears" and these percepts are of course truthful to me, but their interpretation is no more than likely and I know well how often I have been mistaken, at least partly. Nonetheless, our outer experience is *very convincing*, but also very *varied* and unequally rich. Dramatists must remember this and many of them consciously narrow down the circle of their audiences to learned people. It is actors and stage directors who need to heed this even more. They create for the "here and now" and must therefore respect the average of their audience's outer experience here and now. Whenever in performance the audience encounters elements that are close to their outer experience, they will understandably ask that said elements resemble it *in the degree corresponding to how determinate they are in the dramatic text* (literary and musical).

> If the personas of the action are "mother and son" and the environment is rather vague, the audience will limit themselves only to their inner experience, but when the action is about a (present day) "builder" and his office, then they apply their outer experience and are justified to require that there be no contradiction in the play, nor in the staging. If Wagner's Siegfried whistles on a pipe he has just made of reed, the onstage reed must not be stylised beyond our recognition.

Learned knowledge on the contrary does not have the limited self-evidence of our inner experience. It is only based on our belief in the truthfulness of the authority we have it from, and even if we are "convinced" of it, it is still just a belief. Learned knowledge is theoretical, not ostensive. It is thin, incomplete, we lack it in many fields, and individuals in the audience differ from one another even more than in their inner experiences. Dramatic works, whose personas and action come from "somewhere and sometime else", usually turn toward such learned knowledge and they are not obliged to respect it in any of its components.

> If the author of a history play studies a certain stretch of history, they do so for their inspiration; if they are aspiring to some "truthfulness", that is very futile effort. It was whichever way the author presents it – or rather, we do not even ask for it. And if we happen to know that it was (allegedly) otherwise, nothing in us protests in such an elementary way as when there is a contradiction with our direct experience. The dramatist therefore has the indomitable right to change "historic reality" but this is only an artistic right. If this is done on purpose (ideologically), they are morally accountable. The same artistic freedom applies to actors and stage directors, but only in respect of this moment, and that even if the work were otherwise realistic. For us in Prague it is unnecessary that the scene (set) for Wagner's *Die Meistersinger von Nürnberg* be a copy of Nürnberg. It can be – but only for the visual and atmospheric value. In contrast, a scene with the Old Town Square market must resemble reality, which *does not rule out* visual stylisation. How could the creator then be bound by such things as, for example, a myth? Similarly with music. If a composer studies the music of a particular nation to characterise the dramatic environment, they do so only for their inspiration: the composer's creative obligation not to simply copy it (e.g., folk songs or dances). Whenever the composer needs to count with the audience's experience, they are only obliged by the resemblance to the degree they have themself determined, but not otherwise. There is so much "oriental" music in European operas; what would people from the Orient say to them? And will the experience of present day audiences become no more than learned knowledge to future audiences, if even that? In contrast, if a composer

wants to portray a storm, they are bound by the resemblance to our current and future experience; but the stylisation is arbitrary.

The result of our discussion is this: *The relative and subjective resemblance between the technical and referential images is necessary for the dramatic work, but only in the signifying sense*, i.e., to assure that the desired referential image is actually evoked in the audience. The *outer truthfulness* obliges the authors of *the literary as well as the musical* text only to the extent that they bound themselves to it by the overall conception of their work. The *same extent* of outer truthfulness is obligatory to all those who co-create this written-down work – whether in the same age and environment or in the future, under other circumstances – which *modifies* their obligation by the fact that the extent of the text's outer truthfulness has changed. The *inner* truthfulness binds everyone absolutely and for good.

This norm resolves clearly the much-disputed and unnecessarily muddled question of how to stage older dramatic texts. As for the *quantity* of the stylisation, follow the extant texts; as for the *quality*, follow the present day and the audience.

10 DRAMATIC STYLES

If we use the word "structure" to refer to the *ostensive form* of an artwork – that is, all the formations (*útvary*) it comprises, from the smallest to the entire work – then we can define artistic style as follows:

Artistic style is determined by a structural unity shared by a set of artworks selected according to specific criteria.

There may be many and various criteria, and so there are also *many and various styles* named after the chosen criteria. Although in this chapter we look only at the styles of dramatic works, it is still impossible to cover all the innumerable styles specifically. We will therefore only focus on the broader stylistic classes and types and will only occasionally look into specific exceptional styles.

Critically, i.e., empirically, styles can be determined by a comparative method.

In this way we may compare all of Shakespeare's plays to determine what they have in common – thus we may speak of *Shakespeare's* style, which is classified as an *individual* style. If we also include the works of his predecessors and successors, we get the *English* style of the Elizabethan era; an instance of a *national* style. Also, if we extend the range of the era's works to cover most of Europe, we get the *Baroque* dramatic style; an instance of a *historical* style. All such styles as well as many others belong to the class of *historical-social* styles.

We may also form groups of plays according to their authors' *grasp* of psychology, which also shows in the effects the plays have on us. For example, by comparing dramas that emphasise the link with actuality we formulate the *realistic* style. With a view to a specific effect plays have we may formulate the *tragic* style, and so forth. Or, with a view to the non-aesthetic purposes of plays, we may recognise the *religious* (*sacred*) style, etc. Naturally, we narrow down our comparisons historically or socially (e.g., Spanish religious drama of the 16th–17th centuries), but it is evident that the aforementioned criteria reach beyond any given time and place; they belong to a class of *psychological* styles.

According to individual components of dramatic works, we may group them by their *textual* nature as verse drama, prose drama; by their *scenic* form as ensemble dramas or chorus dramas; by their *music* as recitativo operas or through-composed operas and so on. All these correspond with styles that form the class of *technical* styles.

The latter class of *technical styles* is the most important, because its individual styles are *the most elementary*, so to speak "stylistic features" (or elements). These elementary features come to form all the styles of the former two classes. After all, each *psychological* style can be transposed to a *particular* combination of technical styles; the combination of which arose through the author's specific psychological focus (*psychologické zaměření*), and that is why it works on the audience in that specific direction. All *historical-social* styles are *a unique set* of certain technical and psychological styles shaped by the era, society and individuals.

Technical *dramatic styles*. These styles capture *on the simplest, elementary level* the variable effects of the act of *"stylisation"*. In the last chapter, we defined *stylisation* as the *purposeful* (intentional; *účelné*) distance of the artwork from the natural and real-world objects it resembles – and must necessarily do so. Therefore we may speak of stylisation only in mimetic arts (*obrazová umění*), including the dramatic art. However, it does not pertain to the referential image, but the *technical* one. A dramatic work has a direct effect on us by means of its ostensive qualities, which we perceive: these are the direct factors of our impression (see above, page 93). It also has an indirect effect on us, by means of associations that our percept causes; this is the indirect cause of our impression. This impression also contains the specifically *dramatic* referential image. It follows that the dramatic effect of the work depends on certain *a posteriori* effects, given by our experiences of nature and life; the dramaticity principle (*princip dramatičnosti*) requires a maximum amount of this dramatic effect (but nothing else) and is thus an entirely aesthetic principle, *not* an artistic one *quite yet*, because we may happen to experience highly dramatic events in the real world or in its reproduction (e.g., in film). The *artistic qualities* of the dramatic work only appear when the work is *purposely formed* (*účelně utvářeno*) *in such a way* that certain *a priori principles* stand out, which are appropriate for the material but usually remain hidden in our everyday perception. The *a priori* nature of these qualities is not absolute; they are "innate" to us as individuals in the sense that we have *inherited* physiological dispositions for them from our predecessors in the lengthy evolution of organisms. What is at play here are the *logical relations* that guide our *thinking*, but not *just* abstract thinking, they also guide *ostensive* thinking, which dominates in the arts – especially when it comes to relations between individual elements of the perception of art. To give a few examples of these *guiding ostensive relations*, there is *affinity* (*příbuznost*; e.g., a harmony of colours or musical notes), *contrast* (e.g., of direction or force) or (ostensive) *similarity*, which may even gradually progress to *sameness* (*stejnost*). The latter sameness, which is necessarily only partial when it comes to more complex formations, we may apply to the highest and most general relation of thinking: *identity*. In temporal arts – and the dramatic art belongs to them – the applied identity principle shows in several typical basic forms: one, as a *repetition* and *return* of "the same" or "partially the same" (i.e., modified); and two, as an (ostensive) *continuity* (*souvislost*) of something that transforms over time and rests on one of its uninterrupted and permanent components. The more complicated the structure of the artwork – which particularly applies to dramatic works – the more it builds not only on the ostensive, but also on the abstract (or generally, logical) relations.

In regard to the aforementioned emphasis of the direct factor in artistic impression as the main carrier of the guiding values, we must point out that in some art forms the indirect factor also takes effect. But this factor *does not* produce referential images, evoked on the principle of similarity, but rather *abstract conceptual* images (*abstraktně významové představy*), which arise in us on the principle of concurrence (simultaneity; *současnost*). For the dramatic work, this applies specifically to speech delivery (*řeč*) as well as to "mimetic music" (*významová hudba*), as discussed above in Chapter 8.

The purposeful modifying of formations (*útvary*) within a dramatic work, as outlined here in brief, effectively means a distancing from how we experience them naturally and in the real world – but only in so far as their similarity remains to some extent at least. Only then can referential images arise, which are the true carriers of the dramatic impression. Therefore, *the principle of* **stylisation** *is always guided by the dramaticity principle as its primary and necessary* condition. Thus, we need to define it as follows:

The dramatic work as a work of art must be artistically stylised in all its components; this may happen in any way, but only in so far as to respect the dramaticity principle.

> The aforementioned "any way" pertains to the quality of the stylisation and is left up to all artists who in turn come to create the dramatic work. As for the quantity of the stylisation, we refer to the principle of *consistent* stylisation (*princip stejnoměrné stylisace*) defined in the previous chapter.

Technical stylisation follows primarily from the *nature of the material* that the artist uses to form their work. Technical styles are thus in principle material styles. Since early in this book we have been asserting that the dramatic work is very complex and varied in this respect, and it presents to our senses several components, even heterogeneous ones. It follows that we need to subdivide our brief overview accordingly. In our discussion of the synthetic theory in Chapter 2, we observed that some components resemble specific artistic disciplines. But these disciplines shape the *same material artistically* – that is, in the sense of their respective *a priori* principles – but their purpose is *other* than dramatic. For that reason every dramatic artist finds in these disciplines a suggestion, a *model* (or example; *poukaz, vzor*) for a possible stylisation of the component of the dramatic work – without disrupting the dramaticity principle, of course. This is how a *practical relation* emerges between a particular component of a dramatic work and its corresponding "mother art". We will later formulate it as a *principle* of sort – albeit a conditional one. An artist may, if it is dramatically convenient, use formations that already exist in the "mother art". But they may equally (and often must) create some that do not exist there – for now at least. The "mother art" may adopt these formations and thus enrich itself – which has often been the case.

A safe indication that a certain component of a dramatic work has been stylised artistically is that if we assess it *in and of itself* – as it were, taken away from the rest of the work – the component has an effect on us with its *purely artistic* qualities, just like artworks of the "mother art" – even though the isolation weakened or even destroyed its dramatic effect. In that way one may assess the isolated verbal and musical text (the play script and the score) and judge their specific *artistic* quality – but not their dramaticity, as we know from the above.

In sum, it follows from the definition of style that only that way of technical stylisation *that carries* out consistently *throughout* the entire component of a dramatic work is its technical style. Conversely, any possible *differences* in stylisation in different parts of the work (e.g., dramatic personas, or situations) cannot count as stylisation but as dramatic characteristics, because as *differences* they associate certain referential images. So, for instance, if all characters in a play speak in prose, this is the play's style, but if it is only servants who speak in prose (such as in Shakespeare), this evokes the referential image of an uneducated individual.

An overview of technical stylisations of a dramatic work according to all its components.

1. *Speech stylisation.* The material of the dramatic text is *human speech*, one of the most important products of human culture; in this case, we are dealing with particular utterances (*konkrétní řeč*) as they appear in the real world. As part of a dramatic work, the lines (utterances, speeches) of dramatic personas *must* be stylised. There is an autonomous art that forms speech artistically: *literature* (lyrical and epic; *básnictví*, i.e., poetry and fiction). Literature is a practical model for the creation (*tvorba*) of specifically "literary" qualities, regardless of their purpose. Thus, the *principle of literariness* states that **a verbal dramatic text must have** *literary qualities*, but **without destroying its dramaticity**.

> This principle is merely an *indication* of verbal stylisation: it does not require the same qualities that we find in poetry (and fiction), although it accepts them on condition of dramaticity; but it merely requires such qualities approximately; calling them "literary" (or "poetic") qualities is a mere suggestion (*poukaz*).

In regard to the literariness principle, a play script itself must give us literary pleasure. This is not in conflict with our discussions defining the position of the text (also applicable to opera composition), because our discussions only considered the text's dramaticity.

It follows from the literariness principle that the creator of a verbal dramatic text, i.e., a *playwright*, must also *have literary talent*.

Why did we refrain then from calling the playwright a poet? Because the *primary* talent of the person writing a dramatic text must be *dramatic* – as is evident from the process of their creative work (Chapter 4) and the fact that the required degree of the text's dramaticity is an absolute. In contrast, the degree of literariness of the dramatic text *may* be higher or lower – in short, it is relative.

The material itself involves various degrees of stylisation: from *actual* speech (*real-world* utterances), which is a *dialect* (in an ethnographic sense), to standardised speech, where we can distinguish between *prose* and *verse*. It is interesting to observe the historical development of drama from verse drama to drama in prose – that is, from higher stylisation to lower; this development is not without its hesitance, first occurring in comedy and only later in tragedy – and, similarly, first in comic opera, and only recently, in our time, in tragic opera. It was also only in our time that drama written purposely in dialect (as opposed to standardised speech) came into existence. When verse and prose is used alternately (e.g., in Shakespeare), this does not serve differences in style but it uses speech differently to characterise dramatic personas and the environment, or to characterise the dramatic action (cf. our discussion of "social dialects" and "psychological dialects" in Chapter 4). In this way, for instance, Gerhart Hauptmann uses dialect in *The Weavers* or in *The Sunken Bell*, where the witches speak it. Thus, a dialect does not always mean naturalism.

All literary (poetic) values found in literature (poetry) – as has been identified in various poetics – are available to make a dramatic persona's speech as long as they do not destroy its dramaticity. As we know from Chapter 4, even purely epic and lyrical speech (emotional as well as reflexive) has its justification in drama. The speech of dramatic personas may be plain or ornate, figurative or even symbolic (i.e., involving two simultaneous referential images) and so on. Particularly typical of dramatic speech is the elementary metaphor, which is a kind of detour that a dramatic persona uses to express their mental state. If an entire play is written this way, it becomes its style; but these various means are available for use in dramatic characterisation, e.g., in Molière's young ladies précieuses or Mercutio's fantastical nature and so forth.

The poetic forms (lyrical and epic) are scarcely applicable in drama, since drama is limited to an exchange of utterances (speech) between personas – perhaps only as parts of the action in the sense of the real-world application of these forms. Examples of this are when a triolet is read out in Molière's *The Misanthrope*, or when Edmond de Rostand's Cyrano composes a ballad during the duel.

2. *The actor's stylisation.* For the actor's total performance, acoustic and optic – that is, the actor's totality principle – there is no corresponding "mother art", as in the case of the text. The correspondence between both components (acoustic and optic) is given in the technical sense by the principle of *coordination* of inner tactile impulses; the persona's unity is up to the principle of coherence of the actor figure (*zákon kontinuity herecké osoby*); and the continuity of action is given by the principle of *exteriorisation* of inner tactile impulses: the three guiding principles of "acting logic", as discussed in Chapter 4. The *physiological principles* of bodily movements direct the actor *instinctively toward a stylisation* of their performance in the sense of its regularity, which manifests itself mainly in a tendency toward periodicity, i.e., repetition (cf. breathing, walking and so on).

a) *Stylisation of* **speech** and of other vocal expressions as temporal formations happens through *rhythmisation*, which subdivides the speech into elementary and more complex (i.e., metric) emphases and pauses, distributed as evenly as possible. The degree of rhythmisation follows the author's formation of the verbal text along this scale: prose – rhythmic prose – free verse – regular verse, which progresses from a loose rhythmisation to a strict one, which requires a subjectively equal duration of beats. The actor must deliver verse *as verse*, i.e., declaim them, not speak them as prose, in a so-called "natural style", i.e., naturalistically. There surely are psychological states in which our speech becomes *spontaneously* rhythmic (e.g., orations). In the stylisation of their speech, the actor comes close to a *reciter*, while observing the differences required by the dramaticity principle (as pointed out above on page 166). Stylisation also involves a careful modification of speech melodies (intonation), which regardless of pauses subdivides and unifies the delivery; and also the actor's work with the dynamics and speed of speech (cadence, in the case of verse), and of course changes and transitions – sudden, i.e., contrasting, or gradual (increase and decrease in intensity) – all of which always needs to depend on the sense of the speech and the dramatic situation. As we know, in all this the actor may take muster in the stylisation of speech into singing, which the composer of sung drama creates and fixes in the score in such a way that the opera singer may only focus on its nuances.

b) *Stylisation of* **mimics**, i.e., of the visible acting, happens in two directions, since it involves, generally speaking, spatial movement. *Temporal* stylisation is again the *rhythmisation* of these movements. The regularity (periodicity) of the gestures subdivides the bodily (physical) performance entirely naturally into a continuous, or intermittent chain of action – i.e., fluent, or broken up by pauses and moments of stillness – alongside distributed emphases of psychologically more significant gestures. This layer (system) runs parallel with speech delivery, but it is principally independent, sometimes supporting speech (especially facial mimics) and more often complementing it in the sense of alternation. As we know, in sung drama the layer of movement ties up with the simultaneous orchestra music, which strictly determines it temporally. As for the actor's work with the intensity and speed (or, tempo) of movement, the same as aforementioned with speech applies here. *Spatial* stylisation applies to larger mimics, i.e., bodily movement, and relates to its trajectory, which appears to us as a line – which may be straight or curved, undulating or zigzag. The scope of the trajectory signals the intensity of the gesture – fully in the sense of the gradation principle of exteriorisation (*gradační zákon exteriorisace*). The stylisation tends towards regularity again – which shows in the case of a single movement a tendency to a line with the simplest, i.e., geometrical shape (a straight line, a circle, a wave, etc.). When there are several simultaneous movements, their correspondence becomes prominent, leading naturally – i.e., by the mechanical setup of the body – to symmetry (e.g., the moving of both arms) and to polarity (e.g., the right arm and the left leg). This stylisation of larger movements of the body (but only that, not the stylisation of facial expressions) comes close to *dance*, as well as to various *rituals*. It needs be said that such "geometric" stylisation of bodily movements hides a danger: in its extreme application, the mimics becomes unintelligible and fails to evoke any referential image, which is essential for a dramatic work. As such, it is useless to the actor. The only exception is ceremonial (ritual) gestures, because they are in the real world linked with a conventional referential image; as such, they are of use. Conversely, the stylisation of an actor's movements into purely *dance* movements is *unacceptable* because *these* movements do not "mean" anything. This, of course, does not apply to the case that is common in opera: that of an actual dance.

Generally it needs to be emphasised that the direct factor that manifests itself in stylised mimics evokes a certain mood in us – but that mood is *ineffable* as it is specifically *"mimic"* (gestural). To compile a "dictionary of mimics" would be not only *dogmatic*, as it would lead to cliché templates (cf. pantomimes!), but also *dilettantist*, as would be an attempt to compile a "dictionary of music" that would indulge in subjective wilfulness and offer to translate the specifically musico-atmospheric effect of certain elementary musical forms into words.

3. *The stage director's stylisation.* As we know, we are dealing with the creative work of the director-conductor, whose function is anticipated by the composer of sung drama, and that of the director-scenic. We will merge both tasks when discussing the spatio-temporal stylisation of the stage work and only keep separate the stylisation of the fixed fill (*pevná výplň*) of the scene.

a) *Stylisation of* **interaction** amounts to the *creation of the regular dramatic form* (both dynamic and agogic; *vytvoření zákonité formy dramatické*) and *of the scenic form* (both positional and kinetic): in other words, the director's task proper is to *stylise* the dramatic action temporally and spatially. It will suffice to refer to our discussions of the director's tasks in Chapters 6 and 7. Let us only remark that the dramatic form in sung drama is determined by the temporal form (the dynamics and movement) of its musical component as created and fixed by the composer. To complement our above conclusions, let us point out typical forms of dramatic (and analogically, musical) *culmination*, i.e., of the climax. This may occur in two ways: one, by a dynamic (*silový*), or a motional (*pohybový*) *contrast*, when the relevant change is abrupt (a reversal; *přelom*); or two, by dynamic or motional *gradual intensification* (by degrees; *gradace, stupňování*), when the relevant change is progressive, incremental (a transition; *přechod*). Both cases entail a change in the sense of "tension – release", or "agitation – calming down". Following the two possible temporal sequences, each of these simple instances can be further subdivided into another two – as illustrated in the four diagrams below, the fourth of which is effectively a "gradual descent" (degradation; *degradace, sestupnění*).

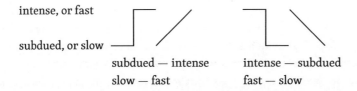

The general *principle of alternation* of impressions – based on the psychological, basically physiological processes of *exhaustion* and *numbness* – calls for a dramatic work to alternate impressions, because long-lasting weak (subdued) impressions will exhaust us, while the intense impressions will numb us. It is thus necessary to *combine* both paired forms, as outlined in the above diagram. This is how the *basic* shape of *temporal* forms emerges – not only the dramatic ones, but also the musical ones. This form combines *culmination* with *relaxation*; the following diagram visualises its typical shape, with a repetition:

Let us notice that the two "waves" are asymmetrical, with the rise being much longer than the fall. This important quality springs from the asymmetry of duration whose movement, ever racing ahead (indicated by the arrow), as if *drags* the culmination as far toward the ending as can be. Let us call this form **"the thrust wave"** (*vržená vlna*): after a gradual rise follows a sudden fall. The points of *culmination* and *relaxation* (the ups and downs of our thrust waves) are often *static*, sometimes containing even longer moments of the highest tension (or agitation) and of the greatest release (or calming down). Culminations that follow one after another tend to differ in intensity and form a unit – for an entire act, and of course for the entire work – that culminates in a higher order, once again in the shape of a thrust wave. It follows from the above that every culmination *necessarily requires relaxation* and *those* are the moments with less dramatic parts of the plot (known as *episodes*) or even with entirely undramatic, purely atmospheric, *lyrical* parts. All such moments, even if seemingly contravening the dramaticity principle, are justified by the *stylisation principle*; naturally, their function within the entire work dissipates when they go on for too long, because their justification does come from them alone, but from the contrast with what immediately preceded them.

Thanks to the relative possibility to measure the dynamics and the tempo in music, we may create *outlines* of the dynamic form for individual compositions (see my book *Symfonické básně Smetanovy*; Smetana's Symphonic Poems, 1924). In principle we can also do this for sung drama. However, in spoken drama the dynamics and tempo of dramatic action is not measurable.

The *overall* tempo may also be stylised in the sense of "fast-slow" (the *presto-grave* style). In opera the scale of such stylisation is much wider than in spoken drama, especially when it comes to slowness: singing and music affect the play (*hra*). For that reason, opera librettos must be more concise than play scripts; that is also possible because they can effectively and quickly set the mood of the scene.

As for the spatio-temporal stylisation of the *scene*, we may refer back to our overview of the scenic kinetic qualities in Chapter 7. Although the scene along the width tends to symmetry, a balanced fill of the two sides of the scene (due to its static nature) is used only in moments of dramatic calmness. Otherwise, the scene is filled only on one side, and alternately, of course. An even arrangement (blocking) of figures along the width (i.e., equal standing), or along the depth (i.e., with decreasing standing in the upstage direction) has a quality generally called "*a visual rhythm*".

b) *Stylisation of the **fixed fill of the scene***. At the start of the scene chapter (Chapter 7) we asserted that from a technical point of view the empty stage is an architectural formation (an interior). If a specific location of the action requires that the scene is built all around and filled with fixed objects that represent something specific, such a scene with these objects (but without figures!) may be viewed as a work of "*mimetic architecture*" (*obrazová architektura*) of sorts. It follows that the fixed material objects (in agreement with the architectonic frame of the scene, naturally) may be stylised according to models from architecture (and from art crafts and industries), with the help of painting – which architecture does anyway. This fact establishes a *visual requirement* (*postulát výtvarnosti*): *any fixed fill of the scene*, including *lighting*, which makes the fill visible, *must have visual artistic qualities*, without *disrupting its mimetic function*, which is necessary for the dramatic work. This requirement is no more than a directive; it does not insist on the same qualities as in the visual arts, merely on the same kind. The fixed fill in question is also no more than conditional and only secondary; the main fill of the scene is the dramatic personas in movement. It follows that the composition of the overall fill needs to consider the temporal changes of the entire scene – in fact, the change that happens with the changes in theatrical lighting. For that reason it is particularly misguided to apply indiscriminately some general principles of the visual arts to the scene (e.g., the *bas-relief*). The visual requirement is thus *rather limited* dramatically speaking; still, it involves various optical qualities, such as colours and shapes; we need to state then that the *director-scenic must have a talent for the visual arts*. If they are not visually gifted – and the talent concerns a sense for the art as well as being inventive when it comes to the visual qualities – the director-scenic must employ a visual artist (an architect) – but one who has an avid dramatic sense because their design (*koncepce*) needs to observe the dramatic, i.e., dynamic human scene.

One can achieve consistent stylisation by selecting *one* (or a few) *visual quality* for each section of the work with its own scene; that visual quality may be a colour or a shape that is characteristic (*příznačný*) in mood or in the visual image (or even symbolically) for action that takes place in the section. The selected visual quality serves then to stylise everything in the scene. This is the *guiding idea* of a production. When designing a scene, one must consider that lighting can change the colour of the scene according to what the dramatic situation requires. The direct visual factor, emphasised by the stylisation, is especially important to enhance the mood of the static moments of the dramatic action (plot) – the aforementioned "relaxations". But one should not emphasise it too much, lest its monotony override the rich diversity of the dramatic action.

The more the visual stylisation becomes distant from reality, the simpler it may be; this is very important for plays with many scene changes. And just like with actor's performance, we need to point at the dangers of extreme stylisation – the geometric, and the expressionist: whenever scenic objects become incomprehensible to us, i.e., when they fail to evoke referential images in us, they become useless for the dramatic work, and as such unacceptable. Their *merely* atmospheric effect as visual objects cannot be a sufficient justification: such a scene becomes lyrical, not dramatic (according to our definition), and the stronger its effect becomes, the worse it is for *drama* (after all, drama must be the main goal and could perhaps even do without this scene altogether). Even our own age, healthily reacting to the preceding era of scenic naturalism, fosters careful visual stylisation of the scene and often brings us productions that are artistic in themselves, and yet quite one-sidedly made "for the eye", "ostentatiously" (*na podívanou*). This is welcome for dance works (ballet).

4. *Stylisation of music.* We cannot speak of "stylisation" of operatic music in the same sense as stylisation of speech or of the actor's performance – with the exception of the *singing* component of opera where, as we know, the declamation may be viewed as the "musical stylisation" of speech. In contrast, instrumental music effectively stands *outside* all stylisation because its material is artificial (*umělý*) and its formations bear no relation to our real-world experience. It is only at the point, such as in sung drama, when it is formed as *mimetic* music, when it *aspires* to bear a similarity with outer and inner experiences, that it gives us the right and opportunity to perceive the *distance* between its formations and its corresponding phenomena as instances of their "stylisation". This "stylisation" thus proceeds in an *inverse direction*

to the previous ones, because it proceeds from *a priori* musical forms to *a posteriori* (experiential) forms. As such, it occupies a different *niveau* which cannot be *compared* to the preceding stylisations, as the following diagram illustrates:

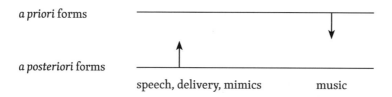

This diagram resembles the "naturalism – realism" figure in the previous chapter (p. 337).

Additionally, mimetic music – despite its "naturalist" tendency – remains in one of the above directions at least firmly rooted in its *a priori* basis, i.e., its *tonal nature*. For that reason, in our discussion of singing, we chose to name this specific kind of stylisation *"musicalisation"* (*zhudebnění*) and the same concept should also be used in all the other cases discussed in Chapter 8: in *tone painting* and *soul painting*.

> This autonomy of the musical component within the dramatic work effectively creates the *musicality requirement* (*postulát hudebnosti*), which we will assert here as self-evident, if not tautological: while it is necessary to stylise the speech of drama in order to make it literary, music in drama should be stylised to become – musical? This goes without saying, and so it may seem that the musical component only obeys the dramaticity requirement. But artistic practice speaks differently (and all the aforementioned stylisation requirements apply to practice). We have characterised above the tendency of mimetic music as "naturalistic"; truly, it runs the *danger* of naturalism: that danger does not reside in its resulting "imitations", which can never be too illusionistic, but rather in the *minimal creative invention* needed to achieve the most "faithful" imitation of speech melodies, of natural sounds and so on. It is against this danger that we assert our requirement emphasising the "relative realism" of the musical component.

The *musicality requirement* asserts thus that **dramatic music (including singing) must possess** purely musical qualities, **without disrupting its dramaticity**. As such, operatic music *on its own* must give a purely *musical* pleasure when read, or played and sung from the score, although its dramatic and general visual effect is weakened in this way, if not wiped out altogether (when the libretto is not involved). The dramatic composer must therefore *have a talent for musical creation* just like any composer of vocal and instrumental music.

No formation of "mere music" is excluded from sung drama as long as it is dramatically justified; otherwise it is unacceptable, no matter how musically great it is. To speak of "purely musical" qualities is again a mere indication, a suggestion (*poukaz*): there are many such qualities to be found in music on its own – throughout history until nowadays. Not only does mere music constantly develop new formations, but it also becomes richer by constantly *adopting* many new formations from mimetic music – programmatic, vocal and especially dramatic: a great amount of musical formations that could hardly emerge *on their own*. The modern symphony can serve as a good example. By "purely musical" elements we refer, in short, to *"musico-logical"* formations that observe the principles of harmony, melody, rhythm, etc.

a) As for **singing**, it is enough to refer to our discussions in Chapter 8. Here we could consider the aforementioned *declamation principle* as a "stylisation" of sorts; but the musicality requirement calls for vocal melodies created in this way to possess a *purely musical* quality. This can be evidenced by the many melodies that composers successfully use even without lyrics as instrumental music in the *orchestra* and even, as we know, as characteristic motifs. The range of distance between singing and speaking may be measured on the "recitativo – cantilena" scale. But, since both forms usually combine in sung drama, we cannot see them as stylistic, but rather as dramatic differences that serve mainly to characterise the plot: recitatives correspond to dramatic speech, and cantilenas to the lyrical. They are simply *different kinds* of human vocal expressions, and as we know from our discussion of melodrama (end of Chapter 8), plain speech can supplement them in opera (e.g., in Smetana's opera *Dvě vdovy*, where plain speech characterises the reading, i.e., the quotation, of a letter). But in scenic melodrama, the systematic use of plain speech is a stylistic marker. When, after a certain section of a sung drama, the plain speech gives way together with the orchestral accompaniment, and the sections become entirely spoken, like in spoken drama – in contrast to sections that are sung throughout – at that point the entire work – known as *conversational opera* (*konverzační opera*) – *falls apart* into *stylistically different* sections. Its stylistic inconsistency comes down to its musical component and does not affect the others; specifically, it does not need to damage the work's dramaticity – as evidenced by the many conversational operas that are dramatically excellent. Nevertheless, composers of these operas sense the fragmentation of the musical component; and so, if they are not trying to "through-compose" their libretto, they at least try to substitute prose with a recitative. Conversational opera belongs to one of the *historic* operatic styles.

In our discussions of singing (in Chapter 8) we pointed out that the declamatory principle is justified not only dramatically – following from what we could call the requirement of relative realism – but also stylistically, in agreement with the material style of actual speech. In opera practice (and even more so in vocal music) there are numerous instances where the vocal singing melody is in fact *absolute*, i.e., conceived as an instrumental melody with *underlying lyrics*. Italian operas provide numerous examples, e.g., Rossini's *Il barbiere di Siviglia* or Verdi's *Aida*. If such singing is characteristic for the dramatic persona, this method is acceptable under the condition that the vocal melody does clash with the prosody of the language it is sung in; in other words, that the "declamation is correct". This needs to be heeded in the translation of operas; it becomes apparent how *nationally conditioned* declamatory melodies are – because these resist having a text in another language the most. The above method has led to two known operatic patterns of the past: the *repetition* of words and phrases, and the *coloratura*. However, we cannot reject the repetition of words if it has dramatic justification as an emotional expression (cf. repetition in lyric poetry) or as a personal characteristic (a chatterbox); nor can we discount the coloratura, which has significant characterising potential, as have previously asserted. Moreover, the coloratura does not contravene the declamation principle because a single syllable in plain speech often spans over a (sequential) series of notes. This is partly because in singing the succession of syllables, especially the long vowels, may be very slow.

b) As for **orchestral music**, we can also measure the stylising distance of musical formations from our experience through *tone painting*. Realistic tone painting is concrete citation, almost a musical photograph, idealised tone painting is part of the musical setting (*faktura*), and though general and unified; sometimes it serves to paint the environment (e.g., a forest) and runs throughout a whole scene or at least its part (such as an aria). *Thematic musical forms* are a different case: in opera, we can only measure their departure from absolute musical forms, and since those are based on *repetition* and *return* (*opakování a návrat*), they are strict forms. In contrast, the dramatic musical form is *thematically free*, only governed by the dramatic action (*děj*) that presses ahead and generally does not repeat or return. In principle, the strict forms are not exempt as long as they correspond to the dramatic situation – for instance, the so-called *"closed"* (*uzavřená*) musical numbers; when a plot segment ends, its music may end too. Even in absolute music there are free, fantasy forms, and the malleable principles of *repetition* and *return* operate in dramatic action (*děj*) as well, in the form of *modified* repetition and return (cf. "characteristic reminiscence"). In Chapter 8, in our discussion of ensemble and chorus, we pointed out how naturally the form of *imitation* serves when several parties agree; we also stressed the importance of *variation* in characteristic motifs. The structure of characteristic motifs, when carried out consistently in sung drama, takes over the *unifying* musico-thematic function. (It is the musical theme that carries that function in pure music.) There are whole operas (e.g., Smetana's *Dalibor*) with a single motif (monomotivism) or with just two, a primary and a secondary one (e.g., Wagner's *Der fliegende Holländer*, Smetana's *The Secret, Tajemství*). To sum up, the stylising range of musico-thematic forms (*hudebně myšlenkové formy*) in sung drama can be measured against their parallel thematic-dramatic forms (*dramatické formy ideové*) in *spoken drama*. The exceptions are polyphonic forms, typical of opera, and as such they are always characteristic of a high degree of stylisation. Sung drama does not exclude even the most typical forms of absolute music, such as the canon and the fugue. The latter can serve as an excellent form of gradation (*gradace*), as I have done in my opera *Vina* (*Guilt*), where it accompanies a purely wordless action of writing a crucial letter.

There is also a third way of considering the stylisation of music. It relates to the musical formations common *also in the real world*. We touched on them at the end of Chapter 8 and their use in spoken drama. The various *songs* (ballads, romances, barcaroles, lullabies, prayers, serenades, etc.) for soloists and the chorus, and singing and music accompanying various *rituals* (weddings, funerals, religious and festive ceremonies, etc.) and *dances*. The opera loves making use of all these: firstly, because such music can significantly strengthen the lyrical effect of songs as well as the motoric effect of rituals and dances, and that heightens atmospheric effect in moments of dramatic relaxation and helps escalate dramatic climaxes from the outside too, while also enhancing the scenic qualities (e.g., the use of feasting and dancing for a finale). Secondly, in such moments the composer may absolutely let go of the reins of their musical imagination without jeopardising the dramaticity (again, with moderation, as we have said several times). It might seem that using music that reminds of the real world is realistic, especially when there are both singers and musicians on the stage (i.e., as actors); this is even referred to as "musical naturalism" in the instances when the music is a truthful reflection of folk music and songs. But the reverse is true because all music of this kind is highly stylised in the sense of using absolute musical forms – even if primitive ones; this will become apparent as soon as we compare it with the music in the rest of the opera. That is, "musical folklore" is not an instance of naturalism, because what it imitates or "counterfeits" is already a work of art; what is at stake here is the composer's *creativity* (creative inventiveness) – and in the extreme cases, when it builds excessively on real-world models, the composer's eclecticism. It is quite strange that *eclecticism* does not come up when the work adopts folk songs and dances; this is probably so because the original authors are anonymous. Stylisation needs to be measured only in relative terms, by comparison with music that is used in such real-world situations; the resulting difference suggests the composer's own "idealisation" of real-world musical forms – especially the folk ones (compare Smetana's operas with Janáček's).

It is only all these three criteria *combined* that determine the degree and kind of musical stylisation in an opera score, and those should then be applied to the acting and the scenic components of the sung drama.

෴ ෴ ෴

Psychological *dramatic styles* spring from an artist's uniform *grasp* (or concept) of the dramatic material – and we deduce it from our *impression* of the work. Objectively speaking, this is always a matter of a typical coexistence of some technical stylisations of various aspects and components of the dramatic work. Sometimes, a single technical style among all others may become the dominant feature of a particular psychological style. In opera, the psychological style of the whole work (its performance) follows from its musical style; that is, from the composer's stylistic conception, which in turn follows at least partially from the librettist's stylistic conception. In spoken drama, the staging (production) follows the indications from the playwright's psychological style (i.e., from their script). It is characteristic of these two categories of psychological styles, which differ qualitatively in the artist's psychological conception, that they typically appear *in pairs* that point to their quantitative *opposition* in the sense of "little – much": they are effectively two ends of a single scale. Let us first give a few instances of such pairs, which apply outside the dramatic arts as well.

1. The *close – distant to our outer experience* concept. This grasp applies to all mimetic arts (*obrazová umění*) and we discussed it in the previous chapter under *"realism – idealism"*, not to mention the above overview of technical styles. To distinguish dramatic works of this kind, there are numerous similar terms, variously nuanced according to the era in which the given style dominated – e.g., impressionist, verist and neorealistic (civilist) drama; as opposed to expressionist, fantastic, symbolist drama, etc.

Let us emphasise that if one *extreme* (i.e., unacceptable) style of this conception is *naturalism*, because it involves minimum creativity (as we have seen), then the other end of the scale is *idealism*, with its own minimum of creativity: *eclecticism*. If the artist does not draw their elements from life and nature, they must take them from art. For that reason this conception has not one, but two *dangerous* extremes:

(naturalism) — realism — idealism — (eclecticism)

Getting stuck in one or the other extreme brings about the well-known alternating reactions in the historical development of the arts.

2. The *earnest – non-earnest* concept: in other words, the grasp of what is serious and humouristic. This appears both in art and in the real world. In the dramatic art, this relates to serious drama, with *tragedy* as one of its kinds, and comic drama or *comedy*, with its many kinds. Sung drama knows the distinction *"opera seria – buffa"*. Tragedy as a term is not commensurate with comedy because tragedy is only ideational (thematic; *ideová*), whereas comedy can also be ostensive. That is why music is never tragic, but only "serious" (*vážná*), while there is purely musical comedy or even a musical joke.

3. The *human – superhuman* concept. This concept grasps the intensity and extensity of the impression. In dramaturgy, there are the *small-scale*, the *generic* (*žánrový*) or the *intimate* styles, as opposed to the *grand*, the *monumental* or the *ceremonial* styles. This corresponds to two different types of *theatre* buildings, with the stage and the auditorium small or large; and to the range of acting and musical devices used: the delivery and the gestures, conversational or grand; the orchestra, small or large, etc.

These principal pairs – omitting a few ideational (thematic) ones, such as optimism–pessimism; intellectualism–emotionalism and others – do not exclude one another, but rather combine and complement one another. In fact, we can classify every single work according to these three conceptions. E.g., Alfred de Musset's *Le Chandelier*: an idealistic intimate comedy; Richard Strauss's *Salomé*: a realistic grand tragedy and so on.

Some *specifically dramatic* stylistic pairs would be of greater interest to our discussion, yet we may no more than list them here. Their characteristic is that their psychological style predominantly springs from one type of single technical style.

a) *The predominant weight* lies on the dramatic *personas* that make action (děj), or on dramatic *action* (děj) that carries the personas. We discussed this difference in the opening of Chapter 6; we speak of *character-* and *situation-driven* drama, respectively. (This is a common distinction especially in comedy).

b) The dramatic personas are either roughly *equally*, or *unequally weighted*. We could call the former *ensemble* drama; the latter further branches out depending on how much *one* persona stands out in the size of their role above others: the *solo concerto* (*koncertní*) drama (in the positive sense of the word, as an analogy to the musical "concerto"; Carlo Goldoni's *Mirandolina* is one example), or conversely, when there are many secondary personas, this may come to form *mass* (*davové*) drama. Heroes (usually the "titular" ones) can come in twos (e.g., Wagner's *Tristan and Isolde*); they generally carry the weight of the play's success; this genre sometimes degenerates into a mere display of virtuosity.

c) The dramatic action (plot) is either *continuous*, or *intermittent*. The action of the drama is generally presented in units called "*acts*" (*akty* or *jednání*), with the action that unfolds in between acts being negligible. Alternatively, the action (děj) of the drama is ideal (*ideálný*) and the drama presents no more than short extracts, suitably called "*tableaux*" (*obrazy*) or "*scenes*" (*scény*) – and these are mere samples, phases of a progress that generally occurs in-between. The drama of the former type generally comes "*in several acts*", while the latter comes "*in many scenes*". The following diagram describes both types: the thick line as real action, and the thin one as the ideal one (which unfolds in-between).

```
Act              I.            II.           III.
                 ▬▬▬▬          ▬▬▬▬          ▬▬▬▬

Tableau (scene) 1.    2.    3.   4.    5.   6.    7.    8.
                ▬▬    ▬▬    ▬▬   ▬▬    ▬▬   ▬▬    ▬▬    ▬▬
```

The first type has a dynamic character and in fact represents *drama proper* – except when it abundantly employs lyricism, often underpinned by music (*lyrical* drama). The second type is common in literary drama; it is clearly static and it relies heavily on scene changes. Even if it does not degenerate to a spectacle (*hra výpravná*), it always betrays its epic origins; it is often a *scenic* (but not a "dramatised"!) *novel*.

Historico-social *dramatic styles*. *Historical* styles are in fact *singular combinations* of the above "concept" styles with selected technical stylisations, as they emerged as products of the spiritual focus (*duchovní zaměření*) of a particular era and of the state of technology – and that not only in the theatre but also in its "mother" arts, especially in literature, music and in the visual arts. They often originate as collective creations of a certain society, especially a *nation*, and they sometimes reach beyond the national boundaries towards an international appeal.

The question of *national* style in the dramatic art is a very complex and challenging issue that cannot be resolved *a priori*, by some norm, but only *a posteriori*, by comparing dramatic works created by a specific nation in a particular *consistent* (*unified*) style (if we are to recognise it as a style, that is). It follows that a national style springs from a *series of individual styles* (of authors from the same nation) *connected by a continuous tradition*. In the early phases a national style is usually comprised of *anonymous* works that generally lack individuality (the nation's *folk* style).

Individual styles in the dramatic art *diverge* into two groups of different character. One group comes from *authors* of verbal and musical *scripts*: the playwright and the dramatic composer. Both are fortunate in that they can *fix* (*fixovat*) their works so that the work will survive them, exempt from time and place, but unfortunate in that they can fix the works they created internally (i.e., in their imagination) only *partially*. Their works as lasting documents of their individualities – that is, of their individual styles – can form the history of the dramatic art. The second group comes from actors with their directors and other theatre collaborators. Their joint work, the theatrical performance, is in fact the *true and complete dramatic work*, but it *dies* with its delivery. This is the tragic fate of acting because it does not leave behind a lasting artwork to document the artistic individualities. There is certain *social justice* in that great actors (just like great musicians) receive much more recognition and fame from their audiences than authors of dramatic and musical scripts. Moreover, even outside of an actor's personal career that wipes out their individual style at their lifework's end; neither can an established acting style (an acting tradition) transcend beyond personal contacts, and as such any *history* of acting is thoroughly imperfect, lacking *direct* artistic documentation. What the individual styles of great actors of the past were, we can learn only very inadequately.

The *permanent* component of the dramatic work – that is, the verbal or musical script (text) – is stylistically rooted in its author and the era. If it is the work of a genius, it contains universally valid, panhuman qualities; after all, the dramatic art is in its object the most human kind of art. Of course, congenial works from other arts have lasting qualities that transcend their era; but their impact *ages* and after centuries we need to approach them historically if we want to understand them fully. A dramatic work is different. Its *variable* (*měnlivá*) component is a product of present day artists, and even if it follows a historic textual style, *it may and must transpose it to present day artistic idioms* (*umělecká mluva současnosti*). The partial textual fixity (*fixace*) is not the work's weakness, but rather its strength. In place of *invariable* eternity, it is endowed with an eternity of *rebirth*.

The interpretive openness (*mnohoznačnost*), caused by the text's partial quality, is the dramatic work's source of life. The freedom of the acting component is so broad that it can achieve an individual synthesis of historic and present day styles. When and where will texts' possibilities be exhausted? It may seem sometimes that even a great dramatic work is defunct and has nothing else to say. But this is often only a seeming death, for a time, resulting from the periodical waves of realism and idealism: with another wave, the work will resurface again, in a new variation. *How many* more variations are hidden in the seed of future times? It is good that a dramatic work cannot be fixed in its entirety: it would grow old too soon. Classical ancient drama can hardly live today; certainly not the way it was produced back then – but it can live truly, not rot. If we manage to record performances mechanically, these will only be historical documents for the museum. Is it the fact that sung drama (*zpěvohra*) can be fixed more extensively that causes so many operas to age? We have asserted that opera's more detailed fixity is its advantage – but each light, it seems, has its shadow. On the other hand, the sung drama tradition is relatively recent in comparison to spoken drama.

The dramatic art, matching the art of architecture in its universality, is one of the most fortunate arts. It is no mere monument of the past; its *ephemeral* (*transitory*) component bursts through the dams between the past, the present and the future. The great dramatic work, *immortal* in its universal, panhuman quality, is equally *ever fresh* in its ever new variations of its overpowering presence.

AFTERWORD

OTAKAR ZICH IN CONTEXT: INSPIRATIONS, INTERPRETATIONS AND ISSUES

(DAVID DROZD)

Since its publication almost a century ago, Zich's *Aesthetics of the Dramatic Art* has gathered a number of interpretations and commentaries mostly in the Czech context and beyond. Its reception has been far from conclusive and it would be a mistake to assume the book's potential for engendering new readings is closed. Zich's *Aesthetics* is a book far too diverse and complex. This is doubly so in the current climate in Theatre Studies with its tendency for methodological plurality and critical revisions, as Zich's *Aesthetics* defies the attempts to narrow itself down to a singular mode of interpretation. Hence, this Afterword offers a series of critical explorations of different aspects of the book. We have divided it into three basic areas signalled in the subtitle: (1) possible inspirations, sources and contexts of the book's inception; (2) the most prominent traditions of interpreting the book; and (3) the problems of translating Zich's terminology into English.

1 ZICH'S INTELLECTUAL WORLD: INSPIRATIONS AND SOURCES

Unlike his other academic works, in which Zich provides references and lists the works cited, in his *Aesthetics of the Dramatic Art* he intentionally omits them. That means that the inspirations, sources and contexts of the book's inception remain hidden or implicit. Zich merely states in his introduction:

> As for the detailed elaboration of this design in the second part, the conception and arrangement of the material are my own. Factually it does not contain – as that would be entirely impossible in a systematic study – only my own thoughts, especially when it comes to spoken drama, which has recently been thoroughly theorised. Nonetheless, specialists will appreciate how many new thoughts and concepts of my own there are here. (56 above)

The second part of *Aesthetics* deals primarily with the issues of inner laws and principles of the dramatic art – the potential and limitations in the creative work of individual artists participating in the making of the dramatic work. Zich acknowledges in this part his allegiance to contemporary aesthetic thinking. It is only logical given that he primarily touches upon contemporary (i.e., modern) theatre practice. It is his original contribution to "the conception and arrangement of the material" that would need a closer enquiry. Zich's phrases, such as "specialists will appreciate", indirectly suggest that rather than academics and scholars, he intended his book for thoughtful practitioners, theatre professionals or critically minded spectators – although we might object that the book is sufficiently complex and challenging for today's academics too. In order to understand what Zich's academic and scholarly contemporaries would have taken for granted and therefore not worth repeating, we will need to undertake an archeological investigation and attempt a reconstruction of the period discourse of theatre scholars and practitioners.

ZICH AS A UNIVERSITY TEACHER

The university lectures Zich delivered in the years *before* the publication of his *Aesthetics* help to gain insight into his own thinking and the connections and contexts of his book. Zich started teaching at the Faculty of Philosophy

(*Filosofická fakulta*) of Charles University in the summer semester of 1911, first as a private (extramural) lecturer (*docent*) and later as a regular staff member. He took over as the department director of the Seminar of Aesthetics after the departure of Otakar Hostinský (1847–1910), a formative figure of the discipline in the Czech context. Zich continued in this position until his death in 1934, but in the years 1921–1924 he also taught at the newly established Masaryk University in Brno, acting as the founding director of the Seminar of Philosophy. Zich's leadership at Masaryk University effectively oriented the department towards experimental psychology, in keeping with his research interests – an approach that may seem surprising a century later.

The principal thematic blocks of Zich's teaching stand out clearly. He gave regular lectures in general aesthetics – for instance, his module of 1911/12, Modern Trends in Aesthetics, comprised (I) Experimental Aesthetics, (II) Psychological Aesthetics, and (III) Physiological Aesthetics. He complemented it with a general overview of the history of aesthetics. His other thematic blocks included the psychology of art – such as his lecture series Psychology of Comedy and Humour (1913), Analysis of the Aesthetics of Perception (1915) or Psychology of the Aesthetics of Perception (1929). Simultaneously and in agreement with contemporary trends, he focused on the issues of artistic creativity and the creative processes – for instance in his modules Psychology of Artistic Thinking (1929) and Psychology of Artistic Creation (1932). Zich conceived his teaching as a set of systemic approaches to the discipline and completed that system by modules dedicated to individual art forms and artistic disciplines, such as Aesthetics of the Dramatic Text (1928), Aesthetics of Opera (1930) or Aesthetics of the Visual Arts (1934). In 1914 he gave the first lecture series offering his own comprehensive take on theatre, in a module entitled Theoretical Dramaturgy. The principal focus throughout his teaching career was general aesthetics, or scientific aesthetics, and the psychology of art.

ZICH AS A CRITICAL READER

According to the available evidence and reports, Zich's lectures were never historiographic in nature – with the exception of the one module on the historic overview of aesthetics, which was surprisingly the only one that explicitly took a historical perspective. However, there is ample evidence that Zich reflected on contemporary theatre practice, occasionally as a reviewer (more on this below), but it seems that he commented on theatre and dramatic literature in his lectures too. His manuscript notes contain an extensive list of playwrights covering up to the 1930s. As is characteristic of the systematic Zich, he arranged the list neatly into categories – according to the country, genre and style. His list contains both standard and idiosyncratic descriptions: *historic drama, social, irreal, expressionist, philosophical, nonrealism, grotesque, noetism, the drama of silence, ideological (plays), civilism, factual, fantasticism* or *the unconscious*. Zich's surviving papers also contain a single page of notes on modern stage directing. These notes are rather fragmentary but provide a solid outline of Zich's breadth of knowledge and interest in contemporary theatre practice. The notes are arranged according to the contemporary understanding of the development of stage directing, starting with the Meiningen Ensemble, followed by a lengthy list of stage directors working in the realistic style. It is noteworthy that Zich names both Otto Brahm and Konstantin Stanislavski as the supreme representatives of psychological realism. He arranges other directors more or less chronologically, adding a few terms to characterise them, such as:

Edward Gordon Craig – *visual-arts-isation*; Max Reinhardt – *sensual externalisation of scene, lighting!*; Leopold Jessner – *expressionism*; Tairov – *(Russian Comm.), unleashed stage* [alluding to the title of Tairov's book], *actor is everything*; Meyerhold – *mechanisation, detheatricalisation*; Piscator – *scenotechnol., rotating scene* [stage], *changeable, projected*.

The list comprises more than twenty other names, including a few Czech directors. In effect, this is a very close look at a period that is referred to today as the Modern, sometimes subdivided into Modernism, Expressionism and Constructivism or the Avant-Garde. Most importantly it shows that Zich was clearly aware of the most recent developments in theatre practice (Tairov, Meyerhold, Piscator) but he remained rather sceptical of them. His conservative aesthetics were a conscious approach critically justified by his aesthetic argumentation.

Zich wasn't the first university academic at Charles University to incorporate theatre and drama into his lectures. His concept of aesthetics as a scientific system derived from his teacher Otakar Hostinský and his lectures of the 1890s, comprehensively reconstructed by Zdeněk Nejedlý in the 1921 book *Otakar Hostinský's Aesthetics: Part I General Aesthetics* (Otakara Hostinského Estetika: Díl 1. Všeobecná estetika). Side by side Hostinský, drama (and later also theatre) emerged in individual philological disciplines – first in classical philology; later it can be found in linguistic modules on classical German drama, Shakespeare, French classicism and even modules on Kalidasa's dramas introduced by Josef Zubatý (the founder of Czech Indology). Václav Tille (1867–1937), who was a decade older than Zich, received his habilitation promotion (*Dozentur*) at about the same time as Zich. He worked in the department of comparative literature and gave lectures that explicitly focused on theatre history. In 1929, Tille introduced a seminar module, explicitly entitled "Theatre Seminar", on the comparative study of dramatic literature and its productions. Next to Zich, Tille played a formative role in the institutionalisation of Theatre Studies as a discipline concerned with the history of theatre productions. Tille, who systematically followed theatrical trends in the Czech lands and abroad, brought to the field his ethnographic expertise as well as his experience as a theatre reviewer and writer. It is worth noting that Tille also mediated the contacts with the burgeoning discipline of Theatre Studies (*Theaterwissenschaft*) in Germany. In 1931 he visited the theatre departments at the universities in Munich and Berlin, and published a detailed and influential report on his experience, including a vivid description of Carl Hagemann's practical classes on stage directing, which were part of Max Herrmann's programme of theatre studies in Berlin. Tille wrote his text to encourage local efforts at establishing the discipline institutionally. Ethnography, as a study of culture, thus served as one of the key points of departure for the academic study of theatre.

SCHOLARLY SOURCES FOR ZICH'S *AESTHETICS*

Not even earlier drafts of his *Aesthetics of the Dramatic Art* available in Zich's archival papers contain explicit references to scholarly sources and criticism. The early drafts include only fragmentary excerpts from sources, but in the book manuscript the wording is so remote from all these excerpts that any clear identification of their provenance is impossible. Anyway, what would be the point of such an identification apart from a positivist proof of a textual connection? After all, the intellectual and conceptual bedrock from which Zich departed necessarily permeates his *Aesthetics*. At the same time, his theoretical originality and intellectual creativity transformed this theoretical context substantially. Despite originality in his aesthetics of theatre, Zich wasn't a recluse outside of any map of contemporary intellectual contexts.

One such map of the period discourse can be derived from the journal *Zeitschrift für Ästhetik und allgemeine Kunstwissenschaft* (Journal of Aesthetics and the General Science of Art), established in 1906 by the German scholar of aesthetics Max Dessoir (1867–1947). As has become clear, this journal played a seminal role in the formation of aesthetics and art studies as they are today. Dessoir was attempting to systematise the discipline and without prejudice gave space in his journal to all new methodological impulses in the area of art studies:

> the content of the articles published in the *Journal* enables assessment of the innovativeness of the emerging literary theory in Eastern and Central Europe, with its special focus on formalism and phenomenology, as they convey the intellectual climate, background and standard toolbox of the era's philosophy of art as well as literary and art

studies. [...] [I]t took the geniuses of the Formalists, the Phenomenologists and, later, the Structuralists to bring about the synergy, as an effect of which the fragments of theory scattered around different issues of the *Journal* unified and solidified into literary theory in its various, but related, forms. (Mrugalski 2023: 119)

All of Zich's methodological inspirations discussed in the present text – such as experimental psychology, formalism or phenomenology – were covered and discussed as the points of departure for "scientific aesthetics" in Dessoir's *Zeitschrift*. The links were very close, as we will see below in Zich's responses to individual texts. This is not to say that Zich was dependent on the contributions to Dessoir's *Zeitschrift* but rather that they shared theoretical questions and methodological challenges. Among such questions was the problem of style in individual arts and the possibilities of studying artistic creativity. It was also Dessoir who introduced a distinction between the artistic and the aesthetic object – a distinction later developed by phenomenology (see Mrugalski 2023: 123). Zich himself dedicated an extensive study to the question: "Hodnocení estetické a umělecké" (Aesthetic and Artistic Evaluation; 1917). Dessoir's theoretical impulses helped shape the academic programme of the nascent departments of art studies: "All these schools tried to pin down the relation between the aesthetic and the technical aspects of artworks, the problem assigned to future generations by Dessoir's watchword" (Mrugalski 2023:123). It is not surprising then that that very same problem is a key question of Zich's *Aesthetics of the Dramatic Art*.

Numerous studies and texts have demonstrated convincingly that the *Zeitschrift* also contributed to establishing Theatre Studies as an aesthetic and historical discipline. Zich reviewed several of the journal issues for the readers of the Czech scholarly journal of philosophy and aesthetics *Česká mysl*. Among Zich's papers can be found his list of studies on theatre and drama published in the *Zeitschrift* in its first 18 years:

I. Helene Herrmann: Ibsens Alterskunst [Ibsen's Late Style];
II. Wilhelm Waetzold: Kleists dramatischer Stil [Kleist's Dramatic Style];
III. Hans Wütschke: Friedrich Hebbel und das Tragische [F.H. and the Tragic];
IV. Ernst Bacmeister: Die Tragödie im Lichte der Anthropogenie [Tragedy in the Light of Anthropogeny];
V. Heinz Schnabel: Über das Wesen der Tragödie [On the Essence of Tragedy]; Hans Heinrich: Hebbels Anschauungen über das Komische nach ihren historischen Grundlagen [Hebbel's Views on the Comic on the Basis of Historical Principles]; Bernhard Luther: Die Tragik bei Ibsen [The Tragic in Ibsen];
VI. Julius Bab: Von den sprachkünstlerischen Wurzeln des Dramas [On the Literary Roots of Drama]; Waldemar Conrad: Bühnenkunst und Drama [Stage Art and Drama];

VIII. Richard Müller-Freienfels: Über die Formen der dramatischen und epischen Dichtung [On the Forms of Dramatic and Epic Poetry];

IX. Wilhelm von Scholz: Das Schaffen des dramatischen Dichters [The Creative Work of the Dramatic Poet]; Robert Petsch: Die Theorie des Tragischen im griechischen Altertum [The Theory of Tragedy in Classical Greece]; Erwin Hernried: Weltanschauung und Kunstform von Shakespeares Drama [The World View and Art Form in Shakespeare's Drama];

X. Christoph Schwantke: Vom Tragischen [On the Tragic];

XI. Willi Fleming: Epos und Drama [The Epic and Drama]; Albert Görland: Die Idee des Zufalls in der Geschichte der Komödie [The Idea of Chance in the History of Comedy]; Johannes Bathe: Leben und Bühne in der dramatischen Dichtung [Life and the Stage in Dramatic Poetry];

XIV. Heinrich Merk: Wilhelm von Scholz als Theoretiker des Dramas [Wilhelm von Scholz as a Theorist of Drama]; Robert Klein: Heinrich Theodor Rötschers Theorie des Schauspielkunst [H. T. R.'s Theory of the Theatre Art]; Friedrich Kreis: Die Begrenzung von Epos und Drama in der Theorie Otto Ludwigs [The Definition of the Epic and Drama in Otto Ludwig's Theory];

XVI. Theodor A. Meyer: Das deutsche Drama und seine Form [German Drama and Its Form];

XVIII. Friedrich Kainz: Zur dichterischen Sprachgestaltung [On the Poetic Formation of Language]; Helene Herrmann: Studien zu Heinrich von Kleist [Studies on H. v. K.]; Kurt Sommer: Über Gruppierung der Gestalten im Drama [On the Grouping of Personas in Drama].

(cited from Ivo Osolsobě's endnotes in Zich 1986: 334)

This list requires at least a brief commentary as most of the authors' names are practically unknown nowadays. However, Helene Herrmann (1877–1944), whose name appears twice in Zich's list, is worth highlighting. Herrmann was the first married woman in Germany ever to study at university. Her husband was the famous theatre scholar Max Herrmann (1865–1942), one of the founders of *Theaterwissenschaft*. Helene Herrmann was a specialist trained in German philology and art history and established herself as a theatre and literary scholar in her own right. Another figure particularly inspirational for Zich was Richard Müller-Freienfels (1882–1949). Apart from his study published in the *Zeitschrift*, Zich also reviewed his book *Psychologie der Kunst* (Psychology of Art, 1912) and praised the book's clarity and concision of writing, the empirical approach to psychological aesthetics and particularly the absence of conventional jargon "so popular in aesthetics". It is apparent that Zich found great interest in Müller-Freienfels's typology of artistic perception and the possible typologies of creative types. Overall, a majority of the studies that Zich lists from the *Zeitschrift* focus on questions of style, and methodologically on contemporary experimental psychology and issues of creativity.

At least one of the authors who contributed to the *Zeitschrift* and appears in Zich's list remains a well-known figure to this day – dramaturg, playwright and theatre critic Julius Bab (1880–1955). On account of Bab's essay "On the Literary Principles of Drama" (1911), Zich asserted that Bab's approach was rather narrow, "ignoring the mimic and scenic aspects of drama" (*pomíjejíc v dramatu stránku mimickou a scénickou*). At the same time, he praised Bab's definition of the playwright as "a poet whose life's feeling focuses on *speaking* people and whose need for *creativity* activates by the experience (*Erleben*) of people *in dialogue*" (*jako básníka, jehož životní cit se orientuje na* mluvících lidech *a u něhož potřeba* tvořiti *vzněcuje se zážitkem* (Erleben) rozmlouvajících lidí; *Česká mysl*, 1912: 93). It is characteristic of Zich to be criticising the tendency to reduce dramatic work to the text; on the other hand, he appreciates Bab's observations that the playwright's creativity works with real-world experience of human communication, which includes not only the words but also the agents themselves – in other words, it works with the real-world experience of a situation.

It was not only articles on theatre and drama in the *Zeitschrift für Äesthetik und allgemeine Kunstwissenschaft* that caught Zich's attention, but especially studies of experimental psychology and on aesthetics inspired by early phenomenology. In many ways, Zich shares Waldemar Conrad's (1878–1915) views expressed in his extensive study "Stage Art and Drama" published in the 1911 issue of the *Zeitschrift*:

> Podstatou dramatu jest auktorovi představovati děje či pochody v citovém a snahovém životě lidském. Prostředkem toho jest slovo a hra (mimika); tím stává se scéna nejvhodnější půdou pro drama a naopak drama nejideálnějším účelem umění scénického. (*Česká mysl*, 1912: 93)
> [For the author the basis of the dramatic text is to represent the actions and processes in the emotional and aspirational life of people. Its instrument is the word and play (mimics); in this way, the scene [or stage] becomes the optimal place for drama, and vice versa, drama becomes the ideal objective of the scenic art.]

This agreement in views shows that Zich not only reported on the contents of the journal but also sorted and classified the texts systematically, and in dialogue with these texts honed his own views. Within the contextual maps of Zich's influences, Waldemar Conrad is a lesser known figure today but in his own time belonged to the highly relevant scholars of aesthetics inspired by early phenomenology. It is a well-known fact that the key figure of phenomenology, Edmund Husserl (1859–1938), never expanded his phenomenological philosophy to the area of aesthetics. It was Conrad, Husserl's student at Göttingen, who ventured in that direction. The very first issue of Dessoir's *Zeitschrift* contains Conrad's lengthy study entitled "The Aesthetic Object"

(*Der ästhetische Gegenstand*), which has been hailed as "the first description of the aesthetic object according to the method elaborated in the *Logische Untersuchungen* of his teacher Edmund Husserl" (Angelucci 2010: 53). Conrad's study on the theatre is virtually unknown today, but could be considered as one of the first attempts to approach theatre from a phenomenological perspective.

Phenomenological aesthetics became one of the recurrent topics in the later issues of the *Zeitschrift*, often emerging as a topical subject of debate. This was very prominent in the 1925 issue (Vol. XIX) that comprises the proceedings from the Second Congress of Aesthetics and General Art Studies (*Zweiter Kongreß für Ästhetik und allgemeine Kunstwissenschaft*), held in Berlin on 16–18 October 1924. Although Zich makes no explicit references to Husserl or those of his students working in the field of phenomenological aesthetics, the very fact that Zich followed it in his reviews and consolidated his system simultaneously with the new subdiscipline is significant. Zich and early phenomenological aesthetics shared a common point of departure in philosophical logic and in experimental psychology. In agreement with Emil Volek's recent claim I would argue that Zich's *Aesthetics of the Dramatic Art* should be read first and foremost as a phenomenological work (see Volek in Zich 2019).

In one of his reports on the *Zeitschrift* that Zich wrote for *Česká mysl*, he comments on new developments in psychological theory:

Nejcennější je článek K. Groosův Das ästhetische Miterleben und die Empfindungen aus dem Körperinnern. Přijímaje teorii James-Langeovu (naše emoce jsou v podstatě tělové počitky, inkluzive libé či nelibé jich zabarvení) jako empirický fakt psychologický, *spatřuje podstatu estetického citu* (nikoli ovšem soudu!) *především v tělových počitcích* — ústrojí zažívacího, dýchacího, hlasového – *vznikajících instinktivním vnitřním napodobením a tedy i "spoluzažitím"* (Miterleben) *předmětu esteticky nazíraného* (např. postoje sochy, spádu hudby atd.) Závěrečný akt tohoto procesu je promítání tohoto našeho *tělesného* "zážitku" aneb, chcete-li, "já" do estetického předmětu, jemuž se tím propůjčuje výraz. (Česká mysl X, 1909: 296–297; emphasis mine)

[The issue's most valuable article is K. Groos's "The Aesthetic Co-Experiencing and Cognition from within the Body". Drawing on James–Lange's theory as an empirical psychological fact, stating that our emotions are basically bodily sensations, with pleasant or unpleasant adumbrations, *Groos finds the basis of the aesthetic feeling* (but not of judgement!) *primarily in bodily sensations* – in the digestive, respiratory or vocal organs; *these sensations arise from instinctive inner imitation and therefore in the "co-experiencing"* (Miterleben) *of the thing that we observe aesthetically* (e.g., the posture of a statue or the cadence in music). The final phase of this process of projecting our *bodily* "experience" into the aesthetic object – or, if you will, of projecting our "self" into it – is that we lend the object an expression.]

Zich's formulation suggests not only his own theoretical interests (James-Lange's theory of correspondence) but its emphasis on inner physiological experiencing of the aesthetic feeling also anticipates what Zich later comes to call *inner tactile perception*.

Other notes and excerpts surviving among Zich's paper helps reconstitute a certain map – albeit fragmentary – of the critical work that Zich knew. The crucial figure among the scholars was naturally Zich's teacher, aesthetician and musicologist Otakar Hostinský – the first prominent representative of scientific aesthetics derived from the philosophy of Johann Friedrich Herbart (1776–1841). It was Hostinský who introduced Richard Wagner's concept of the *Gesamtkunstwerk* (total artwork or synthetic work of art) to Czech culture. At the same time, Hostinský belonged to a generation that naturally operated in a bilingual environment. His treatises *The Beautiful in Music and the Gesamtkunstwerk from the Point of View of Formal Aesthetics* (*Das Musikalisch-Schöne und das Gesamtkunstwerk vom Standpunkte der formalen Aesthetik*; Leipzig, 1877) and *Herbart's Aesthetics and Their Fundamental Parts Introduced and Articulated with Reference to Sources* (*Herbart's Aesthetik in ihren grundlegenden Teilen quellenmässig dargestellt und erläutert*; Hamburg, 1891) contribute simultaneously to the German tradition of Herbartian philosophy, systematically expanding it towards aesthetics and to Czech academic studies, to which Hostinský introduced the system in his lecture series. In the Czech context, Hostinský pioneered the development of aesthetics as a systematic, empirical discipline. Among his students it was primarily Otakar Zich who carried on in this intellectual tradition. (For a broader context of the links between Czech aesthetics and Herbartism, see Steiner 2017 and 2023.)

ZICH AND THE FORMATION OF *THEATERWISSENSCHAFT*

Reconstructing Zich's critical reading, it transpires that German-language scholarship dominates his bibliography, such as the book by the theatre critic Sigmund Bytkowski (1866–1923), *Gerhart Hauptmanns Naturalismus und das Drama* (Hamburg, 1908). Zich seems to have followed the work of his colleague from the Prague German University, Arnulf Perger (1883–1955): his early work *The System of Dramatic Technique* (*System der dramatischen Technik*; Weimar, 1911) or his later books *Unity and Disunity of Place in Drama* (*Einortsdrama und Bewegungsdrama*; Rohrer, 1929) or *Transposition of Action as an Artistic Principle in Drama* (*Die Handlungstransponierung als dramatisches Kunstprinzip*; Rohrer, 1932), which are effectively contemporary with Zich's *Aesthetics* and also share the effort of an analytical classification of drama and theatre. Both Zich and Perger emphasise the playwright's work with time and space, and their central theoretical category is *action (Handlung)*.

Zich also made excerpts from such books as Ernst Hirt's *Formal Principles of Epic, Dramatic and Lyrical Poetry* (*Das Formgesetz der epischen, dramatischen und lyrischen Dichtung*; Leipzig and Berlin, 1923), Walther Lohmeyer's *Dramaturgy of the Masses* (*Die Dramaturgie der Massen*; Berlin, 1913), Käte Friedemann's *The Role of the Narrator in the Epic* (*Die Rolle des Erzählers in der Epik*; Leipzig, 1910) or T. A. Meyer's *Stylistic Principles in Poetry* (*Stilgesetz der Poesie*; Leipzig, 1901).

Zich made many notes on the works of the theatre scholar and director Carl Hagemann (1871–1945), especially on his books *Modern Stage Art* (*Moderne Bühnenkunst*; 4th edition, 1916–1918), *Theatre Art and Theatre Artists* (*Schauspielkunst und Schauspielkünstler*; Berlin, 1910) and *Opera and the Stage* (*Oper und Scene*; Berlin, 1905). Hagemann can serve as a helpful illustration of the intellectual world Zich inhabited: graduating in 1900, Hagemann was an early student of Max Herrmann, Helene Herrmann's husband and one of the founders of German theatre studies. Hagemann became a literary critic and theatre historian, and later also a respected stage director and Intendant (company manager). Years later, theatre scholar Carl Niessen hailed him as the best educated stage director of his generation (Niessen in Altmann 1964: 4). Hagemann's stage directing style goes beyond descriptive realism and illusive naturalism, experiments with different ways of simplifying the performance space, often with the help of lighting. It was Max Reinhardt (1873–1943) who had the strongest impact on him – as well as on his other theatre contemporaries, such as Jaroslav Kvapil (1968–1950) at the National Theatre in Prague. In effect, all these artists were occupied with the same questions that Zich tried to explore as a theorist – overcoming the literal and mechanical depictions of realism towards a consistent stylisation, and the originality of the actor's creative work. Arguably, Hagemann's practice-based reflections had significant influence on the second part of Zich's *Aesthetics* that deals with the artistic questions of stage directing and opera.

Although there is no tangible evidence that Zich knew Max Herrmann's texts, the fact that he read and studied Carl Hagemann, Julius Bab and Helene Herrmann is sufficient proof that Zich and Herrmann shared an intellectual context.

It is beyond the scope of this Afterword to summarise the origins of German theatre studies (*Theaterwissenschaft*) as a discipline (for that, see Quinn 1991 or Fischer-Lichte 1999), but the key formative figures of the process were Max Herrmann (1865–1942) in Berlin, Artur Kutscher (1878–1960) in Munich and Carl Niessen (1890–1969) in Cologne. Each of them approached the task of establishing and justifying the discipline differently – founding it in different theoretical and disciplinary principles and giving it different grounds for methodological autonomy, independent of literary studies, literary history, modern philology or ethnography.

Max Herrmann was the first to make the fundamental distinction between drama and theatre, under the influence of contemporary theatre practice, namely the practice of Max Reinhardt. For Herrmann, the new discipline of *Theaterwissenschaft* was:

> the study of the non-literary aspects of theatre, which were resolved for him, primarily, by a focus on reconstructing the conditions of past theatre performances (with specific emphasis on theatre buildings). (Quinn 1991: 127)

The historical reconstruction of a theatre performance with a special view to the audience and the social dimension of the event became a crucial method. Although Herrmann wrote extensively, his approach still can't be understood as a holistic and systematic approach to theatre studies. His student Hans Knudsen wrote of him later:

> ...denn er war weit mehr ein Problemsucher als ein Problemlöser. Es war ihm nicht so wichtig, dass in seinen Übungen "Ergebnisse" herauskamen, es war ihm nur entscheidend, dass die Wege zu den Lösungen gefunden wurden. (Knudsen 1950: 59)
> [...since he was more of a problem seeker than a problem solver. It wasn't so important for his explorations to arrive at "results"; the decisive thing was that the path to the solutions was found.]

At the University of Cologne, Carl Niessen established a university institute and an extensive collection that contained artefacts from a range of performative activities, far beyond the narrow limits of theatre. His approach was more broadly ethnographic or anthropological – without a rigorous theoretical system – and his research focused on:

> all kinds of performance from various cultures and historical periods, ranging from performances from classical drama to festivals, rituals, ceremonies and games – what we would today call cultural performances. (Fischer-Lichte 2014: 13)

ARTUR KUTSCHER AND HUGO DINGER AS ZICH'S CONTEMPORARIES

Munich's Artur Kutscher contributed a more systematic concept of theatre studies.

> [Kutscher] focused on the mimic and expressive quality of performance and [his] research extended to the non-literary folk and religious theatre traditions in Southern Germany and Europe. (Fischer-Lichte 2014: 13)

The approaches of the three foundational figures of German *Theaterwissenschaft* also differ in the way in which they approach the discipline historically – as a sum of facts, often of a positivist kind – or in their effort to establish it *vis-à-vis* modern theatre practice as a complex theoretical-historical discipline on a par with other aesthetic disciplines. In this respect, Otakar Zich is closest to Artur Kutscher and his concept of *Theaterwissenschaft*.

Kutscher derived his approach from the work of the little-remembered scholar Hugo Dinger (1865–1941), who was a professor at the University of Jena. Of an age with Max Herrmann, he is considered one of the founders of the discipline and, according to Michael Quinn, he shares with Herrmann the primacy of delivering "[t]he first lectures on theatrical art in Germany [...] in 1900 at two universities, Jena and Berlin". On account of his early influence, Quinn adds:

> Dinger's work, impressive in length and in the complexity of its Neo-Kantian arguments, has long been overlooked, though his course at Jena in 1914 was the first full course in theatre in any German institution of higher education. (Quinn 1991: 124)

And yet his work has been mostly forgotten. Rather uniquely, his treatise *Dramaturgy as Science* (*Dramaturgie als Wissenschaft*; Part 1, 1904; Part 2, 1905) has received a passing mention in Janek Szatkowski's *A Theory of Dramaturgy*:

> Hugo Dinger presents not only the first attempt to reflect dramaturgy as a science, but also hints at the difference between systems (science and art). (Szatkowski 2019: 122)

In his brief but succinct summary Szatkowski emphasises Dinger's aspiration to link theatre theory with contemporary experimental psychology. In this way Dinger could well have served as an inspiration for Zich.

In keeping with the period efforts at a rigorous and systematic approach to aesthetics – vehemently promoted in the German-language academia by Max Dessoir in his *Zeitschrift* and through an infrastructure of congresses and seminars – Hugo Dinger tried to formulate "dramaturgy" (i.e., the theoretical study of drama and theatre) as a scientific activity. He expanded the concept of dramaturgy beyond its usual remit inherited from the 18th and 19th centuries that understood dramaturgy purely as relating to the dramatic text. Dinger views dramaturgy in broader terms as a theory of "the dramatic art", which is:

> Darstellung in der sinnlichen Anschauung, nicht der abstrakten Vorstellung, ist nicht erzählte Handlung, sondern angeschaute. Durch abstrakte Vorstellung als Mittel wirkt vermöge der Intuition und Assoziation die Kunst der Dichtung, in konkreter "Vorstel-

lung" – das Wort buchstäblich genommen im Sinne von Vorführung – die dramatische. (Dinger, Part I, 1904–05: 242)
[a performance in the sensual perception, not in the abstract presentation; it is not narrated action, but visually perceived action. In abstract presentation as a medium the art of poetry works by means of intuition and association, whereas in concrete "presentation" – the word *Vorstellung* taken literally in the sense of *presenting* – what works is the dramatic art.]

Dinger views the dramatic art as identical with live theatre performance, whereas dramatic literature or poetry (*dramatische Dichtung*) – the dramatic text, that is – is no more than an abstract concept or a "project". (The metaphors Dinger uses are telling: the text is to the dramatic art what the architectural project is to the resulting building or what the score is to live music.) It follows from Dinger's approach that he refuses to see the roots of theatre and drama in literary art forms (or in their combinations), but rather relies on contemporary ethnography to trace theatre back to the physical imitations made by humans – that is, dance. Dinger offers a working hypothesis that rejects the idea that theatre had stemmed from one place – i.e., the notion that the origins of (European) theatre lie in ancient Greek culture; he proposes an investigation that would test the claim that theatre (or the dramatic art, as Dinger terms it) emerges spontaneously and independently at a certain level of development of any national culture from various physical, choreographic or ritualistic practices.

From today's perspective Dinger's book appears rather inaccurate in its terminology as Dinger is inconsistent in his own definitions. At the same time his approach goes against the usage of terms as they were established later. So, in the volume entitled *Texts on Theatre Theory* (*Texte zur Theorien des Theaters*, 1991), probably the most recent collection that reprints extracts from Dinger's book, the editors felt compelled to note:

Nicht nur der Titel von Dingers Buch ist erläuterungsbedürftig. Die komplette Darstellung leidet an terminologischen Defekten, die dem heutigen Leser erhebliche Verständnisschwierigkeiten bereiten dürfen. Das ist Schade. Denn Dingers "Versuch" ist der erste deutschsprachige Beitrag zur Begründung der Theaterwissenschaft. (Balme and Lazarowicz 1991 : 51)
[It's not only the title of Dinger's book that needs explanation. The entire discourse suffers from terminological flaws that present today's reader with considerable difficulties for comprehension. That's a pity since Dinger's *Attempt* is the first German contribution to the establishment of theatre studies.]

Authors who take Dinger as a point of departure therefore make significant shifts in their use of terms. Most prominent among them, Artur Kutscher in his treatise *The Principles of Theatre Studies* (Grundrisse der Theaterwissenschaft, 1949) follows Dinger's concept of the dramatic art as a concrete temporal and spatial art form (Kutscher 1949: 137).

It certainly won't go unnoticed that Dinger's definition of the dramatic art has much in common with Otakar Zich's concepts, including their use of similar analogies and metaphors. However, significant differences separate them. While both of them are concerned with establishing the "dramatic arts" as an autonomous aesthetic phenomenon with its own specific working methods and principles, Zich practically avoids using any historical, diachronic perspectives to make his arguments. In that he is strictly empirical and ahistoric, analysing what it is here and now that we perceive as dramatic art. At the same time, Zich narrows down the area of dramatic art and restricts it to only a partial segment of theatre art. In so doing, he eschews the terminological jumble that riddles and eventually also dooms Dinger. Dinger's theory clearly influenced Zich and one can trace the continuity, especially when Zich adopts Dinger's taxonomies and gives his own book the subtitle of "theoretical dramaturgy". At the same time, Zich is entirely independent in the elaboration of his theoretical system, far exceeding Dinger in the detail and integrity of his theory. (As a side note, the inaugural issue of Dessoir's *Zeitschrift* printed a review of Dinger's book. Zich clearly read it.)

Zich's working papers also contain commented excerpts from Artur Kutscher's *The Art of Expression on the Stage* (Die Ausdruckskunst der Bühne; Leipzig, 1910). In this early work Kutscher reflects theoretically the state of the art in the theatre at the turn of the nineteenth and twentieth centuries. Kutscher is rather selective in his view of history – highlighting the progressive and modernising efforts that started with the Meiningen Ensemble, proceeding to Otto Brahm's Freie Bühne Theatre and concludes with Max Reinhardt. His perspectives on theatre derive substantially from Edward Gordon Craig (1872–1966) viewing theatre as a unified and elaborated organism that necessitates a director as its supreme controlling creator. From that point of view Kutscher foregrounds the most recent Modernist theatre trends and interprets them as a qualitative change – from a theatre of comedians to an artistic and poetic(!) theatre. Although he views poetry (i.e., dramatic poetry) as no more than one of the components of theatre, he places it highest in the hierarchy, arguing that theatre is "the place for the presentation of poetry" (*der Ort der Darstellung von Dichtung*; Kutscher 1910: 12). I would argue that Zich derived most of his knowledge of contemporary German theatre practice from Kutscher – either directly, or through the mediation of other reviewers of Kutscher. He also agrees with the view that modern theatre in its complexity and artistic elaboration is qualitatively different from the theatre of preceding eras. (Zich also shared Kutscher's critical view of "low" theatre genres and theatre entertainment.)

They both understand drama differently but these differences are more or less a circumstantial matter of perspective – Kutscher refers to the dramatic text, whereas for Zich, the dramatic work is the performance, conceived in outlines by the playwright but then completed by other creators along the lines of the text's indeterminacies and lacunas. The dramatic text is central in this process for Zich, but he views it as a performative conception, to use today's term. It is also worth noting that both Kutscher and Zich dedicate a great deal of attention to the issues of artistic stylisation. On the one hand they require that art moves beyond naturalism, which they view as a mechanical approach lacking in creativity. On the other, they call for a style that is consistent as an expression of a conscious creative activity. To a great extent, Kutscher's book critiques contemporary German theatre finding fault with Max Reinhardt – who was, at the time, unconditionally venerated – suggesting that his productions are somewhat fragmented both externally and stylistically.

KUTSCHER'S SYSTEMIC *THEATERWISSENSCHAFT*

Kutscher's next significant book, *An Outline of Theatre Studies* (*Grundriß der Theaterwissenschaft*), published only in 1932, differs in its principles substantially from his first treatise. Naturally, this second book couldn't have influenced Zich's *Aesthetics*, which had come out the previous year, but the direct lines of influence and questions of "progeny" are less important here than the mutual entanglement of intellectual contexts within which Zich operated. From that perspective a comparison of the two books is worthwhile given that Kutscher and Zich as contemporaries, only a year apart, shared and responded to the same trends of modern European theatre.

Kutscher's *Outline* is, in a way, an introduction to theatre studies as well as the first systematic treatment of the new discipline – and not only in the German-speaking world. In this aspect there is no point looking for similarities with Zich, as his *Aesthetics* follows a very different agenda. However, as far as the dramatic work is concerned, Dinger serves Kutscher as a point of departure. Equally, Kutscher sees the anthropological root of theatre in the *mimus* (mime) – that is, in the universal human ability and need to physically depict and externalise inner processes (such as ideas and feelings) and Kutscher projects this onto his concept of drama, just like Dinger (and also Zich). For Kutscher, the dramatic text is no more than a capturing of the conception that is to be performed on the stage. In contrast to a literary and reductively textual perspective, drama should be understood dramaturgically, argues Kutscher with a reference to Dinger:

Eine *Bewertung* des Dramas von rein literarischem oder philologischem Standpunkte aus ist nur für einzelne nebensächliche Fragen berechtigt, im ganzen aber ungemäß; es muß vielmehr *dramaturgisch* Stellung genommen werden. Die literarisch-dichterische Leistung geht die Kritik nur an, insoweit sie die dramatische stützt. Uns handelt es sich um Stil. Die dramaturgische Frage lautet: inwiefern ist das Drama dramatisch? Was gibt der Wortlaut für die Aufführung her? Welche Darstellungsmöglichkeiten bestehen für dies Stück? Entspricht die textliche Form der szenischen? Die äußere der inneren? Wo sind Deckungen? Brüche? Das Gemäße? Das Ungemäße? (Kutscher (1949 [1932]: 138)

[An *appraisal* of drama from a purely literary or philological perspective is suitable only in respect of a few secondary issues, but generally it is inappropriate. A *dramaturgical* approach needs to be taken. The literary-poetic achievement interests criticism only insofar that it supports the dramatic. The issue is the style. The dramaturgical question then is: To what extent is the dramatic text dramatic? What does the sound of words contribute to the performance? What staging opportunities arise from the piece? Does the textual form correspond with the scenic one? The outer with the inner? Where are the congruences? Where the discrepancies? What is appropriate [for the stage]? What inappropriate?]

These questions mirror Zich's approach in the first part of *Aesthetics*, namely in Chapter 2 where he discusses what constitutes the *dramaticity* of the dramatic work and formulates the so-called *theatrical paradoxes* (78 above). I leave it to the reader to size up the differences between Kutscher and Zich and between the elaboration of their arguments.

There are also remarkable similarities between Kutscher's *Outline* of 1932 and Zich's *Aesthetics* of 1931, particularly in the passages on the stage director's role in creating the theatre production – following logically from a similar concept of the dramatic work. Both also deal with a crucial issue that has accompanied modern stage directing since the beginnings: the appropriateness and measure of updating or *aktualisace* (bringing the play closer to the present) and the director's right for the autonomy of the stage interpretation. Kutscher allows a certain amount of updating but imposes limitations:

Jede Zeit hat ihr eigenes Daseinsgefühl und ihre eigene Gebärde. Aber eine "Aktualisierung" der Dramatik, besonders der klassischen, kann nicht Aufgabe des Theaters sein. [... Ein] Drama sei ein in seiner Ganzheit gegebener Organismus, der auch im Sinne seiner Entstehungszeit bedingt bleiben müsse. Man könne ihn nicht völlig hinüberreißen in die Gegenwart. (Kutscher 1949 [1932]: 227)

[Every era has its own sense of existence and its own attitudes. But the "updating" of the drama, especially of the classics, cannot be the objective for the theatre. A play in its integrity is an organism in its own right that needs to remain within the logic of its time of creation at least partly. One shouldn't completely shift it over to the present.]

Since Kutscher did not understand drama from a narrowly literary perspective but as a holistic scenic project of the playwright, he argues that this concept should be respected in its integrity:

> Das Drama ist also für die Regie Ausgangspunkt. Aber es gibt für die Bühne kein absolutes Drama, kein Werk von objektivem Charakter und Dauerwert. Kein Drama besteht als bloßer Text; jedes ist an die Schauspielkunst und mit ihr an den Raum gebunden, und zwar zuletzt an einen sehr bestimmten. (Kutscher 1949 [1932]: 227)
> [The drama is therefore the point of departure for stage directing. However, there is no absolute drama for the stage, no artefact that has an objective character and eternal value. No drama exists purely in the text, but it is tied to the art of acting and to the space, and that is true in a particularly concrete way.]

KUTSCHER AND ZICH VS. THE AVANT-GARDE

While the Kutscher of 1910 had been rather critical of the external effects of Reinhardt's directing techniques, the Kutscher of 1932 disapproved of the Avant-Garde directing methods of Leopold Jessner, Erwin Piscator or Alexander Tairov. He stipulates the principles of stage directing in the spirit of the early Modern, citing Carl Hagemann as the supreme authority:

> Künstlerisch erfreulicher sind im allgemeinen die Ideen, die *aus dem Drama selbst entstehen*; sie sind mehr innerer Art und wechseln von Fall zu Fall. Hagemann fordert vom modernen Regisseur "nicht überhaupt irgendeinen Bühnenstil zu betätigen, sondern für jedes Drama den Stil zu erfühlen und zur Gestaltung zu treiben, dessen Normen das einzelne Stück und seine Gattung in sich birgt, nach einer modernen, den besten und tiefsten Geistern seiner Zeit entsprechenden Welt- und Kunstanschauung, in einer großen, durchhaus unbeschränkten Freiheit künstlerischen Schaffens". (Kutscher 1949 [1932]: 230)
> [Artistically more pleasing are generally those ideas that *derive from the drama itself*; they are more of an inner kind and vary from case to case. Hagemann requires that the modern stage director "should operate not only in any stage style whatsoever but intuit a style for each drama and derive a structure whose norms are contained in each piece and its genre, and all that with a modern world view and artistic views that tally with the best and most profound minds of the times, in a great and entirely unhindered freedom of artistic creation."]

Like Zich, Kutscher distinguishes between inner and external techniques of updating. He views the external as negative; the positive approach, he argues, lies in "inner stage directing" (*innere Regie*). He sees the Avant-Garde, "excessively directorial" directors-producers as usurpers of the actors' creativity. Citing Carl Hagemann once again, he admonishes sharply:

> Schon Hagemann schreibt: "Der Schauspieler ist immer das, was der Regisseur aus ihm macht." Für Jeßner war der Schauspieler das Instrument, auf dem der Regisseur spielt, für Piscator die Puppe, die der Marionettenspieler am Draht leitet. Hier war die selbsttätige Regie an ihrem Pole angelangt, sie hatte sich emanzipiert, wie vom Drama, so auch von der Schauspielkunst. Sie war zu Ende in ihrer ganzen Entwicklung.
>
> Das umgekehrte Verfahren wäre genau so schädlich: man kann auch der Individualität des Schauspielers nicht die Zügel überlassen. Die Theatergeschichte warnt davor. Der Urtrieb des Mimen muß dem Theater erhalten bleiben, er ist notwendig und in den richtigen Zusammenhängen schöpferisch, er muß aber eingeordnet und kultiviert werden. Das "entfesselte" Theater is anarchie! (Kutscher 1949 [1932]: 233-234)
> [Already Hagemann wrote: "The actor is always whatever the director makes of them." For Jessner, the actor was an instrument on which the director can play; for Piscator, the actor is a puppet that the puppeteer leads on the strings. Here, the self-controlling stage directing has arrived at its extremes, having emancipated itself both from drama and from the art of acting. It has reached the end of its own development.
>
> The opposite tendency would be as damaging; one cannot hand over the reins to the individuality of the performer either. Theatre history warns against it. The mime's basic instinct needs to be preserved in the theatre as it is necessary and productive in the correct interactions, but it needs to be ordered and cultivated. The "unleashed" theatre is anarchy!]

It is symptomatic of Kutscher's radical proclamation that he cites Jessner and Piscator by name but only refers indirectly to Tairov by alluding to the title of his book *The Unleashed Theatre* (published in English as *Notes of a Director*).

Zich occupies himself with the same question in several places in his book, particularly in Chapter 9 on stylisation. Inducing from the inner structure of the dramatic work and reflecting on the principles of stylisation from the creator's and spectator's points of view, Zich takes a different path, a more analytical one, but arrives principally at similar conclusions:

> *The relative and subjective resemblance between the technical and referential images is necessary for the dramatic work, but only in the signifying sense*, i.e., to assure that the desired referential image is actually evoked in the audience. The *outer truthfulness* obliges the authors of *the literary as well as the musical* text only to the extent that they bound themselves to it by the overall conception of their work. The *same extent* of outer truthfulness is obligatory to all those who co-create this written-down work – whether in the same age and environment or in the future, under other circumstances – which *modifies* their obligation by the fact that the extent of the text's outer truthfulness has changed. The *inner* truthfulness binds everyone absolutely and for good.

> This norm resolves clearly the much-disputed and unnecessarily muddled question of how to stage older dramatic texts. As for the *quantity* of the stylisation, follow the extant texts; as for the *quality*, follow the present day and the audience. (356 above)

Whereas Kutscher formulates a normative and a somewhat prescriptive aesthetic position, Zich carries out a systematic analysis of what today's theory would call "places of indeterminacy" in the structure of the dramatic work and studies the inner structural logic before he, also somewhat normatively, stipulates that this logic needs to be respected. Zich carefully – one could say, phenomenologically – describes how the impression of the work's outer (or inner) truthfulness or verisimilitude is evoked in the audience, and how much this is influenced by different kinds of the spectators' experience – their outer experience (i.e., in relation to the real world), their inner experience (i.e., their emotional and intellectual understanding) and their experience with various forms of artistic stylisations (i.e., how much and what art they have been exposed to).

Zich's and Kutscher's affinity in views illustrates well the interconnectedness (or inseparability) of the Central European theatre space that served both theorists as a springboard for their thought systems. On the anecdotal level, it shows on their categorical rejection of Tairov – only with Zich, this detail can't be found in his *Aesthetics* where Zich meticulously tries to avoid the particular and abandons concrete references in favour of a general, holistic theory. However, in an interview given after the publication of his book, Zich makes a very explicit reference – although much less sharply, given his nature: "I defend [drama] against Tairov and others" (*hájím proti Tairovovi a jiným*; Novák 1933: 465). In the following part of the interview, in response to the question why he had chosen that subject for his book, Zich adds:

> Předně jsem chtěl podpořiti herectví. Zdá se mi, že proti dřívějším dobám [...] je teď zatlačeno z obecného zájmu přílišným kultem režie. [...] I režiséry mám rád, ale ne ty naduté, kteří považují herce jen za "materiál" pro své veledílo. (Novák 1933: 466)
> [Firstly I wanted to write in support of acting. It seems to me that, compared to earlier times, [...] a general emphasis is placed on the excessive cult of stage directing. [...] I like stage directors as well but not the self-important ones who treat actors as a mere "material" for their magnificent work of art.]

Rejecting the Avant-Garde view of theatre was more than a fashionable aesthetic whim. It had grown from a profound paradigmatic difference between different concepts of the work of art as such. Whereas Zich, Kutscher, Appia or Craig work with the concept of a work of art as an organic, coherent and necessarily organised integral unit, Avant-Garde theatre practice stands on entirely different principles. Avant-Garde theatre works of art primarily emphasise the inner dialectical tensions between individual features and components. It is radically more dynamic and aesthetically pluralist or even heterogenous in its concept of the aesthetic object. While these sit well with the Prague School functional-structuralists and later with Theodor W. Adorno and the Frankfurt School, Otakar Zich with his aesthetics views wasn't ready to accept this as artistic.

Zich's theory had an immense impact on the theoretical work of his younger contemporaries, who readily applied their theories to Avant-Garde artistic practice. Martina Musilová (2020) has analysed in detail the relationship between Zich's attitude to the Avant-Garde and to acting methods in particular, with a view to contemporary psychological theories. However, at the time, this application of their theories on the more progressive theatre makers was beyond Zich (or Kutscher).

ZICH AND THE INTELLECTUAL HORIZONS OF HIS AGE

Zich's *Aesthetics of the Dramatic Art* and his theoretical *oeuvre* relates closely to the scholarly and artistic environment of his age. His work runs parallel with trends that emerged as intellectual companions of modern theatre, such as the efforts to establish theatre studies as an independent discipline and provide them with a scientific and philosophical basis – a trend that also coincides with the development of experimental psychology towards phenomenology. It would be futile to mechanically trace any direct influences of scholarly trends from "abroad" on Zich; that would implicitly nourish a pseudo-colonial notion that local reception is no more than derivative epigonism of established authorities. Zich's own thought is autonomous and original and grew out of a range of impulses of the Central European intellectual, artistic and cultural milieu, in which he organically participated all his life.

This milieu has clear sites and boundaries: two universities, a Czech one and a German one, co-existed in Prague, and as for the theatre culture, the artistic worlds of Central European languages mingled actively too, as can be demonstrated on two mutually independent publications in the Czech language – a collection on new Czech theatre and a theatre encyclopedia.

In the years surrounding the publication of Zich's *Aesthetics* (1931), theatre critics and highly knowledgeable intellectuals Josef Kodíček (1892–1954) and Miroslav Rutte (1889–1954) edited several volumes of a collection entitled *Nové české divadlo* (New Czech Theatre, 4 volumes; Prague, 1926, 1927, 1929 and 1932). Although their project produced only four volumes, it almost amounted to establishing a scholarly theatre journal. Individual volumes of *Nové české divadlo* contain specialist analytical and historiographical texts, such as portraits of stage directors, actors, documents, lists of roles and productions, and academic book reviews. They also printed texts written by theatre makers, presenting their artistic reflections and programme manifestos. As a matter of course, Czech theatre practice is viewed here against a backdrop of European theatre, especially the German-language practice – a cultural region ranging roughly from Vienna through Munich to Berlin. Several texts also cover theatre events in France, Soviet Russia or Poland. In other words, local culture is seen as an integral part of a broader, Central European space. This perspective translates also into the reports on scholarly publications, with many of the aforementioned names appearing in *Nové české divadlo* as innovative researchers and academic authors. Zich himself contributed two articles on modern opera and their musical composition – analytical case studies he later incorporated into his *Aesthetics*.

The other publication project – which would also end up as a torso – had started even earlier: a specialist dictionary. Between 1888 and 1909, the Otto Publishing House had produced a general encyclopedia, *Ottův slovník naučný* (Otto's Learned Dictionary). As a follow-up project, Otto attempted a special encyclopedia dedicated to the theatre and its history. Although *Divadelní slovník* (Theatre Dictionary) came out only in the years 1914–1919 and ended with the letter F, it ran into over 1,000 pages and contains remarkable entries. Among them were two, *Dekorace* (décor) and *Divadelní budova* (theatre building), written by stage director and (by this very act) theatre historian Jan Bor (1886–1943). Bor wrote his two entries as extensive historical studies covering the history of theatre architecture and scenography from their beginnings in ancient Greece until the very contemporary experiments from the time of the encyclopedia's publication: Bor included Craig's theories, the relief-scene experiments of Munich's Künstlertheater or directorial approaches of Otto Brahm and Max Reinhardt. Bor's entries contain extensive lists of mostly foreign critical works, including the names of theatre practitioners and scholars discussed above. Craig's writings are listed in both their English and German editions, and also include his journal *The Mask*. In other words, what else could serve as a standard summary of contemporary theatre scholarship than such a meticulously referenced encyclopedia?

It is a great pity that the project didn't reach the letter R, and so we haven't got the entry on *Režie* (stage directing) written by a leading specialist (most likely Jan Bor again). That would have allowed a comparison between the standard period understanding of modern stage directing and Zich's theory in the *Aesthetics*. In other words, when Zich writes in the introduction to his book that the specialists among his Czech readers will recognise what his sources are, he isn't exaggerating: Zich relies on the body of critical literature surrounding *Divadelní slovník* and *Nové české divadlo* – a body that comprised all key theatre makers and specialists relevant to the local, multilingual culture, and one that established a certain canonical standard (instantiated by the bibliographies of Bor's two encyclopedic entries).

The last two examples demonstrate the unity of the Central European cultural and intellectual space, in theatre practice, in academia and in print. It is in this context that Zich wrote his *Aesthetics of the Dramatic Art*, side by side with his German-language colleagues' efforts to emancipate the academic study of theatre and give it a rigorous scientific framework. In this sense, Zich's book is part and parcel of this transnational intellectual organism, complementary to the other intellectual and artistic initiatives.

Using Erika Fischer-Lichte's concepts of theatre studies (Fischer-Lichte et al. 2014: 375–382; entry "*Theaterwissenschaft*"), Zich would certainly fall into the concept of *Theaterwissenschaft als Kunstwissenschaft* (theatre studies as art studies). This shows not only in his view of the dramatic text (and of the dramatic art as such) but also in the emphasis Zich places on distinguishing between the auditorium and the stage as well as on his vehement exclusion of the cabaret and the circus from the dramatic art. For the same reason, it seems, Zich never asks about the origins of the theatre. In so doing, he shuns the inconclusive discussions that occupy his colleagues who relied on ethnography to trace the origins of the theatre in dance, ritual, movement, or – like Kutscher or Niessen – in mime (*mimus*). These discussions combined Nietzsche's concept of tragedy, the thoughts of the Cambridge ritualists and the discussions of the *mimus* prompted by Hermann Reich's book *Der Mimus* (1903), as Peter Marx has summarised (Marx 2017: 149–157). Even though Zich understood drama as live performance, he never adopted any of these ideas. In contrast to most others who took literary studies as their point of departure (and naturally tended towards theatre history or an ethnographic approach to theatre), Zich as an aesthetician and musicologist is closest to Hugo Dinger's philosophical standpoint. His approach bears all the signs of scientific aesthetics as championed by Max Dessoir – the aesthetics and theory of theatre. But there is a significant difference between Dessoir and Zich. In Chapter III "Tonkunst und Mimik" (Sound Art and Mimic) of his influential study *Aesthetik und Allgemeine Kunstwissenschaft* (Aesthetics and General Art Studies, 1906), Dessoir dedicates only one subchapter of about 15 pages to theatre ("Mimik und Bühnenkunst"). Zich, in contrast, wrote an elaborate book-long treatise on theatre as part of his scientific aesthetics. His contribution to the Central European discourse on theatre studies as a discipline is purely synchronic (ahistoric), yet systematically theoretical.

ZICH AND THE CASE OF...

Let us shift the perspective and view Zich in relation to several key figures and theoretical trends. I intentionally do not limit the reach of theatre theory and history but try to match Zich's aesthetic and philosophical outlooks by selecting thought systems, concepts and tendencies that continue to form the broader context of the era. What follows then is an attempt at correlating Zich's work with others. In some cases, the correlations will not only be ones of affinity and justifiable connections but also of principal difference and a lack of compatibility.

...ROMAN INGARDEN AND PHENOMENOLOGY

In the context of the 1930s the thoroughness and elaboration of Zich's theoretical system dedicated exclusively to theatre (or the dramatic art) is unique. It bears comparison only with the influential literary theory of the Polish phenomenological aesthetician Roman Ingarden (1893–1970), published in German as *Das literarische Kunstwerk* (The Literary Work of Art) in 1931, in the same year as Zich's *Aesthetics*. The relationship between these two books, published simultaneously only 250 kilometres apart, deserves a brief comment.

On several occasions in the Introduction to this volume as well as in this Afterword, I have emphasised those elements of Zich's theory that focus on audience reception and I have interpreted them in agreement with Emil Volek's recent discussions of Zich's relationship to phenomenology. Volek argues convincingly against reading Zich as a late representative of nineteenth-century psychologism – a view overwhelmingly common throughout the 1900s, propounded by such Zich scholars and critics as Jan Mukařovský (1891–1975) or Ivo Osolsobě (1928–2012). Against this trend, Volek interprets Zich as an early phenomenologist and in so doing redefines his position on the map of Czech (and possibly European) aesthetic theory:

> Instead of remaining a work that "fell short" or that perpetuated an exhausted tradition, Zich's project emerged as a standalone and unsurpassed phase of Czech aesthetics and as a hitherto missing link in the early development of the phenomenological movement. (Volek's introduction to Zich 2019: 352)

Volek argues that Zich constitutes the "missing link" that anticipates, among others, Jan Mukařovský's attempts at incorporating Edmund Husserl's concept of meaning into functional-structuralist thought.

From this point of view, the coincidental publication in 1931 of the two foundational books, Zich's *Aesthetics of the Dramatic Art* and Ingarden's *The Lit-*

erary Work of Art, invites a more sustained discussion. Firstly, a comparison of the two is complicated at face value by the fact that both works are written in very different styles, so one might be tempted to assert that the two books are perfectly transversal in their objectives and conclusions. Secondly, Zich and Ingarden apparently handle different subject matter – theatre and the dramatic art in one case, and the literary work in the other – and they overlap thematically only in their discussions of the dramatic text. Interestingly, Zich and Ingarden differ significantly on this issue, even though Ingarden's concept of drama as a liminal case of a literary work (i.e., an artistic literary creation of a specific kind) doesn't appear to disagree with Zich's on the surface. They both acknowledge the specificity of the dramatic text but Ingarden sees the text as *dual in nature* (existing as a literary text *and* as a performance text), whereas Zich refuses to accept the autonomous existence of the dramatic text as a literary work.

Ingarden offers a meticulous analysis of the structure of the literary work of art to establish *how* a literary work exists as a work of art. This ontological question becomes his primary objective. To Zich, such a question may seem marginal as he deals with the ontology of performance (i.e., of the dramatic art) relatively simply as that which "we perceive (see and hear) in the course of a performance in the theatre" (60 above) and proceeds to analyse the structure of the work of art as it is perceived by the spectator. However, when Zich gets to discussing the creative work of the playwright, he must necessarily ask in what way the actions, places and personas of the play exist – in what sense is it *ontic*, to use the phenomenological term (see Chapter 4). He makes a fundamental – and in fact ontological – distinction and asserts that whereas in poetry or prose (a novel) these objects are only imaginary, *ideal* (occasionally phenomenologists use the term *ideational*), in the dramatic work, during a theatrical performance, they are *real* (or *ontic*) in the sense that they are presented directly, ostensively, for our senses to perceive them in real time and place. In a formulation that comes close to early phenomenological logic he states:

> Ideální děj není vlastně už ani dějem, nýbrž jen pojmem děje, a jeho časovost není jeho živoucí vlastnost, nýbrž pouhým logickým znakem.
> [Ideal action is in fact no action any more, merely a concept of action and its temporality is not its inherent characteristic, but only a mere logical feature.] (113 above)

In close reading one can trace how the antithesis of *ideal* and *real* forms one of the fundamental, truly ontological distinctions of Zich's theory – where *ideal* (ideational) refers to an object that exists only in thoughts, as an imaginary idea, and *real* (ontic) refers to an object that is perceptible to the senses and ostensively presented. In contrast with Zich, Ingarden – as will be apparent to

1 ZICH'S INTELLECTUAL WORLD: INSPIRATIONS AND SOURCES

anyone who has had the courage to delve into his book at least a little – never arrives at such a simple ontological distinction. Instead, Ingarden builds on the late work of the phenomenologist and his teacher Edmund Husserl and elaborates a much more complex system of ontological categories. Zich's distinction is perhaps closer to Waldemar Conrad, another of Husserl's students of an earlier generation, for whom phenomenology was a form of logic of psychological phenomena. Ingarden departs from their theories – with all due respect paid to Conrad as a relevant predecessor in the field of phenomenological aesthetics. There is, nevertheless, a certain affinity between Zich's and Ingarden's discussions of the ontological status of things (entities) represented in a work of art. Of theatrical reality Zich states:

> Je to skutečnost se životní skutečností sice paralelní, jí odpovídající, ale *noeticky jiná, různorodá.*
> [It is an actuality that is parallel with real-world actuality, corresponding to it, but *noetically other and heterogeneous.*] (349 above)

Like Ingarden, Zich also tends to establish the ontological status of the "reality" (or actuality) of the work of art, but his solution of the issue differs terminologically from Ingarden, who applies a special concept of the *quasi-real* introduced by Husserl.

Another question arises in comparing Zich's and Ingarden's theories: Could Zich's concept of the duality of *the conceptual image* (*významová představa*) be understood as reflecting the ontology of the (mimetic) work of art? (The dual conceptual image refers to the realisation that as spectators we are able to retain in our minds both the image of what we perceive sensually on the stage *and* the imaginary action that is represented. In other words, we can simultaneously think *this is theatre* as well as retain the fiction of the play.) Zich discusses this question not only in the first part of his book but also in the last part, in Chapter 9 on theatrical illusion and style. Here he deploys his concept of the conceptual image to lay out how the spectator perceives the dramatic work and in so doing refines his initial pragmatic definition of the dramatic work, adding the aspect of audience reception:

> Podstata tzv. divadelní iluse *je v divadelním zaměření*, jež, jako speciální případ zaměření obrazového, potlačuje cit skutečnosti a vybavuje k vněmům dvojí představu významovou, technickou a obrazovou.
> [The basis of the so-called theatrical illusion *lies in the theatrical focus*, which – as a special case of the mimetic focus – suppresses the sense of reality and evokes to perceptions a dual conceptual image, the technical and the referential.] (344 above; my emphasis)

This exceeds a definition of *the theatrical illusion* and its analytical delimitation as such. For Zich, the theatrical illusion *establishes* the dramatic work of art – since a dramatic work needs to be recognised as a mimetic work of art (i.e., art that imitates something). The notion of *the theatrical focus* is uniquely Zich's original concept. Zich uses it to refer to the spectatorial mindset – the spectator's readiness, an "attunedness" with which we access a work of art – and recognises that this is an active contribution on the part of the spectator. Audience perception had interested Zich long before his work on the *Aesthetics* and he dedicated several of his earlier studies to its detailed analysis on a wide range of material. In his essay "Estetická příprava mysli" (The Aesthetic Preparation of the Mind, 1921), for instance, he uses examples from music, the visual arts and the theatre to analyse how spectator habits and knowledge serve to create receptional conventions for consuming works of art. Crucially for Zich, the spectator or auditor is not a passive recipient of the art but an active (but not interactive!) co-creator of the meanings that are communicated, and, by extension, an active co-creator of the work of art proper.

Jaroslav Etlík discussed this theoretical tradition of audience engagement in detail in his study "Theatre as Experiencing" (Divadlo jako zakoušení; Etlík 2011 [1999] translates as "Theatre as Experience"). Etlík has pointed out that many semiotic theories operate with a mechanical, passive concept of the spectator as someone who merely decodes prior significations, whereas Zich, in contrast, treats the spectator as an active participant of the process of making meaning in the course of the dramatic work – that is, during the performance. So while Zich doesn't use explicitly phenomenological terms, his discussions of audience perception work with the concept of the dramatic work as something that is conditioned by the spectator's *theatrical focus* – or to rephrase it in phenomenological parlance to highlight the parallels, by the specific intentionality of the spectator's consciousness. Very importantly, Zich presupposes a spectator with a certain awareness of theatre, or at least of the general conventions of art, and with a certain type of spectatorial habit or (as we would say now) of "cultural capital". Of course, where Zich speaks of conceptual images (that is, of concepts in the minds of the recipients), phenomenologists would probably use the term *intentional objects*. In this regard, our comparison of Zich and Ingarden hits against the barrier of a paradigmatic divide. The two thinkers move in widely divergent directions and have surprisingly little in common, apart from a shared interest in a phenomenological approach to works of art.

The originality, importance and efficacy of Zich's theory of the theatrical focus, with its emphasis on the knowledge of conventions, which shapes it, will stand out if we confront it with Ingarden's later study, devoted specifically to drama. In this short essay, entitled "The Function of Language in Theatre" (German in 1958, English in 1973), Ingarden makes a number of subtle findings based on the fact that language in theatre during a performance simultaneously has a dual effect: on the persona and on the spectator. But he focuses his analysis predominantly on the working of language within the represented situation – a narrowing of view for which Jiří Veltruský criticised him (Veltruský 2016 (1976): 406). Moreover, when towards the end of his essay Ingarden tries to come to terms with stylised, non-naturalistic theatre – such as Shakespeare or classical tragedies – he arrives at ridiculous conclusions. He claims that if a play is in verse, then:

> The represented persons in turn behave as if they do not notice that these verses and declamations are often not at all appropriate to the situation. (Ingarden 1973 (1958): 395)

He draws a flawed comparison between theatrical stylisation and a nebulous, intuitive idea of "naturalness" and "natural functions of the speech". In a footnote he adds another bizarre example:

> This occurs to a much greater extent in modern opera, where the "heroes" – participants in a bourgeois drama, e.g., *Madame Butterfly* – do not seem to be at all aware that they are continually singing when they should be simply speaking. (Ingarden 1973 (1958): 395)

Such a simplifying and rather naive view of theatre is surprising, especially from a renowned philosopher, whose model spectator is blithely ignorant of any theatrical conventions or knowledge. In retrospect, Ingarden's initially marginal note in his *Das literarische Kunstwerk* where he purports focusing on spoken drama, omitting "musical drama or musical comedy" (Ingarden 1973 (1931): 318) turns from a minor detail into a more significant issue. If one studies spoken drama only, one can – to a great extent – work with the modern, predominantly realism-oriented theatre and its objective of a "natural behaviour" – whatever that may mean. But all forms of musical drama are by definition stylised and work within obvious cultural conventions. Ingarden's theoretical approach cannot be applied to it – which significantly undermines the validity of his theory in relation to theatre and performance as such.

For the above reasons, it is all the more important that Zich views the dramatic art as one integral whole and it is only its individual parts or kinds that distinguish between spoken and sung drama. In this sense the theory of theatrical conventions and stylisation permeates Zich's book in its entirety and prevents Zich from falling into the trap of naive realism/illusionism. The theory comes to the fore most prominently in the final chapters of *Aesthetics*. In that sense, Zich's concept of the spectator's *theatrical focus* allows him to elaborate on the impression of "realness" that is evoked in the spectator's reception – and Zich manages to do that without the naive simplifications that are still common in theatre theories. The spectator actively creates the impression of "realness" by comparing the work they are watching with their inner (emotional and intellectual) and outer (lived) experience, bringing into the equation their knowledge of theatrical conventions. In this, Zich creates a potent theoretical tool that allows a close reading of a dramatic work of art (a performance, a production) across a wide range of styles and with various types of stylisation, without judging them simplistically on the basis of how "natural" or "distant" they appear in relation to the real world. It is no wonder then that the subchapter on theatrical stylisation was the first to come out in English. Emil Volek and Andrés Pérez-Simón selected and translated it as an extract for journal publication (Zich 2019). The excerpt can work as a self-contained study and it presents a truly refined concept that stands no comparison with other concepts of stylisation, realism or presentation.

Unsurprisingly – and perhaps inevitably – this brief comparison of Zich's theory and Ingarden's phenomenological aesthetics only raises more questions and opens other problems, which would far exceed the scope and objectives of this Afterword. They would require examining phenomenological aesthetics in its entirety and the details of its development as a subdiscipline before one could appraise its possible links with Zich's theory.

Nonetheless, let us sketch out the possible directions of thought. One of the reasons why Czech scholarship has not sufficiently studied the connections between Zich and phenomenology is due to the prevailing understanding of the Czech phenomenological tradition.

> Phenomenological incursions into Czech literary scholarship are associated with the structuralism of the Prague Linguistic Circle in the second half of the 1930s. It is owing to Jan Patočka, who had inspired the 1934 foundation of the Cercle philosophique de Prague pour les recherches sur l'entendement humain [Pražský filosofický kroužek] with its focus on phenomenological enquiry, that a visit to Prague was undertaken, between 11 and 25 November 1935, by Edmund Husserl. (Vojvodík 2023: 323)

Husserl's presence, on the invitation of his first direct student Jan Patočka (1907–1977), is perceived as a symbolic moment, a watershed of sorts, as if phenomenology had not existed beforehand and had not even registered. But the opposite is true: several overviews and outlines had mentioned phenomenology before Husserl's arrival on the scene. To name one instance, the influential Czech philosopher and later politician František Krejčí (1858–1934), who had also taught Zich, mentioned Husserl's early works in his book *Filosofie posledních let před válkou* (Philosophy in the Last Pre-War Years, 1918), namely in the subchapter devoted to the current trends in German idealist philosophy. But Krejčí was a representative of realist and positivist philosophy and seems not to have been willing or able to appreciate Husserl's contributions to knowledge. Krejčí does not deny Husserl's importance but understands his work merely as a new wave of Hegelian philosophy. Given Krejčí's influence we could assert that his assessment slowed down the reception of Husserl in the Czech context. However, this assertion might obscure the possible appeal that Husserl's early works – namely his *Logische Untersuchungen* (Logical Investigation, 1901 and 1906) – could have had to Otakar Zich in their logico-mathematical foundations. In other words, Zich could well have received and incorporated impulses from Husserl – as Emil Volek has identified (Zich 2019).

Additionally, the phenomenological features in Zich's work have been broadly overlooked as Zich has been read primarily within the discipline of aesthetics, or aesthetics and theatre theory. The links with broader philosophical concepts have been in the shadows of the dominant disciplines. Phenomenological philosophy rarely exists independently and it often intertwines with other methodologies and disciplines. It has become standard to read several critical works as instances of such an intertwining, for example Jan Mukařovský's study "Umění jako semiologický fakt" (Art as a Semiological Fact, 1934). Mukařovský's students picked up the impulse, as Josef Vojvodík has recently pointed out:

> During the 1970s and 1980s, various followers of Mukařovský, above all Milan Jankovič, Květoslav Chvatík and Oleg Sus, but also Zdeněk Mathauser, looked at the interference between phenomenology and structuralism. Zdeněk Mathauser stressed, for example, the transcendentally phenomenological hinterland of the structuralist approach and the problem of time. (Vojvodík 2023: 336)

In the context of Czech theory of literature, the works of Zdeněk Mathauser can be seen as:

> an amplification of the structuralist aesthetics, poetics and ontology of the work of literature as art upheld by the Prague School in its dialogue with phenomenology, a dialogue begun inspiringly in the mid-1930s and then interrupted for years to come at the end of the 1940s. (Vojvodík 2023: 336)

If we were to revert to this point of view, we could interpret such an "interference" or "dialogue" not only in relation to Mukařovský but perhaps even more to Zich and several of his works, namely his *Aesthetics of the Dramatic Art* as well as his essays on rhythm in poetry and on the temporal perception of music. The topic of temporality in the arts opens further overlaps between Zich's theory and phenomenology.

This shift of perspective presupposes that in talking about phenomenology we abandon the idea of a singular phenomenological tradition or a single method in the field of art theory – as Patrick Flack has convincingly argued. Phenomenology, especially in its early phases, was characteristic of

> its own inner diversity [as well as] the recurrent and essential role it played in the dynamic system of exchanges and transfers that powered both the rise and the evolution of literary theory as a discipline. At various points in time and to varying degrees, phenomenological ideas provided impetuses that were crucial to the development of many of the major traditions of literary theory (Russian and German formalism, structuralism and post-structuralism, materialist dialectics, hermeneutics, reader-response criticism, deconstruction, etc.). (Flack 2023: 309)

If we extend this reading of the link between phenomenology and literary theory and include theatre theory and general art theory, it is possible to build on Emil Volek's observations on the phenomenological aspects of Zich's thinking and revisit the question of what would a phenomenology of theatre look like today.

…ARISTOTLE AND STRUCTURAL POETICS

The question underlying this subchapter is simple: What "Aristotle" should we relate Zich to? The philosophical and aesthetic tradition of interpreting Aristotle is very extensive, to say the least. What matters for our present purpose is to ascertain which of the strands of Aristotelian tradition – or more specifically, which school of poetics – should Zich be related to? Lubomír Doležel's book *Occidental Poetics* (1990) is as good a point of departure as any for approaching the diversity of Aristotelian tradition.

In *Occidental Poetics* Lubomír Doležel (1922–2017), who is best known for his theory of fictional worlds, brings together the theoretical and historical approaches to the question of poetics. In brief, he has written a history of structural poetics from Aristotle to the Prague School. Logically, Zich's *Aesthetics* is missing in Doležel's account as he concentrates on literary poetics, especially those that were available in English at the time of his writing, but in a sense Zich fits perfectly within the frame of Doležel's concepts of what constitutes *structural poetics*, and Doležel's theory of *literary poetics* aligns with Zich's concepts well.

Doležel takes Aristotle's literary theory, especially his *Poetics*, for the foundational structural poetics in the Western (Occidental) tradition. He argues persuasively that Aristotle was the first to study the art work as a whole comprised of parts that have specific relations to one another – hence, a study of "poetic structures" (Doležel 1990: 24). At the same time, he understands Aristotle as both an empiricist and logician. He reads his *Poetics* as a somewhat ambivalent treatise that is simultaneously theoretical (in that it creates a logical system of concepts) and critical (in appraising and classifying existing works of art). Doležel also views *Poetics* as an essay that turns directly towards creative practice: "Poetics as a productive science is not only a theory of poetry but also a significant factor in its practice" (Doležel 1990: 14). At this abstract level, Zich's treatise can easily fit in with Doležel's theory as Zich also constructs a logical system – and in this sense, Zich is also an Aristotelic theorist who creates systemic thought. Simultaneously, Zich in the second half of his book reflects on contemporary practice and tries to generalise it. Doležel argues that the tension between criticism as a temporal matter and poetics as a scholarly aesthetic discipline plays a key role in Aristotle's treatise. In the subchapter "Criticism versus Poetics" (29–30), Doležel describes the principles as well as limitations of Aristotle's method:

> Aristotle's theory is not an *a priori* construct; it is based on a thorough knowledge of extant Greek tragedies. But the explicit process of theory formation is preceded by a silent intuitive axiological operation; by means of this invisible aesthetic filter a few tragic works are selected into a privileged set, the corpus on which (and for which) the theory will be constructed. *Poetics of the ideal structure is a theory of the poetician's favorite artworks.* (Doležel 1990: 29; my emphasis)

It is in this sense that we may speak of Zich – as we have done repeatedly in the Introduction and this Afterword. For one, Zich doesn't work with *a priori* constructs, an approach he declares in his methodology at the outset of his introduction to *Aesthetics*. Second, he also carries out "a silent intuitive axiological operation" when he determines that he will only be drawing on high-quality artworks for his case studies. In this Zich is far from free of judgemental prejudice. Similarly, the contemporary context intervenes in his book, especially in its central parts, and along with them Zich's personal predilections and tastes. Doležel argues this as a general aesthetic principle in his discussion of Aristotle:

> Aristotle tackled the basic dilemma of poetics: poetics as a science has to be descriptive, but because it studies aesthetic phenomena, it cannot escape axiological assumptions. (Doležel 1990: 33)

The same holds true for Zich. He can't – and clearly doesn't want to – escape from what Doležel calls the inseparable link between poetics and criticism. Zich declares in his introduction that his writing will interweave theoretical and aesthetic approaches – that is, combining poetics and criticisms exactly as Doležal observes in Aristotle. For that reason Zich opens with an admission that his analyses will focus only on selected works – "a selection restricted to those that are truly valuable" (57 above) – and such selections are always partly subjective and partly given by an aesthetic consensus. From today's perspective this selection necessarily (but not incorrectly) comes across as being "of its time".

Doležel also creates a continuous interpretive tradition of individual occidental poetics, beginning with Aristotle and following through to the twentieth century.

> The advance of the mereological model from a *logical* to a *morphological* to a *semiological* stage represents the main thread of the history of poetics. (Doležel 1990: 6)

Although Doležel focuses primarily on strictly literary poetics, Zich could easily enter his discussions as one of the transitional phases that predate an explicitly structural-semiotic phase of semiotics. Throughout this Afterword, we have already done this but it's worth emphasising that Zich fits integrally within a very long theoretical tradition – even of literary theory as outlined by Doležel. Besides, there are parallels on the level of individual partial concepts: Aristotle's "postulate of completeness", as Doležel outlines it (1990: 23), is close to Zich's "postulate of the totality of actor's performance" (*postulát totality hereckého výkonu*). Similarly, Aristotle's concepts of tragedy that emphasises *plot* and of tragedy (i.e., theatre) understood as "imitation of action" (1990: 27), are both close to Zich, who stresses the category of human interaction and essentially derives all of his following discussions from it. These parallels between Aristotle and Zich are all the more significant in that Zich defines his theory against Aristotle, rejecting him as a normative and normalising thinker, a common interpretation of Aristotle in the late nineteenth century. If we approach Aristotle from an angle different to Zich's, the similarities between the two stand out all the more clearly. This direction of inquiry is very productive and promises many new research opportunities. Petr Osolsobě (2020) and Herta Schmid (2020) have pursued the path and have come up with a number of partial findings.

… FRIEDRICH NIETZSCHE AND SIGMUND FREUD

It may seem logical today to inquire into the relationship between Otakar Zich's theory and the ideas of Friedrich Nietzsche (1844–1900) and Sigmund Freud (1856–1939). Nowadays some of their concepts form a central part of the theoretical apparatus of theatre, and Zich's creative life coincided with the early phases of reception of the two thinkers' legacy. A reader of Zich's *Aesthetics* could equally pose the reverse and equally justified question:

Since there are no clear traces of Nietzsche or Freud in Zich, why should we compare them at all? Simply for exactly that reason: a conscious omission is as significant as an explicit inclusion. The paragraphs that follow look into Zich's position on a historical map of intellectual trends through the lens of absence. In other words, the underlying question is: What does the absence of Nietzsche's and Freud's ideas in Zich's work suggest?

Given the closeness of the Czech and German cultures, the Czech reception of Freud and Nietzsche did not depend on translations. Nietzche's ideas found their readers and commentators as they were being published. Probably the earliest trace of Nietzsche's influence in the Czech cultural space appeared in 1893 in the correspondence between the writers Julius Zeyer (1841–1901) and Karolína Světlá (1830–1899), who found interest in Nietzsche's "mysticism". Nietzsche's ideas appealed strongly to the literary generation of the 1890s that emerged around the journal, symptomatically called *Moderní revue* (The Modern Revue). This generation strove to push against the petit-bourgeois dilution and laxity of the national revival, with a programme of individualism, modernism and decadence. Nietzsche served as a welcome opponent to nationalist collectivism and sober and grey democratism. His influence is very prominent, for instance, in the work of the leading literary scholar and critic František Xaver Šalda (1867–1937), who approached art in a distinctly Nietzschean way as an individual and personal titanic gesture. Nietzsche's elitism and subjectivism were viewed as supremely creative values (for details in Czech see Novák 1912; in German, Novák 1914). The literary generation's fascination with and even adoration for Nietzsche found an early outpouring in 1896 in the translation of selected chapters from his influential *Also sprach Zarathustra* (Thus Spoke Zarathustra, 1883–1885).

Alongside this burgeoning Nietzschean cult came academic attempts at coming to terms with the provocative philosopher. In 1902, František Krejčí published a short treatise called *Bedřich Nietzsche* (Bedřich is the Czech variant of Friedrich). Giving it the subtitle "from popular lectures", Krejčí apparently wrote the booklet as a popularising work for a wider public. That in itself suggests Nietzsche's appeal to the culture at large. While Krejčí was a proponent of very different philosophical principles, he clearly took it upon himself as a philosophy professor of Charles University to comment on Nietzsche. In his book *O filosofii přítomnosti* (On Present-Day Philosophy, 1904), he dedicated an entire 80-page chapter to his work. Krejčí saw Nietzsche, alongside Herbert Spencer and Leo Tolstoy, as the most significant representative of modern philosophy:

> Bedřich Nietzsche jest zjev neobyčejný. Dojmem, který způsobil, jest ustrnutí, z něhož jsme se dosud nevzpamatovali, ač již více než deset let tomu, co poslední jeho spis vyšel. (Krejčí 1904: 279)

[Friedrich Nietzsche is an extraordinary phenomenon. The impression he caused is one of astonishment, from which we are yet to come around although it has been over ten years since his final treatise appeared.]

Krejčí's words capture well the period mood: Nietzsche's work is incoherent, hard to conceive, and full of contradictions. At the same time it is captivating especially in its literary qualities and poetic visions. It is also a work that has immeasurable and awe-inspiring features. And more importantly: interpretations of the work are still ongoing and still too fresh. With the pedantism of a positivist philosopher, Krejčí describes Nietzsche's work in accurate contours, but he comes short of doing justice to it as an interpreter – not to mention Krejčí's uninspiring and detached commentary. Krejčí takes the concept of "Wille zur Macht" (the will to power) as Nietzsche's central tenet and interprets it as a positive call to a confident and creative life. At the same time, Krejčí fails to relate to Nietzsche as a personality – clearly due to the limits of his own outlook: as a rational positist, a sober democrat and a humanist, he was able to describe Nietzsche objectively but was unable and unwilling to engage with him on a more immediate and more intimate level. Nietzsche simply did not fall into his philosophical system.

Later books on Nietzsche came much closer, but these also originated with the next artistic and philosophical generation. Two books appeared in close proximity: one in 1912 by philosopher Lev Borský (1883–1944) and another in 1913 by literary theorist, Germanist, theatre critic and dramaturg of the Prague National Theatre Otokar Fischer (1883–1938), who promoted Nietzsche's work in translation and interprets him as a visionary and a poet (see Zittel 2020). Broadly speaking, Nietzsche's philosophy appealed especially for its antimoralism, its vision of the Übermensch and its social critiques of petit-bourgeois culture and of Christianity. That is to say, Nietzsche arrives not as a systematic philosopher but as a provocative free thinker. It is very likely that when it comes to Nietzsche, Otakar Zich shared the view of his university teacher and senior colleague František Krejčí. Like him, Zich tended towards sober, systematic and rationalist thought.

Nietzsche also appealed as an aesthetician and it was Zich's contemporary and university peer, the musicologist Zdeněk Nejedlý (1878–1962), who offered a critical assessment in that respect. In his short history of aesthetics, *Katechismus estetiky* (A Catechism of Aesthetics, 1902), Nejedlý mentions Nietzsche briefly, dedicating two pages to Nietzsche's views on Richard Wagner, portraying him as a "mere" representative of Romantic aesthetics and a disillusioned Wagner admirer (Nejedlý 1902: 115–116). While Nejedlý viewed Nietzsche as a relatively marginal figure within a systematic overview of aesthetics, a decade later he dedicated a book to him. Nejedlý's *Nietzschova tragedie* (Nietzsche's Tragedy, 1913) came out almost simultaneously with

Borský's and Fischer's books. His book adopts a biographical approach that portrays Nietzsche's life through the prism of his tragic relationship with Wagner and his wife: an idealistic dreamer's clash with the pragmatics of the theatre industry. The biographical account is interspersed with snippets from Nietzsche's works and Nejedlý's own (rather subjective) interpretations, which he presents in a heightened style somewhat imitative of Nietzsche's own poetic diction. In so doing, Nejedlý tried to come close to his subject and mediate him through his own words, as if it were from within a troubled soul. To achieve this, Nejedlý argued that Nietzsche was "umělecká duše, tvořící si fikce úžasnou intuicí, ale přitom jen umělecký ideolog" (an artistic soul forging fictions with its immense intuition, and yet little more than an artistic ideologist; Nejedlý 1926: 40) and repeatedly emphasised that "Nietzsche nebyl vědec, byl umělec" (Nietzsche was not a scientist, he was an artist; Nejedlý 1926: 64). In keeping with the principles of systemic, i.e., scientific aesthetics, Nejedlý (as well as Zich) approached Nietsche's aesthetic concepts as expressions of an original and complex creative personality. They viewed these expressions as an artistic commentary, a vision or a manifesto, rather than a contribution to a scientific investigation of the aesthetic principles of art.

Nietzsche's distinction of the Apollonian and the Dionysian principles was read in a very narrow sense, as a commentary on Wagner's work, namely his concept of the chorus. It is questionable if at that point in the history of ideas Nietzsche's principles were viewed as general aesthetics paradigms to be reckoned with at all. His speculative distinction between the two creative principles – and indeed, life principles – has no correspondence with Zich's typology of creatives (playwright types and actor types) which he presents in his *Aesthetics of the Dramatic Art*. Zich based his types not on the study of speculative theories of other authors (among them Nietzsche) but on his own empirical observations, his introspective phenomenological insight and his analyses of very concrete, specific material – in contrast to Nietzsche, who strives to be a universalist and provide overarching visions.

Nietzsche's book *Die Geburt der Tragödie aus dem Geiste der Musik* (The Birth of Tragedy Out of the Spirit of Music, 1872) can be read as an aesthetic analysis of Wagner opera. Nietzsche's assertion that tragedy (that is, new music theatre) is born out of the chorus and out of music must have come to Zich as simply too particular and basically alien. Zich's brief polemical footnote on account of Richard Wagner's work in *Aesthetics of the Dramatic Art* might be read as an implicit commentary on Nietzsche's views as well. While Zich acknowledges the influence that Wagner's music theatre has had, he finds his Ring Cycle in particular too epic (narrative), and as such argues that the work is not a dramatic work in the true sense of the word. Zich evidently does not adulate Dionysus as the god of ecstasy, of musical trance and of dissolution of individuality in the primal unity of the chorus. In more general terms it could be said that Zich has little sense for the metaphysics of music as Nietzsche tried to assert it. For Zich, music is a question of material, and he pursues the rather technical issue of what music can express from the realm of human action (both inner and outer). The opening of Zich's chapter on opera perhaps could not be more distant from Nietzsche's theories, as Zich remains essentially faithful to the concepts of the Austrian music critic and theorist Eduard Hanslick (1825–1904).

At an even more abstract level we could argue that Nietzsche's and Zich's notions of *mimesis* (and by extension of the meaning of art) are entirely incompatible. A small instance will help illustrate this: Nietzsche's writings on music and movement became a lifelong inspiration for the dancer and choreographer Isadora Duncan (1877–1927), who sought new means of expression through movement and its representative capacities – in the sense in which Nietzsche viewed this category. In contrast, Zich's more or less Aristotelian conception of *mimesis* views dance as a non-mimetic, non-representing art (see p. 96 above). Zich leaves out Nietzsche on purpose since their conceptual theories of art are irreconcilable. The only reference to Nietzsche in *Aesthetics* is polemical and respectfully brief. Zich cites Nietzsche's infamous outcry that actors are "ideal apes" – an outcry that gave vent to Nietzsche's frustration with the sordid pragmatics of theatre practice and justified his break with it. Zich adopts a very different approach: seeking ways in which acting can be appreciated and acknowledged as an autonomous creative art. This stands as a fine example of the sharp difference between Nietzsche as an idealistic visionary and Zich as a sober practitioner. Let us acknowledge at the same time that Zich belongs to the first generation of Nietzsche's critical recipients. Nietzsche's work, seen at close quarters by his near contemporaries, may have seemed fascinating – even though it was no more than a mere episode.

Equally symptomatic is the absence of Sigmund Freud's theories. In the 1920s, Freudian ideas were immensely fashionable in the arts, and drama and theatre were no exception. Especially the popularity of Arthur Schnitzler's plays grew from the ingenious ways in which Schnitzler operated with the subconscious motivations of his dramatic personas. The abovementioned Otokar Fischer observed in a 1925 text that fashionable trends also bring about parodies: the ultimate proofs of cultural reception. As an instance Fischer mentions the ironic comments about the omnipresent libido made by the Viennese writer Karl Kraus or the parodic one-act play *La Psychoanalyse* staged at the Švanda Theatre by Jean Bard's recitation group. Fischer does not look down upon psychoanalysis but rather points out the number of novelists and dramatists (among them Hermann Hesse, Arthur Schnitzler, Hugo von Hofmannsthal and Thomas Mann) who have clearly been inspired by the method. He further develops his observations and points out the possible incorporation of the psychoanalytical method with literary theory and aesthetics. While he remains somewhat cautious, he concludes his text with an exhortation:

> Jako Nietzsche, směřující ze zcela jiného východiska ke zcela jiným cílům, Freud je literárnímu badateli návodem a povelem, aby se nespokojoval s jevy povrchu a uvědomoval si, že pod obrazným světem umění, zvlášť tragédie, jsou tajemné propasti. (Fischer [1925] 2014: 81)
> [Like Nietzsche, who takes different points of departure and pursues other objectives, Freud serves the literary critic with an instruction and a command not to content himself with superficial phenomena but to realise that underneath the evocative world of the art, especially of the tragedy, there are mysterious abysses.]

It is a testimony to Fischer's perceptiveness that he beckons at a possible link between Neitzsche and Freud, which would later manifest itself more clearly.

In regards to Zich's *Aesthetics*, Fischer's suggestion registers in two aspects. Zich does not ignore psychoanalytical subjects in drama. In his notes on modern drama he operates with the category of the "subconscious" (*podvědomo*) where he locates Schnitzler, among others. While apparently accepting the subject matter, his psychological analysis of creativity and of the dramatic persona stays with the James-Lange associationist theory of emotions (promoted also by the above mentioned František Krejčí).

> Associationists reduce the process of associations and the interpretation of impulses to the sphere of consciousness, thus denying Freudian or Jungian concepts of the unconscious. In associationism, the sphere of psyche and consciousness is identical, with mental processes conceived as a series of successive psychological elements; emotional and volitional operations are thus accentuated. (Musilová 2020: 82)

Martina Musilová has analysed Zich's starting points in the context of the changing acting aesthetics of his time, as influenced by new psychological theories. It is also through the absence of the most recent developments that we can interpret Zich's resistance to or perhaps distance from the Avant-Garde theatre:

> Rooted in empirical methods, Zich's aesthetics has its limits, as it does not reflect contemporary changes in modern psychology nor the new concepts regarding the human psyche (Freud, Jung, behaviourism, Gestaltpsychologie). From this point of view, Zich could not accept Tairov's *plastic and phonetic forms* concepts of acting that are analogical to the abstractionism in visual arts of the 1920s and the 1930s. (Musilová 2020: 86)

In other words, Zich remains on the pre-Freudian positions. With a bit of licence, we could argue that Zich leaves untouched the vitalistic, psychoanalytical and irrationalist concepts (to use the period terminology), which we understand today through the works of Friedrich Nietzsche, Sigmund Freud or Henri Bergson. Zich does so because there is no way of incorporating them into his systematic aesthetics. Whether we view this omission as an instance of Zich's methodological rigour, or his methodological conservatism is a matter of our choice and present-day tastes. Notwithstanding, Zich had the supreme right for that resolution.

Let us conclude these reflections with one last example, this time from artistic practice. Zich clearly could not have ignored the influence Friedrich Nietzsche had on music – and it is characteristic of Nietzschean reception that it first took root in the arts, and only then, more conceptually, in aesthetics and philosophy. Among such artistic examples are Richard Strauss's symphonic poem *Also sprach Zarathustra* (1896) and Gustav Mahler's first four symphonies, starting with Symphony No. 1 "Titan" in D Major (1889). Zich had great admiration for Mahler as a composer and conductor and even translated the lyrics of his *Das Lied von der Erde* (The Song of the Earth, 1907–1909) into Czech. He also wrote an obituary for Mahler where he confessed a profound admiration of the composer's genius. Zich claimed that modern time had only two true geniuses: Auguste Rodin and Gustav Mahler. In this obituary, Zich took leave of Mahler as a visionary of symphonic music:

> Dílo je tedy zastaveno; a nám možno aspoň potud, pokud lze posouditi díla současná díla, jež znamenají tepnu moderní hudby, promluviti o jeho odkazu. Jen jedno jest *zcela jisto*, co lze o jeho umění říci, že patří budoucnosti. (Zich 1911: 514)
> [His art is now complete. And we are able – at least as far as we can assess contemporary works of art that constitute an artery of modern music – to speak of his legacy. One thing to say about his art is *beyond certain*: it belongs to the future.]

In addition, the obituary serves Zich as a pretext to give a working analysis of Mahler's compositional methods, but that exceeds my present objective. What matters here is Zich's marginal self-reflective note: he admits that in his own creative and scholarly work he holds a very different position himself. In contrast with Mahler, Zich calls himself "a proponent of tranquil positivism" (*vyznavač klidného positivismu*; Zich 1911: 513). This passing remark in which Zich characterises himself may help us interpret why Zich chooses to include some philosophies in his system of thought, while excluding others – notably Freud and Nietzsche among them.

THE *WHAT IF* OF ZICH'S RECEPTION

It would be counterfactual to speculate how theatre studies would have developed if Zich had lived long enough to publish his *Aesthetics* in German. The fact remains that a manuscript German translation, made by an unidentified Czech translator probably shortly after Zich's premature death (1934), was discovered by Martin Bernátek in the Otakar Zich archive at the National Museum in Prague only in 2017. The question now is irrelevant given that Zich's *Aesthetics of the Dramatic Art* is about to come out in Herta Schmid's German and in our English translations almost at the same time. Nevertheless, were it not for the coincidence of Zich's unexpected death, the abandoned publication of his book in German and the reception of the Czech original cut short by the political turmoils of the 1930s and the catastrophe of World War II, theatre theory would look very different today. As one Czech scholar has quipped provocatively, Otakar Zich is the greatest German theatre scholar writing in Czech. His holistic theory of theatre and the dramatic art as such – covering not only spoken drama but also opera, musical drama and other genres – redefines the fundamentals of theatre studies as a discipline with its central cruxes: the relationship between the stage director, the actor and other creators of performance; the ontology of the dramatic text and its position between literature and drama; the decisive role of the performance space and scenography; the questions of realism, stylisation and theatrical styles...

Erika Fischer-Lichte's genealogy of theatre studies proper, starting with Max Herrmann and his concept of *Theaterwissenschaft* as the study of performance (see Fischer-Lichte's *The Routledge Introduction to Theatre and Performance Studies*, 2014: 12ff.), is fundamental here. There is little doubt about the validity of her arguments. Nonetheless, the question remains whether narrowing down the beginnings to a single personality, a single point in the history of culture as a starting point, is not reductive given the complexity of the intellectual and artistic culture that led to the establishment of theatre studies as a new discipline. It would be probably more inclusive and pluralistic to acknowledge the network of influences, inspirations and initiatives that helped consolidate the intellectual and artistic community that engaged simultaneously in theatre practice and its theoretical reflection. To name one instance of this overlap, the aforementioned Arthur Kutscher was also crucial for his close contacts with theatre practitioners, including Bertolt Brecht. The origins of the discipline are much more inconclusive and much more interpersonal than a single genealogy can ever capture. That Otakar Zich hasn't registered on those genealogical maps is a matter of historical and personal accident; notwithstanding that, his place within that intellectual world is indelible and deserves full acknowledgement. Adding Zich with his background in aesthetics to the map with the others – such as Herrmann, Nielsen or Kutscher, who are grounded in literary history or ethnography – calls for a revision of the whole reading of the origins of *Theaterwissenschaft*.

2 READING ZICH IN CZECH AND BEYOND: INTERPRETING THE BOOK

Having placed Zich within a contemporary intellectual world, let us sketch out individual approaches to and traditional ways of interpreting his work. Starting with the earliest published reviews I will attempt to outline how Zich has been read through the lens of structuralism and (later) semiotics. In Czech, of course, Zich is an indelible part of the curriculum in university courses on theatre studies and especially dramaturgy. I will also summarise what Zich's reception has been abroad – almost exclusively in connection with the Prague School (and the Prague Linguistic Circle) – and what the consequences are for the interpretation of his concepts.

...IN EARLY PUBLISHED BOOK REVIEWS

The period book reviews were naturally rather brief, often no more than announcements and reports. But they can illustrate the early reception of *Aesthetics of the Dramatic Art*. The contemporary assessments and comments document the aesthetic preferences and predilections of individual reviewers in relation to theatre practice of the day. Along those lines, one reviewer, Bedřich Slavík (1911–1979), comments on the scholarly, specialist nature of the book, somewhat hinting at the limited scope of Zich's case material:

> Aby vynikla přísná soustavnost, s níž Zich rozvádí princip dramatičnosti a stejnoměrné stylisace, bylo by třeba přepsati obsah knihy, která – *i když především sleduje divadlo realistické a ilusionistické* – uvádí k nám prvé a zásadní dílo o teoretické dramaturgii. (Slavík 1932)
> [In order to highlight the strict method with which Zich analyses the principle of dramaticity and consistent stylisation, one would need to revise the contents of the book that – *although following primarily realistic and illusionistic theatre* – represents the first and fundamental work on theoretical dramaturgy.] (my emphasis)

In contrast, actor and stage director Prokop Laichter (1898–1975) welcomes the book enthusiastically and almost uncritically, putting it into context not just with present day theatre practice but also with the state of theatre education in the Czech lands:

Docílili jsme své dramatické konservatoře, ale nebyl nám jasný ani systém výuky ani nebylo patřičných pomůcek. [...] Vítáme proto dílo Zichovo, jež je jednou z prvých dokonalých učebnic, která objasní příštím adeptům divadelního umění cesty a uvědomí ho o pravém poslání. (Laichter 1932: 53)
[We have achieved the establishment of our dramatic conservatoire but we have not had either a clear idea of the curriculum, nor the appropriate accessories. [...] Therefore we welcome Zich's work as one of the first definitive textbooks that will light the path to future learners of the dramatic art and make him [sic] aware of its true objective.]

The reviewer appreciates in particular that Zich:

s plným zdarem obhajuje herecké umění nikoliv, co umění výkonné, nýbrž tvůrčí. Zdůraznění práce hercovy je v řadě statí skvěle doloženo proti mylnému názoru nezasvěcených, kteří řadí herce mezi umělce reprodukční, právě tak, jako se svého času stával herec režisérům pouhým materiálem. (Laichter 1932: 53)
[...succeeds in defending the art of acting not just as a reproductive art but a creative one. The emphasis laid on the actor's work is excellently documented in a number of chapters, in defiance of the mistaken view of the uninitiated who group actors with reproductive artists, just like when the actors used to be no more than mere material for the directors.]

Towards the end, Laichter contextualises Zich with contemporary discussions about the relationship of the actor and the stage director:

Herec byl dobou utopen v problémech režisérských, stával se částí jevištní mašinerie, mnohdy dekoraci byla přidělena větší úloha než jemu. Daleko zaváděl od práce Brahmovy Reinhardt své druhy, s nimiž si samolibě zahrával až dospěl ke stanovisku dokončenému diktátem Jessnerovým. Copeau ve Francii, Stanislavskij v Rusku osvobozovali herce k vlastní práci. (Laichter 1932: 53)
[At times the actor was drowned in directorial problems, becoming a part of the stage machinery, with the decoration often playing a more substantial role than the actor. Far from Brahm's work did Reinhardt lead his peers, playing with them smugly before arriving at the stance fully accomplished by Jessner's dictate. Copeau in France or Stanislavski in Russia have liberated their actors to their own work.]

An apparent agreement in his views on modern and Expressionist theatre leads Laichter to an unabashedly enthusiastic conclusion:

Svým rozborem dává Zich herci plné vědomí jeho práce. Proto právě v hereckých rukou a v jejich knihovnách měla by se tato kniha ocitnouti. Zodpoví jim nejen otázky jejich práce, ale i otázky celku, práce režisérovy, pohyb scény, práce činohry i opery. Bude jejich kapesním naučným slovníkem. (Laichter 1932: 53)

[Through his analysis, Zich gives the actor a full awareness of their work. It is particularly in the actors' hands and in their libraries that this book should find its place. It will answer not only questions over their work but also questions over the whole, the stage director's work, the dynamics of the scene, the workings of spoken drama as well as opera. It will become their pocket encyclopedia.]

It is characteristic of his review that apart from the "strictly scientific" treatment Laichter praises Zich's approach to the dramatic art and sees it as part of contemporary debates over the relation between the actor, the stage director and the playwright. Whether Zich's book truly could or couldn't work as "a pocket encyclopedia", I prefer to leave without comment.

Some reviews contain polemical moments that will help us see Zich's book in contemporary context. Theatre and film critic J. J. Paulík (1895–1945) responds to Zich's strict view that it is intolerable to erase the boundary between the stage and the auditorium:

Ano nebo ne k této pasáži je ovšem věcí zásadního názoru na umění, odpovědí na otázku o funkci umění vůbec a divadla zvlášť, tedy zde nejde jen o jevištní prostor. Neboť 1.) je neustálá oscilace mezi životem a uměním, život se neustále v umění přelívá a naopak. 2.) divadlo zvláště citlivě obráží změny stavu společnosti v té nebo oné době, jeho společenská funkčnost je zvláště živá a naléhavá. Nelze, myslím, *a priori* odmítnout jako uměleckou absurdnost např. setření hranice mezi jevištěm a hledištěm na základě jeho rozporu s jistě dobře vypracovaným pojmem dramatického umění. Neboť i pojmy se mění zároveň se svou látkou, jíž je společenský život, a nelze jim přiznati absolutní platnosti. (Paulík 1932)

[Whether yes or no, on this issue, is naturally a fundamental matter of how we view art, how we answer the question of what is the function of art generally and of theatre specifically; so this is not just about the stage space. Because (1) there is an unceasing oscillation between life and art; life pours into art and vice versa. (2) Theatre is particularly sensitive to the changes in society in one age or another, and its societal function is especially vivid and insistent. For that reason, I believe, it is impossible to reject *a priori* as an artistic absurdity, say, the erasing of the boundary between the stage and auditorium on the basis that it contradicts his [Zich's] surely well-elaborated concept of the dramatic art. For concepts undergo change hand in hand with their matter, which is public life, and they cannot be ascribed absolute validity.]

The most substantial criticism came from the Czech Germanist, theatre critic, playwright, dramaturg of Prague National Theatre and member of the Prague Linguistic Circle, Otokar Fischer. In his review, Fischer commends Zich highly for trying to establish the dramatic art as an autonomous art form and for emancipating drama from the realm of literary forms. He contextualises Zich's approach with other critical views on the position of theatre and drama within literary studies and art. Fischer writes:

> Při své polemice proti obvyklému členění estetických druhů nejde však Zich tak daleko jako někteří moderní teoretikové divadla, kteří drama přiřazují k výkonům artistů a uznávají primát scény jakožto takové. (Fischer 1932)
> [In his polemics with the traditional categories of aesthetic types, Zich doesn't go as far as other modern theatre theorists who attach drama to the theatre artists' performance and acknowledge the primacy of the scene as such.]

In this Fischer places Zich at a distance from the even more progressive theories, such as the concepts of Avant-Garde theatre makers. As a literary and theatre historian he also sees certain limits in Zich's theoretical concepts:

> Zich vybírá z četných projevů divadelnictví právě jen dva, činohru a zpěvohru, stanoví jejich společné zákony, úmyslně vylučuje ze svého zkoumání film a kabaret, němohru a tanec, ba i historicky tak význačné etapy, jaké jsou určovány pojmy commedia dell' arte a mimus. Kdo se na otázky divadelní dívá s hlediska vývojového, uchová si reservu k nejednomu vývodu, ježto Zichovi jde myšlenková úplnost a systematičnost [...] nad konkrétnost a složitost mimických rozborů. (Fischer 1932)
> [Out of the numerous manifestations of theatre making, Zich selects only two, spoken drama and sung drama, establishes the shared laws that govern them, purposely excluding from his discussions such forms as film, cabaret, pantomime and dance, and even such historically significant phases as were determined by the commedia dell'arte and the mimus. Whoever views questions of theatre from a developmental point of view will necessarily be wary of several of his deductions since Zich values the completeness and system of his thought [...] over the concreteness and complexity of mimic analyses.]

Fischer's comment precisely pinpoints the limitations of Zich's system of thought that are crucially tied up with Modernist aesthetics. Zich's failure to appreciate film as an autonomous art is understandable given the position of the sound film in 1931. From today's perspective, Fischer raises a much more significant critical objection in pointing out that Zich doesn't give appropriate acknowledgement to improvised and several comedic forms of theatre. Fischer's review is proof that these shortcomings were known at the moment of publication. Zich's theory derives from a starting point that the current theatrical forms – be it the opera or spoken drama – are the supreme and most elaborate, and as such they should serve as the points of reference, and all the preceding developmental forms are viewed as obsolete.

Zich formulates these assumptions only implicitly in *Aesthetics of the Dramatic Art*. But in his 1922 lecture, in which he presents his working theses, he was very articulate about them.

> [m]usíme bráti v úvahu jen dramatické umění naší doby, neboť jen to známe tak, jak požadujeme, tj. prováděné. [...] O způsobu provádění tehdejšího jsme zpraveni jen velmi nedokonale, ačli vůbec. Historické hledisko tedy pro naše úvahy estetické nemá významu a nemá ceny, neboť nám jde o to, odvoditi zákony dramatického umění přítomnosti, zákony, jež by se mohly uplatniti v nynější umělecké praxi. To nám káže i širší stanovisko estetiky (a vědy vůbec), býti životnou vědou. (Zich 1997: 13–14)
>
> [we must limit our consideration to the dramatic art of the present, since it is the only theatre we know in the way required, that is, as produced. [...] Our information on historical performance practices is very imperfect and sometimes lacking completely. Hence the historical perspective is of no relevance and of no value for our aesthetic reflections since the objective here is to deduce the laws of today's dramatic art, laws that might be employed in current artistic practice. This is also the broader requirement of aesthetics (and of scholarship generally) – to be living scholarship.] (Zich 2016: 38)

Zich clearly focuses on the principles of contemporary theatre, but in his own tendency towards an objective approach he omits his own aesthetic preferences. Fischer points that out concisely in his review:

> Zich výslovně se dovolává jen takových příkladů, jež jsou mu doklady dobrého nebo správného umění, kdežto historik by si všímal bedlivěji těch ukázek a přechodů, jež jsou zdánlivými výjimkami z předpokládaných pravidel. (Fischer 1932)
>
> [Zich explicitly refers only to those case studies that serve him as examples of the good and correct art, while a historian would pay much greater attention to the instances and borderline cases that appear to be exceptions to the hypothetical rules.]

It is symptomatic of contemporary reviews of Zich's book that it was viewed from different angles – as a contribution to the discussion of the state of present day theatre practice, especially stage directing and acting, or as a contribution to the general, "strictly scientific" aesthetic theory. Likewise Zich's *Aesthetics of the Dramatic Art* didn't escape criticism for its apparent disregard of theatre history.

...BY STRUCTURALISTS

No other period book review has been as influential as Jan Mukařovský's extensive, 10-page commentary in the scholarly journal *Časopis pro moderní filologii* (Journal of Modern Philology). Mukařovský's review launches the tradition of the structuralist reading of Zich. It is as early as his opening paragraph that Mukařovský appropriates Zich for the "structuralist" cause, arguing that in his book:

> je kladen veliký a stálý důraz na sémantiku dramatického umění a významovou stránku jeho složek. Při každé příležitosti se zdůrazňuje "obrazová představa", navazovaná jednotlivými složkami a nesoucí celý kontext dramatického díla. Tato obrazová představa není nic jiného než velmi složitý a mnohonásobně zvrstvený *význam*. (Mukařovský 1933: 318–319)
> [great and constant emphasis is placed on the semantics of the dramatic art and the referential [meaning-related] side of its components. On every occasion, the *referential image* is emphasised, linked to individual components and carrying the entire context of the dramatic work. This referential image is nothing else but a very complicated and many-layered *meaning* [*significance*].]

Mukařovský's review brings a meticulous and positively biased report tending towards a structuralist approach to Zich's book, presenting in turn the key arguments of each of his chapters. Mukařovský repeatedly demonstrates that the book's central topic is the making of meaning – the semanticisation of individual components of the dramatic work. In fact, he views the dual concepts of *technical conceptual image* and *referential conceptual image* through the lens of his own structuralist and linguistic theory and interprets them as identical with *sign* and *meaning (significance)*. The second feature Mukařovský highlights, which clearly brings Zich's theory close to the structuralists, is his analysis of the static and the dynamic in a work of art. Logically, Mukařovský highly praises Zich's dynamic conception of the dramatic space (dramatic scene) as a force field.

In his 1941 lecture "On the Current State of Theory of Theatre" (K dnešnímu stavu teorie divadla; Drozd et al. 2016: 59–75), Mukařovský hails Zich as a director predecessor of the Prague School. The key passage of Mukařovský's text – his definition of the theatrical artefact – is principally a translation of Zich's definition of the dramatic art into structuralist terminology:

> Divadlo přes všechnu hmotnou hmatatelnost svých prostředků (budova, stroje, dekorace, rekvizity, množství personálu) je jen podkladem nehmotné souhry sil sunoucích se časem a prostorem a strhujících diváka do svého měnlivého napětí, do souhry, kterou nazýváme jevištním výkonem, představením. (Mukařovský 1941)
> Despite all the material tangibility of its means (the building, machinery, sets, props, a multitude of personnel), the theatre is merely the base for a non-material interplay of forces moving through time and space and sweeping the spectator up in its changing tension, in the interplay of forces we call a stage performance. (Mukařovský 2016 (1941): 61)

At the same time, Zich didn't escape numerous partial criticisms from the members of the Prague School. Jiří Veltruský (1919-1991) takes fundamental theoretical issues with Zich's anti-literary conception of drama – a polemic expressed in full in his treatise *Drama jako básnické dílo* (1942), reworked and published in English as *Drama as Literature* (1977). Petr Bogatyrev (1893-1971) points out the inaccuracies and biases in Zich's understanding of puppet theatre and criticises Zich for overrating the importance of consistent stylisation in theatre – see Bogatyrev's essay "A Contribution to the Study of Theatrical Signs" (1937-1938; in Drozd et al. 2016: 91-98). Jindřich Honzl (1894-1953) takes the standpoint of modern Avant-Garde theatre and rejects Zich's conviction that the stage space must be architectonically fixed and that the stage must be strictly divided from the auditorium. Honzl returns to Zich's dictum repeatedly in his essays "The Mobility of the Theatrical Sign" (1940), "The Hierarchy of Theatrical Devices" (1943) and "Spatial Concerns in Theatre" (1933-1934; all printed in Drozd et al. 2016: 129-146, 157-164, 290-302, respectively).

I will refrain from a detailed discussion of all the polemics and criticisms since all the relevant texts are available in English and only sketch out the intellectual context: A cosmopolitan group of young scholars in Prague is trying to establish themselves and their new theoretical way of thinking. In 1926, they found the Prague Linguistic Circle (Pražský lingvistický kroužek) and in 1929 they present themselves publicly with their *Theses* at the congress of Slavists. Their basic intention is naturally to elaborate a functional-structural approach, extend it from a purely linguistic to a broadly aesthetic system of thought and tackle art as a fact in its own right. (For more reference literature on this huge issue see Drozd et al. 2016). At that point, a renowned peer academic of the previous generation publishes a volume entitled *Aesthetics of the Dramatic Art* in excess of 400 pages in length, in which he tackles many of the issues that have been, metaphorically, waiting on their desk. At that point, Otakar Zich, a full professor at Charles University and head of the Seminar of Aesthetics, is fifty-two. A leading structuralist, Jan Mukařovský, who would succeed Zich in his position, is twelve years his junior (for the academic relationship between Zich and Mukařovský, see Sládek 2014: 124-125). For the members of the Prague Linguistic Circle, Zich is of course a highly respected senior colleague, who has already given papers as part of the Circle as a guest, and such an extensive and conceptually thorough work presents a challenge that can't be left without commentary.

The challenge that the publication of Zich's *Aesthetics* gave to the Circle was, logically, a polemical one to start with. It is inevitable therefore that in their responses the Circle's members initially pointed out the limitations of Zich's system and of his conception. In another sense they are not just polemics but also notes on the margins of a major systematic treatise. In a way, our anthology *Theatre Theory Reader: Prague School Writings* (Drozd et al. 2016) as a whole can be to some extent viewed as one half of the critical dialogue with Zich's theory – or as a volume complementary to the one you are reading now, and vice versa. Further contexts and impulses for a broader understanding of this dialogue are offered in the relevant subchapter in the afterword to the anthology, particularly "Prague School Theatre Theory and Otakar Zich" (Drozd et al. 2016: 616–620).

Entirely independently of the Structuralist readings of Zich, the art history professor at Charles University, Růžena Vacková (1901–1982), published a book entitled *Výtvarný projev v umění dramatickém* (Visual Expression in Dramatic Art, 1948). In her scholarly work, Vacková primarily focused on classical Greek and Roman art, but since the 1930s she had also been active as a theatre critic. Her 1948 book brings together her expertise in both fields. As her point of departure, she takes Zich's assertation that the visual component of the theatre should follow the principles of visual arts, but only as long as it is dramatically (i.e., scenically) effective. Vacková brought her expertise in art history to elaborate on Zich's theses and analyses the "logic" that governs the "dramatic visual expression" – what we would refer to nowadays as *scenography*. She follows up on Zich's assertion that the most important measure of space in the theatre is the human figure, with its height and movement. In so doing Vacková elaborates on Zich's proto-anthropological theory of the theatrical space. Her book *Visual Expression in Dramatic Art* thus becomes one of the earliest systematic attempts at a theory of scenography in the central European context.

Růžena Vacková's work is little known – a lasting legacy of her political discrimination. Vacková was a Catholic intellectual and a vocal opponent of the Communist totalitarian regime that seized power in 1948. In a show trial of 1952, Vacková was sentenced to 20 years in prison. In 1967, she was released and, in 1969, rehabilitated, but she was never given a chance to work publicly. Her work still remains unpublished in part and it is still waiting for a full recognition and critical assessment. In respect of theatre criticism, it was theatre scholar and classical philologist Eva Stehlíková (1941–2019), professor at Charles University and Masaryk University, who built on Vacková's writings on classical drama and its potential for modern staging (Stehlíková 2012).

…BY SEMIOTICIANS

When the intellectual thaw arrived after World War II along with the ideological repressions of the postwar decades, the next generation of scholars continued to respond to Zich's impulses. It was primarily the theoretical work of Oleg Sus (1924–1982), Ivo Osolsobě (1928–2012) and Miroslav Procházka (1942–1997) that came to the forefront of Czech semiotics from the 1960s.

Oleg Sus studied Zich especially in the context of Czech aesthetics, an effort that resulted in several articles and a lengthy introduction that accompanied a reprint of Zich's *Aesthetics of the Dramatic Art* (Würzburg, 1977). Three of his essays have been published in English as well, forming a loose triptych of Zich scholarship: "Poetry and Music in Psychological Semantics of Otakar Zich: From the History of the Czech Formal Method and Pre-Structuralism" (Sus 1969); "On the Genetic Preconditions of Czech Structuralist Semiology and Semantics: An Essay on Czech and German Thought" (Sus 1972); and "On the Origin of the Czech Semantics of Art: The Theory of Music and Poetry in Psychological Semantics of Otakar Zich" (Sus 1973).

Sus views Zich strictly as a representative of the Czech formalist school and refers to his method as *psycho-semantics* or *psychological semantics*, merely an early phase of systematic, integral structuralism. He highlights Zich's roots in experimental psychology and the link to Johannes Volkelt and his somewhat psychologising theory of the concept of *Bedeutungsvorstellung* (the conceptual image; for a more detailed discussion see Lánská 2016). Sus also points out the idiosyncratic specialty of Zich's aesthetic theory, which doesn't derive from literature or the visual (or plastic) arts, but from music, and is therefore much more sensitive towards meanings that are hard to semanticise. Sus views Zich's work primarily as a point of inspiration and a developmental phase, a mere forerunner of structuralism and semiotics, and argues that Zich's *Aesthetics* has articulated a lot, but:

> mechanismy sémantizace bylo a je třeba odkrývat, rekonstruovat, neboť v Estetice dramatického umění z roku 1931 vystupují do popředí složky v užším smyslu sémantické – psychosémantické – totiž významové představy zahalené do psychologického pojmosloví, kdežto složky sémiologické a s nimi širší, domýšlené teoretické konkluze jsou zazávorkovány, zčásti naznačeny, zčásti nerozvinuty. (Sus 2010 (1977): 243)
> [the mechanisms of semanticisation needed and still need to be uncovered, reconstructed, because *Aesthetics of the Dramatic Art* of 1931 foreground the components that are narrowly semantic – or psychosemantic – that is, mental images that are shrouded in psychological terminology, whereas the semiological components and with them the broader, deduced theoretical conclusions, are left in the margins – partly sketched, partly undeveloped.]

Zich's historical significance is fundamental and Sus declares towards the end of his introduction that:

> [Zichovi] patří čestné místo průkopníka ve vývoji sémantických teorií aplikovaných při rozboru uměleckých děl, a to nejen v dějinách českého myšlení, nýbrž i evropského, třebaže zůstal po celá desítiletí za hranicemi své vlasti skoro neznám… (Sus 2010 (1977): 243)

[Zich deserves a place of honour as a pioneer figure in the development of semantic theories applied to the analysis of works of art, in the history of not just Czech thought, but European, although he has, for whole decades, remained almost unknown outside the borders of his country...]

From a broader perspective, it is symptomatic that Sus, a literary theorist and semiotician, appreciates Zich but views the psychological and introspective aspects of his theory as period residues that have been surpassed by the ensuing development of structuralism and semiotics. Whereas, from today's point of view, critics tend to see these aspects as part and parcel of Zich's phenomenologically oriented method. It may seem that Sus underestimates the originality of Zich's theory. This is probably down to the fact that Sus aims at outlining the Czech tradition of aesthetics and presenting it as genuinely autonomous. Within this framework, Zich comes across as a component of a longer developmental process. Sus emphasises the links and affinities between Zich and Structuralist literary theory that followed. The fact that he calls Zich a *pre-Structuralist* makes sense within his narrative of a genealogy of aesthetics – without trying to belittle the unique value of Zich's theory.

Ivo Osolsobě and Miroslav Procházka were close friends and collaborators, working together on a new, fully annotated edition of Zich's *Aesthetics of the Dramatic Art* in Czech and, like Sus, dedicated much attention to the interpretation of Zich's work. Osolsobě opens his seminal study "Dramatické dílo jako komunikace komunikací o komunikaci" (Theatre Work as Communication of Communications about Communication; 1970) with a characteristically self-effacing modest remark that he brings no more than a translation or rewording of Zich's definition of the dramatic art. For Zich's individual concepts Osolsobě finds new equivalent terms from the realm of semiotics and communication theory. In so doing, he effectively actualises Zich's theory in the context of 1960s theoretical discourse and launches a new phase of critical reception of Zich's work. On that ground he is able to make the radical statement in his most extensive study of Zich:

Nepochopili jsme Estetiku dramatického umění, jestli jsme ji nepřečetli jako sémiotiku. [...] Jeho kniha je sémiotika *avant la lettre* bez ohledu na to, že o sémiotice či sémiologii v ní nepadlo ani slovo. (Osolsobě 2002 (1981): 218)
[We have failed to understand *Aesthetics of the Dramatic Art* unless we've read it as semiotics. [...] His book is semiotics *avant la lettre*, irrespective of the fact that it makes no single mention of semiotics or semiology.]

With that he proceeds to offer a convincing interpretation of *Aesthetics* from a semiotic perspective. (The basic points of Osolsobě's argument can be found in our Introduction to this book.)

Miroslav Procházka, in his studies, collectively edited in the volume *Znaky divadla a dramatu* (The Signs of Theatre and Drama; 1988), views the relationship between Zich, the Prague School and theatre semiotics from a historical perspective. From a distance, he re-evaluates the period polemics and points out their limitations and prejudice. Procházka's essay that compares Otakar Zich's and Jiří Veltruský's views on the nature of drama in relation to theatre and literature is also available in English under the title "On the Nature of Dramatic Texts" (Procházka 1984).

Jiří Veltruský takes a similar approach in his 1980s studies "The Prague School Theory of Theater" (1981) and "Drama as Literature and Performance" (1985). In contrast to his earlier, youthfully intransigent polemical criticism from the point of view of Avant-Garde theatre (see Veltruský's 1941 essay "Structuralism and Theatre" in Drozd et al. 2016: 76–85), his later texts, written after a gap of some four decades, emphasise Zich's thorough and refined systematic thought, appreciating his analytical probes into individual issues. In these later works, Veltruský effectively views Zich as part of the Prague School's theatre theory.

...BY SCHOLARS ABROAD

Only a fraction of Zich's text mentioned above has been available in English. Still, Zich's influence has permeated international contexts in connection with and by means of the Prague School theatre theories. These made a significant impression in the 1970s and 1980s through individual studies and several collected editions, such as *Semiotics of Art: Prague School Contributions* (1976) and *Sound, Sign and Meaning: Quinquagenary of the Prague Linguistic Circle* (1976), both edited by Ladislav Matějka, or *The Prague School: Selected Writings: 1929–1946* (1982), edited by Peter Steiner. Unfortunately, all these publications present Zich in a reductive perspective, simply as a predecessor of the Prague School. The complexity of the reception of Zich in the 1980s can be demonstrated on the passage from Keir Elam's book, cited already in the Introduction to this volume – only here presented more extensively:

> The year 1931 is an important date in the history of theatre studies. Until that time dramatic poetics – the descriptive science of the drama and theatrical performance – had made little substantial progress since its Aristotelian origins. The drama had become (and largely remains) an annexe of the property of literary critics, while the stage spectacle, considered too ephemeral a phenomenon for systematic study, had been effectively staked off as the happy hunting ground of reviewers, reminiscing actors, historians and prescriptive theorists. That year, however, saw the publication of two studies in Czechoslovakia which radically changed the prospects for the scientific

analysis of theatre and drama: Otakar Zich's *Aesthetics of the [Dramatic Art]* and Jan Mukařovský's ["An Attempt at a Structural Analysis of an Actor's Figure (Chaplin in *City Lights*)"; Drozd et al. 2016: 192-198]. The two pioneering works laid the foundations for what is probably the richest corpus of theatrical and dramatic theory produced in modern times, namely the body of books and articles produced in the 1930s and 1940s by the Prague School structuralists. Zich's *Aesthetics* is not explicitly structuralist but exercised a considerable influence on later semioticians, particularly in its emphasis on the necessary interrelationship in the theatre between heterogeneous but interdependent systems (see Deák 1976; Matejka and Titunik 1976; Sławińska 1978). Zich does not allow special prominence to any one of the components involved: he refuses, particularly, to grant automatic dominance to the written text, which takes its place in the system of systems making up the total dramatic representation. Mukařovský's 'structural analysis', meanwhile, represents the first step towards a semiotics of the performance proper, classifying the repertory of gestural signs and their functions in Charlie Chaplin's mimes. (Elam 2005: 5)

Elam's appreciative passage is characteristic of the 1980s reception in several ways. Zich's extensive and complex book, the result of about 15-20 years of systematic research, comes on a par with Mukařovský's groundbreaking, but effectively initial pilot study of 6 pages that applies the structuralist method to acting (note: to film acting, not to theatre acting!). Zich's contribution is stressed on the one hand, but on the other slips probably too easily into a stepping stone "towards a semiotics of performance proper". Of course, it would be unfair to fault Elam: while Mukařovský's short essay was available in English, Zich's lengthy book only existed in Czech – and in an unpublished and unfinished English manuscript translation in Ivo Osolsobě's office.

For the sake of the history of ideas and the politics of science, let us acknowledge those on whom Elam relies: František Deák (*1940) and Ladislav Matějka (1919-2012) were Czechoslovak émigrés who succeeded in establishing themselves in the US academic world and brought into that context a knowledge of the Prague School, taking a lion's share in making a place for it in Anglo-American (or international?) scholarship. (For more details, see Sládek 2015). Another source for Elam came from Poland: Irena Sławińska (1913-2004) was a leading Polish literary and theatre scholar. Unlike many other academics from the Socialist bloc, she managed to create and sustain working links with Francophone and Anglophone scholarly circles. In the 1960s she came to prominence in the European academic context as a theorist of a semiotic-anthropological bent. Thanks to the fact that Polish and Czech are both Slavic languages, Sławińska's theoretical work naturally incorporated Czechoslovak trends, especially the Prague School. It was Irena Sławińska who stated that the Prague School was "semiotics in statu nascendi" (Sławińska 1977).

Scholarship's paths through the twentieth century, between political regimes and across national and cultural borders, were far from straightforward. It is all the more commendable that Keir Elam, knowing the theory secondhand, without having direct access, awarded Zich's work the status of a foundational oeuvre. And that at the turn of the 1970s and 80s, a point in history when theatre semiotics reached its peak. The Prague School gained its first acknowledgement internationally, recognised as an important link in theoretical tradition that started with formalism and culminated with contemporary semiotics. Within that narrative, Keir Elam gave Otakar Zich and his *Aesthetics of the Dramatic Art* a place of almost symbolic significance. However, since no one mustered the courage to translate the book as a whole, *Aesthetics* remained unknown and unassessed in its specifics and its detail, and until recently has always been read through the lens of the Prague School theorists and their appropriations of Zich's theory. That prism, however, fails to do justice to it and makes it very difficult to see the conceptual thoroughness of Zich's *Aesthetics* as a systemic theory. Inevitably, reading *Aesthetics* from a semiotic-structuralist perspective is reductive *vis-à-vis* Zich's integral thinking. The international reception of the Prague School theory on its own terms faced a challenge as it had to counter the impact of Victor Erlich's influential and decisive book *Russian Formalism: History – Doctrine* (1965). Erlich provided effectively the first critical account of Russian formalism and of the Prague School in the English-speaking academic world. Unfortunately, Erlich reduced the Prague School to a mere mechanical development of the Russian predecessor. Many of the commentaries of Czech and Slovak academics after the publication of Erlich's book were polemical and tried to correct his distorted and far too influential account. As Ondřej Sládek observes:

> The Prague School and Czech Structuralism are often misunderstood as a mere "branch" of Russian formalism or an advanced form of Saussurean structuralism. Although theoreticians "genetically" akin with Czech structuralism (Lubomír Doležel, Ladislav Matějka, Thomas G. Winner and others) have been attempting to rectify this misunderstanding for several decades, the situation has scarcely changed. (Sládek 2015: 25)

Naturally, academic debates of the 1970s and 80s that led to the international establishment of the Prague School as an autonomous theoretical movement with its unique methodologies and aesthetics, left little time for a more refined discussion of the differences between Otakar Zich's theory and the thinking of a member of the Prague Linguistic Circle (PLC), both of whom worked in the geographically and chronologically distant context of interwar Czechoslovakia. Thomas Winner's study "Otakar Zich as a Precursor of Prague Literary Structuralism and Semiotics" (1989) is a case in point. Winner brought to the Anglophone context detailed information on Zich, introducing his work in its entirety and outlined individual themes of his *Aesthetics of the Dramatic Art*. However, Winner also interpreted Zich primarily in connection with the Prague Linguistic Circle. Summarising the broader philosophical contexts, he stated:

> [T]hus Western scholars who do not read Czech remained largely uninformed concerning an important epistemological strain underlying Czech structural aesthetics and semiotics. (Winner 1989: 229)

Winner presented Zich as a direct precursor of semiotics and repeatedly emphasised that "Zich combines a mixture of psychological and semantic concepts" (232) and that "Zich's theory of the dramatic performance is not only based on the psychology of sensory perceptions and associations, but on semantic problematic as well" (234). In the conclusion of his detailed interpretation of Zich, Winner stated:

> [Zich] came close to many semiotic concepts and ideas, so that we can clearly call Zich a pre-semiotic thinker, since many of his thoughts anticipate, or in his last work – *The Aesthetics of Dramatic Art* – parallel, those of the Prague Linguistic Circle. (Winner 1989: 239)

Michael Quinn, in his book *The Semiotic Stage: Prague School Theater Theory* (1995), devoted attention to Zich, and in so doing further strengthened the structural-semiotic reading and reception. As a theatre and Czech scholar, Quinn worked directly with the original and grounded his understanding in the Czech theoretical tradition – working with criticism by the above-mentioned scholars, Oleg Sus, Ivo Osolsobě and Miroslav Procházka, among others. Quinn viewed Zich's theoretical concepts as crucial points of departure for the later theories of the PLC members. Quinn's view of Zich is captured in the title of one of the book's subchapters: "From Zich to Theater Semiotics".

It may seem from this overview that there has been ample information on the PLC's and Zich's theories in English-language academic scholarship. This begs the question why they have not been more influential in a theatrical context. Possibly, this lack of impact may have come from its specialty and its particularity, or perhaps from the fragmentation of the academic discourse since most of the above studies appeared in journals and series of Anglophone Czech or Slavic studies, rather than in theatre studies periodicals. These specialist outlets have a limited reach, within an atomised scholarly community.

The situation changed after 1989, and in the late 1990s after the collapse of the Communist regimes in Europe. The discussion of the Prague functional-structuralist method reopened and the local and international scholarly traditions could meet directly and start reintegrating. At that point, the Prague Linguistic Circle had no need of introduction. The scholarly debates focused on more detailed discussions of the diversity of conceptual thinking within the Prague School, which was far from uniform and enclosed. In that context discussions appeared that addressed the affinities as well as the differences between the PLC and Zich. Our previous publications belong to these initiatives, most prominently our critical anthology *Theatre Theory Reader: Prague School Writings* (2016) and the volume you are currently reading.

This summary of international reception focuses primarily on the Anglo-American context, especially because this book aims at the English-speaking world. But we shouldn't forget that the reception of the Prague School had often occurred first in other languages and cultures. In the German-language context, the Prague School has been the principal focus of the Czech and Slavic Studies scholar Herta Schmid. Her theoretical work centres on the links of Czech structuralism and semiotics in the sphere of theatre theory – such as in her conference proceedings *Moderne Dramentheorie* (1975), *Semiotics of Drama and Theatre: New Perspectives in the Theory of Drama and Theatre* (1985) or *Drama und Theater: Theorie Methode Geschichte* (1991). Since Schmid is not only a structuralist and a literary semiotician but also a Slavic scholar, Otakar Zich's theory forms an integral part of her interpretation of Czech structuralist thought. It is in her and Jan Jiroušek's forthcoming German translation of Zich's *Aesthetics of the Dramatic Art – Ästhetik der dramatischen Kunst* – that her scholarly interest in the Prague School logically culminates.

The German theatre scholar Erika Fischer-Lichte also has a "Czech chapter" in her rich expertise, particularly in her 3-volume *Semiotik des Theaters: Eine Einführung* (1983). The same is true of the French theatre theorist Patrice Pavis – as his *Dictionnaire du théâtre: termes et concepts de l'analyse théâtrale* (1980) and its index show. Manfred Pfister's *Das Drama: Theorie und Analyse* (1977), a book that continues to appeal to readers today with its analysis of drama, builds on the tradition of the Prague School and its semiotic and structural theories. While Zich's name doesn't appear in Fischer-Lichte's, Pavis's and Pfister's books, they have reached the English-speaking world in numerous English editions and have shaped the foundation of the Anglophone reception of Zich. The book we have mentioned repeatedly, Keir Elam's *Semiotics of Theater and Drama* (1980), written in the same era and in Italy, forms another important part of the period context.

For the sake of completeness and for the benefit of readers of other languages, let us add that Emil Volek has included a section of Zich's *Aesthetics* in his anthology *Teoría teatral de la Escuela de Praga: de la fenomenología a la semiótica performativa* (2013), as he views Zich as the direct predecessor of the Prague School. To the best of our knowledge, Otakar Zich is available in

French only in a translation of his general aesthetics study *Hodnocení estetické a umělecké* (Aesthetic and Artistic Evaluation) in an anthology compiled by Carole Maigné, entitled *Formalisme esthétique : Prague et Vienne au XIXᵉ siècle* (2012). For a thorough understanding of Zich as a composer, Brian S. Locke has brought an invaluable historical analysis in his book *Opera and Ideology in Prague: Polemics and Practice at the National Theater, 1900–1938* (2006). Here Locke portrays a broad and detailed picture ofthe musical culture in early twentieth-century Prague. It is in that context that Zich's theoretical and practical work took shape and came to be. Locke has also published a critical edition (2014) of the score of Zich's 1922 opera *Vina* (Guilt), providing it with a detailed annotation that allows the reader insights into what Zich thought of music's dramatic possibilities and potential.

…BY THEATRE PRACTITIONERS

Almost all period reviews of the *Aesthetics of the Dramatic Art* appreciated Zich's insights into theatre practice, and several reviewers recommended the book as essential reading that should be found on every actor's shelf. Zich's impact on practical theatre should be a point of reassessment too. This presents a specific challenge – not necessarily because his views may appear as conservative; conservatism is a relative notion. A major challenge is the relation between Zich and the early Modernist reforms in theatre, such as the loosening up (dynamisation) of the stage space (viz Adolphe Appia's scenographic treatises from the late 1890s and early 1900s, or Edward Gordon Craig's innovative visions) or the modern theories of stage direction, especially of opera direction. As for the potential of Zich's theory for acting, Martina Musilová has discussed the topic in her essay "Zich on Dramatic Acting" (2020). She points out the limitations of Zich's psychological theories, which intentionally ignored the most recent advances in psychoanalysis, and outlines the consequences of this omission for the theories of acting.

A particular line of legacy in the Czech context has been developed by Jaroslav Vostrý (*1931) and Jan Císař (1932–2021), both practising dramaturgs, theorists and academics. In opposition to or rather in polemics with the structural-semiotic view, Vostrý and Císař emphasise the dependence (non-independence) of drama as a literary kind and stress Zich's approach to theatre, to theatricality and to "theatrical reading" – that is, reading the dramatic text for its staging potential. Their publications are grounded in decades of teaching theatre dramaturgs and directors. Jan Císař presented his theory comprehensively in his *Člověk v situaci* (The Human in the Situation; 1st edition 2000, 2nd edition 2016). He uses a purely theoretical language to develop Zich's thesis on dramatic action and dramatic situation – that is, ostensive action in a situation as the basis of all dramaticity. As a teacher of practical dramaturgy (and as a theatre dramaturg himself) he positions himself implicitly against recent efforts to promote postdramatic theatre as the dominant model of theatre culture.

Since the late 1990s, Jaroslav Vostrý has been presenting his theoretical approach as a self-standing discipline called *scenology* (*scénologie*). He has published numerous essays and books; his crucial work that presents his theory comprehensively is *Scénologie dramatu* (The Scenology of Drama, 2010). In a sense, Vostrý develops Zich's theory beyond the point that Zich refused to cross, namely in regards to modern psychological realism and illusiveness in the theatre, and Vostrý applies the theory across a range of twentieth-century drama. Vostrý reaches for his theoretical inspiration to Zich's teacher Otakar Hostinský. Hostinský formulated a thesis on the dual source of theatre. Unfortunately, he presented his thesis only in lectures in the late 1890s, which remained unpublished until 1981. Hostinský argues that theatre finds its sources (1) in imitation, playacting, comedian mime, and (2) in literary origins such as public speeches, and rhetoric or lyrical poetry recitation. He treats both sources as of equal importance and even criticises trends that give preference to one "face" of theatre over the other. The connecting point that brings the two into balance is acting, which is by definition the only inherently dramatic art – an artistic creation that brings together the word and the body that embodies the emergent word. As Vostrý puts it:

> Ano, slovo se chce stát znovu tělem, bez jehož bezprostředního působení lze jen těžko mluvit o skutečném (diváckém) prožitku se všemi jeho potenciálními konsekvencemi. (Vostrý 2010: 62)
> [Indeed, the word once again wants to become flesh, the body without whose immediate activity one can hardly speak of a genuine (spectating) experience with all its potential consequences.]

Vostrý apparently insists on the indivisibility and autonomy of the dramatic art – a Zich-like notion that hearkens back to the *Aesthetics of the Dramatic Art*, such as the actor's totality principle. In polemics with literary-semiotic approaches to theatre, which he sees as too reductive, Vostrý argues:

> Vytyčené dva póly nebo prameny [...] jsou svébytnou projekcí toho, co od sebe teoreticky a – nakonec! – i prakticky nelze oddělit. (Vostrý 2010: 104)
> [The outlined sources or antipoles... are a specific projection of what cannot be theoretically, nor – ultimately! – practically separated from one another.]

Taking lead from Vostrý and Císař, Jaroslav Etlík (*1956) has developed his original theoretical approach in his study "Theatre as Experience: On the

Relationship Between the Noetic and Ontological Principles in Theatre Art" (2011 [1999]). He pitches his interpretation of Zich as a polemic with theatre semiotics and structuralism, criticising it for being too centred on the text and for adopting a rather static concept of the sign that derives from linguistics. He views highly Zich's emphasis on the active involvement of the spectator in the process of meaning making that emerges in the course of the performance, in the very act of reception. Etlík follows through a point that he claims Zich fundamentally underestimated, namely the fact that the actor, as a physical person, is present during the presentation of his or her art. For Zich, the actor effectively does not exist as an empirical person; as spectators, we view the actor always as an acting actor and perceive them as the actor figure. Etlík argues for an ontological difference between the theatre and other arts and proposes that it lies in the shared physical presence of the empirical creator (the actor who realises the artwork in real time) and the recipient (the spectator). Etlík enriches Zich's theory with the issues of non-intentionality (and even randomness) and of the phenomenological presence of the actor. In his hands, the theory opens towards a performative approach to theatre.

Dramaturgical interpretations highlight Zich as a reflective theatre practitioner and emphasise his concept of the dramatic text as a projected/intended theatrical staging. Unsurprisingly, all the cited scholars that interpret Zich along these lines (Císař, Vostrý and Etlík in particular) work in close connection with theatre practice as dramaturgs and/or as teachers of dramaturgy. One could say that throughout the twentieth century Czech culture always featured a prominent tradition of theorising dramaturgs who combined creative practice and its theoretical reflection. Our previous publication, *Theatre Theory Reader: Prague School Writings* (2016), is a case in point: a significant number of the anthologised authors were theatre practitioners.

Our mapping of how Zich's theory has been received needs to necessarily remain incomplete, but it shows all the principal crossroads and contact zones that relate to this book's historical contextualisation, to current theatrical practice and to its theoretical reflection. Our objective in publishing this translation is not just to fill a gap in the reception of Czech theatre theory, but more importantly it is to respond to a new impulse towards rethinking and repositioning theatre theory as such. Zich's book offers a unique opportunity to return to the conceptual origins of modern critical approaches to theatre and in so doing to refine our current theatre theories. This Afterword has followed a simple, though potentially far-reaching ambition: to suggest how to take Zich's integral theory, which inherited its desire for completion, complexity and system from the Enlightenment tradition, and bring it to bear on our pluralist, post-Enlightenment age.

3 ZICH'S WORLD OF WORDS IN CZECH AND IN TRANSLATION

In the final part of the Afterword we would like to reflect on three points: the historical circumstances of the translation; the challenges of translating Zich; and a few formal features of Zich's writing and typography. While this book's Introduction and the Afterword until this point have primarily been an invitation to different ways of reading and interpreting Zich's magnum opus, what follows is more of a "how to use this book" guide.

A BRIEF HISTORY OF TRANSLATING ZICH'S *AESTHETICS*

Our translation is far from the first attempt at rendering *Aesthetics* into a foreign language. An as-yet-unidentified translator made a German version of the book shortly after Zich's death in the 1930s, probably on the request of Zich's wife Milada to whom the German translation is dedicated. Unfortunately no other information has survived that would clarify who took up this colossal undertaking and why they did so. It is only on inner evidence, based on the textual analysis of the translation, that we can surmise that the translator was a Czech native with a highly competent knowledge of German. Nor do we know why this translation remained forgotten and unpublished in Zich's papers. The second attempt was an English translation by Ivo Osolsobě and Samuel Kostomlatský. Their manuscript has survived, unpublished again, in Ivo Osolsobě's papers and has served as a reference and a source of inspiration for our version. As we are completing our edition, a new German translation *Ästhetik der dramatischen Kunst* by Herta Schmid and Jan Jiroušek is also forthcoming.

It was Ivo Osolsobě (1928–2012) who initiated the first English translation of Zich. It resulted logically from his systematic scholarly interest in Zich's work, to which he dedicated a large part of his theoretical and editorial life. We have discussed his scholarly activities above when introducing his second, annotated edition of *Aesthetics* (1986). Throughout the 1960s and 1970s, during the short-lived thaw in the socialist bloc, Osolsobě also managed to establish a significant network of international contacts, with Roman Jakobson nominating him to the executive board of the International Association for Semiotics Studies (IASS-AIS) in 1971. Osolsobě lived outside the well-worn paths of Czechoslovak academia (as a musical theatre dramaturg in Brno) and so somewhat outside the main searchline of the centralist ideological control. As a result, he took part in many semiotic conferences and numerous publications – among others, he contributed crucial entries to the *Encyclopedic Dictionary of Semiotics* (Sebeok 1986: 656–60). As such, Osolsobě had an ideal position to export Zich's work to international academic circles.

Osolsobě approached Samuel Kostomlatský (1895–1984), a retired university lecturer of English from Brno, and invited him to cooperate on the translation. Kostomlatský made and typed up the first translation draft, and Osolsobě edited it. We have no evidence of the two scholars actually getting together to work on the text, but we may assume from various publications by Osolsobě (Osolsobě 2007a (1975) and Osolsobě 2007b) that Kostomlatský had finished the first draft of his translation as early as 1975, and it was from then on that Osolsobě used every opportunity to discuss their English version with anyone who was willing and available. So, while on a year-long research scholarship in the Netherlands in 1980/1981, he ran a seminar at the Netherlands Institute for Advanced Studies (NIAS) at Wassenaar to discuss the unpublished translation. Once at Wassenaar, in August 1980, Ivo Osolsobě established contact with Jiří Veltruský, who was living in Paris, and asked him for advice and expert consultation on the translation. From the letters they exchanged we learn that Peter de Ridder Press had been interested in publishing the translation but had no finances for it. The manuscript was, at that point, with Thomas Sebeok and Thomas Winner, but there was hope that Ladislav Matějka might manage to publish it. (Matějka was executive head of the Michigan Slavic Publications series at the time.) Jiří Veltruský was enthusiastic and very supportive on the translation, and together with his wife and scholar Jarmila F. Veltrusky (who was effectively a native-English speaker), they were expecting to review the translation for a publisher before publication.

Several decades later, in an interview of 2001, Osolsobě summed up the history of publishing Zich in English as follows:

> Nejvíce mě mrzí, že jsem nedokázal dotáhnout věc americko-holandského vydání Zichovy Estetiky dramatického umění. Dokázal jsem sehnat peníze na její překlad, překládal to pan profesor Kostomlatský, jedna z nezapomenutelných postav české anglistiky – ale překládejte autora, který je natolik spjatý se středoevropským myšlenkovým prostorem, že přeložit ho do angličtiny je skoro nemožné. [...] Anglická terminologie je prostě jiná, angličtina se brání, takže překlad je sice hotov, ale vypulírovat ho do brilantní podoby, což bylo na mě, na to jsem se pořád dost necítil. Nebo to byla jen lenost? Mezitím se změnily poměry, iránská krize obrovsky zvedla nejen ceny nafty, ale i papíru, vůbec všech surovin, holandská nakladatelství pracující pro zámořský univerzitní trh se položila včetně Moutona a jeho Approaches to Semiotics, všecko sice zachránila

fúze s berlínským De Gruyterem, ovšem ediční politika se změnila, Zich se najednou ocitl v konkurenci se záplavou podřadných, i když aktuálních prací na podobné téma, zkrátka se Zichem, jsem to prohrál. [...] Místo hnusných, nepoctivých blábolů, které dnes reprezentují strukturalistickou a poststrukturalistickou sémiotiku, tu mohlo být dílo geniální, lucidní, systematické a průzračné. Ta kniha ve světovém jazyce mohla situaci projasnit. (Osolsobě 2001: 10)

[What I am most sorry about is that I failed to pull through the affair of the US-Netherlands edition of Zich's *Aesthetics of the Dramatic Art*. I was able to raise the funds for the translation, made by Professor Kostomlatský, an unforgettable figure of Czech English Studies – but go on, try to translate an author who is so closely embedded in the Central European mental world that it makes an English translation highly impossible. ... English terminology is simply different. English resists. So the translation is ready, but to polish it to its final glitzy form, which was down to me to do, I simply didn't feel up to the job. Or was it just laziness? In the meantime, the circumstances had changed, the Iranian crisis brought about not just the soaring prices of oil, but also of paper and of all raw materials, the Netherlands publishers that served the overseas university market went bust, including Mouton and their Approaches to Semiotics series. A fusion with the Berlin-based De Gruyter threw them a lifeline, but the editorial policy got an overhaul. Zich found himself in competition with a deluge of inferior but current books on a similar topic. The long and short of it is that I lost the battle over Zich. ... Instead of the disgusting and disingenuous waffle that represents structuralist and post-structuralist semiotics nowadays, there could have been a work of genius, lucid, systematic and crystal clear. That book in a global language could have brought light to the state of affairs.]

Kostomlatský and Osolsobě's manuscript translation that survives in Osolsobě's papers – and was kindly provided by his son, the aesthetics scholar Professor Petr Osolsobě – is machine-typed on A4 sheets in a clean and perfectly legible copy. Ivo Osolsobě's notes, some of them very extensive, appear on the first 70 pages. These pages contain the first three chapters of the book. The remainder of the copy bears only minor corrections, though we can only speculate why Osolsobě refrained from correcting the rest of the text, as there are evident terminological inconsistencies in Kostomlatský's draft, requiring the editor's attention. Still, no other versions of Zich's text in English survive, so we have no chance to compare manuscript versions. As we have already published a detailed discussion of Osolsobě's approach (Kačer and Drozd 2020), let us only briefly summarise the basics. Osolsobě tends to use the semiotic terminology characteristic of the 1970s and 1980s. One example will illustrate this: their translation of Zich's key concept of *významová představa* (*Bedeutungsvorstellung*; in our version, *conceptual image*). Kostomlatský tends to use (somewhat inconsistently) *semantic image* or *meaning image*, while Osolsobě clearly preferred *significatory image*. Osolsobě's approach gives

Kostomlatský's translation a more precise terminological focus with clearly delineated contours. But it moves away from Zich's pre-semiotic terminology, derived from German idealism and Herbartism; Zich's concepts are often literal translations of German terms into Czech and had entered the language with Hostinský's aesthetics at the turn of the nineteenth century. We may say that given the time of its creation, the Kostomlatský and Osolsobě translation would fit into the theoretical context of the 1980s, typical for its semiotised language (such as Elam 1980). The translation also bears traces of the semiotic circles in which Osolsobě moved as a theorist of the time. As such, it has also aged. Many of the semiotised concepts that Osolsobě opted for have continued to develop and have become loaded with additional meanings. Necessarily, the manuscript translation feels dated for today's reader.

About halfway through our own lengthy work on this book, we took time to summarise the challenges of translating Zich. Until that point, we had understood our work as a thorough editing of the existing translation by Kostomlatský and Osolsobě (for details, see Kačer and Drozd 2020). However, it was becoming increasingly clear that the translation required a much more radical approach. Particularly the second half of Kostomlatský's translation, practically untouched by Osolsobě's editing, was frequently very clumsy. Translating from scratch turned out to be the easiest option. Our final translation version uses Kostomlatský and Osolsobě as a mere springboard and reference. Their efforts entered ours as indelible constituents but the resulting translation is entirely ours, both stylistically and terminologically.

After several years of editorial work and discussions it turned out that the most logical option would be to remain as close as English allows us to Zich's idiosyncratic formulations. Our definitive versions are often radically literal. In our translation we attempt to grasp, interpret, and reconstruct Zich's terminology in English from within – from its own logic – without relying on or adapting any current theoretical trends. In this approach we try to apply a logic similar to Zich's own methodology in order to reconstruct his system of thought. We have also capitalised on our collaboration of more than a decade, of translating and editing Prague School texts and Otakar Zich. Positive responses to our *Theatre Theory Reader: Prague School Writings* (2016) have encouraged us and seem to suggest that these texts do not just work in English as historical documents but also contribute to ongoing theoretical discussions. Over the years, the translatorial-editorial team has consolidated and we play to our individual scholarly and professional strengths. The general editor David Drozd (Masaryk University, Brno, CZ) contributes his expertise in the history of theatre theory, archival research and practical (and theoretical) dramaturgy; he has refined the terminology, provided historical and philosophical contextualisation, and formulated our histories of theatrical ideas and concepts. Tomáš Kačer (Masaryk University, Brno, CZ) is an expert on British and American drama and has a background in philosophy; he is also a translator from English and a playwright. Pavel Drábek (University of Hull, UK) has expertise in theatre history and theory, with a background in English literature and maths; he is also a theatre translator, playwright, dramaturg and practical theatre maker based in the UK. We have collaborated with two native-English theatre makers: in the early phases with Mark McEllan (formerly Leeds Beckett University), who worked closely on the opening three chapters; later with playwright and experienced copy-editor Josh Overton, who has combed through the remaining chapters and revised the entire manuscript. Jules Deering (Queen Mary University London, UK), a scholar of Czech scenography, kindly read through the manuscript and made valuable comments. We have also drawn on the expertise of numerous other colleagues, experts, and peer-reviewers – most prominently Brian S. Locke (Western Illinois University, USA; for the chapter on musical drama), Veronika Ambros (formerly University of Toronto, Canada; for terminology), Martin Revermann (University of Toronto, Canada; for theatre history) and Peter W. Marx (University of Cologne, Germany; on German *Theaterwissenschaft*). Also, our students have played a key role: in reading and disputing the texts – and being inspired as well as angered by them. The translation has emerged as a team effort and we hope that the complementarity of the team has helped us capture the complexity of Zich's thinking.

KEY CONCEPTS IN TRANSLATION

In the Introduction we discussed most of Zich's key concepts. Here we would like to return to a few central ones and trace the deliberations that led us to the English renderings we have opted for. In the case of theoretical concepts it's truer than ever that their translation is inevitably an interpretation. It is therefore a matter of courtesy and transparency towards the reader to spell out the interpretive logic of our translation. In the first occurences of key terms and in crucial repetitions, we include the Czech original terms in the form of Zich's first edition of 1931.

Zich's key concept of *názorný* (ostensive) – and its derivative noun *názornost* (ostension or ostensiveness) – corresponds neatly with the German term *anschaulich*. The *názorný–anschaulich* pair is one of the instances of the closeness between Czech and German philosophical terminology. As such, it brings a substantial challenge in translating it. English offers a number of partial solutions in words such as *legible, graphic, demonstrative, manifest, evident, tangible, clear, visible, visualised, observable* and *empirical*. Almost all of these appear as provisional versions in Kostomlatský's and Osolsobě's unfinished translation. Very late in our process *empirical* came as a *heureka* of sorts, as it would tally with Zich's inductive method that follows in the tradition of empirical aesthetics. Nonetheless, it is a philosophical term that would bring in a complex history, potentially confusing for its links to specifically English empirical philosophy. In the end we opted for the term *ostensive* (and *ostension*). Although not as easygoing as its Czech and German equivalents, it captures most accurately what Zich tries to convey: the theatrical art and the mental images it evokes are available for the senses to perceive and grasp. In using this term we also pay homage to Ivo Osolsobě, who devoted great effort to develop the concept of *ostension* in his semiotic theory to show the channels of communication that happen outside of language and outside of sign systems. Osolsobě also contributed a lengthy, exhaustive entry for "Ostension" to the *Encyclopedic Dictionary of Semiotics* (Sebeok 1986: 656–60), in which he incisively summarised the concept's multiple histories. It seems, however, that he still considered the term too much of a neologism requiring commentary and clarification to use it in a translation. Also, Zich's *názorný* is a stylistically unmarked word. It is a common Czech word derived from the semantic root -zor- (view, seeing), so *názorný* means *viewable, legible, obvious, apparent* or even *available to the senses*. While our English equivalent, *ostensive*, is far from an easy choice, it is precise. With a view to present-day scholarly English, the term *ostension* is sufficiently established and also much more in use than was the case half a century ago. This development since the late 1970s clearly (ostensively?) shows the progressive development of theatre terminology towards inclusivity and openness to new theoretical impulses.

The term that has required the most discussion and deliberation appears with Zich's thorough elaboration in Chapter 3: the notion of *významová představa* (literally *an imagination, semantic imagining* or *meaning concept*), which we translate as *conceptual image* (or simply *image*). Once again, the Czech term stems from German, namely from experimental psychology, and specifically from Johannes Volkelt's theory. The German equivalent, *Bedeutungsvorstellung*, is a composite word that refers to a *mental image* (or *an imagination*; *Vorstellung*) that carries a *meaning* (*Bedeutung*). All the available versions to date translate *představa* (*Vorstellung*) as *image*, in the sense of *mental image*. We also toyed with the word *idea* as a possible translation but *idea* is too broad, vague or even abstract to work in Zich's theory. The same could be said about *mental image* and *mental concept* as both have their cognitivist associations we wished to eschew. The issue was the necessary adjective that would qualify the word *image* and give it specificity. Osolsobě and Kostomlatský considered *meaning image* and *significatory image*; Emil Volek uses *semantic representation*. We have found all these renderings too semiotic for the pre-semiotician Zich. We have considered both *semantic image/idea* and *conceptual image/idea* but opted for the latter. The notion of *conceptualis-*

ing a sensory percept – that is, the process of turning what the senses have perceived into a formed meaning or concept – agrees with Zich's argument. Zich sees the outcome of the conceptualising process to be the *významová představa* (conceptual image) in the recipient's mind. In that sense, the term *conceptual image* accurately captures Zich's theory of meaning formation as a psycho-semantic process. At the same time, the adopted English term doesn't carry the burden of semiotic or cognitivist connotations.

Zich further splits the notion of the *významová představa* (*conceptual image*) internally and distinguishes between (i) our awareness that we are, technically speaking, perceiving a material artwork (i.e., we are aware that we are perceiving a stone, colours on a canvas or a moving actor), and (ii) the fact that we are creating a fiction in our mind and that the artwork shows or represents something as well. What Zich calls *technická významová představa* can easily be translated as *technical image*. Translating the other, complementary one – *obrazová významová představa* (or *významová představa obrazová*) – poses a substantial challenge; the word *obrazový* is an adjective of *obraz* (picture or image), and as such emphasises the notion that the mental image (*představa*) that forms in our minds *portrays* or *pictures* something. In English we can also say that an image *signifies, symbolises* or *refers to* something. For its specificity, we have opted for *referential image*. Again, we were trying to find a term that wouldn't be too semiotic and that would capture Zich's argument that a *mental image* is an audio-visual image, not only a visual one. For that reason we abandoned the variant *picturing image* as purely visual. We found the variant suggestion, *symbolic image*, too vague and unfocused; the words *symbol* and *symbolic* would require further clarifications. We also eschewed specifically semiotic terms such as *signifying image* or *semantic image*. The issue of translating the nuanced and complex notion of *významová představa* has kept a number of Zich scholars busy. Petr Osolsobě has summed up the lengthy deliberations:

> Kostomlatský translated the term významová představa obrazová as *pictural image*. Ivo Osolsobě suggested *meaning image* and Mirek Čejka *significatory image*. Ambros and others use *semantic image*, Volek uses *semantic representation*, Drozd, Drábek and Kačer simply, *the image*. I settled on *referential image* in contrast to *technical image*, both concepts referencing *the significant mental image* (významová představa). (Osolsobě 2020: 31)

Petr Osolsobě's summary accurately reflects the state of our discussions in 2020. While we eventually decided for *conceptual image* as a wholly different solution of the umbrella term *významová představa*, it was its subdivision *obrazová významová představa* that provoked the most protracted and complex debates.

We believe that the term *referential image* brings out an important aspect of Zich's theory: the idea that the fictional mental image we create in our mind on the basis of the *technical image* very crucially *refers* or *relates* to a phenomenon known from our real-world experience. In our mind, we work with sensory percepts, moulding them into mental images that we relate to the memories of our past experiences. On that front it is apparent how heavily Zich's term *obrazová významová představa* relies on a specific contemporary understanding of the relation between art and reality. Our solution offered itself only when we approached the concept from a broader context of Zich's theory. Zich deploys the concept to differentiate between art forms that represent something (and in so doing evoke *referential images* in our mind), such as painting, theatre and literary forms (lyrical or narrative poetry, the *belles-lettres* novel, short stories, etc., which he simply calls *the epic poetry*); and between non-representing art forms, such as architecture, dance or music. It is important to note that Zich does not consider drama proper (in the sense of play texts or dramatic works) as an artistic literary form at all. He argues that drama's true domain is the theatre and that its core art is not *verbal* but *interactional*. Zich's aesthetic theory is, from today's point of view, truly old-fashioned and simply distinguishes between art forms according to whether they represent something or not. This is a genuinely traditional aesthetic issue of representation – i.e., *mimesis*. For these reasons we opted for *referential image* as our translation of the concept.

The same reflection directed us towards a translation solution for Zich's *obrazová umění* (i.e., picturing, portraying arts or image-arts), i.e., the art forms that evoke the *dual conceptual image* – one that contains both a *technical* and a *referential image*. We refer to *obrazová umění* as *mimetic arts*. We believe that the word *reference* (or *referential*) is the closest we were willing to come to semiotic terminology without running the danger of over-semiotising Zich's own terminology. The simple use of *mimesis/mimetic* in its first, and essentially Aristotelian, meaning offered our translation an elegant and subtle way of signalling Zich's own rootedness in period terminologies. At the same time, it helps emphasise Zich's central argument: that theatrical performance (as we would call it) is an autonomous art form based on its unique aesthetic core: the dramatic art of *human interaction*. For Zich, just like for Aristotle, representation (i.e., imitation or mimesis) is far from a simple, mechanical copying of the outer appearance of things. For Aristotle, Tatarkiewicz has argued that:

> imitation meant [...] not faithful copying but a free approach to reality; the artist can present reality in his own way. [...] To Aristotle "imitation" was, in the first place, the imitation of human activities; however, it gradually became the imitation of nature, from which it was supposed to derive its perfection. (Tatarkiewicz 1980: 268)

Similarly, Zich thought of *imitation* in non-literal terms. Throughout *Aesthetics*, he repeatedly rejects naturalism based on replicating the real world as superficial and mechanical, and therefore un-artistic. It would be inappropriate and anachronistic to bring into the translation process the entire discussion that unrolled over the twentieth century regarding the concept of *mimesis*. That would complicate it out of all proportion. For the same reason, ironically, it would be foolish to eschew this term just because it's too contentious or unsustainable today. Without further commentary we adopted its use, also to historicise as well as estrange our translation appropriately in regards to today's terminology.

The example of *mimesis* also serves to illustrate how coherent Zich's system is and how individual translation solutions need to be considered in context – a process that often brings great benefits. We should also note, for completeness, that in editing the thematic issue of *Theatralia* dedicated to *Otakar Zich and a Structural Approach to Art* (*Theatralia* 2020/1), we intentionally gave our contributors a free hand in their individual solutions of Zich's terminology in English. Individual contributions to the issue may also serve as an archive of sorts that records the prolonged discussions. At the same time, we would like to disclaim any finality of our solutions and wish to offer them only as propositions that necessarily forego a closure and will continue to stay open to further interpretive discussions.

A much less precarious as well as explosive term, though no less conceptually crucial, is *jednání*, which can seemingly easily be translated as *action* or *activity*, but also as *behaviour* or *performance* (in the sense of *performing an action*) – in many ways like the Aristotelic notion of *praxis*. However, Zich uses the term very frequently and very specifically at that. For Zich, *jednání* is always a conscious and intentional activity, and as such it is primarily human (or it is anthropomorphised as part of the artistic form). Simultaneously it is always an activity in relation to someone else. Very often, the term appears as *vespolné jednání* – where *vespolné* is a now-dated word meaning *social*, *mutual* or *communal*. So *vespolné jednání* could be loosely rendered as *mutual action*. It is also crucial for Zich that the dramatic art deals with ostensive human activities; *jednání* and *vespolné jednání* as activities are also relational, mutual, two-way and interpersonal – and as such potentially conflicting and therefore dramatic. We have therefore decided to consistently use *action* and *(human) interaction*, respectively, as our translations. In so doing, we followed the lead of Ivo Osolsobě, who suggested in his seminal essay "Dramatické dílo jako komunikace komunikací o komunikaci" (Dramatic Work as a Communication of Communications about Communication; Osolsobě 2002 [1970]) that Zich's *vespolné jednání* could easily be replaced by the term *interaction*. In adopting *interaction*, we have opted for a more modern (but we believe a much more precise) expression.

Rather than theoretical, it was more of a linguistic question as to how to translate Zich's dual concepts of *dramatická osoba / herecká postava* – in our rendering, *dramatic persona / actor figure*. In the case of the fictive *dramatic persona* represented on stage we decided to eschew the common English term *character*. That would point too narrowly towards an idea of a psychologically elaborate "character", while a dramatic persona may entirely lack interiority or a notion of self (such as supernatural beings or highly stylised creations). In the case of the actor's onstage creation, denoted by Zich's term *herecká postava*, numerous possible translations have been suggested – such as *actor's persona*, *actor's figure* or *stage figure* – the latter offered with some hesitation by Jiří Veltruský:

> The literal translation of Zich's own term, *herecká postava*, would be the "actor's figure", an utterly misleading expression. I chose the somewhat barbarous "stage figure" because in my view it is the only possible term if confusion with the actor on one hand and with the character on the other is to be avoided. (Veltruský 2016 (1976): 378).

The central binary is well captured in the pair *persona / figure*. The concept of *persona*, apart from its etymology in Latin and originating in the Greek theatre mask, captures the idea that we can create and flesh out the mental image of the fictive persona with substantial, even psychological, complexity, whereas what the actor creates on stage is intentionally shaped, formed and constructed almost like a statue – that is, a *figure*. It was the qualifiers that became the challenge. The variant *actor's figure* is semantically quite accurate but stylistically rather clumsy: the *figure* doesn't belong to the actor but it is their creation, not to mention the awkward straits we would run into when Zich does refer to a particular actor's *herecká postava*. Veltruský's suggested *stage figure* is somewhat radical but it captures accurately the fact that the *herecká postava* is by definition present on stage and the audience perceive it exclusively there. However, the implications of *stage figure* edit out the actor as the figure's creator – which may agree with Veltruský's semiotic interpretation of Zich but it fails to meet our own objectives in keeping Zich un-semiotised. Finding the right qualifier that would fit stylistically became a major point of debate: *actor's*? *actorly*? In the end, we decided to launch *actor figure* as a new compound with the hope that it will float.

Let us add one more example. The concept of *dramatický děj* spans in its meaning from *dramatic onstage action* to *dramatic plot*; the semantic field of *děj* (literally *happenings, that which occurs*; in German, *die Handlung*) is broad and the English equivalents we use have to be understood contextually and functionally. The principal problem with the translation of *jednání* (we use *action*) and of *děj* (often *action*, occasionally *plot*) is that Zich views the two as closely linked. He asserts that "the central concept of dramatic art is human action" (183 above) and argues that this claim is a sufficient definition of the semantic aspect of drama. It is the specific feature of dramatic art that *děj* (*action, plot*) or *příběh* (*story, storyline*) grow directly from the dramatic personas' action – that is, from their interaction. That is, Zich clearly distinguishes between *jednání postav* (*action of personas, personal action*) and the *děj* or *zápletka* (which we translate, depending on the context, as *action, plot*, or *storyline*). In a similar vein, Aristotle defines *plot* as an arrangement (*synthesis*) of incidents (*pragmaton*). Early in Chapter 6, Zich defines the relation most accurately and stresses that in literary fiction there is no such close link: a novel, for instance, does not need to contain *dramatic action*, but only *action* of any kind. In dramatic art (i.e., in theatrical performance), the two concepts – *jednání* and *děj* – are so closely intertwined that they may seem interchangeable and Zich may seem to use them as synonyms. With a view to the structure of the dramatic work, they are not, as *děj* originates from *jednání*, and as such is subordinate to it. Although we often translate both as *action* – an English term with its own complexity in theatre theory (see Scanlan 2020: 49–71) – we try to make it contextually clear what the significant distinction is (and also include the Czech term in brackets).

As for other terms (and their translations) we hope that they are self-explanatory in their contexts and define themselves by their usage. There are many such cases – such as *spoken drama* for the Czech *činohra* (literally *action play* but denoting "straight" or "spoken" theatre) and its musical counterpart *sung drama*: *zpěvohra* (literally *sung play*), a term that covers not only opera but also other kinds of theatre that combines music and singing as well as potentially speaking or dance. We occasionally take risks and use less common expressions – such as *percept*, to refer to a single, one-off sensory perception.

Our translation naturally respects that English – unlike Czech or German – tends to create shorter units, be they sentences or paragraphs. We tend to break up Zich's convoluted sentence constructions – which were in vogue as signs of scholarly style – into shorter structures, while retaining of course Zich's patterns of thought, logic and his hierarchy and line of argument.

AN ANNOTATED GLOSSARY

(PAVEL DRÁBEK AND DAVID DROZD)

This glossary offers concise definitions and explanations of the key concepts, terms and notions Zich uses in his *Aesthetics of the Dramatic Art*. Each term is given with its Czech original. Where relevant, the corresponding German term and occasionally an alternative English term. While the definitions accurately follow Zich's logic and his entire aesthetic theory, the formulations try to operate independent of his idiosyncratic language. An asterisk (*) marks the words that have their own separate entries in the glossary (e.g., *dramatic work*, *melodrama*). When appropriate, entries refer to the chapters and passages where Zich discusses the term in detail. The final section of the above Afterword discusses several key concepts in greater detail, with a special view to the challenges of finding a suitable English equivalent – such as *významová představa* (conceptual image), *názorný* (ostensive), *herecká postava* (actor figure), *dramatická postava* (dramatic persona) or *action* (*jednání, děj*).

The Annotated Glossary complements and works alongside the book's extensive and analytical list of contents. The contents list offers the reader a clear overview of the building blocks of Zich's theory; we include these building blocks in the glossary too with a page reference to Zich's text. Those building blocks are of two principal kinds: one, terms that help analyse and describe the structure and the construction of the work of art; and two, principles (also spoken of as postulates, laws or guidelines) that Zich derives from the inner logic and qualities of the material of dramatic art.

action (*jednání, děj*; *Handlung*) is a key term in Zich's theory, adopted from the Aristotelic tradition. *Action* involves more than mere acts or deeds (as these are individual, one-off, self-contained) but builds on them, on behaviour and on realised intents (cf. Aristotle's notion of *praxis*). Zich defines *action* (*jednání*) as a person's *ostensive act that is intended to have, and also has, an effect on another person. Zich makes a careful distinction between *action* (*jednání*) and acts or deeds (*skutky, činy*) to highlight the processual character of *action* as a category. Through this distinction, Zich appears to be thinking performatively, taking *action* as a purposeful activity that realises certain *aspirations. That is a first step towards conceptualising the more specific category of *dramatic action, the central building block of *dramatic art.

Only as a side note: the word *jednání* in Czech (just like *Handlung* in German) also means *act*, a subdivision of an entire play – as in *a tragedy in five acts*. Luckily, the use is so specific that this meaning of *action* tends to be apparent from the context. (For a detailed dramaturgic discussion on *action*, see Scanlan 2020: 49–71.)

actor figure (*herecká postava*; *die Schauspielergestalt, Gestalt*; also *stage figure*) is what the audience sees and hears when watching an actor's performance. The *actor figure* is the product of the actor's creative work: the actor fully formed in their role. In Zich's terminology, the *actor figure* is the *technical image* associated with the *referential image* (see **conceptual image*), i.e., with the **dramatic persona*. The actor figure is of a physiological kind: it is the formed actor themself, and it builds on the actor's movement, gesture and **mimics* (nonverbal expressions), as well as on their costume, their **mask* (the actor's visage) and on their **delivery* of the lines. Zich views the actor's lines, the words written by the playwright, as part of the dramatic persona. But their delivery – i.e., how the actor performs them – is the actor's creative work, and as such the delivery is part of the *actor figure*. The *actor figure* is the actor's performance (interpretation) of the persona as conceived by the playwright and as imperfectly (i.e., only partially) rendered in the text of the play.

It is an important specific of the actor's creative work that the actor uses their own live body as the material for their creation. As such, Zich argues, actors are the only artists who are existentially identical with their work: they are "inside" their creation. The same holds for dancers, but only the actor uses their body fully, in the totality of its expressive means, including their voice. (See Ch. 3.)

Zich argues an important distinction: For the audience, the *actor figure* is mainly a visual and an acoustic percept – in part also an inner-tactile or kinaesthetic percept (we empathise with the actor's efforts and experience). For the performing actor, the *actor figure* is primarily their bodily perception (i.e., how they feel their own psychosomatic experience); more precisely, it is a set of the actor's inner-tactile perceptions and mental states. As such it is both of a physical and a psychological nature. The physical and psychological aspects of the actor's self-perception are linked by *psychophysiological correspondences*, e.g., an angry facial expression bonds with anger as an emotion (see Ch. 5, p. 161 above).

aesthetic effect (*estetický efekt*; *die ästhetische Wirkung, der ästhetische Effekt*) is the emotional response of the recipient, who perceives the artwork. The *aesthetic effect* is the recipient's subjective feeling, of aesthetic sensation evoked in the recipient's mind (consciousness). The *aesthetic effect* occurs at a distance from what caused them; we (as recipients) are able to spectate (observe, watch) *disinterestedly* and enjoy an artwork, an action or an event. (The concept of *disinterested pleasure* follows Immanuel Kant's philosophy.) We are capable of enjoying (having *aesthetic pleasure* in) various things, such as turbulent storms or agitated fights, as long as we can watch them, *disinterestedly*, i.e., from an aesthetic distance. In this, Zich is a representative of psychological aesthetics (a scholarly discipline concerned with aesthetic states of consciousness). That is why he understands the *aesthetic effect* purely as an emotional response (both pleasant and unpleasant) and makes a distinction between the aesthetic and the artistic value of an *artwork.

a posteriori effects (*aposteriorní účinky*) are, in Zich's theory, those effects that arise from the *artwork retrospectively, only once we start relating the experience of the artwork with our own lived experience. The *aesthetic effect* (e.g., *catharsis*) is actually an *a posteriori effect*. In his analysis of the *dramatic art, Zich strictly distinguishes between *a priori principles (given and often logically necessary qualities and principles of the art form) and *a posteriori effects*, which incorporate the recipient's subjectivity, the variations in their inner and outer experiences, and their knowledge of art as such. (For more see Ch. 10.)

a priori principles (*apriorní zákonitosti*). As a formal aesthetician, Zich assumes that every artistic *material has its unchanging qualities and follows certain *principles. The material and the principles predetermine the *artwork*. In Chapter 10, Zich elaborates on this theory and asserts – clearly following Kant and his philosophy of *a priori forms of perception* – that these are *a priori principles*, i.e., preexisting, predetermined or given principles, that may not be absolute but have their apparent and *ostensive logic, out of necessity. As recipients we are predisposed by our physiological capacities and our artistic-aesthetic experience (upbringing, education, training) to perceive relations between individual components of an artwork; depending on how well versed we are in the art, we understand how individual *formations come together to build the artwork as a whole. Zich uses the concept of *a priori principles* to name and describe such relations. These can be of various kinds: there are abstract logical relations, such as causality or temporal sequence; and there are ostensive relations (i.e., relations that are available to the senses: to view, to hearing, etc.), such as affinity (harmony in colours, in music, in shapes), contrast (of intensity, of direction), similarity and others. (For more details see Ch. 10, section "Technical Dramatic Styles", pp. 358ff. above.)

All the partial principles – or *postulates*, if you will – which Zich identifies as the principles of the *dramatic work are effectively concrete instances of such general *a priori principles*. The artistic value of a work depends then on the way and measure in which the artist purposely, consciously and intentionally creates the artwork and allows the *a priori principles* of the material to stand out (become ostensive), which would otherwise remain hidden or indistinct.

A priori principles operate also in the structure of *a priori art forms*, such as musical forms (fugue, rondo, sonata) or poetic forms (sonnet, rhyme royal, ballad, triolet); the structure of these art forms demonstrate several *a priori principles* of their material.

artwork (*umělecké dílo*; *Kunstwerk*; also *artefact*, *work of art* or *artistic work*) is a thing (a phenomenon) purposely created to have an *aesthetic effect. An *artwork* can have different forms and different arts: it can be a statue, a poem, a dramatic work, the creation of an *actor figure, a performance in *reproductive arts, etc. In his aesthetics, Zich claims that an *artwork* has its own specific aesthetic value – a judgement that is relatively subjective, as it is based on an emotional response. An *artwork* also has its artistic value, which in turn is objective and can be identified through formal analysis of the *artwork*'s specific structure and logic that derives from the specific artistic *material proper to the art. In trying to understand the principles of *artwork*, Zich states that aesthetic analysis, which breaks up the *artwork* into its individual components, should go only as far as the particular component still retains its aesthetic efficacy – its ability to have an *aesthetic effect.

aspiration, aspirational (*snaha, snahový*; also *effort, related to effort*). *Aspirations* are motoric responses (reflexes) to impulses, many of them *emotional. In Zich's theory, *aspirational* behaviours are *intentional action* and form a crucial component of *ostensive, i.e., *dramatic action, as the spectators can immediately perceive them in the actor's *mimics, i.e., physical, nonverbal expression. (See also *emotion.)

cause-and-objective nexus (*kauzálně finální nexus*; also *causal nexus*) relates to principles of *dramatic action, *interplay and acting. The term is effectively a principle that helps Zich articulate certain observed qualities of dramatic art. The *cause-and-objective nexus* is a bond between, or a series of, affections, aspirations, motivations and actions that lead to a particular goal. Zich distinguished the inner *cause-and-objective nexus* that helps actors to build a *dramatic persona as a coherent individuality, and the outer *causal nexus*, which is a series of actions and reactions in the *interaction of two (or more) personas.

components (*složky*) are the parts or aspects of a dramatic work that are not self-standing (they would not work on their own). These components may resemble or be related to other arts – Zich calls them their "mother arts":

e.g., the stage and the set in their spatial structure relate to architecture; the verbal art of a dramatic text resembles (and could be considered) literature; scenic art (scenography) relates to the visual arts; *sung drama connects crucially with vocal music. But for Zich, the artwork exists as an organic unity of components, with its unique integrity, and although individual components could be linked to their mother art, as part of the dramatic *artwork, they need to follow the principles and the logic of the *dramatic work, not of their mother arts. Otherwise, they could be beautiful architectural, literary, visual, or musical works, but would fail to serve the dramatic purpose and the *dramatic action – or, the *dramaticity of the *artwork.

conceptual image (*významová představa*; *Bedeutungsvorstellung*; also shortened to *mental image* or *the image*) arises in our mind on the basis of our perception. It is a subjective mental image (or mental concept) that our mind associates with what we perceive through our senses. Another way of understanding the term *conceptual image* is to ask the question: "What is it that I see or hear?" The conceptual image evoked by our perception – often on the basis of similarity – tends to merge with the percept itself. The percept and the *conceptual image* blend to such a degree that the conceptual image in our mind is able to retain the percept's *ostensive quality. This is a universal psychological process; in theorising it and applying it to the theatre, Zich builds on James-Lange associationist theory.

Our perception of an artwork, Zich argues, is a special case. The *conceptual image* of our perception of artworks can have a dual structure: the *image* divides into the *technical image* and the *referential image*. The *technical image* (*významová představa technická*; *die technische Bedeutungsvorstellung*) works on our awareness that we are experiencing an artwork; it requires us to have some experience with art and be aware of its conventions. The *technical image* builds on the *artifice*, i.e., on the "way the art is made" (the *techne*). The *referential image* (*významová představa obrazová*; *die bildliche Bedeutungsvorstellung*) is our idea of what the artwork represents, what it refers to or what it *pictures* (*zobrazuje*; see also *mimetic arts). For instance, the shapes or colours of a painting have their own artistic quality: our perception evokes the *technical image*, i.e., the awareness that this is as an artwork. The shapes or colours also associate a specific reference (e.g., a shape in the painting represents a tree or a figure; the colour red represents blood, green represents growth or life).

The *technical-referential* pair plays a crucial role in Zich's theory. He applies this dual *conceptual image* to the distinction between the *scenic space and the *dramatic space; between the *actor figure and the *dramatic persona; or, between the actors' *interplay and the *dramatic interaction. (For more, see Ch. 3 and the Afterword.)

AN ANNOTATED GLOSSARY   451

delivery (*mluva*, occasionally *řeč*; also *speaking, speech* or *talk*) refers to the way an actor performs their lines. *Delivery* includes all aspects of vocal performance that the actor controls: the rhythm and tempo, accentuation, timbre, intonation and others. While the words written by the playwright belong to the *dramatic persona, the *delivery* is part of the *actor figure* – a result of the actor's creative work.

dramatic action (*dramatické jednání; dramatische Handlung*). Zich defines *dramatic action* as an intentional (purposeful) activity, *ostensive *action in drama, that has an effect on another *dramatic persona*. It follows that *dramatic action* results from the interaction of personas (people or personifications) and comprises not only physical action, but also the personas' speech, no matter if in dialogue or in monologue, as long as it is truly dramatic: i.e., as long as it affects another dramatic persona. Zich is very strict in using the term *dramatic*. There are intuitive, popular uses of the word "dramatic" to refer to things that contain tensions, sharp contrasts or great intensity, such as a "dramatic" view, a "dramatic" storm or a "dramatic" speech or oration. Zich excludes these uses from his discussions and strictly distinguishes *natural* (*přirozený*) *dramatic action* – i.e., real-world interaction, such as a quarrel, a dispute or an altercation – from *artificial* (*umělá*; constructed) *dramatic action*, which is the *dramatic action* of *dramatic personas* (i.e., imagined characters) as performed by actors.

Analytically speaking, Zich defines *dramatic plot* as a chain of *dramatic action*, but in his discussions he often fluently shifts from one to the other and it may seem that he equates the two. However, there is a difference in category: for him, *dramatic plot* (*dramatický děj*) is that which comes from the *interaction of *dramatic personas* – in today's parlance, we often speak of the *story*, the *storyline* or the *narrative* (but see Scanlan 2020: 17). In other words, in following *dramatic action*, the spectator perceives and understands it as a more-or-less consistent effort that builds a storyline; both *dramatic action* and *dramatic plot* are a realisation of personas' intents and *aspirations. (See also the discussion of *dramatic action* in Ch. 3 and the section on "Key Concepts in Translation" in the Afterword.) For Zich, *dramatic action* is the proper material and contents of dramatic art. He argues that mimetic, *ostensive representation of human *interaction by means (in the form) of the *interplay of actors is the necessary and sufficient condition of dramatic art. In other words, dramatic art is – by virtue of its material, i.e., live performance of live humans – especially suitable for portraying human interaction: that is *dramatic action*. (For a full discussion see Ch. 6.)

dramatic art (*dramatické umění; die dramatische Kunst*). Zich defines this concept as a specific, autonomous art in its own right. For him, *dramatic art* is the sum of all *dramatic works, i.e., all performances on stage. In its breadth it includes various art forms of *spoken drama, *sung drama, as well as other dramatic art forms and genres. *Dramatic art* is a subcategory of theatrical art, which includes any kind of performance on stage (e.g., monodrama, cabaret, *pantomime). In intuitive and everyday use, *dramatic art* is shortened to *drama* (e.g., in the traditional British use). However, this turns *drama* into a polysemic word that refers to too many different things and prevents a sufficiently nuanced, critical discussion. Zich differentiates kinds of *dramatic art* by their modes of dramatic action (see *dramatic work and *dramatic action). For Zich's own definition, see especially Ch. 3, pp. 102–103 above.

dramatic persona (*dramatická osoba; die dramatische Persona*; also *character*) is the imagined character in the spectator's mind. It is the creation of the spectator's imagination upon watching the actor's performance. Or more precisely, it is a mental image the recipient builds on their perception of the *actor figure (see Ch. 3, p. 94 above). For Zich the *dramatic persona* is a *referential image* (see *conceptual image): an essentially subjective, psychological phenomenon that exists only in the spectator's mind. The *dramatic personas* imagined by different spectators may vary in nuances because in watching the mental processes of association are individual. The psychological process of creating a *dramatic persona* incorporates the spectator's personal experience – both outer (i.e., from the real world) and inner (i.e., from their inner world) – as well as the spectator's knowledge and experience of art, theatre and theatrical conventions. (See Ch. 3 and the Afterword.) People often say that we have an idea of a dramatic character from merely reading the play. Zich is sceptical about that. He argues that in reading our mental associations are very vague, incomplete and random, because the text can only fix the playwright's vision partially: the dramatic text is no more than an imperfect record of the character's lines and a partial outline, a blueprint, for the *dramatic action. Robert Scanlan writes concisely: "The *words* in a script are misleading because they make action claims, but they mask the action as frequently as they reveal it" (Scanlan 2020: 47). The only person who has a complex image of the *dramatic persona* is the playwright, who first imagines the personas and their action, and then captures this imagination in the text as accurately as possible. See also Zich's discussion of the dramatic author's creative tasks in Ch. 5.

dramatic space (*dramatický prostor*) is the fictional space where imagined *dramatic action takes place. The audience imagine (or associate) the *dramatic space* on the basis of the *scenic image* (or *scene) that they see and hear (that is the *technical image*; see *conceptual image). Unlike the physical, non-representing space of the *stage, which is measured in metres, the *dramatic space* operates in *spatial relations* or the intervening space between individual components (e.g., furniture, onstage objects, doors) and what these components afford or evoke for the **dramatic action*. In other words, Zich views the *spatial relations* as *lines of force* for potential action. Analogically, he sees the *dramatic space* as a *field of force*, with its specific affordance for the **dramatic action* of the **dramatic personas*.

dramatic work (*dramatické dílo; das dramatische Werk*) is what we (as spectators) perceive by our senses in the course of a performance in the theatre. Zich (Ch. 1, p. 60 above) defines it as an audio-visual and spatio-temporal art – i.e., an art that is seen and heard (Zich later adds other senses to perceive space and action). The art is clearly defined in time and space by its duration and by its venue: in other words, it exists only when it is being performed. The *dramatic work* is temporal and transitory; it is ephemeral in nature. Zich views the coexistence of the two sensory components – the optical and the auditive – as the defining feature of the dramatic art. For Zich, the two components are heterogeneous (each appeals to a different sense) and inseparable (they happen simultaneously and are complementary). For that reason, Zich excludes literary drama (i.e., dramatic literature that is read, not being performed), as well as dance and **pantomime* (as these art forms exclude speech and do not root itself in full dramatic interaction). For Zich's discussion, see pp. 62, 96ff., and 100 above respectively.

emotion, emotional (*cit, citový*; also *feeling, related to feeling*). Zich draws on contemporary psychological theory and understands *emotion* as the direct cause (or motivation) for any **action*. Emotions then lead to **aspirations* (or effort) as their motoric reflex or response. Importantly for Zich's theory, *emotions* are not always just mental, but also physical, and very often motoric experiences. This is significant for **ostensive*, i.e., **dramatic action*, in that the **dramatic persona*'s *emotional* expressions show in the actor's performance. *Emotions* – unlike *aspirations* – are static in nature. As such, *emotional *mimics* are only lyrical, whereas *aspirational* behaviour leads to **dramatic action (plot)*.

In the opening of Ch. 8, Zich points out that music is very well suited for evoking and portraying a dramatic persona's *emotions* and *aspirations*. Zich argues that while thoughts or ideas may underpin action, they are always *emotionally* tainted. Any action – no matter how spontaneous or premeditated – has its *emotional* base. (For a detailed discussion of different forms of action, spontaneous and intentional, and the relation between emotions, aspirations and conscious and rational motivations, see Ch. 6.).

focus (*zaměření*) is a psychological state of concentrating one's attention and even physical energy intently in a particular direction or a particular field.

Zich establishes *focus* in a practical example in Ch. 5 (163–164 above) and points out how a person's *focus* is not merely a result of one's individual will but comes from suggestion from others. He uses that concept to analyse creative processes in the theatre. The *actorly focus* (*herecké zaměření*) comes from the actor's *interplay with their stage partners and from their own "purposely prepared self-induced suggestion" (164 above). Analogically, Zich speaks of a *theatrically focused* audience (Ch. 7), one that is in the mindset of and intent on watching a theatrical performance. It also needs to be said that the audience mindset builds on previous experience of art; knowing the conventions and understanding how to read the work is part and parcel of cultural consumption. Zich further elaborates on this process of experiencing art in his discussion of the theatrical illusion (in Ch. 9, pp. 343–344 above). Zich refers to an *aesthetic focus* (*estetické zaměření*), occupied with a beautiful object; an *artistic focus* (*umělecké zaměření*) that more specifically focuses on an artwork; and a *mimetic focus* (*obrazové zaměření*) that is intent on the portrayal (imitation) of things. A special, and unique type is the *theatrical focus*. When watching a performance, Zich observes, the audience perceives onstage action in a uniquely dual way: spectating evokes (1) the *technical image* (*významová představa technická*), i.e., our awareness that we are watching an artwork, and (2) the *referential image* (*významová představa obrazová*), which has *mimetic* qualities and represents some *ideal *action. The audience's *theatrical focus* is, in many ways, the spectators' psychosomatic experiencing of the theatre and the part they play in creating *dramatic art.

Theatrical focus creates a perception of *theatrical reality*: an actuality that is parallel with real-world actuality, corresponds to it, but is noetically different and heterogeneous.

formation (*útvar*) is a term Zich uses to refer to parts of an *artwork. The Czech word, *útvar*, means "something that is shaped or formed" (*ú-* suggests finite completion; *tvar* means *shape*, etymologically from *tvořit*, to create, to make). A *formation* is a structural component purposely formed (*účelně utvářeno*) by the artist in the creative process. A *formation* to the *artwork* is what a brick, the groundplan or the plaster colour are to a building. In keeping with Zich's formal aesthetics, a *formation* can be material or immaterial; it is a single creation that helps give shape to the whole.

ideal (*ideálný*; also *imaginary*, e.g., *ideal persons, place* or *action*). Zich makes a clear distinction between phenomena that we only imagine and those presented to us *ostensively. He calls the imagined ones *ideal*, as they are merely ideas in our mind. This distinction is crucial for his theory and he argues a clear, *material difference between the *action presented and observed on *stage, or a *dramatic persona performed by an actor, and the same fictive action or persona that we imagine when reading a text. The former is presented *ostensively (directly through our senses), and so our associated *conceptual images keep its ostensive character (performance is real action in a real space); while the latter, emerging from reading, are imagined: in Zich's phenomenological terminology, they are *ideal*, as the material that evoked them were mere *ideas*, not *real* things.

Zich's distinction applies to dramatic work as well: a *dramatic persona that never appears on stage (e.g., Laius in Sophocles' *Oedipus Rex* or Rosaline in *Romeo and Juliet*) remains *ideal*, because it is only through the words of other personas that they are evoked, as opposed to dramatic personas that actually, *really* appear, presented by actors on stage. The same distinction holds for *action: if an action happens off stage (e.g., the shipwreck in *The Tempest* or the death of Cordelia in *King Lear*), it is *ideal*; if on stage, it is *real*. The *ideal-real* binary serves to distinguish the *materiality* (the *material nature) of phenomena: direct *vs.* indirect speech in literature; locations (*dramatic spaces* of action) presented *vs.* merely described, etc. Their respectively different *material determines the artistic logic (the *principles) that structures the form of the artwork. (For a detailed discussion see Ch. 4.)

interaction (*vespolné jednání*; *gemeinsame Handlung*) is Zich's central term and he asserts that *human interaction* – joint action between people – is the artistic essence of *dramatic art. In his definition of *human interaction*, he equates it with *dramatic action or *plot* (*dramatický děj*). It follows from his definition of *dramatic action* – i.e., a persona's action that is intended to have, and also has, an effect on another persona – that the *dramatic work is necessarily a collective work. Technically speaking, *interaction* comes from the actors' *interplay.

interplay (*spoluhra*; also *actors' interplay*) is the actors' collective creative work. Actors use the affordance of their bodies – their *material – and interact (see *interaction), which results in the *interplay*. This *interplay* portrays (represents) *dramatic action (*dramatický děj*). (For more, see Ch. 3, p. 94; Ch. 5, p. 177; and Ch. 6, pp. 216–228 above.)

mask (*maska*; also *visage*). Zich uses the word *mask* idiosyncratically, in a more general sense: not only to refer to an actual mask an actor wears on their face, but also to speak of the actor's physical appearance or visage as a whole, far beyond the mere face. In this broader sense, the *mask* includes any application of make-up, prosthetics and padding, hairstyling, millinery and wigs, and of costume. Zich's *maska* anticipates Jacques Lecoq's experiments with neutral facial masks that made one "look at the whole body; [...] the 'face' becomes the whole body" (cited in Sennett 2012: 243).

material (*materiál*; also *artistic material* or *medium*). The notion of *material* is central to any aesthetics with a formal orientation, from Kant to the Prague School. Zich distinguishes between individual arts not on a thematic or ideational basis, but on the basis of the *material* from which their artwork is created – e.g., stone, wood, paints, words, sound or the human being. Each material offers a potential and gives creative opportunities and affordances. In today's terms, we could say that every *medium* has its *properties*. At the same time, the *material* specifically limits artistic creativity as it has different capacities for evoking or depicting various themes (cf. the discussion of the capacities of mimics in Ch. 5, or of the mimetic capacities of music in Ch. 8). Zich argues that as a crucial part of their talent, artists need to develop the ability to think (imagine, create) in and through the material of their art; that is, they need to conceive their ideas in concrete "matter", materially. Zich considers *artistic thinking* concrete, *material* and **ostensive*, not abstract or speculative.

For Zich and other formal aestheticians, the task of systematic (or scientific) aesthetics is to describe and analyse the specific **principles* (or postulates), logic, laws, and rules of each art as they follow from the art's particular *material*. Zich argues that the material of dramatic art is **dramatic action*, i.e., **ostensive* human **interaction*.

melodrama (*melodram*; *das Melodrama*) is a specific genre of musical drama (music theatre). In *melodrama*, actors speak to an underlying instrumental accompaniment. The musical score co-creates the impression and enhances the mood (the atmosphere) and the dramatic tension. This genre was prominent in the long nineteenth century, starting with Jean-Jacques Rousseau's *Pygmalion* (c.1762) and Jiří Antonín Benda's *Ariadne auf Naxos* and *Medea* (both 1775). The genre culminated in the Czech context in the late nineteenth-century monumental scenic melodrama, the *Hippodamia* trilogy (1888–1891), by composer Zdeněk Fibich and dramatist Jaroslav Vrchlický. Otakar Zich also composed several shorter melodramas based on Czech poetry. In 1938, Arthur Honegger premiered his dramatic oratorio *Jeanne d'Arc au bûcher* (on the lyrics by Paul Claudel) with sung and spoken parts – a modern development of *melodrama*.

This genre of *melodrama* must not be mistaken with the nineteenth-century spoken dramatic genre of melodrama (e.g., Elizabeth Braddon, Dion Boucicault), which is based on spectacular staging and sensational reversals of expectations and emotions.

mental transfiguration (*předuševnění*; *die Umbeseelung*, *die Umbegeisterung*; in specific contexts also *character identification*, *mempathy*, or historically *metempsychosis*) is a special part of the theatre maker's dramatic talent, necessary for the playwright, the actor, the director, and the dramatic musical composer. Based on empathy – the processes of feeling oneself into another being – *mental transfiguration* is our ability to feel "with" others and imagine being "in their shoes". It happens in the real world when we imagine what others are experiencing or when we daydream about different possibilities of our own personality. In creative practice, it can become an artefact in its own right – as long as it is autotelic (done for its own sake, playfully), and independent of personal stakes in our wish to be another person. *Mental transfiguration* results in the joyful, playful, and creative pleasure of becoming (*mentally transfiguring* into) personas of any kind. The process involves empathising with the person's motoric sensations – what their body feels when they assume postures, make gestures, and undertake *ostensive actions.

Zich argues that *mental transfiguration* is key to the playwright's creative work in that the playwright empathises with the personas they create in their play. In contrast with the novelist, who empathises with the fictional persona's senses (sight, hearing, touch, smell), the playwright very specifically activates also the *dramatic persona*'s inner-tactile, kinaesthetic sensations: the physical (bodily, somatic) playing out of the action. (The modern psychological term equivalent to Zich's *inner-tactile sensation* is *proprioception* or *inner kinaesthesia*.) The playwright imagines the dramatic persona to be *real, to become embodied (*transbodied) by the actor. In that, the playwright anticipates that the actor playing the dramatic persona will assume a persona different to their own individuality (he calls this process *transpersonation*; *přeosobnění*), with that new persona's physical, bodily individuality. In other words, unlike the novelistic creative process, dramatic *mental transfiguration* involves a *motoric quality*, and the playwright's creative process is materially, substantially different and unique. *Mental transfiguration* and *transbodiment are complementary processes: the playwright engages in the former, while the actor participates in both while creating the *actor figure*.

It is *mental transfiguration* with its motoric, physical quality that allows the playwright to create *dramatic action* – i.e., *ostensive *interaction of different and autonomous *dramatic personas*, each with their diverse and often conflicting individuality. Zich argues that for the playwright to create their dramatic personas and dramatic action properly, their *mental transfiguration* should be as complete and thorough as possible. (For more on the playwright's creative work and on the motoric qualities and the motoric effect of artwork, i.e., its ability to evoke inner-tactile perceptions in us, see Ch. 4.)

mimetic arts (*obrazová umění*; *bildliche Künste*; also *representing arts* or *image-arts*) are a category of arts that *represent* (mimic, mediate, convey) an image or portrait of reality. This image may be visual, audible, or audio-visual, but its core is in its *picturing*, i.e., *imitating* of reality. For that reason, our translation of *obrazová* (picturing, image-making, image-using) opts for the word *mimetic*. *Mimetic arts* include painting, sculpture, literature, but also the theatre. Conversely, non-mimetic arts include architecture, dance or music, as these are not concerned with creating image representations of reality but operate in their own independent media. The instances of music and dance as art forms are of course more complicated: Zich distinguishes between *pure music* (or *absolute music*) and musical genres that are somewhat *mimetic*. Among the mimetic musical genres are symphonic poems (e.g., Berlioz's *Symphonie fantastique*), programmatic music (e.g., Mussorgsky's *Pictures at an Exhibition*), vocal music (e.g., oratoria, Bach's *Johannes-Passion* or *Mätthaus-Passion*) and all genres of *sung drama (opera, operetta, etc.). The same distinction applies to dance: the romantic ballet and the *pantomime would fall under mimetic arts based on movement. Zich further develops this distinction: only the *mimetic arts* generate *conceptual images that assume a double structure and include both the *technical image* and the *referential image*. (See also Ch. 3 passim. The mimetic capacity of music – *mimetic music*; *hudba obrazová* – is the subject of the first section of Ch. 8.)

mimics (*mimika*; also *nonverbal expression*) is another idiosyncratic term Zich uses. It refers to the actor's physical behaviour, comportment and nonverbal actions. In today's terms, we would speak of body language, but Zich uses *mimics* more broadly: not only to refer to facial expression, but also to physical, nonverbal expressions of the actor's entire whole body, such as gestures, postures and physical action. Zich argues that *mimics* is especially effective in reflecting and expressing the persona's *emotions, moods and *aspirations (efforts), but it cannot convey intellectual meanings, such as the motivation of a behaviour or an emotion, or a reflection of a mood. An actor can *mimically* portray emotions and moods, and how they lead to aspirations. This is important because the physical, mimic *action of the actor's performance is *ostensive: it is *dramatic action proper. (For a full discussion of *mimics*, moods, *emotions and *aspirations, see Ch. 5.).

ostensive, ostension (*názorný, názornost; anschaulich, Anschaulichkeit*). When something is *ostensive*, it is available to the senses, empirical: it is visible and/or audible, or tactile, or psychologically accessible through *inner-tactile perception*, etc. *Ostension* is the act of showing or demonstrating something. It is also the quality of being available to the senses (*ostensiveness*). The *ostensive* quality is an important distinctive feature of some *real phenomena (e.g., real persons, actions, etc.), as well as of imagined phenomena: Zich calls them *ideal as they only exist in the realm of ideas. When we perceive an *artwork that has a *real, material basis (a painting, a statue or an actor's performance), the associations or *conceptual images, evoked by this artwork in our mind also have an *ostensive* quality. It makes such mental images different from those evoked by reading: the material of literature is words, and while literature evokes **conceptual images*, they lack the *ostensive* quality. Such images remain **ideal*, i.e., imagined in our mind only, without the material basis of *ostension*. See also **dramatic action*. (See also the discussion of *ostension* in the Afterword.)

pantomime (*pantomima*) is a specific form of movement theatre Zich discusses. He refers to the nineteenth-century art form also known as the Romantic French pantomime or "the white pantomime", represented by such artists as Jean Gaspard Deburau. The *pantomime* replaces the spoken word with conventionalised and stylised language of gestures. Zich does not include modern developments of the art form (Marcel Marceau, Étienne Decroux), which would probably question some of his conclusions. In other words, Zich uses *pantomime* in the then traditional sense, and his distinction of the *ballet-pantomime* (*action ballet*, *ballet d'action*) and the *dramatic pantomime* is now dated and untenable.

poetic (*poetický, básnický*) is a term Zich uses in a very specific way, in keeping with systematic aesthetics. *Poetic* as a critical descriptive term denotes any verbal **formation* that is capable of having an **aesthetic effect*, i.e., create and/or leave an impression on the recipient. This use of *poetic* needs to be kept separate from the common, intuitive use of *poetic* to mean *lyrical, evocative* or simply "created by a poet" or even "stylised" in the use of figurative or non-literal language. Analogically, Zich uses *epic poetry* (*epické básnictví*) to refer to narrative literature (or *belles lettres*; in English, unhelpfully, *fiction*), such as novels or short stories. See the opening of Ch. 4, where Zich enumerates different intuitive, vague and popular uses of the word *poetic*. See also **verbal art*.

principle (*princip, postulát, zákon, zákonitost*). Zich is a formal aesthetician and he builds his theory inductively and incrementally. Just like an artist creates an **artwork* in several steps, first creating **formations* within components, then giving the entire artwork its integrity, so does the theorist study a theory first from the **material*, identifying and theorising the material's potency; then articulates the art form's laws or *principles*; and eventually formulates an integral aesthetics. *Principles* are not only logical arguments but also qualities and, truly, laws of certain arts. They are the building blocks in Zich's systemic theory. Zich uses the Latinate term *postulát* interchangeably with the Romance word *princip* and the Czech *zákon* (law) or *zákonitost* (logic, inevitability, rule), and makes incremental assertions on the nature and quality of the subject he is discussing. Once he asserts a *principle* (e.g., the *actor's totality principle* or the *dramaticity principle*), he uses it, inductively, as a building block in his systemic theory.

Very importantly, Zich is writing his theory for practitioners. He argues that every artist needs to have a sense of the inner logic, i.e., the relations of the material elements, of their art (e.g., colour, tones, gestures, words), and he builds his theory on that logic. Zich assumes that artists already operate within the means and "think through their **material*" – within the properties of the medium. His theory only helps them to articulate the *principles* of their art, because every art has its logic and rules, as do its methods. Zich refers to the logic and rules as postulates or *principles* of a given art. The very logic of his assertions is **ostensive*: it follows self-evidently from the practical experience of the art in question.

real (*reálný*; also *actual*, e.g., *real persons, place* or *action*). Zich theorises the concept of the *real* in opposition to the **ideal*. The *real* is that which is **ostensive*, accessible by the senses; that which is actually seen or heard or performed before the audience. Zich uses the *ideal-real* binary to distinguish between different *materiality*, i.e., different modes of mimesis. (For more details see **ideal*.)

referential image (*významová představa obrazová*), see **conceptual image*.

reproductive art (*výkonná umění*; *ausübende Kunst, reproduktive Kunst*). In keeping with standard discourse, Zich uses the term *reproductive art* to refer to artistic performance practice that is based on delivering a text or a score. The *reproductive artist* – e.g., the reciter, the singer or the instrumentalist – delivers a unique spatio-temporal performance of a text (a poem, a musical score). The pre-existing text determines and limits their performance; it sets relatively clear and strict parameters (expression, tempos, dynamics) for their execution, and the *reproductive artist*'s creativity is located in performative nuance and individual, idiosyncratic qualities (timbre, accents, contrasts in tempos and dynamics, emotional expressiveness, etc.). Zich does not use the term *reproductive art* in a judgmental way; he holds reproductive artists, as well as creative artists, in very high esteem.

scene, in keeping with the Czech word *scéna* (and the German *die Szene*), has two principal meanings and uses in Zich:

scene (I) (also *scenic space*) is the **stage* equipped with scenic elements, decorations or stage objects (props) – purposely so, in order to support **dramatic action*. The *scene* (I) is a space evoking or a referring to a **dramatic space*: the fictional place, the *location* where the action takes place. In Zich's terminology, the *scene* is the *technical image* associated with the *referential image* (see *conceptual image) of the *dramatic space. So, for instance, the stage can be furnished and stylised as a *scene* (I) (or a *scenic image*) to look like a royal hall for a production of *King Lear*; that *scene* (I) evokes the idea (*referential image*) of the play's opening *location*, the *dramatic space of King Lear's royal palace.

scene (II) or full scene (in Czech also *výstup*), is a structural part of a script. A *scene* (II) refers to continuous *dramatic action between two moments when the stage – strictly speaking, *scene* (I) – is empty, and there is a break in the dramatic action. During this break between two scenes, the time and location may change. This is the standard word used in English drama; e.g., the opening scene of *Hamlet* starts with the meeting of the sentinels Barnardo and Francisco, who are later joined by Marcellus and Horatio, and then the Ghost, and ends with Horatio, Marcellus and Barnardo leaving with the intention (*aspiration) to inform Prince Hamlet of the Ghost's apparition. The next scene follows at a different time and in a new location.

For his structural analysis of drama, Zich also uses a subcategory of *scene* (II), the **french scene** (*výjev*; *die Auftritt*). The *french scene* is a sequence (a movement or a passage) of a *scene* with the continuous presence of the same characters on stage: Zich defines it as a successive synthesis of dramatic situations with the same *dramatic personas on the *scene* (I). This is a common way of indicating new scenes in the French tradition. English theatre scholarship rarely operates with this term (cf. Scanlan 2020: 28ff.). We have adopted the usual term, *a French scene*, and idiosyncratically use it in the lower case: *the french scene*.

spoken drama (*činohra*; *Schauspiel, das gesprochene Drama*; also *straight drama*) is an art form of *dramatic art or theatre. In *spoken drama* actors interact and deliver their lines speaking without musical accompaniment, as opposed to singing (in opera or *sung drama), the *melodrama (which accompanies speaking with a musical score), dancing (e.g., ballet) or miming (e.g., *pantomime). While *spoken drama* may contain songs and musical segments, its central mode of expression is speaking. Commonly, *spoken drama* is shortened to plain *drama*, but Zich uses the term *drama* in a broader sense and makes a clear distinction between *spoken drama* and *sung drama* (of which opera is one form). Zich uses this distinction to highlight that *opera* and other forms of *sung drama* (e.g., vaudeville or singspiel) are also full dramatic forms.

stage (*jeviště*). Zich views the *stage* as an empty space and defines it merely as an architectural space that does not depict or refer to anything. Zich takes the proscenium stage as the standard, so his default architectural structure is a theatrical space with the actors (who create fiction in the *scene) and the audience (real-world spectators in the auditorium) strictly separated by the proscenium arch. Zich's theory sees the stage as an analogy for the actor who is not performing; the *scene as the *actor figure; and the location as the *dramatic persona.

stylisation (*stylisace*). Zich uses *stylisation* to describe the relationship between the art and the real-world reference. He views *stylisation* in the sense of their distance, and the extent and degree of their mimetic difference. Mimetic artworks *stylise* their correspondences, the natural and even artistic objects they represent.

From another perspective, *stylisation* is the relationship between our perception of the *artwork on the one hand and our inner as well as outer experience on the other. The inner experience involves our inner life as well as our awareness and knowledge of artistic conventions (including other artistic representations of the themes and objects in question). The outer experience relates to how we know the themes and objects from the real world. Since an artwork should aspire to be an organic whole with integrity, *stylisation* needs to be consistent and follow through all the components of the artwork. Zich argues that every artwork is *stylised*, otherwise it is not artistic. He claims that naturalism in the strict sense, as a style aiming to portray the outer face of reality as seen, is merely mechanical, and as such *un*-artistic.

In artistic practice, Zich observes two basic tendencies. He refers to them as *realism* (not to be mistaken for realism as a historic style) and *idealism*. While *realism* tends towards representing and imitating the outer semblance of reality, *idealism* aims to imitate inner reality, depicting the outer only in abstraction, in contour, or symbolically. Zich argues that all creators of the *dramatic work are *relative realists*: the artwork must connect to our experience at least to some extent. That means the dramatic work must resemble *relatively* our empirical reality – no matter if the inner or the outer one.

In Zich's analytical theory, *stylisation* describes the relation of the *referential image and the *technical image. (For more see the final paragraphs of Ch. 9.)

sung drama (*zpěvohra*; *der Singspiel*; also *musical drama*) is an art form of *dramatic art or theatre. In *sung drama* singers (who are also actors and vice versa) interact and deliver their speeches singing. Zich prefers using *sung drama* as a broader term: it includes opera, operetta, vaudeville, singspiel and other forms of music theatre. Nowadays, we might include the musical, as well as some Western and non-Western dramatic music forms.

technical image (*technická představa obrazová*), see *conceptual image.

temporal art, non-temporal art (*časové, nečasové umění*; also *time-arts*). Zich draws a distinction between types of art on the basis of their material. Some arts exist in real time – for instance, music, drama or dance; these arts are transitory (ephemeral) and Zich refers to them as *temporal arts*. The artefacts of other arts have a lasting existence, such as painting, sculpture or architecture. It is interesting that Zich does not specify where literature would sit in this distinction. This is clearly because he distinguishes several types of literature. Some of them, like poetry, are *temporal arts*, especially when recited. Although he never makes this explicit, fiction would fall under the *non-temporal arts* because the artefact (e.g., a novel) is not transitory and can be revisited by the reader at their leisure.

theatrical acoustics (*divadelní akustika*) is a novel concept devised by Zich to capture the paradoxical nature of the dramatic text. Zich refers the reader to their own theatrical experience, without defining it excessively. He observes that no matter how poetic and how literarily exquisite a text might be, this does not guarantee the dramatic (theatrical) efficacy of the work *when performed in the theatre*. The same holds for the *purely musical* or the purely visual qualities of the theatre (see **mimetic arts*); while the music (or the visuals) can be supreme art in its own right, that does not necessarily contribute to the *dramaticity* of the **dramatic work*. See Zich's discussion of the theatrical paradoxes in Ch. 2. See also **theatrical reading*.

theatrical illusion (*divadelní iluse*) is the result of the audience's *theatrical *focus*. *Theatrical illusion* builds on the dramatic art's ability to suppress the sense of outer reality and evoke the dual **conceptual image* in the audience's perception: the *technical image* and the *referential image*. Note the difference of Zich's theory of the *theatrical illusion* from Coleridge's reductive notion of suspense of disbelief. In other words, *theatrical illusion* is not a lie at the expense of reality, but a wholly different type of reality. In modern terms, we could speak of a high level of *mentalising* (Dunbar 2022: 112ff.) or the notion of *blending* in cognitive theatre studies. For more on *theatrical illusion* see Ch. 9.

theatrical reading (*divadelní čtení; theatralische Lesen*) is a strategy for reading dramatic texts during which the reader tries to imagine what a potential live performance (staging) could be, as vividly as possible and in maximum complexity and with a view to **theatrical acoustics*. Zich argues that *theatrical reading* requires a specific dramatic sense (or talent) if the dramatic reader is to succeed. *Theatrical reading* is relatively rare and belongs to the craft of a professional theatre maker, be it the playwright, the stage director, the actor, the conductor, the scenographer, etc.

transbodiment (*přetělesňování*) is effectively Zich's neologism – although other, more intuitive use of *přetělesňování* can be occasionally found in Czech theatre writing of the 1920s and 30s (e.g., in K. H. Hilar). Sometimes *transbodiment* appears as more or less synonymous with *vtělení* (embodiment). But Zich diverts from all previous uses and provides a rigorous, conceptual definition of the term. Zich proposes the term to refer to the complex bodily process the actor engages in when assuming the physical traits of the **dramatic persona* they are performing: the process of *transbodiment* starts with the **mask* (the visage), involves a change in the bodily posture, a choice of specific gestural language and also requires working with a specific timbre of voice, with intonations and accents. In other words, *transbodiment* is the sum of all the actor's physical expressions in creating the **actor figure*: it is the combined bodily **focus* on the qualities needed to present (perform) the **dramatic persona*. *Transbodiment* needs to make the actor figure – and by extension the dramatic persona in performance – specific and characteristic enough. There is artistic technique involved, which we perceive as the *technical image*, as we need to know that the actor is not playing themselves but a dramatic persona. (For Zich's term *actorly focus, zaměření hercovo*, that arises through the actor's purposely prepared and self-induced suggestion, see Ch. 5, p. 164 above.)

In Zich's theory, acting is based on the psychophysiological correspondence between the inner (mental, psychological) processes and their corresponding outer (external, physical, bodily) expressions, such as behaviour, body language, ways of speaking etc. For that reason Zich sees the dual processes of **mental transfiguration* and *transbodiment* as complementary, alongside the resulting **transpersonation** (*přeosobnění*) – the actor's creative portrayal of the **dramatic persona* by means of the actor's unique **artwork*: the **actor figure*.

It may appear that Zich's analysis of an actor's preparation of their role is similar to Stanislavski's. Especially in Czech, since the word *přetělesnění* (transbodiment) is almost identical with *vtělení* (translated into English as *embodiment*), but the two concepts need to be distinguished. To prevent any confusion, we carefully retain the prefix *trans-* (*pře-*) in rendering in English Zich's three related terms: *transfiguration / transbodiment / transpersonation*. Zich's psychological concepts are essentially rational and material, so adopting the idea of *vtělení* (embodiment) would be beyond his conceptual frame. But he often stresses the necessity for the actor to mentally *trans-fer* or *transition* into the mind of the dramatic persona they are performing, and to bodily *trans-form* into the motoric vision of the dramatic persona.

verbal art (*slovesnost, básnictví*; literature) is, for Zich, an art form built on words as its material, nowadays briefly referred to as *literature*. Zich, in his systematic aesthetics, tends to use *verbal art* as the more abstract, inclusive term, which was standard in contemporary discourse. In his discussions, Zich uses *slovesnost* (verbal art) and *básnictví* (literally, *poetry*) as synonymous notions that refer to literary works. See also **poetic*.

BIBLIOGRAPHY

Altman, Georg. 1964. *Vor fremden und eigenen Kulissen* [In front of foreign and our own stage flats]. Emsdetten: Lechte.
Ambros, Veronika. 2020. "Otakar Zich and Prague's 'Semiotic Stage': reading performance avant la letter." *Theatralia*, vol. 23, no. 1, pp. 13-29.
Angelucci, Daniela. 2010. "Waldemar Conrad (1978-1915)." In Hans Rainer Sepp and L. Embree (eds.), *Handbook of Phenomenological Aesthetics*. Dordrecht: Springer, pp. 53-56.
Aristotle. 2018. *Poetics*, trans. James Hutton, *The Norton Anthology of Theory and Criticism*, 3rd edition, ed. Vincent B. Leitch. New York and London: W. W. Norton & Company.
Balme, Christopher B. 2008. *The Cambridge Introduction to Theatre Studies*. Cambridge: Cambridge University Press.
Bentley, Erik. 1965. *The Life of Drama*. London: Methuen.
Bogatyrev, Petr. 2016 (1937-38). "A Contribution to Study of Theatrical Signs." In Drozd et al., *Theatre Theory Reader: Prague School Writings*, pp. 91-98.
Bogatyrev, Petr. 2016 (1938). "Theatrical Signs." In Drozd et al., *Theatre Theory Reader: Prague School Writings*, pp. 99-114.
Burian, Jarka M. 2002. *Leading Creators of Czech Theatre*, London: Routledge.
Burian, Jarka M. 2000. *Modern Czech Theatre: reflector and conscience of a nation*, Iowa: University of Iowa Press.
Císař, Jan. 2016. *Člověk v situaci* [Human in a situation]. Prague: NAMU.
Dessoir, Max. 1906. *Aesthetik und Allgemeine Kunstwissenschaft in den Grundzügen dargestellt* [Aesthetics and general art studies]. Stuttgart: Ferdinand Enke.
Dinger, Hugo. 1904-1905. *Dramaturgie als Wissenschaft* [Dramaturgy as science]. Leipzig: Veit & comp.
Doležel, Lubomír. 1990. *Occidental Poetics. Tradition and Progress*. Lincoln and London: University Nebraska Press.
Drozd, David, Tomáš Kačer and Don Sparling (eds.). 2016. *Theatre Theory Reader: Prague School Writings*. Prague: Karolinum Press.
Dunbar, Robin. 2022. *How Religion Evolved: And Why It Endures*. London: Penguin Random House UK.
Dykast, Roman. 2009. "Otakar Zich: Aesthetic and Artistic Evaluation, Part 1." *Estetika: The Central European Journal of Aesthetics*, vol. 46, no. 2, pp. 179-201.
Elam, Keir. 2005 (1980). *Semiotics of Theatre and Drama*. London and New York: Routledge.
Erlich, Viktor. 1965. *Russian Formalism: History, Doctrine*. The Hague and Paris: Mouton.
Etlík, Jaroslav. 2011 (1999). "Theatre as Experience. On the Relationship Between the Noetic and Ontological Principles in Theatre Art." *Czech Theatre Review 1989-2009*. Prague: Arts and Theatre Institute, pp. 181-223.
Fischer, Otokar (Ot. F.). 1932. "Teoretická dramaturgie" [Theoretical dramaturgy]. *Lidové noviny*, vol. 40, no. 241 (12. 5. 1932), p. 9.
Fischer, Otokar. 2014 (1925). "Psychoanalýza a literatura" [Psychoanalysis and literature]. In *Literární studie a stati I*. Prague: Univerzita Karlova, pp. 77-81.
Fischer-Lichte, Erika. 1999. "From Text to Performance: The Rise of Theatre Studies as an Academic Discipline in Germany." *Theatre Research International*, vol. 24, no. 2, pp. 168-178.
Fischer-Lichte, Erika, Doris Kolesch, and Matthias Warstat (eds.). 2014. *Metzler-Lexikon Theatertheorie*, 2nd edition. Stuttgart and Weimar: J. B. Metzler.

Fischer-Lichte, Erika, 2014. *The Routledge Introduction to Theatre and Performance Studies*. London: Routledge.

Flack, Patrick. 2023. "Phenomenology in German-Speaking Areas and in Russia." In *Central and Eastern European Literary Theory and the West*, eds. Michał Mrugalski, Schamma Schahadat and Irina Wutsdorff. Berlin and Boston: De Gruyter, pp. 307–322.

Havlíčková Kysová, Šárka. 2015. "Metafory, kterými hrajeme: perspektivy a meze české kognitivní teatrologie" [Metaphors we act by: prospects and limits of Czech cognitive theatrology]. *Theatralia*, vol. 18, no. 1, pp. 65–84.

Honzl Jindřich. 2016 (1933–34). "Spatial Concerns in Theatre." In Drozd et al., *Theatre Theory Reader: Prague School Writings*, pp. 290–302.

Honzl, Jindřich. 2016 (1940). "The Mobility of the Theatrical Sign." In Drozd et al., *Theatre Theory Reader: Prague School Writings*, pp. 129–146.

Honzl Jindřich. 2016 (1943). "The Hierarchy of Theatrical Devices." In Drozd et al., *Theatre Theory Reader: Prague School Writings*, pp. 157–164.

Hostinský, Otakar. 1981. *Otakar Hostinský o divadle* [Otakar Hostinský on theater], Prague: Theatre Institute.

Hostinský. Otakar. 1887. *Das Musikalisch-Schöne und das Gesamtkunstwerk vom Standpunkte der formalen Aesthetik* [The Beautiful in Music and the Gesamtkunstwerk from the Point of View of Formal Aesthetics]. Leipzig: Breitkopf und Härtel.

Christiansen, Paul. 2004. "The Meaning of Speech Melody for Leoš Janáček." *Journal of Musicological Research*, vol. 23, no. 3–4, pp. 241–263.

Ingarden, Roman. 1973 (1931). *The Literary Work of Art*, translated by George G. Grabowicz. Evanston, Illinois: Northwestern University Press.

Ingarden, Roman. 1973 (1958). "Functions of Language in the Theatre." *The Literary Work of Art*, translated by George G. Grabowicz. Evanston, Illinois: Northwestern University Press, pp. 377–396.

Jakubcová, Alena, Jitka Ludvová, and Václav Maidl (eds.). 2001. *Deutschsprachiges Theater in Prag: Begegnungen der Sprachen und Kulturen*. Prague: Theatre Institute.

Jandová, Jarmila and Emil Volek (eds.). 2013. *Teoría teatral de la Escuela de Praga: de la fenomenología a la semiótica performativa*, translated by Jarmila Jandová and Emil Volek. Madrid and Bogotá: Fundamentos and RESAD Universidad Nacional de Colombia.

Kačer, Tomáš, and David Drozd. 2020. "(Re-)translating Zich's aesthetics into English: a work in progress." *Theatralia*, vol. 23, no. 1, pp. 199–213.

Kačer, Tomáš, Emil Volek and Andrés Pérez-Simón. 2020. "Interview with Emil Volek and Andrés Pérez-Simón, translators of Zich's 'The Theatrical Illusion'." *Theatralia*, vol. 23, no. 1, pp. 151–156.

Krejčí, František. 1904. *O filosofii přítomnosti* [On present-day philosophy]. Prague: Jan Laichter.

Knudsen, Hans. 1950. *Theaterwissenschaft: Werden und Wertung einer Universitätsdisziplin* [Theatre studies: the establishment of an academic discipline]. Berlin: Christian-Verlag.

Kutscher, Artur. 1910. *Die Ausdruckskunst der Bühne* [The expressive art of the stage]. Leipzig: Fritz Erhardt Verlag.

Kutscher, Artur. 1949 (1932). *Grundriss der Theaterwissenschaft* [The principles of theatre studies], 2nd revised edition. München: Kurt Desch. Available at: http://nbn-resolving.org/

Laichter, Prokop.1932. "Otakar Zich: Estetika dramatického umění" [Otakar Zich: Aesthetics of the Dramatic Art]. *Naše doba*, vol. 40, no. 1, pp. 52–53.

Lánská, Dita. 2016. "Meaning(s) of Otakar Zich's Concept of the 'Semantic Image'." *Theatralia*, vol. 19, no. 2, pp. 103–121.

Lazarowicz, Klaus, and Christopher Balme (eds.). 1991. *Texte zur Theorie des Theaters* [Texts on theatre theory]. Stuttgart: Reclam.

Locke, Brian S. 2006. *Opera and Ideology in Prague: Polemics and Practice at the National Theatre, 1900–1938*. Rochester, New York: University of Rochester Press.

Ludvová, Jitka. 2012. *Až k hořkému konci: Pražské německé divadlo 1845–1945* [To the very bitter end: Prague German theatre 1845–1945]. Praha: Academia.

Maigné, Carole (ed.). 2012. *Formalisme esthétique: Prague et Vienne au xixe siècle* [Formalist aesthetics: Nineteenth-century Prague and Vienna]. Paris: Vrin.
Marx, Peter W. (ed.). 2017. *A Cultural History of Theatre in the Age of Empire*. New York: Bloomsbury.
Mrugalski, Michał. 2023. "Journal and Society of Aesthetics and the General Science of Art." In *Central and Eastern European Literary Theory and the West*, ed. Michał Mrugalski, Schamma Schahadat and Irina Wutsdorff. Berlin and Boston: De Gruyter, pp. 115-136.
Mukařovský, Jan. 1933. "Estetika dramatického umění" [Aesthetics of the dramatic art]. *Časopis pro moderní filologii*, vol. 19, no. 3-4 (July 1933), pp. 318-326.
Mukařovský, Jan. 2016 (1941). "On the Current State of Theory on Theatre." In Drozd et al., *Theatre Theory Reader: Prague School Writings*, pp. 59-75.
Musilová, Martina. 2020. "Otakar Zich on the Dramatic Acting", *Theatralia*, vol. 23, no. 1, pp. 81-88.
Nejedlý, Zdeněk. 1902. *Katechismus estetiky* [A catechism of aesthetics]. Prague: Hejda a Tuček.
Nejedlý, Zdeněk. 1926 (1913). *Nietzscheova tragédie* [Nietzsche's tragedy]. Prague: Bedřich Bělohlávek.
Novák, Arne. 1912. "Bedřich Nietzsche v Čechách" [Friedrich Nietzsche in Bohemia]. *Národní listy*, no. 109 (21 April 1912), p. 17.
Novák, Arne. 1914. "Nietzsche und die Tschechen" [Nietzsche and the Czech lands]. *Das literarische Echo*, vol. 16, no. 23 (1 Sept 1914), pp. 1613-1616.
Novák, Bohumil. 1933. "Rozhovor s Otakarem Zichem" [An interview with Otakar Zich]. *Čin*, vol. 4, pp. 465-469.
Osolsobě, Ivo. 2002 (1967). "Ostenze aneb zpráva o komunikačních reformách na ostrově Balnibarbi" [Ostension or a report on reforms in communication at the island of Balnibarbi. In *Ostenze, hra, jazyk* [Ostension, play, language]. Brno: Host, pp. 15-42.
Osolsobě, Ivo. 1979. "On Ostensive Communication." *Studia semiotyczne*, vol. 8, pp. 63-75.
Osolsobě, Ivo. 1986. "Zichova filosofie dramatického tvaru" [Zich's philosophy of dramatic structure]. In Otakar Zich, *Estetika dramatického umění* [Aesthetics of the dramatic art]. Praha: Panorama, pp. 373-400.
Osolsobě, Ivo. 2001. "Považuju divadlo za zázrak přírody zrovna tak jako včelí úl" [I consider theatre a wonder of nature, just like a beehive]. *Divadelní noviny*, vol. 10, no. 16, pp. 10-11.
Osolsobě, Ivo. 2002 (1970). "Dramatické dílo jako komunikace komunikací o komunikaci" [Dramatic work as communication of communications about communication]. In *Ostenze, hra, jazyk* [Ostension, play, language]. Brno: Host, pp. 90-137.
Osolsobě, Ivo. 2002 (1981). "Semiotika semiotika Otakara Zicha" [The semiotics of the semiotician Otakar Zich]. In *Ostenze, hra, jazyk* [Ostension, play, language]. Brno: Host, pp. 213-38.
Osolsobě, Ivo. 2007a (1975). "Sémiotika v Tampě a okolí, poslouchaná divadelníkem" [Semiotics at Tampa and nearby, as witnessed by a theatre maker]. *Principia parodica*, Prague: NAMU, pp. 235-246.
Osolsobě, Ivo. 2007b. "Dg.: Semiotica Theatralis Chronica." *Principia parodica*. Prague: NAMU, pp. 259-264.
Osolsobě, Petr. 2020. "The Aristotelian Perspective in Otakar Zich's *The Aesthetics of Dramatic Art*." *Theatralia*, vol. 23, no. 1, pp. 30-43.
Paulík, Jaroslav Jan [P]. 1932. "O. Zich: Estetika dramatického umění" [O. Zich: Aesthetics of the dramatic art]. *Rozpravy Aventina*, vol. 7, no. 32 (28 April 1932), p. 264.
Procházka, Miroslav. 1984. "On the Nature of Dramatic Text." In Herta Schmid and Aloysius Van Kesteren (eds.), *Semiotics of Drama and Theatre: New Perspectives in the Theory of Drama and Theatre*. Amsterdam and Philadelphia: John Benjamins, pp. 102-126.
Quinn, Michael. 1991. "Theaterwissenschaft in the History of Theatre Study." *Theater Survey*, vol. 32, no. 2, pp. 123-136.
Quinn, Michael. 1995. *The Semiotic Stage: Prague School Theater Theory*. Pieterlen and Bern: Peter Lang.
Scanlan, Robert. 2020. *Principles of Dramaturgy*. Abingdon and New York: Routledge.

Schmid, Herta. 2020. "Aristotelism in Czech Structuralism: Jan Mukařovský and Otakar Zich." *Theatralia*, vol. 23, no. 1, pp. 44-53.
Schmid, Herta, and Aloysius van Kesteren. 1975. *Moderne Dramentheorie* [Modern theatre theory]. Kronberg: Scriptor Verlag.
Schmid, Herta, and Aloysius Van Kesteren (1985). *Semiotics of Drama and Theatre: New Perspectives in the Theory of Drama and Theatre*. Amsterdam and Philadelphia: John Benjamins.
Schmid, Herta, and Hedwig Král. 1991. *Drama und Theater: Theorie Methode Geschichte* [Drama and theatre: Theory, methods, history]. Munich: Otto Sagner.
Sebeok, Thomas A. (ed.). 1986. *Encyclopaedic Dictionary of Semiotics*. Berlin, New York, Amsterdam: Mouton de Gruyter.
Sennett, Richard. 2012. *Together: The Rituals, Pleasures & Politics of Cooperation*. London and New York: Allen Lane.
Sládek, Ondřej. 2014. "Jan Mukařovský and Theatre." *Theatralia*, vol. 17, no. 2, pp. 122-136.
Sládek, Ondřej. 2015. *The Metamorphoses of Prague School Structural Poetics* (Travaux linguistiques de Brno, 12). Munich: LINCOM.
Slavík, Bedřich [B. S.]. 1932. "Z nové naučné literatury" [From recent scholarship]. *Archa*, vol. 20, no. 4, p. 295.
Sławińska, Irena. 1977. "La sémiologie du théâtre in statu nascendi: Prague 1931-1941" [Theatre semiology in statu nascendi: Prague 1931-1941]. *Roczniki Humanistyczne*, vol. 25, no. 1, pp. 53-76.
Štědroň, Miloš. 2009. "Direct Discourse and Speech Melody in Janáček's Operas." In Paul Wingfield (ed.), *Janáček Studies*. Cambridge: Cambridge University Press, pp. 79-108.
Stehlíková, Eva. 2012. *Co je nám po Hekubě* [What's Hecuba to us]. Praha: Brkola.
Steiner, Peter. 1976. "The Conceptual Basis of Prague Structuralism." In Ladislav Matějka (ed.), *Sound, Sing and Meaning: Quinquagenary of the Prague Lingvistic Circle*. Ann Arbor: University of Michigan, pp. 351-385.
Steiner, Peter. 1982. "The Roots of Structuralis Esthetics." In Peter Steiner (ed.), *The Prague School: Selected Writings: 1929-1946*. Austin: University of Texas Press, pp. 174-219.
Steiner, Peter. 2017. "From the History of the Pre-Marxist Aesthetics in Bohemia: Herbartian Formalism." *Comparative Literature: East & West*, vol. 1, no. 1, pp. 40-50.
Steiner, Peter. 2023. "Herbartian Aesthetics in Bohemia." In Michał Mrugalski, Schamma Schahadat and Irina Wutsdorff (eds.), *Central and Eastern European Literary Theory and the West*. Berlin and Boston: De Gruyter, pp. 200-211.
Sus, Oleg. 1969. "Poetry and Music in Psychological Semantics of Otakar Zich." *Sborník prací Filozofické fakulty brněnské univerzity*, series H, vol. 18, no. H4, pp. 77-96. Avaliable at: <http://hdl.handle.net/11222.digilib/111961>.
Sus, Oleg. 1972. "On the Genetic Preconditions of Czech Structuralist Semiology and Semantics: An essay on Czech and German Thought." *Poetics*, vol. 4, pp. 28-54.
Sus, Oleg. 1973. "On the Origin of the Czech Semantics of Art: The Theory of Music and Poetry in Psychological Semantics of Otakar Zich." *Semiotica*, vol. 9, pp. 117-139.
Sus, Oleg. 2010 (1977). "Průkopník české strukturně sémantické divadelní vědy: (psychosémantika a divadelní umění)" [A pioneer of Czech structural semantic theatre studies: (psychosemantics and theatre arts]. *Theatralia*, vol. 13, no. 2, pp. 218-243.
Szatkowski, Janek. 2019. *A Theory of Dramaturgy*. London: Routledge.
Tatarkiewicz, Władysław. 1980. *A History of Six Ideas: An Essay in Aesthetics*. Warsaw: Polish Scientific Publications.
Tyrrell, John. 2007. *Janáček: Years of a Life*. 2 vols. London: Faber and Faber, 2006 and 2007.
Vacková, Růžena. 1948. *Výtvarný projev v umění dramatickém* [Visual expression in dramatic art]. Prague: Václav Tomsa.
Veltruský, Jiří. 1977. *Drama as Literature*. Lisse: Peter de Ridder.
Veltruský, Jiří. 1981. "The Prague School Theory of Theater." *Poetics Today*, vol. 2, no. 3 (Spring 1981), pp. 225-235.

Veltruský, Jiří. 1985. "Drama as Literature and Performance." In Erika Fischer-Lichte (ed.), *Das Drama und seine Inszenierung*. Tübingen: Niemeyer, pp. 12-21.

Veltruský, Jiří. 2016 (1976). "A Contribution to Semiotics of Acting." In Drozd et al., *Theatre Theory Reader: Prague School Writings*, pp. 376-423.

Veltruský, Jiří. 2016. "Structuralism and Theatre." In Drozd et al., *Theatre Theory Reader: Prague School Writings*, pp. 76-85.

Vojvodík, Josef. 2023. "Phenomenology in Czechoslovakia (Jan Patočka, Přemysl Blažíček)." In Michał Mrugalski, Schamma Schahadat and Irina Wutsdorff (eds.), *Central and Eastern European Literary Theory and the West*. Berlin and Boston: De Gruyter, pp. 323-339.

Volek, Emil. 2012. "Theatrology an Zich, and Beyond: Notes Towards a Metacritical Repositioning of Theory, Semiotics, Theatre, and Aesthetics." *Theatralia*, vol. 15, no. 2, pp. 168-186.

Vostrý, Jaroslav. 2010. *Scénologie dramatu: úvahy a interpretace* [The scenology of drama: reflections and interpretations]. Prague: Kant.

Wingfield, Paul. 1992. "Janáček's Speech-Melody Theory in Concept and Practice." *Cambridge Opera Journal*, vol. 4, no. 3, pp. 281-301.

Winner, Thomas. 1989. "Otakar Zich as a Precursor of Prague Literary Structuralism and Semiotics." In *Issues in Slavic Literary and Cultural Theory: Studien zur Literatur-und Kulturtheorie in Osteuropa*. Bochum: Universitätsverlag Dr. Norbert Brockmeyer, pp. 227-42.

Zapletal, Miloš. 2016. "From Tragedy to Romance, from Positivism to Myth: Nejedlý's Conception of the History of Modern Czech Music." In Sławomira Żerańska-Kominek (ed.), *Nationality vs Universality: Music Historiographies in Central and Eastern Europe*. Newcastle upon Tyne: Cambridge Scholars Publishing, pp. 99-124.

Zich, Otakar. 1909. "Zeitschrift für Ästhetik und allgemeine Kunstwissenschaft" (review). *Česká mysl*, vol. X, pp. 282-83.

Zich, Otakar. 1911. "Gustav Mahler." *Novina*, vol. IV, pp. 513-515, 562-564.

Zich, Otakar. 1912. "Zeitschrift für Ästhetik und allgemeine Kunstwissenschaft" (review). *Česká mysl*, vol. XIII, pp. 91-92.

Zich, Otakar. 1921. "Estetická příprava mysli" [The aesthetic preparation of the mind]. *Česká mysl*, vol. XVII, pp. 150-162, 193-204.

Zich, Otakar. 1923. "Podstata divadelní scény" [The basis of the theatrical scene]. *Moravsko-slezská revue*, no. 5, pp. 129-38.

Zich, Otakar. 1927a. "Dramatické možnosti opery" [The dramatic possibilities of the opera]. In Josef Kodíček and Miroslav Rutte (eds.), *Nové české divadlo 1918-1926* [New Czech theatre 1918-1926]. Prague: Aventinum, pp. 84-91.

Zich, Otakar. 1927b. "Jak se komponuje opera" [How opera is composed]. In Josef Kodíček and Miroslav Rutte (eds.), *Nové české divadlo 1918-1926* [New Czech theatre 1918-1926]. Prague: Aventinum, pp. 86-89.

Zich, Otakar. 1931. *Estetika dramatického umění: teoretická dramaturgie* [Aesthetics of the dramatic art: theoretical dramaturgy]. Prague: Melantrich, 1st ed.

Zich, Otakar (ed.). 1977. *Estetika dramatického umění* [Aesthetics of the dramatic art], ed. Oleg Sus. Würzburg: JAL-reprint. Sus's foreword is also avaliable in Sus 2010.

Zich, Otakar. 1986. *Estetika dramatického umění: teoretická dramaturgie* [Aesthetics of the dramatic art: theoretical dramaturgy]. 2nd ed. Prague: Panorama.

Zich, Otakar. 1997. "Principy teoretické dramaturgie" [Principles of theoretical dramaturgy]. *Divadelní revue*, vol. 8, no. 1, pp. 12-24.

Otakar, Zich. 2009. "Aesthetic and Artistic Evaluation", *Estetika: The Central European Journal of Aesthetics*, vol. 46, no. 2, pp. 179-201, vol. 47, no. 1, pp. 71-95.

Zich, Otakar, and Jaroslav Hilbert. 2014. *Vina: Opera in Three Acts*, ed. Brian S. Locke. Middleton, WI: A-R Editions.

Zich, Otakar. 2015 (1923). "Puppet Theatre." Translated by Pavel Drábek. *Theatralia*, vol. 18, no. 2, pp. 505-513.

Zich, Otakar. 2016. "Principles of Theoretical Dramaturgy." In Drozd et al., *Theatre Theory Reader: Prague School Writings*, pp. 34-58.

Zich, Otakar. 2019. "The Theatrical Illusion," introduction and translation by Emil Volek and Andrés Pérez-Simón. *PMLA*, vol. 134, no. 2, pp. 351-358.
Zittel, Claus. 2020. "Don Juan der Sprache': Otokar Fischer und die tschechische Nietzsche--Rezeption" [The Don Juan of words: Otokar Fischer and the Czech reception of Nietzsche]. In Václav Petrbok, Alice Stašková, Štěpán Zbytovský (eds.), *Otokar Fischer (1883-1938): Ein Prager Intellektueller zwischen Dichtung und Wissenschaft*, Kohl: Böhlau Verlag, pp. 407-426.

EDITORS AND TRANSLATORS

David Drozd is Associate Professor of Theatre Studies at Masaryk University in Brno, Czech Republic. He is a dramaturg, translator and theatre theorist. His main research fields are performance analysis with a focus on modern and postmodern Czech theatre culture, especially directing, and structural and semiotic theatre theory, with a special focus on the Prague Linguistic Circle and the history of Czech theatre theory as such. He has edited the *Theatre Theory Reader: Prague School Writings* (2016).

Pavel Drábek is Professor of Drama and Theatre Practice at the University of Hull, United Kingdom. He publishes on theatre theory, early modern theatre history, and drama translation and adaptation. He is also a playwright and translator in spoken drama, radio, and opera. He has collaborated with Prague Quadrennial as a member of the International Team since 2017, co-curating PQ Talks and PQ Best Publication Award.

Tomáš Kačer is Associate Professor of English Literature at Masaryk University in Brno, Czech Republic. His main research interests lie in eighteenth- and nineteenth-century American theatre and performance culture, American and British Modernist theatre and twentieth-century playwrights. He is the author of the first Czech-language history of early American drama before 1916. He is also a translator of fiction, non-fiction and plays.

Josh Overton is Artistic Director of From Below Theatre, a Sunday Times award-winning playwright and a poet, a writer of musicals and opera, a director of theatre, a hip hop lyricist, a dramaturg, a musician, a YouTube scriptwriter, a fire spinner and circus performer, a part-time master's student, a copy editor for theatre journals and theatres across Europe and was, briefly, a voice of local radio. At the moment he is working on an opera libretto, a musical and two plays.

NAME INDEX

Adorno, Theodor W. 396
Ambros, Veronika 7, 46, 439, 441
Appia, Adolphe 9, 30, 44–5, 395, 432
Aristotle 12–3, 18, 23, 90, 406–8, 412, 427, 442, 443, 445–6
Auber, Daniel François Esprit 99, 286, 303, 317, 324, 326

Bab, Julius 381, 383, 386
Bacmeister, Ernst 381
Bahr, Hermann 42
Bach, Johann Sebastian 67, 458
Balme, Christopher 19, 24, 389
Bard, Jean 412
Bassermann, Albert 42
Bathe, Johannes 382
Beethoven, Ludwig van 37, 72, 146, 270, 320, 323–4, 328
Benda, Jiří Antonín 456
Bentley, Eric 24
Berg, Alban 43
Bergson, Henri 414
Berlioz, Hector 67, 288, 458
Bernátek, Martin 7, 415
Bernhardt, Sarah 40
Binet, Alfred 117
Bizet, Georges 286, 313
Böcklin, Arnold 79
Bogatyrev, Petr 423
Boïeldieu, François-Adrien 274, 282, 315
Bor, Jan 397–8
Borský, Lev 410–1
Brahm, Otto 41, 379, 390, 397, 418
Brecht, Bertolt 415
Brod, Max 43
Burian, Emil František 8
Bytkowski, Sigmund 176, 385

Calderón de la Barca, Pedro 128
Čech, Svatopluk 36, 312
Císař, Jan 432–4
Charles University (Univerzita Karlova) 34–5, 45, 55, 378–9, 409, 423–4

Charpentier, Gustave 326
Chekhov, Anton 44
Chvatík, Květoslav 405
Coleridge, Samuel Taylor 32, 463
Conrad, Waldemar 381, 383–4, 401
Coquelin, Benoit Constant 117, 176
Craig, Edward Gordon 9, 30, 44–5, 239, 379, 390, 395, 397, 432

Deák, František 428
Deering, Jules 7, 439
Dessoir, Max 380–1, 383, 388, 390, 398
Destinn, Emmy (Ema Destinnová) 346
Deutsch, Ernst 42
Diderot, Denis 116, 181
Dilthey, Wilhelm 171
Dinger, Hugo 387–91, 398
Doležel, Lubomír 406–8, 429
Dubos, Jean-Baptiste 90
Dumas, Alexandre 139
Duncan, Isadora 412
Duse, Eleonora 40
Dvořák, Antonín 34–5, 37, 270
Dykast, Roman 38

Eisenstein, Sergei 29–30
Elam, Keir 13, 427–8, 429, 431, 438
Erlich, Victor 429
Etlík, Jaroslav 46, 402, 433–4

Fechner, Gustav Theodor 143
Fibich, Zdeněk 35, 37, 247, 270, 274, 290, 323, 328–9, 456
Fischer, Otokar 410–3, 419–21
Fischer-Lichte, Erika 386–7, 398, 415, 431
Flack, Patrick 406
Flaubert, Gustave 172
Fleming, Willi 382
Foerster, Josef Bohuslav 35, 37, 270, 286, 290, 308, 317, 325–6
Frejka, Jiří 8
Freud, Sigmund 408–9, 412–4

Friedemann, Käte 386
Fuchs, George 79

Gluck, Christoph Willibald 37, 262, 270, 279, 285, 305, 308, 322, 324-5, 328
Gobineau, Joseph Arthur, comte de 67
Goethe, Johann Wolfgang von 67, 72, 78
Gogol, Nikolai Vasilyevich 147
Goldoni, Carlo 128, 346, 372
Görland, Albert 382
Groos, Karl 384

Hagemann, Karl 380, 386, 393-4
Halbe, Max 41
Handel, George Frideric (Georg Friedrich Händel) 307
Hanslick, Eduard 412
Hauptmann, Gerhart 176, 351, 361, 385
Havlíčková Kysová, Šárka 7, 46
Haydn, Joseph 67
Hebbel, Christian Friedrich 258, 381
Hegel, Georg Wilhelm Friedrich 15, 405
Herbart, Johann Friedrich 385, 438
Hernried, Erwin 382
Herrmann, Helene 381-2, 386
Herrmann, Max 380, 382, 386-8, 415-6
Hesse, Hermann 412
Hilar, Karel Hugo 42-3, 464
Hilbert, Jaroslav 36, 195, 202, 322
Hindemith, Paul 43
Hirt, Ernst 386
Hofmannsthal, Hugo von 42, 412
Honzl, Jindřich 8, 423
Hostinský, Otakar 32, 35, 37, 49, 55, 75-6, 81, 270, 275, 298, 323, 329, 378-9, 385, 433, 438
Husserl, Edmund 383-4, 399, 401, 404-5

Ibsen, Henrik 17, 36, 40-1, 44, 136, 186-7, 195-9, 205, 212-5, 225, 232, 266, 352, 381
Ingarden, Roman 399-404

Jakobson, Roman 435
Jakubcová, Alena 41
James, William 25, 117, 148, 180, 384-5, 413, 450
Janáček, Leoš 35, 37-8, 43, 270-1, 296, 314, 370
Jankovič, Milan 405
Jessner, Leopold 42, 379, 393-4, 418
Jirásek, Alois 42
Jiroušek, Jan 431, 435

Kainz, Friedrich 382
Kant, Immanuel 15, 388, 448, 456
Klein, Robert 382

Kleist, Heinrich von 381-2
Knudsen, Hans 387
Kodíček, Josef 396
Korngold, Erich Wolfgang 43
Kostomlatský, Samuel 435-41
Kovařovic, Karel 36
Krásnohorská, Eliška 147
Kraus, Karl 412
Kreis, Friedrich 382
Krejča, Otomar 8
Krejčí, František 25, 35, 404-5, 409-10, 413
Krenek, Ernst 43
Kutscher, Artur 386, 387-96, 398, 415-6
Kvapil, Jaroslav 34, 40, 42, 386
Kvapilová, Hana 40

Laichter, Prokop 417-9
Lange, Carl 148, 180, 340, 384-5, 413, 450
Langer, František 122
Lánská, Dita 7, 38, 425
Lattuada, Felice 36
Legouvé, Gabriel-Marie 117
Lessing, Gotthold Ephraim 33, 116, 181
Littmann, Max 79
Locke, Brian S. 7, 37, 38, 43, 270-1, 432, 439
Loewe, Karl 72
Lohmeyer, Walther 386
Lope de Vega, Felix 128
Lortzing, Gustav Albert 309, 316-7
Ludvová, Jitka 36, 41-3
Ludwig, Otto 116-8, 382
Luther, Bernhard 381

Maeterlinck, Maurice 226, 348, 352
Mahler, Gustav 36-7, 39-40, 43, 88, 270, 347, 414
Maigné, Carole 432
Mann, Thomas 412
Marceau, Marcel 459
Marlowe, Christopher 128
Marschner, Heinrich 327
Marx, Peter W. 7, 398, 439
Masaryk, Tomáš Garrigue 35
Masaryk University (Masarykova univerzita) 7, 378, 424, 438-9
Matějka, Ladislav 427-9, 436
Mathauser, Zdeněk 405
Meiningen Theatre 41, 379, 390
Merk, Heinrich 382
Meyer, Theodor A. 382, 386
Meyerhold, Vsevolod Emilyevich 30, 379
Mickiewicz, Adam 35, 67, 317
Mitterwurzer, Friedrich 175

NAME INDEX

Moissi, Alexander 42
Molière (Jean-Baptiste Poquelin) 36, 78, 120, 128, 153, 206, 246, 248, 311, 361
Monteverdi, Claudio 307
Moreto, Agustin de 193
Mozart, Wolfgang Amadeus 35, 97, 146, 246, 299, 310, 313–5, 317, 320, 328, 346
Mrugalski, Michał 381
Mukařovský, Jan 13, 45, 399, 405, 421–3, 428
Müller-Freienfels, Richard 116, 382
Münchner Künstlertheater (Munich Art Theatre) 42, 79, 239, 397
Musilová, Martina 7, 46, 396, 413, 432
Musset, Alfred de 371

National Theatre in Prague (Národní divadlo, Praha) 34, 36, 40–3, 170, 193, 195, 220, 313, 323, 346, 386, 410, 419
Nejedlý, Zdeněk 37–8, 270–1, 379, 410–1
Neruda, Jan 35, 40, 46
Neumann, Angelo 41–2
Niessen, Carl 386–7, 398
Nietzsche, Friedrich 171, 398, 408–14
Novák, Arne 409
Novák, Bohumil 395

O'Neill, Eugene 167
Osolsobě, Ivo 7, 17–8, 20–1, 26, 33, 39–40, 46, 181, 382, 399, 424, 426–8, 430, 435–8, 439–41, 443
Osolsobě, Petr 7, 408, 441
Ostrčil, Otakar 36–7, 43, 270, 317

Patočka, Jan 404
Paulík, Jan Jaroslav 419
Pavis, Patrice 431
Pérez-Simón, Andrés 32, 404
Perger, Arnulf 385
Petsch, Robert 382
Pfister, Manfred 431
Pirandello, Luigi 147
Piscator, Erwin 379, 393–4
Plato 123
Plautus, Titus Maccius 146
Prague Linguistic Circle (PLC, Pražský lingvistický kroužek) 13, 40, 404, 417, 419, 423, 429–31
Preissová, Gabriela 290
Procházka, Miroslav 181, 424, 426–7, 430
Purkyně, Jan Evangelista 280

Quinn, Michael 386–8, 430

Radok, Alfréd 8
Raynal, Paul 220
Reich, Hermann 398
Reinhardt, Max 9, 41–2, 379, 386–7, 390–1, 393, 397, 418
Revermann, Martin 7, 439
Rodin, Auguste 414
Rossini, Gioacchino 307, 314, 328, 368
Rostand, Edmond 117, 139, 176, 361
Rutte, Miroslav 396

Sabina, Karel 64
Šalda, František Xaver 409
Scheinpflugová, Olga 170
Schiller, Friedrich 190, 196, 205, 211, 232, 261, 323, 353
Schmid, Herta 408, 415, 431, 435
Schmoranz, Gustav 42
Schnabel, Heinz 381
Schnitzler, Arthur 42, 412–3
Scholz, Wilhelm von 116, 118, 382
Schönberg, Arnold 43
Schubert, Franz 72, 88, 284
Schwaiger, Hanuš 341
Schwantke, Christoph 382
Scribe, Eugène 117, 194, 206
Sebeok, Thomas 436, 440
Shakespeare, William 17, 40, 42, 64, 78, 98, 101, 128, 133–5, 139, 146–7, 153, 157, 167, 187, 198–9, 205–6, 212–5, 225, 233, 255, 258, 266, 268, 317, 338, 344, 346, 357, 360–1, 379, 382, 403
Shaw, George Bernard 17, 132, 187, 232
Sheridan, Richard Brinsley 134
Sládek, Ondřej 423, 428–9
Slavík, Bedřich 417
Sławińska, Irena 428
Smetana, Bedřich 34–5, 37–8, 46, 64, 97–8, 114, 146–7, 255, 270–1, 273–4, 279, 281, 283–92, 303, 308, 310–7, 319–22, 324–5, 327–8, 330, 346, 352, 365, 368–70
Sophocles 195, 352, 455
Sommer, Kurt 382
Spencer, Herbert 409
Stanislavski, Konstantin 9, 28, 40, 44, 347, 379, 418, 464
Stehlíková, Eva 7, 424
Steiner, Peter 385, 427
Strauss, Richard 43, 97, 312, 352, 372, 414
Strindberg, August 44, 338, 353
Suk, Josef 37, 270
Sus, Oleg 405, 424–6, 430
Světlá, Karolína 409
Szatkowski, Janek 388

Taine, Hippolyte 340
Tairov, Alexander 45, 128, 180, 379, 393-5, 413
Tatarkiewicz, Władysław 442
Tille, Václav 379-80
Tolstoy, Leo 409

Vacková, Růžena 424
Veltrusky, Jarmila F. 436
Veltruský, Jiří 403, 423, 427, 436, 444
Verdi, Giuseppe 368
Vojan, Eduard 346
Vojvodík, Josef 404-5
Volek, Emil 32, 46, 384, 399, 404-6, 431, 440-1
Volkelt, Johannes 425, 440
Vostrý, Jaroslav 432-4
Vrchlická, Eva 220
Vrchlický, Jaroslav 206, 247, 290, 317, 456
Vydra, Václav 220

Waetzold, Wilhelm 381
Wagner, Richard 18-9, 37, 41, 44, 74-5, 79, 261, 270, 273-4, 279, 280-1, 289-90, 292, 299, 302, 304, 306, 308, 312, 316, 318-9, 324, 326, 328, 352, 355, 369, 372, 385, 410-1
Weber, Carl Maria von 80, 286, 310, 312, 316, 325, 328
Wedekind, Frank 42
Wilde, Oscar 96
Winner, Thomas G. 429-30, 436
Wolf, Hugo 72
Wutschke, Hans 381

Zapletal, Miloš 37, 270
Zemlinsky, Alexander 43
Zeyer, Julius 409
Zubatý, Josef 379